INVARIANCE AND VARIABILITY
IN SPEECH PROCESSES

Edited By

Joseph S. Perkell
Dennis H. Klatt
Massachusetts Institute of Technology

LEA LAWRENCE ERLBAUM ASSOCIATES, PUBLISHERS
1986   Hillsdale, New Jersey   London

This book was produced at M.I.T. on a Xerox Dover
laser printer using the TeX programmed language
developed by Donald Knuth at Stanford University.

Lawrence Erlbaum Associates, Inc., Publishers
365 Broadway
Hillsdale, New Jersey 07642

Library of Congress Cataloging-in-Publication Data
Main entry under title:

Invariance and variability in speech processes.

   Proceedings of the Symposium on Invariance and
Variability of Speech Processes met at M.I.T.
   "In honor of Kenneth N. Stevens"
   Bibliography: p.
   Includes index.
   1. Speech—Congresses.   2. Language and languages—
Variation—Congresses.   3. Stevens, Kenneth N.,
1924–   . I. Perkell, Joseph S.   II. Klatt, Dennis H.
III. Stevens, Kenneth N., 1924–   . IV. Symposium
on Invariance and Variability of Speech Processes
(1983 : Massachusetts Institute of Technology)
P95.I55   1986   001.54'2   85-27557
ISBN 0-89859-545-2

Printed in the United States of America
10 9 8 7 6 5 4 3 2 1

PREFACE

Background

In 1952 a conference on speech communication was held at M.I.T. (Firestone, 1952), and the theoretical classic, *Preliminaries to Speech Analysis* by Jakobson, Fant and Halle (1952) was published. Vocoding, synthesis-by-rule and automatic recognition of speech were among the challenges which were causing the field to grow. Interaction among communication engineers, phoneticians, linguists and psychologists stimulated these budding efforts to understand the speech code, and put such understanding to practical use. Now, thirty-three years later, the vitality of the field of research in speech communication remains undiminished, and it has been stimulated further by the VLSI (very-large-scale-integration) chip revolution. Forecasts for industrial applications of speech technology have never been so optimistic as for the 80's. Rudimentary automatic voice response systems and recognition devices are commercial realities, and considerable resources are being devoted to the refinement and proliferation of such systems. Aids for the handicapped are being developed in the wake of the rapid evolution of hardware and signal processing techniques.

Is the present boom due also to the fact that we have now reached the necessary, and much-longed-for level of scientific understanding of the speech code? Is it due to the emergence of a theory of speaking and listening that satisfactorily integrates observations on the linguistics, psychology, physiology and physics of speech behavior? Although we do not want to play down the highly significant theoretical contributions that have given us better insight into sound patterns of languages and quantitative descriptions of the acoustics of speech, our answer must be no. In fact, there is a real possibility that the lack of a comprehensive theory of speech production and perception will still turn out to be a major stumbling block in current engineering approaches to man-machine interfaces and aids for the handicapped. We might even speculate that a technologically-driven proliferation of applications which are not developed from a basic understanding of speech could eventually result in a partial rejection of such technology, because of unsatisfactory performance (Pisoni & Hunnicutt, 1980).

Thus, a major theme motivating applied as well as fundamental speech research efforts continues to be the quest for an integrated theory which accounts for all aspects of the speech code. Presumably such a theory would incorporate definitions of fundamental units of speech communication and their relationship to signal characteristics and observable behavior, along with a comprehensive and successful accounting of *invariance and variability of speech processes*. What is the nature of invariance? What are the sources and function of speech variability? There are as yet no established answers

i

to these questions, but they are likely to be crucial to the long-term success of our efforts to address human and social needs.

If there is one finding which can be said to most universally characterize speech processes, it is the finding of variability. Variability in the acoustic manifestations of a given utterance is substantial and arises from many sources. These include: (a) recording conditions (background noise, room reverberation, microphone/telephone characteristics), (b) within speaker variability (breathy/creaky voice quality, changes in voice fundamental frequency, speaking-rate related undershoot in articulatory targets, slight statistical variation in articulation that may lead to significant acoustic changes, nasality propagation into non-nasal sounds) and (c) cross-speaker variability (differences in vocal-tract anatomy, dialect, detailed articulatory habits). The accumulated effect of all of these sources of variability is so great and our understanding of variability is so limited, that current systems designed to recognize the digits 0 to 10 have difficulty doing so in a speaker-independent manner (Klatt, 1983). On the other hand, the underlying nature and information-transmitting function of speech communication argue compellingly for some kind of invariance. Thus, for both scientific and practical reasons, the search for invariant aspects of the speech code continues to be a major focus of research in speech communication.

There are numerous points of view on invariance and variability in speech, depending on where one looks. Phonetic theories as embodied in the IPA standards for a phonetic alphabet or formulations based on universal sets of binary oppositions (Jakobson, et al., 1952; Chomsky & Halle, 1968) implicitly take the stance that there are invariant, discrete segmental (and subsegmental) units that make up the speech code. On the other hand, findings in prosody, sound change, and sociolinguistics call into question notions of discreteness and invariance based on universal oppositions (c.f. Labov, et al., 1972). Some speech physiologists argue that speech motor programming is context-dependent and based on invariant targets (MacNeilage, 1970; Perkell, 1980), but others posit a different kind of unit in which context dependencies are incorporated as parts of the units and production is a "direct" process without the need for any transformations (Fowler, et al., 1980). Still others argue that the assumption of any kind of unit impedes physiological research (Moll, et al., 1977), but this point of view is countered by psychologists who interpret speech errors as solid evidence for the existence of discrete sublexical units such as morphemes and phonemes in the planning process (Fromkin, 1971; Shattuck-Hufnagel & Klatt, 1979).

There continues to be lively debate on the extent to which there are invariant characteristics in the acoustic signal, with some researchers suggesting that the invariance issue will appear less formidable once we succeed in identifying the appropriate acoustic dimensions (Stevens & Blumstein, 1981). Views on perception have a wide range. Some hypothesize property detectors for invariant acoustic attributes (Eimas & Miller, 1978), and some look to the development of models of the representation of speech in the auditory periphery (Carlson & Granstrom, 1982). These views of peripheral mechanisms are consistent with the ideas of those psychologists who suggest that perception is basically a process for which perceptual mechanisms have evolved to match properties of the stimuli rather closely and operate "intelligently" in a direct "bottom-up" fashion. An alternative point of view emphasizes that speech perception and understanding are active processes: listeners make up for the lack of invariant information in the speech signal by invoking hypothesis-driven, "top-down" mechanisms (Cole, 1979). Automatic speech recognition schemes represent various degrees of compromise between these two opposing approaches (Lea, 1980), but some choose apparently different methods such as statistical analyses of most-likely paths through a decision network based on acoustic templates (Jelenek, 1976). What is the relationship between such an approach to dealing with variability and the way humans do it? Finally, when we look at language acquisition, we find evidence for units of different "size" at different stages of development and differences between production and perception which make us wonder about the nature of "invariant" units (Yeni-Komshian, et al., 1980).

A SYMPOSIUM ON INVARIANCE AND VARIABILITY
OF SPEECH PROCESSES

The important implications of speech variability for the future of speech-related technology, in combination with the multifaceted debate about invariance among speech scientists, make this a most appropriate time to evaluate the state our knowledge in this area. On October 8-10, 1983 researchers from the fields of production, perception, acoustics, pathology, psychology, linguistics, language acquisition, synthesis and recognition met at a symposium at M.I.T. on *invariance and variability of speech processes*. This volume is the Proceedings of the symposium.

Each chapter of the book consists of a "focus paper" followed by some comments. The comments range in scope from short formal presentations on the subject matter of the focus paper to brief direct comments on the focus paper. There are also some responses of focus paper authors to the comments. Drafts of the focus papers and many of the comments were distributed to participants well in advance of the symposium, so much of the material in the book represents somewhat more interaction and interchange of ideas than usually occurs at such a meeting.

We feel that the book presents a good cross-section of the "state of the art" of ideas on invariance and variability from a variety of perspectives. It is clear that from every perspective, there is a great deal to be learned, and we hope that this volume helps to highlight important issues and possible directions for future research and cross-fertilization of ideas.

B. Lindblom, J.S. Perkell and D.H. Klatt

DEDICATION

The idea for this book sprung in part from the desire of a small organizing committee (Gunnar Fant, Dennis Klatt, Björn Lindblom, Joe Perkell, Stefanie Shattuck-Hufnagel and Victor Zue) to celebrate the 60th birthday of a special friend, respected colleague, and leader in the field of speech communication research, Professor Kenneth Stevens of MIT.

The scientists who were invited to participate in the conference and prepare manuscripts were uniformly enthusiastic about this motivation (as well as endorsing the topic chosen for the conference, which is closely tied to much of Ken's recent research). They related many public and private expressions of congratulations to Ken on this occasion, and share in the feelings of the dedication presented here.

Ken was born in Toronto, Canada in 1924. He obtained Bachelor's and Master's degrees in Electrical Engineering from the University of Toronto, and a Sc.D. from the Massachusetts Institute of Technology. His doctoral thesis "The Perception of Sound Shaped by Resonant Circuits" was supervised by Leo Beranek.

Ken has been a faculty member at MIT since 1951. He became a full professor in 1963, and currently holds the Lebel chair in the Department of Electrical Engineering and Computer Science. He is the head of the Speech Group, a set of 5 faculty and staff plus about 15 graduate students and postdoctoral fellows who are housed in the Research Laboratory of Electronics. As a leader, Ken is known for his devotion to students and his miraculous ability to run a busy laboratory while appearing to manage by a principle of benevolent anarchy.

Ken has performed pioneering research in the areas of speech production, analysis, synthesis, perception, and recognition. A major early contribution (with Arthur House) was the development of a quantitative description of vowel articulation and the resulting acoustic output. This was followed by studies of the perturbations to vowel articulation by consonantal context, and by acoustic analyses of English fricatives. These papers are often reprinted and serve as standards for students entering the field today.

In recent work, Ken has proposed the view that speech has a quantal nature which is inherent in the way it is produced as well as in the way it is perceived. Certain articulations result in stable distinctive acoustic properties, while other articulatory gestures result in acoustic outputs that are very sensitive to small perturbations in the articulation and/or do not contain acoustic properties that are distinctive to the auditory system. These ideas reinforce existing thought that there exist a small set of universal preferred sounds in the languages of man, and that it might be possible to define a universal phonetic framework in terms of a small number of distinctive features. These features group sounds together into sets that have the same unique acoustic and articulatory manifestations. Furthermore, Ken believes that the acoustic manifestations, if defined properly, will be invariant across phonetic contexts (e.g., the acoustic correlates of the labial feature for /b/ in "beet" will be the same as in "boat" and the same as for the /m/ in "meet"), and thus lead to simple perceptual strategies for acquiring speech and language skills. Ken has worked with Morris Halle and others to refine a universal phonetic framework, and has worked with Sheila Blumstein and others to discover invariant acoustic properties of stop consonants (which are the class of speech sounds believed to have acoustic properties that change dramatically depending on vowel context). It remains to be determined the degree to which the phonology of language is constrained by articulatory and psychoacoustic factors, and the extent to which perceptual invariance exists, but the contribution of Ken in directing attention to these important theoretical issues, as well as his thoughtful solutions to specific problems, is immense.

Ken has published scientific papers on other topics such as (1) noise generation in the vocal tract, (2) analysis-by-synthesis strategies for speech recognition and for formant extraction, (3) vocal tract modeling, (4) acoustic-phonetic descriptions of English and other languages, (5) the questionable reliability of voice identification in courts of law, (6) community noise abatement, and (7) speaking and listening aids for the deaf. Over 30 of these publications are in the Journal of the Acoustical Society of America.

One of Ken's most significant contributions, and the one that is dear to his heart, has been the training of speech researchers. Over the years, Ken has supervised some seventy graduate students, including James Flanagan, Hiroya Fujisaki, Larry Rabiner, and Victor Zue. The Speech Group at MIT has also been the home of many postdoctoral fellows who have gone on to make significant contributions to the field. Ken gives himself selflessly to teaching and to his students. His patience, guidance, compassion, his unassuming personality, and his unique ability to inspire high standards in those around him has won the respect and affection of all. In addition, Ken has also devoted considerable amounts of his time to teaching outside MIT, including several summer short courses on speech science to psychologists, linguists, speech pathologists, and engineers from various universities and research institutes. His public service contributions include having been chairman of the Communication Sciences Study Section of the National Institutes of Health and he is currently a member of the National Advisory Neurological and Communicative Disorders and Stroke Council.

Ken has served the Acoustical Society of America in the role of President (1976-1977), President-Elect (1975-76), Vice President (1971-72), Vice President-Elect (1970-71), member of the Executive Council (1963-66), Associate Editor for Speech Communication (1957-59), and as a member of several committees. In 1983, he received the Silver Medal of the society. The citation read "For his contributions to our understanding of the production, acoustic-phonetic properties, and the perception of speech, and how we may join speech and technology in ways useful to man."

Strikingly, along with all of his accomplishments, Ken has always lived modestly. He can be seen riding an old three-speed bike through the streets of Cambridge between home and MIT, both in the heat of summer and the slush of winter. In his few idle moments, he might be practicing early music on his harpsichord or attending a concert, and on his vacations he is most likely to be found biking through the countryside with one or more of his four children.

The contributors, organizing committee and editors dedicate this book to Ken Stevens. May he continue to inspire all of us by his ideas and his humanity.

D. Klatt

In honor of

Kenneth N. Stevens

ACKNOWLEDGEMENTS

The organizing committee for the Symposium on Invariance and Variability of Speech Processes consists of Gunnar Fant, Dennis Klatt, Björn Lindblom, Joseph Perkell, Stefanie Shattuck-Hufnagel, Kenneth Stevens and Victor Zue. Members of this committee were responsible for inviting participants, obtaining funding, organizing and presiding over sessions, and initial post-conference editing of manuscripts.

The Symposium was supported by major grants from the National Institutes of Health and the National Science Foundation and a small grant from the Research Laboratory of Electronics of the Massachusetts Institute of Technology (Jonathan Allen, Director). Organizational and logistical help was provided by Gayle Fitzgerald and Sarah Clere of the M.I.T. Special Events Office, and Alan Morrison was responsible for the audio visual work. Additional help was given by Marie Southwick and Charla Scivally of the Speech Communication Group of the Research Laboratory of Electronics. In order to help minimize the cost of the Proceedings, all royalties have been waived. The manuscript was prepared in camera-ready form by Amy Hendrickson of TeXnology, Inc. using the TeX formatting system. Photographic work was done by John Cook of the Research Laboratory of Electronics.

J.S.P and D.H.K.

Table of Contents

Comments:

Comments:

Comments:

CONTRIBUTORS

JAMES H. ABBS⋆
Speech Motor Control Laboratories
Waisman Center
University of Wisconsin
Madison, Wisconsin 53706

JONATHAN ALLEN⋆ †
Research Laboratory of Electronics
Massachusetts Institute of Technology
Cambridge, Massachusetts 02139

CORINE BICKLEY
Speech Communication Group
Research Laboratory of Electronics
Massachusetts Institute of Technology
Cambridge, Massachusetts 02139

MATS BLOMBERG
Dept. of Speech Communication and
    Music Acoustics
Royal Institute of Technology
S-10044 Stockholm, SWEDEN

SHEILA E. BLUMSTEIN⋆
Department of Linguistics
Brown University
Providence, Rhode Island 02912

SYLVAIN BROMBERGER
Dept. of Linguistics and Philosophy
Massachusetts Institute of Technology
Cambridge, Massachusetts 02139

ROLF CARLSON⋆
Dept. of Speech Communication
    and Music Acoustics
Royal Institute of Technology
S-10044 Stockholm, SWEDEN

J. C. CATFORD⋆
Department of Linguistics
University of Michigan
1076 Frieze Bldg.
Ann Arbor, Michigan 48109

JOHN CLARK⋆
Speech and Language Research Centre
School of English and Linguistics
Macquarie University, North Ryde,
N.S.W. 2113, AUSTRALIA

ANTONIE COHEN⋆
Phonetics Department
Utrecht University
Trans 14
3513 ER Utrecht, NETHERLANDS

RONALD COLE⋆
Department of Computer Science
Carnegie-Mellon University
Pittsburgh, Pennsylvania 15213

BERTRAND DELGUTTE⋆
Centre National D'Etudes
    des Telecommunications
BP 40
22301 Lannion, FRANCE

KJELL ELENIUS⋆
Dept. of Speech Communication
    and Music Acoustics
Royal Institute of Technology
S-10044 Stockholm, SWEDEN

JEFFREY ELMAN⋆
Department of Linguistics
University of California, San Diego
La Jolla, California 92093

GUNNAR FANT○
Dept. of Speech Communication
and Music Acoustics
Royal Institute of Technology
S-10044 Stockholm, SWEDEN

CHARLES A. FERGUSON⋆
Department of Linguistics
Stanford University
Stanford, California 94305

CAROL FOWLER⋆ •
Department of Psychology
Dartmouth College
Hanover, New Hampshire 03755

OSAMU FUJIMURA⋆
AT&T Bell Laboratories
600 Mountain Avenue
Murray Hill, New Jersey 07974

EVA GÅRDING⋆
Department of Linguistics
Lund University
Helgonabacken 12
S-223 62 Lund, SWEDEN

BJÖRN GRANSTRÖM⋆
Dept. of Speech Communication
and Music Acoustics
Royal Institute of Technology
S-10044 Stockholm, SWEDEN

MORRIS HALLE⋆
Dept. of Linguistics and Philosophy
Massachusetts Institute of Technology
Cambridge, Massachusetts 02139

KATHERINE HARRIS⋆ •
Dept. of Speech and Hearing Sciences
Graduate School
City University of New York
33 W. 42nd St. New York, NY 10036

JOHN N. HOLMES⋆
Joint Speech Research Unit
Princess Elizabeth Way
Cheltenham
Gloucestershire GL52 5AJ, UK

PETER JUSCZYK⋆
Department of Psychology
University of Oregon
Eugene, Oregon 97403

HARUKO KAWASAKI
Voice Processing Corporation
1 Broadway
Cambridge, MA 02142

J. A. SCOTT KELSO◇
Haskins Laboratories
270 Crown Street
New Haven, Connecticut 06511

RAYMOND D. KENT⋆
Dept. of Communicative Disorders
University of Wisconsin
1975 Willow Drive
Madison, Wisconsin 53706

DIANE KEWLEY-PORT⋆
Dept. of Speech and Hearing Sciences
Indiana University
Bloomington, Indiana 47405

SAMUEL J. KEYSER★
Dept. of Linguistics and Philosophy
Massachusetts Institute of Technology
Cambridge, Massachusetts 02139

NELSON YUAN-SHENG KIANG★
Eaton Peabody Laboratory
Massachusetts Institute of Technology
Harvard Medical School
Massachusetts General Hospital
Massachusetts Eye and Ear Infirmary
243 Charles St.
Boston, Massachusetts 02114

PAUL KIPARSKY★
Dept. of Linguistics and Philosophy
Massachusetts Institute of Technology
Cambridge, Massachusetts 02139

DENNIS H. KLATT○ †
Speech Communication Group
Research Laboratory of Electronics
Massachusetts Institute of Technology
Cambridge, Massachusetts 02139

KLAUS J. KOHLER★
Institut für Phonetik
Universität Kiel
Olshausenstrasse 40
2300 Kiel, WEST GERMANY

PATRICIA KUHL★
Department of Speech
   and Hearing Sciences
University of Washington
Seattle, Washington 98195

WILLIAM LABOV★
Department of Linguistics
Univ. of Pennsylvania
3812 Walnut St.
Philadelphia, Pennsylvania 19104

PETER LADEFOGED★
Phonetics Laboratory
Department of Linguistics
University of California, Los Angeles
Los Angeles, California 90024

MOSHÉ J. LASRY
Dept. of Electrical and
   Computer Engineering
Carnegie-Mellon University
Pittsburgh, Pennsylvania 15213

ILSE LEHISTE★
Department of Linguistics
Ohio State University
1841 Millikin Road
Columbus, Ohio 43210

ALVIN M. LIBERMAN★ ◇
Haskins Laboratories
270 Crown Street
New Haven, Connecticut 06511

PHILIP LIEBERMAN★
Department of Linguistics
Brown University
Providence, Rhode Island 02906

MONA LINDAU★
Department of Linguistics
Phonetics Laboratory
Univ. of California, Los Angeles
Los Angeles, California 90024

BJÖRN LINDBLOM○
Department of Phonetics
Institute of Linguistics
Stockholm University
S-10691 Stockholm, SWEDEN

LEIGH LISKER★ •
Department of Linguistics
University of Pennsylvania
Philadelphia, Pennsylvania 19104

ANDERS LÖFQVIST★
Dept. of Logopedics and Phoniatrics
Lund University
S-221 85 Lund, SWEDEN

JAMES LUBKER★
Department of Phonetics
Institute of Linguistics
University of Stockholm
S-10691 Stockholm, SWEDEN

PETER F. MACNEILAGE★
Department of Linguistics
University of Texas, Austin
Austin, Texas 78712

JOHN MAKHOUL
Bolt Beranek & Newman Inc.
10 Moulton Street
Cambridge, MA 02238

EDITH M. MAXWELL
Kurzweil Applied Intelligence, Inc.
411 Waverly Oaks Rd.
Waltham, Massachusetts 02154

JAMES L. MCCLELLAND★
Department of Psychology
University of California, San Diego
La Jolla, California 92093

PAULA MENYUK★
School of Education
Boston University
665 Commonwealth Avenue
Boston, Massachusetts 02215

JOHN J. OHALA★
Phonology Laboratory
Department of Linguistics
University of California, Berkeley
Berkeley, California 94720

SALLYANNE PALETHORPE
Speech and Language Research Centre
School of English and Linguistics
Macquarie University, North Ryde
N.S.W. 2113, AUSTRALIA

JOSEPH S. PERKELL○
Speech Communication Group
Research Laboratory of Electronics
Massachusetts Institute of Technology
Cambridge, Massachusetts 02139

DAVID B. PISONI★
Speech Research Laboratory
Department of Psychology
Indiana University
Bloomington, Indiana 47405

LOUIS C.W. POLS★
Institute of Phonetic Sciences
University of Amsterdam
Herengracht 338,1016 CG
Amsterdam, THE NETHERLANDS

ROBERT F. PORT★
Department of Linguistics
Indiana University
Bloomington, Indiana 47405

PATTI J. PRICE
Speech Communication Group
Research Laboratory of Electronics
Massachusetts Institute of Technology
Cambridge, Massachusetts 02139

BRUNO REPP★
  Haskins Laboratories
  270 Crown Street
  New Haven, Connecticut 06511

RICHARD SCHWARTZ★
  Bolt Beranek and Newman Inc.
  10 Moulton St.
  Cambridge, Massachusetts 02238

STEPHANIE SENEFF
  Speech Communication Group
  Research Laboratory of Electronics
  Massachusetts Institute of Technology
  Cambridge, Massachusetts 02139

STEFANIE SHATTUCK-HUFNAGEL○
  Speech Communication Group
  Research Laboratory of Electronics
  Massachusetts Institute of Technology
  Cambridge, Massachusetts 02139

MARY SMITH●
  Department of Psychology
  Dartmouth College
  Hanover, New Hampshire 03755

RICHARD M. STERN
  Dept. of Electrical and
    Computer Engineering
  Carnegie-Mellon University
  Pittsburgh, Pennsylvania 15213

KENNETH N. STEVENS○ †
  Speech Communication Group
  Research Laboratory of Electronics
  Massachusetts Institute of Technology
  Cambridge, Massachusetts 02139

MICHAEL G. STUDDERT-KENNEDY★ ●
  Department of Communication
    Arts and Sciences
  Queens College
  City University of New York
  Flushing, New York, 11364

BETTY TULLER●
  Division of Cognitive Neuroscience
  Cornell University Medical College
  515 E. 71 Street
  New York, New York 10021

JACQUELINE VAISSIÈRE★
  Centre National D'Etudes
    des Telecommunications
  F-22301 Lannion, FRANCE

VICTOR W. ZUE○ †
  Speech Communication Group
  Research Laboratory of Electronics
  Massachusetts Institute of Technology
  Cambridge, Massachusetts 02139

★ Invited Participant, Symposium on Invariance and Variability of Speech Processes

○ Member of Organizing Committee, Symposium on Invariance and Variability of
    Speech Processes

● also of Haskins Laboratories, 270 Crown St. New Haven CT

◇ also, Prof. of Psychology, University of Connecticut

† also of Dept. of Electrical Engineering and Computer Science, M.I.T.

1

Toward a Model of the Development of Speech Perception

Peter W. Jusczyk
Department of Psychology
University of Oregon

From the infant's point of view, the task of sorting out the varied array of sounds directed toward him or her into a coherent set of signals appears to be a formidable one. The sources of variation in utterances produced by even the same speaker in the same context would appear to be overwhelming. The problem is only confounded when one considers the variations produced in noisy environments, by different adults of the same sex, by children and adults, or by males and females. Yet, somehow during the course of the first year of life, infants act as if they understand certain words, and a few months later are producing their own words. Perhaps, we should not be too surprised by this since similar feats of perceptual constancy appear to be presented in the visual domain (Day & McKenzie, 1973; Spelke, 1982), and even intermodally (Meltzoff, 1985; Rose, Gottfried, & Bridger, 1983). Nevertheless, the demonstration that invariance is found in other sensory modalities does not free us from the need to explain the instances of invariance that appear in connection with the infant's perception of speech sounds. Two speech perception phenomena would seem to require the infant's capacity to perceive an invariant relation across different tokens. The first is the well-known phenomenon of categorical perception; the second is the capacity to recognize the same utterances produced by different speakers. Both of these phenomena have been the object of investigation in studies of infant speech perception. In what follows, we review briefly some of the major findings in the field of infant speech perception. We consider the possible mechanisms that might underlie the infant's basic capacities, and then discuss the ways in which these capacities might develop during the course of language acquisition.

1

INFANT SPEECH PERCEPTION CAPACITIES

Discrimination of Simple Speech Contrasts

One of the most important findings in the early studies of infant speech perception was Eimas, Siqueland, Jusczyk, & Vigorito's (1971) demonstration of the existence of categorical discrimination of voicing cues. This result indicated not only that infants were capable of discriminating certain speech sounds, but that their ability to do so was similar to that of adults in a very important way. Previously, investigators had invoked explanations based on acquired distinctiveness and learned equivalence of cues to account for categorical perception—i.e., the fact that adults are sensitive to subtle acoustic differences between members of different phonetic categories but relatively insensitive to differences of the same magnitude occurring within a particular phonetic category (Liberman, Harris, Kinney, & Lane, 1961). The basic argument was that through extensive practice in producing and perceiving speech, listeners would, in time, learn to treat variants of a particular phonetic segment as being the same and as different from variants of other phonetic segments. In particular, the perceived sounds would be referenced with respect to the articulatory gestures used to produce them. In effect, acoustic variations that arose in the attempts to produce the same articulatory gesture would be ignored in perception. A key factor in this process was extensive practice in assigning the same label to the variants of a particular phonetic segment; this presumably contributed to the difficulty which adults had in distinguishing one variant from another on standard speech discrimination test such as ABX. However, the Eimas et al. results indicated that such categorical effects were present in the response of infants who had not been subjected to a long period of discriminative training. Hence, many researchers began to view categorical perception as a consequence of the way in which the human perceptual system is structured right from birth (Eimas & Corbit, 1973). Moreover, because at the time categorical perception was thought to occur only for speech sounds, these findings were taken to be an indication of an innate linguistic capacity (Cutting & Eimas, 1975; Eimas et al., 1971).

In the following years, many studies were undertaken to determine the variety of contrasts that infants are capable of perceiving. These studies indicate that infants are capable of discriminating virtually every type of phonetic contrast that they have been tested on (for a complete review, see Aslin, Pisoni, & Jusczyk, 1983). For example, there is evidence that infants are sensitive to place of articulation differences between stops (Eimas, 1974; Miller, Morse, & Dorman, 1977; Moffit, 1971; Morse, 1972; Till, 1976), fricatives (Holmberg, Morgan, & Kuhl, 1977; Jusczyk, Murray, & Bayly, 1979), glides (Jusczyk, Copan, & Thompson, 1978), and nasals (Eimas &

Miller, 1977). Similarly, infants have been shown to discriminate manner of articulation contrasts such as those between stops and nasals (Eimas & Miller, 1980a), stops and glides (Eimas & Miller, 1980a; Hillenbrand, Minifie, & Edwards, 1979; Miller and Eimas, 1983), liquids (Eimas, 1975), and nasalized and nonnasalized vowels (Trehub, 1976a). Also, infants are able to discriminate a variety of vowel contrasts including [I]–[i] (Swoboda, Kass, Morse, & Leavitt, 1978; Swoboda, Morse, & Leavitt, 1976), [a]–[i] (Kuhl, 1979; Trehub, 1973), [a]–[ɔ] (Kuhl & Miller, 1982) and [i]–[u] (Trehub, 1973). Therefore, it is quite apparent that the underlying capacities which infants possess for discriminating speech sounds extend well beyond those required for the detection of voicing contrasts.

Moreover, the infant's capacity for discriminating phonetic contrasts does not require specific experience with the sounds to be discriminated. Lasky, Syrdal-Lasky, & Klein (1975) found that infants from a Spanish-speaking environment showed sensitivity in the same region of the voice-onset-time (VOT) continuum as did Eimas et al.'s subjects, despite the fact that the VOT boundary for adult speakers in the same environment differed considerably from that of English speakers. Likewise, Streeter (1976) found that the discrimination performance for infants from a Kikuyu-speaking culture corresponded well to that of infants in Eimas et al.'s study. Moreover, other research suggested that cross-language commonalities in perceptual boundaries for infants are not limited to the perception of VOT differences. In one experiment, Trehub (1976a) found that 1- to 4-month old infants from English-speaking homes were capable of discriminating the fricative contrast ([řa]/[za]) that occurs in Czech but not English. In a second experiment, she obtained a similar result for the discrimination of the nasalized/nonnasalized contrast between ([pã]/[pa]), a contrast that is phonemic in Polish and in French but not in English. More recently, Werker and Tees (1983) have reported that 6- to 8-month old infants from English-speaking home are capable of discriminating contrasts from Hindi and from an American Indian language, Thompson. Interestingly enough, a follow-up study suggested that by 8- to 10-months old, the capacity of infants to discriminate these contrasts is attenuated. Evidently, the influence of the infant's native language-learning environment during the latter portion of the first year of life may desensitize the infant to those contrasts not indigenous to the native language. In this sense, specific experience appears to play a role in the maintenance of, as opposed to the acquisition of, discriminative capacities in the infant.

Discrimination of Speech Contrasts in Different Utterance Contexts

In addition to tracking the variety of contrasts that infants are capable of discriminating, a number of researchers have investigated the way in which various contextual factors affect the infant's discriminative capacities. One approach has been to look at the effect of varying the location of the phonetic contrast in an utterance. The early studies in the field had all employed contrasts between the initial segments of single syllables. Hence, there was no way of determining from these investigations if infants processed information beyond the initial segment. Jusczyk (1977) attacked this problem in a study in which he looked at infant's ability to detect a |d|–|g| contrast occurring in either the initial or final segment of CVC syllables. His results indicated that infants are capable of processing phonetic differences beyond the initial segments of syllables (see also Williams & Bush, 1978). Moreover, there was no evidence that the syllable-final contrastswere any less discriminable for infants than syllable-initial ones. Interestingly, this latter result contrasts with findings observed for studies of phonemic perception in infants 1 year of age and older (Garnica, 1973; Shvachkin, 1973). Possible reasons for this discrepancy are considered below.

Additional studies have explored the infant's discrimination of phonetic contrasts in multisyllabic utterances. Again it was found that infants have the capacity to detect contrasts between segments occurring in other than the utterance-initial position (Jusczyk, Copan, & Thompson, 1978; Jusczyk & Thompson, 1978; Trehub, 1976b; Williams, 1977a). Studies with multisyllabic tokens also make it possible to examine how discrimination is affected by the presence of information regarding syllable stress. To date, there is no indication from young infants that unstressed syllables are any less discriminable than stressed syllables (Jusczyk, Copan, & Thompson, 1978; Jusczyk & Thompson, 1978; Williams, 1977a).

Perceptual Constancy

Equally important as the ability to discriminate phonetic contrasts regardless of their position in an utterance is the ability to recognize the same phonetic segment when spoken by different speakers or with a different inflection. The acoustic characteristics of speech sounds vary greatly from speaker to speaker, yet the adult listener is able to ignore such differences in recognizing the identity of a given word. In effect, perception of the phonemic segments is invariant across these differences. Kuhl and her coworkers have looked at the infant's capacity to ignore irrelevant differences in speaker's voice and intonation patterns in making phonetic discriminations. They first trained infants to discriminate between single tokens of two different syllables spoken by the same speaker. Then, in successive phases of the experiment they introduced new tokens of the syllables spoken by different speakers and with varying intonation contours. The infants were deemed to have achieved some degree of perceptual constancy for the phonetic segments being tested if they could successfully maintain the discrimination between the two types of segments in the face of the irrelevant changes introduced by adding new tokens varying the intonation patterns and speaker's voice. Kuhl found evidence that 6-month old infants are able to ignore changes in intonation patterns and speakers voices for both vowel (Kuhl, 1979; 1983) and fricative (Holmberg, Morgan, & Kuhl, 1977) segments.

Infant Speech Perception Capacities: Summary

Infant speech perception studies have revealed a number of things regarding the infant's perceptual capacities. First, categorical discrimination along certain phonetic continua is present for infants as well as adults. Second, the infant is able to successfully discriminate a wide variety of contrasts within the first 2 or 3 months of life. Third, little or no experience appears to be required for making phonetic distinctions because the infant is able to discriminate contrasts that are not present in the native language-learning environment. Fourth, the infant is able to process information about phonetic segments in noninitial positions of utterances. Fifth, the infant is sensitive to phonetic contrasts occurring in unstressed as well as stressed syllables. Sixth, the infant displays some capacity for perceptual constancy in that he or she is able ignore differences in speaker's voices and intonation contours in making phonetic discriminations. Therefore, the infant possesses many of the perceptual capacities required for analyzing the acoustic stream of speech and recovering the phonetic structure of the native language that he or she will be trying to acquire. In particular, the young infant seems to be well-equipped to cope with the variability present in the speech signal as evidenced by the demonstrations of both categorical discrimination and perceptual constancy across changes in intonation and talker.

ON THE QUESTION OF PHONETIC CAPACITIES

The Case for Specialized Phonetic Processing Mechanisms in Infants

Given the complement of abilities that the young infant possesses for discriminating speech sounds, one is tempted to conclude that there is very little in the way of development of speech perception, save for the attenuated abilities with foreign contrasts. Hence, one could argue that the infant comes equipped with specialized phonetic capacities. As noted earlier, when Eimas, Siqueland, Jusczyk, & Vigorito (1971) conducted their study they concluded that the infant was endowed with mechanisms specialized for processing language. However, this claim was based on an assumption, now known to be false, that categorical perception occurs only with speech sounds. Since that time, there have been numerous demonstrations of categorical perception with nonspeech stimuli (Miller, Wier, Pastore, Kelly, & Dooling, 1976;

Pastore, Ahroon, Buffuto, Friedman, Puleo, & Fink, 1977; Pisoni, 1977). Moreover, there have also been indications that categorical perception for speech dimensions can be found in nonhuman species such as the chinchilla (Kuhl & Miller, 1975; 1978). Hence, the mere demonstration that infants exhibit categorical discrimination for speech would not appear to provide sufficient grounds for claiming specialized speech perception capacities exist in infants.

Nevertheless, there are other grounds on which one might base a case in favor of the existence of specialized speech processing mechanisms. A reasonable way to support a claim for specialized speech mechanisms would be to demonstrate that infants process speech sounds differently than they do nonspeech sounds. Some evidence in favor of such a speech-nonspeech processing difference was reported in studies conducted by Eimas (1974; 1975) and Till (1976). Eimas used nonspeech patterns called "chirps" which were truncated versions of the speech syllables that he employed. Specifically, the chirps consisted of only the second (Eimas, 1974) or third (Eimas, 1975) formant transition portion of the speech syllables. Since the only source of acoustic variation which occurred between the speech syllable pairs were differences in the second or third formant transitions, Eimas reasoned that the chirps served as appropriate nonspeech controls. In particular, he argued that the acoustic differences that infants had to discriminate were the same in the speech and nonspeech test pairs. The results of his investigations indicated the infants processed the chirps and speech syllables differently. Discrimination performance for the speech contrasts tended to be categorical in that between-category contrasts (e.g., [ba] vs. [da]) were discriminated, but within-category contrasts (e.g., [ba$_1$] vs. [ba$_2$]) were not. By comparison, discrimination of the nonspeech contrasts was continuous with no differences in performance evident for between-category and within-category contrast. Till (1976) found similar results in his study which employed a different set of nonspeech controls.

An Alternative Explanation: Infant Speech Perception Mediated by General Auditory Mechanisms

The results of these studies involving speech-nonspeech comparisons would appear to provide two grounds for contending that infants possess specialized speech processing mechanisms. First, categorical discrimination was obtained only with speech contrasts. Second, the same acoustic information was apparently processed differently in speech and nonspeech contexts. However, subsequent research has undercut both of these theories. First, it has been demonstrated that categorical discrimination does occur with certain nonspeech contrasts (Jusczyk, Pisoni, Reed, Fernald, & Myers, 1983; Jusczyk, Pisoni, Walley, & Murray, 1980). Hence, for the infant, as well as the adult, categorical discrimination is not limited to speech. Second, the assumption that the same acoustic information is available in both nonspeech chirps and speech syllables has also been challenged (Jusczyk, Smith, & Murphy, 1981; Pisoni, 1976). In particular, Jusczyk, Smith, & Murphy (1981) have suggested that the omission of first formant transition information from chirp stimuli deprives the listener of a context against which to evaluate differences in second or third formant transition differences. They found marked differences in the way in which adults processed nonspeech chirp stimuli with and without accompanying first formant information. Hence, it cannot be assumed that infants are processing the same acoustic differences in the syllable and chirp stimuli, especially if the perceptual analysis is conducted not on the individual formants, but on the relationships between the formants. Therefore, the more recent studies of nonspeech processing by infants (Jusczyk, Pisoni, Walley, & Murray, 1980; Jusczyk, Pisoni, Reed, Fernald, & Myers, 1983) would seem to favor a common explanation for speech and nonspeech processing by infants.

Similarly, the discovery that infants display perceptual constancy across different talkers is actually better handled by an explanation in terms of general auditory capacities rather than specialized speech capacities. Studies such as that of Peterson and Barney (1952) have shown that there is a great deal of acoustic variation in tokens produced by different speakers; at first glance, it would appear that the only commonality that exists in tokens of the same syllable uttered by different speakers is phonetic rather than acoustic. However, nonhuman mammalian species such as the dog (Baru, 1975) and the chinchilla (Burdick & Miller, 1975) are apparently capable of adjusting at least to variations in speaker's voice and intonation contour. Hence, the mechanisms that extract constancies of this sort appear to be generally available in the mammalian auditory system, suggesting a basis in some measure of the overall similarity of the acoustic patterns rather than an analysis into speech-related component dimensions.

Recently, another type of finding has been offered as evidence of specialized speech processing by infants. Eimas and Miller (1980a) found that the infant's discrimination of formant transition duration differences used to signal a contrast between [ba] and [wa] depended upon contextual information in the form of syllable duration even though the information for syllable duration came well after the transition information. The argument that the infants' behavior in this setting is indicative of specialized speech processing mechanisms rests on certain assumptions drawn from a study with adults by Miller and Liberman (1979). Specifically, the latter found that the context effects were not simply attributable to an overall increase in stimulus duration, because changes in overall duration that were not associated with changes in speaking rate (such as adding a new phonetic segment) did not produce the context effects. Instead, only a change in duration associated

with a change in speaking rate (e.g. lengthening the vocalic portion of the
syllable) yielded the context effects. Eimas and Miller (1980a; see also, Miller
& Eimas, 1983) employed similar logic in arguing for phonetic processing effects in their study with infants. Unfortunately, unlike Miller and Liberman
(1979), they were not able to assess the consequences of substituting an
additional consonant in place of an increased vowel duration for their long
duration syllables. Hence, there is no way of knowing for the infants whether
the context effect depended on the composition of the syllable itself or merely
its overall duration.

The most convincing argument against the view that any specialized
speech processing capacity is responsible for the effects observed by Miller
and Liberman (1979) and Eimas & Miller (1980a) comes from recent research
with nonspeech contrasts. Pisoni, Carrell, and Gans (1983) have demonstrated that effects similar to those observed by Miller and Liberman with
adults can be obtained with nonspeech sinewave stimuli, including the different directions of boundary shifts induced by adding either steady-state
or transition-type information. Hence, the perceptual adjustments that listeners make in accommodating to different speaking rate probably reflect a
more general tendency in auditory processing to adjust to changes in the rate
of event occurrence. Furthermore, Jusczyk et al. (1983) have found that 2-
to 3- month olds show shifts in the discrimination of frequency transitions
with changes in overall stimulus duration, paralleling the results of Eimas and
Miller (1980a). Therefore, it appears that the type of compensation observed
by Miller and Liberman is a general feature of human auditory processing
rather than a specific response to a change of speaking rate.

In summary, there is very little support for attributing to the infant specialized speech processing mechanisms. Instead, it appears that the early
speech perception capacities observed in studies with infants are likely the
product of general processes and mechanisms of the human auditory system.

IS THERE A SPECIAL SPEECH MODE IN ADULTS?

Data in Support of Specialized Speech Processing by Adults

Having dismissed claims for the existence of specialized speech processing
mechanisms in infants, it might seem as though the the concept of a specialized speech mode could be dismissed altogether. However, there exists a
substantial body of data from research with adults that is very difficult to
explain without assuming that speech sounds undergo some form of special-

ized processing. In particular, there are a number of studies that demonstrate that the same sounds can be processed in quite different ways, depending upon the listener's set to hear them as speech or nonspeech signals.

For example, consider the phenomenon of "duplex perception" which results from the dichotic presentation of different portions of a speech syllable simultaneously (Liberman, Isenberg, & Rakerd, 1981; Rand, 1974; Repp, Milburn & Ashkenas, 1983). When the third formant transition is played to one ear while the remaining portion of the syllable is played simultaneously to the other ear, subjects report hearing both a syllable and a chirp. Thus, the information in the third formant contributes to the perception of the whole as well as standing alone as a chirp. Moreover, Liberman et al. (1981) showed that listeners were able to make independent judgments about the speech and nonspeech qualities of the stimuli. For example, varying the intensity of the third formant transition affected only judgments about the perceived loudness of the chirp, and not the overall syllable. The implication is that the third formant transition undergoes two modes of processing simultaneously, and that one of these modes is used in the perception of speech (see also Nusbaum, Schwab, & Sawusch, 1983).

Further evidence for the view that speech sounds undergo special processing comes from studies that have employed ambiguous stimuli (Bailey, Summerfield, & Dorman, 1977; Best, Morrongiello, & Robson, 1981). Bailey et al. created a set of nonspeech stimuli by replacing the formant structure of synthetic speech syllables with frequency- and amplitude-modulated sinewaves. Of most interest was their finding that perceptual boundary shifts occurred when subjects were instructed to hear the stimuli as speech rather than nonspeech sounds. Unfortunately, Bailey et al.'s results are clouded by the fact that in a second experiment there was little evidence of a difference in the performance of subjects who heard the sounds as nonspeech. However, a more recent investigation by Best et al. (1981) upholds Bailey et al.'s original finding of differences under speech and nonspeech expectations. More specifically, Best et al. observed a trading relation between two cues—the onset value of the first formant and the duration of a silent closure interval following an initial fricative sound—only when subjects perceived the sinewaves as speech. No subjects who interpreted the sinewaves as nonspeech stimuli gave any evidence of employing a trading relation between the first formant onset value and silent closure interval. This finding suggests that subjects are employing different criteria in evaluating speech and nonspeech signals.

The Speech Mode as an Interpretive Scheme

To the extent that listeners weight the information available in the acoustic signal differently when they are set to interpret it as speech, it becomes sensible to refer to a special mode of perception for speech. The studies involving duplex perception and ambiguous sinewave stimuli are suggestive of such specialized processing. There are at least two possible ways by which specialized processing of speech might occur. First, the speech signal might undergo some form of special sensory coding. Second, no special perceptual mechanisms may be involved; instead the special processing may take the form of certain strategies used when treating the acoustic signal as a linguistic message (phonological categorization). As noted earlier, the available data from the infant and animal studies would seem to favor the second explanation for the existence of a special speech mode of perception. By this latter view, the speech mode of perception develops as a consequence of trying to attach linguistic meaning to speech. The speech mode is not the result of a set of specialized innate perceptual mechanisms; it is an interpretive scheme for weighting the acoustic information gained via general auditory processing mechanisms. In other words, the difference between speech and nonspeech modes of perception lies solely in the weightings assigned to various aspects of the acoustic signal. A similar view of the differences between speech and nonspeech processing has been expressed by Oden and Massaro (1978).

THE RELATIONSHIP BETWEEN INFANT SPEECH PERCEPTION CAPACITIES AND LANGUAGE ACQUISITION

Modifications of Innate Capacities that Arise in Acquiring a Language

The research that we have reviewed to this point suggests that when infants approach the task of acquiring a language, they are already in possession of a number of important speech perception capacities. For example, categorical discrimination and perceptual constancy provide the infant with a means of coping with the variability that exists between speech tokens of the same type when produced by different speakers or by the same speaker on different occasions and at different speaking rates. The fact that such categories exist for infants reduces what otherwise would be an infinite variety of different types of speech sounds down to a manageable few. If languages differed only in which subset of categories they include and *not* in where the boundaries for the same categories are drawn (i.e. the spectral and temporal characteristics of the categories themselves), then the task of acquiring the sound structure of a language might be reduced to determining the correct subset of the categories and the appropriate rules for combining them. However, the available data suggest that the situation is more complicated than this. Although research on this problem has been extremely limited, there is some evidence that differences do exist in the location of the perceptual boundary for certain phonemic contrasts. For example, Williams (1977a) has shown that the perceptual boundary for voice-onset-time differences occurs at about the +4 msec for Spanish speakers, but at about +25 msec for English speakers.

Cross-linguistic results for adults stand in marked contrast to those obtained for infants. Infant studies indicate a relatively uniform perceptual boundary for discriminating voice-onset-time differences in infants of different language backgrounds (e.g. English [Eimas, Siqueland, Jusczyk, & Vigorito, 1971], Spanish [Lasky, Syrdal-Lasky, & Klein, 1975], and Kikuyu [Streeter, 1976]). Together, the findings for infants and adults suggest that infants must learn not only which categories their language includes, but also how the category boundaries are drawn in their language. Thus, any attempt to relate early speech perception abilities to the process of language acquisition must take into account the fact that these capacities are themselves shaped by the nature of the phonemic categories of the language being learned.

The Nature of the Infant's Representational Units for Speech

Putting aside, for the moment, the fact that the sound properties of the language being learned will ultimately affect the nature of the perceptual categories, what can we say about the nature of the infant's earliest representations of utterances in a given language? At first glance, it might seem reasonable to assume that the earliest representations are directly equivalent to categories based on the finest discriminations that infants are capable of making. However, even if one were able to counter arguments that test conditions in infant speech perception experiments seldom replicate those of the infant's natural environment, it would not necessarily follow that the infant's representation of speech sounds would be equivalent to units corresponding to the minimal contrast discriminable between any two utterances. Thus, the finding that infants are able to discriminate between two utterances that differ by only a single phonetic feature does not necessarily imply that they represent the utterances as collections of features, or even as a series of phonetic segments. A global representation of the utterances is also a possibility, provided that it serves to differentiate them.

In fact, discrimination data alone will not permit us to determine the units that the infant uses to represent speech. For, although these data might inform us of the fact that the infant is able to discriminate the occurrence of a given phonetic segment, say [b], in all possible syllable contexts from every other type of phonetic segment, it does not necessarily follow that the infant perceives the [b]'s in [ba], [bo], [bi], or [bu] to be the same element. The only way to determine the latter is from studies that explicitly test categorization.

Unfortunately, attempts to do so directly have been unsuccessful up to now, and what indirect evidence there is that the infant might recognize the same consonant (e.g. |b|) across different syllable contexts (e.g. |ba|, |bi|, etc.) is, at best, equivocal (Katz & Jusczyk, 1980).

The first issue to be considered is what form the basic representational units for infant speech perception might take. There seems to be some agreement in the field that the stretch of information that the infant deals with in processing speech has a duration of at least one syllable length or longer (Aslin, Pisoni, & Jusczyk, 1983; Bertoncini & Mehler, 1981; Eimas, 1983; Jusczyk, 1982).[1] The chief grounds for arguing in favor of the syllable comes from two sources. First, there is the failure to produce clear-cut evidence that infants recognize the identity of phonetic segments in different syllable context, e.g. the [b] in [bi], [ba], [bu], [bɔ] (Jusczyk & Derrah, in preparation; Katz & Jusczyk, 1980). Second, Bertoncini and Mehler (1981) found that infants were better able to discriminate speech patterns that conformed to lawful syllable structures than those which violated such structures (e.g. when the stimuli consisted only of clusters of consonants).

Consideration in Devising an Efficient Means for Word Recognition

One fundamental prerequisite for acquiring a spoken language is to be able to identify the different words of the language and to be able to discriminate them from one another. In other words, the infant must begin by acquiring some sort of vocabulary in the language. To be sure, the infant will also have to learn the rules for lawfully relating the words of the language to one another in complex utterances, but the first step has to involve learning to recognize the vocabulary items that will be related to one another. Moreover, another consideration is the speed with which the words can be recognized. The skilled listener is normally able to understand speech spoken at rates of three or four words per second. Thus, a constraint on language learners is that they must arrive at some sort of organization that makes it possible to understand speech produced at such rates. Clearly, a process for recognizing speech that involved exhaustively comparing the incoming signal serially to all elements in some mental lexicon would not be a plausible procedure given the time constraints. Hence, one expects that there is pressure on the infant to organize the items-to-be-learned in such a way to facilitate the rapid recognition of words. Undoubtedly, the infant's innate endowment, particularly the basic speech perception capacities, is a critical factor in determining how the items in the recognition vocabulary will be organized. In addition, it is likely that the sound properties of the language

---

[1] Whether the infant's representational unit may actually be longer than the syllable is addressed in the comment papers and my reply to them.

being learned also constrain the form of the organization that the listener employs. Indeed, it may be that the attempt to find the optimal organization for processing words in a particular language is ultimately responsible for the cross-language differences in perceptual boundaries that have been observed for adult listeners. Finally, within a given language, words often take on multiple forms and the relationships between these forms are generally lawful (e.g., the relationship between singular and plural forms of the same word). For the average listener such variations apparently pose no great difficulty, even on first hearing a new variant of some familiar lexical item, provided that the context is appropriate. Thus, the underlying organization for the word recognition process should be structured so as to permit these generalizations to occur naturally.

The Relationship of Infant's Representation of Words to Speech Perception Capacities

From the point of view of the perception of speech, when infants learn a particular word, they must store some form of representation of that word that can be used to check against information available from the auditory analysis of incoming utterances. When there is a satisfactory match between the output of the analysis and the stored representation for a given word, then the particular word will be recognized. There are two important points to be made here. First, it should be obvious that the auditory analysis of utterances goes on even before the infant has "learned" a word. In fact, it is this analysis that is the source of the infant's discrimination of speech sound contrasts in the typical speech perception experiments. Second, the information that is stored as the representation of a word is only an approximation of that available for the auditory analysis. Thus, the infant might begin by selectively storing from the information in the auditory analysis only a few highly salient properties of the word such as its prosodic structure and overall acoustic shape. Later this representation would be augmented by the addition of other information from the auditory analysis that would help serve to distinguish it from other words with similar sound properties. In effect, the information contained in this representation would constitute a prototype of the sound properties of the word.

It is useful to consider the nature of the information available in the analysis of the incoming acoustic signal. The speech signal itself is transformed in various ways by the peripheral auditory system. The transformations involved are a consequence of such things as the temporal resolution of the auditory system, the sensitivity of the ear to different frequencies, auditory masking, and the like. Analytic processing routines applied to this transformed signal provide a description of the important acoustic characteristics present in each utterance. In essence, these analytic processing routines comprise the dimensions on which any acoustic stimuli- speech or nonspeech—might be compared. Categorical decisions are based on the outputs of each of these analytic processing routines. The routines are part of the innate endowment of the infant, which explains the similarities observed in the early processing of speech sounds by infants from different language backgrounds.

The Development of a Word Recognition Network

The analytic processing routines yield an auditory description of the incoming acoustic signal which forms the basis for any representation of a word that the infant might develop and store. At first, new words might be stored as separate entities with no particular organization relating them, other than that they are language items. Consequently, whenever the infant attempts to identify a particular word, it would be necessary to search exhaustively through the set of stored items until a match was obtained. Whereas such a procedure might be workable as long as the number of items to be searched remained small (say less than 50), it would soon become unwieldy as the number of items greatly increased. At this point, some sort of systematic organization of the representations of the vocabulary items would be required. It is reasonable to suppose that this organization is based on characteristics of the information available in the representations.

One suggestion is that information about the spectral characteristics of the onsets of words could provide the basis for the organization (Jusczyk, 1985; Klatt, 1979a). According to this view, words having similar spectral onset characteristics would occupy positions relatively close to one another. The obvious reason for choosing an organization on the basis of onset characteristics is that this matches the temporal sequence of the input string, and would allow the perceiver to begin processing the incoming utterance before it has been completed. In addition, there is evidence to suggest that the rapid transitions present in the onset of CV syllables are perceptually salient (Stevens, 1975). An organization of this sort, whereby processing can begin immediately, allows the listener to cope with the speed with which successive words are presented under normal speaking conditions. The perceiver essentially narrows the size of the set of the items to be searched during word recognition to a smaller set having similar onset characteristics.

Given our original assumption of a representational unit on the order of a syllable, it would follow that syllables having similar onset characteristics would be grouped together, and especially that multisyllabic words having the same initial syllable would occupy adjacent locations. For multisyllabic words, the spectral onset characteristics of noninitial syllables would further constrain the location of these words in the growing recognition network. For example, the fact that "cancer", "candy", "candidate", and "cantankerous" share the same initial syllable would ensure that they would be located in the same general area in the network. In addition, the information about the spectral characteristics of the second syllable would serve to locate "candy" closer to "candidate" than to "cantankerous." Although we have posited an organization for the recognition network based on the spectral onset characteristics of syllables, it is certainly plausible that some other aspect of the information available through the analytical processing routines is selected.

Developmental Changes in the Representation of Words

Let us consider in more detail the nature of the representations employed in the network. As noted earlier, the initial representations are likely to be quite global, incorporating a limited number of salient features of the auditory form of the word. In this respect, our view parallels that of researchers studying the acquisition of phonology who have suggested that the initial phonological distinctions occur between global features of whole words, with a gradual progression toward more fine-grained units such as phonemes (Ferguson, 1978; Menyuk & Menn, 1979; Moskowitz, 1973). As the size of the vocabulary grows, there will be increasing pressure to make the form of the representation more specific, in order to differentiate it more readily from similar words. Then the specific nature of the sound structure of the language itself begins to have an impact on the relationship between the acoustic characteristics of a word and its representation by the infant. Specifically, from the information available through the analytic processing routines, the language-learner must devise a representation for a particular word so that it has the greatest number of properties in common with the various tokens of that word, yet the fewest number in common with utterances of different words. In other words, the language-learner's representation will take the form of a prototype (Hyman & Frost, 1975; Posner & Keele, 1968; Rosch, 1978). As Osherson and Smith (1981) have noted, representations in the form of prototypes are particularly well-suited for identification procedures that require rapid decisions about category membership.

The prototype associated with a particular word would likely undergo continual refinement as the infant mastered the phonological structure of the language. In refining a prototype, the infant might learn to weight the information available through the analytic processing routines in certain ways. Certain aspects of the information available from the analytic processing routines will be deemed as more important indicants of distinctions between words in the language than others. In effect, the perceiver prioritizes which sources of information are to be checked and the relative importance of each in matching the input to the prototype during word recognition. In some cases, it is possible that the analytic processing routines themselves undergo some modification. For example, the criterion value used to determine which of the possible acoustic descriptions that the routines will select would be

reset from some initial default value to another one given the nature of the
language input. (For a suggestion as to how such retuning might come about,
see Aslin & Pisoni, 1980.) Thus, in order to refine the prototype in an appropriate manner, the infant develops a scheme or prescription for weighting the
information to be used in recognizing words in the language. This scheme,
which is specific to the language being learned, will be directly reflected in
constraints that guide the formation of the representations to be used in
recognition.

Let us consider how the phonological structure of a given language might
influence the weighting scheme that the infant develops. Voicing differences
signal contrasts between words in many languages. However, as Lisker (1978)
has noted, there are many different acoustic correlates of voicing information.
In any given utterance, several of these different correlates are likely to occur in various combinations. Consequently, as studies of cue trading have
demonstrated (Repp, 1982), perception of such features as voicing is a complex function of the particular combination of correlates that are available in
the utterance.

It is reasonable to suppose that languages differ in the exact manner in
which such correlates are used to signal voicing changes so that different
languages select different aspects of the acoustic signal. A case in point concerns voicing changes in English and Spanish. In Spanish, the determination
of voicing contrasts between words is largely dependent on whether voicing is
present at the onset of a segment, whereas in English many so-called voicing
contrasts are cued by differences in the amount of aspiration (voiced sounds
being unaspirated and voiceless ones generally aspirated as Ladefoged [1971]
has noted). In addition, the duration of the voiced first formant transition
tends to correlate with the English voicing contrast (Stevens & Klatt, 1974).
On the other hand, Macken (1980) has reported that Spanish speakers substitute a stop-spirant distinction for voicing contrasts in utterance initial
positions 30–40 percent of the time and that Spanish-learning children first
employ the stop-spirant for this purpose in their early productions as well.
Therefore, given the present view, one would anticipate that English and
Spanish speakers have developed different means of weighting information
relating to voicing contrasts. The available perceptual evidence is certainly
consistent with this view, since it is known that the category boundary for
voiced–voiceless contrasts differs for the two languages (Williams, 1977a, b).
It follows that the cross-language differences found in studies of adult speech
perception are a direct consequence of the development of the weighting
schemes incorporated into the prototypes.

Not only does the present view account for cross-language differences in
speech perception, but it also helps to account for similarities and differences
that occur in speech and nonspeech processing. For example, since categorical perception is attributable, at least in part, to the analytic processing

routines, it is not surprising that it will be present for certain nonspeech contrasts as well as for speech contrasts. Moreover, since the information available through such routines will be weighted in special ways for speech contexts, some differences might be expected in the way in which the same acoustic information is perceived in speech and nonspeech contexts. In effect, the specialized phonetic processing of speech that has been observed in various experimental settings (Liberman, 1982) is the natural outcome of developing a weighting scheme for recognizing words in a particular language.

The Word-recognition Network and Phonological Development

Having considered some aspects of the way in which the structure of the representations of the individual words develop, we turn to a further examination of the word-recognition network and its relation to phonological development. One important issue concerns the way in which the ability to analyze words into component phonemes arises. Recall that the perceptual units that we postulated are of syllable length. The organization of the word-recognition network helps to explain how the ability for phonemic segmentation might arise. Words that share common initial segments would tend to be located in close proximity to each other owing to similarities in their acoustic characteristics at onset. Pressure to implement some further segmentation of the perceptual units could possible lead to a search for commonalities between items in the same general vicinity in the network.[2]

Common characteristics shared by a large number of items in the same general vicinity might serve as an initial basis for developing a means of representing individual phonemic segments. Once again, this would amount to developing a prototype, only in this instance for a phonemic segment. The phonemic prototype in this instance would be used either to match the output from the analytic processing routines in the case of new words to be analyzed or to match the information encoded in the prototype for the whole word when decisions regarding previously stored items are required. One important caveat is necessary here. Although phonemic segmentation might arise as a result of operations performed on the word-recognition network, it would not necessarily follow that the network would be reorganized so as to provide a segment-by-segment analysis of words during the course of online processing. Instead a segment-by-segment analysis might constitute an entirely independent process occurring only in special circumstances (e.g., when encountering a nonword or an unfamiliar word).

It is difficult to say exactly when the child begins to engage in phonemic segmentation. It is improbable that this type of process is one that infants

---

[2] Such pressure might come about in the context of language play (e.g., games or rhymes) or in connection with learning to read.

would use. There is some suggestion that the ability to perform phonemic segmentation is one that arises in conjunction with learning how to read (Liberman, Shankweiler, Fisher, & Carter, 1974; Walley, Smith, & Jusczyk, 1980). In fact, Morais, Cary, Alegria, and Bertelson (1979) have reported that illiterate adults were unable to learn a task that involved segmentation into phonemes even though they were able to master the same task when it involved manipulating syllables.

Although we have not presented an explicit time frame for the development of the word-recognition network, it is likely to be a rather lengthy process perhaps beginning as young as 9 months of age (Werker & Tees, 1983), lasting several years and covering much, if not all, of the period studied in investigations of the acquisition of phonology. In this regard, it is worth noting that the present proposal is compatible in a number of respects with much recent theorizing about phonological development. More specifically, there has been a recognition of the need to separate rules that relate to output constraints on what the child is able to articulate from those that relate to generalizations about the sound structure of language (Ingram, 1974; Kiparsky & Menn, 1977; Menn, 1980). Much of the early behavior of the child is best viewed as the acquisition of rules for pronunciation, rather than as acquiring rules' regarding generalizations about structural properties of the language. Changes in pronunciation tend to occur first for individual words and only later does there appear to be an attempt to generalize the potential rule to other words in the child's vocabulary (Ferguson, 1978). The latter tendency is apparently responsible for the instances of overgeneralization and regression in pronunciation that have often been observed (Kiparsky & Menn, 1977; Smith, 1973). There is a tendency for the representation of words to undergo increasing phonological organization during the course of development.

It is quite likely that developments in pronunciation rules would affect the word-recognition network that is proposed here. For example, the effort to generalize rules for pronunciation may be a factor that leads to the search for commonalities between different words resulting in the development of representations for individual phonemic segments. Knowledge gained about phonological regularities in the language might be directly incorporated into the network in ways that might help to facilitate word recognition (e.g. by providing shortcuts or alternative routes as Klatt [1979a] has suggested). One consequence of this reorganization would be that, during on-line processing, it would not be necessary to postulate the explicit application of phonological rules. Instead the apparent application of such rules would be a by-product of the way in which the recognition system is structured—i.e., the rules would be "pre-compiled" into the network. The effort involved in organizing the network in this way might be considerable, yet the payoff would come in terms of the increase in speed that it would permit in on-line speech processing.

CONCLUSIONS

The model that we have presented here is highly speculative and preliminary. There are a number of issues that we did not address; the ones that were discussed are supported by data that is by no means conclusive. For example, we have had little to say about the relationship between representations for perception and production. Nor have we provided any specific examples of the kinds of phonological rules that might be expected to change the weightings given to the outputs of the analytic processing routines. Still another problem that requires attention is the manner and degree to which information about stress patterns is represented in the word-recognition network. More precise information is also needed about just what information is included in the earliest representations of words. Despite these shortcomings, we believe that the present account is a reasonable first step in viewing the transition from prelinguistic to postlinguistic speech perception capacities.

Patricia K. Kuhl: Reflections on Infants' Perception and Representation of Speech

Developmental speech perception is noted for its phenomena. These phenomena show that the perception of speech by infants is highly structured. Phonetic boundaries are upheld, discriminably different members of phonetic categories are equated, and it appears that the auditory and visual concomitants of speech sounds are cross-modally matched. (See Kuhl, In press a, for review.) That we can now form such a list of facts about infants' perception of speech is laudable. Unfortunately, the ease with which we have uncovered the phenonoma has not been matched by equivalent success at building a model of the development of speech.

In his paper, Jusczyk attempts to remedy this by taking an initial step towards model building. In the process, he provides a review of the studies on infants' perception of speech, and the classic issues that those studies address. He takes on a very difficult task by attempting to link developmental speech perception and developmental phonology. Jusczyk's paper is organized in three parts: (1) a review of studies illustrating infants' speech perception capacities; (2) comments on a classic issue in the field—namely, are the mechanisms underlying speech perception in infants ones that evolved specifically for speech?; and (3) speculations on the principles by which infants organize and represent the initial lexicon. In the remarks that follow I will comment on selected portions of Jusczyk's paper, and discuss findings from my own laboratories that further extend our knowledge of infants' and animals' perception of speech. My comments will focus on four points. They are: (1) the representation issue—specifically, do the available data suggest that the unit of analysis is the syllable, and that the syllable is represented as an unanalyzed whole?; (2) the contribution of two kinds of studies to the "special mechanisms" debate—specifically, do non-speech studies and studies on the perception of speech by animals test equivalent hypotheses?; (3) the current conclusion regarding infants' speech perception abilities—specifically, do they involve the use of special mechanisms?; and (4) the model issue—specifically, can we meaningfully relate the literature on infants' perception of speech to that on infant's production of speech in order to build a formal model of speech development?

INFANTS' SPEECH PERCEPTION ABILITIES

It is most appropriate that the conference participants have reminded us that speech does not lack variability. What seems remarkable regarding infants' perception of speech, therefore, is not that infants display an ability to hear the differences between speech events, but that they demonstrate an ability to perceive the similarities among them to sort them into categories. Thus, Jusczyk begins by citing two examples of the infant's ability to perceive speech-sound categories.

Categorical perception: The perception of differences

The first example involves the classic studies of categorical perception in infants under 4 months of age (Eimas, Siqueland, Jusczyk, & Vigorito, 1971; Eimas, 1974, 1975). These studies show that when sounds are synthesized such that a set of properties underlying a single phonetic feature is manipulated in small steps, infants discriminate phonetically different sounds while failing to discriminate phonetically equivalent sounds. Moreover, recent studies by Eimas and Miller (1980a) show that the boundaries between categories shift appropriately when the duration of the utterance is altered. Thus, a longer syllable necessitates a longer formant transition before adults hear [b] change to [w], and infants' perceptual boundaries are located such that they are consistent with these shifts. This sensitivity to contextual variation is of great importance in the organization of sounds into linguistically relevant categories.

Categorization: The perception of similarity

In addition to the infant's ability to perceive the appropriate differences between sounds, more recent data suggest that infants are also capable of perceiving the similarities among sounds belonging to the same phonetic category. My own studies (Kuhl, 1979a, 1980, 1983, 1985) show that 6-month-old infants preserve a "constancy" of sorts, similar to that seen in the classic object constancies in visual perception. The studies show that infants have the ability to perceive the identity of a sound across changes in the size of the vocal tract producing the sound, across changes in the characteristics of speakers' voices, and across changes in the pitch contour used by the speaker.

This work is different from that on categorical perception because rather than measuring the infant's ability to perceive the *differences* between sounds, the work has focused on measures of the infant's perception of their *similarities*. The question addressed in these studies is whether infants perceive similarity among discriminably different instances representing a category. The studies show, for example, that 6-month-old infants recognize that discriminably different instances of a vowel, such as the vowel |a| spoken by men, women, and children using different pitch contours, are similar, and distinct from another vowel, such as |i|, produced by an equally varied group of talkers (Kuhl, 1979a). More impressively, the ability to preserve these speech-sound constancies extends to spectrally similar vowel categories, such as |a| versus |ɔ| (Kuhl, 1983).

Infants also do this for consonants in CV or VC syllables when the vowel's context is altered and when the syllables are produced by different talkers. For example, we have shown that infants recognize that the syllables [sa], [si], and [su], when spoken by four different talkers (2 male, 2 female) are similar, and that they differ from the syllables [ša], [ši], and [šu] spoken by the same four talkers (Kuhl, 1980). Similarly, they recognize that [is], [as], and [us] are similar to one another and that they differ from [iš], [aš], and [uš] (Kuhl, 1980). In the same lab, Hillenbrand (1984) demonstrated that infants perceptually separated syllables beginning with [m] from syllables beginning with [n]. Hillenbrand's (1983) work also showed that infants can recognize the similarity among syllables whose initial consonants share a phonetic feature, such as a group of syllables beginning with a plosive ([ba], [da], [ga]) versus a group of syllables beginning with a nasal ([ma], [na], [ŋa]). Apparently, infants are capable of detecting some relation among the members of these categories, which causes them to group the stimuli together.

Basis of category recognition: Phonetic segment representation?

What is the basis for this category recognition? Do infants' abilities specify a particular kind of representation of these sounds? Do the findings clarify the unit of analysis question?

Infants' perception of similarity does not result from a failure to discriminate. These infants readily perceive the differences between [si], [sa], and [su]; yet, they can also perceive their similarities. What does this indicate about infants' representation of speech? Does it mean that infants represent these syllables as being comprised of two phonetic segments–[C] and [V]–and that categorization derives from the recognition that [si], [sa], and [su] share the consonantal segment [s]? It is possible; these data are fully consistent with the idea that infants have access to a segment-level analysis and in fact, comprise the first evidence, allowing one to entertain such a claim (Kuhl, 1985). However, while infants' abilities can be explained by a phonetic-segment representation, they do not mandate such a representation. When infants recognize that [si], [sa], and [su], though discriminably different, are similar, they must be able to break the syllables down into some kind of subunits that allows them to detect similarity at the beginnings (or ends) of the syllables in spite of differences at the ends (or beginnings) of syllables. In order to do this, infants' underlying representations must allow them to isolate *portions of syllables*, independant of the contexts in which they occur, and to detect that the portions are similar. At the very least, the ability to perceive such similarities must rely on a representation of units that allows the beginnings and endings of CV and VC syllables to be isolated and compared across syllables.

Thus, we claim that infants' representations of syllables allow them to break the syllables down into "parts." These "parts" could be phonetic segments or features, in which case infants' detection of similarity is based on the perception of a common identity at the phonetic-segment level ($|s|$ and $|š|$) or at the phonetic-feature level. However, it is also possible that infants could succeed at the task without having access to segment- or feature-level representations. They could be referencing the representation of a larger unit, such as a syllable, as long as the representation is comprised of subunits that allow infants to detect a similarity between syllables whose initial portions are identical, but whose final portions are not.

In summary, the studies show that infants categorize as similar phonetically identical vowels, syllables whose initial or final consonants are the same, and even syllables that share a common feature. These data are consistent with the notion that infants represent speech using phonetic segment- or feature-level units. However, the data do not rule out other possibilities. Any form of representation that allows *portions of syllables* to be isolated and compared can account for the data. Thus, if the syllable is *the unit of representation*, it is not an unanalyzed whole. It must be comprised of *units of analysis* that allow the detection of similarity for parts that are smaller than the syllable. Future research must be directed toward identifying whether these "parts" are phonetic segments, phonetic features, or something else. Regardless of the eventual explanation, we have established that infants are capable of perceiving such similarities by 6 months of age, and this must aid the acquisition of phonology.

ARE THERE SPECIALIZED

SPEECH-PROCESSING MECHANISMS?

To what do we attribute infants' speech perception abilities? This question was taken up by Jusczyk in the second part of his paper. The classic issue is this: Are the infant's abilities attributable to special mechanisms that evolved for speech perception or to other more general auditory perceptual mechanisms? Jusczyk dismisses the claim that infants' abilities reflect the operation of a specialized speech processing mechanism in infants. He uses two lines of evidence to support the suggestion: (1) data demonstrating the replication of speech effects using nonspeech signals, and (2) data replicating speech effects in animals.

My own position (Kuhl, In press a, b; Kuhl & Padden, 1982, 1983) is that it is premature to rule out the possibility that mechanisms especially evolved for speech exist in human infants. The data simply are not yet in. The difference between Jusczyk's willingness to rule out specially evolved mechanisms and my hesitancy to do so rests on the interpretation of tests involving nonspeech signals. Jusczyk treats the nonspeech tests as though they provide critical data concerning the existence of specially evolved mechanisms. As explained below, I think there is a logical problem with invoking nonspeech experiments in this regard.

Nonspeech Tests Versus Cross-Species Comparisons:
Different Contributions to the Special-Mechanisms Debate

It is important to clarify the way in which two different lines of evidence, tests on nonspeech and tests on animals, address the special-mechanisms debate. The two contribute in different ways. Tests on nonspeech address the "tuning" rather than the nature of the mechanisms underlying speech perception. Tests involving animals do not address the tuning issue, but determine whether the existence of a phenomenon *necessitates* specially evolved mechanisms.

There is at present some confusion regarding the contribution of tests involving nonspeech signals. The confusion is due, in part, to the interchangeable use of two terms. The term "speech-specific" has come to be synonymous with "specially evolved for speech." The two are not equivalent. Mechanisms may have evolved especially for the perception of speech without being designed to exclude nonspeech signals. If such mechanisms exist, they would be described as having evolved "specifically for the perception of speech," but they would not be "speech-specific" because nonspeech signals are sufficient to trigger them.

Studies show that the "phoneme boundary effect" typical of categorical perception can be replicated with nonspeech. Given these data, we could conclude that general auditory mechanisms are responsible for both the speech and the nonspeech effects. But it is just as reasonable to argue that mechanisms specially evolved for speech are responsible for both effects. That is, we could argue that the mechanisms responsible are ones that evolved especially for speech, but that the mechanisms are not so narrowly tuned as to exclude nonspeech signals that mimic the critical features in speech.

By this account, nonspeech tests that replicate speech effects serve to equate speech and nonspeech processing and thus tie the two to a common mechanism. But rather than address the mechanism itself (i.e. whether or not it is one that evolved especially for speech), these tests address the selectivity, or "tuning" of the underlying mechanisms. What I am suggesting, then, is that if feature-detecting or other special mechanisms exist, they could be "fooled" by nonspeech sounds mimicking the critical parameters (Kuhl, 1978).

Animal studies contribute to the debate in a different way. They do not address the tuning of the mechanisms underlying speech perception, but the necessity for positing the existence of mechanisms that evolved especially for speech. The successful demonstration of phoneme boundary and other speech effects in animals provides definitive proof that it is possible for the phenomenon to exist in the absence of mechanisms that evolved specifically for speech. This claim cannot be unambiguously supported by the results of nonspeech studies. While tests on animals do not rule out the existence of specially evolved mechanisms in humans, they remove the necessity issue as the sole argument in support of them. As such, successful replications in animals serve as "existence proofs"—they demonstrate the existance of the phenomenon in the absence of specially-evolved mechanisms. They prove that specially-evolved mechanisms are not *necessary* to obtain the phenomenon (Kuhl, 1979b).

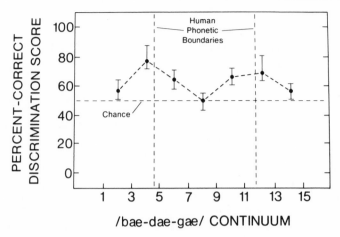

FIG. 1a.1.   Discrimination performance for pairs of stimuli on a [bæ-dæ-gæ] continuum by macaques (Kuhl and Padden, 1983).

To summarize, nonspeech studies address the "tuning" of the mechanisms which underlie speech perception, rather than their origins. Nonspeech tests do indeed examine whether the mechanisms underlying speech perception are "speech spe-cific," but not whether mechanisms evolved "specifically for speech." As such, nonspeech tests do not address the nature and origins of the underlying mecha-nisms, only their exclusion criteria. Conversely, animal studies do not address the tuning of the mechanisms, but directly address the necessity issue. They determine whether a phenomenon can exist in the absence of mechanisms that evolved specif-ically for speech. If animals demonstrate the phoneme-boundary effect, they serve as existence proofs which allow us to state unequivocally that specially evolved mechanisms are not necessary to explain the phenomenon.

Taking these points into account, we can now focus on the speech phenomena that have been replicated in animals. For these cases, it is clear that there is no need to invoke the special-mechanisms argument. Studies on the perception of speech by animals (Kuhl, 1981, in press-b; Kuhl and Miller, 1975; 1978; Kuhl and Padden, 1982, 1983) have focused on the phoneme-boundary effect demonstrated in Eimas' early studies on infants. The data show that the effect can be replicated, both for the VOT and the place of articulation continuua. In our most recent study on macaques (Kuhl and Padden, 1983), discrimination of sounds on a two-formant place of articulation ([bæ–dæ–gæ]) continuum was tested. Figure 1a.1 displays discrimination performance for pairs of stimuli along the continuum. The adult boundaries between the [b–d] and [d–g] categories are marked with vertical dashed lines. As shown, macaques also demonstrate enhanced discriminability at the phonetic boundaries between [b–d] and [d–g].

These demonstrations suggest that the existence of simple phoneme-boundary effects in human infants are not in themselves sufficient to warrant claims for the ex-istence of specially evolved speech-processing mechanisms (Kuhl and Miller, 1975). What remains to be seen is how far animals' abilities extend. We have not com-

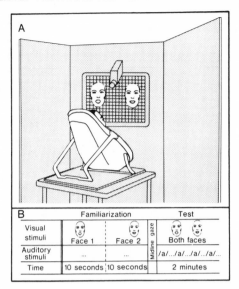

FIG. 1a.2.   A. Auditory-visual speech perception test. B. Experimental procedure (Kuhl and Meltzoff, 1982).

pleted tests on the more complex contextual effects, such as those involving changes in the rate of speech (Eimas and Miller, 1980a), that have been shown in infants. The fact that the rate effects have been replicated in infants using nonspeech stimuli (Jusczyk, Pisoni, Reed, Fernald, & Myers, 1983) is not sufficient evidence to rule out the existence of mechanisms that evolved specifically for speech in infants. The evidence is simply not in. Nonspeech studies will not be sufficient to resolve the issue of the nature and origins of the mechanisms underlying infants' speech perception abilities.

Going Beyond Auditory Tests:
Infants' Cross-Modal Perception of Speech

Infants' abilities to perceive speech go beyond tests involving auditory perception. Recent findings from our lab (Kuhl and Meltzoff, 1982, 1984-a) suggest that speech information may be represented cross-modally in infants. We reported a study showing that infants relate the auditory and visual concomitants of articulation. Figure 1a.2 illustrates the technique. Four-month-old infants were shown two filmed images, side by side, of a woman articulating two different vowel sounds. One image displayed productions of the vowel [a], the other the vowel [i]. A single sound, either [a] or [i], was auditorially presented from a loudspeaker located midway between the two facial images. The two facial images articulating the sounds moved in perfect synchrony with one another.

Infants' visual fixations to the two faces were recorded. The hypothesis was that infants would prefer to look at the face that "matched" the sound. The results confirmed this prediction; infants looked longer at the face that specified the vowel they heard. The effect was very strong—of the total looking time, 73% was spent on the matched face ($p < 0.001$); 24 of the 32 infants looked longer at the matched face ($p < 0.01$). There were no other significant effects—no preference for the face located on the infant's right as opposed to the infant's left side, or for the |a| face as opposed to the |i| face. There was no significant difference in the strength of the effect when the matching stimulus was located on the infant's right as opposed to the infant's left (see Kuhl and Meltzoff, 1984-a, for full details.)

Thus, 4-month-olds perceive auditory-visual concomitants for speech. They act as though they know that |a| sounds go with wide-open mouths and |i| sounds with spread lips. What accounts for infants' cross-modal speech perception abilities? Have infants simply learned to associate an open mouth with the sound pattern /a/ and retracted lips with /i/? We do not favor a simple learning account for the phenomenon, whereby an arbitrary pairing was forged by associative learning (Kuhl & Meltzoff, 1984-a). But if not associative learning, then on what basis is the match between sound pattern and facial configuration made? Two possibilities present themselves. One account argues that the effect derives from a phonetic representation of speech, the other that the effect occurs wholly independently of speech.

The "phonetic account" is itself complicated, with more than a single means by which a perceived match between the information presented to the two modalities can occur. In the simplest case, a perceived match between the optic and acoustic information occurs when identical phonetic information is picked up by both modalities. In this case, the recognition of a common phonetic identity constitutes the basis of a perceived match. Another possibility exists, however, one not requiring the equivalence of information picked up by the two modalities; here the perceived link occurs at a higher ("supramodal") level of representation (Kuhl and Meltzoff, 1984-a). Regardless of the specific alternative, the main postulate of the phonetic account is that the perceived match between the acoustic and optic streams is based on infants' knowledge of phonetics—in this case, their knowledge about the auditory and visual instantiations of phonetic units. Thus, the "phonetic account" suggests that phonetic information per se is represented intermodally.

The second account argues very differently. It holds that the detection of a match is based on "something else," something "wholly independent of speech." By this account, the auditory and visual byproducts of speech are related by some other property, one directed by simple physics. Our current experiments are aimed at separating the physics and phonetics explanations (Kuhl and Meltzoff, 1984-b). We are testing whether some aspect of the formant configuration of |a| (for example, its "compact" nature) is related to an open mouth, and similarly, an aspect of the formant configuration of |i| to spread lips. If this is true, then pure-tone analogs of the three-formant vowels should reproduce the cross-modal effect.

For the purposes of argument, let us suppose that pure-tone analogs were sufficient to reproduce our cross-modal effect. Could we then conclude that the effect occurs "wholly independently of speech"? One could surely conclude that the cross-modal matching effect was not "specific to speech" (since nonspeech sounds were sufficient to reproduce the effect). One could also suggest that rather than phonetic information per se, more general properties relating mouth postures to sounds were represented intermodally. But whether a cross-modal matching effect involving sine-wave analogs and faces could be said to occur "wholly independently of speech" would be difficult to determine for the same reasons provided above in our discussion of nonspeech tests. The non-speech analogs may work because they replicate the critical features in speech.

Under these conditions, it would be an interesting test for our macaques. Should the effect be replicated in macaques (other cross-modal effects, tactile-visual for example, are robust in macaques), then one could claim that the detection of a cross-modal match does not necessitate a phonetic representation of speech. We could then say the effect can exist "wholly independently of speech."

INFANT SPEECH PERCEPTION

AND THE ACQUISITION OF PHONOLOGY

Investigators studying infants' speech perception capabilities and those studying infants' acquistion of phonology have long realized that the phenomena that the two approaches capture and need to explain are different. Perception theorists need to explain infants' exquisite skill at differentiating the sounds of speech, and the extent to which perception appears to be adult-like. Production theorists need to explain infants' nondifferentiation of speech-sound classes, as evidenced by speech errors, and their tendency to preserve prosodic rather than phonetic detail in the production of utterances. Both groups have commented on the difficulty involved in linking the important phenomena in one area to those in the other.

The differences in the phenomena that have been observed by developmental speech perception and speech production investigators are not surprising when one considers the methodological differences inherent in their approaches. These methodological differences fall into three categories. First, the ages of the populations providing the data are different. The bulk of the data on infants' perception of speech has been collected on infants under 6 months of age. The data on production is collected on infants in the transition from infancy to early childhood, typically between 12 and 36 months. Second, the nature of the data being collected is very different. On the one hand we have data concerning the ability to discriminate and categorize speech sounds, usually in simple CV syllables. On the other, we have data concerning the attempted production of meaningful utterances. Third, the experimental questions and the styles in which the tests are conducted are different. Tests of infant speech perception use techniques that maximize performance. Alternatively, measures of speech production occur in natural settings and infants are in the process of communicating rather than demonstrating the limits of their speech production capabilities.

Given this, any attempt to link the two areas is a difficult but important endeavor. So when Jusczyk undertakes a model that tries to incorporate the two, it deserves our attention. Jusczyk focuses on the infant's initial lexical representation.

In so doing, he points up what may well turn out to be a critical distinction between the infant's capacity to discriminate and the capacity to represent speech information.

He discusses a lexical representation based on the assumption that the syllable is the unit of analysis. Words are at first represented by their most salient properties—their prosodic structures and overall shapes. The hypothesis is that the detailed acoustic information discriminated by infants is not contained in the stored representation of speech. Only later is the representation is elaborated by increasingly detailed information. Eventually, the word is represented by a prototype. At first, items form a list, which is searched exhaustively when the infant attempts to identify a word. As the list grows, some systematic organization of it becomes necessary. Jusczyk hypothesizes, along the lines of Klatt's (1980) model of lexical access (LAFS), that the lexicon becomes organized by the spectral characteristics of the onsets of words. As in LAFS, words with similar spectral onsets reside close together. Eventually, the recognition of these common initial segments leads to further segmentation, and finally a representation of phonemic units, also in the form of prototypes, is developed.

The model is an interesting one, and it should be applauded as a first attempt. Phonologists welcome it, not only because it represents one of the first attempts to bridge the gap between two disciplines, but because it incorporates some of the major facts of phonological research. Phonologists have long suggested, based on production data, that phonological distinctions occur between global features of whole words, with a gradual progression towards the resolution of more fine-grained units. It also incorporates the notion that prosodic information is highly salient, another observation based on infants' production of early speech.

The model needs experimental support. It rests on some critical assumptions— that analysis starts at the more global level, perhaps at the level of the syllable, and only later resolves more refined information. The question is: What kinds of experiments can be used to support the notion? What data can be used to determine the units of representation and of analysis? Does the model predict that production and perception rely on the same representation? If so, why are infants' perceptual abilities and their productive capacities so different? What kind of experiments would lead us to tie perception and production to a common representation rather than to two distinct ones?

Another axiom of the model is that words are represented as prototypes. We can offer no information on word prototypes, but have begun studies in our lab which attempt to define a prototype around which infants' vowel categories are organized. I turn now to a short description of those studies.

There is adult work, stemming from the original adaptation studies of Eimas and Corbit (1973) and extended by Miller, J. (1977), suggesting that some exemplars of speech categories are more "potent" than others. These studies show that some stimuli are more effective adapters in adult perceptual adaptation experiments, and more effective competitors in dichotic competition experiments. In vision, the prototypes of natural categories have also been shown to be "preferred" (Bornstein, 1979).

We (Grieser and Kuhl, 1983) set out to examine the internal structure and organization of infants' vowel categories. Our previous data (Kuhl, 1979-a; 1983; 1985) showed that infants recognized vowel categories, but the studies did not aim to specify the organization of these categories. The question addressed in our current studies was whether we could demonstrate an effect of stimulus goodness in infants by testing whether the ability to form categories was affected by the goodness of the stimulus that infants were trained to respond to.

First, we chose a variety of points in an F_1/F_2 coordinate vowel space corresponding to different locations in the [i] vowel category. We had adults rate the "goodness" of these vowels on a scale of 1 to 7. We choose a "good" and a "poor" exemplar of [i]. Around the good and poor stimuli, we created variants that formed "rings" around them. The rings were located at 30, 60, 90, and 120 mels from these points. On each of the four rings, eight stimuli were synthesized, for a total of 32 variants. We then measured goodness for the variants around each of the points.

Our tests on infants were designed to examine whether generalization around a "good" stimulus differed from generalization around a "poor" stimulus. We used a conditioned head-turn technique to examine infants' generalizations to variants around the two points. The results showed that generalization around the good stimulus was significantly broader than generalization around the poor stimulus. Moreover, the subtleties we saw in adults' goodness judgments—the fact that goodness around points was not defined solely in terms of psychophysical distance as measured in mels—were also replicated.

We believe these studies show that some points in vowel space are ideal candidates for category centers, since they are associated with perceptual stability over a broader array of category variants. Other points in vowel space are poor candidates, since perception is not stable and generalization to novel exemplars is weak. These data support the notion first expressed by Ken Stevens (1972), who argued that vowel categories were organized so as to take advantage of the quantal nature of perception.

Thus, the results show an effect of stimulus goodness in 6-month-olds that mimics that shown by adults. It could indicate that infants organize vowel categories around a central good stimulus, and this would be consistent with prototype theory. Further tests involve examining whether the prototype requires experience in listening to or in producing the language. If it does not, the constraints might be innately determined. To examine the nature of inherent constraints, we would attempt to test these effects in animals. If the constraints are purely auditory in nature, then the effects ought to be replicable in animals, but if they are due to inherent knowledge of articulatory dynamics or specific listening experience, then animals should not replicate them.

In summary, infants enter the transition from infancy to early childhood armed with a set of constraints on the organization of sound. Perception is highly structured. Boundaries are upheld, categories are recognized, and these categories may exhibit a high degree of internal organization. The detection of equivalences in speech information presented auditorily and visually suggests that the representation is specified in both optic and acoustic terms. The question is, how is all of this exquisite detail put to work in "Phase 2," when the infant begins to use this information to represent meaningful linguistic entities? My guess is that before we can relate the phenomena of infant speech perception to the acquisition of phonology we will have to map out infants' perceptual abilities during the transition from infancy to early childhood. Hopefully, these efforts will bring us one step closer to building a model of the development of speech.

ACKNOWLEDGEMENTS

The author and the work described here were supported by grants from the National Science Foundation (BNS 81 03581) and the National Institute of Child Health and Human Development (HD 18286). The author thanks Andrew N. Meltzoff and Carol Stoel-Gammon for comments on earlier drafts of this manuscript.

Charles Ferguson: Comment

I found Jusczyk's speculative model for the development of speech perception on the whole plausible, and, as he notes himself, it is compatible with current models of phonological development based on production data. I would like to suggest some additional elements in the model, in the same speculative spirit.

First, it is likely that there are mechanisms operating in addition to the ones Jusczyk proposes. His principal mechanism is that of word-prototypes increasingly refined by virtue of the need to identify more and more words. (This is incidentally quite similar to Lindblom's suggestion (this volume) that phonological development results from the interaction of vocabulary growth and performance constraints.) Jusczyk also proposes the development of a "weighting scheme" to hierarchize the phonetic information used in the child's word-recognition network; this is a valuable addition since it explicitly allows for the important role of the sound system of the input language, which is not sufficiently emphasized in Lindblom's model. Finally, Jusczyk proposes a mechanism of interaction between the growing production repertoire and the recognition lexicon.

These mechanisms provide a plausible account of the gradual, orderly aspects of phonological development (especially when supplemented by Kuhl's notion of focal sounds or "good stimuli"), but they do not attempt to explain the great differences in phonetic accuracy in the production of early words. We would need to add a notion of affective or attentional salience which would allow some words to have much more accurate early prototypes than other words. I would speculate that the kinds of differences that are found in word productions also occur in the perceptual prototypes. Further, I would raise again the possibility that the child's playfulness might also contribute to refinements in word representations apart from the need to distinguish larger numbers of vocabulary items. This playfulness is closely related to the analytic creativity in phonology that is well documented for some children (Ferguson & Macken, 1983; Macken & Ferguson, 1983).

The minor reservations that I would express about the Jusczyk model are ones I would also have about other models of phonological development—the assumption of a crucial role for the syllable somewhat earlier in the infant's development than the evidence calls for and the insistence on unique lexical representations. It seems more likely to me that the child may very well often have multiple representations of the same word, and this possibility should not be excluded just because of the traditional linguistic fondness for parsimony in model building.

In closing, let me note again that the model is speculative and requires data confirming some of its main points as well as more data to flesh out the details. I am continually impressed by the methodological ingenuity of the infant perception researchers and I hope they will turn their attention to what I think is the most promising research area in child phonology—the study of perception between the period of infancy and the later time of fairly full phonology.

Edith M. Maxwell: Comment

There is room for children's creativity and hypothesis-formation, in speech perception as well as in speech production. Children certainly form hypotheses about what is linguistically important in adult speech, and such hypotheses may well be formulated at the perceptual level. If, for example, there are multiple acoustic cues to a particular linguistic contrast, a child listening to those cues may pick up on one of the nondistinctive features as the one important to that contrast, and ignore the rest. This kind of wrong hypothesis should be reflected in perceptual tasks, and might also be reflected in the child's speech production. Weismer, Dinnsen, & Elbert (1981) discuss several misarticulating children who, although they did not produce word-final obstruent consonants, nevertheless maintained differential vowel durations appropriate to the phonemic voicing of the missing obstruent. Vowel duration has been shown to be a strong perceptual cue to the voicing feature of a following obstruent in English and other languages; these children may have decided that paying attention to the vowels was all that was necessary for the language they were hearing.

Philip Lieberman: Comment

Jusczyk develops a plausible and testable hypothesis for the evolution of hypothetical species-specific speech perception mechanisms in humans. The problem has always been that the continuity of evolution argues against the appearance of completely novel perceptual mechanisms in a species. If an entirely new set of neural mechanisms suddenly appear, like perceptual mechanisms tuned specifically to the acoustic characteristic of human speech, then how did they get there? Noam Chomsky simply throws his hands up and argues that new mechanisms like the putative neural "fixed nucleus" that is supposed to structure the syntax of human languages simply appeared suddenly by some process outside of the scope of evolutionary biology. Jusczyk provides an explanation that is essentially another example of Charles Darwin's theory of preadaptation. The Darwinian theory of preadaptation involves the fortuitous possibility for a change in function of an organ that gradually evolved for another purpose. The change in function can follow from a small isolated event. Thus, the respiratory system of terrestrial animals evolved from a system that had been gradually evolving in fish to serve a very different function. The addition of a small slit in the pharynx, the larynx, enabled terrestrial animals to use a system that had been devised for flotation in water, the swim bladders, for respiration. Once terrestrial animals began to use this system for respiration, new selective pressures caused the rapid divergence of terrestrial animals away from fish. The respiratory system started with a comparatively minor change—addition to the swim-bladder system.

One of the interesting effects that we find in the perception of speech is the presence of effects that do not seem to follow from audition. The integrating effects noted by Joanne Miller and the cueing of manner distinctions for stop consonants from the amplitude of the burst and aspiration as well as VOT are, for example, effects that do not appear to have an auditory basis. Jusczyk suggests that neural mechanisms that initially evolved to meet the selective pressures of audition were rearranged for use in speech perception. This is a powerful hypothesis in that it proposes a minimal change that starts the process of evolution of species-specific speech perceiving mechanisms. I think that Jusczyk's hypothesis has more merit as an evolutionary theory than as a description of the present state of homo sapiens. The initial stages of speech perception may have simply involved the rearrangement of neural devices that previously existed to effect auditory distinctions, e.g., sound localization. However, once the process started, once hominids began to use these mechanisms for speech perception, new selective pressures would have entered into the process of natural selection giving us a neural substrate that is in part designed to perceive speech.

I quite agree with Jusczyk and Kuhl in that the neural mechanisms that we use to perceive speech are not so finely tuned that they don't also respond to auditory signals that have some of the characteristics of speech. Data like the perception of the pure tone analogs of speech used by Remez and his associates for example, demonstrate that we will respond to these nonspeech signals as though they were speech signals. The relevant tests of Jusczyk's theory and the putative presence of species-specific neural mechanisms adapted to speech in homo sapiens is likely to come in animal studies.

One last comment on Kuhl's data on the perception of place of articulation by monkeys is perhaps worth noting. The peaks in the discrimination functions that she derived for both her human listeners and monkeys are so low that we cannot be certain that categorical perception is taking place in either population. It will be necessary to replicate this experiment perhaps using synthetic stimuli that have more than two formant frequencies, that establish categorical discrimination in the control human population. Moreover, Kuhl's data are not consistent with earlier data, e.g., that of Morse which show high within-category discrimination of place of articulation for rhesus monkeys.

Peter W. Jusczyk: Some Further Reflections on
How Speech Perception Develops

I would like to take the opportunity to respond to a number of points raised by Professors Kuhl and Ferguson. In particular, I shall discuss (1) the strengths and weaknesses of using data from nonspeech and animal studies to evaluate claims about specialized speech perception mechanisms; (2) the nature of the basic speech perception unit for the infant; and (3) ways of testing the model which I proposed.

First, Professor Kuhl suggests that data from nonspeech and animal studies address different issues concerning the nature of of the mechanisms underlying speech perception. She argues that the nonspeech studies contribute to our understanding of the tuning of the underlying mechanisms but that such studies "will not be sufficient to resolve the issue of the nature and origins of the mechanisms underlying infants' speech perception abilities." On the other hand, animal studies do not rule out the existence of specially evolved mechanisms in humans, but they determine "whether a phenomenon can exist in the absence of mechanisms that evolved specifically for speech." I agree with Professor Kuhl's point that the nonspeech and animal data address different issues regarding the underlying mechanisms. However, I do not agree with her suggestion that only animal studies can bear on the question of the existence of specialized speech processing mechanisms. Rather, I believe that neither type of study can be definitive regarding the existence of specialized speech perception mechanisms. Instead, it is the overall pattern of results from both these domains that presents the most serious challenge to the view that infants are born with specialized speech processing mechanisms. Nevertheless, even in the case of complete agreement between findings from nonspeech and animal studies, it would still be possible (though I would argue quite implausible) for someone to claim that we have not completely ruled out the existence of innate speech perception mechanisms.

The reason why animal studies cannot provide a definitive answer concerning specialized speech perception mechanisms is because, as Osherson and Wasow (1976) have noted, questions about task specificity within a species (i.e., whether a common mechanism underlies performance on different tasks) are logically independent of questions about species specificity (i.e, whether the same mechanism mediates performance on the same task by different species). The two kinds of questions have potentially different answers. Hence, although the demonstration that animals exhibit the same speech perception phenomena as humans would indicate that such phenomena do not require specialized speech perception capacities, it would not prove that in humans such capacities are not used. In other words, it is possible that different sorts of mechanisms produce the same phenomena in both humans and animals.[1]

Professor Kuhl's comment that nonspeech studies address only the issue of the tuning of the underlying mechanisms carries the implication that this issue is not

---

[1] EDITOR'S NOTE: See discussion by Menyuk of differences in human and nonhuman learning conditions, Chapter 4a.

the pertinent one for determining whether the mechanisms are specific to speech or not. I would argue that just the opposite is true. Ultimately, the question of specialized mechanisms hinges on the range or breadth of situations in which these mechanisms operate. Indeed, it is always possible to claim that some specialized speech perception mechanisms were "tricked" into processing a narrow-range of nonspeech signals that closely mimic speech sounds. However, if it can be demonstrated that the range of nonspeech signals so processed is quite broad so as to be encountered in many nonspeech auditory situations in the life of the organism, it seems curious, at best, to label the underlying mechanisms as speech-specific.

Unfortunately, at present we are a long way from determining just how broadly tuned the underlying mechanisms are. To the extent that it is possible to demonstrate that phenomena such as categorical perception, context-effects, and cue trading relationships are widespread auditory phenomena, it will be possible to claim the underlying mechanisms are general rather than specific to speech. For the present, however, we can only base a case on grounds such as plausibility and simplicity. Thus, it is the attraction of being able to provide a single explanation for the speech, nonspeech, and animal studies that favors one based on general auditory mechanisms to account for the perception of speech during the initial state of the infant's life. As I noted in Chapter 1, there is reason to believe that some specialized processing of speech does develop as language is acquired.

Second, both Kuhl and Ferguson raise questions about the nature of the basic speech perception unit for the infant and how one might go about determining it. In some sense, my choice of the syllable as the basic unit is a consequence of the kinds of stimuli used in most infant speech perception studies. An overwhelming majority of these studies have employed contrasts between different syllables. However, it is plausible that the infant might begin with a different sort of unit. If this is so, then it must be a larger unit on the order of the words as Professor Ferguson suggests. Starting with the word as opposed to the syllable as the basic unit would not greatly alter the model which I have presented. The reason why I favor a unit of syllable size or larger has to do with the fact that there is at present little evidence that infants detect commonalities between elements smaller than a syllable. We have attempted several studies in which infants are required to group syllables on the basis of a shared phonetic segment (e.g., [b] in [bi], [bɛ], [bɔ], [bo]) and have not met with any real success (Katz & Jusczyk, 1980). In addition, work by Bertoncini and Mehler (1981) suggests that infants are better able to discriminate stimuli which are arranged into syllabic as opposed to nonsyllabic structures.

In fact, I think that we will be able to gain a better estimation of what the basic processing unit is for the infant as a result of some work that Jacques Mehler and I are concurrently engaged in. We have adapted the HAS procedure to present infants with multiple syllable tokens before shift (e.g., [bi], [ba], [bʌ]). Following habituation to their set of stimuli, we introduce a new token to the set—either a new instance from the same phonetic category (e.g., [bu]) or a new instance from a new phonetic category (e.g., [du]). By comparing the postshift performance of subjects in these two conditions we are able to determine whether the infants recognize any inherent similarity between members of the same phonetic category. By employing the same procedure with multisyllabic tokens, we can determine whether infants will detect similarities between different utterances that contain the same syllable (e.g., [dabi], [bimo], [subi], [bilʌ], etc.). By pinpointing the level at which the infant detects similarities between different utterances, we can begin to ascertain the basic unit of analysis. Depending on the results we obtain with young infants, we can follow any developmental changes that occur in the size of the unit.

I have just alluded to one way of testing some of the predictions of the model; there are other ways as well. For example, Professor Kuhl asks whether one could determine the salience of prosodic information over phonetic information. One problem here is the difficulty in scaling prosodic differences against phonetic ones. However, there are some ways in which we might hope to attain some information regarding the salience of prosodic cues for infants. We are currently investigating the extent to which infants can use the prosodic structure of utterances to assign them to different languages. By carefully filtering the stimuli or alternatively resynthesizing their prosodic characteristics, we can independently vary prosodic and phonetic cues. This will help us to determine the relative salience of each.

Professor Ferguson raised a number of issues pertinent to the model that are worthy of empirical investigation. I was particularly intrigued by his suggestions that affectively salient words might have more fully developed representations than other words and that certain items might have multiple representations. I think that both issues are potentially testable once we obtain a clearer understanding of just what information is typically included in the earliest representations of lexical items.

Finally, I think that one critical area for empirical investigation concerns the extent to which there is evidence for modifications in perceptual boundaries and cue-trading relationships that are concurrent with the acquisition of the phonological structure of a particular language. What is necessary here is to obtain longitudinal data from infants prior to, during, and after the attainment of important landmarks in phonological development. It is a key assumption of the model that important reorganization of basic speech perception capacities will be closely linked to developments in the acquisition of phonology.

2

Discovering Sound Units and Constructing Sound Systems: It's Child's Play

Charles A. Ferguson
Stanford University

Research on child language development generally proceeds under the assumption that the adults of a speech community have a language system that the children of the community gradually acquire. The researchers investigate the path of progress toward the assumed adult target system and relate their empirical findings to the conceptual framework they bring to the study. Thus, structural phonologists have tended to find phonemes, distinctive features, and distributional constraints in phonological development, and generative phonologists have found unique lexical representations and phonological rules operating on them. Such model-influenced findings may contribute to the understanding of processes involved in phonological development as well as to improvement in models of adult phonology; however, the present paper does not start with a theoretical model and apply it to child phonology. Instead, it is written from the perspective of examining striking phenomena in the acquisition of phonology in order to proceed toward the construction of models of phonology or of speech perception and production.

From children's first recognizable words, and even before that, until the time when their pronunciation has pretty well stabilized, there is a tremendous amount of variation in the sounds of their speech. Some of the variation may well reflect the state of flux of a changing, developing system, but some must also reflect children's efforts to arrive at any system at all, i.e. to learn what units at what levels are relevant and what kinds of variation they are supposed to show or are allowed to show under what conditions. This paper will examine some aspects of the child's identification of appropriate *units* of representation or processing and some types of *variation* that frequently appear.

36

UNITS

One central focus of research on child phonology in the last 15 years has been the analysis of the sound systems of individual children, aged 2 to 4 years, as shown by their speech productions (Smith, 1973). The other central focus has been on speech-sound perception by young infants (Yeni-Komshian, Kavanagh, & Ferguson, 1981). The relation between these two lines of inquiry is problematic. Both lines of research have generally taken for granted a phonological unit corresponding to the "segment" of contemporary phonological theories, even though researchers have sometimes been familiar with the problems of relating such abstract units to the processes of speech perception and production. A few authors, however, have raised the question of the child's phonological units in a direct way. Moskowitz (1973) proposed a model of phonological development that provided for the child's successive "discovery" of new units, beginning with the intonation-bearing sentence, ending with the distinctive feature, and placing the syllable as the "phonological elementary unit" somewhere along the way. Each of these units is discovered by the child first as a unit of perception/recognition, then as a unit of production. Each unit remains operative as the child gradually learns to segment it and use smaller units. Also, the capacity to make use of the earlier units remains and leaves important neuromuscular patterns in place: "The fact that [the syllable] was at one time the basic unit of phonological organization leaves its imprint forever on the adult system."[1]

Moskowitz's claims about phonological units were not well supported by empirical evidence. For one step in the process, the child's progression from full reduplication $(C_iV_iC_iV_i)$ to partial reduplication $(C_iV_iC_iV_j)$ or $(C_iV_iC_jV_i)$, she was able to draw on three case studies (Burling, 1959; Leopold, 1947; Moskowitz, 1970), but on the whole her model was speculative. Her account is, however, still worth reading in connection with the issues of this volume: She was explicitly concerned with the child's discovery of "phonetic invariance," her model followed the question of phonological units from infancy to adulthood, and several of her observations foreshadowed later research. Her model emphasized the active, creative role of the child, the existence of extra-systemic "phonological idioms," and the range of individual differences in development, all of which later became important issues in child phonology research. But, her theorizing was too narrowly structuralist in perspective: "[Allophonic] phonetic details rightly do not belong to the structure of language in any way. The child's attention is focused on discovering the completed system upon which is based the structure of phonology." Before progress could be made toward understanding the early stages of phonological development and in particular the organizational units

---

[1] ED NOTE: See Jusczyk's discussion in Chapter 1 for another point of view.

employed by the child, more observations of younger children were needed as
well as more useful analytic techniques than traditional phonemic analysis.

Ferguson and Farwell (1975) examined longitudinal data on the early language development of three children, roughly between 1 and $1\frac{1}{2}$ years of age
(one, H, taken from Leopold, 1947; the other two, T and K, newly recorded).
They added the technique of "phone-tree" analysis to the methodological
armory of child phonologists.

Phone-tree analysis is a technique that makes it possible to follow the
development of sounds in relation to their occurrence in words. After the
child speech samples have been phonetically transcribed, all renditions of a
given word at a given session (or time period treated as a unit, e.g. weekly or
monthly aggregates) are grouped together and all variants of the consonants
in a certain position (e.g. word-initial) in those renditions are noted.[2] Then
all words beginning with the same phone or set of variant phones are put
together. The set of consonantal variants of each of these groups of words
constitutes a "phone class," and is represented by the appropriate phonetic
symbols in a box. Thus an initial-position phone class $\boxed{d \sim t^h}$ consists of
the initial consonants of all those words whose initial consonant sound varied
between [d] and [t^h]. All the phone classes of one child at one session are
represented by boxes in a horizontal row, arranged roughly in order of place of
articulation. Thus a child might show three phone classes of initial consonant
at a particular session:

The phone classes of different sessions are constructed according to the
occurrences of the same word. With each session making up a horizontal
level, solid vertical lines are drawn between successive phone classes if they
contain the same word. If successive phone classes do not contain the same
word but are related to phone classes that do, they are connected by dotted
lines.

Dotted lines are also used to connect phone classes that are each well motivated and are phonetically close or identical but share no words in common.
These diagrams connecting corresponding phone classes of successive stages
are "phone trees"; from them one can see at a glance the child's path of
phonological development during this early period and compare it with the
paths of development of other children.

---

[2] The use of such terms as "consonant" and "phone" is not intended to imply segmentation
by the child. They are used for convenience to refer to stretches of speech sound or the
articulatory movements producing them even if these are not analyzed by the child as
entities at some abstract level of language programming.

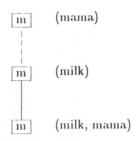

This whole procedure is in principle automatable and the analyses could be presented in other formats, but the explicit relating of words and sounds avoids some of the pitfalls and biases that may appear in other descriptions, notably imputing to children phonemic contrasts not in their production repertoire. For explanation and justification of the technique, see Ferguson & Farwell (1975).

Word Units

One finding of the Ferguson & Farwell (1975) study was that the unit of contrast in production at that period of development is predominantly the whole word rather than the syllable or the segment. The term "word" is used here in the sense of any apparently conventionalized sound-meaning pair, whether based on an adult word or created by the child with no obvious adult model. If the word is based on an adult model, the target may in some instances be a string longer than an adult word or it may be an adult onomatopoeia or other vocal symbol not usually regarded as a word. For example;

	Child's word	Source
from adult model		
word	[ba]	ball
larger-than-word	[kju]	thank-you
vocal symbol	[š:]	sh!
no adult model	[di:]	("look at that")

Given the limited focus of the study—the relation between words as entities and their consonantal beginnings—the evidence for the whole word as the unit of contrast in production was plentiful and of at least three kinds.

(a) *Variable stability.* The consonantal onset may be stable in one word and variable in another even though the two words seem comparable in articulatory difficulty or begin with the same consonant in the adult source word (e.g. H had stable *Carolyn* [da-da] for months but unstable *ball*; T had stable *book* but unstable *baby*).

(b) *Segmental mismatching.* Consonantal onsets of the child's words may show splits and combinations with respect to the adult initial consonants. For example, K had an "m" phone class of words starting with m but occasionally with n in adult words, a "b" class of words starting with b or occasionally with m in the adult models, and a small "n" class of words beginning with adult n).

(c) *Prosodic variability.* A child's word sometimes shows such variation in articulatory features and their position in the word that the child seems to have located such features as somewhere in the word rather than in particular segments in a particular order. K in a half-hour session produced the following ten forms for the new word *pen*: [mã̃ə] (imitation), [ˋṽ] (imitation), [dɛᵈ̩ⁿ], [hln], [ᵐbõ], [pʰln], [tʰn̩ tʰn̩ tʰn̩], [baʰ], [dʰauᴺ], [buã̃]. She seemed to be trying to sort out features of nasality, bilabial closure, alveolar closure, and voicelessness.

Phonological Idioms

A second finding was that early word shapes may be more accurate that later pronunciations of the same words. Although some early words may be considerably modified from the adult target, others may start out in a relatively accurate form that may in the course of time be replaced by modifications that seem to be regressions but represent the partial incorporation of the word into the child's developing sound system. Thus these phonological idioms are not extrasystemic but rather part of the foundation on which the system is being built. For example, H has [ʔələ] for *hello* from 1;5 to 1;10 when it became [jojo]; the change of [l] to [j] represents the operation of a "liquid reduction rule" that is coming into operation at 1;10 and the other changes bring the word into H's set of reduplications.

Lexical Diffusion

Some of the developmental changes in the child's pronunciation proceed through the lexicon in much the way that lexical diffusion sound changes proceed in the history of languages. The same phoneme is not affected simultaneously in all words; the sound change moves from one phonetic environment to another and from one lexical item to another. Such changes in this early period of development may contribute to the gradual establishment of segmental units in the phonological organization of the child's speech. For example, initial voicing spreads through H's lexicon between 1;0 and 1;4, affecting one word at a time, first with labial stop onsets (p- b-) then alveolar (t- d-), leaving a few unchanged relic items until the voiced–voiceless production contrast becomes segmentally established later on.

Individual Differences

A fourth finding relevant to the question of invariance is the individual differences in the path of development and in the phonological strategies that
the children seem to be using in their system building. The three children
agreed in certain aspects of the order of acquisition of initial consonantism;
e.g. all had labial and alveolar stops first, then nasals and semivowels, and
fricatives later still. But the children also had striking differences. One child
had sibilant fricatives and affricates as "favorite sounds": words beginning
or ending with these sounds were welcomed into her vocabulary and used
often although with much variation. The same child seemed to build up her
velar-stop words more than the other two children. A second child developed her active vocabulary slowly and apparently systematically, seeming to
gain control over words beginning with certain consonants and then adding
words to those types; she also whispered many of her words, apparently using
this device to separate homonyms in her output. The third child seemed to
employ an avoidance strategy in the acquisition of labial-stop onsets.

Subsequent studies of the same developmental period, early phonology or
the so-called "50-word stage," using the phone-tree technique, confirmed and
extended these findings (Leonard, Newhoff & Mesalam, 1980; Shibamoto &
Olmsted, 1978; Stoel-Gammon & Cooper, 1984).

In summary, the basic phonological production unit in the period of early
phonology is the whole word shape. The phenomena that point to the existence of smaller (and larger) phonological units than the word are either incipient or nonexistent at this stage. Certain important commonalities appear
in the phonetic shapes of these early words and their phonological development, but each child has a unique pattern of development, as determined by
the particular input received, individual patterns of playing with the input
and the child's own output, the nature of the communicative interaction in
which the child participates, and the various acquisition strategies used.

Ferguson & Farwell (1975) suggested that these early phonology characteristics also remain basic in adult phonology:

> A phonic core of remembered lexical items and articulations which
> produce them is the foundation of an individual's phonology and
> remains so throughout his entire lifetime...though it may be heav-
> ily overlaid or even largely replaced by phonologically organized
> acquisition processes at a later date.[3] ...an adult's ability to
> pronounce his language at any point in his life constitutes a stage
> in his phonological development... Further, since children have
> different inputs and utilize different strategies, the gradual devel-

---

[3] This suggestion was an informal version of a production model resembling the perceptual
model of lexical access proposed by Klatt (1979a).

opment of phonological organization and phonological awareness may proceed by different routes and at different rates; hence adult phonologies may differ from one another just as the lexical stocks of individuals may differ [pp. 437–38].

On the basis of the phone-tree studies already cited as well as detailed diary studies of this stage (e.g., Scollon, 1976, which is independent of the literature cited, and earlier studies, such as Lewis, 1951), we can summarize the early word shapes as follows. They are often open monosyllables. If disyllabic or with final consonant, they often show consonant and/or vowel harmony. The beginning of the word is the position of maximum distinctness where the largest number of different consonantal phone classes is found, new consonant phones tend to appear first, and the consonantal onsets are the most stable. Certain consonantal types are much commoner than others. All 20 children of the phone tree studies reported here had [m- b- d-] as consonant onsets. The next most common were, listed in descending order of frequency [k- w- n- g- p- h-], which were in the lexical repertoires of 11 to 16 of the children; the k- and g- showed more variation than the other phones (in voicing and with alveolar stops; on the precedence of [bdk] in acquisition, see Ferguson, 1975). No other initial consonant phone appeared in more than 6 of the children's repertoires. As an illustration of a set of early words, here are Brenda's at age 1;1.22, presented in a transcription that represents their "most frequent shape" (Scollon, 1976, p. 47):

Child's word	Gloss
awəu	I want, don't want
nau	no
dædi	daddy, baby picture in magazine
dæyu	down, doll
nene	liquid food
e	yes
mæmə	solid food
ada	other, another

Of the phonological acquisition strategies utilized in the period of early phonology, that of reduplication has been discussed the most (e.g. Fee & Ingram, 1982; Ferguson, 1983; Leopold, 1947; Schwartz, Leonard, Wilcox & Folger, 1980). Some amount of at least partial reduplication is very widespread but children differ considerably in the extent to which they make use of it. Reduplication can be seen as an acquisitional strategy that assists in several aspects of phonological development. One possible function is that argued for by Moskowitz (1973): to enable the child to operate with a smaller unit than the word, such as the syllable, as a step toward full phonemic segmentation and specification. Another is that it helps the child to acquire polysyllabic words without having to cope with their internal phonetic complexity. Still another is that it helps in acquiring syllable-final consonants. Some evidence has been found to support each of these developmental functions, but much more investigation is needed.

Some acquisition strategies run counter to the typical trends in development, and their use by particular children is thus very noticeable. For example, as has already been mentioned, in typical early phonology the initial position is the strongest or most salient, i.e. it has the greatest variety of phones, the phones in it are most stable, and the target phones are least likely to be omitted or assimilated. Some few children, however, utilize a strategy of making the final position most salient for consonant variety and stability. Daniel in the Stoel-Gammon & Cooper (1984) study is one such child: At the point when his production vocabulary reached 50 words, he had 8 phone classes in final position, representing 19 words, whereas most English-learning children at that point have perhaps 2 or 3 unstable consonantal codas. For him the initial position still had greater variety of consonant phones but it was "weaker" than medial and final positions in that it suffered more deletion and assimilation.

Daniel (Menn, 1971) gave even greater salience and strength to final position; for him new complex phones (fricatives, affricates, and clusters) made their first appearances there (on the contrasting initial and final strategies, cf. Kiparsky & Menn, 1977). The persistence of such strategy differences between ages 1 and 3 is being examined in a current Stanford project.

Many acquisition strategies seem designed to reduce the complexity of the output, although some seem merely preferences for some alternatives over others without simplification. In any case, these acquisition strategies in early phonology are forerunners of the more segment-oriented phonological production rules that the child constructs between the ages of 2 and 5. Whatever the origins of these strategies in perception, articulation, cognition, affect, or playfulness, they are early instances of the creative effort of the child to discover useful units, construct rule systems facilitating speech production, and get more satisfaction out of the use of language.

A more general phenomenon that can be mentioned in connection with individual differences and acquisition strategies is the use of "proto-words"— items of less phonetic and semantic stability than early words and typically created without adult models. Children vary in the number and characteristics of such proto-words (e.g., exceptional number used by Will in Stoel-Gammon & Cooper, 1984, and by Nigel in Halliday, 1979), but they are quite widespread (each of the ten children in a current Stanford study had at least 2 or 3). This phenomenon is instructive for the child phonologist, not least because it shows the degree of independence possible between recognition and output lexicons. Proto-words most often have the shape CV(C) with a preference for alveolar stops and the glottal [h] and [ʔ], but they may include syllabic sonorants or fricatives, click sounds, and the like that are rare in the world's languages (e.g. Will's [ŋ ŋ] to refer to cars or bicycles).

What I am suggesting in this brief account of units in early phonology is that the child starts with sound-meaning pairings of word size and must actively construct such units as phonological segments and phonological features. I would reject the notion expressed in Gleitman and Wanner's 1982 study on language development that for children "no learning apparatus is required for an initial segmentation of the acoustic wave into discrete phones. The segmentation has been provided in the nervous system [p. 16]."

I would favor the opposite notion expressed by Bowerman (1982) in the same book:

> Forms that to adults have a complex internal structure—that is, consist of subunits with independent combinatorial potential— can be used correctly by language learners before they are aware of their structure ... forms that are initially learned independently of one another can later become integrated into a common rule system [p. 323].

VARIATION

"One of the hallmarks of early language development is phonetic variability," (Leonard, Rowan, Morris & Fey, 1982, p. 55). It is only recently, however, that the great variation in the child's pronunciation of his or her words has become the focus of linguistically oriented research (Ingram, 1979; Leonard, et al., 1982; Menn, 1979; Scollon, 1976). For linguists viewing phonological development as the acquisition of phonemic oppositions (Jakobson, 1968), or the refinement of realization rules (Smith, 1973), variability was an inconvenience to be.acknowledged but not attended to. Neither structuralists nor generativists were interested in the acquisition of allophonic variation or "low level" phonetic rules, surely one of the most impressive feats of the child. To the extent that allophonic variation in any language is not natural or inevitable, it must be learned by the child; since subphonemic differences are by definition not necessary to distinguish words, there is no obvious incentive for the child to acquire them (Ferguson, 1977). Similarly, child phonologists were not interested in the acquisition of the range of phonological variation that marks the speaker as coming from a particular region or social group or marks a conventional style or register of the speech community, although all this is also a part of the phonology-to-be-learned.

Variability in input is present from the beginning, reflecting in part dialect and register differences, but the reaction of the child to such variation has only occasionally been noted (Local, 1983). Input variability is probably less important, however, in accounting for the child's phonetic variability than inherent variability, i.e. that which results from processes internal to the child. The child's inherent variability is of several kinds; these will be discussed from a synchronic point of view in spite of the fact that the child's phonology is always in a state of flux in which the changes come more rapidly and pervasively than in individual adult phonologies or in the phonological systems of whole languages. Each of these types of inherent variability may be viewed also as a stage in what Menn calls "second order long-term variation" (Menn, 1979, p. 170), i.e. the way the variation itself changes over time. In the following discussion, examples will usually be taken from Scollon (1976).

Free Variation

Free variation is simply variation in which no external condition or internal intentionality seems to be determinative. The child repeats what appears to be the same word on different occasions, or successively on the same occasion, with different pronunciations. Brenda's proto-word ⟨awəu⟩ "I want," "I don't want" at age 1;1.22 (or 1 year, 1 month, 22 days) was one item out of an attested production lexicon of 8. Seven different renditions out of 49 occurrences were noted in a half-hour recording:

awʌ	(playing with ice cubes)
avau	(reaching for Suzanne's necklace)
awa	(reaching for necklace again)
awə	(trying to pick up ice cube)
æwəu	
awəu	
avə	(reaching for Suzanne's necklace)
awa	

Brenda's word ⟨bʸæu⟩ 'bear' age 1;7.2 (session lexicon contained 44 items):

bæu	(said while sitting on a toy bear)
biæu	
bʸæ	

In cases like these, the word-shape is apparently not well specified in the output lexicon. The first item ⟨awɔu⟩ has no clear adult model although *I want* and *away* are possible contributory sources. It has achieved the form of non-high vowel + glide + non-high vowel ± [u]; the variation includes [a] or [æ] as first vowel, [w] or [v] or [1] as the medial glide; Brenda only rarely said it without the final vowel, [aw]. The wordshape has become less variable than it was earlier; at 1;0.2 it varied from [awawawa] to [aː] and its renditions included [aba] and [alⁿ].

The second item has a definite adult model *bear* and the variability is limited and shows signs of regular correspondences, e.g. final -r of Brenda's recognition lexicon appears as final [ʔ] [o] or [u] (note that -r varies with 0 in her parents' speech). Menn (1979) subdivides these occurrences of free variation into "local scatter," where the variation indicates lack of articulatory control and "floundering," where the variation reflects the child's inability to specify the item in his or her recognition and/or output lexicon. The difference between the two is clear in definition but often difficult to decide in practice.

Attentional Variation

Many instances of variability in the pronunciation of a word seem to reflect the child's giving extra attention to the pronunciation of the word (or part of it) in relation to an available internal or external target. One subtype is where the child is clearly trying to improve pronunciation in order to be understood or for self-satisfaction. An example of this *clarification/practice* subtype is Brenda's attempt to say *shoe* at age 1;7.2:

š	(Brenda holds up her mother's shoe)
šI	
š	
šIš	
šu	
šuʔ	
šuš	
	(Suzanne says "Shoes!")
š̥i	(whispered)
š̥I	(whispered)
šuʔ	(the "best" pronunciation)

Scollon calls this "production variation" as opposed to "allophonic variation."

Another type, which has been called *trade-off* (Garnica & Edwards, 1977) is where the child pays so much attention to one part of a word that another part of the word is pronounced less accurately or even omitted. An example from Ferguson & Farwell (1975) is the pronunciation of milk as [b̃vʔ] and [ʌk] at the same session, where we assume the child was attending to the beginning of the word in the first variant, the end in the second. Scollon (1976) gives an example where a word is pronounced less clearly when it is said after another one in a presyntactic collocation ("vertical construction"). Brenda at 1;8.21 (session lexicon-71 words) said spontaneously several times [hɛtʰ] for *head*. Scollon then said, "Poor Brenda. Poor Brenda bumped her head. It hurt?" and she responded [bɔmp.hɛ] without the final t. This kind of variation may reflect difference in attention or simply the problem of coping with greater phonetic complexity in the utterance.

Leonard et al. (1982) report three experiments with intraword variability in early phonology in which they asked each child to perform a little bit beyond his or her apparent capabilities at the time, and trade-off variations appeared. The most unusual was the behavior of some subjects in Experiment III, who were asked to imitate specially designed nonsense words and produced two kinds of variants: (a) "production of a limited portion of the word with either accurate production of the target consonant(s) or a production reflecting a simplified process previously seen in the child's spontaneous speech (e.g. [dit] for [ditʃə])" or (b) "a shape that matched or approximated the target shape, but the consonants...were quite unlike both the target consonants and the consonants the child ordinarily used in place of these consonants in his or her spontaneous speech (e.g. [wiwə] for [ditʃə]) [p. 66]."

A third subtype is that of *imitation* versus spontaneous utterance. Often there is no apparent difference between imitated and spontaneous pronunciation, but sometimes the imitated one is more accurate than the spontaneous. Examples can be found where the pronunciation deteriorates (becomes more like the output lexicon target?) as the model recedes in time. Brenda at 1;8.21 said her usual [haidi:] for *hiding*. Scollon said "Hide? What's hiding?" and the dialogue continued:

brũ	
	Oh, the balloon? Where?
	Where is it? Where is it?
haidiŋ	
	Where?
haidi	
	The balloon?
haidih	
haidi:	
haidi:	
haidʸi	

Schema Conflict

Some variation seems to result from the child's subsuming the same word under different schemas; as the child's schemas become more segmental, this variation could be called "rule conflict." One common subtype is the variation that represents a new schema/rule varying with an old one, typically as a transition stage that ends with the victory of the new. As such this is a familiar type of variation in human language, when a change is in the process of spreading. Another subtype is the variation where two or more schemas/rules can all apply. The variation in Hildegard Leopold's pronunciation of *hello* is an example.

Blending

Some variation in the pronunciation of a word is modification toward phonetic characteristics of a neighboring word. This seems to occur most often when the words succeed each other as one-word utterances but are semantically connected (vertical constructions), and for this reason they are usually not noticed by the investigator, who is not looking for such connections. For example, Brenda at 1;7.16 was drawing with her older sister Charlotte, who drew a picture of a girl with long legs and polka dots on her dress. Brenda said *tall* [tʰo] three times, then *Brenda*. Then she said

$$t^h ɔ$$
$$t^h ɔ$$
$$t^h aʔ$$
$$k^h aʔ$$
$$k^h ǝãũ$$
$$k^h ̃ɔ̃ãũ$$

The first repetitions were *tall*, the last ones were *clown* on the basis of her other pronunciations of that word, and the intermediate ones were blends. Brenda was apparently saying *tall clown* in her one-word-at-a-time way and the two words interfered with each other.

Pre-patterning

Leopold (1953) coined the term "pre-patterning" to refer to phonetic characteristics in a child's words that are precursors to a phonemic contrast that will be developed later. Thus in Brenda's first three words ⟨aweu⟩, ⟨nene⟩, and ⟨da⟩, the initial vowel in the first varied between [a] and [æ], the vowels in the second varied along the scale [e] [ɛ] [æ], and the vowel of the third was stable. At this early stage only wordshapes were contrasted (a Jakobsonian phonemic analysis would be /aba/, /nana/, /da/) but the phonetic values of the vowels were closer to the adult models: Japanese baby talk *nen-nen* "sleep" and English *doll*. An allophonic analysis of the vowel variation (e.g. /a/ raised and fronted after a nasal) would be artificial and unrealistic (discussion of such futile phonemics in Ferguson, Peizer & Weeks, 1973; Scollon, 1976, pp. 148–153), but the vowels of ⟨nene⟩ and ⟨da⟩ were like their respective adult models.

Pre-patterning is not a type of variation as such, but it is an useful label for the process of phonetic matching and gradual phonetic approximation to adult models that may operate with or without the development of commutable oppositions at the syllable or segment level. The extreme cases are the phonological idioms that seem beyond the child's output capability or outside the phonological system at the time. For example, Brenda at 1;0.9 said [čoda] based on her mother's Japanese *chodai* "please give it to me" in both pronunciation and use, and a month later at 1;1.8 said [laulau] for *flower*.

BEFORE AND AFTER EARLY PHONOLOGY

This picture of early phonology emphasizes the whole wordshape as the basic contrastive unit of production, individual differences in the utilization of acquisitional strategies, and some general phonetic tendencies. The preceding and following stages can also be characterized in terms of contrastive units, individual differences, and universal tendencies.

The preceding stage, which overlaps with early phonology, is babbling and the transition from babbling to speech. Recent research has established important continuities between babbling and speech (Ferguson & Macken, 1983; Oller, 1981; Stark, 1981) disputing the strong discontinuity position of Jakobson (1968) and others. There is no clear-cut contrastive *unit* in babbling, since this unit is the defining characteristic of speech. Babbling vocalizations differ from early words both by having less meaning and by being more variable phonetically, and they are less stable over time. They show developmental trends in all three respects, however, and investigators find many borderline cases in which highly arbitrary criteria must be used to distinguish them from early words. Children may acquire an adult-model word and then use it playfully in babbling, or they may use a particular babbling vocalization only in certain contexts until it seems clearly to be a proto-word and then shift its meaning or form drastically or drop it altogether.

Individual differences in babbling and the transition period are comparable with those of early phonology and include preferred sequential structures and preferred consonantal onsets (e.g. monosyllables vs. polysyllables, d-favorite). Perhaps the most striking difference is between the extremes of

the jargon babblers who hold lengthy monologues or "conversations" with
natural sounding intonation and prosody but no words, and those who babble
very little but have early proto-words. Often the babbling patterns continue
into the early word strategies (e.g. an unusual child who babbles many [l]-
words acquires [l]-sounds early on in words, and a monosyllabic babbler is a
later non-reduplicator). The Stanford Child Phonology Project is currently
analyzing such persistence of individual differences.

Universal tendencies are present in babbling, e.g. stops are commoner
than fricatives, CV vocalizations commoner than CVC, and reduplicated
babbling precedes "variegated babbling." Finally, we must not forget that
at this stage expressive and communicative events of the infant include head
and body movements, facial expressions, and intonation in addition to the
segmental vocalizations, and these may be combined in various ways. Different ones may have primacy for different children (e.g. one child may build
up a larger repertoire of gestures; another, vocalizations).

The period following early phonology is the time of constructing most
of the segmental phonology and has had the most attention given to it. A
number of competing theoretical models have been proposed to account for
the processes of phonological development (reviews in Edwards & Shriberg,
1983, pp. 163–178; Ferguson & Garnica, 1975). Those currently in the as-
cendancy are cognitive models that emphasize the active hypothesis-forming
role of the child (e.g. Kiparsky & Menn, 1977; Macken & Ferguson, 1983;
Menn, 1976, 1983a). The cognitive theories were developed in reaction to
universalist/innatist models such as those of Jakobson (1968) and Stampe
(1969, Donegan & Stampe, 1979), in the light of such empirical evidence as
individual differences, overgeneralization of phonological rules, and the creation of patterns for which there is no adult counterpart. Although these
models deal more with phenomena at the stage when the existence of segmental contrasts is much in evidence, they do make some claims about the
transition from early phonology.

During this transition, the phonological *units* on the one hand become
more complex phonetically, e.g. the wordshapes lose the severe constraints
typical of early phonologies (consonant harmony, fronting, final devoicing,
etc.); on the other hand, smaller units (syllables, clusters, segments) become
more definitely located within the word and become more commutable. This
whole process is followed in detail for one child acquiring Spanish in Macken
(1979). For that child the basic phonological unit was the word from 1;7 (beginning of the study) until 2;1; between 2;2 and 2;5 the data "could be described adequately in terms of phonemic contrasts, allophonic relationships,
and phonotactic constraints" (p. 44) and there was some weaker evidence
for features as units (for a recent general account of the whole process, cf.
Menn [1983a]). *Individual differences* in order of acquisition, overall learning
style, and details of the mapping rules between recognition and production

lexicons are considerable, and as a consequence *universal tendencies* are the result not only of general human perceptual and articulatory capabilities but also of similarities in the human cognitive processes available for use in analyzing language.

SUMMARY

This chapter, in asserting the relevance of child phonology phenomena for the investigation of invariance and variability of speech processes, has focused on only one period in development: the early phonology or "50-word" stage. It has approached this period from the perspective of units, individual differences, and universal tendencies, under the general assumption that phonological development consists in large part of the child discovering appropriate units and constructing sound systems. Although later periods may be closer to adult speech in the nature of invariances and variability, this early period is worth consideration because the basic production unit seems to be the whole wordshape, and the variant pronunciations of the same word reflect a wide range of processes. Any theoretical models of invariance in the processes of speech perception and production must take account of evidence that children begin with a phonological unit of word size and gradually shift to smaller units, that they show great individual variation in their patterns of acquisition of such units, and that they show certain universal tendencies in preferred phonetic shapes and syllabic structures.

Michael Studdert-Kennedy: Invariance: Functional or Descriptive?

The variability discussed by Ferguson in Chapter 2 is quite different from the variability that has been the focus of much speech research since its inception, and especially of research by Stevens. This focus has been on what we might call "lawful variability": The goal has been to discover the invariants presumed to underlie regular variations in the articulatory and acoustic structure of phonetic elements as a function of stress, rate, and context. On the other hand, Ferguson's concern is with the seemingly unlawful (certainly unpredictable and therefore, in effect, random) variability of early child speech, both within and across children. Moreover, Ferguson's work is mainly concerned with production, while Stevens' interests (at least as they bear on child phonology) (e.g. Stevens, 1975) have largely been in the problem that acoustic variability poses for perception. Finally, even the unit of variation that occupies Ferguson, namely the word, differs from the familiar units of concern in speech research. In spite (or because) of these differences, I believe that the work Ferguson discusses may carry the seeds of a new and fruitful approach to the notorious puzzles of segmentation and invariance.

My purpose here is to trace some implications of what Ferguson describes, as he follows the emergence of the child's first words over roughly the third half-year of life. The unit of contrast at this stage, Ferguson tells us, is the word defined as "any apparently conventionalized sound-meaning pair." The emphasis on function is important. The word is a unit of contrast because it is a unit of meaning, offered by the surrounding language and commensurate with the child's cognitive grasp. This does not imply that other structures are not already being put to contrastive use; for they certainly are, as Menn's (1978a) study of early intonation, for example, has shown us. However, it is Ferguson's hypothesis that the word is the simplest nonprosodic unit with which a child can begin to accomplish some part of its communicative intent.

An important implication of the claim that the word is the unit of contrast is that smaller units—phone-sized segments and features—are not. This does not mean that acoustic correlates of phones and features cannot be described in the utterances of a child. Nor (as we shall see shortly) does it mean that words are perceived by the child as unanalyzed integers. All that it means is that these smaller units have not yet taken on, for the child, the systemic function of contrast that they serve in the adult. To elaborate these notions somewhat, let us speculate briefly on how the child perceives and produces words. Most early words are open monosyllables, or reduplicated syllables, formed by the child's closing and then opening its mouth, usually while its vocal cords vibrate. What must the child do, if it is to close and open its mouth in such a way that the acoustic consequences will count as a word? (I disregard here so-called "proto-words," recurrent phonetic structures that cannot be traced to an adult model.) First, of course, the child must execute the act in some appropriate set of circumstances—a remarkable cognitive achievement that we will set aside. Second, from a phonetic point of view, the child must find, in the acoustic structure of an adult word, information that will specify its own articulators' movements (cf. Browman & Goldstein, In preparation). Third, the child must execute those movements.

At the risk of laboring the obvious, let us roughly spell out the process. Suppose, for example, that a child utters [mɛ], while reaching for a cup, and that an observing adult happily recognizes an attempt at [mɪlk]. Evidently, the acoustic structure of the adult word specified at least the following gestures in a more or less precise temporal arrangement: (1) set larynx into vibration; (2) raise jaw and close lips; (3) lower jaw and open lips; (4) raise velum; (5) raise tongue. Thus, the perceptual representation that controls the child's movements must already have been "segmented" to the extent that it specified the actions of distinct and partially independent articulators.

We may view these actions and their acoustic specifications as precursors of systematic phonetic features, if we wish. But we should not be misled thereby into assuming that the child classifies speech sounds perceptually according to invariant properties shared across contexts. Indeed, evidence for this capacity in infants is quite equivocal (for discussion, see Chapter 3).

Consider the ideal case of a child's first word or first imitation of an adult segmental sound pattern. If the event follows the model sketched above for [mɛ], the child has no need to have "recognized" that components of the acoustic information belong to classes of components whose members occur in other contexts. All that is required is that the acoustic information specify a pattern of articulator action in this word. Thus, for the child, its first word (and indeed every word in its early repertoire) is phonetically unlike every other word in almost every respect. This is the implication, it seems to me, of the claim that the word is the unit of contrast.

To elaborate, let us take the syllables [dæ] and [di], treating them, for present purposes, as items in a child's repertoire. The first syllable of the adult models may have had flat or falling, the second rising second and third-formant transitions, a frequently cited example of a lack of invariance. However, in the present view, we need not suppose that the perceptual representations controlling the syllable onsets, when the child combines them to utter [dædi], are identical. Rather, if the child is tracking the gestures in the speech it hears, it will find a slightly retracted alveolar contact followed by backward movement of the tongue in the first syllable, and a slightly fronted contact followed by forward movement of the tongue in the second, and so will produce just the so-called "coarticulated" pattern it has heard. As the range of contexts in which a child hears and produces alveolar closure and release widens, an auditory-articulatory class may be formed. However, the class qua class initially has no function. Any particular instance of alveolar closure and release is perceived or produced as an idiosyncratic articulatory routine contributing to formation of the particular word to which it belongs. I will not speculate further on the processes by which recurrent articulatory routines or gestures may crystallize into classes of control structures, or phonemes, contrasting systematically in terms of their defining features. These are matters for the child phonologist. But I have two brief disclaimers.

First, the notions sketched above in no way cast doubt on possible functions of features and phonemes in later language. The function of the phoneme, for example, as a control structure in speaking, is demonstrated by the fact that most normal children can learn to consult their own productions and to write alphabetically (sometimes even before they can read). A system of behavioral notation (as in the alphabet, music, and dance) could only serve as a set of instructions to behave, if the instructions matched already existing control structures. Just as the bicycle was a technological discovery of new behaviors implicit in the cyclical mode of human locomotion, so the alphabet must have been a discovery of new behaviors, reading and writing, implicit in the motor control of human speech.

My second disclaimer is that the view taken here has any bearing on whether we may or may not be able to arrive at satisfactory descriptions of invariant classes in the articulatory and acoustic structures of speech. My intent is merely to raise the possibility that such invariants would be simply descriptive, an outcome rather than a condition of development. Invariants, as invariants, may have no necessary function for the child learning to speak.

ACKNOWLEDGEMENTS

Preparation of this comment was supported in part by NICHD Grant HD-01994 to Haskins Laboratories.

Edith M. Maxwell: Comment

Acoustic analysis can be of use in assessing a child's phonological system. There are various cases in the literature where children maintain acoustic distinctions in their speech which correspond to adult linguistic contrasts but which are not apparently perceptible to adult listeners. Macken and Barton (1980) discuss young normally developing children who maintain a difference in voice-onset-times corresponding to the adult English voice contrast in initial stop consonants. The difference was contained, however, within the short lag VOT region, and so was not perceptible to adult listeners (speakers of English). Maxwell and Weismer (1982) found similar results for an older (4 years) misarticulating child. This phenomenon has been seen as well with other instances of apparent collapse of adult contrasts. Examples of this include (1) two kinds of [w] (different formant locations) used for /r/ and /w/ (Kornfeld and Goehl, 1974); (2) the absence of word-final obstruents but duration differences in the resulting word-final vowels (Maxwell, 1982; Weismer, Dinnsen & Elbert, 1981); and (3) a reduced inventory of fricatives but spectral distinctions maintained, e.g. different spectra corresponding to [θ] for /s/ vs. [θ] for /θ/ (Daniloff, Wilcox & Stephens, 1980; Weismer and Elbert, 1982). These are all cases where a phonological analysis based on transcribed speech alone would have failed to represent accurately the child's attempts to produce an adult contrast.

Corine Bickley: Comment

I offer more data which support some of the points made in the Ferguson paper. These data on children's vowel productions give insight into the development of the height and backing distinctions for vowels.

Acoustic measurements were made of the vowels in fifteen children's spontaneously produced words [see also, Bickley (1984a)]. The children were participants in the Language Indices Development project at Children's Hospital in Boston in which each child was observed and recorded on audio tape at one to three month intervals at home. Each utterance was glossed and verified by a speech clinician. Words with known referents were used in this study so that the target vowel could be determined. Only words containing as a target vowel one of the vowels [i], [I], [u], [U], [a], or [ɔ] were analyzed. For the analysis of the height and backing distinctions, these vowels were grouped into three pairs: [i] and [I], [u] and [U], and [a] and [ɔ]. Thus, tenseness was disregarded.

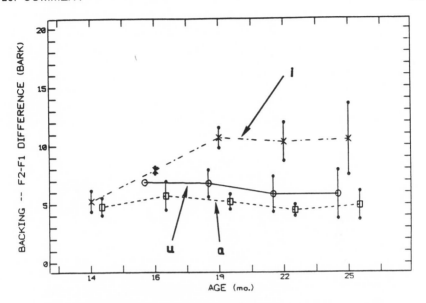

FIG. 2c.1.   Development of front-back distinction.
Development of the vowel backing distinction as measured by the difference in bark between the second and first formants $(F_2 - F_1)$ is shown above. Crosses represent average values of $F_2 - F_1$ of high, front vowels ([i], [I]) at each of five consecutive sessions. Circles and squares represent average values of $F_2 - F_1$ of high, back vowels ([u], [U]) and of low vowels ([a], [ɔ]), respectively. Two standard deviations, calculated for groups of three or more, are shown by vertical black bars.

Utterances were grouped by target vowel according to the word gloss, not by transcribed vowel. For example, an utterance which was glossed as "ball" was grouped with the [a] and [ɔ] utterances, regardless of whether it sounded like "bʌ" or "bi" or "bɔ." For each child, five consecutive recording sessions were analyzed. The initial session was the session in which the child first produced at least five words containing one of the specified target vowels. A maximum of five vowels in each pair was chosen from one recording session. Therefore, from five to fifteen vowels were analyzed from each session.

For each vowel, formant frequencies of the steady-state portion were estimated from narrow-band discrete Fourier transforms. The first formant frequencies and second formant frequencies were converted to a critical band or bark scale. For each child, the average of the first formant in bark and the average of the difference between the second and first formants in bark were calculated for each vowel group (high-front, high-back, and low) at each selected month. The standard deviations were calculated for groups of three or more as a measure of dispersion of formant bark values.

Figure 2c.1 shows an example of the development of backing for one child, as measured by the difference in bark between the second and first formant frequencies $(F_2$ and $F_1)$. Five months of data for child B are shown: months 14, 16, 19, 22, and

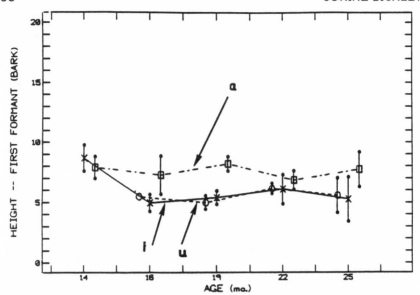

FIG. 2c.2.   Development of high-low distinction.
Development of the vowel height distinction as measured by the first formant (F_1) in bark is shown above. Crosses represent average values of F_1
of high, front vowels ([i],[I]) at each of five consecutive sessions. Circles and
squares represent average values of F_1 of high, back vowels ([u], [U]) and
of low vowels [a], [ɔ], respectively. Two standard deviations, calculated for
groups of three or more, are shown by vertical black bars.

25. The average values of $F_2 - F_1$ are shown for each vowel group. Two standard
deviations about the average are shown by a vertical black bar for each vowel
group at each month. For this child, the productions of front vowels and back
vowels overlap in the $F_2 - F_1$ dimension at months 14 and 16. Front vowels begin
to separate from back vowels at month 19. Front and back vowels are maximally
separate at month 22.

Figure 2c.2 shows the first formant data for the same child. Control of first
formant frequency corresponds to control of the height distinction. The productions
of high and low vowels overlap in the F_1 dimension at month 14 and then separate
from 16 through 19 months.

These data show that the height distinction is acquired before the backing distinction for this child. Child B acquired the height distinction by age 16 months
and the backing distinction by age 19 months.

Each child showed some deterioration of the ability to differentiate vowels in
terms of formant frequency value at some time during the five month sequence
(see, for example, month 22 in Figure 2c.2). This deterioration can be interpreted
as an example of some early word shapes being produced more accurately than later
pronunciations of the same words, as mentioned by Ferguson and Farwell (1975).

In a population of 15 children judged normal in articulatory skills at 3 years,
acquisition of the height distinction clearly preceded the backing distinction for 13

of the 15 children. For two of the children, height and backing control appeared by the same session. For no child did backing precede height control. Thus, although there was variability in the ages at which the height and backing distinctions were seen and in the lag in time between these two events, the pattern of control of height preceding control of backing was evident in normal children.

3

Sources of Variability in Early Speech Development

Michael Studdert-Kennedy
Queens College and Graduate Center, City University of New York, and Haskins Laboratories

This paper considers the origins of differences among children, and within a child from time to time, in the early development of speech. The paper is biased toward viewing these differences as special cases of general variability in animal behavior and its development. Some variability among children is surely genetic in origin (Lieberman, Chapter 4); this is the stuff of natural selection. Other variability is precisely what we expect in a system growing from an open genetic program (Mayr, 1974), that depends on loosely invariant properties of the environment to specify the course of development (for elaboration, see below, and for an excellent brief discussion, see Lenneberg, 1967, Ch.1). Finally, variability within a child is a precondition of the adaptive biological process that we term "learning" (Fowler & Turvey, 1978). However, I will come to all these matters only in the last section of the paper.

My first concern, and the topic of the early parts of the paper, is the apparent differences between capacities of infants and older children. Ferguson (Chapter 2) notes two main areas of research in child phonology: speech perception in infants and the sound systems of individual children aged 2-4 years, as shown by their speech productions. The relation between these two bodies of work is, indeed, "problematic," as Ferguson remarks. For, on the one hand, we have an infant apparently capable not only of discriminating virtually every adult segmental contrast with which it is presented, but also of discriminating speech sound categories across speakers and perhaps even across intrinsic allophonic variants (for a comprehensive review, see Aslin, Pisoni & Jusczyk, 1983). On the other hand, we have an older child producing a bewildering variety of sounds in its attempts to reproduce a particular adult word.

The discrepancy is not simply between perception and production. For we also find the older child, even up to the age of 5 or 6 years, making substantial numbers of perceptual errors on consonant contrasts (voicing, nasality, place of articulation) that would, seemingly, have caused no difficulty at all when it was an infant (see Barton [1980] for a review). Of course, these are cross-sectional comparisons. But the data are well established, and would usually be taken to reflect the child's course of development rather than sampling error.

How then are we to resolve the paradox? The first step is to acknowledge that different tasks place different demands on infant and older child: to detect the difference between two patterns of sound (discrimination) is not necessarily to recognize each pattern as an instance of a category (identification) (Barton, 1980, p. 106). Moreover, even when the tasks assigned to infant and older child are the same (i.e. discrimination), different behavioral measures may give different results: Recovery from habituation to a nonsense syllable upon presentation of a new syllable, as measured by high amplitude sucking or by heart rate, may not draw on the same capacities as choosing which of two nonsense words refers to a particular wooden block (Garnica, 1971). If we assume, as seems reasonable, that the older child has not lost capacities for discriminating between sounds of the surrounding language that it possessed as an infant, we must conclude that those capacities are not sufficient for more explicitly communicative tasks (Oller & Eilers, 1983; Oller & MacNeilage, 1983).

Yet the origin of the paradox is more than methodological. It also arises because infant speech research has "... generally taken for granted a phonological unit corresponding to the 'segment' [or, we may add, feature] of contemporary phonological theories, even though researchers have sometimes been familiar with the problems of relating such abstract units to the processes of speech perception" (Ferguson, Chapter 2). Ferguson has a different and, I believe, more fruitful approach. For rather than viewing the child as "acquiring" its phonology from the adult, Ferguson sees the adult's phonology as growing out of the child's (cf. Locke, 1983; Menyuk & Menn, 1979). Moreover, like Moskowitz (1973), and in accord with sound biological principle (Waddington, 1966), Ferguson sees this growth as a process of differentiating smaller structures from larger. The child does not build words with phonemes: phonemes emerge from words. In short, Ferguson shuns the preformationist view (long banished from embryology, but still thriving in psychology) that attributes adult properties to the child; he seeks rather to trace the epigenetic course from child to adult.

In the next few sections, I will sketch a view of infant speech development over roughly the first year of life that attempts to resolve the problematic relation between the apparent capacities of infant and older child. Broadly, my view is that two wrong turns have led into the impasse. First, a too narrow notion of development has encouraged undue concentration on the infant's initial state. For the biologist, development begins with the first division of the fertilized egg and ends with death. At each moment, the organism is sufficient for adaptive response to current internal and external conditions. Birth is certainly an occasion of abrupt discontinuity and of radical changes in conditions, but prenatal and postnatal development do not differ in principle: The infant's state at birth is simply the first state that psychologists can conveniently study.

Of course, we may treat the whole process teleologically, seeing the end in the beginning. That, in my view, is the second wrong turn. For the habit of describing infants' presumed percepts (and articulations) in linguistic terms has diverted attention from the central problem of early speech development, namely, imitation. We have been easily diverted because it seems natural that, if an adult speaks a word or grasps the air with a hand, a young child can repeat the word or imitate the hand movements. But how, in fact, does the child do this? What information in the acoustic or optic array specifies the executed movements? How is the information transduced into muscular controls? We are far from even imagining an answer to the last question. But we may gain leverage on the former (the very question to which the infant, learning to speak, must itself find an answer), if we couch our descriptions in auditory and motoric, rather than in linguistic, terms. We begin then with a brief summary of what is known about speech perceptuomotor processes in adults.

CEREBRAL ASYMMETRY FOR LANGUAGE IN ADULTS

Brain lateralization offers a window through which we may view the early stages of imitative processes essential to language development. To justify this claim my first assumption is that the association between lateralizations for language and manual praxis in more than 90% of the human population (Levy, 1974) is not mere coincidence. Second, I assume that lateralization of hand control evolved in higher primates to facilitate bimanual coordination by assigning unilateral control to a bilaterally innervated system (Mac-Neilage, Studdert-Kennedy & Lindblom, ms.). Third, I assume that speech and language exploited the already existing neural organization of the left hemisphere to develop a characteristic structure, analogous in certain key respects to the structure of coordinated hand movements.

I have no space to develop the analogy here (for elaboration, see Mac-Neilage [1983] and MacNeilage, Studdert-Kennedy & Lindblom [1984]). In any case, for present purposes, the necessary assumption is simply that language evolved in the left hemisphere for reasons of motor control. The assumption is consistent with studies of aphasics (Milner, 1974), of split-brain patients (Zaidel, 1978) and of the effects of sodium amytal injection (Borch-grevink, 1983; Milner, Branch & Rasmussen, 1964), showing that in most right-handed individuals the right hemisphere is essentially mute: The bilaterally innervated speech apparatus is controlled from the left side.

My final assumption is that a capacity to perceive speech—more exactly, to break its patterns into components matched to the motor components of articulation—evolved alongside the motor system in the left hemisphere. The assumption is consistent with numerous studies of dichotic listening (Kimura, 1961, 1967; Studdert-Kennedy & Shankweiler, 1970), and has drawn further support from studies of split-brain patients. Levy (1974) showed that only the left hemisphere of these patients can carry out the phonological analysis needed to recognize written rhymes; Zaidel (1976, 1978) showed that, while the right hemisphere may have a sizeable auditory and visual lexicon, only the left hemisphere can carry out the auditory-phonetic analysis necessary to identify synthetic nonsense syllables or the phonological analysis necessary to read new words.

In short, the stated assumptions and their supporting evidence justify the claim that the speech perceptuomotor system is vested in the left hemisphere of most normal right-handed individuals. Let us turn now to the development of this system over the first year of life.

CEREBRAL ASYMMETRY FOR SPEECH IN INFANTS

Perception

A number of perception studies has demonstrated dissociation of the left and right sides of the brain for perceiving speech and nonspeech sounds at, or very shortly after, birth. For example, Molfese, Freeman, and Palermo (1975) measured auditory evoked responses, over left and right temporal lobes, of ten infants, ranging in age from one week to 10 months. Their stimuli were four naturally spoken monosyllables, a C major piano chord and a 250–4000 Hz burst of noise. Each stimulus lasted 500 msec and was presented about 100 times, at randomly varying intervals. Median amplitude of response was higher over the left hemisphere for all four syllables in nine out of ten infants, higher over the right hemisphere for the chord and the noise in all ten infants; the one child who responded to speech with higher right hemisphere amplitude had a left-handed mother. Molfese (1977) has reported similar asymmetries for syllables and pure tones in neonates.

Segalowitz and Chapman (1980) studied 153 premature infants with a mean gestational age at testing of 36 weeks. They measured reduction of limb tremor over a 24-hour period, at the end of a daily regimen of exposure to 5-minute spells of speech (the mother reading nursery rhymes) or music

(Brahms' "Lullaby"), presented six times a day at 2-hour intervals. Tremor in the right arm (but not in the right leg, nor in the left arm or leg) was significantly more reduced by speech than by music or by silence (control group). The mechanism of the effect is not understood, nor whether it is due to cortical or subcortical asymmetries.

Finally, Best, Hoffman and Glanville (1982) tested forty-eight 2-, 3- and 4-month old infants for ear differences in a memory-based dichotic task. They used a cardiac orienting response to measure recovery from habituation to synthetic stop-vowel syllables and to Minimoog simulations of concert A (440 Hz) played on different instruments. In the speech task, a single dichotic habituation pair (either [ba-da] or [pa-ta]) was presented nine times, at randomly varying intervals. On the tenth presentation, one ear again received its habituation syllable, while the other received a test syllable (either [ga] or [ka]), differing in place of articulation from both habituation syllables. An analogous procedure was followed in the musical note task. The results showed significantly greater recovery of cardiac response for right ear test syllables in the 3- and 4-month olds, and for left ear musical notes in all age groups. The authors suggest that right-hemisphere memory for musical sounds develops before left-hemisphere memory for speech sounds, and that the latter begins to develop between the second and third months of life.

Neither these nor any of the several other studies with similar findings (see Best et al., 1982 for a brief review) indicate what properties of the signal mark it as speech. We may note, however, that those properties are evidently present in isolated syllables, natural or synthetic, and do not depend on the melody or rhythm of fluent speech. Moreover, the results of Best et al. (1982) invite the inference that infant speech sound discrimination, attested by numerous studies, engages left-hemisphere mechanisms no less than does adult speech sound discrimination.

Production

Evidence for early development of the production side of the perceptuomotor link is tenuous, but suggestive. Kuhl and Meltzoff (1982) showed that 4- to 5-month old infants looked longer at the video-displayed face of a woman articulating the vowel they were hearing (either [i] or [a]) than at the same face articulating the other vowel *in synchrony*. The preference disappeared when the signals were pure tones matched in amplitude and duration to the vowels, so that infant preference was evidently for a match between mouth shape and spectral structure. Similarly, MacKain, Studdert-Kennedy, Spieker, and Stern (1983) showed that 5- to 6-month old infants preferred to look at the face of a woman repeating the disyllable they were hearing (e.g. [zuzi]) than at the synchronized face of the same woman repeating another disyllable (e.g. [vava]). In both of these studies, infant preferences were for natural structural correspondences between acoustic and optic information. Since these two sources of information have a common origin in the articulations of the speaker, we may reasonably infer that the infant is sensitive to information that specifies articulation. (For related work on adult "lip-reading," see Campbell & Dodd, 1979; Crowder, 1983; McGurk & MacDonald, 1976; Summerfield, 1979).

Two more items complete the circle. First, Meltzoff and Moore (1977) showed that 12- to 21-day old infants could imitate both arbitrary mouth movements, such as tongue protrusion and mouth opening, and (of interest for the development of manual sign languages) arbitrary hand movements, such as opening and closing the hand by serially moving the fingers. Here mouth opening was elicited without vocalization; but had vocalization occurred, its structure would necessarily have reflected the shape of the mouth. Kuhl and Meltzoff (1982) do, in fact, report as an incidental finding of their study that 10 of their 32 infants "... produced sounds that resembled the adult female's vowels. They seemed to be imitating the female talker, 'taking turns' by alternating their vocalizations with hers" [p. 1140]. Of course, we have no indication that this incipient capacity, demonstrated under conditions of controlled attention in the laboratory, is actively used by 5-month old infants in the more variable conditions of daily life.

The second item of evidence is a curious aspect of the study by MacKain et al. (1983), cited earlier: Infant preferences for a match between the facial movements they were watching and the speech sounds they were hearing were statistically significant only when they were looking to their right sides. Fourteen of the eighteen infants in the study preferred more matches on their right sides than on their left. Moreover, in a follow-up investigation of familial handedness, MacKain and her colleagues learned that six of the infants had left-handed first- or second-order relatives. Of these six, four were the infants who displayed more left-side than right-side matches.

These results can be interpreted in the light of work by Kinsbourne and his colleagues (e.g. Kinsbourne, 1972; Lempert & Kinsbourne, 1982). This work suggests that attention to one side of the body may facilitate processes for which the contralateral hemisphere is specialized. If this is so, we may infer that infants with a preference for matches on their right side were revealing a left hemisphere sensitivity to articulations specified by acoustic and optic information. Thus, we have preliminary evidence that 5- to 6-month old infants, close to the onset of babbling, already display the beginnings of a speech perceptuomotor link in the left hemisphere.

Here we should strike a note of caution. The evidence reviewed up to this point does not demonstrate that specialized phonetic processes are occurring in the infant. In fact, whatever mechanisms for imitating articulation may be developing in these early months seem to be no different, in principle, than corresponding specialized mechanisms for imitating movements of hand, face,

and body. What distinguishes the speech perceptuomotor link at this stage
of development is first, its locus in the brain, and second, its modality. The
capacity to imitate vocalizations seems to be peculiar to certain birds, certain
marine mammals, and man.

SPEECH PERCEPTION IN INFANTS

0-6 months[1]

As is well-known, infants in the first 6 months of life discriminate almost
any adult segmental contrast on which they are tested. Particularly striking, in the early years of this work (initiated by Eimas and his colleagues
[Eimas, Siqueland, Jusczyk & Vigorito, 1971]) was 1- and 4-month old infants' discrimination of synthetic syllables along a stop consonant voice-onset
time continuum. Discrimination was measured by recovery (or no recovery)
of high-amplitude sucking on a nonnutritive nipple, in response to a change
in sound (or no change for a control group), after habituation to repeated
presentation of another sound. Like adults, infants readily discriminated between acoustically different items belonging to different (English) phonetic
categories, but not between acoustically different items belonging to the same
category. This finding, fortified by similar results on continua of stop consonant place of articulation (Eimas, 1974), consonant manner (Eimas and
Miller, 1980 a, b), and the [r]–[l] distinction (Eimas, 1975) for example, encouraged the hypothesis that "... these early categories serve as the basis for
future phonetic categories" (Eimas, 1982, p. 342).

However, there is a confusion here between two different types of category. On the one hand, we have categories comprising more-or-less random
variations in the precise acoustic properties of a single syllable, spoken repeatedly with identical stress and at an identical rate by the same speaker:
These are the patterns mimicked by a synthetic series, varied along a single
acoustic dimension. On the other hand, we have the categories of natural
speech, comprising intrinsic allophonic variants, formed by the execution of
a particular phoneme in a range of phonetic contexts, spoken with varying
stress, at different rates, and by different speakers. The latter are presumably
the "future phonetic categories" to which Eimas refers, while the former are
auditory categories to which infants, chinchillas (for VOT, Kuhl & Miller,
1978), and macaques (for place of articulation, Kuhl & Padden, 1983) have

---

[1] The periods used here are not fixed stages of development. They are simply convenient
headings that correspond roughly to a period before babbling (0–6 months) on which much
infant perceptual researcher has focused, and a period of babbling (7–12 months) on which
there has been little perceptual research.

been shown to be sensitive in synthetic speech studies (see also Kuhl, 1981). The proper interpretation of these studies would seem to be that infants (and an open set of other animals) can discriminate the several contrasts tested, if they are presented in an invariant acoustic context.

Evidence for phonetic categories from studies of contrasts across varying acoustic contexts differs depending on the nature of the variation. Talker variations, at least on the few contrasts that have been tested, seem to cause little difficulty for infant (Hillenbrand, 1983; Kuhl, 1979a), dog (Baru, 1975), cat (Dewson, 1964), or chinchilla (Burdick & Miller 1975). Cross-talker categories, then, seem to be auditory rather than phonetic. (We may note, in passing, that such findings present a puzzle for accounts of speaker normalization that rest on the listener's presumed knowledge of the speaker's phonetic space [Gerstman, 1968; Ladefoged & Broadbent, 1957]).

Studies of contrasts across variations in phonetic context have given less consistent results. Warfield, Ruben, and Glackin (1966) trained cats to discriminate between the words *cat* and *bat*, but found no transfer of training to other minimal pairs beginning with the same segments. Holmberg, Morgan, and Kuhl (1977) studied fricative perception in 6-month old infants. They used an operant head-turning paradigm, in which the infant was conditioned to turn its head for visual reinforcement when repeating sounds from one category were changed to repeating sounds from another. They found that infants discriminated [f]/[θ] and [s]/[š] across variations in vowel context (e.g. [fa], [f ɨ], [fu]) and syllable position (e.g. [fa], [af]). Kuhl (1980) reports similar results for an infant trained to discriminate [d]/[g].

Katz and Jusczyk (1980), cited in Jusczyk (1982), reasoned that a more stringent test of infant phonetic categorization would be to show that infants more readily learn to discriminate between (that is, to generalize within) phonetically-based groupings than arbitrary groupings of the same syllables. In a head-turning study of 6-month old infants, they found that most infants learned to discriminate between sets of syllables, paired for consonant onset, but differing in vowel (e.g. [bi] and [bɛ] versus [di] and [dɛ]), but not between sets, arbitrarily paired, differing in both consonant and vowel (e.g. [bɛ] and [di] versus [bi] and [dɛ]). However, none of the infants learned to discriminate either phonetic or arbitrary groupings of [b] and [d] followed by four vowels ([i, ɛ, o, ʊ]). Jusczyk (1982) interprets the results as providing some "... weak support for ... perceptual constancy for stop consonant segments occurring in different contexts" [p. 378].

Before commenting on this study, let us compare its results with those of Miller and Eimas (1979), who used a similar set of stimulus materials to ask a different experimental question: Are infants sensitive to the structure of syllables? That is to say, do infants perceive syllables holistically, as seamless, undifferentiated patterns, or do they perceive the structure of syllables, analyzing them into their component segments (consonants and vowels)? Miller and Eimas used a high-amplitude sucking paradigm to test 2-, 3- and 4-month old infants. One group of infants successfully discriminated between sets of syllables, paired for consonant onsets, but differing in vowel ([ba] and [bæ] versus [da] and [dæ]), as did the infants of Katz and Jusczyk. However, another group also discriminated between sets arbitrarily paired, differing in both consonant and vowel ([ba] and [dæ] versus [bæ] and [da]), which the infants of Katz and Jusczyk did not do. Miller and Eimas interpreted their positive outcome as evidence that infants are sensitive to the segmental structure of syllables.

A similar conflict in results emerges at a "feature" level when we compare a study by Hillenbrand (1983) with the second and third experiments of Miller and Eimas (1979). Hillenbrand used a head-turning paradigm to test the capacity of 6-month old infants to discriminate between sets of syllables differing on a single feature (oral–nasal, as in [ba] and [da] versus [ma] and [na]) and sets of syllables differing on arbitrary combinations of two features (oral–nasal and place of articulation, as in [ba] and [ŋa] versus [na] and [ga]). He found that infants were significantly better at discriminating the single feature phonetic groups than the arbitrary double feature groups. He concluded that infants were sensitive to the auditory correlates of consonantal features. Miller and Eimas (1979), on the other hand, tested 2-, 3- and 4-month old infants with a high amplitude sucking procedure on single-feature phonetic groups analogous to those of Hillenbrand (voicing versus place of articulation; oral–nasal versus place of articulation), and on the corresponding double-feature sets where the two features were arbitrarily combined. Pooling data from the two experiments, they found that infants assigned to experimental conditions displayed significantly more recovery from habituation than control infants, and that there was no significant difference in recovery for the two types of syllable set. They concluded from the lack of reduction in performance across set types that infants were sensitive to the structure of consonantal segments, that is, to their particular combinations of features.

We have then a conflict in data from the three studies: 2- to 4-month old infants, tested with high amplitude sucking, discriminate between arbitrary sound classes that are indiscriminable for 6-month old infants, tested with operant head-turning. If the results are valid, and not mere sampling error, we have a paradox similar to that for infants and older children with which we began. We may resolve the paradox on the same two fronts. Methodologically, we must acknowledge a commonplace of psychophysical testing for many years (e.g. Woodworth, 1938, Ch. 17): Different behavioral measures may give different results, even in the same individual, at roughly the same time. Moreover, since demonstrating a capacity takes precedence over demonstrating its absence, and since 6-month old infants are unlikely to have lost capacities for discriminating among the sounds of the surrounding language that they possessed at 3 months, we must conclude that high-amplitude sucking is a more sensitive measure of infant discriminative capacity than operant head-turning. Thus, the two head-turning studies failed to reveal infant conditioning to arbitrary groupings of syllables because task difficulty and behavioral measure interacted— a possibility raised by Jusczyk (1982, p. 379).[2] The attempt to develop a more stringent test of infant consonant categorization across vowel contexts than that used by Holmberg, et al. (1977) for fricatives was therefore not successful.

Beyond the methodological issue lies the matter of interpretation. Consider, first, the conclusion from Miller and Eimas (1979) that infants are sensitive to the segmental structure of syllables and the featural structure of segments. Unfortunately, the conclusion is not forced by the data, since, as Aslin et al. (1983) point out, an infant discriminating, say [ba] and [na] from [da] and [ma], has simply to detect that one (or both) of the syllables in the second set is different from either of the syllables in the first set. In other words, the infant can discriminate the patterns holistically without analysis. Miller and Eimas (1979) recognize this fact ("... we know of no way to make this distinction [holistic/analytic] experimentally with infant subjects"), but justify their preference for the analytic interpretation, because "There is ... rather extensive behavioral as well as neurophysiological evidence for an analysis into components or features in human and non-human pattern perception" [both quotations from p. 355, footnote 2]. I do not doubt this evidence, but it does not justify our attributing analytic capacities to the 3-month old—particularly when, by doing so, we create a paradoxical discrepancy between the capacities of infant and older child.

Consider, next, the evidence that infants can form "phonetic" categories across a variety of acoustic contexts. Here again the data are overinterpreted. Since every phonetic contrast is marked by an acoustic contrast (if it were not, how would the infant learn to talk?), phonetic and auditory perception cannot be dissociated in the infant (though they can be in the adult: Best, Morrongiello & Robson, 1981; Best & Studdert-Kennedy, 1983; Liberman, Isenberg & Rakerd, 1981; Mann & Liberman, 1983; Schwab, 1981). This fact is recognized by Miller & Eimas (1979, p. 365), and by Aslin, et al., (1983). What we are left with then is evidence that infants, in their first 6 months of life, can detect auditory similarities across certain adult phonetic categories. Incidentally, apart from the study of cats mentioned above (Warfield, et al.,

---

[2] This interpretation assumes that arbitrary groups were, in fact, more difficult to discriminate than "phonetic" groups. Perhaps it is easier to detect a difference between groups, if all members of one group differ from all members of another group on the same dimension ("phonetic") than if each member of one group differs from each member of another on a different dimension (arbitrary). The difference in task difficulty might then be great enough to show up, if the criterial response is itself relatively difficult (head turning), but not if the response is relatively easy (high amplitude sucking).

1966), we have no evidence, so far as I know, that other animals cannot do the same. Of course, proving the null hypothesis for animals is a thankless task.

Finally, we may ask what role categories, whether auditory or phonetic, are presumed to play in the infant's learning to speak. Eimas (1982) argues that "... the acquisition of the complex rule systems of linguistics requires that the young child treat all instantiations of a phonetic category as members of a single equivalence class" [p. 346]. He adds in a footnote, "... if the child treats each possible member of the two voicing categories of English as separate entities and not as perceptually identical events or at least as members of the same equivalence class, then acquisition of the rule for pluralization will necessarily be painfully slow, if ever learned" (p. 346, footnote 5). Eimas goes on to justify the search for perceptual constancy in infants on grounds of parsimony, because "... it would effectively eliminate explanations based on receptive experience" (p. 346).

There are several things wrong here. First is the implication that accounts of biological development calling for experience to direct its course are somehow not parsimonious, perhaps even not "biological." In fact, just the reverse is true. Precisely because full genetic specification is costly, even the lowliest behaviors of non-human animals may depend on broadly invariant external conditions to guide development (see Immelmann, Barlow, Petrinovich & Main, 1981; Lenneberg, 1967, Ch. 1; Mayr, 1974; and the brief discussion below). Second, the notion of rule is prescriptive, as though speakers applied rules much as they do in a game of chess. In fact, a phonological rule is simply a description of regularities in speech; the processes by which these regularities arise are completely unknown (for discussions, see Menn, 1980; Menyuk & Menn, 1979). Finally, once again, the outcome of development (the formation of phonological structures that control adult speaking) is posited to be already in place at a time when development has scarcely begun. I do not doubt that infants can form auditory categories, but there is no evidence that this capacity is either needed for or brought to bear on early speaking.[3] If it were, we would be hard put to explain the word-by-word development of adult phones that Ferguson (Chapter 2) describes, or the relatively slow accumulation of the first 50 (or so) words. We may indeed suspect that the emergence of auditory-motoric categories, around the beginning of the third year, is a factor in triggering the explosive growth of the child's vocabulary

---

[3] Jusczyk (1982) makes the same point, proposing the "...possibility [that]...recognition of phonetic identities is not achieved until the child is engaged in learning how to read" (p. 365, footnote 3). If "recognition" here means "metalinguistic awareness," Jusczyk may be right. But functional categories surely predate the alphabet, both ontogenetically and historically. The alphabet (like dance notation) can only succeed because its units correspond to functional units of perceptuomotor control. The task for the child, learning to read, is to discover these units in its own behavior.

(at an average rate of perhaps 5–10 words a day) over the next 4 or 5 years (Miller, 1977, pp. 150 ff.).

In short, we can resolve the paradoxical discrepancy between the capacities of infants and older children if we refrain from regarding precursors of a behavior as instances of the behavior itself. No doubt, infant kicking (and stepping when the infant is held erect) are precursors of walking and, with normal growth in an appropriate environment, will develop into walking (Thelen, 1983). But infant kicks and steps are not strides.

7–12 months

None of the foregoing should be interpreted as claiming that phonetically relevant development of the infant's perceptual system is not going forward during the first 6 months of life. However, the first (and still sparse) behavioral evidence of such development comes from older infants.

Eimas (1975) showed that 4–6 month old English infants discriminated between English [r] and [l]. On the assumption that Japanese infants would have done the same, and given the well-known fact that native Japanese speakers, who know no English, do not make this discrimination (Miyawaki, Strange, Verbrugge, Liberman, Jenkins & Fujimura, 1975), Eimas suggested that learning the sound system of a language may entail loss of the capacity to discriminate contrasts not used in the language. Similar suggestions have been made by Aslin and Pisoni (1980), and Locke (1983).

Werker, Gilbert, Humphrey & Tees (1981) have traced the onset of perceptual loss to the second 6 months of life, a period when the infant is perhaps first attending to individual words and the situations in which they occur (Jusczyk, 1982; MacKain, 1982). Their initial finding was that 7-month-old Canadian English infants, tested in a head-turning paradigm, could discriminate between naturally spoken contrasts in Hindi as English-speaking adults could not. Werker (1982) followed this up by tracking the decline of discriminative capacity in cross-sectional and longitudinal studies. She used a conditioned head-turning paradigm to test three groups of infants on two non-English sound contrasts: Hindi voiceless, unaspirated retroflex versus dental stops (cf. Locke, 1983, pp. 90–92), and Thompson (Interior Salish, an American Indian Language) voiced, glottalized velar versus uvular stops. On the Hindi contrast, the number of infants successfully discriminating were: 11/12 at 6–8 months, 8/12 at 8–10 months, 2/10 at 10–12 months; for the Thompson contrast the results were essentially the same. (An infant was classified as having failed to discriminate only if it had successfully discriminated an English contrast both before and after failure on a non-English contrast). Finally, Werker (1982) reports longitudinal data for six Canadian English infants on the same two non-English contrasts. All six discriminated both contrasts at 6-8 months, but at 10-12 months none of them made the discrimination. By contrast, the one Thompson and two Hindi infants so far tested at 10-12 months could all make the called for discrimination in their own language.

Perceptual loss is not permanent, since capacity can be recovered by adults learning a new language (e.g. MacKain, Best & Strange, 1981). Nor can the effect be general, since sufficiently salient foreign contrasts can presumably be discriminated even by adults. We may suspect then that loss is focused on relatively fine auditory contrasts, specifying slight differences in the space-time coordinates of a single articulator's movements, and that it arises as a side effect of the infant's developing "attention" to closely related contrasts in its own language. This is not to suggest that the younger infant is not "attending" to speech during its early months. Rather, its search for meaning and communicative function (Trevarthen, 1979) may initially be guided by the rhythm and melody of speech (Mehler, Barrière and Jasik-Gerschenfeld, 1976). Only when these larger patterns have begun to take form (Menn, 1978a) are the infant's capacities for segmental discrimination, readily demonstrated in the laboratory, brought to bear on the speech it hears at home.

SPEECH PRODUCTION IN THE INFANT

The infant, by definition, does not speak (Latin: *infans*, not speaking). But there is now ample evidence that the discontinuity between babble and speech, posited by Jakobson (1968), is not real. Oller (1980) provides a taxonomy of the emerging stages from phonation (0–1 month) to variegated babbling (11–12 months). Oller, Wieman, Doyle & Ross (1975) describe similarities between patterns of babbling and early speech (cf. MacNeilage, Hutchinson & Lasater, 1981). Vihman, Macken, Miller, Simmons, & Miller (in press) demonstrate parallels in the distribution and organization of sounds in speech and babble during the period (roughly 9–15 months) when they overlap.   .

What is the origin of this continuity? The first possibility is that the sound distributions of babble and early speech are similar because the infant begins to learn the sounds of the language around it and to practice them during its second 6 months of life. Locke (1983, Ch. 1) has marshalled evidence against this view. First, he has collated data on the babbling of 9- to 12-month old infants growing up in 14 different language environments, distributed across some half dozen language families (Locke 1983, Table 1.3, p. 10). These infants were certainly old enough to have begun to discover the sound patterns of their languages and, indeed, if the data on perceptual loss reviewed above have any generality, perceptual discovery had already begun. Yet of the 143 consonantal sounds entered in Locke's table, over 85% correspond to one of the twelve most frequent sounds in the babbling of English children, a strikingly homogeneous distribution. Second, Locke has reviewed some dozen studies that have looked for drift in the sounds of infant babbling, during the second 6 months of life, toward the sounds of the surrounding language. Most of the studies either found no evidence of drift or were inconclusive. Finally, Locke has reviewed available studies on the babbling of deaf infants and infants with Down's syndrome. Despite the common belief that deaf babbling fades before the end of the first year, several studies agree that it may continue well into early childhood (5–6 years). But what is remarkable is that the developmental course of babbling up to 12 months is similar in deaf and hearing infants, and, incidentally, in Down's syndrome infants. For example, the relative proportions of labial, alveolar, and velar consonants follow essentially the same course: Only after the 12th month does the expected preponderance of labial movements in deaf children begin. The three strands of evidence converge on a process of articulatory development, independent of the surrounding language and common to all human infants.

We are left, then, with the second possible account of the continuity between babble and speech, namely that, as Locke proposes, the phonetic proclivities of adults and infants are similar. Both are largely determined by anatomical and physiological constraints on the signaling apparatus. What these constraints may be has only recently come under scrutiny (Kent, 1980; Lindblom, 1983a; Ohala, 1983b).

Of course, this hypothesis immediately raises the question of language change: If all adult speakers develop from a common infant base, why do languages differ? The question is too large, and my competence too small, for adequate treatment here. However, I note several points. First, as Locke (1983) has shown, many infant biases (e.g. for open rather than closed syllables, for stops over fricatives, for singleton consonants over clusters, and so on) are indeed preserved by many groups of adult speakers (i.e., languages); it is this fact that the continuity of babble and speech reflects. At the same time, infant preferences are not rigid, because, as Darwin taught, no animal structure specifies a unique function. A structure (e.g. the vocal apparatus) permits an unspecifiable, though presumably limited, range of functions, and the natural variability of behavior offers this range for selection. Second, infant articulatory capacities are a subset of the capacities of mature speakers. As skill develops, the range of response, available for selection by a variety of sociocultural forces, widens. Certainly, the exact course of historical change will never be fully specified for language, any more than for, say, clothing, cuisine, or social organization. Nonetheless, there would seem to be no reason, in principle, why we should not develop a cultural–evolutionary account of language diversity (Lindblom, 1984), compatible with relatively fixed infant articulatory proclivities.

In short, perceptual and motor development of speech over the first year of life, as manifested in infant behavior, may justly be seen as parallel, independent processes. No doubt, physiological changes in the perceptual and motor centers of the left hemisphere are taking place to prepare for the ultimate connection between the two systems. These processes may be analogous to those in songbirds, such as the marsh wren, in which the perceptual template of its species' song is laid down many months before it begins to sing (Kroodsma, 1981). But behavioral evidence of the perceptuomotor link appears only with that song, just as behavioral evidence of the link appears in the infant only with its first imitation of an adult sound.

FROM BABBLING TO SPEECH

The transition from babbling to speech is a murky period. At this stage we see the first clear evidence of a perceptuomotor link, but know little about what the child perceives. Even when the perceptual data come in, it will be a delicate task to determine their relevance. For, as we have noted, a capacity demonstrated in the laboratory does not tell us how, or even if, that capacity is put to use in learning to speak. Consequently, we may have to place as much weight on shaky inference from the child's productions as on firm evidence from perceptual studies.

At this stage, we also find it increasingly difficult to refrain from describing the child's productions by means of phonetic transcriptions. Of course, we do not want to refrain: Transcription is our readiest mode of description, because children have vocal tracts very like adults' and make sounds like adults' sounds. Yet transcription is a double-edged blade. For it is precisely in order to understand the apparently segmented structure of speech (and the resulting adult capacity to transcribe) that we are studying its ontogeny. As is well known, phonetic segments are not readily specified either in articulation or in the signal, so that their functional reality has had to be inferred, in the first instance, from adult behaviors, such as errors of perception (Browman, 1978) and production (Shattuck-Hufnagel, 1983), backward talking (Cowan, Leavitt, Massaro & Kent, 1982), aphasic deficits (Blumstein, 1981) and, not least, use of the alphabet. By relying on a descriptive apparatus that derives from characteristics of mature speakers, we put ourselves in danger of attributing to the child properties it does not yet possess.

Despite these difficulties, headway has been made, and a view of the child as something other than a preformed adult is beginning to emerge (see especially Menn, 1978a, b, 1980, 1983; Menyuk and Menn, 1979). A striking aspect of this view, though not a surprising one, is the lavish variability of the child's productions. In these last few paragraphs, I will briefly consider how we might approach this variability.

Variability within a child

Ferguson (Chapter 2) presents compelling arguments for regarding the word as the unit of contrast in early speech; he defines a word as "... any apparently conventionalized sound-meaning pair." The definition is important, because it draws attention to the fact that a word is not simply a pattern of sound, but a pattern of sound appropriate to a particular situation (Menyuk and Menn, 1979). To discriminate one word from another, to recognize a word, and to use it correctly, entails discriminating and recognizing various nonlinguistic properties of a situation. Thus, a child's failure to discriminate or recognize a word in a perceptual test may reflect nonlinguistic as much as linguistic factors. Moreover, many of the child's spoken variations may reflect variability in the situations in which the child has heard the word and in the varying salience of its phonetic properties in those situations. The same adult word may then be a different word to the child in different situations.

Nonetheless, highly variable productions of a given word do occur within essentially the same situation. Ferguson (Chapter 2; Ferguson & Farwell, 1975, p. 423, footnote 8) lists ten different attempts by a child (K at approximately 1 year, 3 months) to say *pen* within one half-hour session. Ferguson comments, "She seemed to be trying to sort out features of nasality, bilabial closure, alveolar closure, and voicelessness." Waterson (1971) describes numerous such instances for her child, P, in similar phonetic terms, noting as a common occurrence that "features" lose their order and become recombined into patterns quite unlike the adult model.

Perhaps, however, we would do well to avoid featural terminology. We might attempt a more direct articulatory description as do Menyuk and Menn (1979), describing one of Menn's (1978a) subjects Jacob's protowords: "... Jacob was varying the timing of front-back articulations against the timing of lowering and raising the tongue" [p. 61]. Of course, this is little more than a gloss on phonetic transcriptions. Yet, in the absence of cineradiographic or even acoustic records, the gloss may "... help us see more clearly what it is the child needs to learn and to look at it in a way less coloured by our knowledge of mature linguistic behavior" (Menyuk & Menn, 1979, p. 61; cf. Kent, 1984). For we then see the speaking of a word not as a bundling of features into concatenated segments, but as a distribution of interleaved movements of articulators over time (Browman & Goldstein, ms.). In the adult, repeated coordination of particular movements in recurrent patterns has crystallized into structures that form the phonological elements of the language. For the child the movements have yet to be organized.

Three points deserve emphasis. First, despite the variability of a child's productions, they also display surprising accuracy. The phone classes of Ferguson and Farwell (1975) show much variability in voicing and manner—due perhaps to unskilled timing of closure and release—yet remarkable homogeneity in place of articulation. Also, K's attempts at *pen* did not include, for example, [gʌk]: Almost every attempt included some recognizable property of the adult word. This means that the acoustic structure of adult words specifies for the child at least some rough pattern of configurations of the vocal tract, necessarily the product of a specialized perceptuomotor link. Yet, second, the link is not precisely predetermined: It must develop. Not only the movements, but their relative timing and sequencing must develop. These are complex processes that almost certainly require active movement for their neural control structures to take form. Perhaps it is the normal function of babbling to promote growth of these structures in the left hemisphere. In any event, we are now led to see, and this is my third point, that genetically programmed variability is a condition of the child's learning to speak. In general, the longer the life span of an animal, the longer the period of parental care, and the more complex the mature behavior, the more likely is the behavior to develop through an open genetic program (Mayr, 1974; though, for an exception, see below). Such a program relies on experience to select and, if necessary, shape the needed behavior from a reservoir of variable responses (Fowler & Turvey, 1978).

Variability among Children

As earlier noted, some individual differences in the course of development are genetic or congenital in origin. MacKain (in press) describes several extreme cases of children born without a tongue who approach a surprisingly normal phonetic repertoire by an idiosyncratic path of development. Yet other differences arise from the plasticity of an open system, sensitive to environmental contingencies and equipped with a variable repertoire of responses. Adaptive response to some particular, short-term aspect of the environment may lead an individual down an idiosyncratic path, because the precise order in which the parts of the system assemble themselves is not preordained. Here we may draw a useful analogy with the self-stabilizing processes in embryological development termed "canalization" (Waddington, 1966, p. 48). Waddington describes how various regions of an embryo differentiate into eyes, arms, legs, and so on. Each region has many possible paths to the same end. The exact path is determined, in part, by chance factors in the embryonic environment; equifinality is assured by fixed constraints inside and outside the developing region. Similarly, we may suppose, no single path is prescribed for the development of a phonological system. Many paths, determined by partially fixed, partially variable perceptual, motoric, and social conditions lead to the same end (Lindblom, MacNeilage, & Studdert-Kennedy, 1983).

Certainly, there may be a "normal" path, the product of articulatory proclivity or "ease" (Locke, 1983) and perceptual salience. But a child can readily be diverted from the path by accidents of the speech it hears or of its physical structure and growth.

For example, if final fricatives become salient for a particular child, due to adult lexicon in some recurrent situation, the child may try them and be successful, yet be unable (through lack of consonant harmony in the target word or other "output constraints" [Menn, 1978b]) to execute the initial consonants of the words. A vowel-fricative routine is then established which the child can bring to bear on words that most children would attempt with the standard stop-vowel sequence, followed by a "deleted" fricative (e.g. Waterson, 1971, p. 185). Yet the deviant child will ultimately come upon the same phonological system as its peers.

Here we should note that even quite simple behaviors in nonhuman animals may develop through an open genetic program. The filial and sexual imprinting of mallard ducklings or domestic chicks on slow-moving objects (such as a walking human, or even a red plastic cube revolving on the arm of a rotary motor [Vidal, 1976]) is well known. The effect is possible because genetic "instructions" are loose; they do not specify the form and color of the mother bird, but only her typical rate of movement. Evolution can afford such imprecision because the normal environment provides the duckling with only one slow-moving object, its mother. If the combination of gross genetic "instructions" and a more or less invariant environment permits essential functions (here, protection from predators and species identification) to develop, there will be no selective pressure for more exact genetic specification.

For the imprinting of precocial birds, the behavior is roughly fixed, while eliciting conditions are only loosely specified. For the development of language, both the behavior and the eliciting conditions are loosely specified.[4] Presumably, the infant has certain minimal, perhaps quite general, capacities (its "initial state"), including sensitivity to the contingencies of its own behavior, the basis perhaps of social responsiveness (Watson, 1972, 1981), while the social environment normally offers the infant certain more-or-less invariant invitations to interact. So, within weeks of birth we find the infant watching intently its mother's eyes, face, and hands, as she talks and plays, and we detect certain inchoate communication patterns in postures of the infant's head, face, and limbs, and in prespeech movements of tongue and lips (Trevarthen, 1979). But at this stage, not even the modality of language is fixed. For if the infant is born deaf, it will learn to sign no less readily than its hearing peer learns to speak. Thus, the neural substrate is also shaped by environmental contingencies; and the left hemisphere, despite its predis-

---

[4] I am not proposing that language can take any arbitrary form. On the contrary, its general form, that is, its two-leveled hierarchical structure of phonology and syntax, emerges necessarily from its function. Innumerable details of form within these levels must result from more-or-less invariant perceptuomotor, cognitive and pragmatic constraints, of which we know, at present, very little.

position for speech, is then usurped by sign (Neville, 1980; Neville, Kutas & Schmidt, 1982; Studdert-Kennedy, 1983, pp. 175 ff. and pp. 219ff.). In fact, recent studies of aphasia in native American Sign Language signers show remarkable parallels in forms of breakdown between signers and speakers with similar left hemisphere lesions (Bellugi, Poizner & Klima, 1983).

The differences between deaf and hearing individuals are certainly gross. Yet every child grows in its peculiar niche with its peculiar anatomical and physiological biases, and must therefore discover its own "strategy" for fulfilling the human communicative function. (The term "strategy" should be stripped of its cognitive, not to say military, connotations in this context, as it is in standard ethological usage.) Indeed, language, as a sociobiological system, exploits the potential for diverse strategies to mark social groups by channeling speakers into distinctive linguistic styles and dialects—to which, of course, children are highly sensitive (e.g. Local, 1983). Thus, individual differences and individual adaptive response make language a force for social cohesion and differentiation. (For examples of stable diversity within species of bee, treefrog, anemonefish, ruff, and other animals, see Krebs & Davies, 1981, Ch. 8).

Finally, individual differences offer an opening for research. Presumably, there are limits on possible strategies. But what these limits may be we do not know. As data from longitudinal studies of individual children accumulate, strategies may cluster, until it is possible to sketch their limits. Such work may lead toward clearer notions of "perceptual salience" and "ease of articulation." Thus, we come back to the constraints on individuals by which phonological elements emerge and phonological systems organize themselves (Lindblom, MacNeilage & Studdert-Kennedy, 1983).

ACKNOWLEDGMENTS

My thanks to Björn Lindblom and Peter MacNeilage for conversations, to Charles Ferguson and Lise Menn for their papers, to John Locke for his book, and my apologies to all of them for any misconstruals. Preparation of the paper was supported in part by NICHD Grant No. HD–01994 to Haskins Laboratories.

S. Shattuck-Hufnagel: Comment: Why We Need More Data

Studdert-Kennedy's paper is an attempt to work the evidence that we have about the early development of speech—evidence that is still sketchy and at times even contradictory—into a coherent story. The story is based on the view that learning to produce the articulatory patterns of a language is central to the language acquisition process, that to perceive speech is to take it apart into its articulatory components, and that adult phonology emerges out of the child's increasing mastery of these skills. The discussion is embedded in a biological framework that gives both genetically- and environmentally-influenced variability an important role in development.

The model in the paper describes several stages of development:

1) The first year of life, during which the perceptual and motor components develop in the left hemisphere. In Studdert-Kennedy's view, the perceptual and motor components develop separately. "The process of articulatory development unfolds independent of the surrounding language, and is common to all infants," while the infant's early perceptual abilities begin to be shaped by the sounds it hears.

2) The stage of early imitation of adult forms, or first words. The perceptual and motor components are now linked together into the special perceptuomotor system for speech, which first extracts from the speech signal the information that specifies the articulatory components that formed it, and then juggles these articulatory components into the right relations for production. This process results in a growing degree of success in imitation of adult forms of words.

3) A 'crystallization' stage, during which phonemic segments emerge out of these now-mastered articulatory patterns as they are repeated over and over in the everyday use of speech.

Clearly this is a model of the development of the child's ability to talk, with other aspects of phonological development viewed as secondary.

This of course is not the only possible view of the development process. One alternative is that the child's early utterances are guided by auditory targets, and that the development of speech abilities includes the slow mastery of the skill of translating these acoustically-based intentions into appropriate motor terms. We will not discuss this alternative further here.

A third alternative is that the child's early utterances are defined not only in terms of auditory or articulatory or even perceptuomotor components, but as abstract segmental representations. In this view, the capacities of the peripheral auditory and articulatory systems shape, but do not fully define, the representations that guide early utterances. These representations are also shaped by the demands of the cognitive systems that analyze, store and plan utterances. On this account, the categories of language elements used by the child are shaped by three forces: the nature of the articulatory control apparatus, the nature of the auditory system, and the nature of the cognitive processing systems that intervene between the two peripheral systems. These three forces have combined over evolutionary time to determine the maturing child's proclivity to construct segmental representations of the words of his language. In this response to Studdert-Kennedy's presentation of a model based on developing perceptuomotor abilities, we will argue that currently-available data do not distinguish between that model and one in which words are represented as sequences of abstract segments, and discuss some of the kinds of data that might do so.

Stated in its strongest form, this third alternative model of early language development makes a very powerful claim: onset of language in the child reflects the occurrence of a significant change in the representations and processing mechanisms that control his behavior. This is not to say that earlier auditory and articulatory operations are irrelevant to the development of language, but rather that these operations are combined in a significantly different way at the moment when the child begins to use language (as opposed to hearing speech wave forms and producing vocal articulations.) Considerable continuity in the observable patterns of pre- and post-language onset utterance is to be expected, since the many of the same influences are at work, but the effects of the shift to structured segmental representations should be evident even through the cloudy lens of behavioral evidence.

What might characterize the combination of processing elements into a new system that makes use of segmental representations? One can hazard a guess that the right description will include the following: production of sound by intentional control of the articulatory apparatus, under the direction of segmental sound structures linked to meaning, according to the patterns of a specific language.

On this view, the articulation of the sound sequence "ba" before and after the onset of language has different accounts. Before language onset, the behavior might be intentional, guided by a plan and communicative, but it is not under the direction of segmental sound structures linked to meaning according to the patterns of the language. After language onset, the representations that guide the behavior are organized into at least rudimentary versions of the structures that adults use. Even a recognizable imitation of an adult word, on this view, would have a different account before and after the onset of language: after language begins, word imitations are based on segmental/structural representations. These structures cannot be inferred from experience in hearing or making speech sounds, but must become available through the maturation of genetically-specified cognitive mechanisms that have evolved over time to fit the demands and capacities of the auditory, articulatory and cognitive processing systems. The contrast between the infant's abilities in acoustic discrimination and the toddler struggling with the sounds of words might then be accounted for by the challenge of learning to operate skillfully with these new structures.

It is a measure of the primitive state of our understanding of phonological development that the data Studdert-Kennedy cites to support his perceptuomotor model could be equally-well accommodated by this segmental model. We will cite two examples.

1. **Word-by-word spread of new allophones.** Studdart-Kennedy notes that a model which relies on acoustic (or, presumably, even abstract) catagories to drive motor control has difficulty in accounting for the fact that a new allophone often appears to spread slowly through the child's productions, one word at a time. If the segment is truly a catagory, the implied argument goes, then when the child knows

that category, he should have control of it in all the relevant words in his lexicon. Yet, nothing in a model that posits segmental representations requires that when a child masters a new segment, he automatically adds it to every lexical item. It is equally plausible that he must hear the word again, in order to add the new segment to its representation, or that he must practice integrating its production with the contextual sounds of each particular word, or even that the new knowledge appears first for newly-learned words, only later having an effect on the forms of earlier-learned items.

In sum, our present understanding of phonic skill can be equally well accommodated in a segmental model. To resolve the issue, detailed studies of the way new segments and distinctions are reflected in a child's productions are necessary. We know that a given segment can emerge in initial position and in final position at separate times; we need to know more about how an initial consonant, for example, spreads through the sets of lexical items where, in the childs production, it is (a) omitted, (b) merged with another segment, or (c) substituted for. These kinds of data have so far resisted systematic collection.

2. **Slowness of initial lexical expansion** A second argument raised in Studdert-Kennedy's discussion is that segmental theories have difficulty accounting for the slowness with which the first fifty words are acquired. Yet this observation might simply reflect a gradual relaxation of constraints on the child's maturing phonological memory, or the child's difficulties in constructing a new motor control pattern for each new early word, even after some form of the word was learned and stored. Again it would be useful to compare perceptual and production data: what is the relation between the number and identity of words recognized, and the number and identity of words produced by a given child at this pre-fifty-word stage? If the word recognition capacity grows much more rapidly than the observable production of recognizable adult words, then the slow expansion of the initial lexicon has different implications.

The fact that almost any existing piece of evidence can be accommodated in either theory is a reflection of how strikingly our theories underspecify the concrete details of the development process, even in terms of the range of possibilities. In this sense, Studdert-Kennedy's paper is particularly useful, because it makes several predictions that can be directly tested. For example, the claim that early perceptual abilities are not phonetic but auditory allows the prediction that preference for matching auditory and optical (face movement) patterns should not be restricted to speech gestures, but should extend to nonspeech sounds made by the human vocal tract, such as whistles, snarls and slow bilabial trills.

A second prediction follows from the claim that articulatory abilities unfold independent of the phonemic shape of the surrounding language. This claim suggests that the babbling of children in their first year should be nearly identical across languages, as long as their speech motor control faculties are intact. This similarity should emerge not just in the general properties noted in this paper but in the acoustic-phonetic details of early babbles. Of course it is difficult to compare the acoustic-phonetic details of articulation patterns for very early speech; it is hard to assign individual utterances to target categories, since we have no idea of what the infant is 'intending'. Nevertheless, we need to find ways around this problem, in order to evaluate the strong form of the independence hypothesis, which predicts that the details of distribution will be constant across infants from different adult language communities. The possibility that individual children may follow different 'routes' to language mastery need not rule out this comparison, but it highlights the necessity of including large numbers of children in the samples.

Finally, Studdert-Kennedy's model predicts that the course of phonological development for non-speaking but normal-hearing children (e.g. those who are mute or suffer from motor-control pathologies) should fall well outside the range of variation for speaking children, since the nature of the task and the tools available to them do not include the imitative practice that Studdert-Kennedy views as central to the development of the perceptuomotor system for speech. Experimental tasks that tap the perceptual and memory capacities of these children can be expected to reveal whether their phonological and lexical knowledge develops in strikingly different ways.

In addition to suggesting several immediate lines of research, the paper raises a number of more diffuse but extremely important questions that need to be addressed by the field. Among them are the following:

1) **The imitation process.** How does imitation occur, and in particular, what is it that improves as the surface form of the child's imitation comes to resemble the adult model more closely? One possibility is that the stored form that the child intends to produce grows more detailed or more accurate: on this view, improvement in imitation accuracy reflects a change in the stored version of the target. A second possibility is that there is improvement in the child's ability to translate the stored form of a word into appropriately ordered and coordinated plan: in this view, imitation becomes more accurate as the child learns how to construct a better utterance plan. Still a third possibility is that the child's ability to use auditory and/or proprioceptive feedback during the articulation gesture matures: on this view, improved imitation comes with development of the child's ability to execute or "run off" a speech plan. Some facts about the observable results of this critically-important aspect of language development are beginning to emerge from patterns of change in the acoustic phonetic details of the productions of individual children, e.g. Maxwell (this volume), Bickley (1984), Kewley Port and Preston (1972), Macken and Barton (1980), Chapin (1983) and others, but concrete progress will be slow until we have the results of coordinated studies of the production, perception, memory and manipulation abilities of many children over an extended period of development.

Still more complexity arises when we consider the details of processing for the following chain of events, described by Ferguson and cited by Studdert-Kennedy: the child hears an adult word and attempts to pronounce it, finds his production unsatisfactory and then immediately makes a series of attempts which come closer and closer to the adult form. What can we infer about the processing steps that underlie this behavior? First, the sound produced by the adult must be processed by the child's auditory system and translated into a form that can be stored. This cannot be the raw acoustic form if, like adults, small children lose the echoic form of an acoustic memory after a second or so. Anecdotal evidence suggests that children go through a "tape loop" stage at which they can immediately imitate adult words of some complexity with great accuracy; it would be very interesting to know what the constraints on echoic memory are for 6-month old infants and how they change during development.

The second aspect of the imitation processing that we can infer is that the child's stored form of the adult word guides the computation of the appropriate plan and motor control pattern for the articulatory gestures that produce the word. In addition it may serve as a benchmark, against which the child can later compare the form of his own output.

Tracking our way through the imitation process, we have so far identified the auditory processing that forms a storable representation, and the construction of an utterance plan based on that representation. Now, in step three, the child executes the plan, producing an acoustic result, and forms a storable representation of his own rendition. At this point a comparison process must take place, and a mismatch must be detected, to motivate a second imitation attempt. This mismatch may implicate the stored form of the word, the utterance plan or the execution of that plan. Once the nature of the mismatch is recognized, there must be a decision about what change will produce a more acceptable result. It is here that a specialized perceptuomotor system for speech like the one proposed by Studdert-Kennedy might be uniquely useful in providing information about the probable acoustic consequences of various changes.

It is clear from this very cursory discussion that our understanding of the imitation process is only in its initial stages. We have a long way to go before we can specify (a) the child's representation of the object he intends to imitate, (b) the process by which this representation guides the computation of an utterance plan, (c) the detection of a mismatch in the result and identification of the nature of that mismatch, and (d) computation of the required changes. Yet, all of these components are necessary to an understanding of the role of the imitation process in speech and language development. Data that explore the interrelations between a child's perceptual, articulatory, mnemonic and imitative abilities may clarify these issues.

2) **Perceptuomotor abilities.** A second important question raised in the paper concerns the definition of the proposed specialized perceptuomotor system, and specification of the abilities it implies. One possibility is a straight-through automatic system, in which any speech signal produced by a human vocal tract could be instantaneously analyzed in terms of its articulatory requirements, and could be accurately reproduced on the first try if it were within the physical range of the listener's vocal apparatus. This is clearly not what Studdert-Kennedy is proposing for the one-year-old child, since the child's early performance reveals that the imitation mechanism operates imperfectly and is still developing. Another possibility, barely sketched by Studdert-Kennedy, is that in its early stages of development this system can extract from the acoustic signal (and reproduce in its motor output) information about the place of closure for the consonants of a word, but has more trouble with the sequencing and timing information.

Whatever its properties, a perceptuomotor link that permits the child to analyze his own spoken output, and compute the changes that must be made in the articulatory gesture to bring it's result closer to the adult form, would provide one step in the complex chain of processing events that underlies early imitation. Such a system might be the precursor to the mechanism that allows adults to compute very rapidly the changes necessary to permit compensation for variations in articulatory conditions, so that even when speaking with a pencil or a bite block in one's mouth or attached to an experimental apparatus that can suddenly apply a displacement force to the lip, the adult speaker achieves something close to the appropriate articulatory and acoustic result.

3) **Word representations.** Finally, this paper raises in challenging terms the question of what counts as persuasive evidence that a child is formulating word representations in terms of discrete phonemic segments. More generally, how is one to know when a child begins to formulate adult-like representations and use adult-like processing in speaking and listening? This question is particularly hard to deal with, as Studdert-Kennedy points out, because in addition to the usual difficulties of determining the elements of cognitive representations from complex and indirect behavioral evidence, we face the problems of describing the child's utterances in a way that doesn't predetermine the answer, and capturing the structure of a rapidly changing system without an extensive and comprehensive survey of the whole system every few days. Studdert-Kennedy reminds us that it is unwise to interpret equivocal evidence for segmental and featural analysis in unequivocal terms, just because such an interpretation fits our convictions about the form that the adult system will eventually take, or because rigorous tests of the segmental hypothesis are so difficult.

On the other hand, there is a substantial body of evidence to suggest that the child's utterances of words do not reveal everything that the child knows, particularly to the adult ear. As Studdert-Kennedy points out with a series of cogent quotes from the literature, immediately-repeated attempts to articulate a given word suggest that the child is exploring the possibilities for organizing the articulation of a stored form that is not fully captured by any one of his attempts. To take another example, if a child systematically says [gʌk] for "duck" and [bɪp] for "dip" yet recognizes the adult form of these words, we can infer that his representation of the initial segments of "duck" and "dip" is not fully reflected in his productions.

Other findings further illustrate the claim that young speakers have representations that are not fully revealed to adult listeners. For example, children sometimes rely on acoustic-phonetic distinctions that adults don't notice, to mark differences between categories (Maxwell & Weismer, 1979; Kornfeld, 1971). Children sometimes object strenuously to adult attempts to reproduce the child's own form of a word, like [fɪs] for "fish" (Berko & Brown, 1960). This may occur because the child distinguishes final /s/ from final /š/ in his own production in a way that the adult imitation fails to capture, or it may be that the child expects the adult to speak the adult dialect rather than the child dialect. In any case, the observation suggests that the adult transcription [fɪs] does not capture everything that the child knows about the sound structure of the word "fish," and points up the need for detailed acoustic-phonetic analyses of child production, combined with perceptual studies.

Other examples: Some children tend to revert to more primitive phonological forms of words just as they begin to combine those single words into longer utterances. For example, the morpheme "come" is pronounced [kʌm] as a single word but [pʌm] in the phrase "come in" or "smoke coming up" (de Villiers and de Villiers 1978). It is unlikely that these children have forgotten the information contained in the more accurate forms; perhaps the exigencies of syntactic and intonational planning leave little time for elaborating those more accurate forms. Whatever the explanation, the observation suggests that a transcription of the word as produced by the child at this word-combination stage may not capture what the child knows about its phonology. Finally, parents often report that children can recognize many words that they never use spontaneously, again suggesting that the study of articulation habits alone is an inadequate measure of the child's developing phonological representations.

Since the observable surface form of the child's utterance may not reveal the full extent of his knowledge of the segments and structure of a word, it seems wise to reserve judgement on whether this knowledge is limited to the dimensions of perceptuomotor control, until we know more about the range of phonemic skills the child has, and can infer more reliably what the form of his knowledge must be. This knowledge can come from studies that explore the child's changing articulatory and perceptual abilities with detailed acoustic-phonetic analyses. For example, it would be extremely useful to have, for a given child at a given point in his phonological development,

a) detailed acoustic-phonetic analyses of a number of utterances of some of his words, including successive attempts at correction, and in both one- and many-word contexts.

b) a survey of the words the child recognizes, as well as experimental data on his ability to distinguish word pairs that differ minimally, and

c) data on the duration of echoic memory, for both speech and nonspeech sounds, and constraints on the ability to transfer information from short-term to long-term memory.

In addition to studies of these aspects of processing ability as they change over time, it would be useful to have day-to-day recorded-speech studies of the spread of new allophones in old and new lexical items, variation in the articulated form of an already-mastered segment in words and phrases of varying complexity, and the form of imitated *vs* spontaneously-produced words.

Even this partial inventory of needed data looks daunting, and will require both patient determination and imaginitive creation of new methods. But without studies that triangulate in on the child's representations by examining several processing abilities at once, we will not make rapid progress toward the goal of modelling phonological development, and accounting for the apparent paradoxes that Studdert-Kennedy wrestles with here.

Though we don't know much for sure about the process of phonological development, we do know, as Studdert-Kennedy points out, that the child must learn to organize his articulatory mechanism to speak. His paper provides a compelling reminder of the complexity of this process, as well as of its central importance for normal language acquisition. It has sometimes been noted that as the child is learning to speak his native language, he is also mastering for the first time the skill of speaking at all. It is a little as if children learned to control their arms and legs by learning to dance Swan Lake. It is therefore not surprising that our understanding of the process advances slowly, particularly since integrated longitudinal data from a variety of tasks, which might reveal necessary links between different developing skills, are so difficult to obtain.

4

On The Genetic Basis of Linguistic Variation

Philip Lieberman
Brown University

Two biological premises structure the form of modern linguistic theory. First, that there is a genetically transmitted, biological substrate that determines human linguistic ability. Second, that this biological substrate, the "fixed nucleus," that determineslinguistic "competence," is uniform throughout the species homo sapiens (Chomsky, 1980). The data that I will discuss are consistent with the first premise, but refute the second premise—that the biological linguistic substrate is uniform for all people.

The premise that everyone has a similar linguistic competence probably follows from an assumption that has been implicit for many years in linguistic, and to an extent in psychological, theory. This assumption is that genetically transmitted biological mechanisms are, by their nature, uniform throughout the population that defines a species. In a gross and simplified sense this is true. Human beings thus usually have two legs and lack wings. However, it is also clear that there are biological differences between the individuals who constitute the population that we would classify as a species. The biological and genetic data that have emerged since Charles Darwin proposed his theory of evolution by means of natural selection are consistent with this view. Genetically transmitted variation is the feedstock for evolution by means of natural selection. There is variation throughout all mammalian populations in all the organs that regulate life. Human beings, like all other animals, furthermore are put together in genetic "bits and pieces." Even when we examine the genetic regulation of closely linked anatomical structures like our upper and lower jaws, or the bones that form the joints of our fingers, we discover that the parts are under independent genetic regulation (Stockard, 1941). Many people, for example, have mandibles that are longer or shorter than their palates. Extreme functional mismatches are, in time, filtered out by the mechanism of natural selection.

85

Variation is present in all of the genetically transmitted attributes of human beings. Some people have blue eyes, others brown. Some individuals can digest the milk of ungulates, others not. Some can perceive all color distinctions, others not. The degree of genetic variation that is present at chromosomal locations in human beings is at least 6.7% (Ayala, 1978). There is always a large pool of variation within the population that defines a species which can allow the species as a population to adapt to changing circumstances. The potential for selection therefore can be viewed as a mechanism for the survival of the species in the struggle for existence. Genetic variation, because it is coded discretely, is not completely predictable in an individual, nor is the pattern of variation completely correlated. Though we can determine the incidence of color blindness in a population, we cannot predict with certainty whether a particular individual will be colorblind. Again, the genetic variation that results in a color perception deficit is not correlated with the genes that regulate other aspects of visual perception. Color deficits moreover, are not correlated with cognitive ability.

The data that we will discuss demonstrate extreme variations that can be viewed as deficits in the identification of the English stop consonants [b], [d], and [g] that differ with respect to place of articulation, and deficits in the identification of the vowels of English. These deficits occur in a dyslexic population that has reading difficulties. None of the subjects had, or has, any auditory deficiencies that can explain these speech perception deficits. Only 5 of the 19 subjects are left-handed; absolute correlation between dyslexia and handedness is thus not evident.

EXPERIMENTS

The subjects were all adults who were voluntarily enrolled in the reading clinic of the Language Disorders Unit of the Massachusetts General Hospital. Psychoacoustic tests were administered to 19 subjects. Four series of vowel identification and consonant identification tests were administered over a period of 27 months. Owing to the clinical situation, only 14 subjects participated in all the psychoacoustic tests. However, 18 subjects participated in the tests on vowel identification, 15 subjects in the psychoacoustic tests involving stop consonants. Case histories of all the subjects were available that noted past or present auditory problems, speech production problems, and other individual traits. A number of clinical diagnostic tests appropriate to the setting of the reading clinic were also administered. IQ measures including separate Verbal and Performance scores and Gray Oral reading equivalent scores were derived using the Revised Wechsler Intelligence Scale. The reading comprehension tests that were given to the subjects range from the Stanford Achievement Battery from primary through high school levels, some parts of the Gates Maginitie Reading tests, and the Nelson Denny Reading test. Different tests were administered to different individuals commensurate with the subject's educational and oral reading level.

Consonants

The psychoacoustic tests were conducted using tape recordings which were presented to the subjects through high quality headphones at a comfortable listening level. Six different tape recordings were used. Three tape recordings were presented to the subjects in which they were asked to identify the initial consonant of a consonant-vowel syllable. These tape recordings were ones that had been used in a previous study (Chapin, Tseng, & Lieberman, 1982) with subjects who have no difficulty in reading. These stimuli were prepared by editing samples of discourse from the utterances of a year and a half child who was talking with her mother. The utterances were converted to digitalized signals and computer edited to obtain short and long duration speech samples that included the first 15 (short) and 135 (long) msec of each consonant-vowel syllable starting from release of the stop consonant. Thirty utterances were edited by computer. All of the editing cuts were made at zero-crossings on an oscillographic display to reduce interfering transients.

A computer program was used to generate tape recordings in which stimuli edited to a particular duration appeared in random order, with each stimulus repeated six times. These tape recordings had been played to listeners who had no reading problems. These listeners were asked to identify each initial consonant as either a B, D, or G (Chapin, et al., 1982). A second series of tape recordings were derived by computer editing thirty consonant-vowel utterances derived from the discourse of the mother addressing her child. These utterances were computer edited following the same procedures to durations of 20 and 135 msec. These tape recordings also had been played to listeners who were asked to identify the initial stop consonant. These utterances included both voiced and unvoiced English stop consonants, i.e. [p], [b], [t], [d], [k], and [g]. In this present study, these four tape recordings were first presented to ten adult dyslexic subjects who were asked to identify the initial consonants by marking an appropriate box on an answer sheet.

Table 4.1 shows the overall percent of correct responses of the dyslexic listeners and the nondyslexic listeners who heard these same tape recordings. Note that the overall error rates are about 30% greater for the dyslexic population. The comparative error rate is about the same for the control group of nondyslexic listeners and the dyslexic listeners for the long and short stimuli. Both the nondyslexic and dyslexic listeners appear to be making use of both encoded formant frequency transition cues to place of articulation

TABLE 4.1
Percent Correct Identification of Place of Articulation of Stop Consonants for Dyslexic and Nondyslexic Subjects

Stimulus Duration

	Long (135 msec)		Short (15–20 msec)	
	Adult	Child	Adult	Child
Dyslexics	57	57	39	36
Nondyslexics	88	93	53	71

present in the long 135 msec stimuli, and short-term onset cues present in the short 15–20 msec long stimuli.

One of the deficiencies of the procedure that we used in this first test is that there is an inherent confound between the transcription ability of the dyslexic subjects and possible perception misidentifications of the test stimuli. We therefore retested the ten dyslexic subjects using a procedure that eliminated the transcription problem. We presented the tape recording of the long computer-edited stimuli derived from the child to the individual dyslexic subjects, who were instructed to immediately repeat the sound that they heard. As each subject repeated what she or he heard, a phonetically trained observer transcribed their responses. The observer made use of visual as well as auditory cues to place of articulation. We also established, by means of psychoacoustic tests that will be described in the pages that follow, that the dyslexic subjects were able to produce these consonantal sounds. All identifications of a stimulus that differed with respect to place of articulation were scored as errors. For the purposes of this experiment, we scored repetitions that differed with respect to voicing as correct if place of articulation was correct, e.g., [p] for [b]. The overall percent correct was 76% using this procedure. Thus we may conclude that part of the high error rate measured using the transcription procedure followed from difficulties that the dyslexic subjects had in making phonetic transcriptions, rather than perceptual errors per se. The error rate of 24% is still significantly greater than the 7% error rate of the nondyslexic control group. However, what was most striking was not the overall error rate of the dyslexic subjects, but the individual differences.

Table 4.2 shows error rates in percentages for each dyslexic subject for the long (135 msec) utterances in both the transcription and the dictation tests. The error rate averaged across [b], [d], and [g] is noted for each subject. Note that the error rates of several subjects are dramatically lower when they dictated their responses. Subjects 1, 2, 4, 5, 7, and 10 fall into this category. Subject 2's error rate is, for example, 60% when he was asked to transcribe

TABLE 4.2

Percent <u>Errors</u> for Place of Articulation for Each Dyslexic Subject

Subject	Dictation	Transcription
1	18	39
2	11	60
3	45	56
4	12	38
5	12	34
6	47	47
7	16	28
8	33	31
9	50	43
10	21	49

the stimuli. His error rate falls to 11% using the dictation procedure. The average error rate of the control group of nondyslexic subjects is 9% and does not differ greatly from that of subjects 2, 4, 5, 7, 15, and 16. In contrast, the error rates of dyslexic subjects 3, 6, 8, and 9 is high for the dictated responses, ranging from 30 to 50 percent.

The pattern of errors according to place of articulation also varied for different groups of subjects. In Table 4.3, errors are tabulated for [b], [d], and [g] for each subject for the responses made using the dictation procedure. Whereas subject 9, for example, has a high error rate for all three places of articulation, subjects 6 and 8 have high [d] and [g] and low [b] error rates. Subjects 2, 4, 7, and 14 have low overall error rates but have high error rates for [b]. Subjects 11 and 13 have high [g] error rates and low overall rates. The error rates are different for the individual subjets and subject groups. It is important to keep in mind the error rates for these stimuli derived from the control group of 16 nondyslexic listeners noted in Chapin, et al. (1982). The error rates for these same stimuli are 8, 5, and 10% respectively for [b], [d], and [g]. Individual dyslexic listeners show error rates are four times greater for the identification of these sounds. The direction of the confusions between consonants also varied for different groups of subjects.

Vowel Identification

One of the observations that is frequently made in connection with the remediation of dyslexic patients is that they have difficulty with vowels. We therefore prepared a series of tape recordings for psychoacoustic vowel identification tests. Three tape recordings were prepared using a computer system adapted for this purpose. One tape recording presented speech signals that

TABLE 4.3
Pattern of Errors According to Place of Articulation

Sub-ject	Sex	Consonant Errors				Vowel Errors		IQ			Oral Reading Grade
		Aver-age	/b/	/d/	/g/	To-tal	w/o /a/O/	Aver-aged	Verbal	Per-for-mance	
1	M	18	22	17	22	27	30	105	97	116	2.0
2	M	11	22	2	4	16	30	93	90	99	3.7
3	M	45	52	60	23	63	71	93	89	99	5.7
4	F	12	23	5	7	31	40	122	122	120	10.3
5	M	12	22	0	13	–	–	85	93	77	9.0
6	M	47	13	53	77	12	16	102	98	106	3.7
7	M	16	28	7	12	45	51	110	111	107	8.7
8	F	33	17	34	50	13	16	91	87	98	2.6
9	M	50	48	43	58	0	9	123	115	131	11.0
10	M	21	27	8	27	38	36	119	118	117	6.4
11	F	10	7	3	20	40	45	106	108	102	5.4
12	F					59	66	89	86	96	5.1
13	F	23	17	15	33	33	37	84	89	80	3.9
14	M	13	27	2	12	21	25	98	93	106	3.7
15	M	11	8	3	20	12	16	108	104	111	9.7
16	M	6	3	3	10	23	26	111	112	107	3.4
17	M					9	11	102	103	100	5.4
18	M					10	15	79	76	86	3.6
19	M					13	23	100	92	110	5.1

consisted of the English words *bat, pet, peat, did, cot, took, Maude, gut,* and *boot* recorded by an adult, phonetically trained native female speaker of American English. The words were carefully produced in isolation and were judged to be good exemplars of the vowels of American English. Words that were judged to be correctly pronounced were converted to digital signals, examined for any signs of distortion using an oscillographic display, and copied onto a test tape by computer programs. Ten repetitions of each of these nine words in random order appeared on the test tape. A second tape was prepared using the same speaker and procedures. This tape recording presented the same nine vowels of American English in the words *had, head, heed, hid, hod, hood, hawed, hud, who'd.* These stimuli approximated the speech signals used in the Peterson and Barney (1952) study.

A third tape recording was prepared in which we presented synthesized vowels. The vowels were synthesized using our computer system as a cascade synthesizer by means of the computer program written by Klatt (1981). We synthesized the nine American English vowels noted above using the average formant frequencies of F_1 and F_2 found by Peterson and Barney (1952). The value of 3300 Hz was used for F_3. The fundamental frequency of phonation started at 135 Hz, which again is the Peterson and Barney (1952) average value for adult male voices. The fundamental frequency was made to drop 10% by the end of the 200 msec long synthesized stimuli to increase their naturalness. Each stimulus was presented ten times in random order on the tape recording that was used in the psychoacoustic tests. We had used these same stimuli in a previous experiment with a group of nondyslexic subjects (Ryalls & Lieberman, 1982). These three tape recordings were presented in separate sessions to 16 adult dyslexic subjects. Seven of these subjects had previously been tested using the consonant stimuli discussed earlier. We again used a "dictation" procedure in which the subjects were asked to repeat the sounds that they heard, recording their responses on a cassette recorder while they listened to the test stimuli over headphones. The subjects' responses were then scored by two phonetically trained, nondyslexic listeners.

With the exception of the [a] and [ɔ] vowel contrast, which is not stable in the dialects of many of our subjects, virtually no errors occurred when they listened to the two tape recordings of natural speech stimuli. These results are similar to the responses of nondyslexic subjects who will identify vowels with virtually no errors if the difficulties of phonetic transcription are circumvented (Kahn, 1978; Assman, 1979). The dyslexic subjects also made virtually no consonantal errors when they listened to and repeated these natural speech stimuli. These tests demonstrate that our subjects can produce the consonantal stimuli under the general test conditions that we used. The errors that occurred when they listened to the 135 msec long stimuli derived from discourse that cannot be ascribed to inherent difficulties in speech production since we used the same interstimulus interval in all our psychoacoustic test tapes.

The dyslexic subjects, however, did differ from our nondyslexic control groups on the computer synthesized vowel stimuli. The overall rate for the nondyslexic subjects who were forced to make phonetic transcriptions of the vowel stimuli was 10%. If we eliminate [a] versus [ɔ] confusions, the error rate falls to 9%. If we compare the dictated responses of the dyslexic subjects to these error rates, some dyslexic subjects cannot be differentiated from normal subjects on this test. Subjects 15, 9, 17, and 18 whose error rates are noted in Table 4.3 thus show low error rates. Other dyslexic subjects, however, have significantly larger error rates. Subject 12's error rate was 59%. Subjects 7 and 11's error rates were 45 and 40% respectively; subjects 10 and 13's error rates were 38 and 33% respectively. Other error rates were in the 20 to 30 percent range. The pattern of the dyslexic subject's confusions involves vowels that have similar formant frequency patterns and do not differ from the pattern of confusion typically reported for nondyslexic subjects since the time of the Peterson and Barney study(1952). The magnitude of the confusions is, however, substantially greater except for the vowel [i] which is almost never misidentified by the dyslexic subjects. Indeed, 15 of the 16 dyslexic subjects *never* misidentified [i]; five [i] errors were made by one subject, number 10. Error rates for the dyslexic subjects excluding the [a] versus [ɔ] dialect confound and [i] responses are perhaps a better indication of the comparative vowel identification deficiency of some dyslexic subjects and are thus noted in Table 4.3.

Retest Procedures

The errors made by some of the dyslexic subjects were so extreme that we instituted a series of procedures to retest and check the validity of our data. We first checked through the clinical records for either past or present auditory deficiencies or instances of trauma that might affect the auditory system. The check revealed no such instances. The dyslexic subjects' responses to the tape recordings of natural speech in the vowel study ruled out any gross speech production or test-taking difficulties, that might prevent their repeating the sounds that they identified. Moreover, we also systematically tested our subjects to see whether they could correctly repeat spoken vowel and consonantal contrasts. They all could do this when an isolated spoken CV or CVC syllable was presented to them.

We also tested our transcription procedure by means of a double blind transcription test in which a specialist in phonetic transcription who has years of experience in the transcription of English, as well as non-Indo-European languages, transcribed the cassette recordings that seven of our dyslexic subjects made when they listened to the computer synthesized vowels. The transcriber did not know either the details of the previous transcriptions or the "correct" answers. To complete the retest of our procedures, we had six of these seven subjects listen to the tape recording of synthesized vowels again. The subjects were again asked to dictate their responses. The error rates and patterns of errors derived from the double-blind transcription of these responses were consistent with our earlier data. The error rates agreed within 5%, tending to be slightly higher except for subject 4 whose error rate increased from 59 to 73%. The errors in our psychoacoustic tests that used the dictation procedure thus, in all likelihood, reflect perceptual deficits.

DISCUSSION OF THE DATA

The data that we have discussed appear to reflect discrete speech perception deficits. These deficits are not present in the entire population of dyslexic subjects, nor is there a uniform pattern of errors in identification of vowels and stop consonant place of articulation. Table 4.3 presents vowel identification error rates as well as consonantal error rates for the seven subjects who participated in the full set of psychoacoustic tests. Though some subjects—e.g., subjects 11, 7, and 10—have higher error rates for both consonants and vowels, other subjects show different patterns. Subjects 8 and 6 thus have high error rates for stop consonants and low vowel error rates. However, these generalizations fail to capture the variation in the pattern of errors of different subgroups of subjects for particular consonantal place of articulation contrasts.

There is no apparent correlation between error rates and the IQ scores derived from the WAIS tests. The data of Table 4.3 show that high vowel and high consonantal error rates occur for subjects whose verbal IQ scores differ by 32 points. Lower Oral Reading Grade Equivalents can be associated with high vowel error rates but note that one subject, number 7, has a high vowel error rate at an equivalent 8.7 Reading Grade. High consonantal error rates occurred for subjects who had high Oral Reading Grade Equivalents; subject 9, for example, had an average error rate of 50% and a reading equivalent grade of 11. High and low consonant error rates also occurred for subjects who had low reading equivalent grades, e.g., subjects 6 and 16. Both of these subjects had about the same overall IQ. A high consonantal error rate also occurred with a comparatively high Oral Reading Equivalent Grade of 11.0 for subject 9 whose overall IQ was 123. All of the dyslexic subjects tested in this study, of course, have reading difficulties which have led them to enroll in the program of remediation at the Language Disabilities Unit.

It is apparent from family patterns that many forms of dyslexia are genetically transmitted. Recent studies, for example, of families with a three-generation history of dyslexia are consistent with a pattern of alletic variation of chromosome 15 (Smith, Kimberling, Pennington & Lubs, 1983). Our data refute theories like that of Tallal and Piercy (1975) that claim that all reading deficiencies follow from a general sensory deficiency involving dyslexics being unable to follow rapid temporal events. Though the errors in stop consonant identification are consistent with a theory that claimed that all dyslexics are deficient with respect to the sensory processing of rapid temporal sequences, the vowel errors occurred for synthesized signals that have steady formant frequency patterns.

The errors of the dyslexic subject on the synthesized vowel stimuli might appear to follow from the relatively short 200 msec durations of these stimuli. However, this explanation is ruled out by the almost perfect identification of the [i] stimuli. The vowel [i] appears to act quite differently than other vowels. It appears to be less susceptible to adaptation effects (Sawusch, Nusbaum & Schwab, 1980) and may function as an optimal vocal tract length calibrating vowel signal (Lieberman, 1975; Nearey, 1978). However, we must recall that the subjects showing vowel identification deficits performed without errors when they listened to carefully articulated natural speech stimuli. The synthesized vowel stimuli differed only with respect to steady state formant patterns. The natural stimuli also differed with respect to patterns of formant frequency variation that are the consequences of diphthongization and duration (Nearey, 1978). The dyslexic subjects may have made use of these additional acoustic cues to phonemic vowel class when they listened to the natural stimuli. It is likely that human languages make use of diphthongization and duration distinctions to help convey phonemic distinctions that otherwise might not be reliably conveyed.

The high error rates of some dyslexic subjects on the 135 msec computer edited Consonant–Vowel stimuli cannot be simply ascribed to the short duration of the stimuli. If the deficit simply followed from the stimuli's short durations, we would expect the effects to be uniform with respect to place of articulation for a given subject. This is not the case; although subjects 6 and 9 have high, almost uniform, error rates for labials, dentals, and velars, the pattern is variable for the other subjects who have high consonantal error rates. Subject 6, for example, has a 13% error rate for [b]'s and 53 and 77% error rates for [d]'s and [g]'s. Subject 3 shows a different pattern: 23% for [g] but 52 and 60% for [b] and [d]. In general, [d] shows the lowest error rate, [g] the highest error rate.

The pattern of errors is consistent with the presence of neural mechanisms that are adapted for the identification of different consonantal place of articulation features. The short 135 msec duration of the stimuli may perhaps stress the system, making comparative deficiencies of "weaknesses" of particular neural "detector" mechanisms in individual subjects apparent. Similar examples can be found in other aspects of human life. It is obvious that human beings differ with respect to the strength of their vertebrae and supporting musculature, and that this variation is in large measure genetically transmitted. These differences might not be evident in our day-to-day sedentary existence, but they would become apparent in an environment that stressed people's backs, e.g., carrying heavy weights continually. Similarly, the short duration of the consonantal stimuli can be regarded as a stress condition. The nondyslexic control group and some dyslexic subjects had little difficulty in identifying these stimuli. Some subgroups of dyslexics, however, had high error rates for particular place of articulation distinctions. One hypothesis that appears to account for the comparative deficits of the subjects is that there is variation in the neural substrate that is involved in the identifying features of consonantal place of articulation from the acoustic signal. Whether these variations involve processing of formant frequency transitions, short-term spectral onset cues, or both is not apparent.

PHONETIC CODING AND READING DEFICIENCIES

Deficiencies in phonetic coding have been linked to reading deficiencies in a number of recent studies. Liberman, Shankweiler, Orlando, Harris, & Berti (1971), Shankweiler, Liberman, Mark, Fowler, & Fischer (1979), and Liberman & Shankweiler (1979) offer an explanation for the phonetic coding hypothesis. The speech perception deficits that are apparent in the data that we have discussed would obviously increase the difficulty of establishing phonetic recoding of orthographic symbols in reading. A child, in acquiring a language, must establish an equivalence class into which tokens of the acoustic signal are grouped to establish a phonetic classification. If a person is not able to reliably identify certain acoustic cues as tokens of a phonetic event, then that phonetic class will not be equivalent to that of other individuals who make use of that particular acoustic cue to signal the phonetic event.

Dyslexic subjects whose identifications of formant frequency patterns were less reliable than those of other individuals could, for example, fall back onto the differences in duration that also play a part in differentiating the vowels of English. They could still perceive speech signals but they would be deficient in using one of the principal acoustic cues to the phonetic class of a vowel. The situation is in some ways analogous to that which would confront a person whose vision was color-deficient, who had to decipher a visual code that made use of color distinctions. Color-deficient individuals might be able to decipher the code making use of differences in luminosity, but their recognition procedure would be different and less robust than that of "normal" individuals who could make use of a full range of color distinctions.

On Variation

In speaking of the "normal" population, it is perhaps necessary to note that we really don't know the distribution of variation in speech perception. It is probable that many individuals who have no difficulty in reading cannot identify certain acoustic cues to phonetic events, as reliably as other individuals. Our pilot experiments show this to be the case. Some "normal," nondyslexic individuals may have perceptual deficiencies similar to some of the dyslexic population. The only way in which we can determine the range of variation in the population at large, is to study variation. Psychoacoustic experiments have traditionally been structured to determine a hypothetical "average" pattern of behavior that implicitly is supposed to be typical of the entire species. Subjects who perform in a mode that is at variance with the rest of the subject population are often treated as "end points" on a distribution that measures a unitary mode of behavior that has been affected by extraneous experimental "noise," i.e., "competence" sullied by "performance factors." Too often we "throw out" subjects whose performance is not up to some "criterion."

The problems inherent in designing experiments that look for variation are not simple to resolve. Aberrant behavior on the part of a subject, or group of subjects, may be the result of their not being able to follow instructions, or interpreting the instructions in some undesired way. The experimental design thus has to establish whether subjects can perform a particular task, e.g., repeating speech sounds. Differences in behavior become significant once we establish that the subjects can perform the task. Again, patterned variation in which a *class of subjects* exhibit a particular mode of behavior that is similar but different from that of other groups is significant. Genetic variation is by its nature discrete and should manifest itself in patterned behavior.

GENETIC ISOLATES, LANGUAGE DIVERSITY, AND LANGUAGE CHANGE

One of the predictions of the modern "synthetic" theory of evolution, a synthesis of the Darwinian theory of evolution by means of natural selection with modern genetics (Mayr, 1942), is the concept of divergence in genetic isolates. Rapid changes that lead to speciation can more readily occur in genetic isolates that are subject to different environments. As the size of an isolate population decreases, genetic variation decreases. Thus the range of possible optimal solutions to a new environmental condition decreases as the effects of chance increase. The data of comparative studies of nonhuman primates (Goodall, 1968), as well as the historical record, are consistent with the premise that particular human languages were in earlier periods spoken by smaller, more uniform groups that more closely approximate genetic isolates.

Given the genetic component of dyslexia (Smith, et al., 1983) it is evident that different human groups who spoke different languages might in an earlier period have had somewhat different neural substates that would yield different phonetic markedness conditions and perhaps different syntactic organization (Lieberman, 1984). So long as language was the "property" of a genetic isolate, a condition of equilibrium would be established. In a population that had a strong [g] "feature detector," there would not be a tendency to reduce the phonetic inventory of [g]. Again a population who could readily perceive the formant distinctions that differentiate vowels could develop a complex vowel system. A different population who lacked these neural mechanisms would more likely develop a linguistic code that minimized vowel distinctions based on subtle formant frequency distinctions. These genetically-transmitted differences might explain some of the divergence of languages that we note today. Genetic factors might also play a part in triggering the process of linguistic change when a language that previously was the property of a particular genetic isolate is diffused through contact or conquest into a wider population in which more genetic variation occurs. The initial conditions that structured markedness relations no longer would hold, opening the system to change.

The linguistic components of genetic variation are perhaps most pronounced at the phonetic level since the particular form of human speech is probably a comparatively recent development. Whereas the cognitive aspects of human linguistic ability probably derive from the more conservative aspects of the human brain which are probably structurally similar to the brains of other animals, the supralaryngeal vocal tract anatomy, neural control, and perceptual mechanisms particular to human speech appear to have evolved in the last 500,000 to 25,000 years (Lieberman, 1984). the likelihood of genetic variation at the phonetic level of language thus is more probable than at the "higher" cognitive aspects of linguistic ability.

CONCLUDING COMMENTS

It is probable that genetically-transmitted variation structures other aspects of human linguistic ability. The ability to perform the automatized articulatory maneuvers that underlie speech may be genetically transmitted and there may be *discrete* differences in the way that people produce speech. Some aspects of rule-governed behavior in language, morphology, and syntax may also involve a neural substrate that is language specific and genetically coded (Lieberman, 1984). Some of the disputes concerning the form of a syntactic description which involve differing opinions on the "grammaticality" of a crucial example, may reflect genetic variation in this domain. Again, recent data indicate that the perception and production of linguistic word stress is not uniform even in a highly literate population (Gewirth, 1983). These differences may reflect different phonological rule structures in different individuals. Some people may have a psychologically "real" bias for word stress, others may lack this aspect of linguistic ability.

The data that we have discussed are consistent with the theory that some forms of dyslexia involve alletic variation in the specific neural mechanisms that are involved in the perception of human speech. Several theories have been developed over the past thirty years that attempt to account for the perception of human speech. Though some investigators claim that speech perception is not very different from other aspects of audition (Kuhl, 1981), it is difficult to account for many of the phenomena of speech perception without hypothesizing neural perceptual mechanisms that are in a sense "special," i.e., neural mechanisms that are adapted to the perception of the specific acoustic properties of human speech (Liberman, Cooper, Shankweiler & Studdert-Kennedy, 1967; Lieberman, 1970, 1975, 1984). These mechanisms appear to be genetically-transmitted insofar as they are manifested in the earliest stages of infancy and appear to be present in all human populations. That genetic variation exists is not surprising.

Linguists often assume that a nativist position regarding the biological basis of language necessarily leads to the claim that linguistic ability—i.e., linguistic "competence" or "la langue"—is uniform throughout the population that makes use of a given language or dialect. This position is simply wrong. Even the most basic and central biologically determined aspects of human life, e.g., the anatomical and neural mechanisms that affect and regulate respiration, vary in the present human population (Bouhuys, 1974). The biological bases of respiration, moreover, have been filtered by the selective forces that are relevant to respiration in terrestrial animals for hundreds of millions of years. Despite this long evolutionary history, we find genetic variation in the biological mechanisms that structure respiration. The specific acoustic parameters that specify the consonantal and vowel distinctions that we have investigated in this chapter, their formant frequency patterns, and onset spectra, in contrast, appear to involve mechanisms which have evolved recently, over the past 500,000 years. Thus, it is not surprising to find genetically-transmitted variation in the ability of human listeners to identify these sounds.

It is likely that some aspects of speech perception as well as other aspects of human linguistic ability are more basic, in that their biological determinants are more uniformly distributed in the present human population. These aspects of human speech and language would, in a sense, constitute its most "universal" aspects. However, the only way that we can hope to determine what aspects of human linguistic ability are most central and basic is to study the actual pattern of variation. The data of this present study can be regarded as an initial step in this program. They establish the presence of genetically-transmitted variation in the identification of consonantal place of articulation and vowel classification—two of the most central distinctions of human speech.

Paula Menyuk: Comment

In his paper, Dr. Lieberman presents several hypotheses, provides his own and other investigators' data in support of these hypotheses, and then makes some suggestions for further research.

The first hypothesis presented is that there is a species-specific innate ability to acquire at least two components of language: phonology and syntax. Those genetically transmitted biological mechanisms that define the species and allow acquisition of these components are, by definition, uniform throughout the population. To support this hypothesis Lieberman points to the fact that nonhuman species lack these abilities. Supporting data are found in his own studies of differences between both the anatomical and neural control mechanisms of the human articulatory apparatus on the one hand and the vocal apparatus of nonhuman primates on the other.

However, the evidence for perception and production of speech sound differences as being a uniquely human ability is mixed. Certainly there is clear evidence that nonhuman primates are incapable of producing speech or speech-like sounds regardless of heroic efforts on the part of trainers. Lieberman suggests that nonhuman primates also cannot perceive speech-sound differences in a human manner. There is evidence that chinchillas (Kuhl & Miller, 1975) and rhesus monkeys (Morse & Snowden, 1975) can be trained to discriminate between speech-sound categories such as [pa] and [ba] and [da] and [ga] in a manner similar to the human. However, although some training is involved in infant speech-sound discrimination studies, the procedures employed are much less strenuous than those used with nonhumans. Rigorous and lengthy training procedures need to be employed (using both positive and aversive reinforcement) to get these animals to perform.

The same differences in learning conditions exist between the human infant's learning of language as a whole and the nonhuman primate's acquisition of a sign system. There is, in addition, some evidence that while nonhuman primates who acquire nonspeech symbol systems can combine elements into a string, these strings are fixed in structure (a small memorized set) or simply chains of randomly juxtaposed items (Seidenberg & Pettito, 1979). The acquisition of syntax then seems an impossible task for the nonhuman. The hypothesis that there is a species-specific ability to acquire some components of language seems well supported by the data obtained thus far.

The second hypothesis presented by Dr. Lieberman further defines his proposed set of genetically transmitted biological mechanisms that differentiates one species form another. Within this set, there is a large pool of variation. This large pool, it is further suggested, is important for survival of the species. Lieberman states, "Genetically transmitted variation is the feedstock for evolution by means of Natural Selection." He points out that this variation is present in "all" of the genetically transmitted attributes of human beings and gives as examples color of eyes, tolerance for certain food substances, and the efficiency of transfer of oxygen into the blood stream. This hypothesis is presented to counter claims by certain theorists that there is a holistic device [for language acquisition] that is similar throughout the population. Lieberman also suggests that these theorists claim that all human beings have the same linguistic ability.

The above hypothesized variation might consist of several aspects. The first is that there is variation within what one might term normal development. The second is that there is variation within what one might term "non-normal" development and the third is that there is variation between normal and non-normal development. It is this last aspect of variation that is dealt with most extensively in Dr. Lieberman's paper, although he does not categorize the data discussed as exemplifying this last type of variation. Rather he places this variation within the large pool. The data discussed throughout the paper are intended to provide support for this large pool of variation in speech sound processing, but they do so with varying degrees of success.

A large proportion of the data discussed was obtained in a study of speech sound identification in a dyslexic population. A number of experiments were designed to examine dyslexic subjects' ability to identify voiced stops ([b], [d], and [g]) and the vowels of English. In addition to hypothesizing variation in language ability, the overall claim being made from the data collected in these experiments is that these subjects have deficits that are local and limited and, therefore, provide evidence that there are genetically transmitted "... neural mechanisms that are adapted for the identification of different place of articulation features."

The data obtained indicate that there are significant differences between dyslexic and nondyslexic subjects. Clearly this supports the notion of group variation in language ability. Two other findings support the notion of individual variation in speech-sound perception *within* the dyslexic group. There were large differences among these subjects in their ability to identify the consonants. Errors ranged from a high of 60% to a low of 11%. In addition, for a majority of the subjects a shift in the response required (from transcription to dictation) had a marked positive effect (from +11 to +49%), no effect for one subject, and a slight negative effect for two others. The data certainly provide evidence of not only differences between normal readers and dyslexics in speech-sound identification, but also of variation among the dyslexics both in this ability and, to some degree, in the conditions under which more or fewer correct responses can be elicited.

Additional analyses of the data further substantiated the hypothesis of individual differences within this population. For some few subjects, there was almost equal difficulty in identifying the voiced stops, but for most there were sharp differences in accuracy of identification depending on the speech sound. For one subject, the order of difficulty was [b], [g], [d], for another [d], [b], [g], and so on. Virtually no errors were made by dyslexic subjects when they listened to and repeated vowel sounds from natural speech stimuli. They did differ, as a group, from nondyslexic subjects in identifying synthetic vowel sounds, but this difference could be accounted for by the responses of only a few subjects. Further, those subjects who were most accurate in identifying consonants were not the ones who were most inaccurate in identifying vowels. In this task number of errors ranged from 0 to 63. Again, there is evidence of difference between the normal readers as a group and the dyslexics as a group. There is also evidence of individual variation within the dyslexic population in speech-sound identification.

It is clear that the data support the hypothesis of individual variation in speech-sound identification for dyslexic persons. However, there is little evidence of such individual variation within the nondyslexic population. The proposed wide pool appears to be limited to the non-normal population. There is no data to support the claim that there are specific neural mechanisms adapted to the perception of "certain" speech events (as opposed to general speech-processing mechanisms), and that these mechanisms are genetically transmitted. Although there were differences in identification of particular consonant sounds among the dyslexic subjects, their identification ability varied depending on task conditions. It is not clear how this could happen if a one-to-one relation exists between a mechanism and a speech contrast. A less strong claim, that neural mechanisms are generally available for determining speech-sound contrasts as well as other acoustic contrasts, and that these mechanisms differ both within the dyslexic population and between dyslexics and nondyslexics, seems more supportable, given the data.

This ability is apparently separate from more general abilities, at least in this population. Both measured IQ and (surprisingly) reading scores appear to be unrelated to particular speech-sound difficulties or degree of difficulty. For example, the subject with the highest grade level reading score (11.0) and a high IQ score (123) makes an average of 50 consonantal errors (the highest number within the population). However, this subject makes no vowel errors. One might hypothesize that vowel errors are more related to reading, but this possibility is weakened by the observation that the subject with the lowest reading score (2.0) and above average IQ score (105) makes an average number of consonantal errors (18) and vowel errors (27). These data, again, support the hypothesis that there are neural mechanisms available for determining speech-sound contrasts and that these mechanisms are distinct from those employed in tasks on IQ tests and in reading. Thus, these mechanisms are both more general than is hypothesized by Lieberman and more specific than higher level linguistic processing.

Thus far the data support the hypothesis of individual variation within a particular non-normal population and difference from normal. This hypothesis can be extended to other non-normal populations. That is, one can find subgroups within the large pool of variation from normal that differ from each other just as they differ from normal. An example of this is the dyslexic population as compared to a learning disabled population. This latter population has more general difficulties than does the dyslexic population. Such subgroups are postulated within the aphasic population (Broca's, Wernicke's, Conductive, for example) on the same grounds; differences in knowledge and use of language. These differences are due to differences in neural substrates and may lead to a different (from each other and from normal) and/or less robust phonetic recognition procedure or phonetic matrix. Thus, although there is individual variation in speech-sound identification within the dyslexic group, there is a more marked distinction between them and nondyslexic subjects. This form of the hypothesis of variation has always been accepted by those who espouse a so called innate LAD (Language Acquisition Device). The claim has never been made that *all* humans are alike in language ability. Indeed differences due to brain "lesion" in interaction with experience are referred to in support of the notion that language development is due to biological maturation (Lenneberg, 1967).

The distinction between Dr. Lieberman's position and those who espouse some form of LAD is Lieberman's notion that variability of an important kind exists within the nondyslexic, nonaphasic, or so-called "normal" population due to differences in the neural substrates that are the bases for speech processing. The data that are used in the paper to support this hypothesis are findings of differences in speech-sound categorization functions for different listeners for stop sounds and variation "in the mode of language acquisition." The latter is described as variation in the rate and manner in which children acquire language.

Undoubtedly, there is variation to some degree within individuals in the "normal" population in the physiological and biochemical substrates that underlie all functions, but the important question is, "What do these differences mean in terms of carrying out these functions?" Some of the differences pointed to by Dr. Lieberman, that are representative of genetically transmitted attributes, seem to make no difference in function, (for example, eye color), others do and require some intervention (for example, differences in food substance tolerances), while still others may or may not make a difference depending on the degree to which they occur (for example, efficiency of transfer of oxygen into the blood stream).

Although there are differences in the rate and manner in which normally developing children acquire their phonological system and use it for the perception and production of speech, there is little indication that these differences result in a different and/or less robust phonetic matrix. Much of the data on individual variation in language acquisition for normally developing children indicate that there are stylistic variations in patterns of acquisition (Menyuk, 1977, Chap. 2). Some children produce chunks of speech while others work on one word at a time proportionately more frequently; still others equally balance the production of the two forms. Some children produce a large proportion of nouns as compared to pronouns, while others do the reverse; still others produce both classes with equal frequency. Some children use language proportionately more to refer, while others use language proportionately more to express needs and feelings.

These behaviors are most frequently referred to in the literature as evidence of individual variation in normal language development. It is important to note that proportion of behaviors is referred to, not presence or absence of behaviors. Further, at about age three, many of the differences observed at an earlier age have disappeared. Differences in rate also change in time during the early years so that some late beginners and slow acquirers catch up with early beginners and fast acquirers (Menyuk, 1979). Finally, and very importantly for any hypothesis concerning the biological bases of language acquisition, many of the differences observed appear to be related to environmental factors such as the style of speech used with the child and the emphasis placed by the environment on the hierarchy of importance of the uses of language to communicate and learn.

On the other hand, children with frank language disorders do not catch up. In fact, the differences between them and normally developing children become more marked with time. This occurs in all components of language development, including phonology (Menyuk, 1978). In this component, several types of behavior appear to distinguish language disordered children from their normally developing peers and from each other, beyond simple rate of acquisition (Menyuk, 1980). The first is the kinds of sound substitutions that occur in both perception and production of speech. For example, children within the language disordered population will, as late as age six or beyond, substitute |g| for |b| in perception and |k| for |p| in production. sounds that are markedly distinct from each other will also be substituted one for the other (for example |b| for |m|). These types of substitutions rarely, if ever, occur in normal phonological development past $2\frac{1}{2}$ years of age.

Children in the language disordered population will vary widely from each other in terms of the substitutions they make and will be inconsistent in the use of these substitutions. Thus, there is variation in terms of sound substitution among and within language disordered children long after such variation among and within normally developing children has disappeared.

The behaviors found in children with language disorders are similar to those found by Dr. Lieberman in his studies of the speech processing of dyslexic subjects. He found marked differences in numbers of errors between dyslexics and nondyslexics in speech-sound identification and he found marked differences among the dyslexics. He did not find marked differences among his nondyslexic population. Similarly, marked variation among normally developing children tends to disappear by about age three. Both sets of data, Lieberman's and those obtained in studies of language disordered and normally developing children, support the hypothesis that within the large pool of variation there are, first, those differences which make a difference; that is, the outcome is different and/or less robust as compared to same and robust enough. Second, within this different group, perhaps because of this difference or fragility, there is a great deal of variation. Clearly one needs to be aware that normalcy is frequently dictated by cultural norms. Nevertheless, there are differences that make a marked difference in an individual's ability to communicate and to use language to learn, and others that are nondetectable in these everyday uses of language.

Dr. Lieberman ends his paper with both a romantic and pragmatic suggestion. The romantic suggestion, if I understand it correctly, is that dyslexics may be descended from individuals who spoke another kind of language. The pragmatic suggestion is that we do more research to determine the place, degrees, and parameters of individual variation. As one who is deeply interested in what differences do really make a difference so that we can do something about them, I can only say, amen.

John J. Ohala: Comment

There is no problem in accepting the claim that not only linguistic ability as a whole but certain types of linguistic abilities or disabilities are genetically determined. The literature in this area is quite vast. For example, it is well known that the incidence of stuttering can be disproportionately high in some families. Furthermore, it is not difficult to accept that there are marked individual differences between people in certain linguistic skills. Again, the literature—and everyday experience—gives ample testimony to this. What we need in the present case is evidence linking these two facts, i.e., that the individual differences found can be traced to a genetic factor. I don't think Dr. Lieberman has adequately demonstrated this connection.

Logically, the differences found between the two groups, granting that they are real, can be due either to genetic or environmental factors. It is necessary to show in a rigorous way that the differences found are not due to this latter cause before we can accept that they are due to the former. For example, could the differences found be due to the two groups' differing abilities in taking the kind of test administered? Would they also show this difference on tests assessing their skill in dealing with nonspeech stimuli? Are the subjects' responses mediated by some sort of orthographic image they form corresponding to the speech stimuli they hear? If so, then obviously dyslexics would have more difficulty than normals, but this difficulty would be due to their reading disability, not their ability to perceive speech. Are there differences of a nonlinguistic sort, possibly neurological in origin, which might affect their test performance? For example, do they have a hard time making decisions or do they make hasty decisions?

Are the case histories of these individuals so complete that we can rule out the effect of postnatal injuries or nutritional deficiencies as the cause of their poorer performance on these tests? Are dyslexics perhaps embarrassed by being part of the reading clinic and thus identified as below normal according to society's standards? Have they thus formed a negative self-image of themselves and do they therefore approach the test as a way of somehow improving that image? In other words, do they bring to the test more than the experimenter would wish, which is simply their inherent speech-perception abilities? It would further strengthen the case for a genetic factor influencing their speech-perception ability if it could be shown that dyslexics' relatives, especially their identical twins (if such cases could be found) also show some measurable deficit in these tests.

Philip Lieberman: Further Remarks

I'd like to note at the start, that these data follow from the work of a number of people: Mary Chatillon and Helaine Schupack of the Massachusetts General Hospital, and Robert Meskill, Judith Parker, and Anne Edwards of Brown University.

The first point that I'd like to address is that of genetic variation and dyslexia. The reference cited in the body of Chapter 4 to the recent work of Smith and his associates (1983), establishes a genetic basis for some, though probably not all, forms of dyslexia. Smith traced the occurrence of dyslexia through three generations and identified an anomaly on chromosome 15. Dyslexia can be regarded as an "experiment of nature," which we can use to study genetic variation in relation to speech and reading.

I also would like to emphasize that variation in the pattern of speech perception has long been noted in the normal population, i.e., that part of the population that doesn't show profound reading disabilities. It's common to find that some subjects can't reach criterion on some particular test. We often ascribe these effects to experimental noise—the inability of the subject to follow instructions, distracting factors, or other procedural problems. These problems obviously always occur and we must be careful to eliminate these confounds from any experiment that is directed towards showing differences between groups of subjects.

In running the experiments that I've noted in the focus paper we tried to avoid artifacts that could introduce differences in the performance of our dyslexic subjects. The perfect identification of stop consonantsand near perfect identification of vowels that occurred when the dyslexic subjects responded to CVC syllables that were carefully articulated, establishes that there were no inherent difficulties associated with the test procedure that can account for the deficits which occurred when the same subjects listened to the computer-edited and synthesized stimuli. The control CVC syllables were presented at the same interstimulus interval, and the dyslexics in all the experiments after the initial run all responded by repeating what they thought they heard. Their responses were transcribed by the same listeners.

We furthermore used a second control procedure which established that the results were not due to either some unconscious bias on the part of our transcribers, or some chance effect that affected the behavior of the dyslexic subjects on the particular day that they listened to these tape recordings. We reran the subjects on the synthesized stimuli which showed high error rates. Their dictated responses were then transcribed using a double-blind procedure by a phonetician who did not know what the correct responses to the tape were. The responses of the dyslexic subjects to the tapes furthermore show that the deficits cannot follow from some extraneous general effect like an inability to respond to short computer-edited stimuli or synthetic speech. Some dyslexic subjects had no difficulty with any consonants; others had difficulty with only one place of articulation, e.g. labials; others with velars; other subjects had difficulty with vowels but not with consonants. It's evident that the deficits of the subjects do not reflect any general aspect of the test situation.

The test procedure that we used undoubtedly stressed the dyslexics speech-perception system. We removed the distinctions in duration and diphthongization that differentiate the vowels of English in our synthesized stimuli which can thus be regarded as rather impoverished compared to the spoken CVC syllables. The short computer-edited consonant stimuli also stressed the dyslexic and normal subjects; however, normals have no great difficulty with these stimuli. Therefore the test provides an appropriate measure of inherent biological differences. The procedure is analogous to that which could be used to determine genetically transmitted deficiencies in the strength of the vertebral column. Under the normal conditions of sedentary civilized life, individuals who had weaker vertebrae might not be in any detectable. However, if people were subject to stress, for example, by carrying 200 pound sacks of sand up an embankment for two days, the subgroup of the population that had inherently weaker backs would show up.

The suggestion that we run sibling studies is good. We would be happy to run such experiments.

The presence of genetically distinct subgroups in the human population who may differ with respect to some of the neural mechanisms that determine the perception of speech offers an explanation for both the diversity of human language and for linguistic change. The pattern of genetically based variation is first of all not random. We would expect to find patterned subgroups within the total population. In a genetic isolate, a group of people living together and speaking the same language who resembled each other more closely, we would expect to find shared genetically transmitted characteristics. The members of the isolate, in other words, would all form a single subgroup. An isolate thus could consist of people who, like subjects 2, 4, 5, 7, 10, and 14 on Table 4.3, had deficits in the identification of labial stop consonants. The feature labial would be less robust, yielding a different markedness convention than it would have in a population that had no difficulty with the identification of this feature, e.g., a population in which people like subjects 15, 16, 11, and 13 lived. Genetic diversity thus could explain some of the diversity of human language.

Genetic diversity also would explain some aspects of linguistic change. The historical record demonstrates that genetic isolates always merge to form a larger population that shares a common language. Once a language becomes the "property" of a larger population in which there is genetic diversity, the original, biologically based, markedness conditions no longer apply, freeing the system for linguistic change.

The comment that the dyslexic data do not address the "linguistic" aspects of the neural substrate of language implicitly claims that some neural mechanisms exist that function exclusively in the human behavioral realm of language. I doubt that any such mechanisms exist: Chomsky (1980) believes that they do, but I don't (Lieberman, 1984). The data of speech perception are consistent with the theory that we have various neural devices that were developed in the course of homonid evolution to enhance communication by speech. However, as I, Pisoni, Jusczyk, Kuhl (see contributions in this volume) and others have noted, these devices also seem to function when human beings listen to nonspeech auditory signals.

I think that a more productive distinction is whether a particular neural mechanism has evolved to meet the selective pressure of vocal communication. It is obvious that the initial stages of vocal communication must have used perceptual mechanisms that had evolved to meet other functions just as the initial stages of the evolution of the lungs involved the use of anatomical and physiologic mechanisms that had evolved for flotation. However, once a new behavioral pattern is established, it will exert new selective pressures. Air-breathing animals thus evolved specializations for more efficient respiration like the larynx under the selective pressures of terrestrial life. Comparative studies have long noted the presence of species-specific neural mechanisms that evolved to enhance the call systems of various species. Human beings are probably the most vocal animals on earth; it is most unlikely that we lack neural mechanisms structured to our call systems.

5 Auditory Models As Front Ends in Speech-Recognition Systems

Mats Blomberg, Rolf Carlson, Kjell Elenius and Björn Granström
*Department of Speech Communication and Music Acoustics,
Royal Institute of Technology, Stockholm, Sweden*

INTRODUCTION

The use of auditory models as speech recognition front ends has recently attracted a great deal of interest. The underlying assumption is that a good model of the auditory system should generate a more natural and efficient representation of speech compared to ordinary spectrum analysis. However, we have to keep in mind that only some of the peripheral processes of sound perception are included in most existing models. It is claimed that three aspects of the acoustic-to-auditory transformation most necessary "to include in any new front-end designs of speech recognizers." The three effects are the mechanical filtering in the cochlea, the mecano-electric transduction, and the temporal adaptation.

In this chapter, we discuss some standard spectral transformations of the acoustic information and also a model based on the dominant frequency concept. We also evaluate the performance of the different representations in the context of a standard speech-recognition system.

AUDITORY MODELS

Basic research has resulted in several models of peripheral auditory processing. The elaboration of Zwicker and Feldtkeller (1967) of the loudness and the Bark concept has become more or less standard in psychoacoustics. Other models, including lateral inhibition and time dependent mechanisms, have also been created (e.g., Chistovich, Lublinskaya, Malinnikova, Ogorodnikova, Stoljarova and Zhukov, 1982). Efforts have been made to include knowledge of the auditory system in practical applications by Schroeder, Atal and Hall (1979) and Lyon (1982). Klatt (1982b) has discussed physiologically related spectral representations in models for lexical access and speech-recognition systems. New models of the peripheral auditory system have been developed based on neurophysiological results (Delgutte, 1982; Dolmazon, 1982; Sachs, Young & Miller, 1982; Seneff, this volume). These positive developments make us believe that in the future we could use such models as the first analyzing steps in a speech-recognition system.

In the present chapter, we try to elaborate some of the basic facts of the auditory mechanisms in the context of such a system. In Figure 5.1, we present the different models/transformations that we have used in the current experiment. Figure 5.2b and Figure 5.2c give examples of computer-generated spectrograms based on two of these models. Figure 5.2a is a standard FFT based wide-band spectrogram included for reference. A pure sinusoid and a vowel are used as test stimuli to illustrate some alternative representations in the amplitude/frequency domain. A conventional analysis consists of an FFT analysis with a constant bandwidth (e.g., 300 Hz, window 25 ms) and a linear frequency scale (*FFT*, Figure 5.1a).

If we use a Bark scale and a bandwidth of one Bark, we will have a psychoacoustically more relevant representation (BARK, Figure 5.1b).

A psychoacoustic masking filter, (Schroeder et al, 1979), rather than a sharp bandpass filter, together with equal loudness curves (phon curves), has been used to derive a phon/Bark plot (PHON, Figure 5.1c and Figure 5.2b). We believe that the visual impression of Figure 5.2b has a much closer relation to the perceived sound than the FFT representation. Note the reduced emphasis on the fricative and the position of the very important second formant in the middle of the spectrogram. The lowest formant occupies more space, commensurate with its perceptual importance.

The phon/Bark representation has been transformed to a sone/Bark representation which often is claimed to give a better description of the perceived loudness (SONE, Figure 5.1d).

In Figure 5.1e, an alternative model (*DOMIN*) is introduced. It is based on our earlier work on vowel perception (Carlson, Fant & Granström, 1975; Carlson & Granström, 1979), and explores the possibility of temporal analysis in the auditory system (Sachs et al, 1982). The model uses the masking filter introduced in Figure 5.1c to find which frequency dominates each point along the "basilar membrane." The dominant frequency is plotted along the y–axis while the x–axis still corresponds to the Bark scale. It may be

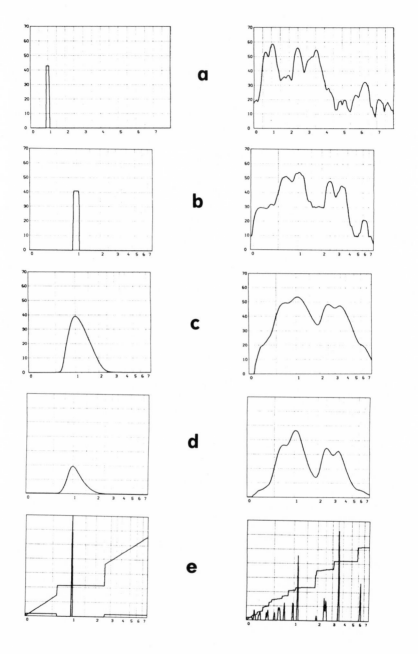

FIG. 5.1.   A sinusoid of 1 kHz (left half) and a vowel (right half) in the different representations explained in the text.

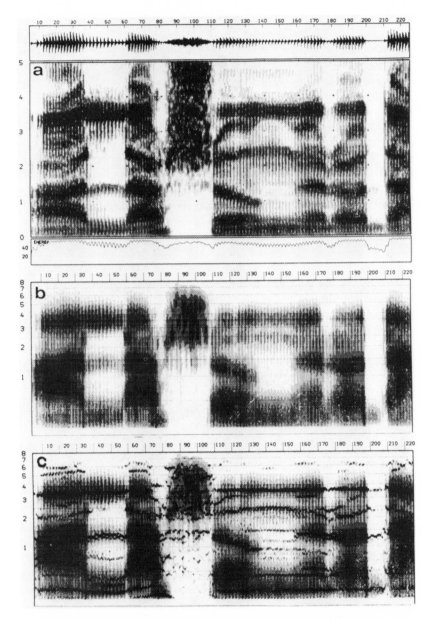

FIG. 5.2.   Three alternative spectrograms of the of the Swedish sentence /ala ʃʊŋɔr ɔ da.../. See text for details.

seen that the sinusoid generates a step in the curve, and that the width of the step corresponds to the degree of dominance. If the stimulus consists of a number of resonances or cutoff frequencies, they will each generate a step in the curve. The size of the step will be dependent on the amount of masking or dominance.

The superimposed narrow peak in Figure 5.1e presents the same information in histogram form; i.e., the y-axis is now the interval along the Bark scale that is dominated by a certain frequency. Intuitively this could be regarded as the number of neurons that respond to the same dominant frequency. At low frequencies each harmonic has a dominating effect, while at higher frequencies the dominating frequency is a complex function dependent on harmonics, masking filters, and formant bandwidth.

Figure 5.2c incorporates the histogram representation of Figure 5.1e with the phon/Bark analysis. The formants are emphasized, and the resonances during the occlusion of [b] may be observed. Since the analysis bandwidth is frequency-dependent and narrow at low frequencies, the first harmonics are well marked, while they disappear at higher frequencies in favour of formants. The intonation and the formant pattern can be studied in the same representation.

The auditory models described so far in this chapter are static, even if time is used as a parameter. No temporal masking effects have been taken into account. These kinds of effects are obvious candidates for future developments of speech recognition front ends.

THE RECOGNITION SYSTEM

The recognition system is based on ordinary isolated word-recognition techniques using pattern matching and dynamic programming (Elenius & Blomberg, 1982). The Euclidean metric is used for calculation of distances between word patterns.

The speech signal is digitized (16 kHz) and processed according to the different auditory models described. In each representation, 74 parameters, evenly sampled along the different frequency scales, are used. A new calculation is made each 20 ms. When a word is detected, it is linearly normalized to 40 sample points in time. This reduces the processing needed for the dynamic programming. A word is hence described by 40 parameter vectors, each having 74 elements.

The intention with this facility is not to make a speech recognition system with the best possible performance; what we intend is a flexible, standard framework to compare different recognition preprocessors and recognition strategies.

TABLE 5.1

Recognition Accuracy in Percent

Model	Vowels		Consonants		Mean
	Male	Female	Male	Female	
FFT	99	96	95	97	97
BARK	99	95	92	95	95
PHON	96	91	88	91	92
SONE	91	93	82	83	87
DOMIN	99	99	90	90	94

Experiment

Two vocabularies were tested. One consisted of the long Swedish vowels in an hVl–context, and the other of the 18 Swedish consonants in an aCa–context. What really was tested, since the context is constant, was the consonant and vowel discrimination ability of the system, though there was no segmentation into phonemes of the words used. The recordings were made in a relatively quiet office room.

Each vocabulary was read 31 times by one male and one female speaker. Seven repetitions of each word were read in a normal way and were used to build the reference templates. The test utterances were read in four different ways: normally, slowly, rapidly, and emphatically. There were six utterances for each speaking style making a total of $24 \times 18 = 432$ test words for the consonants and $24 \times 9 = 216$ test words for the vowels. The reason for varying the manner of speaking was to increase the error rate in order to make the differences between the models more pronounced. Rate differences were within the normal range, (variations less than $\pm 25\%$). No extreme phonetic variation was observed.

Results

The results are displayed in Table 5.1 where the recognition performance of each auditory model is shown separately for consonants and vowels for each speaker. The mean for each model is also given.

The FFT-based recognition is surprisingly accurate, especially for consonants (97.5% for vowels and 96% for consonants). The number of parameters (74), however, is greater than what is normally afforded in speech-recognition systems. Furthermore, the intervocalic position of the consonants bypasses the endpoint detection problem.

When the auditory-inspired transformation of the speech spectra grows more complicated (BARK-PHON-SONE), the recognition results deteriorate progressively for both consonants and vowels. The DOMIN, which is a model of a rather different kind, does not follow this general tendency. The performance for vowels is excellent, but for consonants it is no better than the PHON representation. This is understandable in the light of the function of DOMIN. In this model, all emphasis is put on the frequency location of prominent regions (formants) which are known to form a good basis for vowel identity decisions. However, all loudness information is disregarded, which could make the discrimination between consonants problematic, especially if they have the same place of articulation. For the SONE model, the difference between performance on vowels and consonants is considerable. The low score for consonants is possibly due to the amplitude transformation involved. The relatively weak consonant segments tend to be disregarded in the distance calculation.

CONCLUDING REMARKS

It is obvious from our experiment that the unqualified assumption does not hold—auditory models used as speech-recognition front ends will not consistently improve performance. Several plausible explanations for our results could be mentioned:

1. All models are based on the FFT analysis. The data will be smeared in frequency and time depending on the chosen approach.
2. The models describe only a few selected ways in which the human auditory system processes data. They may be based on experiments which are too specific, capturing ways of processing the signal that are not very important for speech processing and missing those that are.
3. There is no match between the human-modelled primary analysis and the rest of the recognition system. If this match is required, the modelling could pay off only if the decision making part of the program models the way the central nervous system looks at the sensory data.

All these explanations may contain some truth. This should, of course, not hold us back from the interesting fields of auditory modelling and speech perception. It might, however, be premature to include our fragmentary knowledge of the auditory system in today's speech recognizers.

Stephanie Seneff:
A Synchrony Model for Auditory Processing of Speech

INTRODUCTION

Our understanding of the peripheral auditory system at the present time is sufficient that it is possible to develop detailed models that attempt to simulate the output of this stage (Allen, 1979; Johnson, 1974). Auditory physiologists have also begun to analyze the response characteristics in the auditory nerve to complex speech-like stimuli (Delgutte, 1980; Sachs & Young, 1980). Sachs and Young presented synthetic vowel stimuli to a large population of nerve fibers along the basilar membrane, and generated a "spectrum" by plotting mean rate response as a function of center frequency. Because of saturation phenomena, broad diffuse peaks appear at the formant resonance frequencies, even for conversational level speech, and thus it would seem that rate response alone is inadequate for vowel identification.

Sachs and Young (1980), explored an alternative approach which took advantage of the phase-locking characteristic of the nerve fibers. Period histograms show that the fibers are able to follow to some degree the shape of the input signal; that is, that they respond in synchrony to the stimulus. By applying a second filter to the output at the peripheral level, to extract only the energy in the period histogram near the center frequency of the fiber, a much more stable spectrum can be generated. This spectrum retains formant information and is much less variable with signal level. The only major problem was a very strong response at the frequency of the second harmonic of the first formant. This response was a consequence of distortion products introduced by the half-wave rectification process.

We describe here a computer system which explores an alternative method for extracting the synchronized response. The system includes a peripheral auditory model, followed by a spectral estimator and an independent pitch estimator. Both estimators make use of a Generalized Synchrony Detector (GSD), which is related to the "second-filter" concept, but does not pick up a distortion component at the second harmonic frequency. There is considerable similarity in the design of the pitch estimator and the spectral estimator, and thus a unified approach to these two tasks is advocated.

SYSTEM DESCRIPTION

The implemented system consists of an initial stage of signal processing, corresponding to the peripheral auditory system, whose outputs are delivered in parallel to the spectral estimator and the pitch estimator. The initial stage processing is a terminal–analog model, emulating the responses of actual nerve fibers as measured through period histograms. The model is not intended to be physically meaningful. In brief, the input speech is processed through a bank of 32 linear filters spanning the frequency range from 200 to 2700 Hz, with approximately critical bandwidths. Each filter output is then processed through a nonlinear amplitude

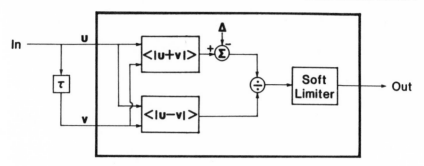

FIG. 5a.1. Generalized Synchrony Detector (GSD).

compression scheme and a half-wave rectifier. The waveforms are never reduced to spike sequences; a value at time t instead represents a probabilistic response.

Both the spectral estimator and the pitch estimator make use of the GSD to detect appropriate periodicities. The spectral estimator processes each of the outputs from the initial stage through the synchrony measure, tuned to the center frequency of the corresponding critical band filter. A sharpening of the peaks in the spectrum is realized by detecting enhanced synchrony at the places tuned to formant frequencies. The pitch estimator first combines all of the outputs of the initial stage processing into a single waveform, which is then fanned out to a series of GSDs to detect periodicities at frequencies appropriate for human pitch. The summing process generally results in a reenforcement of the periodicities at the pitch period at the expense of periodicities at the formants.

A block diagram of the GSD algorithm is given in Figure 5a.1. The two input waveforms, u and v, consist of a signal and that same signal delayed by a specific time, τ. A sum and a difference waveform are constructed from u and v, and the full-wave rectified outputs of both of these are passed through identical lowpass filters, to obtain an envelope response. A small threshold, δ, is subtracted from the sum envelope, whose value is slightly greater than the spontaneous rate. The sum envelope is then **divided** by the difference envelope, so that, in the event that the two signals are very similar, a response approaching infinity is obtained. Finally, a soft limiter (arctan function) is included in order to clamp the potentially infinite output when the denominator is near zero.

In order to obtain a "pseudo spectrogram," the output of each of the 32 channels of the initial stage processing is compared with itself delayed by a "center tau", equal to the inverse of the center frequency of the channel, as shown in Figure 5a.2. The comparison is made by feeding the waveform and the delayed waveform through a GSD, and the output of the GSD is recorded every time a new spectral image is desired. The pseudo spectrogram is constructed from a time sequence of the 32 pseudo spectral samples, using the output of the GSD as the intensity dimension.

Figure 5a.3 illustrates the ability of the GSD algorithm to enhance spectral peaks. The input is a 1000 Hz tone, whose amplitude increases step-wise by a fac-

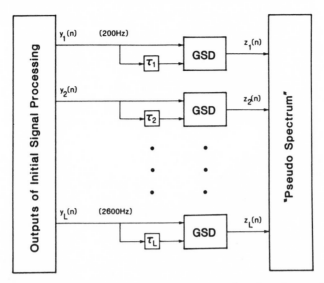

FIG. 5a.2.   Block diagram of Spectral Estimator (32 channels spaced by 1/2 Bark).

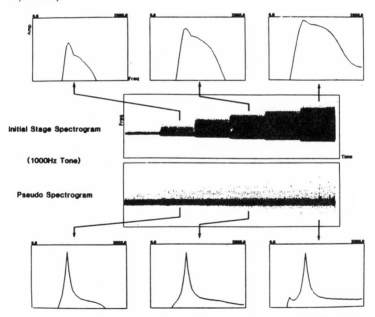

FIG. 5a.3.   Spectrograms and spectral cross sections at selected points in time of the initial stage output compared with the outputs after processing through the GSDs, when the input signal is a 1000 Hz tone whose amplitude increases in steps by 6 dB. In all cases, the frequency range is from 0 to 2.7kHz.

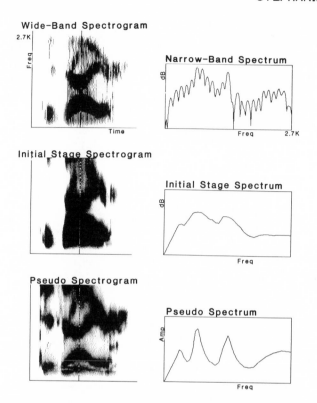

FIG. 5a.4. Comparison of standard spectral analysis (top) with log magnitude spectra taken from the outputs of the initial stage model (middle)
and spectra obtained from the outputs of the GSDs (bottom), for the
word "desire" spoken by a male speaker. The spectral cross sections are
all taken at the time slice indicated by the vertical line on the spectrogram.
The wide-band spectrogram was computed using a 6 msec Hamming window, and the narrow-band spectral cross section used a 25 msec Hamming
window.

tor of two in quantal stages over a two second time interval. The upper spectrogram
is produced from the envelope of each channel output, $y_i[n]$, of the initial stage processing. As the amplitude increases, the response pattern expands upward above
1000 Hz, because critical band filters have a slow fall-off on the low-frequency end,
an effect that is compounded by the saturation of filters near the tone frequency.
Filters below 1000 Hz do not pick up the signal because of the steep slope on the
high end. The lower spectrogram displays the outputs of the GSDs. There is a narrow peak at 1000 Hz that is maintained constant as overall amplitude is increased.
This constancy is achieved because there is an effective energy normalization procedure inherent in the divide of the GSD. These effects are also demonstrated in
cross-section at three different amplitudes, as indicated at the top and bottom of
the figure.

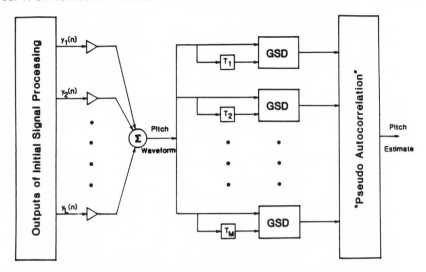

FIG. 5a.5.   Block diagram of Pitch Estimator

Figure 5a.4 shows a comparison of the GSD output (bottom), with the output of the initial stage (middle), and with standard spectral analysis procedures (top), using a sample of natural speech. On the right are cross-sections taken at the time slice indicated by the vertical bar on the spectrograms, in the /a/ of the word "desire". The vertical lines in the wide-band spectrogram are pitch striations, due to the fluctuations in amplitude over time as glottal pulses pass through the 6 msec Hamming time weighting window. Such fluctuations are eliminated in the middle spectrogram because of integration over a broader time window. However, the peaks at the formant frequencies have become somewhat obscured due in part to saturation phenomena. The bottom spectrogram shows the outputs of the GSD as the intensity dimension. The temporal pitch striations and the harmonic structure in frequency have both been eliminated, and the formant peaks are more prominent than in the initial stage outputs. Note also that, because of amplitude normalization, the second formant in the initial unstressed syllable has been emphasized by the GSD algorithm.

A block diagram of the pitch estimation process is given in Figure 5a.5. The process is quite similar to the spectral estimator, except that the outputs of **all** of the channels are **summed**, and the resulting pitch waveform is passed to each of the GSDs for synchrony processing. The delays for the GSD v-inputs (c.f. Figure 5a.1) span the periods appropriate for pitch in speech, from about 2 msec to about 16 msec. A "pseudo autocorrelation" is constructed by plotting the outputs of the series of GSDs as a function of the time delay. The pitch period is determined as the first prominent peak in this pseudo autocorrelation function.

Figure 5a.6 shows three examples of the original waveform and the pitch waveform generated by adding all the channel outputs. At the top is a portion of the vowel in "red" spoken by a male speaker. The middle pair shows a sample of female speech in the vowel portion of "cost." At the bottom is a portion of "cow" spoken

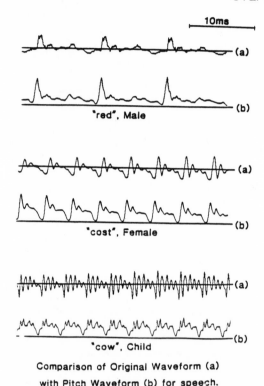

Comparison of Original Waveform (a)
with Pitch Waveform (b) for speech.

FIG. 5a.6.   Comparison of pitch waveform with original waveform during the vowel in three samples of natural speech, for a wide range of fundamental periods. The pitch waveform is created by summing all channel
outputs of the initial stage processing.

by a 3-year old child. In all cases, the pitch waveform resembles the original waveform, but is shifted above the origin, and the formant periodicities are reduced in
prominence relative to the fundamental periodicity.

Figure 5a.7 shows the complete pitch estimation procedure applied to the word
"glass" spoken by a male speaker. Because of the adaptation and saturation effects
that were implemented in the first stage of the model, the pitch waveform tends
to begin more abruptly at an onset of a voiced region than the original waveform.
This abrupt onset results in a more exact periodicity of the first two glottal periods, allowing for an accurate estimation of the onset pitch. At the bottom of
the figure is the original waveform on a compressed time scale, and above that is
the aligned pitch track that is produced by the estimator. The voiced/unvoiced
decision was made by examining the overall level of the pitch waveform and the
relative prominence of the peak in the pseudo autocorrelation.

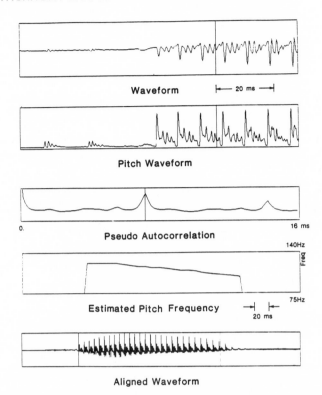

Waveform |— 20 ms —|

Pitch Waveform

0.   16 ms

Pseudo Autocorrelation

140Hz

Estimated Pitch Frequency   75Hz
20 ms

Aligned Waveform

FIG. 5a.7. Illustration of Pitch Estimator applied to the word "glass" spoken by a male speaker. The output of the pseudo autocorrelation centered at the mark is shown below the pitch waveform. At the bottom the estimated pitch frequency is shown aligned in time with a compressed version of the original waveform.

SUMMARY

The system described here is potentially useful both in terms of obtaining a good speech processing system and in leading to a better understanding of the human auditory system. System design strategies were intentionally limited to devices that required simple operations that seemed reasonable given our present understanding of the auditory system. In the GSD algorithm, for example, the divide could be interpreted as an excitatory-inhibitory process, and the arctan function could represent a saturation effect. The difference waveform could be generated through an XOR gate, if the two inputs are spike sequences, and leaky integrators could perform the lowpass filtering.

The pitch estimator is attractive as a possible model for auditory pitch processing because a single procedure is applied to pure tones and harmonic sequences in low or high frequency regions, without requiring a high level moderator that decides among ambiguous pitch estimates from multiple processors. Furthermore, with a single waveform from which to extract the pitch, the problem of variability in synaptic delays as an argument against time-domain methods is irrelevant. As long as the delays were implemented as a tapped delay line, relative pitch but not absolute pitch could be measured regardless of synaptic variability. From an engineering standpoint, most waveform pitch processors attempt some spectral flattening (such as center clipping [Sondhi] or inverse Linear Prediction [Markel, 1972]) prior to the periodicity detection. The pitch waveform is derived through a highly nonlinear procedure; however, it can be conjectured that a form of spectral flattening is achieved as a consequence of saturation effects in the initial stage processing.

These results are necessarily preliminary, and it remains to be demonstrated whether on the one hand the performance of the system in any practical task is better, and on the other hand whether the central auditory system processes its input in a way that is at all similar to what is done here.

Nelson Kiang: Comment

I can understand the enthusiasm of theoreticians who would like physiologists to find correlates for the components of functional parsing schemes, but I shall try to explain why such a program would be unlikely to prove successful with present schemes.

In any complicated system (and the brain is certainly one), the operating machinery is likely to involve many functional subunits interconnected in multiple networks. The overall behavior of such systems can frequently be represented by fairly primitive functional models in simple situations, but will not work in more realistic circumstances. For example, the nuances in the symptomatology of sensorineural deafness cannot be accounted for by the simple additive models such as are satisfactory for describing conductive losses.

In the case of the auditory system, sufficient anatomical and physiological information is already available to reject any simple theoretical model for speech perception. It is not the lack of formal models that hampers our study of speech and language processing; it is the inability to monitor brain activity in functioning humans as they perform such tasks. Present methods lack sufficient temporal and spatial resolution but as new ones become available, we should see rapid increases in our knowledge.

6

Speech Perception as "Vector Analysis": An Approach to the Problems of Invariance and Segmentation

Carol A. Fowler and Mary R. Smith
Haskins Laboratories
and Dartmouth College

INTRODUCTION

Two central problems for a theory of speech perception are those of segmentation and invariance. The segmentation problem is to partition the acoustic signal into the phone-sized segments reported by phoneticians and (literate) listeners. The invariance problem—in the aspect that interests us here—is to explain why acoustically distinct, apparently context-sensitive, versions of a phonetic segment may sound free of contextual influences to listeners. We call this the problem of "perceptual invariance."

We suggest that the invariance problem arises in part from assumptions made to resolve the segmentation problem, and that different assumptions imply a novel solution to the problem of perceptual invariance. We approach the problem of segmentation with two hypotheses, one concerning the natural structure of the acoustic signal, and one concerning the nature of perceptual systems. These hypotheses allow us to understand why listeners credit acoustic signals with phone-sized structure, and why they can report perceptual invariance for acoustically different signals.

The Problems of Segmentation and Invariance

Language is said to have "duality of patterning" (Hockett, 1960)—a relatively large number of meaningful linguistic units composed of a relatively small number of meaningless phonological constituents. Compatibly, speakers and listeners behave as if acoustic speech signals are composed of separate and serially-ordered phonetic segments. For example, speakers misorder phonetic segments in spontaneous speech errors and speaker–hearers learn to use alphabetic orthographies. However, in most instances, analysis of the signals has not revealed invariant acoustic correspondents of separate and ordered phonetic segments.

Analysis does reveal acoustic segments, however (Fant, 1962). For example, in spectrographic displays, certain salient changes in the signal provide markers of the edges of acoustic segments. The difficulties are that for many signals, the acoustically defined segments outnumber the phonetic segments attributed to the signal (Fant, 1960, 1962); further, across different phonetic contexts there may be differences in the *kinds* of acoustic segments identified with a given phonetic segment, not just their number; and within the borders of an acoustic segment, typically there is information about more than one phonetic segment.

When researchers adopt a solution to the segmentation problem—for example, for purposes of measuring the durations of phonetic segments (Fowler, 1981a; Klatt, 1975, 1976; Lindblom & Rapp, 1973)—generally, they partition the signal into temporally discrete segments by drawing segmentation lines perpendicular to the axis of time. It is probably accurate to say that segmentation lines are drawn where influences of one phonetic segment cease to predominate visibly in the signal and those of the next segment take over. This manner of segmentation is illustrated in Figure 6.1a. The figure presents a schematized display of a syllable consisting of three segments with time along the horizontal axis and a provisional dimension, "prominence," along the vertical axis. The prominence of a phonetic segment refers to the extent to which the acoustic signal takes its character from properties of that phonetic segment. For example, an interval of frication is identified with a fricative consonant and not with a coarticulated vowel even though the frication may bear spectral evidence of the vowel. Therefore, during a period of frication, a fricative consonant has more prominence than a coarticulating vowel. As illustrated in Figure 6.1b (i), a consequence of segmentation along prominence lines is that the acoustic interval identified with a phonetic segment is context-sensitive. A perceptual theory is required to explain why listeners treat distinct acoustic signals as tokens of the same phonetic-segment type, and, why intrinsic allophones of a phoneme *sound* free of contextual influences to listeners. This is the problem of perceptual invariance.

Proposed resolutions to both the segmentation and invariance problems have come either from reexamining the acoustic basis on which perception rests (Stevens, 1981b), or from invoking special perceptual mechanisms and strategies in the listener (Oden & Massaro, 1978). We take a tactic here that requires us to look *both* at how the signal is structured and at how the listener may accomplish the task of perception.

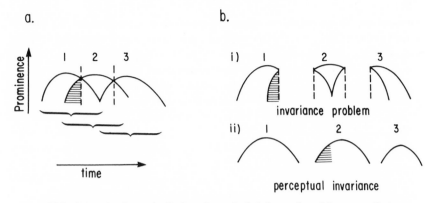

FIG. 6.1. A schematic display of coarticulated speech and two ways that it may be segmented.

The Structure of the Signal and Two Strategies for its Perception

Talkers coarticulate neighboring phonetic segments in speech—that is, their productions of neighboring phonetic segments overlap, as illustrated in Figure 6.1a. In Figure 6.1b, we illustrate two possible perceptual strategies for partitioning such a signal into phonetic segments: strategy (i) was described above as conventional for researchers measuring durations of phonetic segments in speech; strategy (ii) follows the natural structure of the speech as produced by the talker. In (i), the signal is partitioned into segments with boundaries perpendicular to the axis of time according to the dashed lines in Figure 6.1a. The resulting segments are discrete and context-sensitive. In (ii), the segmentation procedure follows natural coarticulatory lines (indicated by the braces in Figure 6.1a). Intervals of overlap among neighboring phonetic segments have, as it were, been factored from one another; therefore, the resulting segments are separate and free of contextual influences. Our research contrasts these two perceptual strategies.

We favor the hypothesis that listeners use a strategy similar to (ii) on two grounds. First, the strategy yields perceptual invariance; potentially, therefore, it can explain why, for example, the [d]s in [di] and [du] sound alike to listeners despite substantial acoustic differences between them. Second, it yields a "realistic" percept in recovering the structure of the segments as produced by a talker. Next, we provide an elaboration of this second perceptual strategy.

Perceptual Vector Analysis

Our proposal that listeners segment speech along coarticulatory lines implies that they will not always group together acoustic events that cooccur in time. Similarly, where appropriate, they will hear temporally successive events as coherent. In short, the hypothesis implies that information for segmentation and its complement, coherence, is not solely temporal succession and simultaneity.

Researchers in other domains confirm that perceivers' parsings of complex events rest on information other than coincidence and temporal or spatial separation. Johansson (1974) and Bregman (1978) show this clearly. We see our proposal as analogous to "perceptual vector analysis" as described by Johansson, and to the process of "auditory stream segregation" as described by Bregman.

Johansson (1974) finds that viewers use common motions of components of an event as important sources of information for coherence of spatially separated components of the event and use distinctive motion as information for segmentation. An attractive aspect of this approach is that it tends to yield a realistic percept. That is, when viewers perceive a vector analysis of motions of point lights filmed on the joints of a walking person or of a dancing couple, they perceive, respectively, a walking person or a dancing couple.

Bregman (1978) offers an analogous analysis of complex acoustic patterns. He describes a number of auditory displays for which listeners report separate "streams" in the signal. As Bregman points out, the principles whereby components are grouped are the same principles whereby components are dissociated or segmented. In Johansson's terms (and the terms we have adopted here), vector analysis captures both the notion of finding the common fate of components and that of segregating the remaining material relative to the unified material. Thus, both coherence and separation among components of a complex event emerge perceptually from a vector-analysis on the stimulus.

Predictions of a Vector Analysis Hypothesis for Speech

Two complementary predictions can be derived from a hypothesis that segmentation in speech perception occurs along natural coarticulatory lines. One is that acoustic consequences of coarticulation will be ascribed to the *influencing* segment. A second is that they will not contribute to the listener's perceptual experience of the *influenced* segment.

Figure 6.1 shows why these are two major consequences of a perceptual vector analysis of speech and why at least the second consequence is not expected if segmentation of speech creates temporally *discrete* segments. In Figure 6.1a, acoustic influences of segment 2 to the left of the dashed line— during a time frame in which segment 1 predominates in the signal—are identified as "anticipatory coarticulation." If listeners were to segment the signal perceptually along the dashed lines, anticipatory coarticulatory influences of segment 2 should not be ascribed to 2 itself, but rather, integrated with influences of 1, should contribute to perception of 1 as a context-sensitive phonological segment as illustrated in Figure 6.1b (i).

Alternatively, if listeners segment the signal along natural coarticulatory lines, anticipatory influences of 2 should be ascribed to 2. For its part, segment 1 should sound invariant to listeners over influences of different neighboring 2s because, by hypothesis, those influences are "factored" from 1. This alternative, labeled "perceptual invariance," is illustrated in Figure 6.1b (ii).

The first prediction has been confirmed in recent research by Whalen (1982) and Martin and Bunnell (1982). Whalen cross-spliced frication noises from CV syllables across different vocalic contexts. Subjects classified the vowels in a choice reaction-time study. They were slower and less accurate when fricative noises or transitions provided misleading information about the vowels than when the information was accurate. Martin and Bunnell obtained a similar outcome when stimuli were VCVs in which the initial vowel had been cross-spliced across different final-vocalic contexts and subjects classified the final vowels.

In themselves, these outcomes are compatible with speech segmentation by the listener into either discrete (i) or overlapping (ii) segments. By strategy (i), the percept of the fricative in Whalen's study and of the initial vowel in Martin and Bunnell's work is context-sensitive, and the nature of the contextual influence can be used by a listener to predict the identity of the following vowel. By strategy (ii), the utterance-final vowel has its onset during the frication in Whalen's study and during the utterance-initial vowel in Martin and Bunnell's experiment. That onset, no less than the later-coming information for the vowel, contributes to identification.

Strategy (ii) would be favored by its convergence with tests of the next prediction—that anticipatory information for a segment does not contribute to the perceptual experience of the segment with which it cooccurs. Rather, it is perceptually "factored" from cooccurring information for an earlier segment. This can be tested using a discrimination paradigm (Fowler, 1981b).

If listeners factor anticipatory and carryover effects of neighboring segments from the acoustic domain of a phonetic segment, then two consequences are expected. First, a given phonetic token should sound different from itself in different contexts because the contexts will cause different information to be factored from the token. Second, versions of a given phonetic type produced in different coarticulatory contexts should sound alike (free of contextual influences) as long as each is presented in its original context so that contextual influences can be factored out. These predictions are tested in the present experiments.

The studies we report are the initial ones in a series that pairs the choice reaction time procedure of Whalen (1982) and Martin and Bunnell (1982) with a discrimination paradigm first used for this purpose by Fowler (1981b). The reaction-time procedure determines whether anticipatory coarticulatory information for a forthcoming segment is ascribed to that segment. The discrimination procedure determines whether it is factored from a phonetic segment with which it cooccurs in time.

THE EXPERIMENTS

To date, we have applied the reaction-time and discrimination procedures to two sets of stimuli, both involving coarticulatory influences of a stressed vowel on unstressed schwa. One stimulus set includes the disyllables [bəbi] and [bəba]; the other includes trisyllables [ibəbi] and [abəba] and, as filler items in the choice reaction-time study, [ibəba] and [abəbi]. In the first stimulus set, schwa receives contextual influences from a following stressed vowel (anticipatory coarticulation); in the second set, contextual influences on schwa are both anticipatory and perseverative.

Materials

Disyllables. Two tokens of the disyllables [bəbi] and [bəba] produced by a female talker were digitized at a 20 kHz sampling rate and filtered at 10 kHz. The stimuli were electronically divided into syllables at the onsets of closure for the second [b] in each disyllable. This created two unstressed [bə$_i$] syllables from the two tokens of [bəbi] (hereafter, a subscript preceding or following [bə] indicates the context in which it originated), two unstressed [bə$_a$]s, and two tokens each of the stressed syllables [bi] and [ba]. Three types of disyllables were constructed from these unstressed and stressed syllables: "original" productions in which an unstressed syllable was appended to the stressed syllable with which it had been produced originally, "spliced" productions in which an unstressed syllable was appended to a different token of the same phonetic type of stressed syllable with which it had been produced originally, and "cross-spliced" productions in which unstressed syllables were appended to stressed syllables different in phonetic type from their original neighbors. These stimulus types are illustrated in Figure 6.2.

Trisyllables. Two tokens each of [ibəbi] and [abəba] and one each of [abəbi] and [ibəba] produced by a male talker were digitized at a 20 kHz sampling rate and filtered at 10 kHz. They were divided into syllables at the onsets of closure for each of the [b]s. The tokens of [$_i$bə$_i$] from [ibəbi] and of [$_a$bə$_a$] from [abəba] were used to create "original", "spliced" and "cross-spliced" stimuli as illustrated in Figure 6.2. The fillers [ibəba] and [abəbi] appeared only as "original" productions in the choice reaction time study to eliminate the redundancy between the initial and final vowels.

Splicing Conditions

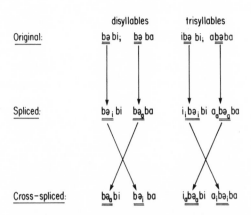

FIG. 6.2.   The splicing conditions of the reaction-time and 4IAX studies.

Test Orders and Procedures

Choice reaction time. Subjects received four blocks of trials, the first serving as a practice block. There were 48 trials per block in the disyllable study and 64 per block, consisting of 32 fillers and 32 test items, in the trisyllable study. Each block included one-quarter original productions, one-quarter spliced productions, and one-half cross-spliced productions of the test stimuli, giving nine responses per subject per test item in the disyllable study and six in the trisyllable study.

Stimuli were presented on-line to listeners over headphones. In both studies, listeners were instructed to identify the final vowel of a stimulus as [i] or [a] by pressing a labeled key on the computer terminal.

If listeners use anticipatory coarticulatory information for the final vowel, choice reaction times should be slowed and accuracy reduced in the cross-spliced condition as compared to the other two conditions.

Discrimination. The paradigm was a 4IAX discrimination procedure. Only spliced and cross-spliced productions served as stimuli. On each trial, subjects received four stimuli, grouped temporally into pairs. Their task was to decide which pair had members that sound more alike one to the other. Two sample trials from the disyllable version of the study are given below:

A: bə$_i$bi---bə$_i$bi---------bə$_i$bi---bə$_a$bi

B: bə$_i$bi---bə$_a$ba---------bə$_i$bi---bə$_i$ba

In trials of type A, within and across pairs, the stressed vowels are the same. In addition, one pair of the two has identical members, whereas the second has members that differ. When the members differ, one member has a spliced and one a cross-spliced unstressed vowel. If subjects are sensitive to the different contextual influences on these two versions of [bə], they should pick the identical pair members (in the example, the first pair) as more similar than the different members.

Trials of type B provide the critical test of our segmentation hypothesis. In these trials, stressed vowels within a pair are different, but, as in trials of type A, stressed vowels do not differentiate the two pairs of stimuli. In addition, in a B trial, one pair has identical [bə] syllables, one spliced and one cross-spliced (in the example, the second pair); the other has two different spliced [bə]s.

In the sample B trials, if listeners segment the speech signal as in Figure 6.1b(i), they should pick the members of the second pair as more similar than the members of the first pair. Alternatively, if listeners segment the signal along natural coarticulatory lines as indicated by Figure 6.1b(ii), then they should pick the members of the first pair as more similar than the members of the second. This should occur because vector analysis of spliced [bə] syllables (as in the first three disyllables in the example above) should leave the same, perceptually-invariant schwa vowel; vector analysis of a cross-spliced [bə] should leave a different residual. In the example, schwa in the last disyllable should sound high because effects of the low vowel [a] will be factored from an already raised schwa vowel.

In the two studies, the test order consisted of three blocks of 64 trials; the first block served as practice. A trials and B trials appeared equally often. Similarly, [bə$_i$] and [bə$_a$] occurred equally often as the more frequent unstressed syllable within a trial. (In the example, [bə$_i$] is the more frequent unstressed syllable.) Finally, if the four stimuli in the sample A and B trials above are given the numbers 1, 2, 3, and 4, then the stimuli within a trial appeared equally often in the orderings: 12–34, 21–43, 34–12, and 43–21.

Subjects were instructed to provide first, a "1" or a "2" signifying respectively that the members of the first or the second pair sounded more alike and, second, a confidence judgment (1: guess; 2: uncertain; 3: certain). Neither response was timed.

Subjects. Subjects were undergraduates at Dartmouth College, who received course credit for their participation. Nineteen students participated both in the choice reaction time study involving disyllables, and, in the same session, in the corresponding 4IAX discrimination study. Ten students participated in the choice reaction-time study involving trisyllables and a different group of 18 students performed the corresponding 4IAX discrimination.

Results

Choice Reaction Time. Results of the two choice reaction-time studies are shown in Table 6.1 collapsed over identity of the stressed vowel. In the

TABLE 6.1

Response Times (in msecs) and Proportion Correct in the Choice of Reaction-time Studies

	Disyllables		
	Original	*Spliced*	*Cross-spliced*
RT	473	464	512
S	46	43	41
Prop. correct	.97	.97	.91

	Trisyllables		
	Original	*Spliced*	*Cross-spliced*
RT	563	568	604
S	39	33	49
Prop. correct	.95	.94	.92

disyllable study, an analysis of variance performed on the response times revealed a significant main effect of splicing condition ($F[2, 36] = 59.71$, $p < .0001$), but no effect of vowel and no interaction (both $Fs < 1$). Analysis of accuracy provided a similar outcome (splicing condition: $F[2, 36] = 21.34$, $p < .0001$; vowel: $F[1, 18] = 2.82$, $p = .11$; vowel by splicing condition: $F < 1$). In both analyses, the significant effect of splicing condition was due to the difference between the cross-spliced and the other two conditions, which did not differ.

The results were essentially the same in the study involving trisyllables. The effect of splicing condition on response time was highly significant ($F [2, 18] = 25.03$, $p < .001$). Neither the effect of vowel nor the interaction reached significance. In the analysis of accuracy, the effect of splicing condition did not reach significance ($F[2, 18] = 2.74$, $p = .09$). The main effect of vowel and the interaction were nonsignificant (both $Fs < 1$).

These results are predicted by our hypothesis that listeners segment speech along natural coarticulatory lines, but this hypothesis is not unique in making the prediction. The special prediction of our hypothesis—that anticipatory information for a forthcoming segment is factored from the phonetic segment with which it cooccurs—is tested by the discrimination studies.

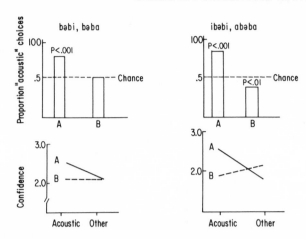

FIG. 6.3. Discrimination (top) and confidence (bottom) judgments in
the disyllable (left) and trisyllable (right) studies.

Discrimination test. Figure 6.3 displays the results for the two tasks.
The top half of the Figure 6.3 presents the proportions of A and B trials
on which listeners select acoustically identical schwas as more similar than
acoustically different schwas. They are predicted to exceed the chance or
no-preference value of .5 on A trials, but to fall below .5 on B trials. The
bottom half of the figure presents subjects' confidence judgments. In view
of the observation that subjects tend to be more confident of their correct
responses than of their erroneous responses, we predicted that they would
be more confident of their selections of acoustically identical schwas on A
trials than of their selections of different schwas; on B trials, their pattern of
confidence judgments should reverse.

In the disyllable study, displayed on the left side of the figure, subjects
selected the acoustically identical schwa vowels as more similar than the
different schwas on .75 of the A trials, significantly more frequently than the
chance value of .5 $(t[18] = 10.97, p < .001)$. Listeners' confidence judgments
also followed the expected pattern.

Subjects were unable to make consistent choices on B trials, however,
selecting acoustically identical schwa vowels on exactly half of the trials.
Their confidence judgments on B trials verify that listeners were equally
unconfident when they made judgments based on acoustic identity as when
they made judgments based on vector analysis.

We know both from the A trials of the present study and the reaction
time study reported above that listeners are sensitive to the anticipatory
coarticulatory information about [i] or [a] in the schwa vowels of the disyllables used there. We ascribe the subjects' chance performance on B trials
in this study to three factors. First, in comparison to A trials, B trials are

difficult because stressed vowels are different within a pair. In A trials, schwa vowels may be compared against an invariant backdrop. Next, as compared to the reaction-time procedure, the 4IAX procedure is relatively insensitive[1] in placing memory demands on listeners not imposed by the reaction-time studies. In addition, the 4IAX procedure is difficult in requiring that listeners make explicit judgments of similarity. In contrast, the reaction-time procedure requires a very easy judgment (classifying the stressed vowel) and looks for subtle influences of the schwa vowels on classification times and errors.

The difficulties with the 4IAX paradigm are less evident using the trisyllabic stimuli in which coarticulatory influences on schwa are bidirectional.[2] Results using trisyllables (a partial replication of Fowler [1981b]) are shown on the right side of Figure 6.3. As in the disyllable study, subjects consistently picked acoustically identical schwas as more similar one to the other than different schwas on A trials. Subjects made that selection on .82 of the trials, differing significantly from the chance value of .5 $(t[17] = 16.58, p < .0001)$. On B trials, as predicted, subjects selected acoustically identical schwas (in different coarticulatory contexts) as more similar than acoustically different schwas (each in its proper coarticulatory context) less than half (.37) of the time $(t[17] = 3.46, p = .003)$.

Subjects' confidence judgments mirrored their discrimination selections. On A trials, subjects were more confident when they chose acoustically identical schwas than when they did not; on B trials they showed the opposite pattern. An analysis of variance on the confidence judgments shows significant main effects of trial type. Subjects were more confident overall on the relatively easy A than B trials $(F[1,17] = 10.97, p = .004)$—a main effect of choice type. They were more confident of their choices of acoustically identical than different schwas $(F[1,17] = 14.28, p = .002)$, and, most importantly, a significant interaction occurred $(F[1,17] = 32.21, p < .001)$. The interaction occurs because subjects are in fact only more confident on A than B trials when choices of acoustically identical schwas are made (A: 2.54, B: 1.89); they are less confident on A than B trials when the opposite selection is made (A: 1.86, B: 2.13). Similarly, the main effect of choice type holds only for A trials; on B trials, confidence is higher when a coarticulation-based

---

[1] By 'insensitive' we mean that the procedure places demands on subjects that may preclude their exhibiting discriminations that they may in fact make.

[2] A reviewer suggested an alternative reason why the results were positive with the trisyllables and not with the disyllables. Possibly perceivers do not work backward to adjust earlier perceptual identifications based on later ones. Therefore, only perseverative coarticulatory influences are subject to factoring. This account, however, is disconfirmed on two grounds. First, if subjects did no factoring in the disyllables, performance should have patterned identically on A and B trials. Second, in a recent study we have found factoring of anticipatory coarticulatory information for a vowel using the 4IAX procedure (Fowler, in press).

(vector analytical) choice is made than when acoustically identical schwas are judged the more similar.

CONCLUSIONS

Our findings suggest that in respect to the stimuli we selected for study, listeners segmented the acoustic signals along natural coarticulatory lines. They used anticipatory coarticulatory information for a phonetic segment as information for that segment. Moreover, they behaved as if they had "factored" those anticipatory influences from the segment with which they cooccured, hearing the influenced segment as free of contextual influences.

We are currently testing the generality of our findings across a broader range of contexts. We turn now to issues that will be important and relevant if our extensions are successful.

Finding Acoustic Support for Segmentation Along Coarticulatory Lines

We have not yet suggested what acoustic support there might be for the segmentation strategy we have observed in our listeners' behaviors. We can only suggest an approach that may be productive.

In effect, the segmentation strategy we have observed indicates (along with other evidence—for example, Fitch, Halwes, Erickson & Liberman, 1980; Fowler, 1979) that listeners use the acoustic speech signal as information about articulation. We see this role of the acoustic signal as analogous to that of reflected light in vision. In visual perception, light reflected from distal objects and events serves as a proximal stimulus providing information about the objects and events. It can provide information about them because, in being reflected from objects and events, it takes on structure specific to them. In Figure 6.4, we show the analogy we recognize between the role of reflected light in vision and that of the acoustic signal in speech perception.

The acoustic signal, structured as it passes through the moving vocal tract, can provide information about the changing shape of the vocal tract and about the articulatory gestures taking place. According to the analogy, the acoustic signal is not the object of perception itself, but rather, like reflected light in vision, is *proximal* stimulation. The "object" of speech perception is the distal source of the structure in the acoustic signal, the moving vocal tract (cf. Gibson, 1966; Liberman, Cooper, Shankweiler & Studdert-Kennedy, 1967).[3] If this analogy is apt, the place to start looking

---

[3] In fact, of course, the moving vocal tract is only the most peripheral of the perceptual objects. The perceptual object of which the listener is most aware is the talker's message.

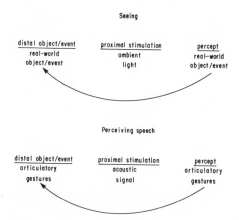

FIG. 6.4. Schematic representation of the analogous roles of reflected light and acoustic speech signals in perception.

for support for the listeners' perceptual reports is in articulation. Then, having discovered the perceived articulatory structure of speech we can look for its reflections in the acoustic signal.

Examination of coarticulated speech may reveal articulatory analogues of the "common" and "relative" motions studied by Johansson (1974). Stressed vowels—produced both during neighboring unstressed vowels, as in our studies, and during neighboring consonants—reveal themselves as relatively slow and continuous gestures of the tongue and jaw that together effect a global change in the shape of the vocal tract. Consonant gestures, produced either relatively independently of vowel gestures (as in bilabial consonants) or superimposed on vowel gestures (as in velar consonants), are rapid, local occluding gestures. Possibly, then, gestures for overlapping segments can be identified as coherent or, alternatively, as separate based on their common or distinctive rates and kinds of movements.

Other Applications of "Vector Analysis" to Speech

Listeners correctly classify phonetic tokens of a type over variations in speaking rate and over variation in vocal-tract size. These "normalizations" may be understood as factoring of invariant information for rate or for vocal-tract size from invariant information for phonetic identity.

A different application of the idea of vector analysis derives from Ohala's proposals (1981) concerning the origins of some sound changes in language. Ohala suggests that some sound changes occur when listeners fail to detect coarticulatory influences of (or, in Ohala's words, "distortions" by) neighboring segments. For example, some languages may have developed tones for linguistic uses when listeners failed to ascribe the tonal influences of consonants on a following vowel to the consonants themselves and interpreted them instead as tones intentionally imposed on the vowels by talkers. We interpret this hypothesis as one that listeners fail to recover the natural segmentation of the produced signal. The raising of low vowels in English particularly before nasal consonants (Labov, 1981) may have a similar interpretation (Wright, 1980). This phenomenon, like the development of tones, may be seen as an inaccurate parsing of the acoustic speech signal along its natural coarticulatory lines.

ACKNOWLEDGMENTS

This research was supported by NSF Grant BNS-8111470 and NICHD Grant 16951-01 to Haskins Laboratories.

Philip Lieberman: Comment

The data of Fowler and Smith are consistent with the theory that there is a syllabic level in the perception of speech that precedes the identification of segmental phonetic elements. The responses of their listeners indicate that they can sort out sequences that are mismatched at a syllabic level. The syllable being in this case a unit of speech in which articulatory preprogramming takes place. Sven Öhman showed in 1966 that the vowels in a CV_1CV_2 sequence were coded together (Öhman, 1966). The formant frequencies of V_1 were affected by V_2. Fowler and Smith demonstrate that listeners at some level of perception are aware of this effect. Their data however, do not appear to address the theoretical issues that were raised.

Carol A. Fowler and Mary R. Smith: Response

We will briefly respond to Lieberman's published comments and then discuss other comments that were raised following the oral presentation of our paper.

Lieberman finds our data consistent with a theory that there is a syllabic level of information extraction prior to extraction of phonetic segments in speech perception. The findings he cites are that "listeners can sort out sequences that are mismatched at a syllabic level." In view of the fact that the same sequences are mismatched at the phonetic segmental level (and, for that matter, at the articulatory level), however, the findings do not particularly address the question of a syllabic level of information extraction; nor, accordingly, do they address the question *when* syllables are extracted, if they are, in relation to extraction of phonetic segments.

Lieberman does not explain why, in his view, our data do not address the issues of segmentation and perceptual invariance. In our view, defended earlier and in a different way below, they do.

Much of the discussion following the presentation of our paper focused on a fundamental question whether our research is misguided from the outset in assuming that phonetic or phonological segments are recovered in speech perception. Although several other interesting and useful comments were made on other topics, we will restrict our response to this very fundamental question.

Stevens pointed out that there is no strong evidence that phone-sized segments are recovered by listeners, and that, in any case, recovery of lexically-specified segments would be difficult from casual-speech productions. (His example was a casual-speech production of the word "international" realized as something like [Inɜˇnaeš n̩ l̩].) Perkell argued that whereas production of speech must be more-or-less exhaustive ("serial" to use his wording), putting into the signal everything that a listener should recover, perception may involve short cuts when information is redundant. In particular, recovery of phonological or phonetic segments may be short circuited. (Stevens' example of "international" suggests that talkers take short cuts too; however, there must be somewhat stronger constraints on the talker's short cuts than on the listener's.) Finally, Lisker suggested that phonemes[1] are constructs derived from words.

The disagreement between at least the first two of these views and the premises of our research is not, we think, as substantial as it may have appeared to Stevens and Perkell. It is not a disagreement between two views of *processing* in speech perception, one (ours) that listeners go through a phonetic or phonological stage of processing in speech perception and another (theirs) that they do not. The premises of our research do not concern *processes* in speech perception, nor is the research designed to uncover any covert psychological processes by which vector analysis may be achieved, if it is. Instead, the premises concern a set of *conditions* that, in our view, must obtain if the essential duality of patterning in language (Hockett, 1960) is to be perpetuated. The conditions define a perceptual and articulatory "realism" (cf. Fowler, 1983) whereby talkers actually produce and listeners actually perceive the units constituting part of their "linguistic competence." Our research supports the view that conditions like these do obtain.

---

[1] We are not always certain what range of phone-sized segments the commentator intended. For example, it is a more radical claim that phonetic segments are constructions than that phonemes are. However, we would disagree with either claim. In the view of articulatory and perceptual "realism" we are working from here (see also, Fowler, 1983 and Fowler, Rubin, Remez and Turvey, 1980), spoken utterances have phone-sized structure despite coarticulatory overlap; the phonetic segments, in addition, are phonological in their deployment. Therefore, units at both levels of abstraction are in the linguistic behavior of the talker and, realized acoustically, are available for the listener to recover.

Relevant premises of our research can be characterized as follows:

1. Talkers realize linguistic units of various types in articulation (see footnote 1). In casual speech, the units they realize may not be precisely the ones they use in formal speech, but in either case, spoken words have a phone-sized segmental structure as evidenced by the occurrence of phonetic segment errors in speech production.
2. The acoustic signal provides information about those linguistic units and serves the role of message carrier about the units to listeners.
3. Listeners extract information about produced linguistic units from the acoustic signal. Among those extracted units can be phonetic units (or, even, we would argue, phonological ones [again, see footnote 1]).

Our research examines a situation in which listeners extract phonetic segments from speech and asks: *when* this occurs, what kind of segmentation do they achieve, and can that manner of segmentation explain the phenomenon of perceptual invariance?

Perkell's comment that listeners ordinarily need not, and do not, bother to recover the segmental structure of speech[2] may be correct. If it is, processing in speech perception is an example among many processes under investigation in cognitive psychology currently that can be characterized as involving an interactive relationship between "top-down" and "bottom-up" processes. Top-down processes may occur in speech, for example, when the listener knows what is forthcoming in the talker's message, and, knowing that, shortcircuits the bottom-up recovery of individual phonetic segments.

We have no particular reason to dispute that, but we find it important that the bottom up recovery of segmental structure in speech is the sine qua non for perpetuation of languages' duality of structure—which, by most accounts, is a universal, special and essential property of the language. Top-down short cuts are overlaid processes that develop based on experience with the language and with the world. As Studdert-Kennedy pointed out, speech errors provide strong evidence that talkers produce phonetic (and/or phonological) segments, our premise (1). For a child to become a talker, information for the existence of segmental structure in words must be available in the acoustic signal, our premise (2), because the acoustic signal is the only (or at least the major) source of evidence the child has. Finally, the would-be talker has to extract the produced segmental structure from the signal, our premise (3).

However, there are apparent barriers to the views that phonetic, and especially phonological, segments are in articulated speech, that they are specified in acoustic speech signals, and, hence, that they can be recovered from the signals by listeners. Some of those barriers are philosophical considerations that these segments are

---

2 There is an assumption here that extraction of phone-sized segments requires more work than not extracting them when the message is redundant. This may or not be the case. It probably is the case if extraction of the segments requires a stage of processing prior to lexical identification. It need not be, however, if listeners extract words directly that have phonetic and phonological structure.

mental kinds of things and, hence, can exist in the mind, but not in the mouth (see, for example, Hammarberg, 1982; Repp, 1981). One of us has discussed these apparent barriers elsewhere (Fowler, 1983), and we will not repeat the discussion here. Two remaining barriers are the problems bof segmentation and perceptual invariance.

If, as we believe, the child must extract segments from the acoustic speech signal, there must be solutions to these problems. Our research examines one solution (viz., perceptual vector analysis) that we believe extends to both problems. We conduct our research with adult subjects rather than with children in part because it is more easier to do so but also because we believe that the capacity to perceive the phonological structure in speech is fundamental to perception at all levels of development. However, our choice of subjects does require us to prevent their normal use of top-down short cuts. We do that by using isolated nonsense words and by giving listeners tasks that coerce them into using phonetic information.

In summary, then, we agree that in conversation listeners may use short cuts and, indeed, that talkers, who say such things as [Inɜˇnaešn̩], count on their doing so. However, in our view, bottom-up extraction of segmental structure is a prior and fundamental capacity. In a world without top-down short circuiting of phonetic or phonological perception, talkers would have to use formal rather than casual speech all of the time, and, perhaps, would have to slow down significantly, but communication would not be prevented. In contrast, in a world limited to top-down processes, there would be no communication, only hallucination.

ACKNOWLEDGMENTS

Preparation of this manuscript was supported by NSF Grant BNS 8111470 and NICHD Grant HD 16591-01 to Haskins Laboratories.

7

VARIATION AND INTERACTION IN SPEECH

Louis C. W. Pols
Institute of Phonetic Sciences
University of Amsterdam

INTRODUCTION

Speech is a dynamic acoustic signal with many sources of variation. Acoustic cues to phonetic segments are multiple and intertwined. In order to study the importance of specific cues, one frequently makes use of manipulated or synthetic, short utterances. Identification of such isolated utterances is a laboratory task of which the results are sometimes too easily generalized. One complicating factor is disregarding the importance of context. Apart from the linguistic aspects of context, the physical aspects of context are also important in order to create a referential framework for correct interpretation of various attributes.

In this chapter, a plosive identification experiment with ambiguous sentences is described, in which context is strongly emphasized. It will be shown that, in an appropriate context and with a realistic identification task, the amount of information in a vocalic transition about preceding or following plosives can compete with that in the plosive burst itself. There is always interaction between, on the one hand, the variation in speech sounds and, on the other hand, the context which sets the referential framework. If there is no context then the listener's reference is ill-defined. Presentation of isolated chunks of speech for identification provides an ill-defined perceptual set, with consequences that are not totally predictable.

This chapter discusses the sources and consequences of variability in the speech percept at the acoustic-phonetic level, and the way this variation interacts with the physical aspects of context. I am going to disregard syntactic, semantic, and pragmatic aspects of speech perception, not because these are not essential to everyday speech perception, but because I want to

140

concentrate here on certain aspects of phoneme identification at the acoustic-phonetic level which up to now have tended to be neglected.

Considering phoneme identification, one can think of the [ba]-[da]-[ga] type of experiments, where various physical parameters are systematically varied (e.g. Liberman, Delattre, & Cooper, 1952). One can also think of vowel identification experiments, whether or not with various speakers or various contexts (e.g. Verbrugge, Strange, Shankweiler & Edman, 1976), or of coarticulation studies using the deletion paradigm (e.g. Pols & Schouten, 1978). These few examples serve to illustrate various lines of approach and types of variables:

Synthetic utterances versus (manipulated) natural utterances.
Isolated presentation versus presentation in context.
Systematic variation of a single variable versus many variables.
Identification, discrimination, similarity judgment, reaction-time measurement, or use of adaptation as experimental procedures.

The variables studied in this type of perceptual experiment, like VOT, F_2-transition, vowel duration, burst characteristics, vocalic transitions, tempo, context, or speakers, are all potential sources of variation in actual speech. A number of levels can be distinguished here:

Phonemic variation; e.g. marked differences between acoustic realizations of the same phoneme.
Position in the word; e.g. an (aspirated) initial plosive differs from an (unaspirated) intervocalic plosive, and from an (unreleased) final plosive.
Local (syllabic) context; e.g. carry-over and anticipatory coarticulation, or progressive and regressive voice assimilation.
Remote (word and sentence) context including prosodic aspects like tempo, stress and accent, and variations like vowel reduction.
Speaker (including sex, style, speaking habits) and language/dialect differences.
Acoustic environment including reverberation and masking.

Many of these sources of variation interact with each other. Identification of part of a speech utterance depends on all the above-mentioned, and probably even more, variables. In normal speech perception, the running context, as well as our knowledge of the present conversational situation, provide us with most of the information necessary to do the appropriate interpretation.

Now consider the situation in most phonetic listening experiments: Subjects are provided with a minimal amount of information, frequently in a not very speech-like presentation, and almost always without the appropriate context. On top of that, the task they have to fulfill is often very far from a natural speech understanding task: They have to perform a forced choice, or a similarity judgment, a scaling, or a fast reaction-time job.

In this paper, I want to concentrate on the consequences of isolated presentation of speech segments out of context. By "context" I do not mean meaningful environment, but physical information sufficient to create a referential framework. Such a referential framework can be built up by one and the same carrier phrase, which nevertheless allows transfer of information with respect to tempo, dynamics of vowel transitions, and vowel duration. A good example of this approach is a recent paper by Johnson and Strange (1982). They studied the identification of vowels in tVt syllables spoken in normal and rapid tempo, always in the context of the same carrier sentence: "Was it the ... sound that you heard?" Intrinsically long vowels [e, æ, a, ɔ, o] in rapidly spoken tVt syllables were identified with greater accuracy when they were presented in their own rapid-rate sentence context (94%) than when they were represented in isolation (68%), or in a normal-rate sentence context (82%). Confusions were mainly in terms of spectrally similar short vowels.

When in a subsequent experiment the sequential order effect was better controlled, and the subjects were informed that the isolated syllables had also been produced as citation-from utterances, identification performance for those isolated syllables improved but was still not as good as it was for syllables presented in their original context. If only *parts* of the carrier phrase were presented, the presence of the stressed word "sound", immediately following the tVt test syllable, appeared to be essential for the accurate identification of intrinsically long vowels in rapidly spoken syllables. The intrinsically short, rapidly spoken vowels [i, ɪ, ɛ, ʌ, ʊ, u] were much less sensitive to context, and all tVt syllables spoken at a normal rate were identified with at least 95% accuracy regardless of the context in which they were presented, even if that was conflicting. Apparently, vowels articulated at the speaker's normal rate are completely specified by the information within the acoustic boundaries of the tVt syllables, whereas at a rate of articulation beyond the preferred rate, extrasyllabic information appears to be necessary to achieve maximum identification accuracy.

This leads to interesting questions about the relation between obtaining knowledge about the speaker's rate of articulation or timing in general, and using this knowledge to normalize the perceptual interpretation of temporal parameters in the stimulus (Fowler, 1980).

Fitch (1981) also studied temporal information with respect to speaking rate, but now in relation to voicing judgments of plosive consonants. She varied the closure duration of an intervocalic plosive as well as the duration of the vocalic section preceding the closure. It is known from the literature that a short vowel duration and a long closure interval are more favorable for the perception of a voiceless stop than for a voiced one. Subjects were asked to judge the speaking rate (by scoring "fast" or "slow"), or the voicing character of the plosive (by scoring [b] or [p]), in various realizations of the word [da$_u^v$i]. It was shown that each of the two types of temporal information (closure duration and vowel duration) can cue voicing differences as well as rate differences. However, when they are presented in combination, a difference in the *ratio* between closure duration and vowel duration affects the judgments of voicing most, whereas a difference in the *sum* of the two affects the rate judgments most. This still leaves open the question whether listeners score a sound because they are aware of the rate, or can judge the rate because they are aware of the sound. Vowel duration itself appeared to be not enough indication; however, the relationship between the duration of the steady-state vowel nucleus and that of the vocalic transition was perceptually salient. The longer the transition and the shorter the vowel nucleus, the shorter was the closure needed to change [b] to [p]. In order to distinguish voicing information from rate information, the listeners apparently use fine-grained temporal relationships in a syllabic context which up to now are not fully understood.

The results of Johnson and Strange (1982) and Fitch (1981) are just two examples of a phenomenon in everyday speech perception which I consider very important. A few basic attributes or cues define in principle the characteristics of speech sounds; however, because of variation in realization, there is no unique relationship. This makes it necessary for the listener to make an intelligent interpretation while taking into account contextual information.

In a recent review paper, Repp (1982) has given an excellent overview of multiple cues, phonetic-trading relations, coarticulation, and context effects. There have been many studies about isolated cues (e.g. VOT, F_1-transition, amplitude of aspiration noise, F_0), or complex cues (e.g. shape of total short-term spectrum) to phonetic distinctions (e.g. voicing of initial plosives), as well as about interactions in terms of trading relations between these cues. What worries me in most of these studies is the use of synthetic stimuli, the unnatural range of variables, and the unnatural task for the listener. But most of all, I am worried about the fact that in almost all of these stimuli a natural context is missing, not so much because it is necessary to place the listeners into a speech mode of perception, but more to create a natural acoustic referential framework to allow them to interpret properties like speaker, rate, F_0-excursion, duration, or transitions. Effects of speaking rate have been thoroughly reviewed by Miller (1981). Rather than duplicating Miller's and Repp's papers, I will describe an experiment which was recently carried out by M. E. H. Schouten and myself (Pols & Schouten, forthcoming). The two experiments mentioned above had to do with the importance of tempo information in the context. The present experiment is about the importance of an additional context factor for the optimal use of information in vocalic transitions for the identifications of plosives.

EXPERIMENTAL PROCEDURE

The experiment studies the identification of intervocalic plosives inshort sentences. At the position of the plosive, the sentences wereambiguous and allowed for two different meanings. The sentences were in Dutch (for instance, "Hij *t*elde twee keer" = "He counted twice" versus "Hij *b*elde twee keer" = "He rang twice"); a comparable example in English could have been "The *b*ar is open" versus "The *c*ar is open." The VCV segments around the critical plosive were isolated and then also presented to subjects for identification of the intervocalic plosive.In the sentences, as well as in the VCV segments, various parts of the utterances were deleted in order to find out more about the relative contributions of bursts and vocalic transitions to plosive identification. The experiment has a number of interesting aspects:

Because of the use of sentences, it is a realistic study of coarticulation with a natural task for the listeners.

Since the isolated VCV segments are also presented, the influence of presence or absence of remote and local context can be studied.

Since the contribution of the burst relative to that of both surrounding vocalic transitions is studied, new data can be added to the dispute about invariance and context-dependence. However, one should keep in mind that what we call "bursts" is not identical to what others call "onset spectra."

It is only fair to say that together with the good things one also has to accept some drawbacks. In the sentence context, only one phoneme in one specific position in the sentence can be studied, furthermore only in one direct opposition ([t] versus [b] in the Dutch example, or [b] versus [k] in the English example). Dutch has only five plosives [p, t, k, b, d] that are all unaspirated. Furthermore, [b] and [d] do not occur in final position. From these five plosives, one can obtain ten plosive pairs. For each pair, we made up five different sentences in which both plosives were about equally probable at one specific intervocalic position in each sentence. A male Dutch speaker spoke all 100 sentences and was very careful in pronouncing both matched sentences, as much as possible, in the same way. The tape-recorded sentences were digitized and stored in a computer for subsequent segmentation and regeneration. With a speech-editing program, any part of the sentences could be made audible and visible. In every utterance, four segmentation points were defined:

1. The middle of the vowel preceding the plosive. For practical reasons, this easily defined point was considered to be the beginning of the vocalic transition towards the plosive. In this way, part of the stationary vowel was probably also included, but that part hardly contributes to plosive identification (Schouten & Pols, 1983).

2. The end of the vocalic part preceding the plosive and the beginning of the closure (silence or vocal murmur).

3. The end of the plosive burst and the beginning of the vocalic transition towards the vowel following the plosive.

4. The middle of the following vowel, which in this chapter is considered to be the end of the vocalic transition.

All segmentation points were chosen as close as possible to the zero line and were smoothed by a 4 ms cosine window to prevent clicks. The part between segmentation points 1 and 4 defines the isolated CVC utterance. With the four segmentation points various presentation conditions were created:

Condition 1: whole utterance intact, no deletions.

Condition 2: deletion of the plosive burst.

Condition 3: deletion of the vocalic transition following the plosive (CV transition).

Condition 4: deletion of the vocalic transition towards the plosive (VC transition).

Condition 5: deletion of both transitions, only burst present.

Condition 6: deletion of VC transition and burst, only CV transition present.

Condition 7: deletion of burst and CV transition, only VC transition present.

Condition 8: deletion of burst as well as both transitions.

Deletion here always means substitution of a silent interval of equal duration. Condition 8 was not used for the isolated VCV segments, since it would have resulted in complete silence. In order not to make the listening session with the sentences too long, conditions 3 and 4 were not presented there; a pilot study had shown that the scores for these two conditions would have been close to 100% anyway.

Twenty-three university students scored all 600 sentences (6 conditions times 50 pairs of sentences), which were presented in a random order. For each sentence, they put a circle around one of the two letters on a sheet showing the complete sentences (e.g. hij ʾₑelde twee keer). At the position of the plosive in the sentence, both alternatives were printed, one in the line space above, and one in the line space below the rest of the sentence. The position (upper or lower) of the two alternatives per sentence was balanced. Subjects were told in advance that bits of particular consonants had been tampered with, but except in condition 8, where nothing of the consonant remained, they noticed hardly any gaps. They considered this an easy and natural task to do.

The same group of subjects also participated in two paper-and-pencil experiments with the same 50 sentences, preceding the listening experiment. First, they were given the sentences with a blank at the position of the plosive, and they were asked to fill in the very first letter they thought of, provided it did not result in a meaningless sentence. Next they were given the sentences again, but now with the two alternatives indicated, and they were asked to circle the preferred one. Both tasks took only a few minutes and were meant to get some insight about response biases. The sheets with the blank position in the sentences were moreover filled out by another 100 people.

A different group of 20 university students identified the isolated VCV utterances presented over headphones. These VCV parts were physically identical to the corresponding parts in the sentences, only the (supposedly redundant) sentence context was missing, which resulted in a loss of naturalness. This experiment was conducted in two parts; half of the subjects did one part first, the other half did the other part first. In part one, the subjects were offered two alternatives to choose from, just as in the sentence condition. On the response sheet, no sentence context was given; only the two alternatives were printed, one above the other. There were ten pairs on a line. After every ten stimuli, a brief tone was given in order to prevent subjects from losing track.

The stimuli in part two were identical to those in part one, but this time the subjects were not limited in their choice to two alternatives, but could respond with any of the five possible Dutch plosives [p, t, k, b, d]. Five of the seven conditions were presented together in a random order; however, conditions 6 (CV transition only) and 7 (VC transition only) were each presented separately. For each of these two conditions, the subjects had to be told where they should try to identify a (missing) plosive, at the beginning or at the end of the stimulus, whereas in all other conditions there was no ambiguity about the position of the consonant to be identified.

EXPERIMENTAL RESULTS

All basic results from the three listening experiments are gathered in Table 7.1. The code for the sentence experiment is SENT, the codes for both experiments with the VCV segments isolated from the sentences are VCV2 and VCV5, depending on whether the listeners had just two alternatives, as in the sentence experiment, or could choose from all five possible Dutch plosives. The eight conditions are labeled in three different ways, first of all with the numbers defined earlier (1 to 8), next with a short description (e.g. "no deletion," or "burst only"), and finally with an indication of which of the three segments were presented (vocalic transition preceding the plosive = VC, intervocalic consonant including closure interval and burst = C, vocalic transition following the plosive = CV).

Percentage correct scores are given per plosive, and for the unvoiced as well as for the voiced group of plosives. All plosive scores are averaged over the 20 occurrences per consonant and over the 23 listeners (sentence experiment), or the 20 listeners (VCV experiments). For VCV5, two scores per consonant are given; the upper score represents the percentage of times the plosive itself was correctly identified, just as in the other experiments, and the lower one tells us how often the place of articulation was correct (e.g. for [p]-stimuli, apart from [p]-responses, [b]-responses were also counted correct). A great improvement from the one score to the other indicates that most plosive errors were voicing errors. In the two-alternatives experiments (SENT and VCV2) it does not make sense to derive place-of-articulation scores, because there the voicing alternative could either not be chosen or was the only alternative.

The last two columns again give scores for unvoiced and voiced groups of plosives,but this time corrected for chance level in order to allow comparison of results between two-alternatives experiments (50% chance level) and five-alternatives experiments (20% chance level). The following simple formula was used for this chance correction: $p = p' - (1/n)/1 - (1/n)$, in which p' is the original score and n is the number of alternatives. It would perhaps be worthwhile to consider d'- or z-scores instead.

For a clear graphical representation and comparison of the data, we will use the scores averaged over the three unvoiced plosives (UV) and the two voiced plosives (V), with chance correction. There are of course differences between the plosives within each group as well as per plosive depending on the vowel environment, but the limited amount of data does not allow a systematic evaluation of these aspects apart from the listeners' preference for bilabial plosives, which we will discuss later.

Figure 7.1 gives the scores for the three different experiments (SENT, VCV2, and VCV5, whenever appropriate. The unvoiced and voiced plosives

TABLE 7.1

Scores per plosive and per group of plosives for eight different conditions and three different experiments

Presence of VC C CV	Expt. code	\multicolumn{5}{c}{Scores per plosive}					\multicolumn{4}{c}{Per group Chance corr.}			
		P	T	K	B	D	UV	V	UV	V
VC C CV (no deletion) 1	SENT	99.8	99.5	100	99.4	98.7	99.8	99.0	99.6	98.0
	VCV2	98.8	95.8	99.7	99.3	98.4	98.1	98.8	96.2	97.6
	VCV5	94.5	94.7	99.2	96.5	94.0	96.2	95.3	95.3	94.1
		98.8	96.9	99.2	99.5	94.3	98.3	96.9	97.5	95.4
VC – CV (– burst) 2	SENT	95.7	73.2	90.4	96.7	97.6	86.4	97.2	72.8	94.4
	VCV2	90.0	36.8	70.8	84.0	83.5	65.9	83.8	31.8	67.6
	VCV5	59.5	15.5	46.1	64.0	55.8	40.4	59.9	25.5	49.9
		87.0	43.4	46.1	87.3	62.0	58.8	74.6	38.2	61.9
VC C – (– CV) 3	SENT	–	–	–	–	–	–	–	–	–
	VCV2	94.8	97.6	98.7	99.3	97.3	97.0	98.3	94.0	96.6
	VCV5	84.5	95.3	96.1	95.3	87.0	91.9	91.1	89.9	88.9
		95.8	96.6	96.1	99.3	89.0	96.1	94.1	94.2	91.2
– C CV (– VC) 4	SENT	–	–	–	–	–	–	–	–	–
	VCV2	99.3	99.4	99.7	99.0	97.6	99.5	98.3	99.0	96.6
	VCV5	93.8	95.3	99.7	92.5	93.5	96.3	93.0	95.4	91.3
		97.5	98.7	99.7	97.5	95.0	98.6	97.3	97.9	96.0
– C – (burst only) 5	SENT	98.3	99.5	98.2	85.7	88.0	98.7	86.8	97.4	73.6
	VCV2	97.8	98.2	99.0	95.3	93.3	98.3	94.3	96.6	88.6
	VCV5	89.3	94.5	90.8	78.8	73.0	91.5	75.9	89.4	69.9
		96.3	96.3	90.8	97.3	83.3	94.5	90.3	91.8	85.5
– – CV (CV only) 6	SENT	96.1	62.2	77.1	89.1	93.5	78.5	91.3	57.0	82.6
	VCV2	84.0	44.1	51.7	74.0	71.3	59.9	72.6	19.8	45.2
	VCV5	53.0	12.9	26.1	40.5	43.0	30.6	41.8	13.3	27.3
		79.0	35.5	26.1	70.8	53.5	46.9	62.1	20.4	43.2
VC – – (VC only) 7	SENT	95.2	48.1	81.2	79.1	67.2	74.8	73.2	49.6	46.4
	VCV2	72.4	57.4	83.6	72.3	55.0	71.1	63.6	42.2	27.2
	VCV5	43.0	33.7	63.4	38.5	31.8	46.7	35.1	33.4	18.9
		69.5	60.8	63.4	74.0	57.5	64.6	65.8	46.9	48.7
– – – (–everything) 8	SENT	92.4	38.9	62.9	70.9	44.1	64.7	57.5	55.9	46.9
	VCV2	–	–	–	–	–	–	–	–	–
	VCV5	–	–	–	–	–	–	–	–	–

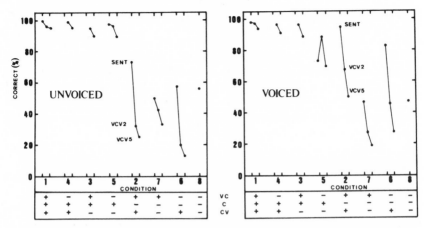

FIG. 7.1. Percentage correct scores for the three experiments (SENT, VCV2, and VCV5). The results for the unvoiced and voiced plosives are shown separately, as well as each of the eight conditions.

are shown separately, as well as each of the eight conditions. In the left-hand panel (unvoiced plosives), we can see that for the four leftmost conditions the score is always very high, with small but consistent differences between the three experiments. In all four conditions, the burst is present. In the other four conditions, where the burst is absent, much lower scores and more variation over the experiments are shown. The large difference between SENT and VCV2 for conditions 2 (minus burst), 6 (CV transition only), and to a lesser extent 7 (VC transition only) is especially interesting, because it illustrates the possible influence of a noninformative sentence context. This context contains no information insofar as it gives no indication for one alternative or the other. However, it does contribute to a more natural stimulus which apparently allows one to draw more information from the VC or CV transition than is possible when exactly the same VCV segment is presented in isolation. Since the scores in Figure 7.1 are corrected for chance, it is also possible to compare the results for experiments VCV2 and VCV5. Obviously there is a consistent, but not very big, difference between both experiments: Even after chance correction, choosing among two alternatives is somewhat easier than choosing among five.

Let us next discuss the scores for the *voiced* plosives, as given in the right-hand panel of Figure 7.1. The big difference between "burst present" (conditions 1–4–3--5) and "burst absent" (conditions 2–7–6–8) is here certainly less evident than with the unvoiced plosives. The burst from voiced plosives is less prominent, and we can see that in the sentence experiment the scores for conditions 2 (minus burst) and 6 (CV transition only) are actually higher than for condition 5 (burst only). This means in fact that CV plus VC transition, and even the CV transition on its own, contain *more* information about the voiced plosives than the vocal murmur plus burst itself does. Here we see a clear example of a situation where the burst is *less* important than the vocalic transition in natural utterances.

The fact that this result has never been shown before is, in my opinion, a consequence of the exclusive use of the short isolated nonsense-syllable type of stimuli. In the present experiments with *isolated* utterances (VCV2 and VCV5), the voiced plosive burst (condition 5) indeed dominates the transitional information (conditions 2-7-6). Only in a more natural listening situation does the vocalic transition appear to carry more weight than the plosive burst for the identification of intervocalic voiced plosives. The fact that the score for condition 5 (burst only) is even lower in SENT than in VCV2 is perhaps caused by the weak plosive burst, which could be masked to some extent by the sentence context.

By comparing the scores for conditions 7 (VC transition only) and 6 (CV transition only) we can see that the CV transition contains more information about the preceding plosive than the VC transition does about the following plosive. The scores for conditions 4 (minus VC) and 3 (minus CV) point in the same direction. However, before making this a general conclusion, one must realize that this is Dutch material and that the structure of most sentences was such that only the second syllable, the one with the CV transition in it, was stressed.

Another difference between the experiments SENT and VCV2 has already been pointed out for the unvoiced plosives: The scores are significantly different in both experiments for conditions 2, 7, and 6, while the relevant VCV parts in both experiments are absolutely identical. The sentence context in experiment SENT apparently creates a more natural setting, resulting in higher correct scores.

One could argue that the sentence context was not as redundant as we consider it to be, which would be sufficient explanation for the higher scores for SENT than for VCV2. However, when all three segments (VC, C, and CV) are deleted (condition 8), the score is only slightly above chance, suggesting that there really is very little information left for correct plosive identification. In Table 7.1, we can see that the better-than-chance scores are caused mainly by the scores for the bilabials [p] and [b]. Despite the fact that we did our utmost to achieve smooth segmentation boundaries and that there were certainly no audible clicks in the stimuli, the subjects still show an irresistible preference for [p-b] responses. This is the more puzzling since this preference was absent in the paper-and-pencil experiments, as is shown in Table 7.2.

TABLE 7.2

Response percentages per consonant for each of the ten
consonant pairs for two paper-and-pencil experiments
and one listening experiment.

Plosive pair	Paper-and-pencil experiment Fill in blank space (100)	(23)	Two altern. (23)	Listening SENT, cond. 8 (23)
p	40	45	44	92
t	51	50	56	28
p	45	54	65	91
k	32	32	35	45
p	49	60	54	90
b	47	37	46	23
p	45	52	60	97
d	31	30	40	14
b	22	24	35	87
t	62	61	65	29
b	44	47	48	90
k	30	44	52	45
b	38	41	44	84
d	43	44	56	44
t	39	50	37	34
k	51	47	63	87
t	57	55	60	66
d	28	40	40	58
d	40	47	64	60
k	47	26	36	71

Table 7.2 gives for each of the ten plosive pairs, averaged over the five
different sentences per pair and over the number of subjects indicated, the
response percentages per consonant. The first two columns of percentages
represent the condition with a blank at the position of the consonant for
the two different groups of subjects. These scores do not add up to 100%
because subjects filled in other acceptable consonants as well, different from
the two we had in mind. The next column gives the percentages for the
two-alternatives condition, which do add up to 100% per pair.

The last column gives the results for condition 8 (everything deleted) in the listening experiment with 100 sentences. Since burst as well as both transitions were deleted, we would have expected a 50–50 score if there had been no bias at all and no remaining information about the deleted plosive. If, on the other hand, still enough information had been available in the remainder of the sentence for a perfect guess, then the scores would have been 100–100. Finally, with a very strong bias towards one of the two alternatives caused by the meaning of the sentence itself, the scores would have become 100–0 per consonant pair. What actually happens is that, for all pairs with a bilabial as one of the options, there is a strong preference for that plosive irrespective of the vowel environment. If both alternatives are bilabial ([p] versus [b]), then the unvoiced variant is strongly preferred. The few remaining pairs show more or less equal scores, although [k] is preferred in the [k–t] pair, but that preference was already suggested in the paper-and-pencil experiments and must be caused by the semantic structure of the five sentences concerned. The strong bilabial preference in the listening experiment cannot be explained by preferences in the sentences themselves because these would have come out in the paper-and-pencil experiments. For the [b–t] pair, it even works the other way around!

For the time being, we can only conclude that any manipulation of a speech signal by deleting parts of it produces a [p]- or a [b]-like sensation in the listeners, which overrules any other preferences. It is difficult to simply remove information: By deleting parts of the signal, we frequently add new information. This bilabial preference in deletion experiments was noted by Pols and Schouten (1978) as well as by Fischer-Jørgensen (1972b). We are well aware of this phenomenon, but so far we do not know how to get rid of it. There is some evidence that adding noise can improve the situation (Pols & Schouten, 1981). "Adding noise" here means that, instead of substituting a silent interval at the position of the deleted segment, one puts in a burst of noise of the same duration. A possible explanation for this improved plosive identification could be that with silence one can "hear" that no information is there, whereas with noise one could imagine that the information is there and can be "heard through the noise." It is probable that with any abruptly starting or terminating manipulated stimulus, like for instance the chirp-type stimuli, this effect plays a part. In our opinion, it would go too far to reject for this reason the deletion paradigm, since the effect is only annoying in the most extreme conditions, which are usually not really interesting. For more details about this experiment with the ambiguous sentences and for a comparison with results for CVCVC stimuli (Schouten & Pols, 1983), see Pols & Schouten (forthcoming).

GENERAL DISCUSSION

In this section, I would like to return to the general topic outlined in the Introduction, variation and interaction in speech. Some aspects of it can be reformulated as follows:

1. There is a great deal of variation in the speech signal; the more frequently that experimental results point in the direction of context-dependent effects, the less probable it will be that dominant invariant cues exist.
2. Context is needed to create a referential framework in order to allow correct interpretation of speech events and in order to create natural listening conditions.
3. For most phonetic contrasts, there exist multiple cues; the possible perceptual importance of specific cues is misinterpreted in certain experiments because of the procedures used.

With respect to the first point (variation in speech), there are of course an endless number of examples. The data from Johnson & Strange (1982) and Fitch (1981) about duration and voicing related to rate are good illustrations of this phenomenon. Even such an advocate of invariant cues as Sheila Blumstein recently had to accept that context-dependent cues play a nonnegligible role in the perception of place of articulation of initial stop consonants (Blumstein, Isaacs & Mertus, 1982).

The second point (the need for context) is illustrated by the experimental results described in this chapter. It is still very useful to do detailed analyses with isolated utterances, as I have done myself many times. However, one must take into account the fact that listeners may use an unspecified kind of default referential framework. Or they may use a reference which is only relevant within the experiment itself, for instance in a categorical perception experiment in which the endpoints of the scale are not always optimal representatives of the sounds of both categories. These problems also play a role in vowel identification experiments with short segments, isolated from conversational speech (e.g. Koopmans-van Beinum, 1980).

A fixed reference, without adaptation to the local circumstances, is also used in almost all automatic speech-recognition systems which use fixed word templates, cluster centers, and the like. In my opinion this also explains why Crystal and House (1982), in their statistical evaluation of segmental durations in connected speech, did not find a strong vowel-lengthening-before-voicing effect. On a local basis this effect, most probably, still exists, but on an average basis this specific effect is lost.

The third point (the perceptual importance of multiple cues) is also demonstrated by the experiment described in this chapter. If we had only had the results from the VCV experiments, we would have concluded that

context-independent information in the burst was dominant for plosive identification. However, from the sentence experiment we have learned that vocalic transitions can be more specific for the plosive than the burst itself.
Actually, it is not really important which part is most specific or contains
most information; what is important is the fact that there are multiple cues
for plosive identification, one of which is the vocalic transition.

This seems to be a very relevant property of speech, since the vocalic
transition is probably more resistant to sloppy pronunciation and masking
than the burst. Crystal and House (1982) found that of the 972 stops they
identified in the running text they analyzed, fewer than 50% were "complete
stops," including a clearly defined hold followed by a plosion release. It seems
fair to suppose that even for the incomplete stops, the vocalic transition will
still be present. It could very well be that hearing-impaired listeners can
make more effective use of vocalic transitions (higher amplitude, low- and
mid-frequency range) for plosive identification, than of the release burst (low
amplitude, high frequency range, not always produced) under many circumstances. In a study about acoustic cues for final stop voicing (Revoile, Pickett
& Holden, 1982) it is concluded that for many hearing-impaired and for all
normal-hearing listeners, the vowel transitions are an important additional
source of cues to final-stop voicing perception. The relevance and importance
of multiple cues in speech perception under realistic listening conditions is
an intriguing area of research.

ACKNOWLEDGEMENT

The author would like to thank Bert Schouten for the many discussions about
this contribution and about the experiment described in it, as well as for his
willingness to correct the English text.

David B. Pisoni: Contextual Variability and the Problem
of Acoustic-Phonetic Invariance in Speech

INTRODUCTION

The bulk of research on speech processes over the last 35 years has been concerned
principally, if not exclusively, with the analysis of features and phonemes in highly
controlled experimental contexts using nonsense syllable test materials. This observation applies equally well to research in both speech production and speech
perception. Such a research strategy is not at all surprising when one begins to
study complex phenomena such as speech and when one tries to understand the

relations between spoken language and its acoustic-phonetic realization as speech. Researchers in any field of scientific investigation typically work on tractable problems that can be studied with existing methodology and experimental paradigms. However, relative to the voluminous literature on isolated phoneme perception, very little is actually known at this time about how the acoustic-phonetic information in the speech signal is used by listeners to support word recognition, sentence perception, or understanding of fluent connected speech. Fortunately, the situation is changing rapidly as shown by the new research reported in several of the chapters in this book.

There are several reasons for this change in research strategy and emphasis over the past few years. First, many more researchers are now actively working on basic questions in speech than 10 to 15 years ago. Second, the cost of doing speech research has dropped quite significantly with the wide spread availability of low-cost digital computers and signal-processing techniques. Thus, many more major universities now have speech-processing labs that are engaged in acoustic-phonetic research. Finally, with more interest in the field of speech and more powerful research tools available, many investigators have turned their efforts to a much wider range of problems to study. Taken together, these developments have directed the focus of speech research well beyond the domain of phoneme and feature perception in isolated highly controlled environments to a number of other problems associated with spoken language understanding in more natural and realistic contexts. Much of this interest was no doubt stimulated by the ARPA (Advanced Research Projects Agency) project which demonstrated, among other things, that a speech understanding system could be built (see Klatt, 1977).

Louis Pols's paper, "Variation and Interaction in Speech," is a good example of this recent trend in research in acoustic-phonetics. While acknowledging the enormous amount of variability in the speech signal and the contributions of multiple cues to perception of segmental phonemes, Pols nevertheless has set out to examine the contextual effects of sentence environments on phoneme perception using a deletion paradigm. In this procedure, parts of the speech signal are carefully removed via digital editing techniques and the effects of these manipulations on listeners' responses is observed. I will first focus my remarks on the major generalizations and implications of Pols's findings for work in speech perception. Then, I will describe two recent studies from our own laboratory that bear very closely on the issues and problems raised by Pols. These two studies deal with the role of context in speech perception and the search for acoustic-phonetic invariance in the speech signal.

NONSENSE SYLLABLES AND SYNTHETIC SPEECH

One of the issues that Pols raises concerns the almost exclusive reliance on the use of nonsense syllable stimuli in perceptual experiments. While much has been learned from these early studies about the minimal acoustic cues to phoneme perception (Fant, 1973; Liberman, Cooper, Shankweiler & Studdert-Kennedy, 1967) and the interaction of these cues in certain well-defined although isolated environments (Liberman, 1982; Repp, 1982; Studdert-Kennedy, 1982), relatively little attention has been devoted in the acoustic-phonetic literature to word recognition, particularly word recognition in sentence contexts or to the processing of connected fluent speech (see Cole & Jakimik, 1980; Foss & Blank, 1980; Marslen-Wilson & Welsh, 1978). Much of what we currently know about the speech cues comes from perceptual studies using highly simplified synthetic speech signals. There is now clear evidence that even high quality synthetic speech is impoverished and less redundant than natural speech (Pisoni, 1982). Both criticisms raised by Pols are, in my view, quite valid and appropriate when one looks over the acoustic-phonetic literature and reexamines the issues that a large number of researchers have focused their attention on over the years (e.g., Lane, 1965; Repp, 1983). In his recent investigations, Pols has made a deliberate and conscious effort to move away from the exclusive use of synthetic speech stimuli to research using natural speech. Pols and others have also made efforts to study the perception of more meaningful stimuli such as words and sentence-length materials (rather than simple nonsense syllables) in more realistic or natural tasks that require recognition or identification.

CONTEXT EFFECTS IN SPEECH

The role of context has been a major problem area not only in the field of speech research but also across almost all other domains of human and animal behavior. We need to learn much more about the sources of variability and the contributions introduced by talker differences, variations in speaking rate, the local phonetic environment, and the linguistic context including syntax, semantics, and pragmatics. These are the major sources of variability known to exist in speech. Several years ago people were quite optimistic that increased attention to prosody in speech research would somehow magically solve the problems of invariance and variability (Cohen & Nooteboom, 1975). Instead, this work has revealed even more sources of variability. The work on prosody in the last few years has been important in the overall research effort to understand human speech processing but it has not proved to be the critical missing link that provides all the solutions to the old problems in speech. The same problems are still with us today as they have been since the earliest days of speech research.

What is needed now are more detailed and systematic studies that examine what these various sources of context do and how they operate in modulating the variability observed in the acoustic-phonetic structure of speech. In many cases, these seemingly troublesome sources of contextual variability are not something just added onto an "idealized" discrete segmental representation of speech as a linear sequence of phonemes. Researchers are beginning to realize that some context effects may be an inherent part of the signal itself, reflecting important properties of the speaker and the linguistic content of the message.

With the recent development of large data bases for measurement purposes and hypothesis testing (Crystal & House, 1982; Shipman, 1982), many of the seemingly difficult questions surrounding the operation of phonological rules or the effects of local phonetic contexts can be studied within a fairly manageable time frame. Years ago, it took several minutes just to make a spectrogram of one utterance from a single talker. Because of advances in the available technology, some research questions in acoustic-phonetics that are practical to address today would not even be conceived of only a few years ago. The ability to test hypotheses at a faster rate will allow researchers to make greater advances in accumulating knowledge about the acoustic-phonetics of fluent connected speech and the effect of different sources of contextual variability in speech (Shipman, 1983).

EFFECTS OF SPEAKING RATE ON PHONETIC PERCEPTION

Over the last few years, a great deal of interest has been focused on the effects of speaking rate. The findings of Port, Fitch, and Miller among others who have studied the influence of speech tempo on the perception of phonetic segments is well-known (see Miller, 1981 for a review). Their work has been interpreted as demonstrating a form of perceptual normalization whereby the listener "compensates" or "readjusts" his or her decision criteria in accordance with the systematic variability and changes introduced by different speaking rates. In one well-known perceptual study, Miller and Liberman (1979) reported that overall syllable duration influences the locations of the identification boundary between the stop [b] and the semivowel [w]. More specifically, they reported that the duration of the vowel in an isolated CV syllable systematically influenced the perception of the formant transition cues for the stop-semivowel distinction. With short syllables, subjects required shorter transition durations to perceive a [w] than with longer syllables. Miller and Liberman interpreted these results as a clear demonstration of perceptual normalization for speaking rate—the listener adjusts his/her decision to compensate for the differences in vowel length that are conditioned by the talker's speaking rate. The listener interprets a particular set of acoustic cues or attributes such as the duration of a transition for a [b] or [w] *in relation* to the talker's speaking rate rather than by reference to some absolute set of contextually invariant acoustic attributes in the signal itself. Although Miller and Liberman used isolated, synthetically produced nonsense syllables in a somewhat unnatural experimental setting, at least according to Pols's criteria, their findings were of some interest to us because of the strong claims made about the underlying perceptual mechanisms.

To evaluate Miller and Liberman's (1969) claims about rate normalization, we carried out several experiments comparing the perception of speech and comparable nonspeech control signals (see Pisoni, Carrell & Gans, 1983). The nonspeech control signals were created with sinewave analogs of the speech stimuli which preserved the durations and temporal relations, although these signals did not sound like speech to naive listeners. The results of these comparisons which are shown in Figure 7a.1 demonstrated comparable context effects for the perception of the duration of a rapid spectrum change as a function of the overall duration of the stimulus for both the speech and nonspeech stimuli. Our findings therefore call into question the rate normalization account offered by Miller and Liberman by demonstrating clearly that context effects such as these are not peculiar to the perception of speech or to the normalization of differences in the talker's speaking rate. Rather, these types of context effects may simply reflect general psychophysical principles that affect the perceptual categorization and discrimination of all acoustic signals, whether speech or nonspeech (see Goldhor, 1983). Indeed, these context effects

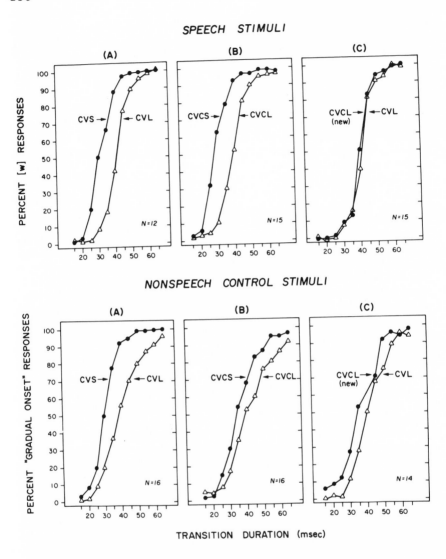

FIG. 7a.1. Labeling data for synthetic CV and CVC syllables (top panels) and nonspeech control signals (bottom panels). Panels A and B in the top display show percent of [w] responses as a function of transition duration in ms. for CV and CVC syllables that differ in overall duration; the filled circles are the short (80 ms) stimuli, the open triangles are the long (295 ms) stimuli. Panel C shows data for CV and CVC syllables that were matched for overall duration. Panels A, B, and C in the bottom display show percent of "gradual-onset" responses for the matched nonspeech control signals. These functions are parallel to the speech labeling data shown in the top panel (From Pisoni, Carrell & Gans, 1983).

may not even be peculiar to the auditory modality but may reflect fairly general perceptual principles operative across all sensory modalities (e.g., Cutting, 1983; Helson, 1964).

INVARIANCE OF THE CONSONANT/VOWEL RATIO

Closely related to this work on speaking rate is a series of studies reported by Port on the consonant/vowel ratio, a presumed invariant cue to voicing of stops in syllable-final position (Port, 1981a, b; Port and Dalby, 1982). It has been known for some time that vowel duration and closure duration enter into a reciprocal relation by providing cues to the voicing feature of stops in this environment. Moreover, it has been shown that each of these cues is affected by changes in speaking rate (Fitch, 1981; Miller & Grosjean, 1981; Port, 1979). Recently, Port (1981a, b) has argued that vowel and closure duration should be considered together as a unitary property or attribute of the voicing feature that remains invariant over changes in speaking rate. Port claims that the ratio of closure duration to vowel duration (e.g., the C/V ratio) should be considered as a "relational" cue to voicing that is contextually invariant. In a number of speech-production studies, Port has found that the C/V ratio appears to remain invariant despite variations in speaking rate, number of syllables in the test word, and vowel tensity. Thus, although all three factors clearly affect the absolute durations of the vowel and closure intervals, the C/V ratios appear to remain constant due to the temporal compensation between the two cues.

In the studies on the effects of speech tempo reported by Port as well as the work of others, test words always appeared in fixed carrier sentences of the form "He said the word ____ again." Recently, in our laboratory, Paul Luce and Jan Charles-Luce (1983) carried out an important test of Port's invariance claims for the C/V ratio by examining the well-known effects of phrase-final lengthening on vowel and closure durations. In their production study, Luce and Charles-Luce were interested in determining if the C/V ratio would remain invariant from nonphrase-final to phrase-final sentence positions. Previous research has shown that the vowel and closure durations are affected by local rate changes due to phrase final lengthening. Would the C/V ratio remain invariant over these transformations?

The C/V ratios from their study are shown in separate panels for CVC test words ending in velars, bilabials, and dentals in Figure 7a.2. The results clearly demonstrate that the C/V ratios are larger for test words produced in nonphrase final position compared to the same words produced in phrase-final position. However, the effect interacted with the voicing value of the final stop, the place of articulation of the stop, and the immediately following local phonetic environment. Despite the contribution of these additional factors, the results demonstrate very clearly that the C/V ratio for syllable-final stops does not remain invariant across all environments.

I have described this study because it is a good example of how important it is to examine the precise effects of known sources of variability in speech production and perception. The use of controlled carrier sentences in Port's earlier work is

DAVID B. PISONI

BILABIALS

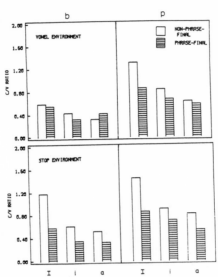

FIG. 7a.2. Mean C/V ratios for word-final bilabial stops. For each
test word, vowel duration and closure duration for the final stop consonant were measured from a digital waveform display. Vowel duration was
measured from the onset of periodic energy to a marked decrease in the
periodic energy in the waveform. Closure duration was measured from this
decrease in periodic energy to the onset of burst frication of the word-final
stop. The upper panel shows the mean C/V ratios for test words ending
in [b] and [p] produced in a vowel environment. The bottom panel shows
the mean C/V ratios for test words ending in [b] and [p] produced in a
stop environment. Mean C/V ratios are shown for each vowel [I], [i], [a],
separately. The open bars refer to the C/V ratios for test words produced
in nonphrase-final position; the hatched bars refer to C/V ratios for test
words produced in phrase-final position. Note the consistent difference in
the C/V ratios across phrase-final and nonphrase-final environments (data
from Luce & Charles-Luce, 1983).

commendable since it avoids the biases introduced by talkers reading lists of isolated
words in citation form. However, the exclusive use of these "neutral" materials may
be quite misleading when one proceeds to generalize the findings beyond the specific
experimental contexts. More research is needed on the contribution of context and
the specific form of variability that different sources of context introduce in the
speech waveform. Much of the work on the effects of speaking rate has been
done by asking talkers to consciously speed up or slow down their speaking rates
when reading controlled experimental materials. The conditioning and variability
of segmental durations observed under these explicit instructions to subjects may
be quite different from the types of durational changes that occur more-or-less
automatically as a consequence of naturally occurring sentence-level phenomena in
speech.

CONCLUSIONS

It is clear from the work in Louis Pols's paper and the results of the recent studies I summarized from our laboratory that the effects of context on variability in speech are enormous and quite diverse in scope. The problems associated with acoustic-phonetic invariance and variability in speech have not yet been solved. However, I am encouraged by the change in direction and attitude of many researchers working in the field. Research efforts appear to be directed toward much broader issues than just a few years ago, issues that involve the study of more meaningful linguistic stimuli in more naturalistic tasks. These studies also employ experimental paradigms that require the listener's active deployment of phonological, lexical, syntactic, and semantic knowledge in assigning an interpretation to the sensory input. There also appears to be a more optimistic attitude about eventually understanding the role of context and its differential contribution to the acoustic-phonetic realization of the speech signal. Speech is a complex phenomenon. As such, it is very unlikely that we will find one simple unifying principle that will serve to rationalize and explain all of the different sources of variability observed across the articulatory, acoustic, and perceptual domains.

ACKNOWLEDGEMENT

The work described in this paper was supported, in part, by NIH research grant NS–12179 and, in part by contract F33615–83–K–0501 with the Air Force Office of Scientific Research, Air Force System Command. I thank H. C. Nusbaum, D. Kewley-Port and P. A. Luce for their comments and suggestions.

J. C. Catford: Comment

I have two comments. First, with respect to the term "natural contexts," I would like to make a comment as a linguistic phonetician, emphasizing the "linguistic" at this moment. It seems to me quite *unnatural* to say things line "say____again," "dis____de nouveau" over and over again, especially when the word inserted in the frame has not previously been said at all. Of course, these meaningless utterances are useful because they provide a more or less invariant phonetic and phonological context, and that is why they care used. But I find it a little odd to call them "natural."

My second comment is really a question. Looking at Table 7.1 in Dr. Pols's paper, I was struck by the fact that the recognition of [t] was noticeably bad in the conditions "minus burst" and "CV only," whereas other consonants were still more or less recognizable in these conditions. Is it perhaps the case that in Dutch, a language supposedly with unaspirated stops, the [t] is actually somewhat affricated or aspirated? Would that account for the fact that it behaved differently from the others in those conditions? If this is the case, it suggests the more general observation that in interpreting such data one has to take into account detailed phonetic characteristics, and not just "global" ones, like the idea that all voiceless stops are unaspirated in Dutch.

John Holmes: Comment

I obviously agree with the importance of using more natural stimuli for speech-perception experiments. However, I am not so happy with the assumption that synthetic speech is necessarily too unnatural, merely because it is synthetic. It is possible, if you take sufficient care in producing synthetic speech, to get signals sufficiently close to natural for them to be mistaken for natural speech. It seems to me that if you can use really good synthetic speech—that is, synthetic speech that will be accepted by subjects as examples of natural speech—then the synthetic stimuli will be much better than natural ones, simply because all their parameters will be under control, you will know exactly what the stimuli are, and you will be able vary them in precisely controlled ways.

Klaus J. Kohler: Comment

Since the context-free VCV utterances in the listening experiments were excised from whole sentences containing them, they contained the contextual sentence-internal prosodies (timing, pitch, intensity). They thus differed in essential aspects from VCV utterances produced (or synthesized) in isolation (as isolated utterances). It is, therefore, not surprising that their identification scores dropped significantly in relation to the scores obtained for the VCV sections in the original sentence context. This procedure introduced a higher degree of artificiality into the experimental design than the use of VCV sequences produced in isolation or in frames of the sort "Say_____again" because it violated the syntagmatic component of paradigmatic differentiation in speech production, although it set out to stress the need for context in natural identification tasks. The results of the experiments speak against the use of such excised sentence sections as stimuli in listening tests, not necessarily against the use of syllable sequences that were produced as isolated utterances. The conclusions from the results should be scaled down accordingly.

8 Analysis of French Stop Consonants Using a Model of the Peripheral Auditory System

Bertrand Delgutte
Centre National d'Etudes
des Télécommunications, Lanion, France

INTRODUCTION

Knowledge of auditory processing should be valuable in a search for correlates of phonetic categories that would be relatively invariant with respect to speaker and phonetic context (Blumstein & Stevens, 1979; Chistovich, Lublinskaya, Malinnikova, Ogorodnikova, Stoljarova & Zhukov, 1982; Fant, 1973; Searle, Jacobson & Rayment, 1979). Psychophysical models based on critical-band filters have been successfully used in speech analysis and recognition (Fant, 1973; Pols, van der Kamp & Plomp, 1969; Searle et al., 1979; Syrdal, 1982; Zwicker, Terhardt & Paulus, 1979). Recent studies of the responses of auditory-nerve fibers to speech-like sounds (Delgutte, 1980; Delgutte & Kiang, 1984a, b; Hashimoto, Katayama, Murata & Taniguchi, 1975; Kiang & Moxon, 1972, 1974; Miller & Sachs, 1983; Sachs & Young, 1979; Sinex & Geisler, 1983; Young & Sachs, 1979) have shown that peripheral auditory processing is considerably more complex than that of linear filter-bank models. These studies used only a minimal number of stimuli from each phonetic category, therefore they could not investigate the variability of speech. In this paper, a functional model of the peripheral auditory system that simulates selected properties of the discharge rates of auditory-nerve fibers (Delgutte, 1982) is used to analyze French stop consonants produced by male and female speakers in several vowel contexts.

Two acoustic events characteristic of stop consonants are the release of the plosive burst and the onset of voicing. The interval between these two events is the voice onset time (VOT), which is a cue to voicing distinctions among stop consonants in many languages including French (Lisker

& Abramson, 1964; Serniclaes, 1979). These two events are also involved
in place-of-articulation distinctions among stop consonants. For instance,
the gross shape of the short-time spectrum sampled at the release (Blumstein and Stevens, 1979; Fant, 1973; Halle, Hughes & Radley, 1957; Zue,
1976a), and the spectral changes occurring between the release and the onset of voicing (Kewley-Port, 1983; Lahiri, Gewirth & Blumstein, 1984) have
been proposed as characteristics that are relatively invariant with respect to
speaker and vowel context. This paper describes a scheme for locating the
consonantal release and the onset of voicing in both voiced and voiceless stop
consonants from the pattern of rapid onsets in frequency channels of the peripheral auditory model. This scheme depends critically on model elements
that simulate the short-term adaptation of auditory-nerve fibers. The paper
will also briefly consider how the auditory model represents the short-time
spectra of stop consonants sampled during these key events.

MODEL OF THE PERIPHERAL AUDITORY SYSTEM

The model of the peripheral auditory system (Delgutte, 1982) consists of
parallel channels, each representing the activity of the auditory nerve fibers
innervating a restricted portion of the cochlea. Channel outputs simulate
post-stimulus time (PST) histograms for auditory-nerve fibers. In order to
examine gross spectral features, we used 28 channels whose center frequencies
(CF) ranged between 0.16 and 6.8 kHz, with a spacing between CFs corresponding to 2 percent of the length of the cat cochlea (Liberman, 1982).

Figure 8.1a illustrates the stages of signal processing in each channel. The
first processing element is a minimum-phase, linear bandpass filter whose
magnitude characteristics were obtained by averaging the tuning curves of
many auditory nerve fibers (Liberman, 1978). These tuning curves were corrected for the transfer ratio of the pressure at the tympanic membrane to the
free-field sound pressure (Wiener, Pfeiffer & Backus, 1966). The magnitude
characteristics of the 28 filters[1] are shown in Figure 8.1b. The filter gains at
the CF rise rapidly with frequency below 0.5 kHz, then more gradually up
to 4.5 kHz where the cat's ear canal has its main resonance. This increase in
gain is reinforced by an increase in filter bandwidths to produce an emphasis
of high-frequency components with a mean rate of 5 dB/octave between 0.5
and 4.5 kHz.

---

[1] The finite impulse response of each bandpass filter was derived from the corresponding curve in Figure 8.1b in three steps: (1) bandwidth-dependent smoothing of the log-
magnitude spectrum; (2) computation of the minimum-phase characteristics by the DFT
method; and (3) windowing of the impulse response.

Each filter is followed by an envelope detector[2] with a time constant of approximately 1 ms (Figure 8.1a). This element smooths out fine time patterns of response, so that the model does not simulate the synchronization of auditory nerve fiber discharges to stimulus components, except for very low-frequency components such as the fundamental frequency of voice. The envelope detector is followed by a saturating, memoriless nonlinearity with a dynamic range of about 30 dB, consistent with physiological rate-level functions (Sachs & Abbas, 1974). The threshold of this element can be varied to simulate auditory nerve fibers with different sensitivities (Liberman, 1978).

The last processing element in each channel simulates the short-term adaptation of auditory nerve fibers (Kiang, Watanabe, Thomas & Clark, 1965; Smith, 1979). Some of the effects of adaptation are illustrated in Figure 8.1c, which shows the response of the 1-kHz channel to two tone bursts at the CF for three different intensities of the first tone, the level of the second tone being fixed. At the onset of the first tone, the response rises above background activity and rapidly reaches a maximum, then decays gradually to a steady level. The response peak becomes more prominent as the level of the first tone increases. At the end of the first tone, the channel output drops to a minimum, then increases again in response to the second tone. The response to the fixed-level second tone decreases when the level of the first tone increases. Thus, two effects of adaptation are (1) to enhance the response to rapid increases in amplitude in each channel; and (2) to decrease the responsiveness of channels that have been stimulated by a relatively long, intense sound.

Because the model contains nonlinear elements, its responses vary with stimulus level, as do the responses of auditory nerve fibers to speech sounds (Kiang & Moxon, 1974; Sachs & Young, 1979). It has been suggested that the central nervous system might normalize for these variations by attending to populations of fibers with different thresholds at different stimulus levels (Delgutte, 1982). For the analysis of stop consonants, we chose stimulus levels in relation to channel thresholds so that the release bursts would generally remain below the saturation level of the memoriless nonlinearity. Specifically, the mean levels of the [a] sounds for each speaker were set 60 dB above the channel thresholds for tones at the CF in the 1-kHz region. The resulting data can be considered to represent the responses of the most sensitive auditory nerve fibers to speech at about 60 dB SPL or, alternatively, the responses of less sensitive fibers to more intense speech.

---

[2] The envelope detector detects local maxima of the bandpass filter outputs, linearly interpolates between these maxima, and convolves the interpolated signal with a Kaiser window. The "time constant" of the envelope detector refers to the half duration of this smoothing window.

(a)

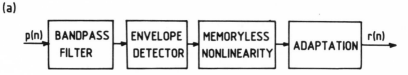

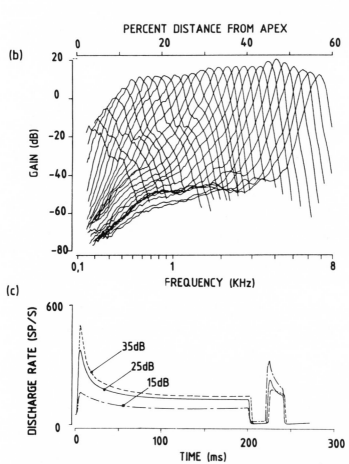

FIG. 8.1. (a) Signal-flow diagram for one model channel. The input signal p(n) is the free-field sound pressure sampled at 16 kHz. The output signal r(n) is the "discharge rate" of the channel sampled at 3.2 kHz and expressed in units of spikes/second.

(b) Magnitude characteristics of the 28 minimum-phase bandpass filters. The top axis represents percent distance from the apex in the cat cochlea, according to the cochlear frequency map of Liberman (1982).

(c) Response of the 1-kHz model channel to two tone bursts at CF for three different levels of the first tone. The first tone has a duration of 200 ms, while the second tone, which starts 20 ms after the end of the first one, has a duration of 20 ms and a level of 25 dB SPL.

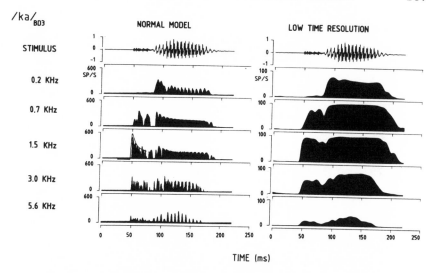

TIME (ms)

FIG. 8.2.   Peak-density analysis for a [kaka] utterance. The top panel shows the waveforms of the stimulus and windows that begin 4 ms before the computed time markers. The second panel shows times of occurrence of onset peaks for the 28 model channels. Specifically, whenever an onset peak was detected in one channel, a vertical bar is plotted at the abscissa corresponding to its time of occurrence and the ordinate corresponding to the channel CF. The height of the vertical bar gives an indication of the peak amplitude. The third panel shows the peak-density histogram for channels with CFs above 0.8 kHz, while the fourth panel shows the histogram for channels with CFs below 0.8 kHz. Each histogram was obtained by dividing the time axis into overlapping 4-ms bins spaced every 0.5 ms, and summing the heights of all onset peaks that occurred in each time bin. The vertical scale has units of discharge rates.

SPEECH MATERIAL

The speech corpus consisted of the CVCV utterances formed by combination of the stop consonants [b], [d], [g], [p], [t], [k] with the vowels [a], [i], [u] and [ɛ̃], each one being inserted in the frame sentence "C'est CVCV çà." Three random presentations of this corpus were read in a quiet room by 4 native speakers of French (2 male, 2 female). The signal from a condenser microphone was amplified, lowpass filtered at 7 kHz, and sampled at 16 kHz. After elimination of recording errors, a total of 271 CVCV utterances were processed by the model of the peripheral auditory system.

Traditionally, French stop consonants are classified into a "voiceless un-aspirated" series ([p], [t], [k]), and a "voiced" series ([b], [d], [g]). A stable acoustic difference between these two classes is the presence of voicing during the closure and, usually, during the burst for voiced stops (Fischer-Jorgensen, 1972b; Serniclaes, 1979; Wajskop, 1979). The top panel of Figure 8.2 shows the waveform of a [kaka] utterance. The consonantal releases and voicing

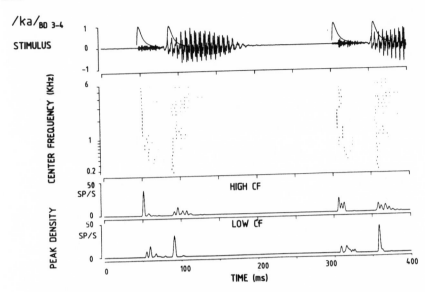

FIG. 8.3.   Same as Figure 8.2 for a [dada] utterance.

onsets are clearly defined, as was usually the case for voiceless stops. As in previous studies for French and other languages (Fischer-Jorgensen, 1954, 1972b; Lisker & Abramson, 1964; Wajskop, 1979) VOTs for voiceless stops systematically varied with the consonant place of articulation and the following vowel. However, these distinctions were often masked by considerable interspeaker variability. For instance the VOTs for [pi] ranged between 7 and 10 ms for speaker AS, and between 28 and 35 ms for JB, while the VOTs for [tu] ranged between 11 and 15 ms for AS, and between 40 and 60 ms for JB. These variations were not obviously correlated with speaking rate. Under such conditions, for the purpose of finding relatively invariant correlates of the place of articulation for stops, it does not seem appropriate to sample the short-time spectrum with a fixed-duration window beginning at consonantal release (Blumstein & Stevens, 1979), because this window would encompass a considerable voiced portion for certain speakers, while it would contain only the burst segment for others. It would be preferable to use two brief windows, one placed at release, and the other one at voicing onset, and to combine the spectral information from both windows (Lahiri et al., 1984).

Definition of release and voicing onset from speech waveforms was considerably more difficult for voiced stops than for voiceless stops due to the presence of voicing during the closure. The top panels of Figure 8.3 and 4 show the waveforms of a [dada] and a [didi] utterance. For all four stop consonants, there is a clear low-frequency periodicity throughout the closure

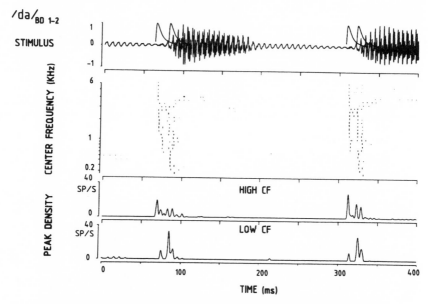

FIG. 8.4.   Same as Figure 8.2 for a [didi] utterance. The vertical scales in the lower two panels are 2.5 times greater than in Figure 8.2.

and the burst, although its amplitude can decrease at the end of the closure. Because this feature was present for virtually all voiced stops in our corpus, it would be improper to define a voicing onset for intervocalic voiced stops in French. However, for the [dada] utterance in Figure 8.4, there is a rapid rise in amplitude and a distinct change in waveform 10-15 ms after each release. Such events will be called "onsets of low-frequency energy". For the [didi] utterance in Figure 8.4, particularly the second syllable, the rise in amplitude after release is smaller and more gradual than in Figure 8.3, and the change in waveform is not so distinct, so that the onset of low-frequency energy is more difficult to define.

DETECTION OF CONSONANTAL RELEASES AND ONSETS OF LOW-FREQUENCY ENERGY BY THE MODEL

The left panels of Figure 8.5 show the outputs of five model channels with different CFs in response to a [ka] syllable. The consonantal release is marked by prominent peaks in the 1.5-, 3.0- and 5.6-kHz channels, while there are peaks at voicing onset in the 0.2- and 0.7-kHz channels. In order to compare the peripheral auditory model with traditional speech-analysis techniques in which the short-time spectrum is sampled with 10–20 ms windows, the same

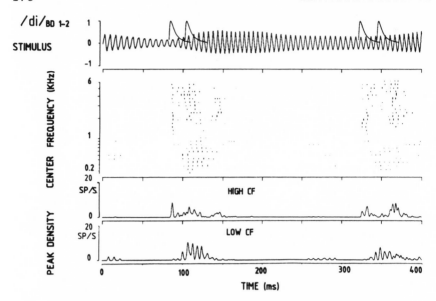

FIG. 8.5. The left panels show the responses of 5 model channels with different CFs to a [ka] syllable produced by a male speaker. The stimulus waveform is shown on top. The continuous line superimposed on the response of the 1.5 kHz channel is the waveform of the matched-filter function used in onset peak detection. The right panels show the same data for a modified model in which the adaptation elements were removed and the time constant of the envelope detector was increased from 1 to 8 ms.

[ka] was also processed by a modified model with a reduced time resolution. Specifically, the data shown in the right panels of Figure 8.5 were obtained by removing the adaptation element in each channel, and increasing the time constant of the envelope detector from 1 to 8 ms (see Footnote 2). The release and the onset of voicing are more difficult to distinguish for the model outputs obtained with low time resolution than for the normal model. Another difference is that the fluctuations in response waveforms at the fundamental frequency are completely suppressed in the low-resolution outputs.

The results of Figure 8.5 suggest that the response patterns associated with rapid onsets in individual channels of the normal model provide information for detecting the consonantal release and the onset of voicing. These specific response patterns, which will be called "onset peaks," ideally consist of a low response sustained for at least 20 ms, followed by an abrupt increase and a gradual decay lasting at least 20 ms. Onset peaks were detected by a "matched filter" method based on the 50-ms function whose waveform is shown superimposed on the response of the 1.5 kHz channel in Figure 8.5. Specifically, the cross-correlation function between the output of each channel and the matched-filter function was computed, all points below a certain threshold were discarded, and onset peaks were defined as local maxima of the clipped cross-correlation function. The clipping threshold was adjusted so that the fluctuations in channel responses at the fundamental frequency would not usually be detected as onset peaks during the steady-state portions of voiced sounds.

The second panel of Figure 8.2 shows the distribution of onset peaks both in time and in CF for a [kaka] utterance. For channels with CFs above 0.7 kHz, onset peaks were detected at consonantal release for both [ka] syllables. Other onset peaks were detected in these channels at the time when the burst of the second [ka] rapidly rises in amplitude, and during the voiced formant transitions. For channels with CFs below 1 kHz, there are onset peaks at voicing onset as well as smaller peaks during the burst for both [ka]'s. Because onset peaks tend to occur simultaneously over wide bands of CFs , little information is lost by reducing the diagram of Figure 8.2 to a low-CF band and a high-CF band. The cutoff frequency was set at 0.8 kHz to roughly separate the first formant from higher formants.[3] For each band of CFs, a peak-density histogram was computed by summing the heights of all the onset peaks occurring within 4-ms time bins. The bottom panel of Figure 8.2 shows the peak-density histogram for the low-CF channels, while the second lowest panel shows the histogram for the high-CF channels. For each syllable, the first local maximum of the high-CF histogram after closure corresponds to the consonantal release, and the highest maximum in the low-CF histogram corresponds well with voicing onset.

Figure 8.3 shows the same diagrams as in Figure 8.2 for a [dada] utterance. Again, for each syllable, the first local maximum after closure in the high-CF peak-density histogram occurs near consonantal release. In addition, the highest maximum in the low-CF histogram corresponds well with the the onset of low-frequency energy in the speech waveform. Figure 8.4 illustrates the peak-density analysis for a [didi] utterance. The releases of both syllables are clearly apparent in the high-CF peak-density histogram, although the histogram amplitude for the second [di] is weak due to the temporal scatter of the onset peaks. The low-CF peak-density histogram shows multiple local maxima of comparable sizes, so that a definition of the onset of low-frequency energy is meaningful only to within 10–20 ms. This pattern was common for voiced stops followed by the close vowels [i] and [u].

The following semi-automatic procedure was used to define two time markers for each CV syllable in the corpus on the basis of the peak-density analysis. First, consonantal closures were roughly determined by visual examination of speech waveforms. Second, Marker 1 was defined as the first local

---

[3] More precisely, there is a gradual cutoff region extending from 0.7 to 1 kHz in which each channel contributes to the peak-density histogram with a CF-dependent weight.

maximum of the high-CF peak-density histogram after closure that exceeded a certain threshold. The threshold is intended to eliminate small peaks occasionally occurring during closure. Third, Marker 2 was defined as the highest local maximum exceeding threshold in the low-CF peak-density histogram during an interval extending from 4 to 110 ms after the first marker.[4] When no such maximum was found (17 cases), Marker 2 was set by applying the same procedure to the peak-density histogram for the entire range of CFs.

In 507 CV syllables out of 542, this procedure successfully placed Marker 1 near consonantal release, and Marker 2 near the onset of low-frequency energy determined by examination of the speech waveforms. As expected, errors in marker placement were more common for voiced stops (25 cases) than for voiceless stops (10 cases). Mean errors rates were similar for all speakers, although certain types of errors occurred more frequently for certain speakers. In five cases, one of the markers could not be defined because the relevant peak-density histogram showed no local maximum above threshold in the specified time interval. In five cases of [p] followed by [a] or [ɛ̃], the burst was too weak to be detected, so that Marker 1 corresponded to voicing onset and Marker 2 to the onset of the second pitch period. In 18 other cases, Marker 2 was judged to be placed too early. This usually happened either when the burst had intense low-frequency components which appeared in the low-CF peak-density histogram (e.g. in [gu]), or when the onset of low-frequency energy was very gradual so that the low-CF histogram showed multiple local maxima of comparable sizes (e.g. in [bu] or [di]). In seven cases, Marker 2 occurred at least one pitch period after the main onset of low-frequency energy. This happened most frequently for [du] (3 cases). Finally, in six cases, although the placement of the markers was not grossly wrong, the low-CF peak-density histogram showed prominent local maxima before the release. In such cases, a description of speech events in terms of a release followed by an onset of low-frequency energy may not be appropriate.

COMPARISON OF THE SPECTRAL REPRESENTATIONS PRODUCED BY THE MODEL WITH OTHER SPEECH-ANALYSIS TECHNIQUES

As a first step in an analysis of place-of-articulation distinctions among stop consonants, the two markers were used to sample the distribution of channel responses across CF near the consonantal release and the onset of low-frequency energy. Specifically, for each channel, the response was multiplied by a selected time window, and the weighted samples were summed over

---

[4] In addition, when two local maxima of the peak-density histogram were separated by less than 10 ms, more weight was given to the earliest peak.

the duration of the window. The summed output of each channel was then expressed as a function of the channel CF to form a "model rate profile." These profiles directly represent physiological rate profiles (Sachs and Young, 1979), and can be compared with physical spectra or psychophysical masking patterns. The right panels of Figure 8.6 show model rate profiles obtained for two 20-ms windows beginning 4 ms before each of the markers[5] for a [pa], a [ta] and a [ka]. The interval between the two markers was 9 ms for [pa], 20 ms for [ta] and 38 ms for [ka]. The profile at the release of [pa] is higher in the low-CF region and lower in the high-CF region than the profiles for [ta] and [ka]. In addition, the profile at the release of [pa] remains below the profile at voicing onset for the entire range of CFs, whereas the release profiles for [ta] and [ka] exceed the corresponding profiles at voicing onset near 2 and 5 kHz. The [ka] syllable differs from [ta] in that the difference between the profile at release and the profile at voicing onset is greater in the 2-kHz region. Some of these features resemble those that have been used in characterizing the short-time spectra of stops with different places of articulation (Blumstein & Stevens, 1979; Lahiri et al., 1984; Kewley-Port, 1983), while others seem to be more specific to this particular spectral representation. It is worthwhile to identify which processing elements of the model are responsible for these differences.

In order to study the effects of adaptation and dynamic range on these rate profiles, the model was modified by extending the dynamic range of the memoriless nonlinearity from 30 to 60 dB in each channel, and removing the adaptation element. These modifications make the model more similar to a traditional channel vocoder. The center panels of Figure 8.6 show rate profiles obtained with this modified model for the same time windows as in the right panels. The effect of varying the dynamic range is seen most clearly in the high frequencies for the release of [pa], where the profile for the normal model deviates little from the baseline representing background activity, whereas the profile for the modified model is falling. Some effect can also be seen in the low-frequencies for the onset of voicing in [pa], where formant peaks are less clear for the normal model than for the modified model due to the saturation of the nonlinear element. Overall, the restriction in dynamic range does not seem to be a major impairment in the study of gross spectral patterns for stop consonants, at least when the channel sensitivities are appropriately adjusted relative to the speech level for each speaker. However, the study of vowels, which are more intense than stops, would probably require a different adjustment of the channel sensitivities (Delgutte, 1982), or a recourse to complex temporal processing schemes (Delgutte, 1984; Young and Sachs, 1979).

---

[5] The 4-ms offset corresponds to the average delay between a step in stimulus amplitude and the corresponding onset peak.

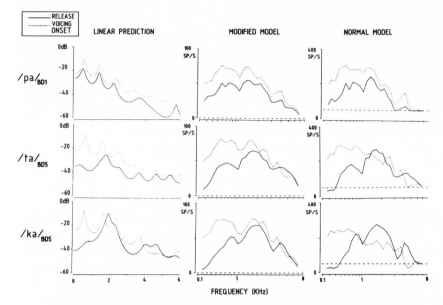

FIG. 8.6.   Right panels: Model rate profiles at consonantal release and at voicing onset for a [pa], a [ta] and a [ka] produced by a male speaker. Each profile was computed using a 20-ms modified Hamming window in which the samples during the first 10 ms were set to the peak value. The horizontal dashed lines indicate background discharge rate.

Middle panels: Same as in the left panels for a modified model in which the dynamic range of the memoriless nonlinearity was extended from 30 to 60 dB, and the adaptation element was removed.

Left panels: Linear-prediction spectra for the same windows as in the right panels. These spectra were obtained using the autocorrelation method with 18 coefficients. Before computing the spectra, high-frequency components were emphasized by taking the first difference of the speech signal.

Figure 8.6 also illustrates some of the effects of short-term adaptation on the model rate profiles. In response to the [ka] stimulus, the rate profiles obtained without adaptation show prominent peaks near 2 kHz both at consonantal release and at voicing onset. When adaptation is introduced, the peaks at voicing onset almost completely disappear because the channels with CFs near 2 kHz are strongly adapted by the intense burst. A similar reduction in response at voicing onset can be seen in the 5-kHz region for [ta]. Such effects are not found so clearly for [pa] because its burst is shorter and less intense than those of [ta] and [ka]. Thus, due to short-term adaptation, the profile at voicing onset contains information about the duration and intensity of the preceding burst, and the contrast between the rate profiles at release and at voicing onset is enhanced.

The model also differs from certain speech-analysis techniques in that the channel bandwidths vary with CF. The effects of frequency resolution can be studied by comparing the rate profiles in the central panels of Figure 8.6 with the linear-prediction spectra shown in the left panels. The low frequencies are more prominently represented in the model rate profiles than in the linear-prediction spectra, so that the first formant appears clearly in the rate profiles at the releases of |ta| and |ka|. In contrast, the high-frequency peaks of the linear-prediction spectra at the releases of |ta| and |ka| are merged into a single peak in the rate profiles. The prominent peak near 2 kHz in the linear-prediction spectrum at the release of |ka| appears broader in the corresponding rate profile. Similar properties have been observed for spectral representations of speech based on critical-band or $\frac{1}{3}$-octave filters (Carlson and Granstrom, 1982b; Kewley-Port, 1983; Klatt, 1979; Searle et al., 1979).

In summary, the present model of the peripheral auditory system differs from traditional speech analysis techniques in frequency selectivity, dynamic range, and adaptation properties. Future work will attempt to determine whether these properties affect the representation the short-time spectrum of stop consonants in a way that makes place-of-articulation distinctions more apparent.

DISCUSSION

This paper demonstrates the effectiveness of a scheme for detecting the consonantal release and the onset of low-frequency energy for syllable-initial French stop consonants: In 507 out of 542 cases, both events were judged to be located with satisfactory precision. The first step in this scheme is to detect the response patterns associated with rapid onsets in individual model channels. Detection of rapid onsets in frequency channels of an auditory model has been demonstrated by Chistovich et al.(1982). In particular, they show the spatiotemporal distribution of onsets and offsets in the same manner as in the displays of Figure 8.2, 3, and 4. Our method for onset detection differs from that of Chistovich et al. by making use of the properties of short-term peripheral adaptation. The effects of short-term adaptation are to emphasize the rapid onsets relative to the steady-state portions, and to provide a stereotyped response pattern, the "onset peak," which is easily detected by a matched-filter method. In principle, the same method could be used to detect rapid offsets, although it might not be so effective because the valleys in discharge rate below background level have a smaller dynamic range than the onset peaks. Detection of offsets might be useful for identifying the instant of closure in stop consonants.

The second step in the procedure for detecting releases and onsets of low-frequency energy is to sum the outputs of the onset-peak detectors over selected bands of CFs. A similar summation is carried out for the time derivatives of the outputs of the frequency channels in the model of Searle et al. (1979). In both the present model and that of Searle et al., precise detection is achieved by means of a considerably finer time resolution than is commonly used in speech analysis (Figure 8.5). On the other hand, such procedures should remain effective if the number of channels was severely reduced because onset peaks tend to occur at the same times over broad bands of CFs.

The scheme for detecting stop release and voicing onset does not explicitly depend on the speaker or the phonetic context, although errors are more common for voiced stops than for voiceless stops. The general form of this scheme might remain valid for languages with aspirated stops such as English, although some parameters might have to be modified, for instance to accommodate a wider range of VOTs. However, this scheme cannot be said to be invariant in an absolute sense. First, it could not be effective for syllable-final stop consonants, which are characterized by a different sequence of acoustic events (Kewley-Port, Chapter 9a). More fundamentally, the relatively invariant properties of the peak-density histograms that are used to place the markers are derived from simpler properties, the onset peaks, whose distribution across CF varies considerably with speaker and phonetic context. In addition, the placement of the markers involves comparison of events separated by intervals exceeding 100 ms. These considerations suggest that a search for relatively invariant correlates of phonetic categories might focus on schemes for integrating various cues distributed over wide time intervals and exhibiting considerable variability.

The principle of recognizing specific patterns in the spatiotemporal distribution of onsets in individual frequency channels of the peripheral auditory model may have more general applications than those of this study. We have previously suggested that the transitions from sonorant to obstruent segments (and vice versa) might be recognized from the distribution of onset peaks across the frequency channels (Delgutte, 1982). Chistovich et al.(1982) show oblique bands appearing in the spatiotemporal pattern of onsets in response to certain formant transitions. Such bands do not appear in Figure 8.2, 3 and 4, perhaps because the limited dynamic range of the model blurs formant peaks in the intense vocalic portions.

At a more general level of discussion, the present approach resembles those of Blumstein and Stevens (1980) and Chistovich et al.(1982) in that it emphasizes the role of discrete events in the auditory processing of speech. These discrete events are hierarchically organized: Simple events are the onset peaks, and perhaps offsets, in individual frequency channels. Complex events are particular patterns in the spatiotemporal distribution of onset peaks, while still higher-order events might combine onset features with certain properties of spectral profiles. This view contrasts with spectrographic models of auditory processing that represent speech more as a continuous sequence of spectral patterns (Kewley-Port, 1983; Klatt, 1979; Searle et al., 1979; Zwicker et al., 1979). The role of continuous spectral changes in the processing of certain speech sounds is not denied by Chistovich et al., who specifically postulate a continuous spectral-processing system proceeding in parallel with the onset-processing system. This assumption is implicit in the present study and that of Blumstein and Stevens (1980), because the onset events are used to sample the continuous output of peripheral auditory system. In general, the identification of the hierarchy of auditory events involved in speech perception may be key in finding relatively invariant correlates of phonetic categories.

ACKNOWLEDGEMENT

I wish to thank J. Vaissière for making valuable suggestions at many stages of this work, P. J. Price and C. Sorin for helpful criticisms of the manuscript, and R. Descout and M. Stella for providing useful computer software.

9 On Acoustic Invariance in Speech

Sheila E. Blumstein
Brown University

INTRODUCTION

In recent years, a theory of acoustic invariance has been elaborated which attempts to account for the speech processing mechanism in man, as well as provide a theoretical framework to characterize the nature of the phonological systems of natural language (cf. Stevens & Blumstein, 1979, 1981; Blumstein & Stevens, 1981). This theory has been guided by two claims. The first is that there is acoustic invariance in the speech signal corresponding to the phonetic features of natural language. That is, it is hypothesized that the speech signal is highly structured in that it contains invariant acoustic patterns for phonetic features, and these patterns remain invariant across speakers, phonetic contexts, and languages. The second claim is that the perceptual system is sensitive to these invariant properties. That is, it is hypothesized that the perceptual system can use these invariant patterns to provide the phonetic framework for natural language, and to process the sounds of speech in ongoing perception.

The detailed evidence in support of such a view of invariance as well as the broader theoretical claims of a theory of acoustic invariance are presented elsewhere (Stevens & Blumstein, 1981). What I would like to consider in this paper are the particular ramifications that a theory of acoustic invariance has for linguistic theory, on the one hand, and speech processing, on the other. My overall objective is to show that a theory of acoustic invariance provides a point of convergence between principles of phonological theory and models of speech processing. The specific issues I plan to address are the following:

For linguistic theory, I hope to show that a theory of acoustic invariance provides a means of explaining some so-called natural rules in phonology, and in particular can account for why certain assimilation rules are more likely to occur than others.[1] To explore this issue, I will review the palatalization process in natural language and discuss the invariant acoustic properties for dental, palatal, and velar consonants with specific reference to the Hungarian language. For theories of speech processing, I hope to show that while the perceptual system may be sensitive to context-conditioned variations in making phonetic decisions, many of these variations will have minimal perceptual consequences when the test stimuli contain the appropriate invariant properties and acoustic parameters found in natural speech. The implication of such a claim is that speech perception may be less "context-dependent" than has been generally assumed. To explore this issue, I will provide evidence from several studies exploring stops and glides and specifically [b] and [w].

LINGUISTIC THEORY AND ACOUSTIC INVARIANCE IN SPEECH

Natural Rules in Phonology

Despite what might appear to be an infinite number of potential sounds used in natural language, it is the case that there seems to be a finite inventory of speech sounds(Greenberg, 1963, 1966). Jakobson and Halle (1956) and Jakobson, Fant, and Halle (1963) elaborated a framework in which theoretically all possible phonological segments occurring in natural language could be defined using an inventory of approximately 12 distinctive features (cf. also Jakobson, 1968; Jakobson & Waugh, 1979). While there has been some question whether this framework captures every possible speech sound that can occur (Ladefoged, 1968), by and large all phonological systems can be characterized with a relatively small number of these features.

Moreover, the sound systems of natural language pattern in similar ways. That is, the phonemic inventories of language tend to group themselves in terms of the phonetic features they share. When classes of sounds group

---

[1] I am not suggesting that all natural rules can be explained solely on the basis of invariant acoustic properties. It is quite clear that a large number of assimilation processes are conditioned by articulatory and physiological considerations (cf. Lindblom, MacNeilage and Studdert-Kennedy, 1983; Ohala, 1981b). What I am suggesting, however, is that in order to define and understand the possible range of speech sounds as well as phonological processes found in natural language, it is necessary to explore the physiological and articulatory properties as well as the auditory and acoustic properties of the human speech apparatus.

in this way, they are called natural classes (Halle, 1964). For example, a language is more likely to have a class of stop consonants, e.g. |p, t, k, b, d, g|, than only one stop consonant in its inventory; it is more likely to have a class of voiced stops, e.g. |b, d, g|, than one voiced stop consonant; and it is more likely to have a class of labial consonants, e.g. |p, b, m, f, v| than only one labial consonant.

It is also the case that phonetic features and natural classes provide the basis for characterizing phonological processes in language. Phonological processes are modifications to the sound structure of a language which usually affect a class of sounds and typically occur as a result of the influence of neighboring phonological contexts. These processes can be shown in either a synchronic analysis of the phonological system of a particular language or in a description of phonological change in the history of a language. To take one example, the phonological shape of the plural morpheme /s/ is conditioned by the phonetic feature of the last segment in the noun stem. Thus, the plural form is the voiceless fricative [s] when preceded by a voiceless consonant; it is the voiced fricative [z] when preceded by a voiced consonant; and it is the syllable [əz] when preceded by a sibilant consonant.

Nevertheless, some phonological processes or rules are more likely to occur than others. For example, vowels may become nasalized when preceding nasal consonants, but never when preceding affricates. It has been hypothesized that these natural rules reflect universal constraints on the phonological systems of natural language, and occur as a result of intrinsic properties of the sound systems of natural language (Chomsky & Halle, 1968a; Donegan & Stampe, 1979).

The example provided above is fairly easy to explain in terms of the phonological properties of the sounds undergoing modification in relation to the phonological properties of the neighboring sounds. Thus, the nasalization of a vowel preceding a nasal consonant reflects an assimilation of the nasality feature of the consonant to the vowel. That is;

$$\begin{array}{ccccc} V & \rightarrow & \tilde{V} & / - & C \\ [-\text{nasal}] & & [+\text{nasal}] & & [+\text{nasal}] \end{array}$$

In contrast, there is nothing intrinsic to the phonological properties of affricates which would affect the nasality of a preceding vowel. It is also the case that assimilation rules require not only that a phonetic feature of the neighboring sound 'move' or assimilate to the modified sound, but that also the original sound and the modified sound also share a number of phonetic features. Thus, a fricative consonant might become a stop, but it would never become a vowel.

Linguistic theory has devised a number of formal devices for attempting to characterize such natural rules in phonology. These devices have included evaluation metrics based on feature counting, markedness conventions, and linking conventions (cf. Chomsky and Halle, 1968a). While many of these procedures have formally defined what should be a more natural segment, syllable, or rule, it is not always clear that the devices *explain* why some rules are more natural than others. That is the rules may give the "right" (i.e. generally accepted) answer, but there is nothing intrinsic either to the rules or the feature specifications which provides an explanation for *why* some rules are more natural than others.

Palatalization processes in natural language provide a case in point. Palatalization is a common assimilation process in which a velar consonant becomes fronted to the palatal or palato-alveolar place of articulation in the environment of front vowels, e.g. [i]. As rule 1 shows, the gravity feature of the vowel [i] assimilates to that of the preceding consonant, changing the velar into the palatal stop [c].[2]

1.   [k]   →   [c]   / –   [i]
      [+compact]   [+compact]   [−compact]
      [+grave]   [−grave]   [−grave]

Although such formal devices as linking conventions "predict" such a process (Chomsky & Halle, 1968a), they do not "explain" *why* velars front to the palatal and palato-alveolar places of articulation, and why the reverse process, a "backing assimilation" of a palatal or palato-alveolar consonant to a velar in the environment of back vowels, as for example [u], never occurs in natural language. That is,

2.   [c]   →   [k]   / –   [u]
      [+compact]   [+compact]   [−compact]
      [−grave]   [+grave]   [+grave]

Rule 2 is parallel to rule 1 in that the grave feature of the vowel assimilates to that of the preceding consonant. Nevertheless, rule 2 is not a natural phonological rule, and this particular assimilation process never seems tooccur in natural language. The question is why is there an asymmetry in the occurrence of rules 1 and 2? There is nothing intrinsic to the phonetic features of the rules which would provide an explanation.

---

[2] The particular feature framework used in this discussion is that of Jakobson, et al. (1963). I have used this system primarily because it has made explicit attempts to provide acoustic definitions corresponding to phonetic features, and a number of the invariant acoustic properties described by earlier researchers (Blumstein and Stevens, 1979; Stevens and Blumstein, 1978) correspond closely to the Jakobson et al. framework. Further, while Chomsky and Halle (1968a) state that their features have both articulatory and acoustic correlates, they have only explicitly defined their features articulatorily. Nevertheless, the discussion below concerning natural rules and the phonological analysis of palatalization, in particular, holds true regardless of the particular framework adopted.

What I hope to show is that considerations of the invariant acoustic properties of the sounds involved in these assimilation processes provides an explanation for the particular direction and occurrence of these rules. Before
considering the palatalization process in more detail, it is necessary to provide a brief background discussion of the invariant properties for place of
articulation in stop consonants.

Invariant Acoustic Properties for Place of Articulation

While a number of research labs have suggested that there is acoustic invariance for place of articulation in stop consonants (Cole & Scott, 1974a,b;
Kewley-Port, 1980, 1983; Searle, 1979, 1980; Stevens & Blumstein, 1981), there
has been some disagreement on the form of invariance proposed. In some
recent research in the Brown University phonetics lab, we have postulated a
form of acoustic invariance for place of articulation in stop consonants called
"dynamic relative invariance" (Lahiri, et al., 1984). The form of this invariance is dynamic in the sense that the invariant properties are determined by
comparing the spectral properties of portions of the signal across the time
domain (cf. also Kewley-Port, 1983). It is relative in the sense that the invariant properties are derived on the basis of relative spectral changes in regions
of high information (cf. also Ohde & Stevens, 1983; Stevens, 1975; Stevens
& Blumstein, 1981). The metric used for determining these properties charts
the relative changes in the distribution of energy at high and low frequencies from the burst release to the onset of the voiced-formant transitions and
compares the differences between the spectral energy at the burst and onset
of voicing at high relative to low frequencies. Labial consonants, defined by
Chomsky and Halle (1968a) as anterior and Jakobson et al. (1963) as grave,
show either a pattern characterized by a relatively sustained spectral energy
in the low frequencies (around 1500 Hz), or a flat distribution of spectral
energy. Dental and alveolar consonants, members of a natural class defined
by Chomsky and Halle as coronal and by Jakobson et al. as nongrave, show
a pattern in which there is greater energy or relatively sustained energy at
the high frequencies (around 3500 Hz).

In essence, there are two invariant properties characteristic of the class of
labial and coronal consonants. These two classes of sounds are distinguished
by a feature of gravity; i.e. the relative distribution of energy in high and
low frequencies. However, they also *share* an invariant acoustic property for
place of articulation, and that property has been defined as diffuse. That is,
at the release burst, there are a number of spectral peaks which are fairly
spread out throughout the spectrum (cf. also Blumstein & Stevens, 1979;
Fant, 1960; Jakobson et al. 1963; Stevens & Blumstein, 1978).

The *functional* importance of the feature [diffuse] is seen when considering
the phonological contrasts between those consonants defined by Chomsky
and Halle as [+anterior] vs. [−anterior] or defined by Jakobson, Fant, and

Halle as [+diffuse] vs. [−diffuse]. In contrast to the diffuse stop consonants in which there are a number of spectral peaks throughout the spectrum, the [−anterior] and [−diffuse] consonants are acoustically compact. That is, at the release of the consonants, there are either one or two peaks dominating the spectrum in the frequency regions between 1200-3500 Hz.[3] As Stevens and Blumstein state, "A peak is 'prominent' if there are no other peaks nearby and if it is larger than adjacent peaks so that the peak stands out, as it were, from the remainder of the spectrum. In this sense, the spectrum is compact" [1979, p. 1006].

While the invariant acoustic property for compact has been considered with particular reference to velar stops in English, the acoustic property of compact does *not* uniquely define velar consonants. Consistent with predictions from phonological theory, there is a class of compact consonants including the palato-alveolar, palatal, and velar places of articulation. Figure 9.1 shows examples of the spectra for the burst and the first three glottal pulses at the onset of the voiced formant transitions for palatal and velar stop consonants from Hungarian produced in the context of the vowels [i, e, a, o, u]. The burst spectra are represented by the solid lines, and the voiced formant transitions are represented by the dotted lines. As can be seen, the burst spectra for both the velar and palatal stop consonants show the compactness property.

However, it is important to note that the distribution of the compact spectral peaks varies as a function of place of articulation and vowel context. Comparing across place of articulation, e.g. [ci–ki], [ca–ka], the frequency of the peaks for the velars are relatively lower than that for the palatals, presumably corresponding to the larger front cavity of the velar in comparison to that of the palatal. And for both velars and palatals, there are several patterns of spectral compactness as a function of vowel context. Velars in front of back vowels, i.e. [o] and [u], display a frequency peak around 900 Hz and a high frequency peak around 4200 Hz, with a noticeable absence of energy in the frequency regions between them. Velars in front of front vowels, i.e. [i], [e], [a],[4] display a fairly broad mid-frequency peak between 2000 and 3000 Hz. In contrast, the burst spectra for palatals in front of back vowels show a mid-frequency peak between 2000 and 2500 Hz, and in front of front vowels show a high-frequency peak around 3500 Hz. These differences in the pattern of spectral peaks for velar and palatal consonants will figure importantly in the palatalization processes to be discussed below.

---

[3] The frequency range specified for compact consonants was defined on the basis of the observations of velar stops in English.

[4] The acoustic properties of velars and palatals before [a] pattern with the front vowels. Hall (1938) describes [a] phonetically as central and somewhat fronted. The phonological status of [a] is less clear, since it can function as either a front vowel or a back vowel in vowel harmony.

Nevertheless, if both velars and palatals are acoustically compact, can they
be distinguished by an invariant acoustic property? In some recent work,
Lahiri and Blumstein, (1983), have attempted to determine what acoustic
properties would distinguish these two sound classes. It turns out that the
same acoustic property used to distinguish the class of labials from dentals
and alveolars also can distinguish the class of velars from palatals. Similar
to labials, velar consonants are acoustically grave in that they either show
a predominance of low frequency energy or a flat distribution of energy in
the spectrum. And similar to dentals, palatals are acoustically nongrave in
that they show a predominance of high frequency energy. Figure 9.1 shows
the changes in the distribution of spectral energy from the burst release
(represented by the solid lines) to the onset of the transitions (represented
by the dotted lines) for velar and palatal stop consonants produced by a
Hungarian speaker. Comparing these changes at high and low frequencies,
we can see that for the palatal consonants (shown in the right column), there
is a large difference in the amount of acoustic energy between the burst and
the onset of voicing in the low frequencies (between 800 and 1800Hz) relative
to the difference in the amount of energy at the higher frequencies (above
3000 Hz). Thus, high-frequency energy is sustained from the burst to the
onset of voicing. In contrast, for the velar consonants (shown in the left
column), the patterns of energy change from the burst to the onset of the
voiced-formant transitions at high frequencies (above 3000 Hz) relative to
the changes at low frequencies (between 800 and 1800 Hz) are quite similar.
Thus, they show a "flat" distribution of energy, in the sense that there is
minimal change in the distribution of energy at high and low frequencies.

These results are consistent with the phonetic feature framework elaborated by Jakobson, Fant, and Halle (1963), and lend further support to the
view that invariant acoustic properties can be derived from the speech signal and that these properties correspond to phonetic features. For place of
articulation, the invariant acoustic properties corresponding to the phonetic
features [compact], [diffuse], and [grave] can uniquely characterize place of articulation dimensions for labial, dental/alveolar, palatal/palato-alveolar, and
velar consonants. The feature classification for these sounds are summarized
below:

	Labial	Dental/ Alveolar	Palatal/ Pal-alveolar	Velar
Diffuse	+	+	−	−
Compact	−	−	+	+
Grave	+	−	−	+

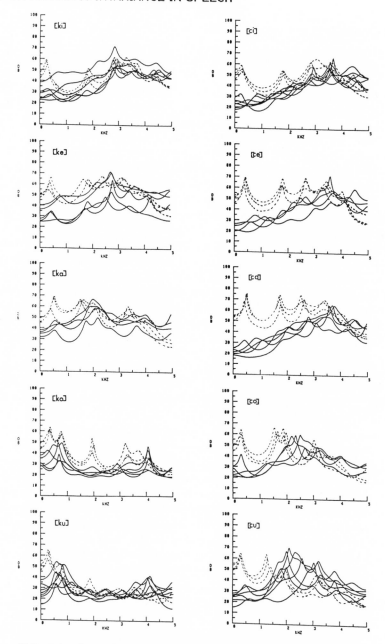

FIG. 9.1. Spectral characteristics for velar (left column) and palatal stop consonants (right column) spoken in five different vowel environments by a Hungarian speaker. The solid lines correspond to the spectra of the burst and the dotted lines correspond to the spectra for the first three glottal pulses of the voiced formant transitions.

On Palatalization and Natural Rules

Given these acoustic properties, we can now turn to the theoretical question introduced earlier. Namely, what is the explanation for the occurrence of assimilation processes such as palatalization, and why are these processes asymmetrical? For a detailed discussion of these issues see Lahiri and Blumstein (1983).

We will first consider the palatalization of [k] in the environment of [i]. As indicated earlier, several conditions must be met for an assimilation to occur. First, the two contiguous segments must share *some* similar acoustic properties. Second, the original sound and the modified sound must also share a number of acoustic properties. As Figure 9.2 shows, both conditions are met for the assimilation of [k] to [c] in the environment of [i]. The top left panel of Figure 9.2 shows the spectra for the burst (represented by the solid lines), the first three glottal pulses at the onset of voicing (represented by the dotted lines), and the vowel steady-state (represented by the circles) for the syllable [ki], and the top right panel shows the same spectra sampling points for the syllable [ci]. Both the consonant spectra for [k]—i.e. the burst spectra and the first three glottal pulses—and the vowel spectrum for [i] share a predominant energy peak in the same frequency region (around 2800 Hz), and in this sense are acoustically nongrave (cf. Jakobsonet al., 1963; Stevens, 1980). Further, the spectrum of the burst for the velar (top left panel) and the palatal (top right panel) share a compact spectrum, although the frequency of the peak is clearly higher for the palatal. Thus, the assimilation of [k] to [c] involves a true assimilation of the acoustic property of gravity from the vowel to the preceding consonant.

If the spectral characteristics of a vowel can condition a change in the spectral characteristics of a consonant, as was shown in the case of an assimilation of a velar to a palatal before a front vowel, we might also expect to find an assimilation of a palatal to a velar in the environment of a back vowel. Looking at the spectral properties of velar and palatal consonants in the environment of [u], however, it becomes clear why such a backing assimilation does not occur. The bottom left panel of Figure 9.2 shows the spectra for the burst, the first three glottal pulses at the onset of voicing, and the vowel steady-state for the syllable [ku], and the bottom right panel shows the same spectra sampling points for the syllable [cu]. As the vowel steady-state shows, [u] is acoustically grave, in the sense that there is a predominance of energy in the low frequencies. However, looking at the acoustic properties of the palatal consonant before [u] in the bottom right panel, it is the case that the major spectral peak for the burst spectrum for [c] is quite different, occurring in the mid-frequency region extending from 1800 to 2400 Hz. Moreover, comparing the acoustic characteristics of the burst of [c] and [k], it is clear that they too are quite dissimilar. In particular, whereas [c] has

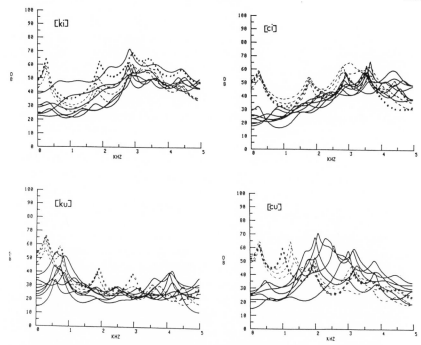

FIG. 9.2. Spectral characteristics for velar and palatal stop consonants spoken in the context of the vowels [i] and [u] by a Hungarian speaker. The Spectra for the burst are represented by the solid lines; the spectra for the first three glottal pulses at the onset of voicing are represented by the dotted lines; and the spectrum for the vowel steady-state is represented by the circles.

a peak dominating the spectrum in the mid-frequency region, [k] has one very low peak of energy at about 800 Hz and a second peak at about 4000 Hz, with a noticeable gap in energy in the mid-frequency region. Thus, the spectral characteristics of [c] and [k] in the context of [u], while both sharing the feature [compact], are quite different. As a result the conditions for triggering assimilation based on shared acoustic properties between contiguous sounds and shared acoustic properties between the modified and original sound are not met. There is, then, a straightforward explanation for the non-occurrence of an assimilation of a palatal to a velar before a back vowel.

SPEECH PROCESSING AND ACOUSTIC INVARIANCE

In recent work (Mack & Blumstein, 1983; Shinn & Blumstein, 1984a, b), the perceptual consequences of invariant properties for phonetic features have been explored by focussing particularly on the phonetic feature for continuant-noncontinuant distinguishing, among other contrasts, the class of stops from the class of glides. This research has been guided by two considerations. The first applies directly to a theory of acoustic invariance and attempts to determine whether the perceptual system is indeed sensitive to the hypothesized invariances corresponding to the continuant-noncontinuant contrast. The second consideration is an outgrowth of the search for acoustic invariance and attempts to determine to what extent speech processing is indeed context-dependent. What we hope to show is that while context-dependent cues for stops and glides play a role in the perception process, the perceptual importance of these cues for making phonetic decisions is minimized when the test stimuli are patterned after natural speech parameters.

Perceptual and Acoustic Invariance for Stops and Glides

Mack & Blumstein (1983) have shown that the amplitude characteristics in the vicinity of the consonant release provide an invariant property distinguishing stops from glides. In particular, we found a large increase in the amount of acoustic energy at the moment of consonant release relative to the acoustic energy immediately preceding or following the release. This large increase in energy reflected the abrupt release of the stop closure. For glides, we found a small increase in the amount of energy at the moment of consonant release relative to the amount of acoustic energy immediately preceding or following the release. This small increase in energy reflected the more gradual release of the glide as the articulators moved into the configuration for the following vowel. Using a measure based on relative energy changes, we were able to correctly classify over 90% of initial stops [b, d, g] versus glides [w, y] in the five vowel environments [i, e, a, o, u] produced by five speakers. Thus, the relative change in acoustic energy in the vicinity of the consonant release seems to serve as an invariant acoustic property distinguishing stops and glides across vowel contexts and speakers.

The obvious question is whether this invariant property serves as a perceptual cue to the stop-glide contrast. In natural speech, [b] and [w] are distinguished on a number of acoustic parameters including presence or absence of burst, formant frequencies, duration, rate, and extent of the formant transitions, and overall amplitude envelope (Mack & Blumstein, 1983). On the basis of the measurements obtained from natural speech stimuli, we synthesized good exemplars of [b] and [w] in the environments of [i] and [a], and interpolated the frequency, duration, and amplitude values between these two endpoints to create a stimulus continuum consisting of 11 stimuli (Shinn & Blumstein, 1984a). The stimuli varied in their formant frequencies, transition rates, durations, and also amplitude envelope. Two other continua were then synthesized with the frequency, formant transition, and duration characteristics as in the first series, but containing either a [w] amplitude

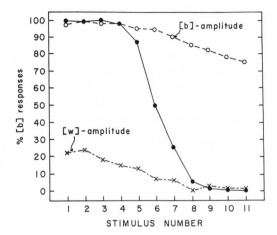

FIG. 9.3.   Results for the perception of three [bi wi] continua. The filled
circles and dotted lines show the percent [b] responses. The open circles
and dotted lines represent the perceptual results for the continuum in
which all of the stimuli on the continuum contain [b] amplitude values, and
the x's and dotted lines represent the perceptual results for the continuum
in which all of the stimuli on the continuum contain [w] amplitude values.

envelope—i.e. with a gradual onset of energy at consonantal release—for the
entire test series, or with a [b] amplitude envelope—i.e. with a rapid onset
of energy at consonant release—for the entire test series.

Subjects were given two tasks. The first was a two-alternative forced
choiced task in which they were required to identify the CV stimuli as either
beginning with [b] or [w]. The second task was a free-identification task in
which the subjects were told to identify the syllable in terms of whatever
initial consonant or consonants they heard.

Perceptual results of the two-alternative forced-choice task for the [i] series
are shown in Figure 9.3. The amplitude manipulations had perceptual effects
on all of the stimuli on the test continua. Namely, with a [w] amplitude
envelope, all of the stimuli on the continuum including the exemplar [b]
stimulus were perceived as a glide initial syllable ranging from 75–98% of
the time. With a [b] amplitude envelope, all of the stimuli on the continuum
including the prototype [w] stimulus was perceived as a stop initial syllable
ranging from 76–100% of the time.   Thus, the context-dependent formant
frequency and formant transition rate and extent cues for the stop versus
glide contrast were overridden by the invariant property based on the relative
changes in the amount of acoustic energy at consonantal release. Similar
results were obtained for the [a] series.

When the subjects were given the free identification task, an interesting
pattern of results emerged. For the continua in which all the stimuli contained the [b]-amplitude envelope, subjects identified all of the stimuli on the

continuum as beginning with a stop between 80-100% of the time in the [i]
vowel series and 60-81% of the time in the [a] vowel series. But for the continua in which all of the stimuli contained the [w]-amplitude envelope, stimuli
on the [b] end of the continuum were perceived primarily as the fricative [v]
and less so as the glide [w], and stimuli on the [w] end of the continuum
were perceived almost exclusively as [w]. Thus, stimuli with an abrupt rise
in acoustic energy at the consonantal release are perceived as stops—i.e.
noncontinuants like [b]—while stimuli with a gradual rise in acoustic energy
at the consonantal release are perceived as continuants [v, w]. These results strongly support the view that the nature of the amplitude envelope in
the vicinity of the consonantal release is a critical acoustic property for the
continuant–noncontinuant contrast, and in particular provides an invariant
property distinguishing the class of noncontinuants of which [b] is a member,
from the class of continuants of which both [w] and [v] are members.

Context-Dependent Cues in Speech Perception

The perception experiment described above showed that the invariant property for the stop-glide contrast relating to the amplitude envelope is perceptually salient, and in fact, can override context-dependent cues of formant transitions and transition duration. However, more recently, Miller
and Liberman (1979) have demonstrated another context dependent effect
for the [b–w] contrast, relating to the duration of the syllable. In particular,
they found that the locus of the phonetic boundary of a [b–w] continuum
varying in duration and slope of the formant transitions changed as a function of the duration of the syllable and in particular of the vowel duration.
Miller and Liberman interpreted their results in terms of listener adjustments to speaking rate. Thus, if a talker were speaking slowly, the duration
of a syllable therefore would be longer and the listener would require longer
transition durations to perceive a [w] than if the talker were speaking more
quickly and the syllable duration were shorter.

This effect has proved to be a stable perceptual phenomenon having been
shown in a number of different experimental manipulations (Miller, 1980), not
only in adults but also in infants (Miller & Eimas, 1983), and not only for
formant driven speech stimuli but also for sine-wave stimuli (Carrell, Pisoni
& Gans, 1980; Jusczyk, Pisoni, Reed, Fernald & Meyers, 1983).

Nevertheless, considerations of the nature of the stimuli used in these
experiments suggest that this effect may be lost when the stimuli contain
acoustic parameters more nearly like those found in natural speech. The implication of this hypothesis is that in ongoing perception, the listener may *not*
have to make such adjustments to the duration of the syllable and presumably
to speaker rate in order to distinguish [b] from [w], since the acoustic distinctions between these sounds are clearly demarcated in the acoustic properties

inherent in each segment. Let us consider this view in more detail.

The basic methodology in the investigation of context-dependent cues in speech perception research has been to pare down the acoustic differences between the endpoint stimuli so that they are minimally different. Such a methodology is reasonable when exploring the minimal cues necessary for perceiving a phonetic distinction and for exploring the limits of the perceptual system. However, it is often the case that the resulting stimuli are not simply *reduced* versions of the exemplar stimuli, as for example, an acoustic continuum for place of articulation containing only formant transitions and no burst. Rather, the acoustic parameters found in natural speech are often *compromised* in synthetic speech, and as a consequence, some parameters are in essence inappropriate for those stimuli, at least at one end of the stimulus continuum. For example, the studies exploring [b, w] typically use the same formant frequency values for all of the stimuli on the continuum. However, acoustic analysis of natural speech shows that [b] and [w] do not share the same formant frequency values (Mack & Blumstein, 1983). The values actually used in the synthetic speech experiments are *unnatural* at least for the stimuli on one end of the continuum. Could the use of such values produce context-dependent effects which would not occur if more appropriate frequency parameters were used?

We decided to explore this question by replicating the Miller and Liberman (1979) effect and then changing the acoustic parameters to be more like those found in natural speech (Shinn & Blumstein, 1984b). A total of four sets of synthetic [ba-wa] continua were made. The first contained parameter values patterned after the Miller and Liberman stimuli. All stimuli contained the same formant transitions and varied in transition duration (and as a consequence slope) from 15–65 ms in 5 ms steps. The second set was based on the same parameters as the first, but also contained a burst at the [b] end of the continuum which was systematically reduced along the continuum until it was totally absent at the [w] end of the continuum. The third set was the same as the first, but also varied in the formant frequency values of the transitions. Both the [b]-endpoint stimuli and the [w]-endpoint stimuli contained appropriate formant frequency values as measured by natural speech. The formant frequencies of the remaining stimuli on the continuum were interpolated between these endpoint values. And finally, the fourth continuum varied in all of the above parameters including formant transition duration, presence or absence of burst, and formant frequency values.

Within each set, five continua were created varying in syllable duration from 102–317 ms. These stimuli were presented to four different groups of listeners for identification as [b] or [w].

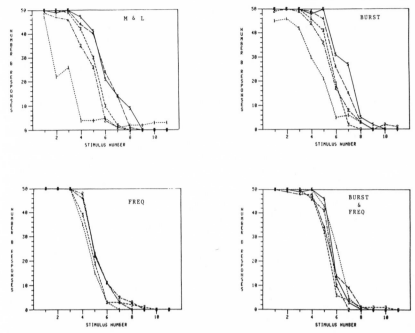

FIG. 9.4.   Perception of a series of [b–w] continua varying in transition duration from 15 ms (stimulus 1) to 65 (stimulus 11). The duration of the syllables in each continua range from 102 ms (represented by the functions labelled 1) to 317 ms (represented by the functions labelled 5). The intermediate labelled functions (numbers 2, 3, 4) correspond to duration values between the shortest and longest syllable durations. The top left panel shows subjects' responses to stimuli patterned after the Miller and Liberman (1979) parameter values. The top right panel shows responses to stimuli based on the first set of stimuli, with the addition of a burst varying in amplitude along the stimulus continuum. The bottom left panel shows subjects' responses to stimuli containing formant frequency values derived from natural speech measures. The bottom right panel shows responses to stimuli containing a burst varying in amplitude along the continuum as well as formant frequency values.

Figure 9.4 shows the results.[5]   As can be seen, the Miller and Liberman (1979) effect was replicated in the set of stimuli patterned after their original stimuli and in the set of stimuli containing a burst. However, the effect is lost *as soon as* the formant frequency values of the stimuli on the continua are changed. Thus we see a dichotomy in the presence or absence of the effect as a function of the nature of the test stimuli. When all stimuli contain the

---

[5] The results presented in this paper correspond to those subjects (n equals 5) who received the stimulus tapes in the order from shortest syllable duration to longest syllable duration. In our study, we found a test order effect, such that those subjects who received the tapes in this order were *more likely* to show the Miller and Liberman effect, than if the test tapes were presented in the opposite order, from longest to shortest syllable duration.

same formant frequency values, the locus of the phonetic boundary for a [b–w] continuum varies as a function of the duration of the syllable. When the stimuli contain different formant frequency values, the locus of the phonetic boundary remains the same across different syllable durations.

In natural speech, stops and glides do *not* share the same frequency characteristics. Although speech rate may affect the duration of formant transitions, for glides, it does not seem to have the same effect for stops (Miller & Baer, 1983). Moreover, speech rate changes will not have significant effects on the frequency characteristics of [b] and [w]. As a result, we are suggesting that rate adjustments may not be required for the perception of the phonetic contrast [b, w] in natural speech. The acoustic parameters of these sounds are sufficiently distinct without the need to invoke context-dependent effects for on-line speech processing.

ACKNOWLEDGEMENTS

Thanks to Kenneth N. Stevens for his comments on an earlier version of this manuscript and for introducing me to the search for acoustic invariance, and special thanks to Aditi Lahiri and Phil Shinn for their collaborative efforts, many helpful discussions, and commitment to these research projects. This research was supported in part by grant NS15123.

Diane Kewley-Port: Converging Approaches Towards Establishing Invariant Acoustic Correlates of Stop Consonants

Many investigators are presently pursuing different approaches to determining invariant acoustic correlates of stop consonants. These approaches fall into three categories which are all represented in this volume. One is that of Blumstein and her colleagues who look at the problem of invariance from a formal linguistic approach. As Blumstein states in her introduction to chapter 9, this approach seeks to relate invariant acoustic properties directly to universal phonetic features as defined by linguists. Two other approaches are derived from an interest in modeling auditory processing of speech. Delgutte and Searle have been developing explicit physiological models of the auditory processing of speech sounds. Finally, Klatt (1982) and Kewley-Port (1983; Kewley-Port & Luce, 1983) have based their work on psychophysical models of auditory processing. The inspiration behind much of this research has been Stevens' ongoing search for the invariant acoustic correlates of phonetic features (Stevens, 1967, 1975, 1980).

An examination of research from these three approaches suggests that they are converging towards a single description of the acoustic correlates for phonetic features associated with stop consonants. In this paper, two issues will be addressed.

First, I will examine the similarities among these three approaches for specifying the acoustic correlates of the stop-release burst, the onset of voicing and place of articulation. Second, I will examine Blumstein's claim that these acoustic correlates are, in fact, *the* invariant properties associated with universal phonetic features.

While a number of recent proposals have been made concerning the specification of the acoustic correlates of stops, the ones to be discussed here are found in the work of Blumstein (Chapter 9; Lahiri, Gewirth, & Blumstein, 1984; Mack and Blumstein, 1983), Delgutte (Chapter 8, and 1981) and Kewley-Port (Kewley-Port & Luce, 1984). One important similarity between all three proposals is that the correlates of stop consonants are described by *dynamic* properties which are based on changes in energy or frequency over time. Naturally, the specific description of the correlates depends on the acoustic processing used: Delgutte based his work on the output of a physiological model, Kewley-Port used a psychophysical model, and Blumstein used a combination of hand-edited waveforms and linear predictive spectra. Besides proposing specific acoustic correlates, all three investigators experimentally tested whether the correlates were invariant over vowel context and, to a lesser extent, talkers. Other sources of acoustic-phonetic variation such as syllable position, speaking rate and language have not been examined in great detail by any investigator yet. It is clear, however, that all three approaches seek to define acoustic correlates of stops as invariant over several of the major sources of phonetic variation.

In order to discuss these proposals in detail, I will refer to some examples of stop-vowel syllables processed by Kewley-Port and Luce's psychoacoustic model (1984) shown on Figure 9a.1. Figure 9a.1 displays the auditory running spectra of the syllables, /pi/, /da/, and /ku/. The spectral sections or frames, updated at 5 ms intervals, are $\frac{1}{6}$ octave critical-band spectra displayed on a Mel scale. In this figure, the first frame was positioned during stop closure between 2 and 4 frames preceding the burst.

First, consider an acoustic correlate of the initial stop burst which is associated with the phonetic feature of manner of articulation (continuant versus noncontinuant). Delgutte's correlate for detecting bursts is the presence of an "onset peak" in the discharge patterns of high-frequency channels. Kewley-Port's correlate is an abrupt increase in energy at high frequencies in the running spectra. Blumstein's correlate is an increase in relative level of energy over all frequencies. While the validity of these correlates was tested in different ways, all three were better than 90% successful in identifying the burst. Thus, all three approaches converge on the observation that an acoustic correlate of release bursts in stops is a detectable change in acoustic energy, a finding that was previously predicted by the acoustic theory of speech production. The primary difference in the approaches is that Blumstein examined energy changes over all frequencies while the other two approaches examined only high frequency energy. This difference may reflect differences in the experimental tasks. Delgutte and Kewley-Port examined both voiced and voiceless stops, while Blumstein examined only voiced stops contrasted with glides.

Both Delgutte and Kewley-Port have proposed an acoustic correlate for the onset of voicing in stops. These correlates were defined analogously to those for burst onset, except low frequencies were examined instead of high frequencies. Delgutte's

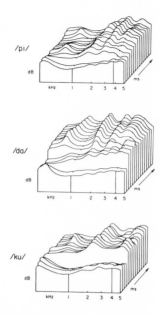

FIG. 9a.1. Critical-band running spectral displays for the syllables /pi/, /da/, and /ku/. Frequency in kHz is represented on the x-axis; relative dB is represented on the y-axis. The spectral frames are offset along the z-axis in 5 ms intervals.

results appear quite successful and superior to those obtained from Kewley-Port's psychophysical approach. Nonetheless, there is agreement that the acoustic correlate of voicing onset is an abrupt change in low-frequency energy in the region of the first formant. While neither of the proposed correlates for the onset of the burst and the onset of voicing are surprising in light of previous research, the importance of the present work is that specific mechanisms for detecting these correlates in the human auditory system have now been experimentally tested.

Blumstein, in collaboration with Stevens (Stevens & Blumstein, 1978, 1981) and other colleagues, and Kewley-Port have been examining acoustic correlates for place of articulation for several years. In their recent formulation of these correlates, many similarities can be observed. First, both approaches define these correlates based on *dynamic* spectral properties, which for Blumstein is a change from her earlier *static* approach (Stevens & Blumstein, 1978; see also Ohde & Stevens, 1983). Secondly, both rely on prior detection of the onset of both the burst and voicing to define a temporal course over which the correlates of place of articulation are assumed to occur. Delgutte is in agreement with this proposal, although he has not formally examined correlates of place of articulation.

In defining the details of the correlates of place of articulation, however, Blumstein's and Kewley-Port's approaches differ in several respects. Consider first the acoustic correlates for distinguishing labial versus alveolar place of articulation. Blumstein proposes that the tilt of all voiceless spectra compared to the tilt of the spectra of the first three pitch pulses is the basis of the correlates. Kewley-Port proposes that a difference in spectral tilt of up to 40 ms of voiceless frames (or 10 ms of voiced frames when the burst is voiced) is the basis of this distinction. Thus, Blumstein's approach requires comparison of spectra over a long temporal interval for the aspirated stops of English. A typical stop with 50 ms VOT for a male talker would require about 80 ms of time for analysis (including the three pitch pulses). Although Blumstein has experimentally validated this correlate for aspirated English stops, it does not appear to be a good candidate for an invariant acoustic cue to place of articulation in speech perception. The results of speech-perception studies have shown that place of articulation can be accurately identified within the first 20 to 40 ms after burst release (Blumstein and Stevens, 1980; Kewley-Port, 1980, Exp. 3B; Kewley-Port, Pisoni, and Studdert-Kennedy, 1983; Ohde and Sharf, 1977; Tekieli and Cullinan, 1979). Thus, Blumstein' correlate for long VOT stops requires analysis time intervals much longer than the 20 to 40 ms needed in perception. On the other hand, Kewley-Port's proposal for analyzing only the first 40 ms of voiceless spectra was made in light of these perceptual studies. Overall, however, the similarities between the two positions are more notable than their differences.

Regarding the velar place of articulation, Blumstein's recent papers have not presented a formal proposal for a velar acoustic correlate. Kewley-Port's proposed velar correlate is the presence of a prominent mid-frequency peak extending over at least 15 ms of the voiceless spectra. While Blumstein's discussion of compact spectral correlates for palatals and velars seems in accord with Kewley-Port's proposal, more research will be needed in this area.

Thus, it is obvious that a number of different converging proposals for defining acoustic correlates of stop consonants have developed from different research perspectives. Furthermore, the three approaches discussed above have specifically tested the extent to which these correlates are invariant over several sources of phonetic variation. There is, however, an important divergence between the claims of invariance made by Kewley-Port's approach based on an auditory processing model and those of Blumstein based on a somewhat more formal linguistic approach. Specifically, Blumstein states in Chapter 9 that invariant acoustic correlates should "remain invariant across speakers, phonetic context, and languages." However, at least in our view, experimental research has not substantiated this claim. For example, consider the claim of invariance over speakers. Of the research reviewed here, only Kewley-Port's has seriously addressed the issue of defining high, low, or mid-frequency ranges for talkers with large differences in vocal tract size (see Kewley-Port, 1983; Kewley-Port & Luce, 1984). While our proposed vocal tract normalization rule to locate a speaker's "mid-frequency" range appears to be a step in the right direction, many more speakers need to be studied. Blumstein's recent research on place of articulation has not specifically examined this problem since she has used only male speakers and did not examine velar correlates.

Perhaps more important from a linguistic point of view, recent work on invariants for stop consonants has not examined their validity over changes in syllable position or consonant manner class. The earlier studies of Blumstein and Stevens (1979) were, for the most part, unsuccessful in experimentally establishing invariant acoustic correlates for both syllable initial and syllable final stops (cf. Kewley-Port, 1983). In fact, it has been our view that it is quite unlikely that acoustic correlates for identifying place and manner of articulation will be physically the same for both initial and final stops. While the three proposals discussed above are very similar, they all depend on detecting the initial burst and voicing prior to identifying place of articulation. Since most syllable-final stops do not have bursts, it is obvious that the putative acoustic correlates simply cannot apply. Clearly, invariance over syllable position is essential to the linguist's definition of invariance over phonetic context. Thus, these acoustic correlates, or even similar ones, cannot be invariant over phonetic context at least with the current definitions of invariance (see Port, Chapter 25).

In conclusion, it appears that Blumstein's contention that there currently exists a theory of acoustic invariance which unites principles of phonology and models of speech processing is premature. On the other hand, models of auditory processing of speech in the nervous system are helping us to discover acoustic correlates which appear to be invariant over several sources of phonetic variation. This is obviously a step in the right direction (see Carlson & Granstrom, 1982). The converging knowledge and methodology from linguistics, hearing and speech sciences, and signal processing is enabling us to uncover invariant acoustic correlates and to further our understanding of human speech perception well beyond where we were just a few years ago.

ACKNOWLEDGMENTS

This work was supported in part by NIH research grant NS-12179 to Indiana University. I thank D. B. Pisoni and M. Studdert-Kennedy for advice and comments on an earlier draft of this paper.

John J. Ohala: Comment

Two comments: First, I accept Blumstein's main point that the reason [ki] often changes to [ci] but [cu] never (or rarely) changes to [ku] is because the former are acoustically similar but the latter are not. However, I don't think this has anything to do with assimilation. It is true that linguists have traditionally labeled the former process "assimilation," but this is simply careless usage which we do not need to perpetuate. Among the things [ki] changes to are [ci], [tsi], [tši], [si] and [ši] (although there may be undiscovered intermediate stages in some of these cases). Many of these changes do not have the "ring" of assimilation to them.

Consider the case of the change of [ki] to [tsi]; for example, Latin *bracchiu* [brakiu] "arm" became Roumanian *brat* [brats]. It cannot be claimed here that the [k] became more like the following [i]; [i] doesn't have a [ts]-like articulation. Not only is the area of tongue-palate contact different, the part of the tongue that is involved— tongue "front" as opposed to apex—is also different. From an articulatory point of view, rather than the place of articulation of the [k] assimilating to that of [i], it actually overshoots it. For these reasons [ki]→[ci] is best regarded as simply a case of one sound changing into another because the two sound alike and listeners were not always able to tell which articulation the speaker used to create the given sound; in some cases they make the wrong choice, implement a different articulation in their own speech, and thus a sound change takes place (Durand, 1955; Ohala, 1974, 1978, 1981b, 1983; Ohala & Lorentz 1977; Sweet, 1874). It is thus similar in character to many other changes which involve acoustically similar sounds, e.g., [p]→[t], [k]→[p], [θ]→[f], and velarized [l] →[w]. These, in addition to [ki]→[ci], are not only well-attested diachronically but, crucial to my contention that they represent what is essentially a listener misapprehension, are also evident as mistakes (confusions) in lab-based speech perception studies (see Winitz, Scheib, & Reeds, 1972).

Once we are clear that what Blumstein has demonstrated for us has nothing to do with assimilation we can also discard the first of her preconditions for assimilation: "...the two contiguous segments must share *some* similar acoustic properties in order for a phonetic feature of the neighboring sound to move...to the modified sound." Given the vast range of speech-sound variation which is legitimately considered assimilation, this simply cannot be maintained. Many examples could be cited but consider just the following. In many languages, e.g., several in the Mayan family, vowels— *any* of the several vowels in the given language—become "tense" or creaky voiced when next to an ejective consonant. The constricted glottis condition appropriate to the consonants is assimilated by the vowels. But what similar acoustic properties do all vowels and ejective consonants share? In fact, they are about as different acoustically as any two segment types could be.

Gunnar Fant: Comment

In my view, articulatory versus auditory anchoring of features is first of all an abstract though legitimate metalinguistic issue in studies of the speech code from the outside. To what extent are our features related to production or perceptual invariance? When it comes to alternative theories of speech decoding mechanisms, the issue becomes less well defined. My scepticism is thus related to the difficulty of finding out just how much and which aspects of perceptual mechanisms rely on or have merely developed in synergy with an internalized structuring of production categories.

Paul Kiparsky: Comment

At the end of her paper, Blumstein remarks that her analysis of palatalization isn't dependent on any particular choice of feature system. I would like to take issue with that and suggest that the *Sound Pattern of English* (SPE) feature system comes out faring rather better when a wider range of cases is taken into account. Bhat's data on palatalization collected for the Stanford Universals Project shows that palatalization works somewhat differently for velars and coronals. The vowel which most commonly triggers palatalization is [i]. For velars the process generalizes along the height dimension, so that the class of front vowels is also a common environment. This could be characterized as spread of either [− back] or [− grave] and so fits both feature systems equally well. For the dentals, however, the process generalizes "along the top," so that the class of high vowels is a typical environment. If we assume Blumstein's features, the process "[t]→[č] in the context of [i,u]," is actually a *dissimilation*, in which consonants become [+ compact] in the context of [− compact] vowels. In the SPE feature system, it is still an assimilation process, namely consonants becoming [+ high] in the context of [+ high] vowels. So at least on the assumption that these are assimilatory changes (which I share with Blumstein and against Ohala), the SPE features are preferable. Of course such relationships between vowels and consonants were among the reasons for revising the Jakobson-Fant-Halle *Preliminaries to Speech Analysis* features in the first place.

As for the asymmetry between [ki]→[či] and the nonexistent change [ču]→[ku], it seems to be a special case of a general tendency for *marked* feature values to spread. It would thus be basically the same thing as vowels becoming nasalized before nasal consonants but not denasalized before nonnasal consonants, or the fact that harmonic processes typically involve the spread of marked feature values such as [+ round], [+ nasal], [+ tense]. Can the account that Blumstein offered of the asymmetry of palatalization versus depalatalization be generalized to this wider range of cases?

Sheila E. Blumstein: Response

At the outset, I would like to state that there is no question that there is a tremendous amount of acoustic/articulatory/phonetic variability in speech. This is not at issue. What seems to be a more controversial question is whether there are any invariant patterns relating to speech, and if there are, what form they take. In my paper, I claimed that there are invariant acoustic patterns directly derivable from the acoustic signal, and that these patterns correspond to the phonetic features of natural language. In this view, a theory of acoustic invariance provides a convergence of phonological theory and speech processing, by presenting a framework for characterizing the sound systems and phonological processes of natural language, and by delineating those acoustic properties which the perceptual system uses in structuring the phonetic dimensions of speech.

With respect to the relation between a theory of acoustic invariance and phonological theory, I have argued that the basis for the asymmetry of some phonological rules, and in particular assimilation processes in palatalization, can be explained in terms of the acoustic similarity between certain properties of contiguous sounds. Thus, to respond to John Ohala's remarks, the assimilation rules are phonological, as traditionally defined, since one phonological feature "assimilates to" or moves to a contiguous segment, thereby changing that segment. However, I agree with his comments that the assimilation process itself is driven by acoustic or phonetic factors, and not by phonological factors per se.

The feature system that we have used to characterize acoustic invariance is that of Jakobson, Fant, and Halle (1963). Paul Kiparsky expressed some doubts whether the Jakobson et al. system and that of Chomsky and Halle (1968a) are comparable in terms of their characterizations of phonological rules. He suggests that the Chomsky and Halle features characterize the palatalization of [t] to [c] before a front vowel more "naturally" as an assimilation, than does the Jakobson et al. framework, which characterizes this process as a dissimilation. I would agree that in this case the Chomsky and Halle features seem to capture the intuitive notion that this process reflects an assimilation rather than a dissimilation. Nevertheless, the Jakobson et al. framework has had the broadest application to a theory of acoustic invariance, as it explicitly defines the acoustic properties relating to phonological features. In contrast, Chomsky and Halle make no such attempt. Those properties relating to place of articulation defined by Jakobson et al. as grave, compact, and diffuse have received empirical support from our acoustic analyses.

The theory of acoustic invariance has been presented in fairly bold terms. Over the past 30 years, the major conclusion of those investigating the acoustic and perceptual characteristics of speech has been that there are few generalized patterns derived from the acoustic waveform. However, more recently, a number of researchers are coming to a converging view that there are in fact invariant acoustic patterns. The question still remains—what do these patterns correspond to, and whether these patterns remain stable across such transformations as changes in vowel context, syllabic context, speaker, and language. With respect to the former question, I would disagree with Kewley-Port in her claim that the frame of reference for these invariances is different across researchers, and in particular, would argue that all have shown that the invariant patterns correspond to phonetic features. Thus, invariant patterns have been found for place of articulation (labial, alveolar, and velar), and these patterns have remained invariant across variations in vowel context, voicing, and speaker. Thus, [p, b], [t, d], and [k, g] each form a class of sounds. Similarly, acoustic invariance has been demonstrated for stops and continuants, and thus distinguishes the class of stops [p, t, k, b, d, g] from fricatives [f, θ, s, š, v, δ, z, ž] and glides [w, y]. Generalized patterns then have been found which correspond to attributes of phonetic segments and these patterns group sounds into natural classes. These attributes and associated patterns correspond to the classic definition of phonetic features.

Whether or not the invariant acoustic patterns generalize across languages and across various syllable positions, as has been claimed, are important questions and need empirical confirmation. We have taken the research strategy of investigating acoustic invariance across languages. Results have shown invariant acoustic patterns for place of articulation (labial, dental and alveolar, and velar) in stop consonants in English, French, Malayalam, Czech, and Hungarian. While there are, to be sure, fine differences in the phonetic manifestation of these consonants, they share the same invariant acoustic properties.

With respect to the generality of invariant acoustic patterns across syllable positions, Ken Stevens and I attempted to quantitatively explore this issue (Blumstein & Stevens, 1979). As Kewley-Port points out, the results were not compelling, as only about 65% of final stops displayed the proposed invariant acoustic properties. However, there are two points worth mentioning. First, in our 1979 paper, Stevens and I looked for invariance using a metric based on the gross shape of the spectrum at the stop release. While this metric was a good first attempt at defining the nature of the invariant acoustic properties for place of articulation, we would now agree that the gross shape of the spectrum is probably not the best means of capturing invariant properties for place of articulation. A metric incorporating a dynamic or time-varying parameter is probably more optimal (cf. Kewley-Port, 1980, 1983; Lahiri, Gewirth, & Blumstein, 1984). Thus, the fact that only about 65% of final stops displayed invariant acoustic patterns may have reflected a limitation of our analysis procedures, rather than a demonstration that invariance does not generalize across syllable position. The second point concerns the actual findings of Blumstein and Stevens (1979). The results showed 76% classification for stop consonants with a burst, but only 53% correct classification for stop consonants without a burst. What is interesting is that the pattern of these results mirrors the data for perception of place of articulation in final stops. Released stops in English are generally perceived well with respect to place of articulation. However, unreleased stops are generally perceived very poorly. Thus, the fact that the measurement procedures so closely paralleled the perception data suggests that the theoretical framework was reflecting appropriately characteristics of the speech-processing system.

10

Invariance and Variability in Speech Production: A Distinction Between Linguistic Intent and its Neuromotor Implementation

James H. Abbs
University of Wisconsin–Madison

The scientific study of phonology and phonetics has been in a state of theoretical crisis for over twenty years. Analyses of the speech-system output (e.g., acoustic patterns, articulatory movements, muscle actions) frequently have yielded patterns that are not consistent with phonological units or features. Complex, elegant, and even metaphysical explanations have emerged in attempts to reconcile this lack of correspondence. Yet other investigators have (1) proposed novel sets of phonological units; (2) chosen to remain agnostic; and/or (3) elected to investigate speech-production behavior from the standpoints of cognitive psychology or information processing. This chapter is aimed at providing a motor control perspective on the apparent incongruity between speech-production system output and its underlying phonological representation. The fundamental argument is that classical physiological analyses have been focused too narrowly, by virtue of the implicit premise that the character of underlying units is discernible in patterns of isolated speech movements or muscle actions. The present chapter re-emphasizes the concept that phonological units are abstract *intentions* which are implemented by generating perceptually acceptable acoustic waveforms (cf. Ladefoged, DeClark, Lindau & Papcun, 1972; Perkell, 1980). From this perspective it is apparent that while speech-motor actions are related deterministically to underlying phonological units, the individual movement and muscle actions are wholly subordinate to the achievement of multiaction goals.

Three lines of evidence will be forwarded to support this point of view: (1) observations of speech movements and speech-muscle activity; (2) results of studies in which unanticipated perturbations have been applied to speech movements; and (3) knowledge of cortical mechanisms involved in speech-motor actions and their associated linguistic functions.

202

OBSERVATIONS OF SPEECH MOVEMENT
AND ASSOCIATED MUSCLE ACTIVITY

In 1971, a strain gauge transduction system was developed that allowed us to transduce simultaneous movements of the upper lip, lower lip, and jaw (Abbs & Gilbert, 1973). With this system, it was possible to obtain samples of these movement patterns from large groups of subjects without restrictions due to radiation hazard. Our expectation at that time was that we would be able to codify the speech-specific behaviors of the labial-mandibular system. We initially took a traditional speech-production analysis approach. Carefully selected samples with canonical speech-sound contrasts were embedded in multiple phonetic environments. For example, lip and jaw movement patterns were observed for rounded and spread vowel productions with differing degrees of openness; jaw opening was observed in labial, palatal, and velar consonant environments. We were soon blessed with a heretofore unobtainable database for evaluating the speech behavior of the labial-mandibular subsystem. In one study alone, we acquired movement data on 480 utterances from three subjects (Abbs, 1973; Abbs & Netsell, 1973).

Unfortunately, these large samples of speech-movement data revealed some shortcomings in previous studies where earlier techniques, particularly cineradiography, had been used. In earlier investigations, due to radiation hazard, samples of speech from a particular subject rarely exceed 2–4 minutes. The modern literature prior to 1971 provided data on a *total* of 25–40 minutes of speech data with only a few subjects per study (cf. Daniloff & Moll, 1968; Houde, 1968; Kent & Moll, 1972; Lubker, 1968; Moll & Shriner, 1967; Perkell, 1969); several of these investigations focused upon movements of a single articulator. Because contemporary theoretical emphasis was on issues like coarticulation, few experimenters reduced the number of phonetic contrasts (within the limited sampling period) to obtain multiple repetitions. Thus, despite large intersubject variability (cf. MacNeilage, 1972), speech-production models were based largely upon a few repetitions of select sequences in one to three subjects. Intrasubject variability was largely unaddressed.

By contrast, since utterance numbers were not limited by strain-gauge techniques, we obtained many repetitions of each utterance and usually studied four to six subjects. Analyses of those latter movement data indicated thatthe intra- and intersubject variability was not merely noise that blurred otherwise robust trends; rather, it appeared that hypothesized patterns might not exist, even for isolated productions. Indeed, movements for isolated CVCs were observed to be more variable than CVCs in carrier phrases (Abbs, 1971). For every apparently consistent movement pattern of a phonetic sequence in a particular subject, there were equal numbers of counter examples in the same and different subjects. Under circumstances where the subjects produced the same utterance repeatedly (10-20 times), the lip or jaw displacement variability for a particular gesture was often as large as 50% of the mean. A related observation was made regarding movement variability in naive subjects as compared to individuals who were phonetically sophisticated; the latter subjects, perhaps as part of their unusual and intensive experience, were far less variable.

Based upon the reasoning that achievement of absolute spatial targets may not be critical for generation of perceptually significant acoustic signals, these observations led us to examine speech-movement dynamics. Acoustic discontinuities (e.g., vocalic transitions, burst transients) are important features in vowel and consonant perception. Thus, it was possible that invariance might be found in articulatory velocities and accelerations rather than articulatory displacements. However, articulatory dynamics were almost as variable as articulatory displacements (Abbs, Netsell & Hixon, 1971; Kuksht, 1975).

These observations led us to question whether individual articulator movements had more than a statistical relation to any underlying segmental unit. For this reason, we chose to investigate the peripheral physiology of the labial-mandibular system; we argued that understanding speech control required a more enlightened view of biomechanical and muscular properties (Abbs & Eilenberg, 1976). Initial foci were the seemingly deterministic relations between activity in a given speech muscle and the articulatory movement that it generated. This rationale suggested that we observe movement and muscle activity simultaneously (Abbs, 1973; Abbs & Netsell, 1972; Kuksht, 1975). However, predicted EMG-movement relationships likewise were violated by substantial degrees of variability. Under some circumstances, muscle activity appeared to relate to select aspects of movement (Abbs, 1973). However, with further quantification, the repetition-to-repetition variability in EMG onset/offset, peak amplitude, and peak-amplitude timing, appeared to be only related moderately to similarly salient aspects of the movement (Abbs & Netsell, 1972; Kuksht, 1975). Muscle activity for a repeated movement had substantial variability in waveform shape as well. Further, a muscle that appeared to be the prime mover for a particular structure would at times practically cease activity without change in the associated movement (Barlow, Cole & Abbs, 1983). It became apparent that even when coarticulatory influences were constant, stereotypic "motor commands" were not associated with particular phonetic units, at least as these commands were reflected in individual muscle actions.

After considerable frustration in search for some degree of consistency in speech movements and associated muscle activity, we came to the realization that analyses limited to individual muscles or movements were not focused

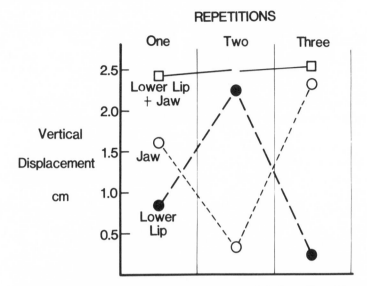

FIG. 10.1.   Magnitudes of vertical displacement of the lower lip and jaw for three repetitions of the vowel [a]. Measures obtained at midpoint of the vowel. After Abbs & Netsell (1973).

appropriately in terms of the intended goals of speech production. That is, after extensive messaging of this database, it appeared that the ubiquitous variability we were observing was due to the fact that our analyses of speech-motor behavior were not focused on the *intended multiple-movement goals*. For example, the position of the jaw for repeated productions of the same lingual consonant in the same vowel context manifests considerable variability. The obvious conclusion from this observation is that when the jaw was low, the tongue, independent of the jaw, must be high, otherwise the consonant could not be correctly produced. In one of the early studies, we found evidence of this kind of trade-off between the lower lip and jaw movements for repeated productions of the same VCV syllable (Abbs & Netsell, 1973). An example of this observation is shown in Figure 10.1.

These data suggested that the controlled output of the speech-motor system was not a parallel series of independent movements, each directed toward a consistent position in three-dimensional target space as suggested by Mac-Neilage (1970). Rather, the goal of this gesture was a complex action; it appeared that only the combination of these potentially independent movements was being controlled. Further evidence of this kind of covariable, interarticulator trade off was apparent in other simple speech gestures (e.g., the upper and lower lip movements for repetitions of [apa], as shown in Figure 10.2.)

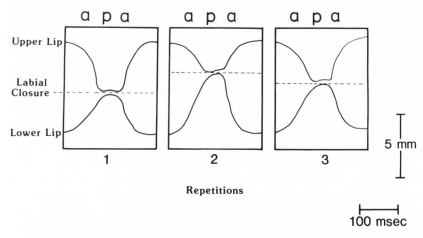

FIG. 10.2. Upper and lower lip movements for three repetitions of [apa],
illustrating motor equivalence between these two articulatory movements.
For these observations the jaw was fixed with a bite-block. After Abbs,
Gracco, & Cole (in press).

A more formal test of this hypothesis was undertaken by observing the
upper lip, lower lip, and jaw for a large utterance set in six naive subjects
(Abbs & Hughes, 1975; Hughes & Abbs, 1976). We asked whether the relative contribution of the upper lip, lower lip, and jaw similarly covaried for
repeated productions of the same vowel in achieving oral opening. The results confirmed the earlier observations. It was found that when the jaw
contributed large displacements to oral opening, the upper and lower lips
contributed smaller displacements, and conversely.

These data reflected the phenomenon of motor equivalence, defined by
Hughes and Abbs (1976) as "the capacity of a motor system to achieve the
same end product with considerable variation in the individual components
that contribute to that output [p. 199]." This phenomenon is not restricted
to speech-motor behavior and has been identified and described for over fifty
years (e.g., Hebb, 1949; Lashley, 1930). However, many earlier observations
of motor equivalence primarily involved observations of limb movements in
two- or three-dimensional space (Bernstein, 1967; Lacquaniti & Soechting,
1982; Morasso, 1981). As noted by Lashley (1930), "every gross movement
of limbs of the body is made in reference to the space system." For speech-
motor actions, the individual articulatory movements would not appear to be
controlled with regard to three-dimensional spatial targets, but rather with
regard to their contribution to complex vocal-tract goals, such as resonance
properties (e.g., shape, degree of constriction) and/or aerodynamically significant variables. This is evidenced by observations of laryngeal height adjustments to lip protrusion during production of vowels where overall vocal-tract

length is the acoustically significant goal (Riorden, 1977) or covariable manipulations of the abdomen and rib cage contributions to total lung volumes for speech (Hixon, Goldman & Mead, 1973; Hixon, Mead & Goldman, 1976; Hunker & Abbs, 1982).

For speech, the significant goals are the aerodynamic and acoustic response properties of the vocal tract (or respiratory system), which only in limited situations correspond to movements of a single structure. Other goals such as degree of labial closure stiffness (not actually involving movement per se) are achieved across multiple repetitions of |p| production via covariations in the magnitude of upper and lower lip muscle contraction (Kuksht, 1975). These latter data point to a prescribed goal of maintaining the labial occlusal seal against rupture during [p] closure. One might predict that the differential actions of velopharyngeal closure associated with voiced and voiceless consonants likewise are related primarily to aerodynamic integrity and only coincidently to position of the velum. Other data that indicate the limitations of simple spatial targets include observations of covariability in the relative velocities of the lower lip and jaw movements, as these two gestures contribute to net lip-elevation velocity to generate perceptually significant vocalic transitions (Hasegawa, McCutcheon, Wolf & Fletcher, 1976). From these data it appears that motor equivalence operates in both the temporal and spatial coordination of the multiple gestures required for speech production. Obviously, recognition of motor equivalence is useful in reconciling the substantial magnitudes of individual movement variability noted previously.

A related issue is whether there is covariance among the multiple synergistic muscles that act in concert to produce a particular movement. Operation of motor equivalence at the intermuscular level offers some explanation for the observations that patterns of muscle activation vary considerably across repetitions of a given movement (Kuksht, 1975). One common observation (cf. Abbs, 1979) is in the activity of the coagonistic muscles which act synergistically to elevate the lower lip (Orbicularis oris inferior and Mentalis) as shown in Figure 10.3.

As is apparent, for the lower-lip elevations where the Mentalis has a large burst of activity (elevations 1 and 3) the Orbicularis oris muscle has a correspondingly small burst. The converse pattern is seen for lower lip elevations 2 and 4. In a recent paper (Gentil, Gracco & Abbs, 1983), the covariable contributions of OOI, MTL, and DLI were analyzed quantitatively in relation to their contributions to lower lip elevation. The results of these analyses (Figure 10.4) revealed that when the magnitude of all three muscles are simultaneously regressed, the coefficient is reasonably high and always greater than any one muscle regressed separately. Folkins (1981) made parallel observations concerning apparent covariable actions among synergistic muscles for jaw closing. Similarly, Fujimura (1981a) proposed a potential motor equivalence trade off between vocalis and cricothyroid muscles in their common

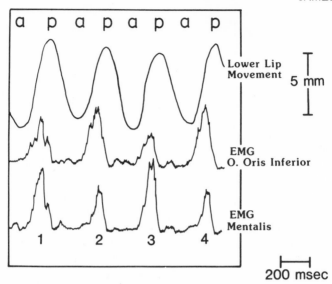

FIG. 10.3. EMG from O. Oris Inferior and Mentalis muscles for a repeated set of lower lip elevation movements. EMG is rectified and smoothed. After Abbs, Gracco, & Cole (1984).

contributions to vocal-fold stiffness. Observations of intermuscle covariability are consistent with findings in the limbs where multiple, agonistic muscles covary in their relative contributions to movements around a single joint (Lacquaniti & Soechting, 1982). Apparently multiple muscles acting to produce a particular limb movement are not constrained to act in a stereotypic manner, but covary from one such complex gesture to another.

Observations of motor equivalence at both intermovement and intermuscular levels address several earlier concepts of speech motor execution. As pointed out previously (Hughes & Abbs, 1976),

> Our results suggest severe limitations on descriptions of speech behavior as a series of consistent articulatory positions. If the phenomenon of motor equivalence is widespread, one could hypothesize that the tongue, lips, jaw, pharyngeal walls, and vertical position of the glottis interact with and compensate for one another, *variably*, from one utterance repetition to another. Certainly this form of compensation is feasible, both physiologically and acoustically [p. 219].

The acoustic and physiological feasibility of these compensations is apparent when the jaw is fixed; compensatory labial and lingual adjustments are almost instantaneous (Lindblom, Lubker & Gay, 1979; Lindblom & Sundberg, 1971). Initially, it is apparent from observations of motor equivalence

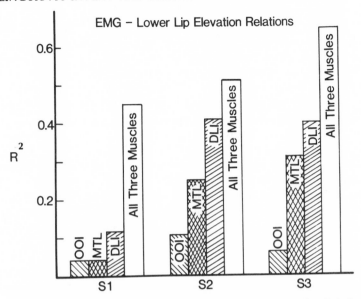

FIG. 10.4.   Regressions between magnitude of EMG in O. Oris Inferior (OOI), Mentalis (MTL), and Depressor Labii Inferior (DLI) muscles and lower lip elevation for [apa]. EMG values are average magnitudes of the EMG bursts obtained from signals that were digitally rectified. Data from three subjects are shown. After Gentil et al. (1983).

that analyses of individual articulatory movement or of individual muscle contractions with regard to underlying linguistic units are likely to yield only statistically discernible trends. That is, *on the average*, low vowels will have lower jaw positions, but given the potential for tongue position to be controlled independently, this characteristic is mutable. Additionally, and in parallel, activity of any given muscle is not likely to show an invariant relation to a particular movement. More importantly, single muscle patterns are even less likely to show a consistent relation to intended vocal-tract goals. That is, inasmuch as individual movements are not invariant with respect to particular phonetic goals, then the muscles that produce those movements (which in themselves appear to be only statistically related to the already variant movement) may show only a very weak relationship.

These observations raise a question as to the teleological basis for the operation of motor equivalence. One consideration is simply flexibility. That is, because the ontogeny and phylogeny of motor systems are not perfect or wholly stereotyped, the complexity of most skilled behaviors requires an inherent ability to accomplish a given goal in different ways. The learning of speech-motor behavior certainly would be more demanding if successful performance was restricted to a single stereotyped pattern of muscle contraction and movement. On a more general plane, the ability to accomplish the same objective in many different ways offers the adaptability necessary for survival in many unusual, unforeseen circumstances, or as a backup for acquired injury and disease. The apparently "normal" speech of someone with a cervical spinal-cord lesion (causing paralysis in several respiratory muscles) illustrates this point. A comparable example is speech with partial glossectomy or following orthodontic modification.

From this perspective, it appears that motor equivalence reduces the control complexity associated with behaviors like human speech. Given the restricted range within which the system has to operate, motor equivalence overcomes the seeming difficulty of exact specification of each of the multiple events; the ability to accomplish the same objective differently relieves the nervous system of the burden of having to prespecify all details of the motor subgestures. One might consider execution of multiple speech movements as comparable to coarse and fine adjustments. That is, a coarse action gets the system close to the desired goal, and a parallel, perhaps slightly delayed action—based upon results of the initial action—predictively makes the fine-grained adjustment. Lacquaniti and Soechting's (1982) observations on upper-limb movements for grasping indicated that the shoulder and elbow movements were relatively consistent across repetitions, while wrist supination and/or pronation (the business end of the complex movement) varied substantially. It is not necessary to couple the wrist movement with the shoulder and elbow movement, and hence its specific temporal properties can vary. In so doing, the control problem of otherwise specifying three joint movements simultaneously is reduced to specification of two joint movements and adaptive adjustment of the third as necessary.

With regard to the multimovement actions of speech, coarticulation may be a manifestation of a process whereby control complexity is reduced by executing the movements asynchronously (cf. Abbs & Cole, 1982). Some of our earlier observations suggest that intermovement motor equivalence adjustments act to reduce the complexity of speech control (Hughes & Abbs, 1976). Quantifying the degree of motor equivalence, we compared its operation under different speaking rates. We assumed that the control requirements are more demanding for faster speaking rates. There was, as predicted, a quantitative increase in the degree of motor equivalence for increased speaking rate for all subjects.

Overall, these observations suggest a nervous-system organization which places a higher priority on acoustically and aerodynamically significant multi-action gestures than on individual movements and muscle actions. However, making interpretations from descriptive analyses of a system output often can be tenuous in terms of actual neural organization. It is critical to constrain and shape the development of such empirically based explanations by testing hypotheses directed at underlying neurophysiological mechanisms. Given the complexity of the nervous system, one must be careful to separate metaphors from physiology (cf. Kelso, Tuller & Harris, 1983). Such analogies, while intellectually stimulating, primarily are empirical abstractions. To overcome this problem, the above interpretations were augmented by studies where certain nervous-system control processes were examined experimentally.

SPEECH-MOVEMENT PERTURBATION ANALYSES

It is critical to further document whether (1) the speech-motor process involves independent control of individual articulators; or (2) these subactions are subordinate constituents of a multimovement speech gesture. An ideal method is to observe compensations when individual speech movements are perturbed, effectively utilizing a sensitivity analysis. To date, unanticipated loads have been applied individually to movements of the upper lip, lower lip, and jaw in various labial-mandibular and lingual-mandibular speech gestures, including [apa], [aba], [afa], and [aza]. If the speech-motor execution process involves parallel, independent control of multiple speech structures, compensatory reponses to loads should be autogenic, viz., observed only in the movement that was disturbed. However, the results of these studies overwhelmingly indicate that the nervous system acts via sensorimotor pathways to preserve the integrity of the combined movement goal; compensatory actions are not confined to the perturbed movements.

For example, when perturbations are introduced on the upper or lower lip immediately prior to or during a bilabial closing gesture [aba], intermovement compensations are most prominent. Lower-lip loads yield primarily upper-lip responses, and conversely (Abbs & Gracco, 1982; Gracco & Abbs, 1982). Similarly, when loads are applied to the jaw during a lip–jaw gesture [apa] or a tongue–jaw gesture [aza], on-line compensatory actions are seen selectively in muscles of the lips and the tongue, respectively (Folkins & Abbs, 1975, 1976; Kelso, Tuller & Fowler, 1982). Indeed, in some of these experiments the *primary* compensatory response was an intermovement sensorimotor action; loads to the jaw during [apa] yielded indiscernible responses in the jaw closing muscles, with the prominent compensations in the upper and lower lips (Folkins & Abbs, 1975, 1976).

Figure 10.5 provides representative examples of upper and lower lip movements for loaded and normal conditions. When the lower lip is loaded and displaced from its normal trajectory, it does not reach its predetermined position; rather, movement adjustments in the upper lip provide the critical compensations (Abbs & Gracco, 1984). Even when loads are introduced 100 msec prior to the onset of the lip movements for bilabial closure with substantial time for autogenic adjustment, upper lip as well as lower lip actions

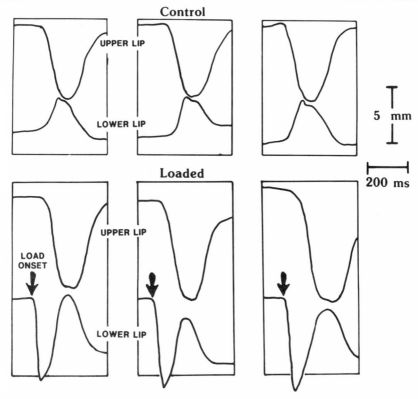

FIG. 10.5. Comparison of upper and lower lip movements for production of [aba] under control conditions (upper panels) and when the lower
lip is loaded (lower panel). Load magnitude for the loaded condition was
40 grams. After Abbs & Gracco (1983).

jointly compensate (Gracco & Abbs, 1982). Parallel observations indicate
that the pattern of these sensorimotor actions reflects dynamically changing
nervous-system goals. As shown, when loads are applied during a combined
upper lip–lower lip gesture [aba], upper-lip responses as well as lower-lip responses are apparent. However for [afa], which does not involve the upper
lip, there is no upper-lip movement when the lower lip is loaded (see Figure
10.6). A similar interpretation is available from the results of Kelso et al.
(1982).

The implication of these observations is that individual speech movements
are only controlled *in relation* to the multimovement gesture. That is, the
spatial targets for individual articulators are wholly subordinate to the significant goals of the combined movement gesture. This point is further manifested in responses to unanticipated loads introduced at various time points
in the speech-movement sequence. If loads to the lower lip are introduced

Differential Upper Lip Control

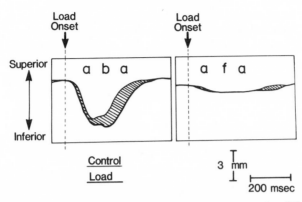

FIG. 10.6. Illustration of upper-lip movement compensation differences (in the same subject) to lower-lip loads introduced prior to movements for [aba] and [afa]. Load perturbation magnitudes for this example were 40 grams. After Abbs, Gracco, & Caligiuri (forthcoming).

early during the first [a] of [apa], there is no compensation during the vowel gesture (Abbs & Gracco, 1982); apparently the lip movements are relatively unimportant for the acoustic achievement of an acceptable [a]. However, if the load is introduced immediately prior to or during labial closure, the movement and EMG compensations are very apparent, even on single-trial comparisons.

Finally, while the multimovement intent and its achievement are acceptably invariant, the details of motor execution (individual movements and muscle actions) are subject to the flexible and dynamic operation of on-line sensorimotor processes. The "normal" operation of sensorimotor actions in speech-intermovement coordination is evidenced by several parallel observations: (1) successful compensation the first time loads are introduced in naive subjects; (2) subject comments indicating that perturbations are coped with by "ignoring them"; (3) subject inability to comply with instructions to "not compensate"; (4) statistically significant compensations to loads as small as 10 gms, producing perturbations in lip or jaw movements as small as 1.0 mm; (5) evidence in over 25 subjects that perturbations (sometimes as large as 15 mm) do not yield a perceptually discernible disruption in the intended speech goals; and (6) clear compensatory reponses to perturbation even after movement is initiated. These moment-to-moment sensorimotor actions appear to underlie the covariability among movement and muscle activity patterns (Abbs & Gracco, 1984). Indeed, such powerful sensorimotor capabilities relieve the nervous system of having to prespecify the motor details, and thus ensure that overall intended goals are accomplished.

The foregoing observations are not specific to speech-motor actions but reflect patterns of organization in most natural motor behaviors. Observations of the limbs indicate that while implementation of motor acts involves a deterministic translation between motor intent and the details of the motor output, this translation does not involve stereotypic specification of motor subactions (Lacquaniti & Soechting, 1982; Morasso, 1981). For example, from observations in multijoint limb movements, it was suggested:

> At higher levels the general structure of a motor act would be defined in abstract terms whose features are only those properties of the motor act which remain invariant under different levels of spatio-temporal transformations. At lower levels of organization, more contingent parameters of the movement (such as the muscles required and their pattern of activation) would be defined on the basis of specific task demands (for instance the speed of execution) and of the current state of the environment and the musculo-skeletal apparatus [p. 408]. (Lacquaniti & Soechting, 1982)

The distinction between the functional intended goals of a motor behavior and its motorsensory implementation offers a basis on which to further consider potential nervous-system correlates. Of particular interest in this context are the multiple motorsensory and sensorimotor representations at the level of the cerebral cortex.

POTENTIAL UNDERLYING CORTICAL PROCESSES

This part of the discussion is concerned with differential cortical processes underlying phonological and speech-motor execution operations, respectively. This evidence augments the neurophysiological distinction between the abstract intended goals (phonological units) and the neuromotor implementation of these goals. In general, it is apparent that at cortical levels, multiple motorsensory and sensorimotor cortical processes underlie different functional subtleties of a given behavior (cf. Woolsey, 1982a, 1982b). The orofacial region is represented at 10–12 different cortical areas, with five sites in the precentral motorsensory regions alone (cf. Muakkassa & Strick, 1979). These multiple orofacial representations are, of course, manifested in the posterior cortex as well, including the posterior parietal region. Acquired cortical lesions in humans yield two expressive disorders that parallel the intention-execution distinction discussed above. While inferences concerning human brain function from lesion data are difficult, certain patterns have emerged. That is, it appears that certain acquired lesions posterior to the central sulcus yield aberrations in the phonological aspects of speech, while lesions anterior to the central sulcus are observed primarily to create speech-motor "programming" problems (Blumstein, 1973; Blumstein, Cooper, Goodglass,

Statlender, & Gottlieb, 1980; Buckingham, 1979; Goodglass, & Kaplan, 1972; Johns, & Darley, 1970).

Nonfluent aphasics (sometimes described as having "apraxia of speech") with apparent anterior lesions exhibit struggle or groping in attempts at achieving phonetic goals as well as extreme degrees of multimovement disintegration (Fromm, 1981; Fromm, Abbs, McNeil, & Rosenbek, 1982; Itoh, Sasanuma, Hirose, Yoshioka, & Ushijima, 1980; Itoh, Sasanuma, & Ushijima, 1979). The subjects having apraxia of speech appear to have a motorexecution problem associated with the anterior lesion. In their purest forms, these patients manifest minimal linguistic aberrations (i.e., few fluent substitutions, no agrammaticism, no agraphia, normal auditory comprehension). Lesions in these rare cases are apparently confined to an area of cortex that is lateral and somewhat anterior to the primary motor strip, viz., Brodman's area 44 or Broca's area (Mohr, 1976; Mohr, Pessin, Finkelstein, Funkenstein, Duncan, & Davis, 1978).

By contrast, patients with conduction aphasia (due apparently to posterior lesions) exhibit normal or near normal comprehension of speech; however, they fluently delete, transpose, add, or substitute sounds in varying degrees, depending on whether the task is repetition, naming, oral reading, or spontaneous speech. While conduction aphasia and apraxia of speech are rare entities in isolation, the general differences in their manifestations, along with the associated data on site of cortical lesions, are generally agreed upon. As such, these human data offer a neuroanatomical basis for the distinction between phonological processes and speech-motor execution.

In relation to the present chapter, the issue is the potential interaction between these two operations and whether it is reasonable to consider phonological processes as coincident with the mechanisms that underlie abstract, intentional motor goals in the generation of speech. For obvious reasons, detailed neurophysiological studies have not been conducted in humans. However, analyses in nonhuman primates point strongly to the viability of this perspective. Certain differences are apparent between the cerebral neocortex of Old World monkeys and humans. However, both cytoarchitectonic and connectivity patterns (to the extent these are known) offer a substantive basis for fruitful comparative analyses (cf. Bonin, 1949; Galaburda, & Pandya, 1982; Porter, 1981). Effectively, as will be discussed, observations in nonhuman primates indicate that (1) the apparent homologue of Broca's area (lateral precentral cortex, areas 6 and 44) are distinctive functionally from primary motor cortex (area 4) and act as a motorsensory center for multimovement orofacial control; and (2) the orofacial region of lateral, posterior parietal cortex (7b) has, as one of its functions, the identification and initiation of abstract, holistic goals, with projections to premotor orofacial areas for motor implementation.

JAMES H. ABBS

It is necessary first to distinguish the function of these lateral cortex regions (area 6 and 44) from the primary motor-face region (area 4). Single-cell
recording in area 6–44 indicates that the neural activity is correlated with
complex, natural, multimovement gestures of the orofacial region; comparable activity is generally not observed in area 4 (Kubota & Niki, 1971;
Lund & Lamarre, 1974). Likewise, cortical stimulation in area 6–44 elicits
natural multimovement orofacial behaviors, while stimulation in area 4 is
more likely to yield contractions of individual muscles (Lund & Lamarre,
1974; Walker & Green, 1938). In terms of sensory projections, afferents from
facial-trigeminal, lingual, and superior laryngeal nerves converge on single
sites in area 6–44 with latencies as short as 7-12 msec (O'Brien, Pimpaneau
Albe-Fessard, 1971). Comparable convergence of sensory inflow is not commonly observed in area 4 (Asanuma & Rosen, 1972). Such somatosensory
convergence likewise is consistent with the hypothesized involvement of this
cortical center in multimovement orofacial gestures. As noted by O'Brien et
al. (1971):

> Common monkey behavior consists of opening the mouth, stick-
> ing out the tongue, raising the eyebrows, curling the lips, ... cells
> in the Broca area were particularly sensitive to stimuli which pro-
> duced these various movements, and the presence of a projection
> from the larynx in this area suggests an integration of vocalization
> with these associated movements [p. 18].

Lesions to the area 6–44 suggest similar conclusions. Several studies (Larson, Byrd, Garthwaite, & Luschei, 1980; Luschei & Goodwin, 1975; Watson,
1974) have focused on the effects of contrastive lesions to the motor face area
4 and to area 6–44. In monkeys with motor cortex (area 4) lesions, Luschei
and Goodwin (1975) found that the animals were able, almost immediately
after surgery, to manipulate food with their hands and mouth. By contrast,
animals with lesions in lateral area 6–44 were unable to manipulate food or
feed themselves for long periods following surgery. These lateral precentral
cortex LPC lesions, as suggested by Larson et al. (1980), appear to "remove
those neurons that seem necessary for complex tongue movements and perhaps as importantly, those necessary for coordination of the tongue, face,
and mandible [p. 649]." These observations, along with evidence on connections to and from lateral area 6 and 44, indicate that this cortical region is
involved in a special way in multimovement sensorimotor coordination of the
orofacial region. These nonhuman primate observations are consistent with
the fact that comparable lesions in man yield disruptions in multimovement
gestures for speech. Indeed, Mohr et al. (1978) note that:

> ...a "restricted" lesion to these areas leads one to view their func-
> tion as "mediating" a more traditionally postulated role as a pre-
> motor association cortex region concerned with acquired skilled

oral, pharyngeal, and respiratory movements, involving speaking as well as other behaviors but not essentially language or graphic behavior, per se [p. 22].

Work by Rosenbek, Wertz, and Darley (1973) indicate a loss of orofacial sensory capabilities in apraxia of speech patients. These observations are consistent also with recent data suggesting that the sensorimotor pathways underlying intermovement coordination have latencies consistent with cortical pathways (Abbs & Gracco, 1983, 1984; Gracco & Abbs, 1982).

The other observations that point to a special function for lateral area 6 and 44 are the connections to other areas of the cortex and to subcortical sites. Based upon observations using axoplasmic tracing techniques, it has been demonstrated that lateral area 6 is interconnected with (1) the primary motor cortex (Muakkassa & Strick, 1979); (2) supplementary motor area (SMA) and posterior regions, including the temporal-parietal region (Galaburda & Pandya, 1982); and (3) a nuclear region of the thalamus that is separate from the thalamic projections to the primary motor cortex or SMA (Schell & Strick, 1983). These neuroanatomical observations further illustrate the functional distinctiveness of area 6, and also suggest that it has a downstream connection from posterior cortex, including the areas in humans where acquired lesions yield disruption of phonological processes. In fact, there appear to be direct projections from the posterior-lateral parietal regions (7b) to lateral area 6; these projections entirely bypass the primary motor cortex (Godschalk, Lemon, & Kuypers, 1983; Jones, Coulter, & Hendry, 1978).

Functions of the lateral posterior parietal area of cortex in those primates that do not utilize oral language also highlight some of the fundamental contributions of this region. Some provocative clues are offered by the landmark investigations of Mountcastle, Lynch, Georgopoulos, Sakata, and Acuna (1975). These authors, based upon single cortical unit/behavioral analyses of posterior parietal function in old world monkeys, noted:

> ...these regions receive afferent signals descriptive of the body in space, and contain a command apparatus... This general command function is exercised in a holistic fashion. *It relates to acts aimed at certain behavioral goals and not to the details of muscular contractions during execution* [p. 871]. (Emphasis in original)

While the observations of Mountcastle and his colleagues were focused on more medial posterior parietal regions, parallel studies by other investigators suggest comparable functions for the more lateral orofacial portion of area 7 (7b) (Hyvarinen, 1982; Leinonen & Nyman, 1979). That is, the more lateral parietal orofacial area (7b) likewise appears involved in identification of movement goals and analysis of holistic, multimodal sensory information for abstract achievement of those goals. For example, more than 40% of the cells in this cortical area fired only in relation to self-generated movements. However, the cell discharge was not related to the details of those movements. This lateral area 7 is thought to involve sensory integration and intended movement goal identification specifically for *personal space* (e.g., exploratory oral manipulation, hand-mouth, or intraoral actions). For example, while the cells recorded were not responsive to peripheral sensory stimulation, they did increase firing when a stimulus (food) was followed by a labial reaching response. Leinonen and Nyman's (1979) comment is relevant in this regard:

> ...this species of monkeys use their mouths for exploratory (mouthing, licking) and communicative (kissing) purposes. The cellular function in the anterior part of area 7 is related to this kind of behavior. Our findings also suggest that meanings of some movements associated with the face are analyzed here, e.g., "towards the mouth" and "threat face" (raising of one's eyebrows). This area may also participate in the motor control of facial expressions [p. 332].

In general, these data suggest a posterior parietal cortex region that may function in *the identification and selection of movement goals.* Abstract orofacial goals in man may include the multimovement intentions associated with phonological processes. As noted by Hyvarinen (1982) in comments on the comparative significance of nonhuman primate observations in parietal cortex:

> In development of the human species, awareness of constructive skills of the hands and speech have acquired a greater degree of *conceptualization of actions.* This "practognostic" awareness of constructive movements may have contributed to the enlargement of the human posterior parietal cortex [p. 1121].

Collectively, these data from both nonhuman primates and man suggest that posterior parietal regions (7b) may function for selection of intentional abstract goals (phonological features in man) and that frontal regions, including area 6–44 and the primary motor cortex (area 4) (in that sequence), operate to carry out the detailed motor execution of these goals.

Despite some obvious issues concerning the specific character of the underlying phonological processes, it seems reasonable that the speech goals are the result of processes whereby communication objectives are transformed into overall speech-motor actions. This transformation may be the essence of phonological processes, deriving from abstract linguistical units. However, these phonological-abstract motor objectives do not prescribe particular movements or muscle actions. What is apparent from the standpoint of speech as a motor behavior is that the phonological goals represent the *intent* of the system to generate an acoustic output that is perceptually acceptable. This concept of speech-motor intent is not different, in principle, from the abstract motor objectives underlying handwriting, sign language, or perhaps even nonlinguistic motor behaviors such as the successful parallel parking of an automobile or reaching for an object in three-dimensional space. In none of these cases does the goal prescribe the specific muscle actions or isolated movements involved in its successful achievement. On this basis, it is of limited value to describe isolated movements or muscle actions of the speech-production system without parallel observation of synergistic actions that may covary in achieving overall system goals.

ACKNOWLEDGEMENTS

The author wishes to acknowledge discussions with Dr. Carol Welt, particularly regarding the interpretations of nonhuman primate neocortical function. Gratitude is also expressed to Marilyn Kerwin for her editorial assistance.

Anders Löfqvist: Comment

I agree with many of the points made by Abbs. The systems approach he advocates and the search for functional units are necessary in studies of speech-motor control. Their neglect has most likely contributed to the theoretical crisis that Abbs refers to. Another factor contributing to this crisis is, I think, a too heavy reliance on the descriptions used by phonologists in analyzing sound systems, in particular an attempt to look for invariance in terms of static entities. This can easily result in an overemphasis of the linguistic side of speech production. One is forced to give a direct and immediate linguistic interpretation of every aspect of articulation, as if the motor system itself made no contribution of its own and was a purely passive transmission device.

I also like Abbs' historical overview of research in speech production over the last decade. Historical references are often very helpful in understanding the present. In addition, they may prevent us from repeating the mistakes of the past.

About 50 years ago in Europe, there was talk about a crisis in speech research. In fact, many of the arguments made at that time are similar to some of the ideas presented in this volume. In that period, students of speech production began to realize that invariance was elusive in speech production. Using the technology of the time, Menzerath and de Lacerda (1933) noticed that the articulatory gestures for one and the same sound (the same phoneme) showed large contextual variability. They also found that it was almost impossible to draw boundaries between adjacent segments in the articulatory records; articulatory gestures for successive segments overlapped.

These findings caused some consternation, since it was generally believed that the same sound would be articulated in the same way irrespective of the context—an assumption that seems to reappear at certain intervals. In particular, a serious discussion started about the relationship between phonetics and phonology. Although the causal links in that discussion are not entirely clear, many people argued for a radical separation between phonetics and phonology. Phonology was thus seen as a mentalist subject, whereas phonetics was a physical science. Part of this debate occurred during the Second International Congress of Phonetic Sciences (Jones and Fry, 1936); other contributions are reprinted in Zwirner and Ezawa (1968).

Such a separation has not proved to be very productive in the past, and there is nothing to suggest that it would be any more so today. It is probably a sound principle in science to avoid making sharp dichotomies.

In his paper, Abbs makes a distinction between the abstract goals of the speaker, his/her phonological intentions, and their articulatory realizations. It is obviously attractive to view speech-motor control as a process where a communicative act successively unfolds itself into greater and greater articulatory detail. On the other hand, such a view requires a very complex set of operations transforming the abstract intentions into articulatory and acoustic results. I am particularly concerned that sooner or later we will have to worry about these transformations in order to provide a more explicit account.

Jacqueline Vaissière: Comment

Abbs has noted that syllables were observed to be more variable in their movement patterns when isolated than when they were placed in a carrier phrase. I would like to comment on the lack of invariance in isolated CVCs.

The observed variance may be explained, first, by assuming the superimposition of gestures unrelated to the linguistic and phonetic aspects of speech. Figure 10b.1 represents the time function of the vertical position of two pellets, one located on a speaker's velum and the other on the lower lip, for the pronunciation of a series of isolated syllables. The data have been obtained with the x-ray microbeam system at the University of Tokyo (Fujimura, Kiritani, & Ishida, 1973) and analyzed using the facilities developed at Bell Laboratories. The tracings illustrate two points. First, the velum is rising prior to and at some points during the realization of the consonant [m]. This gesture is antagonistic to the articulatory requirement of the nasal feature. Articulatory patterns in speech cannot thus be explained in terms of segmental features only, but they have to be integrated into a global view of speech activity. Second, the onset of elevation of the velum (designated by the letter T on the figure) is not fixed relative to the segmental events, but highly context-dependent as exemplified on these three tracings. The height or the velum pellet at the beginning of voicing for the [m] (designated by the letter H on the figure) is dependent on such onset timing; the earlier the onset, the higher the velum peak. The fact that the initial consonant is a nasal determines an upper limit for such an elevation, to keep the velopharyngeal port open.

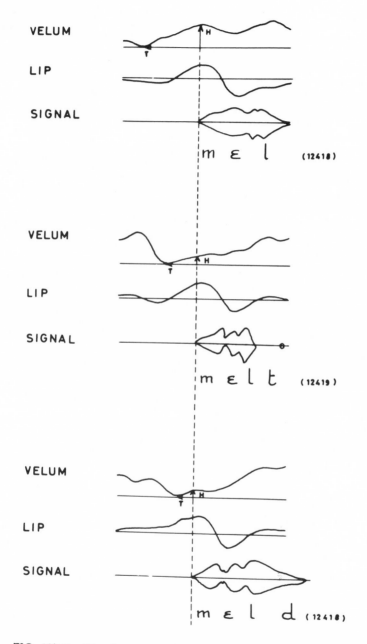

FIG. 10b.1. Time function of the vertical position of the velum pellet, the lower lip pellet, and envelope of the speech signal for three syllables with the initial consonant [m] and vowel [ε]. *T* indicates the onset of the elevation of the velum, and *H* the height of the velum pellet at the voicing onset of the [m].

The tensing of muscles involved in speech production prior to speech is a common observation. This so-called "speech-ready gesture," is highly variable in nature. Its effects can disappear before the first phoneme in an utterance, or can be maintained during the entire beginning of the utterance (or the first CVCs in a list). Similarly, a "speech-relaxation gesture" (a lowering of the velum in this case) before the end of the utterance or after its completion may be observed on the last CVCs just before a pause, and its onset is not readily predictable. Besides the speech-ready gesture and the speech-relaxation gesture, data often illustrate a tendency for articulatory patterns of intermediate CVCs to reflect a decreasing fundamental frequency (related to the so-called declination line in sentences), a lower and lower velum position, and decreasing magnitude of the jaw excursions. These effects represent a general relaxation of the articulators with time. Such a tendency can be counteracted in a repetition of the same list. The speech-ready gesture, the relaxation gesture, and declination effect complicate the interpretation of the data, since such phenomena are not predictable from the linguistic content of speech, and they obscure the relationship between the segmental features and articulatory and EMG patterns.

The speaker's "semantic" interpretation of the speech material that is read can also cause observed articulatory variability. It is well known that in conversational speech, speakers tend to focus on the elements of speech (a feature, a syllable, a word) that they feel are important. Such a tendency is valid not only for meaningful speech but also for nonsense speech, in isolation or in carrier sentences. In other words, in a series like [ted, ted, ten], speakers tend to overarticulate the final consonants to contrast them optimally, while in a series like [ted, ned, med], they will tend to place more emphasis on the syllable-initial consonant. As a consequence, the way of articulating the same syllable [ted] may be slightly different depending on the context and its position in the list.

In summary, the lack of invariance in movements patterns form one repetition of an isolated CVC to another may be partly explained by the interference of nonlinguistic factors, and by context-dependent articulatory "weights" assigned by the speaker to different parts of the syllable.

Katherine S. Harris: Comment

This comment is directed solely at the very beginning of Abbs's paper. Abbs states that "the scientific study of phonology and phonetics has been in a state of theoretical crisis for over 20 years ... [because of] a lack of correspondence between phonological units and what is observed at the speech production output .... The present perspective reemphasizes the concept that phonological units are abstract intentions with a primary objective of generally perceptually acceptable acoustic waveforms."

While Abbs's paper is an admirable review of his own pioneering work, as well as that of others, in bringing a motor-systems perspective to speech, I believe he has misidentified the theoretical crisis which has plagued us since the early 1950s, when systematic investigation of the relationship between perception and the acoustic waveform began. The problem alluded to by many authors in this book is the lack of an invariant acoustic output to correspond to phonological units.

The interest of Abbs's work has been to show us just how well speakers can marshall the activities of a set of articulators to arrive at a particular vocal-tract position, even though the roles of the various components are quite flexible in their contribution to the final target (Abbs, 1979; Folkins & Abbs, 1975). In the same vein, Hixon, Goldman, and Mead (1973) have shown that adjustments of chest wall and thorax can be made interchangeably to attain any particular lung volume. These generative properties of the articulatory system can be shown to be analogous to those of other motor systems.

However, while speakers can attain a given position by multiple means, they can be shown to deviate from constant targets in a systematic way. These are the phenomena which are commonly described as coarticulation. Many authors have argued that these coarticulatory effects are rule-governed, although no one is yet able to describe the rules.

It seems to me that it is the lack of spectral invariance for a given phone that generated the theoretical crisis of 20 years ago rather than the fact that speakers use variable articulatory means to attain a very approximately constant vocal-tract shape. Indeed, given the preoccupation of the researchers of that period with the acoustic level of description, perhaps they would not have noticed the variability of physiological implementation if it were not for their desire to find an explanation of phenomena associated with acoustic variability.

James Lubker: Comment

The contention that classical speech physiological analyses have been "focused too narrowly" on isolated speech movements and muscle actions is, I think, well taken. So, also, is Abbs's view that such individual goals are subordinate to the attainment of larger scale "multi-action goals." The concept of motor equivalence which he stresses is, indeed, a potentially important one. His emphasis on the importance of the speaker's efforts to produce "perceptually acceptable waveforms" is also to be applauded. Further, his advocacy of a holistic and systems theoretical approach is both refreshing and valuable.

Given my overall positive response, I nevertheless have some comments and qualifications which I believe should be considered within the framework of the propositions made by Abbs.

While stressing my general agreement with Abbs, I don't feel entirely comfortable with a blanket indictment of the study of "individual" movements since I believe that such study, when properly designed, may provide valuable input within a holistic and "perceptually acceptable" production framework. I don't argue with Abbs's view that it is not individual muscles and perhaps not even individual artic-ulators which are addressed in motor control, but rather *groups* of muscles. From this point of view, *sets* of articulators contributing to a *total* movement should be studied whenever possible. However, some qualifiers might be added. For example, the lip section of the tube during vowel productions can be effectively varied in two ways: (1) cross-sectional area; and (2) length. Variation in either of these two parameters can have strong effects on formant frequency locations. Degree of labial protrusion should be expected to have a high degree of correlation with changes in length of the labial section of the acoustic tube. Thus, single (or double) articulator observations should be expected to provide valuable information regarding a speaker's control of one important aspect of the acoustic tube. I realize that I am guilty of a little hair-splitting here and that such single (or at most double) articulator observations may prove to be more variable and/or less valuable than would some *set* of observations from a larger number of articulators. I suggest only that there are times when we really are only concerned with one, or very few articulators, and that we should not reject out-of-hand all such "limited" studies.

As Abbs himself suggests, motor equivalence can lead to a sort of infinite regress. Again considering the labial section of the acoustic tube as an example, we have observed that for the lip rounding gesture, lip separation is no less variable than either the upper or the lower lip positions. Is such an observation contrary to motor equivalence? Probably not, since if one takes a holistic view it may not be only Area A that is important but rather A/l, as suggested by acoustic theory. However, if we take a truly holistic view then not even A/l would be expected to be especially free from variability since in von Bertalanffy's (1973) terminology the "equifinality" goal would involve the *total* acoustic tube. But since we know that the acoustic product of the shaping of the acoustic tube is highly variable, then we must assume that the "equifinal" goal of the shape of the acoustic tube for a given vowel must allow a great deal of variability. Does this mean that the study of physiological phonetics, motor control, or whatever, no matter how holistic or systems theoretical in nature, is doomed to failure because of inherent variability? I think not, as I show below.

We might ask how variable the acoustic wave, or the shape of the acoustic tube or its various components, really is in terms human-perceptual abilities. In visual perception, we are often given the example that the information arriving on the retina of the observer's eye regarding the construct "table" varies as a function of distance, size, shape, angle of observation, and so on, to the extent that an almost infinite set of retinal images all result in an observer making the decision "table." Visual stimuli, then, might be described as far more variable than acoustic ones if we compare visual stimuli for something like a table and acoustic stimuli for something like a word. Is it not possible that we are quibbling about an amount of variability in the acoustic wave which really is not especially important to the listener?

This brings me to my final point, which is to simply emphasize the distinctiveness theory proposed by Lindblom in Chapter 23 and in a number of other papers. Basically, Lindblom argues that speakers are as variable as the listeners and speaking conditions allow them to be. Lindblom suggests that we consider three questions which anyone dealing with "phenomena in living organisms" should ask: (1) the question of mechanism (how does it work); (2) the question of adaptation (what does it do for the system); and (3) the question of embryology and evolution (how did it come about). I submit that in dealing with variability in speech production we have only come as far as a partial look at the first of these questions and that we might gain by considering the remaining two. For example, Abbs refers to the work by Lindblom and Sundberg (1971) on tongue and jaw adjustments and notes: "... on the average low vowels will have lower jaw positions associated with them, but given the potential for tongue position to be controlled independently, this character is mutable." In reference to the same work, Lindblom, Chapter 23, goes rather further and states:

> There is no unique combination of values for the position of the jaw and the elevation of the tongue body in producing [i], [a] or [u] since no matter where the jaw is positioned tongue raising can be invoked compensatorily to the appropriate degree to achieve the cross-sectional area function required for these vowels. The automatic derivation of articulatory interpretations of the predicted vowel qualities would accordingly encounter this non-uniqueness were it not for the following conditions on minimal displacement which can be seen as a manifestation of an economy of effort principle: Select that jaw position which would minimize the deviation of the tongue from its neutral position!

Lindblom suggests that from such a rule it follows that "the dimension of opening in vowels arises as a consequence of an interaction between two speech performance constraints: perceptual contrast and articulatory economy," thus approaching the questions of "what does it do for the organism and how did it come about."

Abbs, in stressing that speakers work to produce "perceptually acceptable waveforms," certainly follows the same line of thinking and I only wish here to underscore its importance.

Thus I do not think that research in physiological phonetics is confined to simply describing control variability. Given that once we have begun to answer the questions of mechanism (how much variability and under what conditions?), we can then move on to the questions of adaptation and evolution. This view fits well, I think, with that taken by Abbs; my main point here is to join in a plea for more holistic approaches to issues such as this one of variability.

11 Relative Invariance of Articulatory Movements: An Iceberg Model

Osamu Fujimura
AT&T Bell Laboratories

INTRODUCTION

Recent studies using advanced instrumental techniques have revealed characteristics of articulatory time courses that escape traditional accounts based on concatenated and smoothed (coarticulated) phonetic (segmental) units. A partial model has been proposed which assumes: (1) relatively invariant articulatory movement patterns of the crucial (place-related) articulator (icebergs) for the initial or final part of a syllable based in part on the demisyllabic specifications of constituent distinctive features; (2) loose timing relations between such events of different articulators; (3) the possible involvement of new temporal organization principles such as dissimilation and repulsion as well as smoothing between consecutive gestures by the same articulator; and (4) strong prosodic effects on variable parts between icebergs (Fujimura, 1981b).

Certain transient movements of the articulators were relatively invariant, and these seemed to be related to the identification of occlusive consonants with place distinctions. It was also suggested that identification of these movement patterns provided a new effective means of comparing temporal patterns of different utterances of (partially) comparable phonological forms in different prosodic environments, particularly with respect to phrasing patterns (Fujimura, 1981b).

In this paper I will discuss some characteristics of the icebergs observed in more recent studies with respect to their variability in limited contexts.

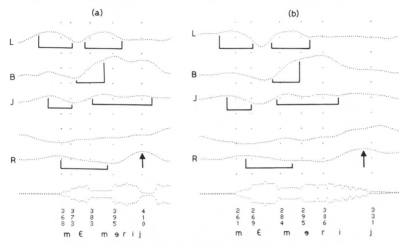

FIG. 11.1.   Comparison of pellet movement patterns for the word 'memory' in a phrase 'memory doesn't' (a), and in isolation (b). *L*: lower lip, *B*: tongue blade, *J*: mandible, *R*: tongue body, all curves representing height as time functions. The unlabelled curve above *R* represents tongue body advancement, and the bottom pattern acoustic signal envelope. Numbers associated with cursors (vertical dot lines) represent frame numbers (about 120 frames per second).

OBSERVATIONS OF ARTICULATORY MOVEMENT PATTERNS

Figure 11.1 compares the word "memory" in a sentence (a) and in isolation (b). The time functions here represent positions of pellets on articulators, as recorded by a computer-controlled x-ray microbeam system (Fujimura, 1973; Kiritani, 1975). The bracketed portions are phenomenologically identified time domains of nearly exact matches (without shifting the curves vertically) between the two utterances for each articulatory dimension. By relating the time values of such matching intervals for individual articulatory dimensions, such as lip height and tongue body front-back movement, between a pair of utterances containing comparable phonetic materials, we can observe an interesting pattern of distortion of temporal structures. In Figure 11.1, for example, the tongue blade movement (labelled *B*) showing a transition from the stressed vowel [ε] to the next apical consonant [r] is almost identical in (a) and (b). But the timing (say, the beginning of the B–bracket) of this event relative to that for matching events in other articulators (say, the beginning of the second L–bracket) is grossly different between the two utterances (a) and (b). That is, in (a), the blade movement precedes the second lip movement considerably (by about 30 msec)[1], whereas in (b), the two movements start simultaneously.

---

[1] The dots composing curves in Figure 11.1 represent time samples, which are about 8 msec apart.

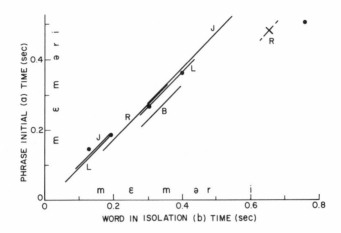

FIG. 11.2. Comparison of timing patterns for corresponding movements. Identical material as in Figure 11.1. Each diagonal line segment
represents the matching part of the curve identified by each of square
braces in Figure 11.1. Dots represent acoustic events (voice onset/offset,
articulatory implosion/explosion).

Figure 11.2 illustrates one way of representing such complex temporal
relations.[2] In this figure, each 45-degree line segment represents the time
stretch for which the movement pattern of the articulator (indicated by the
capital letter) matched. Thus each line segment corresponds to a bracket in
Figure 11.1. Since the relative timing between the two utterances for the
same event (i.e. the bracketed pattern in Figure 11.1) varied from event
to event, not all the line segments fall on a common line in Figure 11.2.
For example, in the middle part of the utterance, the line segments labeled
J (jaw) and B (tongue blade) are about 50 msec apart (horizontally or
vertically). This is a considerable asynchrony in comparison, for example,
with the acoustic duration of the stressed vowel, which is estimated at 80
msec from m–explosion to m–implosion in utterance (a). The jaw gesture in
the beginning of the word is also relatively ahead of the tongue body gesture
(labelled R) for the isolated word utterance.

Unlike the conventional depiction of temporal patterns of speech (such
as concatenated phonetic segments after coarticulatory smoothing), it can
be seen that speech production is inherently multidimensional. It involves
different articulators that move to a significant extent independently of each
other, showing a deviation from the classical notion of the "simultaneous
bundle" of distinctive features. Their phonetic manifestations seem to show

---

[2] A corresponding figure (Figure 3) in Fujimura (1981b) contained some errors which are
corrected here.

considerable variation not only in terms of undershooting, depending on the context, but also in relative timings of events for different articulators.

In general, many corresponding movement patterns are identified as time marks when we compare two utterances of similar phonetic material. For example, the center of each bracket in Figure 11.1 may be used as such a mark for timing comparison. But if we use those time marks as indications of segmental boundaries (as we often do in duration measurements using acoustic events such as voice onset or implosion) we have inconsistent segmental domains depending on the particular articulator we choose. Furthermore, the "distortion" of the segmental patterns is not ascribable to inherent dynamic characteristics of particular articulators. The timing relation observed among a pair of articulators varies in an intricate manner (e.g., due to an apparent repulsion between consecutive gestures by the same articulator), depending on the (articulatory) context (see Fujimura, 1981b).

As we become capable of obtaining abundant data with a quantitative accuracy, due to new observation techniques, we now discover that real phenomena are substantially different from what a simple coarticulatory model might predict based on the distinctive feature matrix representation of phonetic forms. While it makes sense to consider acoustic subsegments for each phonemic segment (Fant 1962), there does not seem to be any justification for the so-called systematic phonetic level of speech description as the output of phonology (Chomsky & Halle 1968a; see for critiques, Dinnsen, 1980; Fujimura, 1970). Unless we 1) consider the looseness of temporal relations between different articulatory dimensions; 2) appropriately construct a multidimensional model of temporal structures; and 3) relate such inherently continuous structures at the concrete level to abstract phonological representations of linguistic forms by a new organization principle of speech, we will not be able to substantiate the validity of linguistically meaningful underlying representations in relation to physical observables.

In addition to assimilatory processes, both of a physical nature (i.e., hard coarticulation) and of a linguistic nature (i.e., soft coarticulation), there seems to be much more to say about reduction and dissimilation in both time (i.e., cohesion/repulsion) and space (Fujimura, 1981b; Fujimura and Lovins 1978). In order to be able to arrive at a correct interpretation of such complex and unknown structures and processes, we must describe phonetic phenomena by a valid and effective framework. The iceberg model, as suggested previously, may provide us with one critical descriptive tool for this approach, or at least exemplify what types of tools we would have to use.[3]

---

[3] Of course, there are other qualitatively invariant phonetic characteristics such as constrictional gestures for obstruents (see Fujimura, Miller & Escolar, 1977).

ICEBERG PATTERNS

The iceberg pattern, a hypothetical elementary gesture, is a relatively invariant articulatory movement pattern (for a given speaker, let us say), into or out of consonantal occlusion, out of or into a specific (perhaps only stressed) syllable nucleus. Such patterns are typically observed in demisyllables (Fujimura, 1976) that involve the particular articulator for an inherent feature that specifies the place of articulation (thus not velum movement, for example).

I refer to demisyllabic context, not because there is a one-to-one correspondence between an iceberg and a demisyllable, but only because, in general, different vowels or additional demisyllabic elements can specify different iceberg patterns for the same occlusive consonant. Some of the matching articulatory movement patterns we observed in Figs. 11.1 and 11.2 (the brackets or short line segments) presumably contain icebergs, but not all of such (coincidental) patterns between a pair of utterances represent icebergs.

The timing of the occurrence of an iceberg pattern presumably is sensitive to its environment, and when it shifts in time, e.g. in another occurrence of the same word in a different phonetic context or prosodic environment, the time shift may not synchronize with or be proportionately related to the time shift for another articulatory movement.

The movement pattern, as observed in the form of time functions representing pellet positions in the x-ray microbeam data, are often remarkably constant, with respect to the absolute position (such as tongue-blade height) and slope, for a portion of the monotonic movement. Such an invariable portion of pattern usually does not include a quasi-stationary position of the articulator. The quasi-stationary position for the vowel, in particular, varies in a very large range, even for the same phoneme in the same phonemic context in its vicinity, if factors such as emphasis, (local) speech rate (depending on syntactic phrasing conditions, for example), or speed of utterance are different. Figure 11.3 compares time functions representing tongue blade height for two utterances of the sentence "It's six five seven America Street," spoken by a female native speaker (with phonetic training) of the Louisiana dialect of American English. One of the utterances (thin line) was spoken with a contrastive emphasis placed on "five," and the other (thick line) with empasis on "seven." It can be seen that the valley representing the stressed vowel is wider and deeper in each of the stressed syllables, showing the emphasis difference. The movement of the tongue blade from [s] to [ε] in the initial demisyllable of [sεv] is shown to be almost exactly the same in a considerable portion of the downward movement. Since the depth of the valley varies greatly, the lowest part of the transition tends to vary more than the uppermost part; but, it is often true that the top part of the transition close

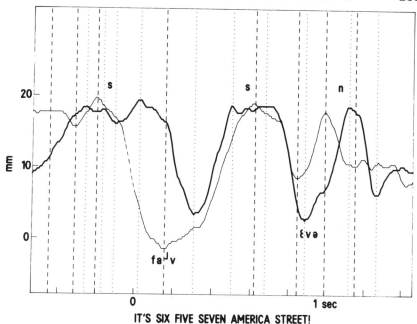

IT'S SIX FIVE SEVEN AMERICA STREET!

FIG. 11.3. Part of the sentence "It's six five seven America Street" as observed in two utterances, (a) with contrastive emphasis placed on "seven" (thick line), (b) with emphasis on "five" (thin line). The ordinate represents tongue blade height, the abscissa, time. Vertical lines dotted for (a) and broken for (b) delimit monotonic (upward or downward) movements, for each of which an automatic comparison procedure was used to find an iceberg region. This display shows a horizontal position adjustment giving rise to a good match of the two curves in the initial demisyllable [sɛ] of "seven."

to the consonantal occlusion, observed as the height of the pellet slightly behind the tongue tip, also varies fairly significantly.

Figure 11.4 shows the variability of the curves representing entire monotonic movement patterns for nine samples of the same initial demisyllable. The sample utterances had the emphasis placed on different words in the sentence, and two of the curves (thick lines) had the word "seven," containing the pertinent stressed syllable, emphasized. The individual curves are shifted along the time scale horizontally (but not vertically) automatically by an algorithm, so that the agreement between each curve and one reference curve (that was selected from the set of utterances to optimize the agreement) is maximized within an empirically determined range of height (given by the two thin horizontal lines). The utterance chosen as the reference is represented by a broken line in Figure 11.4. We have analyzed a number of tongue-blade movement patterns involving apical occlusive consonants, and found a portion of each transitional movement to be fairly stable.

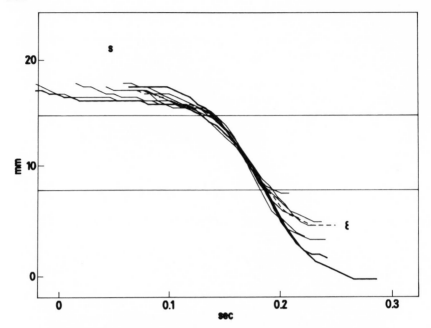

FIG. 11.4.   The [sɛ]–movement patterns for tongue-blade height recorded in nine utterances, two of which had emphasis on "seven" (thick lines).
An automatic algorithm was used to choose one of the curves as the reference, with which all others were compared in terms of the vertical distance,
time sample by time sample, so that every curve is horizontally positioned
appropriately to yield a minimum overall (square sum) distance between
the curves. The distance measure was evaluated over an "iceberg" range of
vertical position, indicated here by the horizontal lines as delimiters. The
"iceberg" region was determined automatically for each of demisyllables
(on things alike showing monotonic movement) by an independent algorithm using the same set of curves, and was defined as the region within
which all pairs of curves, when positioned optimally with respect to each
other, showed relatively small distance (according to a certain statistical
criterion). An optimal choice of the reference curve (shown by the broken
line) was made by comparing the results of trying different curves as the
reference.

The variation in terms of pellet height for all time samples within such (automatically) identifiable iceberg regions was found to be an order of magnitude
smaller than a comparable measure of variation for the minimum height for
stressed vowels, and about one third of that for the maximum height for the
consonantal occlusion, in the material of similar forms spoken by the same
speaker. Other microbeam material obtained from the same and different
speakers is being analyzed.

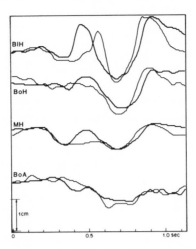

FIG. 11.5. Comparison of two sets of time functions representing (from top) tongue blade height (BlH), tongue-body height (BoH), mandible height (MH), and tongue-body advancement (BoA). One utterance, shown in thick lines, represented a nonexisting phrase "bet aught" which was actually pronounced with an alveolar stop in the intervocalic position (without a specific instruction to do so), and the other, shown in thin lines, "bed aught" actually pronounced with a "flap" (tap; see Laferriere, 1982 for some details). The relative horizontal positioning was adjusted approximately to minimize the overall difference between the two sets of time functions for the mandible and the tongue-body dimensions.

Figure 11.5 represents a comparison between a stop version and a (so-called) flap version of the intervocalic apical stop produced by the same speaker (Louisiana dialect of American English) in isolated word (or phrase) utterances, revealing free variation. The material included nonexisting English phrases [bɛtɔ:t] and [bɛɾɔ:t]. A moderate match can be obtained between the two cases with respect to the gross pattern, except for two major differences. The first difference is in the jaw and tongue-body movements. Both articulators (MH and BoH) show a significant rising gesture for the true stop but not for the flap, as discussed by Laferriere (1982). (There is also some concomitant difference in tongue-body advancement, BoA). The second point pertains to a gross difference in timing of the vertical movements of the tongue blade. The tongue-blade gesture (BlH) may be interpreted as containing two relatively invariant movement patterns (i.e. [ɛt] and [tɔ] icebergs) that are common to the two allophonic versions of the consonant, but the timing pattern, both in their average timing with respect to other articulator's movements and the timings of the two transitions relative to each other, is considerably different.

Whether this variability is of continuous or discrete nature is an interesting question for future investigation. It may shed some light on the nature of phonetically meaningful constituent elements of units such as syllables, and hence what kind of units should be useful for a phonological representation if the phonetic realization rules are to be as transparent and as natural as we would like them to be. One possible answer may be, for example, that the constituent units are a set of distinctive features (stop, labial, tense, spirant, lateral, low, spread) for a demisyllable ([spla]), and the realization rule, in part, relates a subset of the features (labial, lateral, low, spread) to its characteristic iceberg pattern for (lower) lip movement. Obviously, there remains much to be studied, even if this speculation were totally correct, since we do not know how other subsets of features are to be specified in terms of their phonetic realizations, and also how the time function of lip or tongue tip/blade movement is to be generated between icebergs.

Ray D. Kent: The Iceberg Hypothesis:
The Temporal Assembly of Speech Movements

ICEBERGS: SOLIDS IN A SEA OF VARIABILITY?

Osamu Fujimura's paper on the "Relative Invariance of Articulatory Movements" represents a venture toward the identification of the basic elements of speech production. He proposes the existence of iceberg patterns, or hypothetical elementary gestures, that occur as relatively invariant articulatory movements, "into or out of consonantal occlusion, out of or into a specific syllable nucleus (and a glide)." These gestures are most readily observed in the context of demisyllables, for which a given articulator represents an inherent feature specifying place of articulation.

I've used the term "relative invariance" myself, and usually with a certain uneasiness, perhaps because I'm not sure of the observational difference between something that is relatively *invariant* and something that is only modestly *variant*. The implication seems to be that all of the elements we use to describe speech movements are variant to some degree (after all, what isn't?), and it is the difference in degree that helps to identify the relative invariances in speech.

ICEBERGS AND ICE CUBES: ADDITIONAL EVIDENCE OF
TEMPORAL INVARIANCE IN SPEECH

Some time ago, Ken Moll and I (Kent & Moll, 1972) evaluated the hypothesis that movements of the tongue body along a particular trajectory within the vocal tract (or movements using a particular combination of muscle contractions) were highly

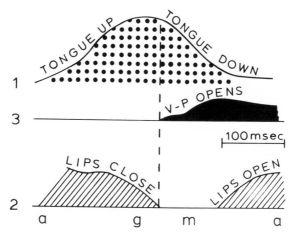

FIG. 11a.1. Movement patterns of tongue dorsum (1), lips (2), and velopharynx (3) during production of [agma].

regular in form even when they served different phonetic ends. For example, we proposed that the tongue-body movement underlying the transition from vowel [i] to vowel [a] was essentially the same whether the tongue-body movement was contained in an utterance like "he honored" or in an utterance like "he monitored." That is, we expected that the tongue body motion would be unaffected by the presence or absence of an intervocalic consonant. Although not all of the data for each speaker confirmed this expectation, the general result was that a given tongue-body movement could in fact have essentially the same dynamic properties whether it underlay a direct vowel-to-vowel transition or such a transition occurring transconsonantally.

One outcome of this study was the demonstration of what has become a frequently replicated regularity in articulation, viz., the principle that velocity of articulatory movement is determined by the distance to be traversed and by the transition time allotted for the manner of production. This brings up one question about the iceberg model. Are the icebergs to be thought of as individually retrievable elementary motor responses or as movements that are shaped according to general rules of motor regulation? Studies of stress variations (Kent & Netsell, 1972) have shown that individual movements for a phonetic transition are modified by stress contrast, again according to the general rule that velocity is related to the magnitude of the movement to be made. Are icebergs reflections of such general rules or are they more akin to phenomena such as "fixed-motor responses" or "modal-action patterns" in the ethology literature?

A very simple hypothesis concerning consonantal gestures is that a basic movement pattern for one consonant can be inserted along with movements for other consonants into movement sequences for a variety of phonetic combinations. For example, the movements in the nonsense utterance [agma] could be formed by appropriate sequencing of the basic component movements identified in the simpler phonetic combinations [aga] and [ama]. The VCNV utterance [agma], as illus-

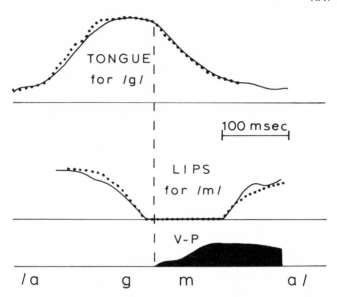

FIG. 11a.2.   Solid lines show movement patterns of tongue dorsum, lips, and velopharynx during [agma]. Dotted lines show tongue dorsum movements from [aga] and labial movements from [aba] superimposed on movement data for [agma].

trated in Figure 11a.1, contains a dorsal consonantal movement (1), and a bilabial movement (2), combined with an appropriately timed velopharyngeal action (3). To test this hypothesis, we can take the consonant gestures from [aga] and [ama] and superimpose them, with appropriate timing adjustments, on the actual articulations observed for [agma]. Cinefluorographic data for one speaker are shown in Figure 11a.2. The solid lines indicate the movements for [agma], and the dotted lines show the movements recorded for [aga] and [aba](which I had to use because [ama] was not part of the speech sample for this subject). The superimposed movement records are highly similar, even to the point of having the same duration of constriction and essentially the same rates of movement.

Results for another utterance are shown in Figure 11a.3. The solid lines show the movements for the utterance [inpi], and the dotted lines illustrate the corresponding lingual and labial gestures from [idi] and [ipi]. The conclusion follows that the basic consonantal gestures recorded from VCV utterances can be assembled to match closely the movement patterns for a VCCV utterance. The individual gestures of the tongue and lips may not qualify as icebergs, but they at least begin to look like ice cubes. I prefer to call them stereotypic articulatory movements (SAMs).

Not every speaker showed such a close within-subject fit of the data, primarily because of differences in the constriction duration or in the velocity of the approach to closure for the second consonant in a VCCV utterance. Notice that in Figure 11a.4 the tongue-tip closing movement for [t] is more gradual than the release movement for the same sound. Some speakers adjust the rate of movement

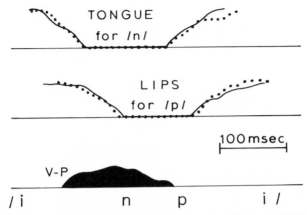

FIG. 11a.3. Solid lines show movement patterns of tongue tip, lips, and velopharynx during [inpi]. Dotted lines show tongue tip movements from [idi] and labial movements from [ipi] superimposed on movement data for [inpi].

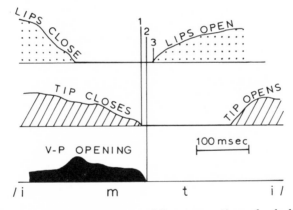

FIG. 11a.4. Movement patterns of lips, tongue tip, and velopharynx during production of [imti].

so that movements occurring during a period of vocal tract closure are slower than a corresponding movement made during an unobstructed period. Still, these subtleties do not detract from the result shown earlier—that a speaker can assemble the movements for an utterance like [agma] from the "pieces" (SAMs) contained in simpler utterances like [aga] and [ama]. A further condition of generality is that a gesture for a nasal consonant highly resembles that for a homorganic voiced stop and is quite similar to that for a homorganic voiceless stop.

Figure 11a.4 also illustrates another important feature of articulation in consonant sequences. Note that three events occur within about 20-30 msec: (1) the achievement of lingua-alveolar closure for [t]; (2) the accomplishment of velopharyngeal closure marking the nasal-nonnasal boundary between the [m] and [t] segments; and (3) the opening of the lips marking the release of [m]. Such intervals of closely timed movements were observed for both VCNV and VNCV utterances. Sometimes there was a virtual simultaneity (at least within the sampling error of the 100 fps time base) of three or more articulatory events. Figure 11a.1 shows an apparent simultaneity of lingual, labial, and velar movements in production of the utterance [agma]. At the instant marked by the vertical broken line the tongue lowers from dorsal closure, the velopharynx opens, and the lips close for [m]. We have reported similar data on timing precision for three-element consonant sequences (Kent & Moll, 1975), in which articulatory events were reliably timed to occur within 10–30 msec of one another. These points of nearly simultaneous articulatory adjustments may be critical hingepoints in the timing plan of speech, because they contain the essential information for timing control of the various movements in the sequence.

For example, to synthesize an [agma] utterance from the basic consonant gestures taken from [aga] and [ama], one needs only to align the two basic movements (SAMs) so that labial closure is achieved as the dorsal constriction is broken. Velopharyngeal opening is timed to begin at approximately the same instant. The articulatory patterns described for VC_1C_2V utterances are consistent with Repp's (1983a) experiment showing that the release burst for C_1 contained information that listeners were able to use in identifying C_2. Repp's result demonstrates that the coarticulation in VCCV sequences has perceptual consequences.

Of course, you don't get very far in life saying things like [agma]. You've got to be able to say things like "Joe took father's shoebench out," "We were away a year ago," or "Next Monday morning, bring three tents for the camping trip." Figure 11a.5 displays for the last declaration data for vertical displacements of a pellet on the lingual dorsum, vertical displacements of a pellet sutured to the knee of the velum, and interlabial distance (mouth opening) measured in the midagittal plane. The phoneme symbols locate salient events in the phonetic string. The actual movement data (smoothed) are shown by the broken lines; the solid lines are best fits using half-cycles of sinusoids. Although the sinusoidal fit is not everywhere exact, the match is quite close for many of the gestures. The sinusoids are simplifications of the actual movements and are intended to model the relative timing of the movements but not the details of amplitude or degree of symmetry. One might think of the sinusoid half-cycles as first-order input to a computer simulation of the speech movements.

Inspection of Figure 11a.5 indicates that velocity constraints are not uniform across articulators. Whereas the dorsal elevating gesture for [k], [ŋ], and [i] has a nearly symmetric shape with nearly equal velocities across occurrences, the gestures of velar elevation are slightly less symmetric and possess different velocities across occurrences. Lip movements are variably symmetric but there seems to be a tendency toward equal velocities for equivalent opening or closing movements.

The stylization of the movement pattern is carried one step further in Figure 11a.6. I want to focus on the events marked by circled symbols. First, compare the relative timing of tongue elevation and velar elevation for the [k] at the left of the figure and the [k] at the right. In the [k] at the left, the two elevating gestures virtually coincide. But for the [k] at the right, which is immediately followed by

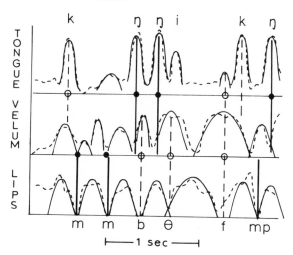

FIG. 11a.5. Movement patterns of tongue dorsum, velum, and lips during production of the sentence "Next Monday morning, bring three tents for the camping trip." The smoothed movement data (broken lines) are fitted with half-cycle sinusoids. The phonetic symbols indicate selected points in the utterance, and the vertical lines serve as alignment references to compare timing of movements.

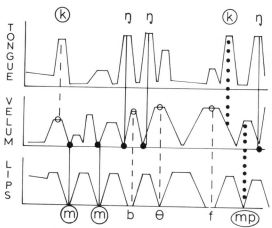

FIG. 11a.6. Stylized movements (derived from the data in Figure 11a.5) showing the timing of articulations of the tongue dorsum, velum, and lips. Attention is drawn to the timing of oral and velar articulations for the circled phonetic symbols. The vertical lines are for alignment reference in comparing the timing of the articulations. Stylized curves were obtained by fitting straight lines to the data curves in Figure 11a.5.

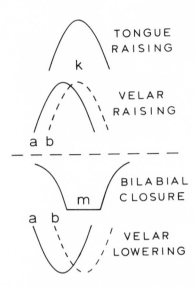

FIG. 11a.7. Timing patterns of oral and velar articulations for [k] segments adjacent to nasal (a) or nonnasal (b) segments (top half) and [m]
segments adjacent to nonnasal (a) or nasal (b) segments (bottom half).

a nasal vowel and consonant in the word *camping*, the maximum elevation of the
tongue is achieved even while the velum is in mid-descent (in fact at the instant
of maximum velocity for the lowering gesture). The same general principle applies
to the timing of velar movement with lip closure for the nasal [m]. Whereas the
two [m] sounds at the left of the figure are characterized by coincidence of velar
lowering and bilabial closure, the bilabial closure for the [mp] combination at the
right occurs during a movement of velar elevation. Similar results can be seen
in the data of Moll and Daniloff (1971) and Kent, Carney, and Severeid (1974).
Obviously, velar movement is variably timed with respect to an associated tongue
or lip movement that forms a nasal or nonnasal consonant.

But the variability in timing is not continuous nor unprincipled. As shown in
Figure 11a.7, the velar-elevating gesture in association with the tongue movement
for [k] usually occurs at one or the other of two times—either in approximate
simultaneity or in advance of the tongue movement. Similarly, the velar-lowering
gesture in association with the bilabial closure for [m] either is virtually coincident
with the tongue movement, or in advance of it. The difference between the two
patterns depends on characteristics of the articulation for the following segment.

I conclude that the articulatory movements in long and phonetically complex
sequences might be modeled using basic component gestures identified in simple
utterances. However, the component movements for a given phonetic target must
be correctly timed with respect to the phonetic context. Acceptable timing relations
are few and seem to be specified with respect to movement onsets, offsets, or velocity
maxima. Examples of these temporal patterns are shown in Figure 11a.8 which

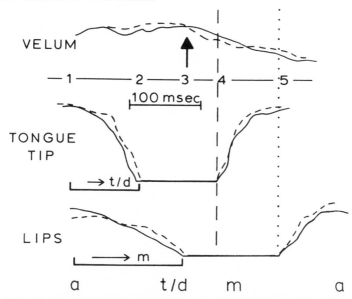

FIG. 11a.8. Movements of velum, tongue tip, and lips during production of the utterances [adma] (solid lines) and [atma] (broken lines).

depicts articulatory movements for the utterances [adma] and [atma]. At the time
points indicated by the numbers 1–5, the articulations are organized as follows: (1)
beginning of the closing movements for both the tongue tip ([d] or [t]) and lips ([m]);
(2) achievement of lingua-alveolar closure for [d] or [t]; (3) achievement of bilabial
closure for [m] and beginning of descent of velum for [m]; (4) release of lingua-
alveolar closure for [d] or [t], which occurs at about mid-descent of the velum; (5)
release of bilabial closure for [m] and completion of lingua-alveolar release for [d]
or [t].

I am sympathetic with Fujimura's search for iceberg patterns, and I believe as
he does that speech production represents a coupling of stereotypic movements
in a liquid environment shaped largely by prosodic factors. The icebergs may be
optimized movement patterns from the point of view of physical economy (Nelson,
1983) and ease of combination into complex movement sequences. It is interesting
that the movement patterns typical of normal speech deteriorate in subjects with
apraxia of speech (Kent & Rosenbek, 1983). The apraxic speakers appear to have
discoordinated movements and a tendency toward longer movement times. These
abnormalities increase in severity with increases in utterance length or complexity.
The temporal distortions that arise in neuropathologies such as apraxia of speech
or ataxic dysarthria indicate that iceberg patterns are not physiologically fixed but
rather are optimized movements for the normal conditions of speech production.

The final point I want to emphasize is that the most important invariance at
the articulatory level may be the basic successional patterns of movement. Certain
combinations of movements in any phonetic string are precisely and reliably timed.

Correct timing is required to produce the critical cues that establish the event code of the acoustic-speech signal. After all, speech is not generated as a linear sequence of equally probable discrete units. Rather, it is a relational pattern in which cue salience is peculiar to the individual phonetic transitions.

James H. Abbs: Comment

As noted in Chapter 10, at one time we (Abbs, Netsell, & Hixon, 1971) also examined speech movement dynamics with the expectation that articulatory velocity and acceleration might be less variable than articulatory position. Our procedure involved the implementation of analog differentiators and examining the time history of velocity and acceleration as well as quantification of the peak values of these derivatives. The data which were presented in 1971 indicated that absolute values of peak velocity and acceleration were as variable as displacement. There was, however, a tendency for a relative invariance in the velocity and acceleration waveform shapes. On this basis we entertained an early version of an "iceberg" model, part of which was presented at the City University of New York Graduate Center in 1972 (Abbs, 1972). This notion was not pursued beyond those initial analyses, primarily because of the lack of enthusiasm with which it was received at that time and the discouraging data noted above.

12 Temporal Invariance in the Production of Speech

Katherine S. Harris[†], Betty Tuller[‡], and J. A. Scott Kelso[‡‡]
Haskins Laboratories
New Haven, CT

A common way of describing speech, or any other kind of movement, is to attribute the output to the execution of a motor plan, into which some form of movable element is slotted. Of course, the argument for the existence of such a plan is circular. The fact that an orderly sequence of movements occurs leads to the assumption that there exists a representation at some level in the nervous system for that sequence. For example, the difference between perceptually fluent and dysfluent speech is attributed to the orderly or disorderly functioning of a speech plan. Thus, the order and regularity we observe in the real world is invested in an inaccessible construct; we make no explanatory gains by adopting such a strategy.

A parallel approach to the study of speech output is to presume that a representation of the static units of phonological description is buried somewhere in it, somehow extracted by the listener by cognitive reshuffling of a migrating feature matrix. To us, it seems more parsimonious to assume that the units of this phonology as they emerge in time exist in the acoustic signal structured, as it is, by the movements of the articulators. In such an approach, we make systematic observations of the properties of speech output when it is naturally manipulated by the speaker, in an attempt to construct a picture of the way speech is produced. In this way, we hope to understand those dimensions of speaking that remain invariant under speech-relevant transformations and those that change. Of course, finding any kind

---

[†] Also Graduate Center, City University of New York.

[‡] Also Cornell University Medical College

[‡‡] Also Departments of Psychology and Biobehavioral Sciences, Univ. of Connecticut.

of invariant in speech has been notoriously difficult. Early work at Haskins Laboratories (e.g., Liberman, Cooper, Shankweiler & Studdert-Kennedy, 1967; MacNeilage & DeClerk, 1969) underscored the problem in both the acoustic and physiologic domain; suprasegmental variables (such as prosodic variations and changes in speaking rate), as well as coarticulatory effects, were shown to affect the acoustic and physiologic realization of the segment. For example, when a consonant-vowel-consonant (CVC) syllable is spoken with primary stress, the muscle activity associated with production of the vowel is of longer duration and greater amplitude than it would be in an unstressed environment. The acoustic duration of the stressed vowel is also longer and the formant frequencies more extreme, than when the same vowel is produced without primary stress. Thus, although the metrics of speech shift constantly, perceptual identity is somehow preserved.

In our work, we hoped that by applying two transformations that are believed to be particularly important for speech—changing syllable stress and speaking rate—we might uncover motoric variables, or relations among variables, that remain unaltered. We have, up to now, performed three experiments, using much the same paradigm. Most of these results have been reported elsewhere (Tuller, Kelso & Harris, 1982a, b, 1983). In the present paper, we will present new data which indicates the generalizability of our approach across articulators.

We approached the problem initially by examining electromyographic (EMG) and acoustic recordings of speakers' productions of utterances in which syllable stress and speaking rate were orthogonally varied. Native speakers of English produced two-syllable utterances of the form pV1pV2p, where Vn was either [i] or [a]. Each utterance was spoken with primary stress placed on either the first or second syllable. The subjects read lists of these utterances at two self-selected speaking rates, "slow" (conversational) and "fast."

When subjects increased speaking rate or decreased syllable stress, the acoustic duration of their utterances decreased as expected, and the magnitude and duration of activity in individual muscles changed markedly. In general, EMG activity was of longer duration and greater magnitude for production of stressed than unstressed syllables. EMG activity was of shorter duration or increased amplitude in syllables spoken quickly compared with those spoken slowly (Tuller, Harris, & Kelso, 1982). Given that there were considerable changes in the absolute duration and magnitude of individual muscle events, we reasoned that there must be some stability in the internal relations between muscle events that underlie the phonetic percept. That is, to the extent that invariances exist, they must be relational in character (Kelso, 1981).

In this regard, it is interesting that for many different skilled activities including handwriting, chewing, and bimanual coordination (see Kelso, Tuller &

Harris, 1983, for review), it is the internal timing relations that are preserved over such transformations as rate and force changes. In the speech experiments, we asked whether the feature of invariant relative timing, specifically the phase relations among internal events, is also an appropriate characterization of speech production.

A first pass at this strategy might be to define a vowel-to-vowel cycle and examine the timing of events associated with intermediate consonants in relation to this cycle. This particular measure may be pertinent to Fowler's (1977) proposal that the vocalic cycle plays an important organizing role in speech production and perception. The stability of this relation can then be compared to other possible measures such as the latency of onset of activity for a vowel in relation to flanking consonants. In our first experiment, we found one very consistent result, namely, an invariant linear relationship between duration of the vocalic cycle (the interval between onsets of muscle activity for successive vowels) and the latency of medial consonant related muscle activity relative to the first vowel. Other possible relationships such as those based on consonant cycles did not show the same degree of stability. There is no need to assume that vowel- and consonant-related activity change by the same or proportional amounts; indeed, they do not usually do so.

The linear relationship results because the small changes in duration of consonant-related activity are correlated with the relatively larger changes in duration of vowel-related activity, when we examine ensemble averages for the two rate and stress conditions. While the same relations should hold across individual tokens within stress and rate conditions, we cannot examine this point in detail using electromyographic data because it is not always possible to define onsets and offsets in individual repetition tokens of an utterance (see Baer, Bell-Berti & Tuller [1979], for a discussion of temporal measures of individual versus averaged EMG records). For these and other reasons, we performed a similar experiment in which articulator movement trajectories were measured (Tuller, Kelso & Harris, 1982b; Tuller & Kelso, 1984). The movement kinematics also can be analyzed on a token-by-token basis.

Briefly, in this kinematic study, four subjects produced utterances of the form [bVCab] where V was either [a] or [æ] and C was from the set of labial consonants [p, b, v, w]. Again, each utterance was spoken with two stress patterns and at two self-selected speaking rates. Ten to twelve repetitions were produced of each utterance type. Articulatory movements in the up–down direction were monitored by an optoelectronic device which tracked the movement of lightweight, infrared, light-emitting diodes attached to the subjects' lips and jaw.

First, we asked the original question about stress and rate variations; does the interval from vowel onset to consonant onset change systematically as a function of a vowel-to-vowel period? To this end, correlations were computed between the period from the onset of jaw lowering for the first vowel to the

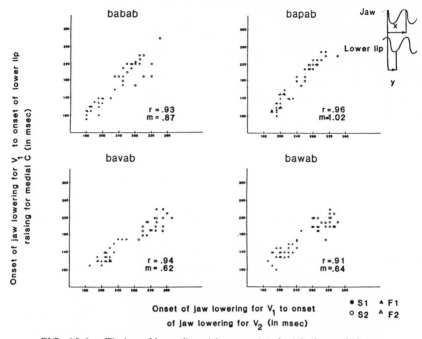

FIG. 12.1. Timing of lower-lip raising associated with the medial consonant relative to jaw-lowering gestures for the flanking vowels. The "period" and "latency," measured as shown in the upper righthand corner of the figure, are plotted on the x and y axes, respectively. In this figure and those following, S1 corresponds to utterances with primary stress on the first syllable, spoken at a slow (conversational) rate; S2 are utterances with stress on the second syllable, spoken at a slow rate; F1 and F2 correspond to utterances with stress on the first or second syllable, respectively, spoken at a faster rate.

onset of jaw lowering for the second vowel and the interval between the onset of jaw lowering for the first vowel and the onset of consonant-specific movement (that is, a close movement analogue of our earlier EMG measure). In separate analyses, the onset of movement for the medial labial consonant was defined either by the onset of upper-lip lowering or by the onset of lower-lip raising (independent of simultaneous jaw movements). Each correlation was based on 35 to 48 data points.

Figures 12.1 and 12.2 show the data plots with the values of r and the slopes for a linear regression for four utterance types, [bapab], [babab], [bawab], and [bavab] produced by two speakers. The measure of consonant production in this case was the latency of lower-lip raising (independent of jaw movement). The r values do not vary systematically with consonant, nor are they affected by a different measure of consonant latency based on upper-lip lowering. For the various measures analyzed so far, the Pearson

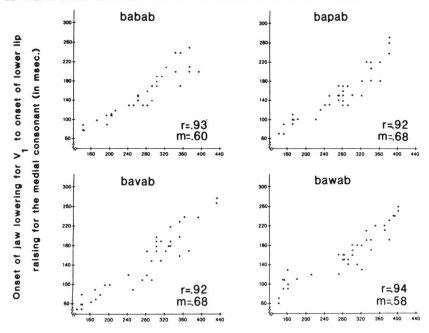

Onset of jaw lowering for V₁ to onset of jaw lowering for V₂ (in msec.)

FIG. 12.2.   Timing of lower-lip raising associated with the medial consonant relative to jaw-lowering gestures for the flanking vowels. Data presented are from a different subject than shown in Figure 12.1.

product-moment correlation values range from $+.84$ to $+.97$ across all four subjects. While the values of m show a trend towards flatter slopes, and thus, earlier onsets for [v] and [w] as compared to [p] and [b], the ordering of slopes is not identical across all four subjects. These kinematic results, obtained from individual repetitions of each utterance type, essentially mirror our earlier EMG findings which were based on utterance ensemble averages.[1]

While these results are interesting, the experiment has a conspicuous flaw. That is, we have not examined the behavior of one of the most important articulators, the tongue, and, for that reason, we have been restricted to examining phone strings in which lips and jaw are primarily involved. We were very grateful to the staff of the Institute of Logopedics and Phoniatrics, and to Osamu Fujimura and the staff at Bell Laboratories, for an opportunity to use the X-ray microbeam system at the University of Tokyo for a third experiment in which we were able to monitor tongue motion as well as lip

---

[1] This work is described in experimental detail in a paper "The timing of articulatory gestures: A relational invariants approach," 1984, *Journal of the Acoustical Society of America*, *76*, 1030–1036.

pi PAP   (conversational rate)

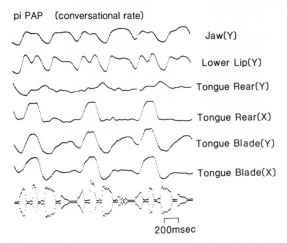

FIG. 12.3.   Representative X-ray display for three tokens of the utterance [pi'pap].

and jaw movement, and to process the results at Bell. In this experiment,
a single speaker repeated the nonsense utterances [pipap], [papip], [pitap],
[pidap], [pikap], and [pigap]. Each utterance, surrounded by schwas, was
repeated about five times at slow and fast rates with the first or second
syllable stressed.

Figure 12.3 shows the output display for one of the utterances of the
experiment, [pi'pap]. In the lower trace is an envelope of the acoustic signal
for three successive tokens of the utterance. The two lowest traces show the
vertical (By) and horizontal (Bx) positions, respectively, of a pellet on the
blade of the tongue as a function of time. Above them are traces of the x and
y coordinates of a pellet on the rear of the tongue, Rx and Ry. The top two
traces show the vertical movement for the lower lip (Ly) and jaw (Jy). The
outputs shown have been subjected to a smoothing program and adjusted for
overall head movement by subtracting the movement of a reference pellet.

We followed our previous strategy of identifying movement onsets for
events associated with the second and third vowels, and with the intervocalic
consonant. In general, onsets were defined from points when the signal began
to depart from zero velocity. A special problem arose with the fast speaking rate utterances; the subject spoke so rapidly that successive utterances
were continuously produced. In some cases, the subject did not articulate
unstressed vowels, or altered the phonetic pattern of the utterance, resulting
in the loss of a few data points.

The measurement of vowel- and consonant-related articulator movement
required some thought. First, we needed traces with as many well-defined
points of zero velocity as possible, over the entire set of four stress-rate conditions. Second, our present model requires the unequivocal separation of

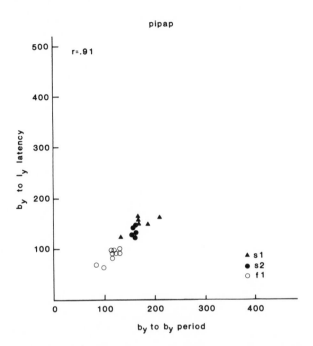

FIG. 12.4. Timing of lower lip movement (Ly) associated with the medial consonant latency relative to tongue-blade movements (By) for the flanking vowels (period) in [papip].

consonant- and vowel-related activity. In observations of tongue movement trajectories, this distinction is hard to make because the tongue rides on the jaw. It is possible to separate tongue and jaw components of tongue movement by assuming a simple hinge movement for the jaw in speech and subtracting the presumed jaw contribution from the pellet trajectories (Edwards, Harris & Tuller, 1983). (We recognize that this model is inadequate since the jaw exhibits both translatory and rotatory movements.) When this subtraction was performed, we found that the X-ray microbeam pellet placements were too far behind the tip for unequivocal association with the tongue tip gesture for [t] and [d]. On occasion, there were possible alternative "movement onsets" which were equivalent on casual inspection. For example, for two tongue pellets there are both x and y trajectories. For each such case, all possible definitions of movement onset were examined. In the description of results that follows, we use the definition that led to the highest correlation.

Figure 12.4 shows the relationship between the tongue-blade movements for the vowel-to-vowel interval and the latency of consonant-associated movement of the lower lip for the four conditions of [pipap]. The abscissa shows

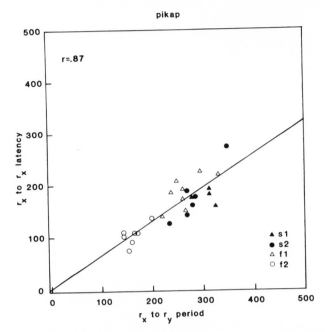

FIG. 12.5. Timing of tongue rear movement backward (Rx) associated with the medial consonant [k] relative to tongue rear movements, forward (Rx) for [i] and downward (Ry) for [a] in [pikap].

the "period" interval between the onset of tongue-blade movement up for the [i], and the onset of blade movement down for [a]. The ordinate shows the time from the movement of the tongue down for the first vowel to the upward movement of the lower lip for the [p]. The distribution of points along the period axis is as expected, with slow utterances at the long end, fast utterances at the short end, and substantial overlap across all conditions. In Figure 12.4, there are no points for fast speech, second syllable stressed, because in this condition, tongue movements were continuous and no points of zero velocity (inflection points) could be determined.

Figure 12.5 shows the results for [pikap]. Notice that we have changed the abscissa; in this case, the period is defined as the time from the movement of the rear tongue pellet forward for [i] to the beginning of the movement downward for [a]. On the ordinate is shown the latency of rear tongue pellet movement backward for [k] relative to the beginning of its movement forward for [i]. The latency-period correlation in this case is .85.

Figure 12.6 shows the same measures for [pigap], with a resulting correlation of .87. The two figures for [k] and [g] can be superimposed indicating that the slope of the regression lines are almost identical ($m = .66$ for [k] and $m = .70$ for [g]).

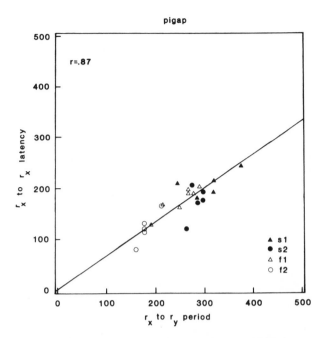

FIG. 12.6.   Timing of tongue rear movement backward (Rx) associated with the medial consonant [g] relative to tongue rear movements forward (Rx) and downward (Ry) for the flanking vowels in [pigap].

The preliminary results of the X-ray microbeam study appear to complement the earlier EMG data and kinematic work. Before offering an interpretation of these results, however, let us mention some caveats regarding the current methodology. First, not only is the phonetic corpus we have examined for tongue movements extremely limited, but, with the X-ray microbeam data, we have problems identifying appropriate points of movement onset using the criterion of zero velocity. This is especially so in cases of rapid articulation, in which tongue movement is often continuous without obvious changes in direction. Clearly we have to come to grips with this methodological problem before we can appropriately describe natural speech. Nevertheless, it should be pointed out that if we define vowel-to-vowel, and vowel-to-consonant relations with regard to the earliest indication of movement, in any dimension of movement, in any relevant articulator, the correlations observed are high. The important point is that the same event be measured in all stress-rate conditions.

Second, we have only looked at phonetically simple strings—single consonants between two fairly robust vowels. Moreover, in all cases the subjects produced the intervocalic consonants in syllable-initial form. If the syllable-final form were used, the interarticulator relations might change. The model says nothing at this time about the vowel affiliation of the consonant, or about the relationships among measures presumed to be associated with the same phone.

In spite of these limitations, the view that a significant articulatory event is the vowel-to-vowel period and that consonant events are temporally related to such periods is appealing as a coherent way of understanding temporal organization. This view is supported by the literature on compensatory shortening and coarticulation. For example, it is well known that intervocalic consonants shorten the measured acoustic duration of the surrounding vowels (e.g., Lindblom & Repp, 1973). This may mean that all aspects of the articulation of vowels are produced in shorter time periods when consonants follow them. Alternatively, it may mean that the consonants and vowels are produced in concert, with the trailing edges of the vowels progressively "overlaid," as it were, by the consonants (Fowler, 1981a). An articulatory organization of this sort was first proposed by Öhman (1966) to explain the changes in formant transitions for intervocalic consonants as a function of the flanking vowels. More recent articulatory evidence that the influence of both preceding and following vowels is apparent throughout the intervocalic consonant (Barry & Kuenzel, 1975; Butcher & Weiher, 1976; Gay, 1977; Harris & Bell-Berti, 1984; Sussman, MacNeilage & Hanson, 1973) might also be interpreted as indicating a significant vowel-to-vowel articulatory period.

In conclusion, we are convinced that these data are compatible with a style of motor organization in which the relative timing among individual electromyographic or kinematic events is preserved in the face of scalar changes in, for example, absolute duration and amplitude of EMG activity or articulator displacement and velocity (for reviews see Kelso, 1981; Kelso, Tuller & Harris, 1983). In fact we believe, with Bernstein (1967), that the behavior of muscles and joints during coordinated activity is best understood as a partitioning of variables into two classes; those that can effect scalar changes in a behavior and those that preserve its internal temporal topology. Temporal invariance across scalar variation may be a design feature of all motor systems and may constitute a natural solution to the problem of coordinating complex systems, like speech, that possess many degrees of freedom.

ACKNOWLEDGMENTS

This work was supported by NINCDS grant NS–13617, US Office of Naval Research Contract No. N00014–83–C–0083, and BRS Grant RR–05596 to Haskins Laboratories, and by NINCDS grant NS–17778 to Cornell University Medical College. We are indebted to Jan Edwards for processing and analyzing the X-ray data reported here. We would like to thank Carol Fowler for her helpful comments.

Peter F. MacNeilage: Comment

In 1971, Kent and Netsell first made the observation that the timing of the onsets of particular articulatory events relative to others may remain invariant across changes in other articulatory parameters. They observed, for example, that regardless of whether stress was placed on the first or second syllable of the word "escort," jaw and lip movements for the second vowel began at about the same time relative to the duration of the [sk] cluster. Jaw movement began at about the time of [k] release and lip movement began about midway through the cluster.

The contribution of Chapter 12 and three other related papers by these authors (Tuller, Kelso & Harris, 1982, 1983, 1984) is to thoroughly document these temporal invariance effects for one particular situation. They have found, in nonsense utterances of the form "that's a $C_1V_1C_2V_2C_3$ again," that the onset latency of C_2 with respect to V_1 is very highly correlated with the V_1-V_2 interval across utterances in which speaking rate and syllable stress location was varied. On the other hand, temporal invariance was not observed in other measures such as EMG peaks or offsets, or V_1 onset in relation to the C_1-C_2 interval.

As the authors note, one of the significant implications of their findings is that speech shares an organizational scheme with many other forms of coordinated activity—e.g. locomotion and certain kinds of bimanual coordination. This is as it should be, although it is only recently that speech has begun to be viewed in the context of motor functions in general.

The purpose of this paper is to raise a number of issues that arise from this work. Perhaps the main issue to raise is: Why is it that it is this *particular* temporal relationship that is observed? In the case of locomotion, it is presumably possible to suggest some biomechanical reason for the fact that the phase relation between flexor and extensor phases of the step cycle remains invariant across a number of conditions which change the absolute duration of the cycle (Grillner, 1975). Is there any analogous explanatory possibility for the speech result? The authors link the result to the hypothesis that the vowel-to-vowel interval is an important and controlled variable in speech, but this emphasis is not altogether convincing. For example, the possibility that the result is due to an overall tempo effect has not been ruled out. This alternative hypothesis could be tested in the following manner. In an expanded version of the utterance ($C_1V_1C_2V_2C_3V_3C_4$) evaluate vowel-to-consonant latencies against a vowel-to-vowel interval that does not contain the consonant; e.g., V_1-C_2 latency against the V_2-V_3 interval, or the V_2-C_3 latency against the V_1-V_2 interval. If high correlations are observed, then an overall tempo effect is presumably involved. The already observed failure to find high correlations between vowel latencies and the consonant-to-consonant interval containing the vowel might be due to one or more of the three events involved not being closely linked with tempo.

As the authors themselves point out, this work needs to be extended to other types of syllable structure. The syllable type investigated so far is the CV syllable. Studies need to be made of VC syllables and syllables with complex intervocalic consonant clusters in which syllable boundaries can be said to fall in various places in the cluster. If consonant timing is simply determined by the vowel-to-vowel interval as the authors suggest, then no effects of syllable boundaries would be expected.

Another issue involves the criterion for segment onset. Many recent studies of coarticulation have shown that the time of onset of a movement for a particular segment can vary considerably as a function of context. In perhaps the most well known case, Benguerel and Cowan (1974) showed that, in French, the onset of the lip-rounding movement for a rounded vowel can range across six segments prior to the vowel, depending on the phonotactic structure of the prior context. Perhaps in any one of these contexts Harris et al could find relative invariance of onset of a consonant across stress and rate conditions where the consonant occurred in a V_1-V_2 interval, including the rounded vowel. But if the rounded vowel were the first in the V_1-V_2 interval and vowel onset were taken to be lip rounding onset, the relative timing of onset of a consonant within the V_1-V_2 interval could vary enormously with the context *prior* to V_1. This is not presented as a counterexample to the findings of the authors, but just as a caution against uncritically adopting the intervowel-onset interval as a simple timing unit in speech production.

Finally, a comment is in order on the implications of the notion of temporal invariance for perception. The authors consider temporal invariance to be a basic property of motor systems which, in the case of speech, happens to make available information leading to perceptual invariance. However, it is not clear what these perceptual invariants are. And it should be noted that the view that perceptual information results solely from the natural operating properties of the motor system is contrary to the widely held view that speech-motor control itself is partially shaped by perceptual constraints on efficient communication (e.g. Lindblom, MacNeilage & Studdert-Kennedy, (1983a); Martinet, 1968).

ACKNOWLEDGMENT

Preparation of this paper was supported by Grant NS 15336 from the Department of Health and Human Services, Public Health Service.

Anders Löfqvist: Comment

If there is articulatory invariance in speech, we have to show it under different temporal and spatial transformations. The approach taken by Harris, Tuller, and Kelso in looking for temporal invariance is clearly productive, as it has proved itself to be in other areas of motor control. I will add some results from other areas of speech production that also illustrate similar instances of articulatory invariance.

In voiceless consonant production, several articulatory gestures occur simultaneously. In the larynx, the glottis opens and closes; in the vocal tract, an occlusion

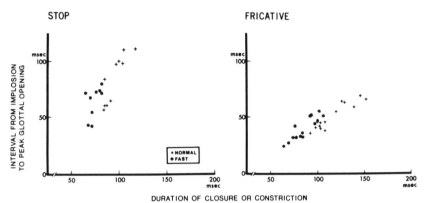

FIG. 12b.1.   Closure/Constriction Duration Plotted against the Interval from Onset of Tongue-Palate Contact to Onset of Glottal Adduction for Dental Voiceless Stops and Fricatives Produced under Variations in Stress and Speaking Rate.

or constriction is made. Studies of the temporal coordination of the laryngeal and oral gestures have provided information with general implications for speech motor control (Löfqvist and Yoshioka, 1980, 1981). Figure 12b.1 is taken from these studies and shows representative results for voiceless stops and fricatives produced under variations in stress and speaking rate.

Figure 12b.1 shows a plot of two articulatory intervals in voiceless consonant production. The x-axis gives the duration of the oral closure or constriction, as measured by dynamic palatography. Along the y-axis is given the duration of the interval from onset of oral closure/constriction to the onset of glottal adduction; records of glottal activity were obtained by transillumination. Results for stops are shown to the left in the figure and results for fricatives to the right. Within each rate condition, the different data points refer to stops and fricatives occurring in positions with different degrees of stress; each data point represents the mean of 10–15 tokens. The subject was a native speaker of American English.

For both stops and fricatives, there is a positive relationship between the two articulatory intervals; they both increase and decrease together. Pearson product moment correlations are 0.87 and 0.61 for the stops at normal and fast rate, respectively; the values for the fricatives are 0.85 and 0.81. Regression analysis showed that $y = 1.71x - 80$ and $y = 1.55x - 53$ for the stops at normal and fast rates; the corresponding results for the fricatives are $y = 0.55x - 14$ and $y = 0.70x - 20$. The differences between the rates were not significant.

In this case, there is, then, a stable relationship between the two articulatory intervals. The ratio between them tends to be maintained under variations in stress and speaking rate.

These results thus add to an increasing body of data indicating that articulatory invariance can in fact be found in speech. Furthermore, the type of relationship found here between articulatory events is very similar to that observed in other areas of motor control such as locomotion or handwriting.

Finally, most evidence from temporal invariance in speech production has been found at the intersegmental level, as illustrated by the work of Harris, et al. for VCV sequences. The results presented here for voiceless consonants illustrate similar invariance at the intrasegmental level.

John E. Clark & Sallyanne Palethorpe: Sources of Invariance and Variability in Temporal Properties of Speech

Investigations of invariance in speech production of the kind described by Harris, Tuller, and Kelso might usefully consider the question of distinguishing among some of the more recognizable sources of potential invariance and variability in the speech-production process.

Specifically, we have in mind an attempt to make quantitative distinctions among sources of variability and invariance motivated by the phonological demands of the language, those due to intraspeaker and interspeaker differences, and those relating to the performance of the speech motor-control system. The first of these relate to properties of the speech-production process which contribute to information-bearing components of the speech code in a formally linguistic sense, while the latter two concern properties of speech production which are determined by such factors as vocal-tract anatomy and biomechanics, and the sum total of habituated skilled motor-control patterns for the articulation of the individual arising from a variety of motives.

In the investigation of invariance properties, it is valuable to know what sort of consistency might be expected within and between individual speakers (for example, in a given articulatory sequence for a protracted series of token repetitions). Such information is important in its own right to the study of invariance, but because it forms an inherent part of the substrate of speech production properties, it can also provide useful information complementing the investigation of linguistically motivated invariance and variability. Equally importantly, identification of the major sources of variability and invariance may help in determining expectations about the actual nature of the invariance and variability properties themselves.

Recently, we have begun preliminary work towards making some of these distinctions in the analysis of acoustic data on syllables containing fricatives (Clark, Palethorpe & Hardcastle, 1982; Clark & Palethorpe, 1983). Some further durational aspects of this investigation may be of interest here.

In brief, the data consisted of durational components from CV, VC, and CVC syllables derived by normal spectrographic analysis from six repetitions of each syllable type by three male speakers. The consonants were the fricatives /s, z, š, ž/ in combination with the vowels /i, a, ɔ/. The duration components analyzed were total syllable, fricative noise, vowel nucleus, and nucleus transition. The object of the analysis was to try and account for some of the sources of variance in the data.

TABLE 12c.1

Percentage of Duration Variance Accounted for by Predictors

Duration Component	Syll	Poa	Voice	Retract	Lip	Spkr	Total Var. Accounted
Vowel Nucleus	3.9	0	25.8	14.8	4.2	0	48.7
Nucleus Transition	5.0	1.5	14.1	9.7	0	3.3	33.6
Fricative Duration	32.5	0	23.7	3.2	0	0	59.4
Total Syllable	9.1	0	1.0	6.1	3.6	2.0	21.8

The first approach was to use stepwise multiple regression (on the CV and VC data only) to provide an estimate of the percentage of variance accounted for in these durational components by a restricted set of phonological features, plus speaker identity, acting as predictors for the regression model. Only results contributing to more than 1% of variance are given here (although a significance level of 0.05 overall was used as the criterion for inclusion in the regression model in the actual analysis). Although the application of stepwise regression analysis to data of this type is a little controversial, we have found it to be capable of yielding plausible results with several forms of speech-production data. The phonological features chosen as predictors effectively include the whole test syllable in the contextual window of the analysis, and the inclusion of speaker identity as a predictor in the regression model allows the possibility for distinguishing phonologically motivated data variance from effects of interspeaker variability.

The predictor set was as follows: SYLL (CV or VC), POA (alveolar or postalveolar fricative), VOICE (voiced or voiceless fricative), RETRACT (front or back vowel), LIP (unrounded or rounded vowel), SPEAKER (subject 1,2, or 3).

Table 12c.1 shows the percentage of variance accounted for in each of the durational components of the syllables by the predictors used in the model. Only main effects are included.

As might be expected, vowel-duration variance arises from two major sources: intrinsic effects in which back vowels are longer than front vowels due to the biomechanical effects of the larger mandibular and tongue movements they require, and phonological conditioning by voicing (which is a well known effect in English). Nucleus transition durations have more complex sources of variability of which the single strongest effect is voicing, and this is due to quite long transitions associated with back vowels in VC syllables. There is also an interspeaker difference effect. Fricative durations show a simpler pattern of variability, with the majority of the variance being due to syllable type and voicing (the latter effect being associated with the voicing conditioning found in the vowel durations). It has also been suggested that the inherently longer duration times for voiceless fricatives observed in this and other studies are due in part to the relatively slow laryngeal myody-namic system requiring time to produce the large glottal areas necessary for the aerodynamic demands of voiceless frication. Total syllable duration (like transition durations) has several sources of variability, although none of them predominate; and they only account for a relatively small proportion of total variance with this measure.

Measures which have a substantial part of their variance accounted for by a single predictor have the greatest potential for invariance, while measures whose variance is accounted for by a number of predictors are those most subject to contextual or other sources of variability. Where only a small proportion of variance is accounted for, either the chosen predictor set is inappropriate, or the variability of the measure itself is inherently unstructured. In the former case of an inappropriate predictor set, potential invariance is not precluded, but it would not be attributed to any of the sources selected for this analysis.

In the present data, a relatively small proportion of both transition and total syllable duration variance is accounted for. In the case of the transitions, this finding probably reflects at least in part the relatively small influence of segmental context. It is also worth noting that in this measure slightly more variance is accounted for by speaker differences than elsewhere, although in no case does this amount to more than a quite minor part of the total variance.

Total syllable duration also shows very little of its variance accounted for either by the selected phonological features or by interspeaker variability as main effects (although there was in fact an appreciable amount of variability in the raw data). It suggests the existence of variability in speaker performance which is not speaker specific, and may be an unstructured example of what Harris, Tuller, and Kelso have called "scalar changes in behaviour."

By contrast, the two major internal temporal components, namely the frica-tive and vowel nucleus durations, have appreciably more of their total variance explained. In each case the explanation predominantly involves two predictors of which one is voicing. This effect reflects a strong trading relationship between vowel and fricative durations durations, vowel and fricative (observable in the raw data, mostly occurring in the VC syllables). Neither duration shows an interspeaker dif-ference effect, despite the fact that this appears in total syllable duration. Overall, this systematic internal variability has only minor effects on total syllable dura-tion, and may be considered as a trend to pattern or relational invariance of a kind which fits in with the notion of "internal temporal 'topology'" discussed by Harris, Tuller, and Kelso.

The second part of this study was to consider interspeaker variability properties alone, this time using univariate analysis of variance (again with an overall signif-icance level of 0.05) to investigate patterns of interspeaker variability in duration component means and variances. CVC data were also included in this analysis.

Although space precludes a detailed presentation of the results of this analysis, some overall observations may be of interest. The majority of cases of significant in-terspeaker differences occur in the means of the durations, with relatively few cases of differences between speakers in their associated variances. VC syllables exhibit the least evidence of interspeaker variability in all measures. Among the individual durational components, interspeaker differences occur most frequently in the means of prevocalic fricatives, and (as might be expected from the regression data) vowel transitions. There is no immediate explanation for this finding, although in the case of the prevocalic fricatives it may be speculated that their temporal programming is under less constraint than that of their counterparts occurring later in the syllable time course. Unfortunately, this hypothesis is not supported by any analogous variability in the VC syllable vowels.

The fact that interspeaker variability occurs more commonly in the means of temporal measures than in their variances suggests that the acoustic outcome of speech motor-control processes results in a stronger tendency to invariance between speakers in their distributions around target values of the temporal measures than in the actual choices of target values for the measures themselves.

Although these data are not sufficiently comprehensive to allow any really strong generalizations to be drawn from them, they do appear to support the general conclusions of Harris, Tuller, and Kelso about the relational nature of observable invariance in the time domain. Both in its phonologically determined structure and speaker determined properties, invariance trends lie not in the absolute temporal component values, but rather in their interrelationships and distributions. It is of interest to speculate why this might be so.

Harris, Tuller, and Kelso have sought an interpretation of the data presented in their focus paper in inherent (and perhaps implicitly necessary) properties of speech motor-control mechanisms. An alternative explanation arising from the "teleological" view of speech production outlined by Lindblom in Chapter 23 and elsewhere (Lindblom, 1983b) should also be considered. Lindblom argues that the principal objective of the talker in speech production is to produce an acoustic output that is as distinctive as the particular linguistic and speaker-listener situation demands it to be. To this end, talkers generally operate well within the limits of their available range of distinctiveness. If this is so, there are good grounds for believing that in many instances speech motor-control mechanisms are operating nowhere near their limits of performance. This would suggest that they are free to function with an appreciable degree of variability (including invoking compensatory strategies) depending on the acoustic distinctiveness required at the time. Such a scenario should make us a little cautious about interpreting articulatory data as reflecting inherent or necessary properties of the speech motor-control system.

Therefore, it is possible to argue that invariant properties in speech are more likely to be found in the end result acoustic signal than in the articulatory processes producing the signal, and that they will be motivated predominantly by communicative requirements.

ACKNOWLEDGMENTS

This work was supported under the Australian Research Grants Scheme (grant F 8015664) and with the assistance of the Macquarie University Speech and Language Research Centre technical staff.

Joseph S. Perkell:

On Sources of Invariance and Variability in Speech Production

Chapters 11 and 12 by Fujimura and Harris, et al. present findings which the
authors interpret as evidence for certain kinds of temporal or kinematic invariance
in speech production. The search for invariant temporal and kinematic elements
is, in part, a reaction to the apparent lack of evidence for other kinds of invariant
units, i.e. "static" articulatory targets which might be the physiological correlates of
distinctive features (cf. Bell-Berti & Harris, 1979, 1981; Fowler, 1980). My purpose
in this comment is threefold: (1) to cite examples of evidence which suggest that
there are limitations on the extent to which any kind of invariance will be found
across a variety of speaking situations; (2) to outline a theoretical framework which
postulates underlying invariant units and allows for systematic phonetic variation;
and (3) to suggest that while data may be found to support any one viewpoint on
invariance in speech, the widespread occurrence of variability, both temporal and
spatial, make it imperative that we systematically analyze much greater quantities
of data before we can argue convincingly for any particular theory.

Figure 12d.1 shows traces of lower-lip protrusion as a function of time from an
experiment on the coarticulation of lip rounding for the vowel [u] (Perkell, 1983).
The figure shows traces for several repetitions of two nonsense utterances, spoken
by three different speakers (with a small bite block in place). The traces in the top
half of the figure are for the utterance [katu] and in the bottom half for [kantu].
From left to right, the plots are from a speaker of English, Spanish, and French.
The utterances were imbedded in carrier phrases appropriate for each language.

The traces are lined up with respect to the onset of voicing of the [u], indicated
by the vertical lines. The symbols on each trace indicate the timing of events as
they were identified either in the time-synchronized acoustic-signal stream or in
the movement signal stream itself. On each trace, from left to right: the diamond
stands for release of the [k], the vertical tick mark stands for protrusion beginning[1],
the circle stands for end of the [a], and the box stands for release of the [t].

Note that in all cases, protrusion beginning occurs just before the end of the [a].
However, other aspects of the movement patterns are quite different for the different
speakers. Protrusion for the speaker of English, at the left, reaches the target for
the [u] just before the [t] release, then a second, more gradual protrusive movement
occurs after onset of voicing for the [u], presumably to produce an appropriate
pattern of diphthongization. The protrusion movement for the Spanish speaker, in
the middle, consists of one single gesture which reaches its extreme after the almost
coincident [t] release and onset of voicing for the vowel. Protrusion for the French
speaker, on the right, reaches a maximum before release of the [t], and gradual
retraction with some hesitation occurs throughout the vowel.

For each speaker, the time from movement onset to onset of voicing for the [u]
is longer in the utterances containing [nt] than it is in the utterances containing
[t]. In addition, peak movement velocities (maximum slopes of the displacement
traces during the protrusion gesture) are higher in the [t] examples for the three

---

[1] Defined by the onset of positive velocity

LOWER LIP PROTRUSION VS. TIME   Line-up point: Onset of voicing for [u]

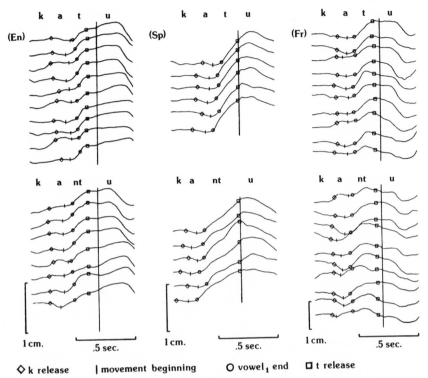

◇ k release | movement beginning   O vowel₁ end   ☐ t release

FIG. 12d.1. Traces of lower lip protrusion as a function of time for the utterances [katu] and [kantu], spoken by a speaker of English (En), Spanish (Sp), and French (Fr).

speakers. Thus, the "invariant" characteristics reflected in these traces are mainly due to competing "static configurational goals": lip spreading is required for the [a] and then lip rounding is required for the [u]. (As noted below, even this kind of invariance is not absolute.)

A possible theoretical explanation for these movement patterns may be given as follows. There are goals for the lips for the vowels [a] and [u]. These goals are defined by articulatory-to-acoustic relationships (Fant, 1960) which may be thought of as being correlates of distinctive features (Perkell, 1980; Stevens, 1972). According to the look-ahead model of anticipatory coarticulation (Henke, 1967; Öhman, 1966), the lips remain spread until near the end of the [a] to maintain its acoustic integrity. Rounding takes place during the consonant string because it has no perceptually-disruptive effect on the acoustics, and rounding is completed during the [u]. This type of explanation has been invoked in one form or another to account for a number of similar findings on anticipatory coarticulation (Lubker, 1981).

The temporal and kinematic aspects of the movement patterns in Figure 12d.1 are hypothesized to be governed by a variety of factors. Speech sounds have intrinsic durations (Klatt, 1976) which are determined by a combination of biomechanical, physiological, perceptual, and linguistic constraints. For some sounds, there may also be kinematic specifications associated with the production of transient acoustic cues (Fujimura, Chapter 11). Such intrinsic temporal specifications are combined with spatial and other types of goals to serve as input information to a set of programming strategies (Perkell, 1980). These strategies include the above-mentioned look-ahead mechanism, movement programming which takes into account biomechanical properties of the articulators (Nelson, 1983) and the use of feedback mechanisms (Abbs, Chapter 10; Perkell, 1980). This programming is variable in nature, and it accounts for the kinematic aspects of the movement trajectories in Figure 12d.1 which show considerable differences among the speakers. One possible source of the variation may be different patterns of diphthongization for the three languages, but there are many other factors which are not suggested by this one example.

The "values" of the targets, the timing of segmental events, and the shapes of trajectories (cf. Fujimura, Chapter 11) are hypothesized to be influenced by a number of additional factors which include whether or not the string is part of natural connected speech, prosody (cf. Harris, et al., Chapter 12), speaking rate and style, distributions of sounds in languages, position in the utterance, paralinguistic, dialectal, and idiosyncratic factors, and perhaps most significantly, the amount of reduction the speaker thinks the listener will tolerate (Koopmans van-Beinum, 1980). The influence of all of these factors should be expressible in sets of rules: universal, language-specific, and individual-specific.

For example, an extreme application of the rules governing reduction could result in a motor program which produces examples of vowels such as [a] and [u] that both sound close to a schwa, with little or no lip rounding or spreading and timing relationships among movements of separate articulators that are different from those of carefully pronounced utterances. For adequate communication with a knowledgeable listener who can take advantage of context, it may be sufficient for the speaker to specify these reduced vowel representations simply with the feature "+ vocalic".

Application of these rules could account in large part for the wide variation that we find in different speaking situations. Along with findings on speech errors (Shattuck-Hufnagel, 1983), the existence of various ways of pronouncing the same utterance, and listeners' ability to understand such pronunciations argue for the existence of fully-specified (feature-like) underlying representations at some level. Sets of rules are used in a "planning stage" to produce a modified, or situation-dependent input specification to the speech motor programming mechanism, resulting in an output which may have a limited number of measurable, absolutely invariant characteristics.

This speculative framework does not preclude the preservation of certain timing relationships under rate and stress manipulation, but it also does not mandate such preservation. Recent evidence that counters the invariance of timing relationships is presented by Al-Bamerni (1983) who examined the coordination of velar and other gestures in speakers of seven languages over changes in speaking rate. Some speakers were found to preserve inter-articulator timing relationships while others did not, with different speakers of the same language demonstrating different strategies.

With abilities to examine ever larger quantities of data on speech patterns, we are uncovering more and more variation. This comment suggests that the variation is systematic, and that we are not really in a state of "theoretical crisis" (Abbs, Chapter 10). We need to methodically accumulate a large body of evidence and understand more about the nature of different sources of variation before we can convincingly support any existing or new theoretical framework. Scaling of temporal relationships as suggested by Harris, et al., (Chapter 12) and the existence of certain invariant kinematic features as suggested by Fujimura (Chapter 11) may be two of a large number of factors which underly speech-motor programming. Considering the complexity and large number of potential influences, it is difficult to know how much weight is given to any one of them. In fact, one source of conflicting experimental findings may be the fact that different underlying factors are weighted differently, depending on the situation or experimental design. The above example of anticipatory coarticulation and the discussion of reduction emphasize the overriding importance of the (individual) speaker's strategy in producing an appropriate, situation-dependent acoustic output (see also Lindblom, Chapter 23).

J. A. Kelso, B. Tuller, and K. S. Harris: Response:
A Theoretical Note on Speech Timing

We wish to make a few comments on Sections 12a–12d and then introduce a representation of interarticulator timing in which time itself is not explicitly involved. To show that such a representation is valid will require a recasting of what data there are on relative timing (e.g., those discussed by Löfqvist in Section 12a) into a geometrical, phase portrait description of articulator trajectories. We have begun to do this. The phase portrait captures the forms of motion caused by an underlying dynamic organization (Abraham & Shaw, 1982; Kelso & Bateson, 1983; Kelso, Holt, Rubin & Kugler, 1981; Saltzman & Kelso, 1984), in which time, as we traditionally measure it (e.g., as duration, latency), is nowhere to be seen. We believe that certain advantages for understanding speech motor control and developing articulatory models accrue immediately from this perspective. But first some comments.

1. We present in Chapter 12 a systematic set of data in favor of relative timing among pertinent articulatory gestures. It is an effort to understand the behavior of an articulatory system that is stable across linguistically meaningful transformations. Some investigators seeking to explore this finding claim not to have observed the same result. However, the measures examined have not been the ones that we are describing here (e.g., Al-Bamerni, 1983). Those who have measured

the relevant variables have provided broad support for our relative timing description (Al-Bamerni & Bladon, unpublished manuscript; Gentil, Harris, Horiguchi, & Honda, 1984; Linville, 1982; Lubker, (chapter 10.d, this volume), Löfqvist, Section 12a; Munhall, submitted). Relative timing, as we propose it, is simply an index of a temporally stable state. It should not be considered as mandatory (Perkell, Chapter 12d) or necessarily inherent (Clark & Palethorpe, Chapter 12c). Clark and Palethorpe set up a binary distinction (acoustic *versus* articulatory) that is not one we have ever subscribed to.

2. We identify the timing of articulatory gestures associated with consonants relative to those associated with flanking vowels. The data presented by Perkell (though interesting) do not pertain to this issue. Other, different accounts exist of coarticulatory effects of the kind discussed by Perkell (e.g., Bell-Berti & Harris, 1979). Many variables are involved in any account of speech production, as Perkell notes. However, to say that the variability in observable output (e.g., trajectories) is accounted for by the variability in programming is circular reasoning at best (cf. Kelso, 1981). Abbs's paper (Chapter 10), MacNeilage (1980), and our experiments (Kelso, Tuller, Bateson & Fowler, 1984; Kelso, Tuller & Fowler, 1982) all converge in showing that the speech motor-control system does not program targets in articulator space, as Perkell claims.

3. Finally, we want to return to the theme of our paper, the relative timing among articulatory gestures. We wish to show how, by examining the data using phase plane techniques, an entirely different conceptualization for the relative-timing finding emerges. We are presently analyzing existing data and conducting new experiments to examine this conceptualization further. Consider the simple case in which the latency (in ms) of onset of upper-lip motion for a medial consonant is measured relative to the interval (in ms) between onsets of jaw lowering motions for flanking vowels. These events are displayed in the idealization of Figure 12e.1A, in which the duration of the V1 to V2 cycle is Jd (in ms) and the latency of upper-lip motion is L (in ms). As we have shown, the two events are highly correlated across rate and stress changes. That is, the lip latency varies systematically with jaw-cycle duration plus an intercept value that seems to change across phonetic context and speaker (see Figure 12e.1B). Note that this is a strictly temporal description. One could posit, in this example, that somehow the system is keeping track of the duration of jaw motion such that when a given amount of time has passed, another articulator, say the upper lip, is activated. Such an account of speech or limb-movement control is not unusual.

A very different view of these events emerges when the articulatory data are expressed as motion trajectories on the phase plane. Two quantities are needed to do this, the articulator's displacement (x) and its velocity $(\dot{x})$. These quantities may be considered to be the coordinates of a point on the articulator in two dimensional space, the phase plane. As time varies, the point $P(x, \dot{x})$ describing the motion of the articulator moves along a certain path in the phase space. Note that time, although implicit and recoverable from this representation, does not appear explicitly in the phase plane description. For different initial conditions, the corresponding paths will be different, and the set of all possible trajectories constitutes the phase portrait of the system's dynamic behavior. Finally, one can transform

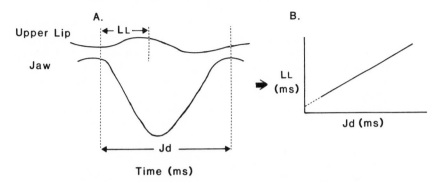

FIG. 12e.1. A. An idealized time series description of jaw and upper lip motion. B. The empirical relation between jaw-cycle duration and upper-lip latency.

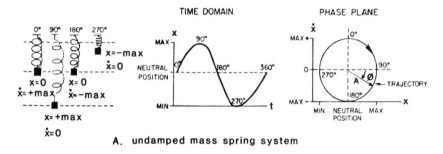

FIG. 12e.2. A. The mapping of a simple undamped mass-spring motion on to the phase plane. B. The jaw cycle of Figure 12e.1A characterized on a "functional" phase portrait; i.e., displacement is on the vertical axis and velocity on the horizontal axis.

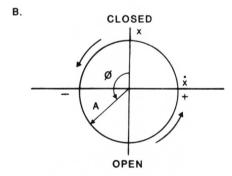

the Cartesian $x, \dot{x}$ coordinates into an equivalent polar form described by a phase angle ($\phi = \tan^1[\dot{x}/x]$), and a radial amplitude ($A = [x^2 + \dot{x}^2]^{1/2}$). In discussions below, the phase angle is a key concept in our interpretation of interarticulator timing phenomena.

Figure 12e.2A illustrates the mapping from time domain to phase plane for a motion trajectory generated by a simple, undamped mass-spring system.[1] In a similar fashion, Figure 12e.2B shows the phase plane trajectory for the idealized jaw motion described as a time series event in Figure 12e.1A. In the phase plane, this jaw motion describes a closed orbit, since the jaw goes from closed to open and back to closed in one cycle. Note that, in comparison with Figure 12e.2A, the axes in Figure 12e.2B have been interchanged in order to express pictorially that the jaw moves vertically in space. In the phase plane, one can plot jaw motions during V1V2 intervals of different duration, and can identify the onset of upper lip motion during each cycle with an onset phase angle for that cycle. Our hypothesis is that the phase angle for upper lip onset should be the same across jaw cycles of different shape, i.e., across different rate and stress conditions. Two idealized examples are illustrated in Figure 12e.3. In one, a small orbit is shown, corresponding to a small displacement of the jaw over time. In the other, a larger orbit is shown. The phase angle of upper lip onset, 0, is predicted to be invariant as shown in the right hand side of Figure 12e.3, though we do not claim it to be the one shown here.[2] Note that the onset of a remote articulator (e.g., the upper lip) is now with reference to the phase angle of another articulator (e.g., the jaw). This angle is therefore a function of the later articulator's position *and* velocity, not merely its absolute position or velocity. Moreover, there is no need to posit any kind of time-keeping mechanism or time controller. In this view, individuals can produce articulatory motions of different durations or magnitudes without affecting the hypothesized regularity in onset phase angle.

To summarize our theoretical points: When representing articulatory motions geometrically on the phase plane, neither absolute nor relative time need be extrinsically monitored or controlled. This fact potentially provides a grounding for, and a principled analysis of, so-called intrinsic timing theories of speech production (e.g., Fowler, Rubin, Remez & Turvey, 1980; see also Kelso & Tuller, in press). Our view is supported indirectly by demonstrations in the articulatory structures themselves of afferent bases for phase angle information (e.g., position and velocity sensitivities of muscle spindle and joint structures), but not for time-keeping information (e.g., time receptors; cf. Kelso, 1978). It might well be the case that certain critical phase angles provide information for orchestrating the temporal flow of activity among articulators (beyond those considered here) and/or vocal tract configurations. Such phase angles would serve as natural, i.e., dynamically

---

[1] Note that the jaw motion, though idealized here, does not have to be (and is not usually) sinusoidal. Thus, different relative timing relations among articulators can give rise to the *same* phase position between articulators and *vice versa*. The determining feature is the shape of the trajectories (for many more details, see Kelso & Tuller, in press).

[2] To date, we have examined this relationship for two speakers and two phonetic contexts, /babab/ and /bawab/. In each case, the phase angle of the upper lip for the medial consonant relative to the jaw trajectory was unaffected by changes in stress and speaking rate.

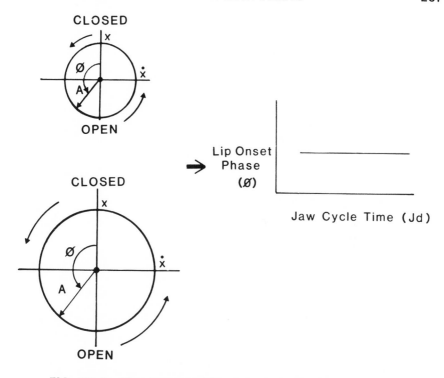

FIG. 12e.3. The phase opposition of the upper lip relative to the jaw cycle for different jaw orbits.

specified, information sources for coordinating speech. Interarticulator speech coordination thus may be captured better with reference to events that are specified by the system's dynamics than with reference to sets of durational rules. These ideas and others are also currently being explored by dynamic modeling (Saltzman & Kelso, 1984).

13 Invariance and Variability in Speech Timing: From Utterance to Segment in German

Klaus J. Kohler
Universität Kiel

INTRODUCTION

It is a fundamental aim of phonetic research to uncover invariant structures for individual languages or—at least with regard to certain aspects—for human language generally, in spite of the great variability of speech processes. Phonological theories since the 1920s assumed that the problem of invariance can be solved by concentrating on sound features taken from their sequential context and viewed as members of a paradigm of sound oppositions. Thus, phonetic phenomena are no longer evaluated simply on the strength of their physical manifestation, but by the relationships they enter into in this paradigm, i.e. in the phonological system. Structural relations between such paradigmatic elements take priority over the observable phonetic substance of elements isolated from the system. Phonetic properties are thus to be reduced to those components which are considered necessary and sufficient for the signalling of such oppositions in a particular language.

Structural relations are, however, not only paradigmatic (between elements in a system), but also syntagmatic (between elements in series). Phonology has overemphasized the former, and although it has put sound elements in the structural perspective of a system, it has also isolated them from their sequential relations, because it has been primarily concerned with sound oppositions for word differentiation. But in speech communication, sound elements not only have to be differentiated from other sound elements in a paradigm, they also have to be identified in a chain, and the identification of a particular paradigmatic element has to rely on its syntagmatic relations. This paper stresses the need for a re-integration of paradigmatic oppositions into syntagmatic structures in the area of speech timing.

268

Phonological elements and structures are abstracted from the temporal course of speech production and perception; they are located outside the time axis. Phonology has never solved the problem of the relationship between such atemporal units and speech processes taking place in time. Building-block synthesis in artificial speech production or building-block analysis in automatic speech recognition realized this thorny problem very quickly, being forced to project the atemporal phonological units onto the time axis of speech. The need to overcome this dilemma led to research into coarticulation and articulatory control. These concepts are based on the structural units of phonology, but are nevertheless designed to adjust them by introducing the time dimension.

In spite of the exclusion of the time axis, phonology has to take duration relations of two kinds into account:

1. Quantity oppositions play an important role in phonemic systems that are set up for a variety of languages.

2. Allophonic duration differences in different phonetic contexts (e.g. lengthening before voiced obstruents) have to be included in phonological descriptions if their aim goes beyond the simple record of the phonemic system of a language.

But in both cases the paradigmatic aspect is still the central issue. The question of the recognition of different quantities in the syntagmatic domain under the prosodic conditions of the utterance is not asked at all. It is, however, decisive when, e.g. the existence of a three-fold quantity opposition is maintained for a language. It is highly improbable that such a paradigmatic relationship could be produced and identified consistently without syntagmatic support in human language, in view of the intervening suprasegmental variables at the utterance level. The language that is always quoted as a clear case in this connection, namely Estonian, does not only have three contrastive quantities in the vowel of the first syllable of a word, but the vowel duration of the second syllable is negatively correlated with the quantity of the first (Lehiste, 1970, p. 50). In this way, the phonological length oppositions are not only signalled by the paradigmatic values in the vowel itself but especially by the contrast within the chain that is realized in time. Because of these duration relationships in the syntagmatic dimension, quantity oppositions can be identified reliably even when the higher-order timing levels of tempo, rhythm, and intonation produce great variability at the segment level and strongly overlapping duration classes. And since the syntagmatic relations can only have the logical values of (approximate) equality or one of two types of clear inequality in the durations of successive segments, three quantities must be the upper limit of what is phonologically possible.

Even in a language with only two quantity levels the syntagmatic relations are necessary to guarantee communication between speaker and hearer. This applies in particular to a language such as Finnish, in which all syllables may contain vowels and consonants in two phonological quantities. Thus the following relationships hold, for instance, in Finnish (Lehtonen, 1970):

(a)

$V_1 C V_2$

$\dfrac{V_1}{V_2} < 1$

$C < V_2$

(b)

$V V_1 C V V_2$

$\dfrac{V V_1}{V V_2} > 1$

$C < V V_2$

The two types of structures are reciprocal: longer V_2 in the first, longer $V V_1$ in the second. In this way, the cases with the same phonological vowel quantity in both syllables (syntagmatic level) are clearly differentiated from one another, the paradigmatic opposition in the first syllable being reinforced. If the temporal relations were $V_1 = V_2$ and $V V_1 = V V_2$, there would be a danger of confusion under the phonetic conditions of the utterance (tempo, etc.).

There is thus a need for the incorporation of phonological quantities into a hierarchy of syntagmatic timing structures from the utterance down to the segment. This paper develops such a top-down timing model for speech production in German. It deals first with the relationship between foot and syllable durations in a so-called stress-timed language, as a function of articulatory complexity and number of syllables in the foot, also taking the influence of different speech rates and intonation patterns into account. It then derives segment durations from the syllable durations generated by this foot-to-syllable algorithm. In a third section, the mathematical formulation of the model is presented, and finally, further timing constraints above the foot are discussed.

FOOT AND SYLLABLE TIMING

Abercrombie (1967, pp. 97ff) following Pike (1946, p. 35), divided the languages of the world into two different types according to their rhythmic structures: one, called "stress-timed," in which the stressed syllables have the tendency towards isochrony, i.e. to equal temporal spacing, and another, called "syllable-timed," in which all syllables have this tendency. English, German, the other Germanic languages, and Slavonic languages, are cited as instances of the first type; French, Spanish, West African languages, and languages of India are given as examples of the second. Stress-timing compression with an increase of the number of syllables in the foot results not only in syllable shortening but also in articulatory reductions (elisions, assimilations, and weak forms) so characteristic of languages such as English and German. This principle of compression is clear and cannot be denied. The question is whether it occurs in its strictest form.

Does the foot duration, i.e. the time from the beginning of one stressed syllable to the beginning of the next one, stay exactly the same irrespective of the number of unstressed syllables in between? This question was raised in a number of experimental investigations concerned with English (e.g. Huggins, 1975; Lehiste, 1971, 1972, 1973, 1977; Uldall, 1971, 1978). The results are rather heterogeneous and certainly do not confirm the strong version of the isochrony theory. There are also certain objections that can be raised on methodological grounds as in the study where Uldall (1971, 1978) recorded the reading of "The Northwind and the Sun" from a single speaker and measured the foot durations from spectrograms. Uldall had to cope with the problems of syllable boundaries and of comparability in a continuous text, quite apart from the fact that the data base was rather small.

I will summarize the results of three experiments which were carried out in the Kiel Phonetics Department to investigate the relationship between foot and syllable timing. Experiment I used strings of nonsense syllables conforming to the phonotactics of German. Experiment II varied nonsense words in accordance with German phonotactics and morphology within a German sentence frame. Experiment III introduced different intonation patterns into the design of Experiment II. Further details of method and data are available in Kohler, Schäfer, Thon & Timmermann (1981) and in Kohler (1983a, b).

Experiment I

In order to demonstrate the trends of rhythmic timing in a stress-timed language, it is necessary to vary a basic foot structure with unambiguous syllable boundaries systematically within a clear time frame set by an external timing device. The purpose of the external timing device is to guarantee that exactly the same time is available for a fixed number of feet with variable numbers of unstressed syllables. In our attempt at Kiel to come to grips with the question of stress-timing, we reversed the strategy of data collection compared to previous investigations. Speech was not produced to be subsequently measured as to its isochrony; rather, an isochronous measure was imposed, and it was checked whether the speaker was able to adjust his or her speech to it by applying the compression principle, and to what extent the speaker was able to carry it through. The procedure of data collection and analysis thus started from the strongest form of the isochrony hypothesis. It was turned into an experimental design to test the expectations of results derived from it, by comparison with the empirical findings.

As external timer, an oscilloscope beam was used with the deflection times of 4s and 2.5s representing two different speech rates. Within these time frames, subjects had to produce chains of five 1-, 2-, and 3-syllable feet, all containing the same syllable structure chosen from the list *pa* [pha:], *ba* [ba:], *bla* [bla:] *pasch* [phaš], *schapp* [šap], and *platsch* [platš]. These logatome syllables were selected according to the phonotactic rules of German and with a view to including different degrees of articulatory complexity.

The results of this experiment are very clear. The most complex syllable chain *platsch* can no longer be compressed into either temporal frame in the case of 3-syllable feet, and in the fast timing 2-syllable feet are not possible either. The articulations become so complex that they are not adjustable to isochrony if no elisions are allowed. But even in the cases of *bla*, *pasch*, and *schapp*, the 3-syllable feet were not producible in the fast timing, and for *bla* not in the slow timing either. Moreover, within the same external time frame, a sequence of *pa* or *ba* feet sounds faster when there are 3 syllables in each foot than when they are monosyllabic. This means that complete compression of an increased number of syllables within the foot to fit the external time measure produces the impression of a higher speech rate for a listener. The concept of stress-timing is, however, proposed on the assumption that the general speed of delivery, as perceived by a listener, stays the same, in spite of articulatory compression. If, on the other hand, the tempo of speaking does not change, complete compression is ruled out.

A second set of data was collected by making subjects listen to their own renderings (in two speech rates) of the German sentence "Max hat Petra *viele schöne Dinge* neu zurechtgemacht," and by making them repeat this sentence with the same tempo replacing the central section by three logatome feet. The logatomes were again *pa*, *ba*, *bla*, *pasch*, and *schapp*. With each syllable target, 1-, 2-, and 3-syllable feet had to be produced.

An auditory judgement revealed that only one subject followed the instructions and used the same speech rate as in the previously recorded sentence. The other subjects changed their tempo in the logatome sections in various ways. One speaker made the 2-syllable foot about twice as long and the 3-syllable foot about three times as long as the single-syllable one; she hardly compressed at all. This proportional expansion results in the auditory impression of a progressive decrease in overall speed of delivery. So, if the perceived tempo of speaking is to stay the same, proportional expansion is also ruled out. There has to be compression to an amount falling within the extreme limits of complete isochrony and proportional expansion.

Linear regression analyses show that the relationship between foot duration and stressed-syllable duration in the case of a repetition of the same syllable type in a chain is linear and proportional, irrespective of the particular syllable structure and speech rate. For the 2- and the 3-syllable foot the slopes are 0.55 and 0.37, respectively. Different syllable types (S_i) with different degrees of articulatory complexity, starting from the least complex syllable S_1 and proceeding in an ascending order, form the ratios ($R_{1...}$ = rhythmic foot duration):

$$\frac{S_1}{R_1} = \frac{S_2}{R_2} = \frac{S_3}{R_3} = \ldots = b. \tag{1}$$

It follows from

$$\frac{S_1}{R_1} = \frac{S_1 + \Delta S_1}{R_1 + \Delta S_1 + \Delta S_1'} \tag{2}$$

where

ΔS_1: duration increment of more complex syllable in stressed position,
$\Delta S_1'$: increment in unstressed position(s)

that

$$\frac{S_1}{R_1} = \frac{\Delta S_1}{\Delta S_1 + \Delta S_1'} = b. \tag{3}$$

Thus, the stressed-syllable and foot increments for different articulatory complexities form the same ratio in this kind of repetitive syllable chain. The same considerations apply to duration changes due to different speech rates.

Experiment II

The speech material in Experiment I conforms to the phonotactics of German syllables but violates the rules of morphological structures. To approach more normal syllable strings the following experiment was carried out.

In the sentence "Nie hat Karl die blöde...durchgestellt," the blank was filled by one item at a time from the following logatome list:

Pinn, Pinne, Pinnige [pɪn, -ə, -ɩgə]
Pahn, Pahne, Pahnige [paːn, -ə, -ɩgə]
Schripps, Schrippse, Schrippsige [šrɩps, -ə, -ɩgə]
Schraabs, Schraabse, Schraabsige [šraːps, -ə, -ɩgə]

The constant syntactic frame consisting of German lexical items gave these nonsense words the status of nouns, which followed common morphological patterns. The logatomes represent different degrees of syllable complexity: single initial and final consonants + short or long vowel, initial and final consonant clusters + short or long vowel. Three subjects (CW (female); KK, GU (male)) produced the whole set of sentences at 3 different speeds of their own choice: normal, slow, fast, 3 times each. They first accompanied the whole corpus by finger tapping to beat the rhythm, and then pronounced it without such a rhythmic timer. The instructions were to keep the speed constant within one chosen rate.

The following sections of each utterance were segmented and their durations measured: sentence, frame I (sentence section before the logatome),

logatome word, logatome stem, logatome ending (– e or – ige), frame II (sentence section after the logatome). The initial stop closures of the logatomes were included in the stem and word durations. In the analysis of the data, it had to be ascertained, first of all, that each speaker used his chosen speech rates (normal, slow, fast) consistently in each production mode (with/without tapping) so that durational differences in the logatomes within one speech rate and production mode were not attributable to tempo fluctuations, but to the factors under investigation: syllable complexity and number of syllables in the foot. For this reason, one-way analyses of variance were carried out over frame I, separately for each speaker, speech rate, and production mode. The results show that the tokens of frame I before all the different logatomes form a homogeneous data set. (There is one exception to this general pattern in CW (with tapping), normal speed: $p = 0.0032$.) Consistency within each intended tempo can thus be assumed.

The means of the foot, stem, and ending durations (see Kohler 1983b for further details) show the following tendencies:

A. 1- and 2-syllable feet of the same syllable structure approach isochrony, most clearly in CW. KK and GU often have a longer 1-syllable foot, thus again demonstrating the compression of the 2-syllable foot.

B. 3-syllable feet are longer; here full compression is not achieved. But the duration differences between 2- and 3-syllable feet, corresponding as to syllable complexity and tempo, are very similar. So there seems to be a constant expansion of the 3-syllable foot compared with the other two foot types.

C. The duration differences between corresponding foot types (same syllable structure and number of syllables) in normal and slow or in normal and fast speeds are very similar and point to a tempo-dependent constant increase or decrease.

D. The syllables [pɪn], [paːn], [šraːps] form a hierarchy of increasing articulatory complexity because [pɪn] only contains single consonants and a short close vowel, whereas [paːn] has a long open vowel, and [šraːps] has consonant clusters in addition to a long open vowel. Similarly, in the series [pɪn], [šrɪps], [šraːps], the second syllable has greater complexity than the first because of its consonant clusters, and [šraːps] is still more complex because of its long vowel. The relative complexity of [paːn] and [šrɪps] is less clear on account of opposing differences in the vowels and the consonants. An inspection of the mean syllable durations shows that these degrees of articulatory complexity are paralleled by duration increments: [pɪn] and [šraːps] are the endpoints of this duration scale in each foot type (i.e. 1-, 2- or 3-syllable feet) and each speech rate; [paːn] and [šrips] are located in between and very close together. Taking these duration differences into account, we may attribute the same degree of articulatory complexity to both [pa:n] and [šrɪps] and set up the hierarchy [pɪn] < [pa:n], [šrɪps] < [šra:ps].

E. The durations of the ending [ə] or [ɪgə] are on a descending scale parallel to the ascending one for stem or foot durations in (D). This is a further aspect of the isochrony principle, which was inevitably absent from the data of Experiment I.

To test these data observations statistically the following procedures were carried out:

1. 3-way Analyses of Variance with the fixed effects Tempo (normal, slow, fast), Number of Syllables (1, 2), Syllable structure ([p_], [šr_]) were performed over the data set [pa:n], [šrips], and over the data set [pɪn], [šra:ps]: i.e. over the syllable structures that differ minimally or maximally, respectively, on the complexity and duration scales described in (D). These statistics aimed at providing answers to the hypotheses set up on the basis of the data observations in (A) and (D), namely:

(1) The durations of 1- and 2-syllable feet belong to the same population in all tempos and syllable structures.

(2) The durations of [pa:n] and [šrips] belong to the same population in all tempos, whereas [pɪn] and [šra:ps] do not.

The results are compiled in tables 13.1 and 13.2. CW structures the data set [pa:n(ə)], [šrɪps(ə)], only along the dimension tempo, thus confirming hypotheses (1) and (2). KK and GU show the additional effect of Number of Syllables, because they tend to have a longer 1-syllable foot, as was pointed out in (A). In the case of the data set [pɪn(ə)], [šra:ps(ə)], GU shows the significant effects Tempo and Syllable Structure; CW (without tapping) is similar, but also has significant interactions. Hypotheses (1) and (2) are again confirmed. These findings point to an articulatory strategy adopted by German speakers: Make 1- and 2-syllable feet (containing the reduced vowel [ə] as an ending) isochronous, and treat the syllable structures [pa:n] and [šrɪps] as equal on the complexity scale. However, these basic patterns may be disturbed by other factors and by factor interactions in the speech production of individual speakers. The above statements (A) and (D) are thus supported.

A 3-way Analysis of Variance with the same fixed effects, but including 3-syllable feet as well, yields significance in the factor Number of Syllables. This, together with the preceding result, shows that it is the 3-syllable foot that fails to achieve full compression (see statement (B) above).

2. 1-way nonparametric analyses of variance (H-tests according to Kruskal-Wallis) with the effects Tempo or Syllable Structure, respectively, were applied to the duration-mean differences between the equivalent 2- or 3-

TABLE 13.1

Results of 3-way ANOVAs with Fixed Effects Tempo (normal, slow, fast), Number of Syllables (1,2), Syllable Structure (/p/, /šr/), over the Data Sets [pa:n], [šrɪps] for Each Speaker. ± = with/without tapping. X = 5% , XX = 1% , XXX = 0.1% .

	CW+	CW−	KK+	KK−	GU+	GU−
Main effects	XXX	XXX	XXX	XXX	XXX	XXX
Tempo	XXX	XXX	XXX	XXX	XXX	XXX
Number of Syllables			X	XX	X	XXX
Syllable Structure						X
Interactions					XX	
T×NS						
T×SS						
NS×SS	X				XX	X
T×NS×SS						
Explained	XXX	XXX	XXX	XXX	XXX	XXX

TABLE 13.2

Results as in Table 13.1 for Data Sets [pɪn] and [šra:ps].

	CW+	CW−	KK+	KK−	GU+	GU−
Main effects	XXX	XXX	XXX	XXX	XXX	XXX
Tempo	XXX	XXX	XXX	XXX	XXX	XXX
Number of Syllables	XX		XX	XXX		
Syllable Structure	XXX	XXX	XXX	XXX	XXX	XXX
Interactions	XXX	XX	XXX	XXX		
T×NS						
T×SS	XXX	XXX	XXX	X	X	
NS×SS	X		XX	XXX		
T×NS×SS	XX					
Explained	XXX	XXX	XXX	XXX	XXX	XXX

syllable feet. This statistical procedure was to test the following hypothesis resulting from statement (B):

> The mean duration increments in the 3-syllable foot as against the corresponding 2-syllable one belong to the same population, irrespective of tempo and syllable structure.

CW and KK confirm the hypothesis, but GU shows a tempo effect.

The nonparametric H-test was applied instead of a parametric analysis of variance because it would have been an arbitrary decision as to which individual tokens of equivalent 2- and 3-syllable feet should be taken to calculate the duration difference. If the test is based on duration means, a nonparametric test was called for because of the small number of data. In the absence of a multi-dimensional nonparametric analysis of variance, effects had to be tested separately. The results of the H-tests suggest a constant expansion from the 1-/2-syllable to the 3-syllable foot, again with individual disturbances of a basic strategy. Thus statement (B) is confirmed.

3. 1-way nonparametric analyses of variance (Kruskal-Wallis) with the effects Syllable Structure or Number of Syllables were carried out over the duration-mean differences between equivalent feet in normal/slow and in normal/fast speech rates, respectively. These statistics were to provide an answer to the following hypothesis resulting from statement (C):

> The duration differences between corresponding foot types in the two speeds normal/slow or normal/fast are homogeneous, irrespective of syllable structure and number of syllables.

With the exceptions of GU+, normal/fast (where the number of syllables has a significant influence) and of CW+, normal/slow (where the syllable structure is a relevant factor), the hypothesis is confirmed. The results support statement (C), although deviations from this basic pattern in individual speakers again have to be taken into account. As regards the application of the nonparametric H-test the same applies as in 2.

4. Spearman rank-correlation coefficients were computed for the pairs of duration variables stem/ending ([ə] or [ɪgə]) and foot/ending. They are listed in Table 13.3 and show strong negative correlations between the variables in almost all cases. The negative correlation is stronger between stem and ending, where all the coefficients are significant, than between foot and ending, where there are also fewer (very) highly significant values. Statements (D) and (E) are thus confirmed: The reduced endings [ə] or [ɪgə] adjust their durations negatively to the time required for the different articulatory complexities of the stem, as a result of the tendency to make feet isochronous. But as this compression cannot be complete, there is also a foot expansion with increasing syllable complexity, resulting in measurable, albeit weaker, negative correlations between foot and ending.

TABLE 13.3

Spearman Rank-correlation Coefficients for Foot/Ending and Stem/Ending in the 6 Data Sets of Experiment II; $n = 12$. $\pm$ = with/without tapping; n./s./f. = normal/slow/fast speed. X = 5%, XX = 1%, XXX = 0.1%.

		foot / ə		stem / ə		foot / ɪɡɔ		stem / ɪɡɔ	
		r	p	r	p	r	p	r	p
CW+	n.	-0.61	X	-0.91	XXX	-0.79	XX	-0.88	XXX
	s.	-0.89	XXX	-0.92	XXX	0.07	n.s.	-0.71	XX
	f.	-0.72	X	-0.85	XX	-0.86	XXX	-0.98	XXX
		($n = 10$)		($n = 10$)					
CW−	n.	-0.76	XX	-0.77	XX	-0.85	XXX	-0.91	XXX
	s.	-0.62	X	-0.75	XX	-0.50	X	-0.76	XX
	f.	-0.30	n.s.	-0.57	X	-0.15	n.s.	-0.50	X
		($n = 11$)		($n = 11$)					
KK+	n.	-0.87	XXX	-0.96	XXX	-0.81	XX	-0.89	XXX
	s.	-0.63	X	-0.80	XX	-0.59	X	-0.72	XX
	f.	-0.65	X	-0.90	XXX	-0.47	n.s.	-0.62	X
KK−	n.	-0.62	X	-0.70	XX	-0.72	XX	-0.86	XXX
	s.	-0.68	XX	-0.72	XX	-0.85	XXX	-0.86	XXX
	f.	-0.55	X	-0.76	XX	-0.76	XX	-0.91	XXX
GU+	n.	-0.75	XX	-0.97	XXX	-0.93	XXX	-0.97	XXX
	s.	-	-	-	-	-	-	-	-
	f.	-0.81	XX	-0.92	XXX	-0.57	X	-0.80	XX
GU−	n.	-0.53	X	-0.58	X	-0.84	XXX	-0.96	XXX
	s.	-0.76	XX	-0.86	XXX	-0.53	X	-0.83	XXX
	f.	-0.93	XXX	-0.95	XXX	-0.88	XXX	-0.93	XXX

Although there are certainly measuring errors due to segmentation problems, they are the same for [pɪn] and [paːn], on the one hand, and for [šrɪps] and [šraːps], on the other; moreover, the constant frame with the initial (devoiced) [d]-closure of "durchgestellt" after the logatome reduces segmentation variability. As will be seen in Experiment III, this procedure also allows the separation of a negative correlation, due to syllable structure, from a positive correlation related to intonation patterns. Ohala's fully justified criticism of Kozhevnikov/Chistovich (Ohala, 1975) and of Wright (Ohala & Lyberg,

1976) is thus not relevant here because approach and aim are different (cf. also Huggins, 1975).

Experiment III

To investigate the influence of different pitch patterns on rhythmic structuring the logatmes *Pinne/Pinnige, Pahne/Pahnige, Schraabse/Schraabsige* were put in the sentence frame "Karl wird die...treten." with the following intonations:

"Karl wird die Pinne treten."

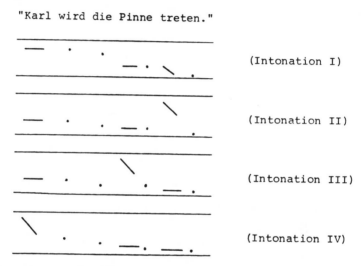

(Intonation I)

(Intonation II)

(Intonation III)

(Intonation IV)

Pinne, Pahne, Schraabse were also put in the sentence frame "Karl hat die...getreten." (with the same 4 intonations) to test the effect of word boundaries (see Kohler, 1983a). The sentences were randomized and interspersed with dummies. One speaker, KK, produced 10 tokens of each sentence type by repeating each of the 4 sets (one for each intonation) 10 times (for further details of method, see Kohler, 1983a). The segmentation was carried out in the same way as in Experiment II.

Linear regression analyses of ending durations ([ə] or [ɪgə], respectively) on foot durations for each pitch pattern yield the intercepts (a) and slopes (b) listed in Table 13.4. The data with/without word boundary in the 3-syllable foot (*Pinnige, Pinne ge-*, etc.) were pooled. The results of the corresponding linear regression analyses for each syllable structure and number of syllables are given in Table 13.5. There is a negative correlation between the duration variables across the syllable types, but a positive correlation across the 4 intonations. This finding adds further support to the statements (D) and (E) in connection with the results of Experiment II. The data from the different

KLAUS J. KOHLER

TABLE 13.4

Intercepts (a), Slopes (b), Correlation Coefficients (r) with Significance Levels (p) in Linear Regression Analyses of Ending Durations on Foot Durations for Each Pitch Pattern of Experiment III.

	$a(ms)$	b	r	p	n
		ə/foot			
Intonation I	168	-0.22	-0.87	0.000	30
Intonation II	147	-0.20	-0.78	0.000	30
Intonation III	146	-0.21	-0.81	0.000	30
Intonation IV	131	-0.19	-0.84	0.000	29
		$\bar{b} = -0.20$			
		$s = -0.01$			
		ιgə/foot			
Intonation I	296	-0.24	-0.79	0.000	60
Intonation II	283	-0.23	-0.74	0.000	60
Intonation III	267	-0.20	-0.74	0.000	60
Intonation IV	255	-0.21	-0.81	0.000	60
		$\bar{b} = -0.22$			
		$s = -0.02$			

syllable structures of Experiment III cannot be integrated into one regression line with a positive slope, although this was possible in Experiment I. This is a reflection of a stronger compression effect in the case of reduced endings: they can adjust their durations negatively to the time requirements of the stem within a much wider margin than can the more complex articulations of the foot remiss in Experiment I. This speaks against the use of reiterant speech (cf. Liberman & Streeter, 1978), when the details of foot structure are at issue, because [ma:]-sequences will not be able to capture these compensatory duration effects between stem complexity and weak ending.

The four intonations covary with parallel shifts of the regression lines (see Table 13.4): Intonations I and IV form the extremes, Intonations II and III lie in between and close together. This relationship is the same for the 2- and the 3-syllable foot. The slopes for these two foot types are very similar altogether. So it looks as if the two endings, [ə] and [ιgə], are simply characterized by parallel shifts of the regression lines. In this case the mean of all the b-values ($\bar{b} = -0.21$), the a-values for [ə] (Intonation I: 168, Intonation II, III: 147, Intonation IV: 131) and an a-increment for [ιgə] ($\Delta a = 128$) can determine the linear regressions. Eqs. (4)—(6) capture the relationships between ending (E) or stem (S) durations and rhythmic foot duration (R).

TABLE 13.5

Intercepts (a), Slopes (b), Correlation Coefficients (r) with Significance Levels (p) in Linear Regression Analyses of Ending Durations on Foot Durations for Each Syllable Structure and Number of Syllables of Experiment III.

	ə/foot				
	$a(ms)$	b	r	p	n
/pɪn/	-11.1	0.26	0.83	0.000	40
/paːn/	-1.6	0.16	0.56	0.000	40
/šraːps/	-39.5	0.18	0.63	0.000	39
	ɪgə/foot				
/pɪn/	34.7	0.34	0.85	0.000	80
/paːn/	25.8	0.28	0.79	0.000	80
/šraːps/	-18.3	0.30	0.77	0.000	80

$$R = R_{pi} + \Delta R_{pa,šra} + \Delta R_3 - \Delta R \text{ II, III, IV} \tag{4}$$

R_{pi} : mean of the least complex 2-syllable foot [pɪnə] with Intonation I

$\Delta R_{pa, šra}$: mean foot increments for [paːn] and [šraːps], respectively

ΔR_3 : mean foot increment for the 3-syllable foot

$\Delta R_{II, III, IV}$: mean foot decrements for Intonations II, III, and IV

$$E = a_i + bR \tag{5}$$

a_i : different intercepts for [ə] and [ɪgə], respectively.

$$S = R - E \tag{6}$$

With R_{pi} = 380 ms, ΔR_{pa} = 74 ms, $\Delta R_{šra}$ = 128 ms, ΔR_3 = 83 ms, $\Delta R_{II, III}$ = 35 ms, and ΔR_{IV} = 65 ms the mean durations for all the different foot types and their parts can be computed. A comparison of the computed means with the empirical ones shows a very good correspondence (see Table 13.6).

The data suggest that the foot duration increments for more complex syllable structures than *Pinne* and for the 3-syllable versus the 2-syllable foot *can* stay constant at different speech rates, and that tempo changes add another additive constant ΔR_T to Equation (4). It may also be assumed that tempo variations have the same effect as intonation on the positions of the regression lines across different stem types, resulting in further parallel shifts.

TABLE 13.6

Empirical and Computed Means of Foot, Stem, and Ending Durations (in ms) in Experiment III. Ft./St./End.=Foot/Stem/Ending.

	Intonation I			Intonation II			Intonation III			Intonation IV		
	Ft.	St.	End.	Ft.	St.	End.	Ft.	St.	End.	Ft.	St.	End.
Pinne	380	294	86	345	268	77	340	263	77	315	246	69
	380	292	88	345	270	75	345	270	75	315	250	65
Pinnige	462	272	190	438	253	185	434	251	183	405	234	171
	463	264	199	428	243	185	428	243	185	398	223	175
Pahne	459	388	71	430	361	69	418	356	62	400	338	62
	454	381	73	419	360	59	419	360	59	389	340	49
Pahnige	525	354	171	504	336	168	498	331	167	475	316	159
	529	344	185	494	323	171	494	323	171	464	302	162
Schraabse	511	458	53	470	423	47	470	424	46	450	409	41
	508	447	61	473	425	48	473	425	48	443	405	38
Schraabsige	584	430	154	559	408	151	563	416	147	538	399	139
	591	419	172	556	398	158	556	408	158	526	377	149

As the data of Experiment II are too few to carry out regression analyses, a further experiment is necessary to test this hypothesis. If a negative ΔR_T for faster speeds than average normal reduces the foot duration to such an extent that the linear syllable/foot and phone/syllable regressions (see the following section) provide phone durations that are below minimal values for the different phone types (Klatt, 1979c), the articulatory control has to be reorganized in such a way that certain gestures are eliminated to suit the temporal constraints. Thus articulatory reductions (elisions, assimilations, and weak forms) are built into this top-down model of speech production.

PHONE TIMING

The data of Experiment I were segmented down to the phone level, and regression analyses of phone durations on syllable durations were carried out across all speech rates and subjects as well as for each speaker separately. Table 13.7 lists the intercepts, slopes, and correlation coefficients with significance levels for the segments within each of the 5 syllable types (stressed

TABLE 13.7

Intercepts (a), Slopes (b), Correlation Coefficients (r) with Significance Levels (p) in Linear Regression Analyses of Segment Durations on Syllable Durations for Each of the Five Syllable Types (Stressed and Unstressed Pooled) and for the Whole Group of Six Subjects in Experiment I.

		a(ms)	b	r	p	n
	p	42.5	0.184	0.797	0.000	1080
	h	8.6	0.092	0.644	0.000	1080
[pa:]	a:	-51.0	0.723	0.977	0.000	1080
	h+a:	-42.5	0.816	0.986	0.000	1080
	b	30.5	0.184	0.839	0.000	1055
[ba:]	a:	-30.5	0.816	0.990	0.000	1055
	b	27.4	0.162	0.827	0.000	881
[bla:]	l	29.8	0.088	0.751	0.000	881
	a:	-57.2	0.750	0.987	0.000	881
	p	13.7	0.233	0.922	0.000	990
	h	15.4	0.051	0.479	0.000	990
	a	15.5	0.258	0.867	0.000	990
[paš]	h+a	30.9	0.309	0.932	0.000	990
	š	-44.6	0.458	0.968	0.000	990
	h+a+š	-13.7	0.767	0.992	0.000	990
	š	6.6	0.414	0.927	0.000	990
	a	10.2	0.226	0.873	0.000	990
[šap]	p	-16.8	0.360	0.913	0.000	990
	a+p	-6.6	0.586	0.962	0.000	990

and unstressed pooled) for all the 6 subjects together. The corresponding values for each speaker were compiled in Kohler, et al. (1981). The relationship is again clearly linear, but contrary to the relationship between foot and syllable in Experiment I, it is not proportional. However, if vowel and closure durations in [šap] are summed, the intercept for this dyad becomes negligible and the scatter around the regression line exhibits a higher correlation between the duration variables. Similarly, if in [paš] the aspiration is included in the vowel, the intercept for the dyad [aš] becomes small enough to be ignored, and again the correlation is higher than for the aspiration, the vowel, and the fricative separately.

TABLE 13.8

Intercepts (a), Slopes (b), Correlation Coefficients (r) with Significance Levels (p) in Linear Regression Analyses of Segment on Syllable and Segment on Dyad Durations for the "Seide"/"Seite" Data of Kohler, et al. (1982); $n = 55$; t, d = stop closure.

	a(ms)	b	r	p
Seide				
z/zaid	9.1	0.187	0.669	0.000
ai/zaid	2.4	0.667	0.926	0.000
d/zaid	-11.5	0.146	0.610	0.000
aid/zaid	-9.1	0.813	0.969	0.000
ai/aid	8.0	0.828	0.964	0.000
d/aid	-8.0	0.172	0.604	0.000
Seite				
z/zait	3.3	0.204	0.593	0.000
ai/zait	16.4	0.537	0.809	0.000
t/zait	-19.7	0.259	0.675	0.000
ait/zait	-3.3	0.796	0.944	0.000
ai/ait	10.9	0.707	0.897	0.000
t/ait	-10.9	0.293	0.645	0.000

The dyad consisting of a vowel and a following obstruent is thus a fairly stable production unit, more so than its component parts, and, just like the syllable within the foot, it changes proportionately within the syllable under the influence of prosodic factors such as tempo, final lengthening, and intonation (Fitch, 1981). The "Seide"/"Seite" data of Kohler, Krützmann, Reetz & Timmermann (1982) provide the linear regressions, summarized in Table 13.8, of phone and dyad on syllable as well as of phone on dyad durations. The proportion of the dyad in the syllable stays the same across the different intonation patterns and sentence positions used in Kohler, et al. (1982), and it is practically also identical for the sequences of [ai] and lenis or fortis stop closures. The global opening-closing-opening gestures from the beginning of the vowel to the end of the consonant are the same in the two cases. It is the internal microstructures of the movements that differ: There is a fast closing movement in "Seite," a slow one in "Seide," captured by the steeper slope of the diphthong/dyad regression in the latter. There seem to be two structural parts within the syllable, viz. the initial consonant (cluster) and the vowel + following consonant, the dyad being in turn broken up into its peak and coda (Hockett, 1955).

A PRODUCTION TIMING MODEL:
FROM FOOT TO PHONE

On the basis of the results from Experiments I–III, the following top-down production timing model is proposed as a set of ordered rules starting from foot durations and working downwards to phone durations.

$$R_{ijkl} = D + C_i + N_j + I_k + T_l$$
$$\text{for } i = 0, 1, 2 \ldots \tag{7}$$
$$j = 1, 2 \ldots$$
$$k = 0, 1, 2 \ldots$$
$$l = 0, \pm 1, \pm 2 \ldots$$
$$C_0 = N_1 = I_0 = T_0 = 0$$

R : rhythmic foot duration

D : duration constant of the 1-syllable foot of the smallest complexity at a neutral pitch pattern and a medium tempo

C_i : additive duration constants for 1-syllable feet of increasing complexity in vowels and consonants

N_j : additive duration constants for feet with more than one syllable

I_k : additive duration constants for feet with other intonations than neutral

T_l : additive duration constants for other speech rates than medium

This rule applies to feet not containing reduced vowel syllables.

$$S^{(S)} = b_{R_j} \times R_{ijkl} \qquad S^{(U)} = R_{ijkl} - S^{(S)} \tag{8a}$$

$S^{(S)}$: duration of stressed syllable

$S^{(U)}$: duration of the unstressed syllables in the foot

b_{R_j} : slopes of the linear regressions of stressed syllable on foot duration, depending on the number of syllables in the foot

This rule applies to feet containing reduced vowel syllables. In this case, $N_2 = N_1 = 0$ in (7).

$$S^{(E)} = a_{N_j} + a_{I_k} + A_{T_l} + b'_R \times R_{ijkl} \qquad S^{(St)} = R_{ijkl} - S^{(E)} \tag{8b}$$

$S^{(E)}$: duration of ending

$S^{(St)}$: duration of stem syllable in the foot

a_{N_j} : intercept of the linear regressions of ending on foot duration, depending on the numbers of syllables in the foot

a_{I_k} : intercept increments depending on intonation; $a_{I_0} = 0$

a_{T_l} : intercept increments depending on tempo; $a_{T_0} = 0$

b'_R : slope of the linear regressions of ending on foot duration

$$SC = a_{P_m} + b_{P_m} \times S^{(S,U,E,St)} \tag{9}$$

SC : duration of syllable component, viz. initial consonant (cluster) and vowel (+ final consonant)

a_{P_m}, b_{P_m} : intercepts and slopes of the linear regressons of syllable component on syllable duration, depending on the type of syllable component; $a_{P_m} = 0$ in $C_1 V C_2$ syllables with $C_2 =$ obstruent

$$P = a_{P_n} + b_{P_n} \times SC \tag{10}$$

P : duration of phone

a_{P_n}, b_{P_n} : intercepts and slopes of the linear regressions of phone on syllable component duration, depending on the phone type.

FURTHER ADDITIONS TO THE MODEL ABOVE THE FOOT

The data of Experiments II and III also show duration adjustments between successive feet. To accommodate the extra time needed for greater articulatory complexity in one foot, the subsequent foot is shortened if its production timing has a wide enough margin, for instance in speech rates that are not too fast and in utterance positions where final lengthening applies. This negative-temporal correlation between feet is a further aspect of the isochrony tendency. Spearman rank-correlation analyses in Experiment II between the mean durations of the different types of logatome cores and the corresponding first or second part of the sentence frame (preceding or following the nonsense word), respectively, provide the coefficients and significance levels listed in Table 13.9. The majority of core/frame I correlations are not significant, and the significant ones are—with one exception—positive. On the other hand, the majority of core/frame II correlations are significant, and they are all negative. These clear results highlight the right-to-left temporal compensation—i.e., the later timing correction for the duration over/undershoot in the preceding foot—as a further aspect of isochrony. The coefficients are lowest in the fast speed where, due to articulatory timing constraints, the duration range for adjustment is very limited anyway.

TABLE 13.9

Spearman Rank-correlation Coefficients (r) and Significance Levels (p) Relating the Mean Durations of the Core Logatome Types (C) and of the Preceding or Following Sentence Frame (FI, FII) in the 6 Data Sets of Experiment II, Separately for Each Tempo; $n = 12$.

		C/FI		C/FII	
		r	p	r	p
CW+	normal	0.27	n.s.	-0.82	0.001
	slow	0.05	n.s.	-0.92	0.001
	fast	0.17	n.s.	-0.80	0.001
CW−	normal	-0.59	0.021	-0.76	0.002
	slow	0.46	n.s.	-0.52	0.040
	fast	-0.27	n.s.	-0.59	0.022
KK+	normal	0.55	0.031	-0.77	0.002
	slow	-0.28	n.s.	-0.79	0.001
	fast	0.32	n.s.	-0.51	0.046
KK−	normal	0.26	n.s.	-0.66	0.025
	slow	0.34	n.s.	-0.86	0.001
	fast	0.46	n.s.	-0.41	n.s.
GU+	normal	0.23	n.s.	-0.15	n.s.
	slow	–	–	–	–
	fast	0.85	0.005	0.14	n.s.
GU−	normal	0.69	0.025	-0.25	n.s.
	slow	0.62	0.05	-0.41	n.s.
	fast	0.25	n.s.	-0.04	n.s.

Pearson product-moment correlations were computed between individual core and frame II durations for each intonation in Experiment III. The coefficients and significance levels are listed in Table 13.10. The correlation is again negative, and it is highest in the step-wise descent of Intonation I, where the overall utterance duration is longer and where a wider margin thus separates the foot duration form the lower temporal boundary determined by minimum requirements for the various articulatory gestures; temporal compensation can therefore operate with less restriction.

TABLE 13.10

Pearson Product-moment Correlation Coefficients (r) and Significance Levels
(p) Relating the Individual Logatome Core and Frame II Durations in the 4
Intonations of Experiment III; $n = 90$.

	Intonation I	Intonation II	Intonation III	Intonation IV
r	-0.63	-0.28	-0.32	-0.34
p	0.000	0.004	0.001	0.001

The effect of utterance-final lengthening also has to be incorporated into
the model. As was shown in Kohler (1983a), the whole utterance-final word
seems to receive a constant duration increment independent of the number of
syllables it contains. The last syllable gets the largest share; the stressed syllable among the nonfinal ones comes next. This utterance-final lengthening is
only a special case of the temporal organization of speech being influenced by
the information structuring the speaker wants to convey by prosodic boundary signals in general. Words and phrases, as well as text cohesion above the
sentence, add further timing constraints on speech production (cf. Kohler,
1983a).

Utterance-final lengthening seems to be a universal phenomenon and has
to be kept separate from compression in stress-timed languages. Jespersen's
reference (1913, p. 180) to a progressive shortening in the vowels of the
German and French series *Zahl, zahlen, zahlende* and *pâte, pâté, pâtisserie*,
respectively (see also Grégoire, 1899), on account of the increasing number
of subsequent syllables, misses the fact that these words were produced in
isolation and therefore in utterance-final position. So they do not primarily
attest to compression in a foot-structure, but to final lengthening, which
affects the last syllable most and shows a decreasing strength to the left.
Therefore *pâte* and *pâté* in French are bound to yield a duration difference
in -â-, because in one case it occurs in an absolute final, in the other case in
a prefinal syllable. Thus these data do not point to the same compression
in French and in German and are no proof of a similar foot structure, and
consequently of stress-timing, in the two languages.

Nonfinal positions in information units are crucial here, and they show
that French behaves differently. A first set of analyzed data suggests that
the compression effect is absent from French and that there is no justification for setting up a foot level in the description of French speech timing.
The concatenation of French syllables is not constrained by a rhythmic su-
perstructure, but the temporal organization is simply governed by syllable
complexity, intonation and tempo. Lindblom and Rapp (1973), Nooteboom
(1972), and Rietveld (1975) also ignored the distinction between compression through a foot structure and final lengthening, and therefore captured

an interaction of decreasing final lengthening from right to left with foot compression in their analyses of Swedish, Dutch, and German.

CONCLUSION

The timing model outlined in this paper integrates phonological quantity oppositions and durational manifestations of other segmental contrasts, such as fortis/lenis, in a comprehensive hierarchy of temporal organization in the speech-production process. Phone duration at the output of this model is not only determined by the phonological units in the phonological system, but also by articulatory constraints on these structural elements and by their positions in the syllable and, ultimately, in the foot. The temporal variability of phonological units—due to articulatory control and coordination, syllabic context, rhythmic structure, tempo, and intonation—is thus built into the system of segmental phonemes, not added as a set of low-level rules, and the paradigmatic elements are viewed in their syntagmatic context right from the beginning. Moreover, this variability is rule-governed and relatable to parameters of invariance at several levels of the utterance. The model no longer distinguishes sharply between invariant phonological formatives and variant phonetic implementations. For instance, different slopes in the linear-regression equations connecting long- or short-vowel quantities with the syllable represent the phonological quantity distinction as well as the phonetic-duration variability in different prosodies. In this way, phonological elements are re-introduced into the time domain of speech production and perception. Invariance and variability thus no longer form an insoluble opposition between discrete and static, on the one hand, and dynamic and continuous, on the other, but are intimately linked, just as phonology is now incorporated into a phonetics laboratory.

ACKNOWLEDGMENT

This research was supported by German Research Council (DFG) Grants Ko 331/16, 17.

Ilse Lehiste: Comment

The paper by K. J. Kohler deals with invariance and variability in speech timing in general, and with timing patterns in German in particular. It argues for the need to approach timing from a syntagmatic point of view, especially in languages that employ contrastive quantity in their phonological systems. Kohler develops a top-down timing model for speech production in German. The model deals first with the relationship between foot and syllable durations as a function of articulatory complexity and number of syllables in the foot; then it derives segment durations from the syllable durations generated by the foot-to-syllable algorithm.

I agree with many of the statements made in Kohler's paper but there are some aspects of the paper with which I disagree. Let me first give a brief overview of the agreements and then mention some instances in which my views differ from those expressed by Kohler.

I am convinced of the validity of the syntagmatic approach to speech timing: Contrastive segmental duration is manifested within the overall temporal structure of a word, the durational structure of a word depends on its position within the utterance, and sentence-level patterns are integrated into patterns characteristic of higher-level units such as paragraphs. In fact, I have been speaking out in favor of this kind of hierarchical approach for quite a number of years.

I also agree that while absolute isochrony of rhythmic feet will probably never be found, a tendency toward giving rhythmic feet more or less equal duration is present in those languages that are traditionally called stress-timed (such as English and German). Kohler has demonstrated that there is an absolute limit to the compression that can be applied to the syllables of which the metric feet consist, and that the articulatory complexity of the syllables is involved in this process: A syllable like [ba] is more compressible than a syllable like [platš], so that at fast rates of speaking metric feet consisting of syllables like [ba] are more likely to remain isochronous than metric feet containing syllables with greater articulatory complexity.

I was interested in Kohler's finding that there seem to be two structural parts within a German CVC-syllable, namely the initial consonant (or consonant cluster) and the VC sequence. The data presented in support of this claim certainly appear convincing; it would be very interesting to have a similar study carried out in languages that have a predominantly CV syllable structure.

I am less convinced that intonation has a direct influence on the duration of metric feet within an utterance. Kohler states that " ... there is a negative correlation across the syllable types, but a positive correlation between the duration variables across the four intonations"; the four pitch patterns which were used in the study caused parallel shifts of the regression lines. I have difficulty seeing the cause and effect relationship between F_0 patterns and temporal structure. The analyzed materials consisted of six test words produced by one speaker (KK) in two sentence frames with four intonation patterns. I doubt whether it is humanly possible to keep everything else constant and change only the intonation applied to a sentence. It seems that the change in the intonation patterns was connected with changes in the degree of stress applied to the different words; but the phonetic manifestation of stress is very complex, and I would hesitate attributing primacy to the F_0 movements and concluding that the temporal structure depends on the F_0 structure in any systematic way. Positive correlations between F_0 and duration patterns may simply mean that both are affected by a third factor in similar ways; the third factor in this case may well have been degree of stress.

What I missed in Kohler's treatment of rhythm is the potential interaction between the rhythmic structure of a sentence and its syntax. In fact, Kohler seems to skip over syntax completely in his model; this is made quite explicit in an earlier paper (Kohler, 1983): "It is superfluous in this generative outlook to have a separate phonological level linking phonetic data with syntactic and semantic structures ... All the relevant features of the communication process can be accounted for by *staying within phonetics and semantics* [p. 131 (emphasis mine)]."

I have shown in several publications (summarized in Lehiste, 1983) that, at least in English, modification of the rhythmic structure of a sentence is used to convey syntactic information. Kohler accepts the presence of utterance-final lengthening, but apparently does not believe in the possibility of preboundary lengthening in the more general sense—where boundary stands not only for utterance boundary, but also for internal, syntactic boundaries within the utterance. I believe that his model needs to be modified to allow for mutual relationships between speech timing and the syntactic structure of the sentence.

Klaus J. Kohler: Response

Ilse Lehiste raises two criticisms:
1. It is difficult to see why there should be a causal relationship between F_O and foot duration in Experiment III. Moreover, the utterances used probably not only differed in F_O, but also in stress, and stress has complex manifestations, e.g. duration.
2. Syntactic factors should have been considered in the discussion of duration control at the utterance level. In particular, other types of final lengthening, outside the utterance-final position, should have been included.

With regard to the first criticism, it must be pointed out that no causal relationship between F_O and foot duration was suggested. What entered into the regression analyses as a statistical parameter was "Intonation I-IV," not F_O. The representation of Intonation I-IV followed the British tradition of intonation analysis and symbolization by dots and dashes. This implies stress besides pitch. Furthermore, data collection also relied on both features: The sentences were read from four lists, one each for the four intonation patterns. In the first list, ordinary typography was used, in the other three, "treten," the logatome, and "Karl," respectively, were typed with capitals, and the instructions were to produce an overall falling pitch pattern with three even stresses in the first case or with one focus each in the other cases.

As far as Lehiste's second point is concerned, there is, first of all, explicit mention that utterance-final lengthening is regarded as a special case of the temporal organization of speech being influenced by a speaker's information structuring. Secondly, the purpose of the paper was to present what might be called the rhythmic component of German utterance timing, independent of syntax and semantics. The latter were only considered in the data to delimit utterances. Utterance-internal duration structures related to syntax and semantics were deliberately excluded from the discussion, and in this connection the reader was referred to Kohler (1983). It was the central aim of the paper to develop a model of speech timing proceeding from foot sequence to foot to syllable to segment, and it turns out that linearity can be postulated for this model based on the statistical analysis of an extensive corpus of data from German. In connection with this central theme, the chapter stressed the need to incorporate the distinctive segment issue into the wider utterance frame, viewing phonological and allophonic length distinctions in a syntagmatic perspective. This is congruent with Vaissiere's (1983b) argument that a combination of prosodic and segmental characteristics determine movement patterns.

Of course, this rhythmic component has to be supplemented by the introduction of syntax and semantics in a more comprehensive model of speech timing, without the independent status of rhythmic-duration control being affected. The speaker's intention, in communicating with a listener, to convey certain information make him choose syntactic and prosodic devices to structure this information and to give relative weight to its components. Syntax and prosody are thus parallel manifestations of this information structuring and weighting. They are the expression of the semantic and pragmatic intention of the speaker; they may converge in their signalling power or they may not. According to this view, it is futile to talk about syntactic relations being expressed prosodically or about syntax having an influence on duration. The semantic and pragmatic intentions of the speaker control both syntax and prosody. Apart from this semantic/pragmatic control of speech timing, the independent rhythmic structuring has to be taken into account, and it is simply the latter this paper is concerned with.

Eva Gårding:
Superposition as an Invariant Feature of Intonation

Kohler's paper deals primarily with rhythmic aspects of prosody and their influence on variation in speech timing. I would like to concentrate on a prosodic feature that implies invariance rather than variability, namely superposition in intonation. To substantiate this point, I shall draw from analyses of languages of varying prosodic complexity. The analyses have been made within the framework of an intonation model which is being developed in Lund (Cf. Bruce & Gårding, 1978; Gårding, 1981, 1983). One of the assumptions of this model is that the accent commands and the sentence-intonation command are largely independent of each other and that they are at least approximately added to each other. This idea of superposition was originally proposed by Sven Öhman (1967) and was later adopted by Hiroya Fujisaki for Japanese (Fujisaki & Nagashima, 1969) and by myself for Swedish in a more qualitative way (1970).[1]

---

[1] For recent, different views of intonation analysis see Cutler & Ladd(1983).

Concepts of the model

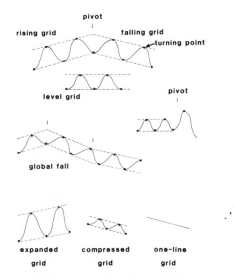

FIG. 13c.1. Concepts of the model, illustrated by schematic FO curves connecting turning points over sonorant segments. Grids are marked by broken lines, pivots by arrows.

The main features of this model, in its present stage, are the grid and the pivots, shown schematically in Figure 13c.1. The vertical FO scale is logarithmic throughout. The grid consists of two lines enclosing the main part of the intonation curve. It represents the general direction of the intonation. With evenly stressed accents or tones, the lines tend to be straight and nearly parallel. They pass through the turning points which are associated with lexical accents or tones. Where the grid jumps or changes position, there is a pivot. A pivot is usually connected with focus and important syntactic boundaries. In the figure, there are examples of grids with normal, expanded, and compressed accents. Note that the grid is meant to exhibit direction and range, not the details of accent patterns.

Superposition is here interpreted in such a way that accents or tones are represented by movements with specified timing and shape that are added to some locally averaged lower bound of intonation (Figure 13c.2). Superposition will be the same under different intonations and in different languages. It will therefore be considered as an invariant principle of intonation.

In my comments, I shall present some features of intonation, collected from languages with different prosodic systems, which speak in favour of superposition. I have labelled these features of intonation *turning-point fixation*, which means that the position of an FO-turning point is tied to a particular phonetic unit—e.g. a vocalic segment or a syllable—under varying sentence intonation and *deformation* of accentual and tonal configurations as a result of the superposition principle.

I will first present examples of turning point fixation effects from a two-tone language like Hausa, a four-tone language like standard Chinese, a two-accent lan-

Superposition

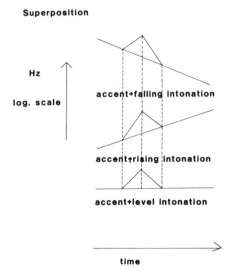

FIG. 13c.2. Superposition. A triangular accent shape is added to different phrase intonations.

HAUSA: MÁALÀM YÁA AÙNÍ LEÈMÓO

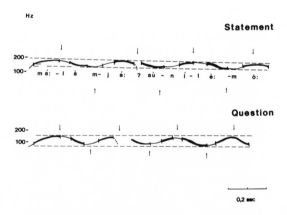

Turning point fixation

FIG. 13c.3. Turning-point fixation in Hausa. Arrows point to high (↓) and low (↑) turning points, associated with the end of syllables which are hyphenated in the transcription. Thick lines denote vocalic segments, broken lines the grid. Glottal stop [ʔ] is used by speaker to avoid hiatus.

STANDARD CHINESE: SÒNG YÁN MÀI NIÚRÒU

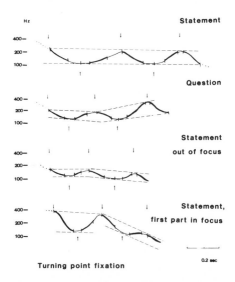

FIG. 13c.4. Turning-point fixation in Standard Chinese. Arrows point to high (↓) and low (↑) turning points caused by falling and rising tones respectively. Their timing in relation to segments (thick lines denote vocalic segments) and grid (broken lines) is constant throughout the different prosodic patterns.

guage like Swedish, and a one-accent language like English.[2] In Hausa (Figure 13c.3), the timing of the highs and lows, indicated by arrows above and below the grids respectively, is tied to the syllable boundary. This timing is shown by the example, *Máalàm yáa aùní leèmóo,* "The teacher distributed the oranges," in statement and question intonation. A high tone gives an FO-maximum at the end of a syllable marked high, and a low gives a minimum with a similar timing. The overall sentence intonation is represented by the grid, that is the broken lines. In the statement these two lines have a very slight fall and in the question they are level. There is, in addition, a raised high in the last syllable of the question, and as a rule the question is quite a bit shorter. All these data are from Lindau Webb (1983).[3]

In Chinese, the timing of the turning points is also fixed to the syllables which in the majority of cases are also morphemes. This timing is independent of the sentence intonation and the focus pattern. Figure 13c.4 shows a sentence with alternating falling and rising tones: *Sòng yán mài niúroù,* "Song Yan sells calf's meat;" in order from the top of the figure: a statement, a question, a statement

[2] The *FO* curves shown are actual observed ones representing means of acoustic records of five to ten utterances by one speaker.

[3] Hausa and Chinese are analyzed at our department in a project supported by the Swedish Research Council.

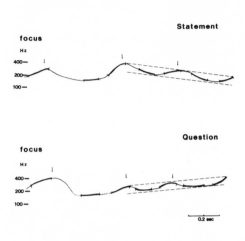

SOUTHERN SWEDISH: MÀNNE MÀNNAR MÀNNARNA

Turning point fixation

FIG. 13c.5. Turning-point fixation in Swedish. Arrows point to high
(↓) turning points caused by Accent 2 and located at the end of the vocalic
segment (thick line) with a slight shift to the left in the focus position of
the question.

out of focus, and a statement with the first part, the subject phrase, in focus. In
the question, the grid is rising after the syntactic boundary, the pivot, and it is
close to level or falling in the statements (Gårding, Zhang, & Svantesson, 1983).

In the Swedish examples (Figure 13c.5), *Mànne mànnar mànnarna*, "Manne
musters the chaps," the highs of the accented syllables, which are all accents 2,
are invariably tied to the same phonetic segment, in this dialect the end of the
accented vowel. There is however, a slight shift of location in the focus position of
the question (See also Figure 13c.8).

My last examples of turning point fixation are English *I heard the BULLS bellow
in the lane* and *Did you hear the BULLS bellow in the lane* (Figure 13c.6). In this case
as well, the timing of the turning points is retained relative to the carrier syllable
"bulls," indicated by the vertical double-pointed arrow. However, the shape of the
focal accent is determined by the global intonation and the position in the phrase.
As a general rule, a high in a falling intonation (the statement) corresponds to a
low in a rising one (the question). This effect is similar to what happens in other
Germanic languages, as in Dutch and German.

The second point that speaks in favour of superposition is the one I have called
deformation of tonal and accentual configurations under varying sentence intonation. This effect is demonstrated by the schematic Figure 13c.7. The effect of
superposition is illustrated by a rising accent or tone in a level, falling, or rising
intonation (A in the figure). The accent (tone) is located in a syllable consisting of
sonorant segments and the high is fixed to the end of the syllable in all the exem-

ENGLISH:

I HEARD THE BULLS BELLOW IN THE LANE

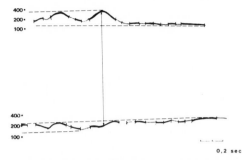

0,2 sec

DID YOU HEAR THE BULLS BELLOW IN THE LANE?

Turning point fixation

FIG. 13c.6.   Turning-point fixation in English. The double-pointed arrow indicates the turning points, high in the statement and low in the question.

DEFORMATION

(A)   Rising accent or tone

Level grid   Falling grid   Rising grid

(B)   Falling accent or tone

(C)Rising-falling accents or tones

Falling grid

Rising grid

Level + compressed,

(D)   falling grid

↑

Pivot focus

FIG. 13c.7.   Schematic drawings of deformation of accents or tones in different kinds of grids.

SOUTHERN SWEDISH: NÌA NÌA NÌA

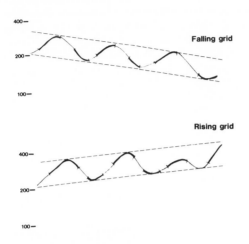

Deformation of accents

FIG. 13c.8. Deformation of accents in Swedish. The locations of the Accent 2 highs are slightly shifted to the left in the rising intonation. The accents sound emphatic and the contour is best labelled surprised question.

plified cases. With a falling grid the rising accent is flattened out, and with a rising grid the slope and the length of the rising movement increase. A falling accent (B) has a steeper slope downwards in a falling grid and is flattened out in a rising one. In the next pair of schematized contours (C), we can compare rising-falling local movements on a falling grid above and a rising one below. Notice that the triangular shape of the accents is different. In the falling contour the tilt makes the left side of the triangle seem shorter, and in the rising contour it is the right side. At the bottom of the figure (D), there is a schematized version of a contour beginning with a level grid followed by a compressed falling grid. The use of a compressed grid after focus is general across languages. In this example, the shape of the intonation curve looks like a sequence of terraces.

Finally, Figure 13c.8 shows some observed curves with features corresponding to the schematic figures. There are two Swedish examples in the figure, *Nìa, nìa, nìa,* "Nine, nine, nine" in military speech, in a falling grid above and a rising one below. The accentual triangles behave as expected. When they are tilted to the right in the falling grid, they seem to have a long righthand side relative to the base, that is, the grid. When they are tilted to the left in the rising grid, it is the lefthand side which becomes longer. In this case, however, all the turning points are slightly shifted to the left relative to the segments in the rising intonation. This may be an effect of emphasis. The accents sound emphatic.

Chinese (Figure 13c.4) has some nice examples of deformation shown in the utterance-final rising-falling tone pattern. The triangular shape of this pattern has almost equal legs in the uppermost statement. In the rising grid, it is tilted in such a way relative to the grid that the left side appears longer than the right one. The carrying syllables, however, have equal durations. The last intonation contour of Figure 13c.4 exemplifies an expanded grid combined with a falling, compressed grid. Here we notice the beginning of a staircase pattern. We must also notice that seen from the grid, perhaps also heard from the grid, this constant-tone movement is rising.

These features, the effects of turning-point fixation and accent or tone deformation, support indirectly the idea that superposition occurs in speech as a general feature, independently of the prosodic system. If superposition is accepted as a principle, it leads naturally to a generative model where the grid—that is, the global expression of intonation—is generated first and the accents and tones, represented by high and low points, are inserted later and fixed to the grid and the segments according to specific rules. Due to the turning-point fixation, these rules can be very simple. The rules pertaining to the grids have to be supplemented by prescriptions for large and fast-pitch movements at the pivots. But it is natural to expect that there is a restricted number of those prescriptions and that they are used in a systematic way for a particular language or dialect.

To sum up: the notion of superposition of accents and tones as defined here makes it possible to predict how different sentence intonations influence the shapes of tones and accents. In this way, their variability is counterbalanced by an invariance feature.

14

The Problem of Variability
In Speech Recognition and
In Models of Speech Perception

Dennis H. Klatt
Massachusetts Institute of Technology
Cambridge, MA, USA

INTRODUCTION

Listeners know, implicitly, a great deal about what acoustic properties define an acceptable pronunciation of any given word. Part of this knowledge concerns the kinds of environmental variability, within-speaker variability, and across-speakers variability that is to be expected and discounted during the process of identification. Current computer algorithms that recognize speech employ rather primitive techniques for dealing with this variability, and thus often find it difficult to distinguish between members of a small vocabulary if spoken by many talkers. An attempt will be made to pinpoint exactly what is wrong with current pattern-recognition techniques for overcoming variability, and suggest ways in which machines might significantly improve their speech-recognition performance in the future by attending to constraints imposed by the human speech production and perception apparatus.

The variability in the pronunciation or words that arises when the task is continuous speech recognition will also be examined. Three similar approaches to continuous speech recognition have been selected for comparison: LAFS (Lexical Access From Spectra)(Klatt, 1979a), the IBM system (Jelenek, 1976) and Harpy (Lowerre & Reddy, 1980). A second-generation LAFS model of bottom-up lexical access is offered as a means for identifying words in connected speech, and as a candidate perceptual model. The refinements concern a more efficient generalizable way of handling cross-word-boundary phonology and coarticulation, and a model of learning that may be powerful enough to explain how listeners optimize acoustic-phonetic decisions and discover phonological rules.

The most successful computer-based speech-recognition devices use pattern-matching techniques to distinguish between a small set of acoustically distinct isolated words spoken by a talker who had previously supplied a set of training data to the computer (see Lea, 1980 for reviews). Nearly all of these systems engage very similar techniques—techniques that seem far removed from the way that we perceive words.

A typical isolated word recognition system might characterize an input speech waveform as a sequence of spectra computed every 10 to 20 msec. Each vocabulary item is typically represented by one or more sequences of spectra derived from training data. Recognition consists of finding the best match between input and vocabulary templates.

Recognition of a small set of words would not be difficult were it not for the remarkable variability seen in the pronunciation of any given word. In the systems we are discussing, within-speaker variability in pronunciation and speaking rate are handled by: (1) including more than one word template if a clustering algorithm or other technique indicates that a single template cannot adequately describe the training data (Rabiner, Levinson, Rosenberg, & Wilson, 1979); (2) using dynamic programing to try essentially all reasonable temporal alignments of the unknown spectral sequence with the spectral sequences characterizing word templates (Itakura, 1975; Sakoe and Chiba, 1971); and (3) using the linear prediction residual spectral distance metric to quantify phonetic similarity between pairs of spectra (Itakura, 1975).

Each of these three techniques represents an important engineering advancement over schemes used previously. However, these techniques are not completely adequate. One must understand the processes by which variability arises and by which listeners have learned to ignore random acoustic variation, yet attend to the minutest acoustic detail that provides information when recognizing words spoken by many talkers. Several ideas for moving in this direction will be developed. Extensions required for continuous speech-recognition are the concern of the second half of the paper.

PERIPHERAL MODELING

We begin the search for new techniques for computer recognition of speech with a consideration of what might be learned by a study of the peripheral auditory system. Many researchers have hoped that much of the mystery concerning speech perception would disappear if the right representation of speech signals could only be found. For example, spectral differences between men and women might be reduced in an appropriate representation. Studies of the transformations accomplished by the peripheral auditory system would be a good place to start the search for an improved representation.

A recent conference on modeling peripheral processing of speech (Carlson & Granstrom, 1982a) provides an excellent review of the issues raised by attempts to specify and simulate the transformations that take place in the early stages of the human auditory system. Their conclusions, as they relate to speech recognition efforts, show that perceptual experiments have provided valuable information by revealing which details in the spectrum cannot be resolved. This has led to the concept of critical bands, the Mel frequency scale, and logarithmic encoding of energy within a critical band (see Zwicker, et al. 1979 for details). Physiological data, on the other hand, have been more provocative than constraining in model-building efforts. One issue concerns whether the average firing rate data on primary auditory neurons is the only information used by the central nervous system when making phonetic judgements, or whether interspike-interval information, which appears to better preserve a representation of formant frequency locations as the signal level is changed (Young & Sachs, 1979), is also used.

Srulovicz and Goldstein (1983) suggest that the "central spectrum" (i.e. the presumed spectral representation in the CNS) differs considerably from that represented by the firing patterns of neurons of the 8th nerve, in that one of the first central transformations consists of a filtering of interspike interval data such that only interspike intervals very similar to the best frequency (of the cochlear filter) of each neural population are passed on to higher centers (see also Chapters 5a and 14a). In these kinds of models, it appears that the central spectrum has two properties that may be important to perceptual normalization for speech: the height of a formant-like peak (1) is insensitive to its physical amplitude over a fairly wide range, and (2) is insensitive to general spectral tilt over a fairly wide range (see Figure 14.1).

These properties are consistent with phonetic distance judgement data (Klatt, 1982a). Thus this transformation may make the central spectrum less sensitive to cross-speaker differences in formant bandwidths and glottal source spectral tilt, although such changes would still be reflected in the average firing rate data and could thus be audible.

Carlson and Granstrom (1979; Chapter 5 in this volume) have also proposed using interspike interval data, and described a method for measuring the dominant frequency components in an auditory representation of speech signals. Unfortunately, this measure seems to be more sensitive to spectral tilt than one involving central filters.

Another difference between the spectral representations used in speech recognition and models of peripheral processing is that auditory models tend to have better temporal resolution than is obtained with, for example, a 25 ms Hamming window. This is particularly true at mid- and high frequencies, where resolution of a few msec is suggested (see Chapter 8). It may be necessary to incorporate less smoothing in processing schemes in order to locate and characterize some brief speech events, while simultaneously using other

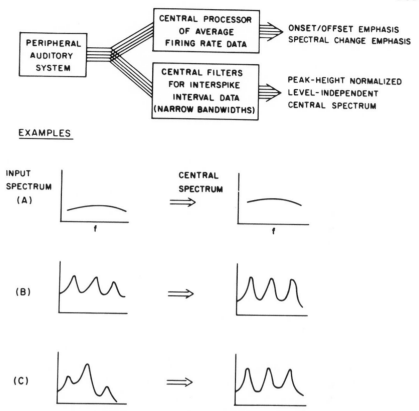

FIG. 14.1. Two ways of processing information provided by the peripheral auditory system (top) and examples of speech spectra and their interspike-interval based central spectral representation according to a model of Srulovicz & Goldstein (1983).

processing strategies with more smoothing in order to satisfy the competing desire to average out pitch-synchronous fluctuations and random background noise.

Finally, the hope has been expressed that a better understanding of peripheral processing constraints might lead to a spectral representation in which the speech of men, women, and children look more similar than is the case with, for instance, broadband spectrograms. However, it does not appear that even critical-band spectral smoothing is sufficient smoothing to merge harmonic locations for high fundamental frequencies and thus make processes such as formant peak-picking a trivial operation (Klatt, 1982b; Seneff, this volume).

It can be concluded that critical-band filtering is a good candidate for the first stage of a speech-recognition device, but much depends on the next

DENNIS H. KLATT

steps in the process—steps (such as those hypothesized in the Srulovicz and Goldstein [1983] model) about which little is known.

THE NATURE OF VARIABILITY

Variability in the acoustic manifestations of a given utterance is substantial and arises from many sources. These include:

1. Recording conditions (background noise, room reverberation, microphone/telephone characteristics).

2. Within-speaker variability (breathy/creaky voice quality, changes in voice fundamental frequency, speaking rate-related undershoot in articulatory targets, slight statistical variability in articulation that can lead to big acoustic changes, variable amount of feature propagation, such as nasality or rounding, to adjacent sounds).

3. Cross-speaker variability (differences in dialect, vocal-tract length and neutral shape, detailed articulatory habits).

4. Word environment in continuous speech (cross-word-boundary coarticulation, phonological and phonetic recoding of words in sentences).

The cumulative effects of this variability are so great that current systems designed to recognize only the isolated digits zero-to-nine have considerable difficulty doing so in a speaker-independent manner. A poor understanding of variability is perhaps the most important stumbling block inhibiting the development of really powerful isolated word-recognition devices.

There is an overwhelminging need for a systematic acoustic study of variability. To cite one example of a step in the right direction, Cole, Stern, Phillips, Brill, Pilant, & Specker (1983) have been working on a speaker-independent system for recognizing the alphabet and digits (the "alpha-digit" task) and have collected recordings of 10 male and 10 female speakers repeating randomized lists of this vocabulary several times. They have shown that listeners perform better than 99.5% correct in identifying these words. On the other hand, the Cole et al. system, although a very good system, produces more than 20 times as many errors, i.e. is correct about 89% of the time.

What processes do we use to speakers trying to distinguish among the highly confusable words from the alphabet: "B, C, D, E, G, P, T, V, Z, 3" as pronounced by unfamiliar speakers? When Cole, et al. made digital spectrograms of all of the talkers repeating these words, they saw no simple answer. However, a number of heuristic acoustic features were devised that, when extracted, contained less variability and led to significantly improved performance over an initial system. These features included formant frequency locations and aspects of the spectrum at critical event times such as voicing onset in a consonant-vowel transition. The features chosen differ in interesting ways from those first proposed as invariant by Blumstein and Stevens (1979). The hypothesis, that there exist computable properties having phonetic cue value and less variability than the raw spectra, is an important conjecture that needs more quantitative study. In fact, quantitative studies of large data bases of the kind collected by Cole, et al. and others (Doddington, 1984) are exactly what is needed to advance the field.

OLD AND NEW TECHNIQUES TO COPE WITH VARIABILITY

In the light of the types of variability outlined above, let us examine some of the standard isolated-word recognition techniques, and what might be done to improve upon them.

Speaker Normalization

As a practical matter, cross-speaker differences can be divided into two types: (1) systematic acoustic effects due to vocal-tract length, sex, or recording conditions; and (2) detailed manifestations of individual phonetic units (dialect and idiolect). Speaker normalization procedures attempt to deal with only the first class of cross-speaker differences. The remaining, often substantial, idiolectal differences must be handled by adaptation/learning at the lexical and/or phonetic level, and will be discussed later (see also Chapter 16).

Variability in vocal-tract length and other factors that modify the distribution of energy over frequencies from one speaker to another or from one session to another for a given speaker require special treatment. For example, some systems try to make the long-term average spectrum of input speech and training data similar, by: (1) prewhitening so that both have the same general spectral tilt; (2) estimation of vocal-tract length and a linear distortion of the frequency scale according to this estimate (Wakita, 1977) or a shift along the bark-frequency scale, resulting in less of a proportional shift at low frequencies, to make spectra from men and women match better (Bladon, 1983); (3) estimation of average formant locations if formants serve as recognition parameters (Nearey, 1977), or use of formant ratios (Miller, Engebretson, & Vemula, 1980); or (4) by permitting small local frequency warps during spectral matching (Sejnoha, 1983). This is an area in need of some basic perceptual research on which to base more sophisticated normalization procedures. Such procedures would perhaps take advantage of formant frequencies as recognition parameters, but somehow avoid the catastrophic errors implicit in the formant extraction process.

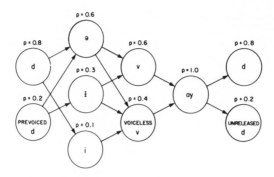

FIG. 14.2.   Several permitted pronunciation variants of the word divide
are illustrated in the form of a network.

Rate Normalization

Variability in speaking rate and details of articulatory timing are usually
handled by considering nearly all possible temporal alignments of unknown
and candidate words, using dynamic programming. Since duration serves
as an important cue to both segmental and suprasegmental structure of an
utterance, future systems must be able to: (1) measure durations of segments
and/or syllables; and (2) interpret durational deviations from expectations
as well as ignoring them when appropriate.

Clustering of Word Templates vs. Phonetic Analysis

An automatic technique devised to discover pronunciation variants in training data has been described by Rabiner et al. (1979). If an "outlier" spectral
sequence differs from the mean word template (spectral sequence) greatly
enough, it is given separate status as a template.

Unfortunately, there are problems with this kind of learning program when
the input has the variability characteristic of human speech. For example,
consider the isolated word "divide." There is a surprising number of ways in
which the word can be (and is) pronounced, as illustrated in Figure 14.2.

The initial [d] may be prevoiced, but probably is not. The first vowel
might be a schwa, a barred-I, or even a short version of the tense vowel [i].
The intervocalic [v] may become devoiced during a portion of its duration.
The final [d] may be released or not. Each of these events has a certain
probability of occurrence for a given speaker (see Chapter 19, this volume).
One such hypothetical set of probabilities is given in the figure. Assuming
that each of the options is independent, one can compute that it is necessary
to collect at least 50 training samples to be 95% confident of seeing at least
one example of each alternative in the training set. More data are necessary

if events are rare. Moreover, if different speakers are also included in the training set, it is not clear whether the clustering algorithm will discover the allophonic variants within all of the other types of acoustic variability.

Of course, there is something very regular and rule-governed going on here, but the clustering algorithm has no hope of seeing the pattern and making appropriate generalizations across all vocabulary items. The only possible way for man or machine to discover the rules and not have to see all variants of all words is to discover the concept of the phonetic segment (or perhaps the syllable)[1] and make up rules for describing allophonic variants of this smaller more regular unit.

A clustering algorithm presupposes that the outliers are true outliers, not speech masked by a cough, or a deviant caused by a malfunction of the alignment and distance calculator. Thus it is important to clustering success both to be able to recognize masking events to be ignored (perhaps the human can do this, at least during training), and to have a matching algorithm that is robust and not prone to occasional serious errors, such as mislocating the beginning or end of a word or misidentifying formant peak locations.

Clustering at a phonetic level requires a large body of phonetically labeled training data. To some extent, children are exposed to a similar kind of large data base—it is not phonetically labeled, but, at least in the beginning, speech contains mostly rather simple CV and CVC forms. It is probably necessary for the child acquiring language to learn to "phonetically label" the auditory input during the process of learning to talk. For example, it has been well established that phonemic categories are manipulated during the sentence production planning process (Fromkin, 1971; Shattuck-Hufnagel & Klatt, 1979). If this is part of the normal language-learning process, then children can presumably process a novel pronunciation of a familiar word by guessing at the intended word, and then comparing the phonetic analysis of the input with the phonemic representation in the pronouncing lexicon, at which point template averaging might be performed, or a new template might be created, or a new phonological recoding rule might be postulated.

In conclusion, it appears that a machine can't be expected to learn the generalizations that humans make about permitted variability in pronunciation unless a very ambitious phonetically-based effort is mounted. On the other hand, it seems both practical and desirable for researchers familiar with acoustic-phonetic details to put more of this kind of information into isolated word recognition systems by hand, through study of large data bases.

---

[1] Some efficiency in rule statement might be gained by going one step further and positing features such as "voiced plosive" which describe three or four English segments that are all subject to the same prevoicing option rule. It would be interesting to see if a test could be devised to measure whether people naturally make such generalizations where there are fortuitous "holes" in phonemic systems, and a naive subject is suddenly exposed to variants of the "hole" phoneme (Ohala, 1974b).

Distance Metrics

Recognition implies the use of a distance metric, although the metric need not make comparisons at the level of raw spectra. Features extracted from spectra might be compared with expectations. Even articulatory parameters estimated from the acoustic data can serve as input to a decision algorithm that employs a distance metric.

Metrics that work best in a recognition system: (1) provide a uniform scoring algorithm, such as probability, in order to compare disparate events; (2) respond in a monotonically increasing way to phonetically increasing distances; and (3) ignore phonetically irrelevant acoustic details, to the extent that this is possible.

Metrics that are currently used in recognition systems fall far short of these goals. For example, a change in fundamental frequency, such that a harmonic is centered on a formant peak or two harmonics straddle the peak, can lead to a 6 dB or more change in formant level that is phonetically irrelevant, but may cause a big change in a metric, such as the linear-prediction residual or the Euclidean distance between two spectra. Similarly, there can be up to a 20 dB change in the relative amplitudes of the first and third formants in [i] depending on vocal effort and detailed frequency values of higher formants.

This kind of variability has led some researchers to propose formant frequency extraction as a necessary step prior to distance estimation (Cole et al., 1983), or to posit the existence of a set of relatively invariant features that must be extracted from the spectra (Blumstein & Stevens, 1979).

Alternatively, one might look for new ways to characterize the raw spectrum without making hard feature decisions that can lead to gross errors (Klatt, 1982a). For example, experiments have been performed using synthetic vowels to determine what aspects of the spectrum contribute to perceptual change (Carlson, Granstrom and Klatt, 1979), and what aspects are ignored when making phonetic judgements (Klatt, 1979b; 1982a). The result of this research was the not too surprising discovery that the frequency locations (and presence/absence) of prominent spectral peaks were most important to vowel quality judgement. Relative formant amplitudes, general spectral tilt, and the effects of highpass/lowpass filtering, while often quite audible, did not influence phonetic judgements much at all. This research shows precisely those ways in which the most popular distance metrics fail to behave in the way that human listeners behave. Overall, both the linear prediction residual and a spectrum-based Euclidean metric pay too much attention to relative peak heights in the spectrum. Improved spectral distance metrics must be found.

I am presently studying the relative advantages of metrics based on spectral slope (Klatt, 1982a) versus a class of metrics based on frequency locations of spectral peaks, weighted by peak prominence. The slope metric, while not

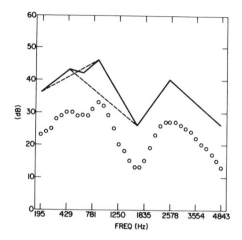

FIG. 14.3. Representation of a vowel-like spectrum in terms of a number of spectral peaks (solid line) and alternative representations that might be applied during the matching process to handle the case where formant peaks merge in the critical-band representation (dashed lines).

ideal, appears to offer some advantages in vowel-like harmonic spectra (Nocerino, 1984). On the other hand, simple Euclidean metrics work best for noise spectra in consonants. This may reflect the dual processing nature of speech perception, where average firing rate data are used for many purposes, but interspike intervals are processed to detect peak locations in vowel-like harmonic spectra.

A variant of formant tracking is illustrated in Figure 14.3. A critical-band spectrum of a vowel (open circles) has been stylized by a number of solid straight lines indicating locations and heights of local maxima and minima. The peaks usually indicate formant locations. However, since a formant can sometimes disappear under the skirt of an adjacent strong spectral prominence, dashed lines are introduced to indicate alternative representations for this spectrum that might be needed when trying to determine if another spectrum with fewer peaks is actually the same.

There is also a need for further experiments to better characterize those aspects of static and dynamic spectra that are important for each phonetic contrast. Some work has been done on cue-trading in consonants (Massaro & Cohen, 1976; Oden & Massaro, 1978; Repp, 1983c; Stevens & Klatt, 1974), but much remains to be worked out.

Another deficiency of most metrics concerns the way that they accumulate distance over time. When discriminating among the words "B, D, E, G, P, T, V, Z, and 3," the vowel can contribute a sum of small distances that outweigh the distance accumulated over the more relevant brief onset of the word, unless one devises an intelligent way to prevent this from happening. One cure is to sum log-probabilities of matches on a phonetic segment by phonetic-segment basis, but this assumes that phonetic boundaries can be found, and that the conversion of a distance metric score to an appropriate conditional probability can be done in a sufficiently accurate way. Alternatively, one might use spectral change as a basis for deciding how important a spectral distance is (large changes in consonants should imply that spectral distance differences are important, while small spectral changes, as in the middle of a vowel, imply less importance of a spectral difference).

No matter what metric is used, distance scores for phonetically similar spectra are usually too big, while those for very different spectra are not big enough. Before summing distances over time, it is therefore a good idea to transform the distance scores into a scale more nearly representing the log probability that the two spectra are phonetically similar (Jelinek, 1976; Klovstad & Mondshein, 1975).

Conclusions, Isolated Word Recognition

To summarize, it is my belief that isolated word recognition systems have attained a plateau in performance that is unlikely to be superseded by mathematical extensions to the already sophisticated pattern-matching techniques available. The variability that prevents significant improvements in performance is unlikely to be "discovered" automatically by any techniques presently conceived in the research laboratory, leaving it up to the designer of the machine to describe this variability in ways that will permit machine optimization of parameters from large data bases. Significant progress can be expected if research effort is directed at studying and characterizing variability in ways that will lead to the design of improved distance metrics, speaker normalization procedures, and the learning of rules characterizing the acoustic manifestations of permitted allophonic variants of phonetic elements.

CONTINUOUS SPEECH-RECOGNITION

I have chosen not to discuss recent efforts to build very large vocabulary isolated word-recognition systems, but rather to jump ahead to the problem of continuous speech recognition. Large vocabulary systems present special problems, which have prompted some investigators to propose two-stage strategies in which the first stage reduces the candidates to a manageable number before detailed analysis is performed (see Huttenlocker and Zue, 1984). In my opinion, the candidate reduction process via simplified heuristics rather than detailed phonetic characterization of all words is of marginal theoretical interest, and will not be required as computational capabilities are enhanced in the future. The real issue is to be able to make the fine phonetic decisions that are required whenever a vocabulary is large enough to have phonetically similar words in it.

There is not as much difference between the problems facing the designer of advanced isolated word-recognition systems and those facing the designer of a continuous speech-recognition device as was once supposed. Both must solve problems concerning distance metrics, speaker variability, and rule governed acoustic-phonetic variability. However, a word is subject to a greater number of permitted variations in continuous speech than in isolation due to variations in stress, duration, and phonetic context specified by adjacent words. Another difference, of course, is the greater search space implied by both coarticulation at word boundaries and ambiguity as to where words begin and end. One question to be considered in this section is how to characterize these processes by rule and use the rule-based knowledge in a recognition algorithm.

The continuous speech-recognition problem can be approached in several different ways. One is to use isolated word templates to spot words in continuous speech, more or less ignoring the coarticulation and phonetic recoding that is known to occur (see Myers & Rabiner, 1981; Sakoe and Chiba, 1971). Another class of systems divides the problem into two stages—phonetic labeling followed by lexical matching (Zue & Schwartz, 1978). These could be characterized as rule-based systems that attempt to embed speech knowledge in a set of explicit decoding rules. These systems are worthy of examination, but I have chosen instead to focus on a third general approach—whole word recognition from a spectrally-based knowledge network.

There are three such systems for performing continuous speech-recognition—LAFS (Klatt, 1979a), the IBM system (Jelinek, 1976), and CMU Harpy (Lowerre & Reddy, 1980).

The IBM and Harpy systems are considered not so much because of their theoretical interest as literal models of human perception, but rather because they work better than a phonetician would ever expect, and it is worthwhile to try to understand why. For example, the IBM system (Bahl et al., 1983), has been applied to the task of continuous sentence recognition using a 5000-word office correspondence vocabulary; word-recognition rate is about 95% for each of 6 speakers who trained the system extensively before use. Harpy is reported to give similar performance (Lowerre & Reddy, 1980), but with a grammar perplexity (roughly the average number of word alternatives at each node in the grammar) of 10 rather than the 90 figure estimated for the IBM task. We begin by considering nine aspects of the design of each system (see Table 14.1):

TABLE 14.1

Systems for Performing Continuous Speech Recognition

Characteristics	LAFS	IBM	Harpy
1. Grammar	all possible word sequences	2nd-or der Markov	artificial syntax
2. Phonetic Unit	diphone	phoneme	phoneme
3. Representation of this unit	subnetwork	hidden Markov model	single spectral template
4. Word	phoneme lattice	phoneme lattice	phoneme lattice
5. Word-boundary recoding	general rules	limited rules	limited rules
6. Input representation	critical band spectra	200 vector-quantized spectra	100 vector-quantized spectra
7. Scoring philosophy	sum of spectral distances	sum of probabilities	sum of spectral distances
8. Tuning	template averaging	probability updating	template averaging
9. Learning	none	probability updating	none

1. All three systems are designed to recognize connected speech made up out of words from a moderately large vocabulary. LAFS will accept any word string, whether it is syntactically and semantically correct or not. IBM uses a probabilistic approach (second-order Markov word-sequence statistics) to bias recognition toward word strings that are more likely to occur, but has no syntactic or semantic constraints to ensure that the recognized word string makes sense. Harpy accepts only well-formed sentences, a desirable property, but Harpy uses a not very habitable grammar (actually, an enumeration of permitted sentences).

2. In all three systems, words are assumed to be made up of a sequence of linguistic (or quasi-linguistic) units drawn from a small set. This is an important assumption because, as we will see, it permits systems to be efficiently tuned from training data without requiring that this training data include several tokens of every vocabulary item. However, for training to succeed,

it is important that an appropriate unit is chosen. This unit should have highly similar acoustic manifestations wherever it appears. For this reason, LAFS has chosen the diphone (and permits use of demisyllables or triphones where needed). IBM and Harpy make the questionable assumption that the phoneme is an appropriate unit when augmented with a small number of pseudophonemes to handle cases where acoustic invariance is known to be poor. The question is whether LAFS, with about 1000 diphone units, can be trained sufficiently, and whether IBM and Harpy, with 50 and 100 pseudo-phonemes respectively, will have good phonetic discrimination capabilities when trained.

3. In all three systems, the basic recognition unit consists of one or more states connected together in the form of a network, as in Figure 14.4. In LAFS, a trained phonetician designs an appropriate network for each di-phone, and each state corresponds to a spectral template. In the IBM system, each pseudophoneme is represented by a subnetwork of the same structure (Figure 4b) and a state has no physical meaning except as a part of a hidden Markov model where each permitted input spectrum has some probability of being associated with the state during recognition. Thus a state is more general than in LAFS in that several acoustically disparate spectral templates could be assigned high probabilities of occurrence for a given IBM state transition. In Harpy, each pseudo-phoneme is represented by a single state, and this state corresponds to a spectral template.

4. In all three systems, a word is initially represented by a lattice of phonemic alternatives. A set of rules is then applied to this representation to automatically expand it into phonetic alternatives (see Cohen & Mercer, 1975). In LAFS, the phonetic lattice must be transformed into a diphone lattice, but this is straightforward. It is obviously important that lexical items be given an initial representation that, following rule application, will result in all reasonable pronunciations being specified in a network.

5. In all three systems, phonetic recoding that occurs across word bound-aries is described by a set of rules, and these rules are expanded into optional network paths that can be traversed to get from the end of one word to the beginning of the next. In LAFS, since the basic unit is the diphone, these rules describe alternative diphone sequences representing deletions, inser-tions, and optional recoding of phonetic sequences. If the diphone inventory is sufficiently rich, many word-boundary phenomenon can be described. In the IBM system and in Harpy, similar rules are permitted, but, of course, must be stated in terms of the pseudophoneme inventory that is available, and therefore may not be able to describe narrow phonetic distinctions.

6. In all three systems, spectra are computed every 10 msec from beginning to end of an unknown utterance. In LAFS, the spectrum is a highly smoothed 40-channel critical-band spectrum. In both the IBM system and Harpy, each input 10-msec spectral frame is matched against an inventory of 200 or 100

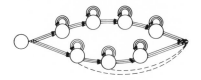

A. EXAMPLE OF A LAFS DIPHONE SUBNETWORK

B. STRUCTURE OF EACH IBM PSEUDO-PHONEME SUBNETWORK

C. STRUCTURE OF EACH HARPY PSEUDO-PHONEME SUBNETWORK

FIG. 14.4 Typical network representation of a LAFS diphone, IBM pseudo-phoneme, and Harpy pseudophoneme. In LAFS, different diphones have different network structures, while in the IBM system and in Harpy, each pseudophoneme has an identical network structure.

well-chosen spectral templates. In the IBM system, the closest template is found, and its name is the only aspect of the 10-msec frame that is used during recognition. In Harpy, the distances from 100 spectral templates are computed and used during recognition. Vector quantization (categorization of input spectra by the number of the template most closely matching the spectrum) is employed as a practical method for speeding recognition. The cost is that a system using too few templates may not be able to resolve important phonetic details. On the other hand, LAFS, with as many as 5000 different spectral templates in its network, confronts the implementation engineer with other practical problems.

One might think that vector quantization places less emphasis on spectral distance metrics since, at least in the IBM system, the distance scores do not enter directly into path scoring. However, the assignment of vector names during input analysis uses a distance metric whose properties determine whether perceptually similar spectra are given the same name or not.

7. In all three systems, the best path through the network is sought, and each input spectral frame adds a cost to the total score for each alternative path that is examined. In LAFS, this cost is the spectral distance between the input frame and the template for a given state. In the IBM system, the cost is the probability of seeing the input spectrum when going to the state in question. In Harpy, the cost is the same as in LAFS, except that the

distance has been precomputed and so the scoring is done by table lookup. Both Harpy and LAFS would probably be improved by a scoring system that attempted to transform spectral-distance scores into log probabilities before summing them over time.

8. In all three systems, the program adapts to the characteristics of a new speaker gradually. Tuning is based on the assumption that the new talker speaks the same dialect or dialects as the system has been designed to handle. In LAFS, when a sentence has been successfully recognized, the templates in the states corresponding to the best path are modified to be slightly more similar to input spectra assigned to them. (In the original LAFS formulation, there was no generalization to other words that share some of the same diphones—I will propose a mechanism for making such a generalization below). In the IBM system, the probability vector associated with each state traversed during successful recognition is adjusted so as to expect spectra identical to the input with slightly higher probability than before.[2] In Harpy, template averaging is used.

The IBM tuning procedure has many advantages over template averaging in that it does not require that the input and template be similar enough that the average is meaningful. The IBM procedure is preferred if there is any chance that the LAFS network or Harpy network do not include paths representing acoustic-phonetic sequences that are going to be encountered in real life. There are other problems with template averaging even when the two spectra are similar: an averaging technique must be employed that does not have the tendency to wash out peaks and valleys, but rather relocates peaks and valleys to appropriate new positions.

9. None of the systems can learn about allophonic variants, e.g. that a poorly matching input sequence is a valid (though unforeseen) way of saying a particular word and therefore the network should grow a path to accept this novel pronunciation. However, the IBM system can approximate this behavior via its normal tuning procedure. Of course, there is a cost, since the novel pronunciation may affect the probabilities for a phoneme that is really not the right phoneme, thereby weakening the overall selectivity of the system. For example, a velar fricative can appear in place of [g] in post-stressed environments, e.g. "toggle," but should not be accepted anywhere a [g] can appear.

Summary Comparison

While I am of course biased in favor of LAFS, it is still not easy to choose between the relative advantages of LAFS and the IBM system. In defense

---

[2] The actual method used to adjust probabilities, the "forward-backward" algorithm, is not incremental in nature, and requires that an entire data set from day 1 be saved and reprocessed offline.

DENNIS H. KLATT

of LAFS, vector quantization (used by the IBM system) may cause a performance decrement (in both single-speaker and speaker-independent recognition) either because too few vectors are chosen, or because the distance
metric is sensitive to perceptually irrelevant acoustic details. Furthermore,
the diphone has considerable theoretical advantage over the pseudophoneme
as a recognition unit that is more nearly invariant as a spectral pattern. But
even given these two criticisms, the use in the IBM system of probability
as a scoring technique and probability updating as a tuning technique may
have considerable advantages. Implementation of a large vocabulary LAFS
network may also require computational compromises that weaken the theoretical advantages. In the remainder of this paper, I will consider some
implementation issues for LAFS and also explore whether aspects of LAFS
and the IBM system can be taken seriously as perceptual models.

PERCEPTUAL MODELS

Networks are appealing models of perception since they seem to involve simple local scoring strategies and little "cognitive" processing.[3] In a previous
publication, I have discussed some of the strengths and weaknesses of a LAFS
network as a perceptual model (Klatt, 1979a). Two modifications to LAFS
are proposed below in an attempt to make LAFS a more realistic model of
speech perception.

Cross-Word-Boundary Phonology

In both LAFS and the IBM system, recoding rules that describe cross-word-
boundary phenomena are fully elaborated (duplicated) at the end of every
word in the lexicon. This is done to ensure that a rule discovered in one
context is applied in all relevant contexts, but it seems to be a perceptually
implausible method of implementation. What, then, are the implications of
assuming that there is really only one physical cross-word-boundary network?

Consider the simplest form that this structure could take in LAFS (Figure
14.5) by assuming for the moment that coarticulation across word boundaries
is restricted to the diphone consisting of the last half of the phoneme at the
end of the word and the first half of the initial phoneme of all words. Then,
instead of creating a large set of paths and states for each word in the lexicon,
so as to connect the end of the word to all word beginnings, it suffices to

---

[3] Newell (1979) argues that cognitive strategies such as analysis by synthesis or hypothesize
and test are too time consuming to be realistic models of human perception, and that one
must find ways of devising highly parallel automatic processes to model speech perception.
A similar view is expressed in the work of Elman and McClelland (Chapter 17).

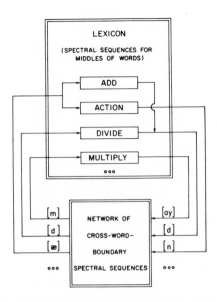

FIG. 14.5. A modified LAFS model of bottom-up lexical hypothesiza-
tion in which cross-word-boundary phonological and coarticulatory effects
are described by a single separate subnetwork.

jump to the appropriate place in a single word-boundary network, carrying
forward a backpointer to the word that would be recognized if this continues
to be the best network path. The word-boundary network specifies spectral
sequences that must be traversed in order to get to the beginning of words
with each possible beginning phoneme.

It is possible to conceive of more general variants of this approach that allow coarticulation and phonological recoding over greater portions of words,
and that might incorporate into this special part of the network regular suffixes such as plural and past, and even incorporate the short highly modifiable
function words, such as "to," "and," "a," and "the." The implications of this
possibility are worthy of exploration, because it may be the case that short
function words are different from other words not only because of their grammatical function and high frequency of occurrence, but also because they are
acoustically so modifiable by context that they must be placed in this special
cross-word-boundary network.

If taken as a perceptual model, the single word-boundary subnetwork
seems to imply that only the best of several alternative word theories at the
acoustic input to the word-boundary subnetwork can be seen. (The state entered can hold only one backpointer to the best-scoring word at that instant.)
Perhaps psychological experiments can be devised to test this prediction.

Tuning

In the IBM system, learning/tuning takes place at the level of the phoneme, and thus may constitute an attractive model of how children first attempt generalizations that depart from whole-word acoustic patterns. In a sense, the IBM system is looking for acoustic invariance in the spectral representations that it sees, and thus the system is in agreement with several current accounts of children's language acquisition (Stevens & Blumstein, 1981), in which it is assumed that each phoneme is characterized by just enough acoustic invariance to get the perceptual system started on the right track. The weakness of the IBM system in making phonemic decisions constitutes evidence against the idea that phonemic invariance is *sufficient* for speech understanding.

The question, then, is: "How great a modification to the IBM model would be required in order to discover more powerful acoustic-phonetic generalizations"? The answer that I propose is surprisingly simple: When a sequence of spectra is mapped onto a particular phoneme in an input utterance (that is correctly recognized), do not update probabilities at all instantiations of a phoneme, as IBM does now, but rather update only probabilities at those network locations possessing the same phonetic environment as is observed in the input. Of course, this is the same as saying "replace IBM's phonemes with a diphone network, as in LAFS." Network states near the beginning of a phoneme definition are tuned only to inputs involving that phoneme preceded by the appropriate phoneme, and correspondingly, network states near the end of the phoneme definition are tuned only to input data having the appropriate following phoneme.

While this is conceptually simple to implement in a computer, it implies a much larger set of probabilities to be estimated and stored than in the standard IBM system. In the standard system, there might be 50 phonemes, 10 network transitions per phoneme (only three with different probability distributions in the current IBM conception of a phoneme), and 200 template probabilities to be estimated for each transition, or about 30,000 probabilities (frequencies) to be estimated and stored (and of these, maybe 90% are zero (or epsilon) and need not be stored). If training is done on the basis of diphones, and the template inventory is increased in order to permit finer phonetic distinctions, the numbers might be about 1000 diphones times, say, five network transitions per diphone times 1000 template probabilities, or five million probabilities to be estimated. A 50-fold increase would imply an impractical increase in required training data as well as a memory greater than is easily referenced in most computers.

Hopefully, it will be possible to create a compromise network where only about 20 probabilities are stored for the 20 most likely templates at each node, and the remainder are considered close enough to zero to be clamped to zero. However, mechanisms are needed to select these favored spectral templates, and to permit experience to modify the set of templates with nonzero probabilities. I hope to report in the future on the success of this approach.

Unsupervised Learning of New Network Configurations

Template probability updating can cause network structures to converge toward optimal performance, but how does one create new network structures to characterize newly discovered phonological rules or unforeseen acoustic-phonetic possibilities? It is necessary to be able to detect when a correctly recognized acoustic input does not match the correct path through the network very well, and furthermore, establish that this acoustic data could be generated by a human vocal tract obeying rules of English phonetics and phonology. Detecting a poor match may not be too difficult for a machine, but to be able to determine whether the deviations are worthy of inclusion as new network paths of local or global import requires expert knowledge of the rules of speech production and their acoustic consequences. It is my belief that the role of analysis by synthesis and the motor theory of speech perception arises exactly here, to serve as a constraint on the construction of alternative network paths during unsupervised learning.[4] Construction of a LAFS-like computer simulation possessing these skills must await progress in understanding the detailed relations between speech production, perception, and phonology.

CONCLUSION

This is a very exciting time for engineers, linguists, and psychologists interested in speech-recognition and speech perception, because we are probably at the threshold of a breakthrough in both understanding and machine performance. It has been argued here that this breakthrough will be expedited by careful study of variability in speech, development of better phonetically-motivated distance metrics, and the description of acoustic-phonetic details within the framework of a recognition algorithm that is both simple and powerful, such as LAFS.

ACKNOWLEDGEMENT

This work was supported in part by a grant from the National Science Foundation.

---

[4] In unsupervised learning, the correct answer is not given explicitly, so a "demon" must decide whether the correct answer is known with sufficient confidence to perform adaptation.

Bertrand Delgutte: Comment

USE OF PERIPHERAL AUDITORY MODELS
IN SPEECH RECOGNITION

In his paper, Klatt suggests that models of peripheral auditory processing might be valuable in automatic speech recognition by providing representations of speech signals in which phonetic categories would have less variable correlates. This theory is based on the fact that human listeners can identify phonetic units more reliably than current recognition systems, particularly when the speech signal is degraded. However, the performance of human subjects is a function of the entire auditory system, not only its most peripheral stages. Therefore, in applying knowledge of auditory processing to speech recognition, it is not sufficient to use a model of the peripheral components as a "front end" to an existing speech-recognition device: One also needs to consider how the peripheral patterns of activity are processed by the central auditory system.

This point is illustrated by the results of Blomberg, Carlson, Elenius, and Granstrom (Chapter 5). They used both peripheral auditory models and more traditional speech-analysis techniques as inputs to a pattern-matching, dynamic-programing word-recognition system. Results showed that the auditory models did not necessarily lead to a higher recognition rate than the traditional analysis techniques. The authors concluded that peripheral auditory models need improvement before they can be useful in speech recognition. It may also be that the relatively poor performance of certain auditory models is due in part to a mismatch between the peripheral processing and the central recognition strategies. In this view, peripheral auditory models would serve as a starting point for developing speech-recognition strategies that would more closely reflect human perception. This approach is limited by the lack of knowledge on the central auditory processing of speech sounds. For instance, as pointed out by Klatt, it is not known to what extent fine time patterns of auditory-nerve fiber discharges are important in the auditory processing of speech. Because this issue is of key importance in how one would practically use a peripheral auditory model in speech recognition, it will now be discussed at some length.

SCHEMES FOR REPRESENTING
THE SHORT-TIME SPECTRUM

The short-time spectrum of speech stimuli might be represented in the discharge patterns of auditory-nerve fibers in several ways. One possible scheme is to express the discharge rates averaged over short times (5–20 ms) as a function of the characteristic frequency (CF) of auditory-nerve fibers. This scheme has been called a "rate-place" representation (Sachs, Young, & Miller, 1982). Alternatively, the stimulus spectrum could be represented in the fine-time patterns of spike activity. These temporal cues reflect the fact that neural discharges are synchronized (or "phase-locked") to frequency components of the stimulus. Several schemes have been proposed to extract phonetically-important parameters from the fine timing information. These schemes differ from the short-time averaging of discharge rates in that they depend strongly on the variations in probability of discharge *within* intervals of 5–20 ms. In one class of temporal schemes, the processing of the discharge patterns is restricted to fibers within independent bands of CFs, so that the tonotopic organization of the auditory nerve is preserved following temporal processing. Examples of such temporal-place schemes are the Average Localized Synchronized Rate (ALSR) of Young and Sachs (1979), or the matched-filter model of Srulowicz and Goldstein (1983). In another class of temporal processing schemes, timing cues from fibers with different CFs are combined, so that the tonotopic organization is not preserved. An example of such a "temporal non-place" schemes is the dominance histogram of Carlson, Fant and Granstrom (1975). Place and nonplace temporal processing schemes have been compared for vowels by Delgutte (1984).

To summarize, schemes to process the discharge patterns of auditory-nerve fibers can be classified in terms of two attributes: (1) the use of fine temporal patterns of discharge; and (2) the preservation of tonotopic organization. In the rest of this discussion, we will focus on the first distinction.

AVERAGE RATES AND FINE TIME PATTERNS OF NEURAL DISCHARGE

Much of the interest in temporal processing schemes originates from the finding that, at stimulus levels well within the normal conversational range, simple rate-place schemes appear to poorly represent the formant frequencies of vowels because many fibers discharge at rates close to maximum (Sachs & Young, 1979). In contrast, fine-time patterns of discharges appear to provide *sufficient* cues for distinguishing between vowels over a wide range of stimulus levels and signal-to-noise ratios (Delgutte and Kiang, 1984a; Voigt, Sachs, & Young, 1981; Young and Sachs, 1979). However, before it can be concluded that fine-time patterns of discharge are *necessarily* used in the coding of vowels, several issues need to be examined:

1. The experiments of Sachs and Young (1979) largely excluded the high-threshold auditory-nerve fibers (Liberman, 1978), which could provide average rate cues at moderate and high stimulus levels (Delgutte, 1982; Sachs et al., 1982)

2. Activation of the efferent projections to the cochlea could reduce the discharge rates of auditory-nerve fibers that would have been saturated in the absence of efferent stimulation (Delgutte & Kiang, 1984a). This mechanism could in principle operate in selected regions of the cochlea to effectively increase the signal-to-noise ratio.

3. At high sound levels, contraction of the middle-ear muscles could reduce the suppression effect of the first formant on the responses to higher formants (Sachs & Young, 1980).

The roles of average rates and fine-time patterns of discharge have also been examined for voiceless fricative stimuli, which have more intense high-frequency components than vowels (Delgutte & Kiang, 1984b). Place-rate schemes seemed to provide sufficient information for discriminating these stimuli, whereas temporal schemes had difficulties at high frequencies where synchrony of discharges becomes minimal.

Psychophysical experiments with patients that have been implanted with a device that electrically stimulates the auditory nerve ("cochlear implant") are also relevant to the role of fine-time patterns of discharge in auditory processing. In these experiments, an electrical sinewave or periodic pulse train is applied to a single electrode, and the patient is asked to scale the pitch of the percept (Bilger, 1977; Eddington, Dobelle, Brackman, Mladejovsky & Parking, 1978; Müller, 1981; Shannon, 1983; Simmons, Mathews, Walker & White, 1979; Tong, Clark, Blamey, Busby & Dowell, 1982). These pitch judgements must be based on temporal cues because rate-place cues seem to be minimal when a single electrode stimulates the auditory nerve (Kiang & Moxon, 1972; Hartmann, Topp & Klinke, 1984).

Results show that there is an upper limit to the frequency range over which pitch judgements are reliable. This upper limit varies between 300 Hz and 1 kHz depending on the patient and the stimulation system. Even in the range of frequencies over which pitch systematically varies with the frequency of the electrical stimulus, the just noticeable difference for frequency is at least an order of magnitude higher than for acoustic tones at the same frequency in normal listeners (Eddington et al., 1978; Fourcin, 1979; Merzenich et al., 1973; Müller, 1981). These results suggest that patients can only make limited use of timing cues in pitch judgements. However, the results do not rule out temporal processing schemes, because the pattern of auditory-nerve activity in such patients must differ considerably from that evoked by acoustic stimuli in a normal ear, and the implanted patients could have considerable loss of auditory-nerve fibers. For instance, if there were a local loss of fibers at the place of the stimulus frequency in the implanted patients, certain temporal-place schemes (Young & Sachs, 1979) should be severely degraded, while certain nonplace schemes (Carlson & Granstrom, 1982a) might remain effective because they do not depend on the exact distribution of the timing cues across the auditory nerve. On the other hand, in case of an evenly-distributed loss of fibers throughout the auditory nerve, the temporal-place schemes might be less severely affected than the nonplace schemes. These examples illustrate that psychophysical results from cochlear-implant patients combined with histological data could place constraints on possible models of processing of auditory-nerve discharge patterns.

In conclusion, the opinions expressed previously (Delgutte, 1982; Delgutte & Kiang, 1984a) remain unchanged: It is not possible at present to assess the roles of average rates and fine-time patterns of discharge in speech processing by the auditory system. Thus, physiological considerations cannot yet specify the central processing schemes to be used in conjunction with peripheral auditory models. From the point of view of speech recognition, different schemes can be compared for how well they achieve a desired signal-processing goal (e.g. enhancing formant peaks), how robust they are to variations in speaker and phonetic context, and how well they predict psychophysical performance for a variety of stimulus conditions.

Jeffrey Elman: Comment

Klatt's paper presents a clear view of the field of speech recognition, as well as some of the recent advances (many of which are the result of his own work). However, I think he is far too sanguine about the prospect of long-term progress. In my view, the current approach in this field is rapidly leading us to a dead end. I would like to mention two problems in particular.

First, I think the prevailing view within the field of speech recognition that the digital computer is an adequate metaphor for the human brain is a fundamental misconception. There are important differences between the architecture of the von Neumann machine and the brain. The von Neumann machine is a serial processor with cycle times measured on the order of nanoseconds; it makes use of random access memory. The human brain is a highly interconnected parallel processor, with many components active simultaneously. Neural transmission times are relatively slow (measured in milliseconds), but the brain takes advantage of content addressable memory. It seems quite likely that the sorts of tasks which are carried out without apparent effort by humans—including speech recognition—may require the special architecture of the brain. If this is so, recognition schemes which accept the digital computer metaphor are doomed to failure.

Secondly, current work in recognition appears to take as given the assumption that the task of the human listener is to "ignore irrelevant acoustic variation." For the sake of argument, let me take the extreme contrary position and claim that there is virtually no speaker-produced variability which is irrelevant to the task of perception. Whether that variability is or is not intentional is another question. But in either event, it is a mistake to assume that the variations are ignored. They provide very useful information about the signal and aid the listener in decoding the speaker's underlying intent. They can also provide important clues about the speaker's identity or the content of the message.

Within a limited context, I think that important and useful goals can be accomplished within the framework that Klatt has outlined. In the long term, however, I think that significant progress in achieving recognition performance which resembles that of humans will require another approach. We should begin to look more seriously at parallel processing models, and we should entertain the idea that variability in the signal is a good thing, not a nuisance. We have accepted for too long the belief that variability in the signal is a problem for listeners and that there must be a hidden invariant behind the "noise." In fact, it may be precisely the variability which enables humans to recognize speech as well and as easily as we do.

John Holmes: Comment

When Klatt discusses continuous recognition he mentions three models—his own LAFS system, the IBM system, and Harpy. He dismisses, for good reason I think, the simple concatenated word approaches that are also being used for continuous speech recognition, because these take no account of coarticulation across word boundaries or higher-level aspects of speech structure.

I believe that the long-term solution to the problem of connected-speech recognition will depend on two future developments. One is a very sophisticated acoustically based model of speech production; this will involve synthesis by rule from linguistic units of some sort, and will copy human performance much more closely than any rule system has so far (and will include the ability to model particular speakers). The second development will be a distance metric for the pattern-matching process that really takes into account the phonetically important properties of the acoustic signal. The process won't detect features, but it will highlight, or make more explicit, those properties that are known to be phonetically significant. Instead of merely working with the output of a simulation of the peripheral auditory system, one would need some functional model of the higher levels that would not make categorical decisions, but would give prominence to such aspects as rapid movements of spectral peaks or sudden changes of level.

If these two hoped-for developments can be combined, I think it should be possible to achieve what might be called analysis-by-synthesis-by-rule for connected speech recognition. At any point in time, the system would postulate all the alternative message components that are appropriate, limited by any known linguistic constraints, but would still use matching algorithms not drastically different from the present-day concatenated word methods. The patterns for matching would be generated by rule as required, and so could automatically deal with coarticulation and higher-level linguistic interactions.

Initially the linguistic constraints would have to be very severe, merely because of the technological problems of processing a large number of candidate patterns. However, this approach opens the way to gradual evolution from the very modest techniques of today to something that might eventually be a very powerful method of continuous speech recognition.

Philip Lieberman: Comment

It's important to note the general failure of recognition procedures that are based on measures of the raw acoustic spectrum. Although various template schemes that compare an input spectrum with stored patterns have limited success when the problem is restricted to a short word list spoken by a particular speaker, these methods do not generalize. They furthermore are sensitive to changes in microphone placement or room acoustics, effects that human listeners are insensitive to. It is apparent that the linguistically salient acoustic characteristics of human speech are somewhat removed from the raw acoustic signal in that they involve "calculations" of parameters like formant-frequency patterns that are not physically present in the acoustic signal. Linguistic systems like the Jakobsonian distinctive features (Jakobson, Fant & Halle, 1952) again operate in terms of these *derived* measures— measures that involve the calculated transfer function rather than the raw acoustic signal. This also applies to recent attempts to derive "invariant" acoustic features that directly specify linguistic contrasts like the work of Blumstein and Stevens (1979; 1980). Such an approach again involves algorithms that operate on a derived transfer function that is implicitly normalized for vocal-tract length.

15

Performing Fine
Phonetic Distinctions:
Templates versus Features

Ronald A. Cole, Richard M. Stern and Moshé J. Lasry
Department of Computer Science
Carnegie-Mellon University
Pittsburgh, Pennsylvania

INTRODUCTION

Despite intensive research in computer speech recognition during the past 10 years, there is still a very large gap between human and machine recognition of speech. Human speech perception is robust and flexible: A person can recognize a novel sentence produced by an unfamiliar talker in a background of other conversations. By comparison, computer speech-recognition systems typically require training to each new speaker and perform well only when word choice is limited to a small number of acoustically distinct items.

Considering the amount of effort that has been devoted to speech recognition research, the "front-end" performance of speech-recognition systems is surprisingly poor. Systems developed during the ARPA speech-understanding project achieved first choice segmental recognition accuracies of 50% to 60% (Klatt, 1977). This is not accurate enough to recognize words unless vocabulary choice is highly constrained, and the items at each choice point are acoustically distinct.[1]

The problem is that computer systems are unable to perform fine phonetic distinctions: Today's systems are unable to discriminate among acoustically similar segments with sufficient accuracy to recognize the words of a language. Failure to correctly identify a single segment can and often will result in word recognition errors (e.g., "big" could be perceived as "pig," "beg," or "bid"). Thus, fine phonetic distinctions must be continuously and accurately

---

[1] The best front-end performance was provided by HWIM (Hear What I Mean), a feature-based recognition system developed at Bolt, Baranek, and Newman (Woods, Bates, Brown, Bruce, Cook, Klovstad, Makhoul, Nash-Webber, Schwartz, Wolf, & Zue, 1976.)

326 Ronald A. Cole, Richard M. Stern and Moshé J. Lasry

performed in order to recognize speech. Until phonetic information can be extracted from speech at levels approaching human performance, it will not be possible to construct truly extensible speech understanding systems.

TEMPLATE MATCHING

Almost all current systems use some form of time-normalized template matching to extract the linguistic information from the stimulus. By template matching, we refer to the time-frame-by-time-frame spectral comparison of an input utterance to a set of reference templates. In this section, we argue that template matching systems are unable to perform fine phonetic distinctions because spectral templates do not capture the acoustic-phonetic events that are necessary to identify most phonetic segments.

In 1975, Itakura published his classic article on isolated word recognition using the dynamic programming (DP) time normalization algorithm (Itakura, 1975; Sakoe & Chiba, 1971, 1978). In essence, the DP algorithm finds the best frame-by-frame spectral match between a test and reference pattern by stretching or folding the temporal axis of either the test or the reference in a nonlinear fashion. For a single speaker, Itakura obtained 97.3% accuracy on a 200-word vocabulary of Japanese geographical names using telephone speech (3 kHz), 8 LPC coefficients, a 30 msec sampling window and a 15 msec sampling rate. These results demonstrated that, even with substantial data reduction, DP template matching can produce high-recognition scores for some vocabularies.[1]

Itakura's research, and many subsequent studies, have shown that DP template matching systems will produce high recognition accuracies in a speaker-dependent mode as long as the vocabulary items are acoustically distinct. The critical importance of the acoustic similarity of the vocabulary items was noted by Itakura: "...the recognition rate is strongly influenced by a particular choice of vocabulary set. For example, if the vocabulary set is the English alphabet and digits, the recognition rate was 88.6% for 720 utterances by the same speaker under the same conditions..." But even this result is misleading, since almost all of the errors obtained in the alphadigit task occurred among a few confusable items. For example, the digits (which are acoustically distinct) were never confused, while the letters M - N, I - Y, and B, D, E, P, T, and V were recognized about 60% of the time.

Following Itakura's study, a number of experiments investigated the performance of template matching algorithms with confusable vocabularies.

---

[1] Template matching systems work well with small vocabularies of unambiguous words. In general, these systems work best in a speaker-dependent mode, but good speaker-independent results can be achieved for small vocabularies by using several templates for each word. The particular set of templates is determined by applying clustering algorithms to a data base provided by many speakers (Rabiner and Wilpon, 1979).

Most experiments used the *alphadigit* vocabulary, the English letters (A) through (Z) and the digits (0) (pronounced "zero") through (9). As Lamel and Zue (1982) point out, the alphadigit vocabulary is one of the most difficult in isolated word recognition (it is also one of the most important for many applications, such as directory assistance). All but three of the items are monosyllabic, so that number of syllables cannot be used to discriminate among the items. Most important, the letters and digits form highly confusable subsets. Rabiner, Levinson, Rosenberg and Wilpon (1979) identify the following six subsets: (a) (B C D E G P T V Z 3), (b) (A J K 8 H), (c) (L M N), (d) (F S X 6), (e) (I Y 5), (f) (Q U 2). Almost all errors occur within these sets; confusions rarely occur across sets.

Table 15.1 summarizes experiments which use template matching with confusable vocabularies. Almost all of these studies include several experimental conditions where effects of different representations and algorithmic variations are explored. Rather than detail each of these conditions, we report the range of results over all conditions.

The results shown in Table 15.1 are consistent across experiments. Recognition accuracy for the alphadigit vocabulary is typically between 60–80% for telephone bandwidth speech and 80–90% for speech sampled at higher rates.[3]

The ability of template matching systems to perform fine phonetic distinctions is illustrated best by recognition rates obtained for the "E set": (B, C, D, E, G, P, T, V, Z, 3). Recognition of these letters is about 60% (Rabiner, Levinson, Rosenberg, & Wilpon, 1979; Waibel & Yegnanarayana, 1981). But even this error rate is an overestimate of the ability of template matching to perform fine phonetic distinctions, since many letter pairs in the E set are not acoustically confusable. For example, B versus C, D versus C, B versus Z, and E versus C, should not be considered fine phonetic distinctions. Examination of the E-set confusions reported by Rabiner et al., (1979) and Waibel and Yegnanarayana (1981) reveals that the letters B, D, E, are recognized at less than 50% accuracy.

One of the main reasons that template-matching systems perform poorly with confusable vocabularies is that all parts of an utterance are given equal weight during recognition. Clearly, in order to discriminate among B and D, we would like to give more weight to information at the beginning of the utterance. Template matching systems give equal weight to each time frame. Thus, when trying to discriminate B from D, irrelevant variation in the vowel part of the utterance can outweigh the more important information

---

[3] The only disparate data point is the 98% accuracy reported by White and Neely (1976). This result represents performance for a single speaker (GW) who is a sophisticated user of speech-recognition machines. As Dixon and Silverman (1981) note, the significant variables in template-matching studies are the vocabulary items and the speakers; all other variables produce small variations in performance. The 98% reported by White and Neely can be attributed to the particular speaker used in that experiment.

Ronald A. Cole, Richard M. Stern and Moshé J. Lasry

TABLE 15.1

Template Matching Studies With Confusable Vocabularies

Experiment	Data	Speakers	Representation	Upper Freq.(kHz)	Recognition Rate(%)
Itakura (1975)	Alphadigit	1	LPC – 8	3.0	87
White & Neely (1976)	Alphadigit	1	LPC – 14 and Filter Bank	5.0	91–98
Rabiner et al.[a] (1979)	Alphadigit	100	LPC – 8	3.2	59–82
Rabiner & Wilpon[a] (1979)	Alphadigit	100	LPC – 8	3.2	65–86
Das (1980)	Alphadigit	8	5 Freq. coeff.	4.5	81–90
Dixon & Silverman (1981)	Alphadigit	22	12 filter bands	5.0	80–82
	Confusable words[b]	22			70–76
Rabiner & Wilpon[a] (1981)	Alphadigit	100	LPC – 8	3.2	84–88
Bradshaw, Cole & Li (1982)	Alphadigit	8	16 mel scale coefficients	4.6	84–93
Lamel & Zue (1982)	Alphadigit	10	27 log scale coefficients	4.8	84–89
E-set results					
Rabiner, et al.	E set[c]				57
Waibel & Yegnanarayana (1981)	E set	8	16 mel scale coefficients	4.6	58–60
Bradshaw, et al.	E set				63–84

[a] Speaker-independent, averaging 12 templates per word determined by clustering algorithms.

[b] B, V, thee, in'valid, inva'lid, dressed, add rest, addressed, saline, sailing.

[c] E set = B, C, D, E, G, P, T, V, Z, 3.

at the beginning of the utterance. Dynamic programming approaches to speech-recognition fail to focus attention on the most informative parts of an utterance.

A possible solution to this problem is to automatically focus on the informative parts of an utterance. Rabiner and Wilpon (1981) developed a two-pass recognition approach for classifying digits and letters. During the first pass, the utterance was classified as belonging to one of the confusable sets. During the second pass, a locally weighted distance was used to provide optimal separation among the words in each class. Recognition improvements of from 3% to 7% were obtained. Bradshaw, Cole, and Li (1982) used a similar procedure to evaluate performance on letters in the "E set." They obtained an improvement in recognition accuracy from 63% to 84%.

Research in acoustic phonetics and speech perception suggests why template matching systems are unable to perform fine phonetic distinctions. These experiments show that there are many different cues to each phonetic distinction, and listeners make use of all available cues (Cole & Scott, 1974b). For example, Lisker (1978) has provided a catalogue of 16 different cues to the voicing of stops in intervocalic position. Moreover, the various cues to a particular phonetic distinction are distributed across both frequency and time. Thus, it is necessary to identify and integrate diverse sources of information to arrive at a phonetic percept.

To summarize, in order to perform fine phonetic distinctions, it is necessary to extract a number of acoustic features from the speech signal—features such as formant frequencies and formant trajectories—and integrate these features to define a phonetic category. Since these features occur at different times in the signal and covary among each other, the information needed to perform fine distinctions cannot be captured by comparing individual spectral slices. We therefore conclude that speech-recognition systems which use template matching technology will not be able to achieve human levels of performance.

FEATURE-BASED RECOGNITION

Feature-based recognition is an alternative to frame-by-frame spectral matching. The idea behind feature-based recognition is to identify and automatically extract those acoustic features from the speech signal that are needed to identify phonetic events.

Figure 15.1 illustrates the advantage of using carefully chosen features and multivariate classification for determining speaker-independent categories for vowels. The figure includes four schematic spectrograms of the vowels "eh" and "ih" that show substantially different formant frequencies for the male and female tokens of each vowel. However, the *relationships* among the formant frequencies define a speaker-independent pattern for each vowel; "eh' consists of equally spaced formants, while "ih" has about twice the frequency

Ronald A. Cole, Richard M. Stern and Moshé J. Lasry

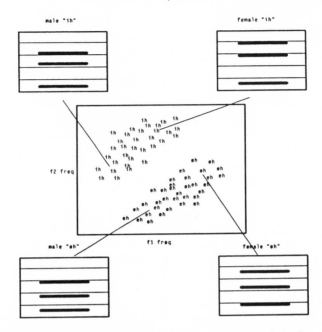

FIG. 15.1. Schematic spectrograms, and comparisons of the first two
formant frequencies, of two vowels from male and female speakers.

separation between the first and second formants as between the second and
third. The central panel in the figure is a two-dimensional projection of
the first two formants. The vowels group into two separate regions that are
speaker-independent descriptions of the vowels "eh" and 'ih'.

The feature-based system described below was motivated by spectrogram
reading experiments performed with our colleague Victor Zue (Cole, Rudnicky, Zue & Reddy, 1980; Cole & Zue, 1980). These studies showed that it
is possible to identify acoustic features on speech spectrograms which form
speaker-independent patterns for phonetic segments. Our studies with Victor
Zue suggested the following strategy for developing a feature-based speech-
recognition system:

- Study various types of visual displays of speech to determine
  the features that are needed to discriminate among phonetic segments. There will be several different features needed for each fine
  phonetic distinction, and these features are likely to be distributed
  across both frequency and time.
- Create algorithms to extract the features from speech.
- Determine the best way to use the featural information to specify
  speaker-independent patterns for phonetic events. The classifier
  must be able to take into account the manner in which features

covary, so that it will be possible to capture trading relations among features.

FEATURE: A feature-based speech recognition system

Research leading to the development of FEATURE began in 1980, when the first author intensively studied speech spectrograms of letters and digits. The goal was to acquire knowledge about the speaker-independent characteristics of English letters and digits. The data base consisted of 2,880 broadband speech spectrograms. The spectrograms displayed 10 tokens of each of the letters A through Z and the digits 0 through 9 produced by four male and four female speakers.

After two weeks of study, the reader was able to identify letters and digits on spectrograms with about 2% error. When a new speaker was encountered, the same pattern emerged. During the first "run" through a set of letters and digits (one spectrogram of each letter and digit) the reader produced one to three errors, and these occurred on confusable items such as P–T, B–D, R–4, I–5. After studying the spectrograms of the confusable items, the reader was able to discover reliable features for each new speaker. We were thus able to show that it is possible to learn to read spectrograms of letters and digits after a short period of intensive study, and to specify the features that distinguish confusable items.

On the basis of knowledge gained during this experiment, we developed a feature-based, speaker-independent isolated letter recognition system. FEATURE consists of the following modules:

- A program that detects the onset of speech and creates a file containing the digitized waveform.
- Signal processing routines that transform speech into a set of representations from which features can be extracted.
- A set of feature-extraction routines that measure formant frequencies, formant slopes, and other features.
- Statistical classification routines that use the feature values to classify letters at each of a series of decision points until a single letter is identified.
- A program that uses feedback to modify the expected feature values at each decision point.

Representation. The signal processing routines produce a set of data structures that are used by the feature extraction algorithms. These vectors and arrays vary as a function of time and include information about (a) the spectrum; (b) pitch; (c) zero crossings; (d) total energy; (e) energy in a low

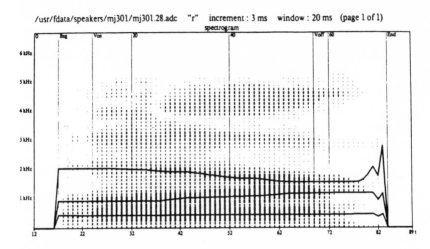

FIG. 15.2.   Spectrogram of the letter "R" using digital spectral representation. The lines are drawn automatically using the formant extraction algorithms.

frequency band; (f) energy in a mid-frequency band; and (g) energy in a high-frequency band.

The spectral representation consists of 54 coefficients compressed from a sequence of 256-point DFTs. The 54 coefficients are computed every 3 msec over 20 msec of speech. The coefficients span the range from 63 to 6,093 Hz. The bandwidth of each coefficient is 250 Hz, and coefficients overlap by 125 Hz. Most of the feature detection algorithms (such as the formant frequency estimators) use this array. Figure 15.2 shows a typical spectrogram of the letter (R) generated from this array. The formant tracks are drawn automatically by our formant estimation algorithms.

Segmentation. Four points are located in each utterance: the beginning of the utterance, the vowel onset, the vowel offset and the endpoint of the utterance. These four points are used as temporal anchors for the feature extraction algorithms.

Feature Extraction. Features were discovered through examination of visual displays of the representations produced by the signal processing routines. The most useful display was the computer-generated spectrogram using the coefficient values in the spectral array. In general, the features used to make fine phonetic distinctions correspond to the acoustic cues reported in the acoustic-phonetic literature. These include:

• The frequencies of the first three formants in the vowel portion of the sound (used to discriminate among different vowels).

• The trajectories of the first three formants in the vowel portion of the sound (e.g., E set versus U set; I versus Y versus R; M versus N).

- The maximum and minimum frequencies of the first three formants between vowel onset and vowel offset (I Y R versus A, L, O),

- The duration of aperiodic energy before vowel onset (voiced versus voiceless stops, CV versus V and VC syllables).

- The duration of aperiodic energy after vowel offset (VC versus V and CV syllables).

- The attack characteristics of the sound (T versus Z; P versus Z; P versus V)

- The ratio of high frequency energy to low frequency energy before vowel onset (B, P, V versus D, T, Z) or after vowel offset (F versus S).

In all, about 50 different features were used to discriminate among the letters of the English alphabet.

Decision Strategy. The hierarchical decision tree shown in Figure 15.3 was used to classify letters. By using a decision-tree structure we were able to reduce the problem of choosing one of 26 letters on the basis of observed values of up to 50 features to a series of decisions between smaller numbers of candidate sets, using a relatively small number of features at a time. For example, at the fourth level, letters are classified into groups of vowels on the basis of formant frequencies. At the later levels, where fine phonetic distinctions are performed, just those measures that are needed to discriminate the confusable letters are used. This approach significantly reduces the dimensionality of the decision space within which the classifications are performed.

The combinations of features actually used at each node of the decision tree were selected automatically. Specifically, a principal components analysis was first performed to reduce the dimensionality of the decision space, and to avoid linearly dependent combinations of the original 50 features. At each node of the decision tree a discriminant analysis was performed to determine sets of linear combinations of features that maximized the ratio of class-to-class covariance to the average covariance within a given decision class. *A posteriori* probabilities of the letters given the observed combinations of feature values were evaluated at each node of the decision tree, using the methods described below. At each subsequent node of a given branch of the decision tree, new linear combinations of feature values were selected that were approximately uncorrelated with the combinations of features that were used to evaluate probabilities at previous nodes along the branch. Because these sets of features were assumed to be uncorrelated, the overall *a posteriori* probabilities of each letter were obtained by multiplying the probabilities calculated at the nodes of the decision tree along the branch ending with that letter. The letter with greatest *a posteriori* probability was the one recognized by the classifier.

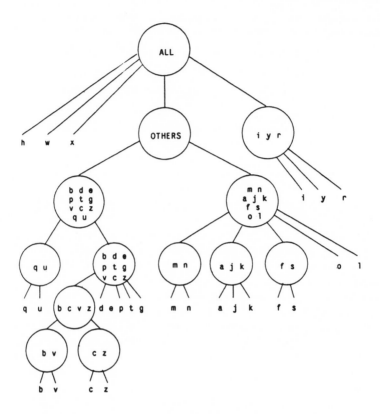

FIG. 15.3. Decision tree used in classifying the letters of the alphabet.

Dynamic Speaker Adaptation. Even when features are designed to be speaker-independent, it is often the case that individual speakers will produce unusual values for some features for some letters. The tuning program produces a running estimate of the expected feature values for individual speakers using maximum *a posteriori* probability (MAP) estimation techniques. After each utterance, the program optimally combines the feature values obtained from the observations thus far with *a priori* statistics obtained from the training data. The amount by which new observations shift the running estimates depends on the sample-to-sample variability of the observed data compared to the speaker-to-speaker variability of the expected feature values. The program also exploits correlations from feature to feature for a given letter and from letter to letter. This component of the system is discussed in further detail in the section "Tuning to Individual Speakers" below.

Performance. The data base used to develop feature extraction algorithms consisted of four tokens of each letter produced by 23 male and 20 female speakers. Data were then collected for a new set of 19 speakers (10 male and 9 female) who also recorded four tokens of each letter.

In evaluating the classifier, the new speakers were divided into subgroups of 10 speakers and 9 speakers. The classifier was trained on the original 43 speakers plus one of the two subgroups then tested on the other subgroup. FEATURE classified the letters of the alphabet with an average error rate of 11.2% across the two groups. The error rate on the E set was 16.7%. This compares favorably to speaker-dependent error rates of 60% obtained with template matching algorithms on the E set.

An important property of feature-based systems is that errors can be analyzed to determine what feature extraction algorithms need to be improved in order to eliminate confusions. For example, the most common substitution that we observed in the E set was P classified as B. Examination of the feature values for these letters revealed that, in each case, the error occurred because of a short Voice Onset Time (more characteristic of B than P). Further analysis revealed that Voice Onset Time was too short because of an error in the automatic location of the vowel onset. If we can eliminate this problem, we will decrease the current error rate by 1%. This seems like a small improvement, but many such improvements will result in a system that can perform fine phonetic distinctions as well as human listeners.

VARIABILITY AND FEATURES

The success of FEATURE depends critically on knowledge of variability in speech. Estimates of the variance and covariance of feature values within letters, across letters, within speakers, and across speakers forms the basis for both the classification of letters and dynamic adaptation to new speakers. Since the theme of this volume is the nature of variability in speech, this section presents a review of the of the sources of variability in speech that are used in classification and dynamic adaptation in FEATURE.

Bayesian Classification

FEATURE classifies letters using Bayesian classification methods. In this section, we briefly review the principles of Bayesian classification, concentrating on the ways in which the optimal classification procedures make use of variance and covariance in classifying data.

Decisions in Bayesian classification are made on the basis of which class of utterance is the most probable, given the specific values of the features that are extracted by the system. We adopt the notation C_i to indicate the ith decision class, the vector x to indicate the set of observed feature values, and

$P(C_i|\mathbf{x})$ to represent the *a posteriori* conditional probability of the decision class C_i being correct given the observed features $\mathbf{x}$. The Bayesian classifier, then, chooses the class C_i for which $P(C_i|\mathbf{x})$ is maximum. This probability is calculated by applying Bayes rule

$$P(C_i|\mathbf{x}) = p(\mathbf{x}|C_i)P(C_i)/p(\mathbf{x}) \tag{1}$$

In most applications it is sufficient to compare the numerators of the above expression for the various decision classes since the denominator is the same in each case.

In order to implement Bayesian classification, it is necessary to estimate or compute $P(C_i)$, the *a priori* probabilities of the various letters, and $p(\mathbf{x}|C_i)$, the probability distribution of each feature vector given that a particular letter has been presented to the classifier. In our current implementation of FEATURE, we assume that letters are equiprobable, and that the statistics of the feature values can be reasonably approximated as jointly gaussian random variables. The gaussian assumption is almost certainly inadequate when large numbers of features are considered at once, but it was adopted as a first working hypothesis because it is the only probability density function that can be easily applied to a large number of statistically correlated features.

Equation (1) can be evaluated directly for the various C_i since explicit analytic expressions for $p(\mathbf{x}|C_i)$ are specified by the multivariate gaussian assumption. Since the general results are available in any standard text on pattern classification (e.g. Duda and Hart, 1973), we will only illustrate through the use of several simple examples how optimal Bayesian classification, and FEATURE in particular, makes use of various types of variance and invariance in recognizing speech.

VARIANCE OF INDIVIDUAL FEATURES

Let us first consider the simplest possible recognition task in which we are recognizing samples from an alphabet of only two letters on the basis of the observed values x of a single feature. Intuitively we would expect that the decision rule for classification should depend on the means and variances of x given that utterances from either decision class 1 or decision class 2 are presented to the system, as well as the *a priori* probability of either class being presented.

If the feature value x has the same variance for the two decision classes, the gaussian assumption leads to the decision rule

Choose class 1 if $x < \gamma$ (2a)

Choose class 2 if $x > \gamma$ (2b)

where $\gamma = (m_1 + m_2)/2 + \sigma \ln [P(C_1)/P(C_2)]$

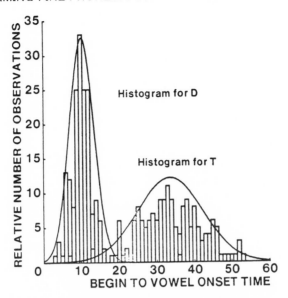

FIG. 15.4. Histograms and Gaussian probability densities for the time between the beginning of an utterance and vowel onset (in arbitrary units) for the letters D and T.

The symbols m_1 and m_2 represent the means of the feature values x given class 1 or class 2 respectively, and σ is the standard deviation of x for the two decision classes. In effect this decision rule partitions the possible values of x into two regions separated by the criterion γ. If C_1 and C_2 are equiprobable, the criterion γ is halfway between m_1 and m_2, so an unknown utterance is assigned to the class with the "closest" mean value along the x continuum. If $P(C_1)$ and $P(C_2)$ are not equal, the criterion γ shifts so as to assign ambiguous samples (i.e. values of x that are close to the midpoint between m_1 and m_2) to the class of letters with greater a priori probability. The amount of criterion shift is controlled by the standard deviation of the feature values σ. Specifically, larger values of σ imply that the particular feature value x is more intrinsically variable. In such a case the criterion is shifted so that the final decision is more heavily influenced by the a priori probabilities of the decision classes, and decisions are less dependent on the specific values of ambiguous observations.

In general, the variance of the feature values will depend on which class of letters is presented. For example, Figure 15.4 shows histograms of values of a feature measuring the time from the beginning of an utterance to the onset of voicing for the letters D and T, with gaussian probability densities superimposed over the histograms. The histograms represent data from 42 speakers, and the validity of the gaussian assumption can be evaluated by comparing the shapes of the histograms to the smooth curves. As can be

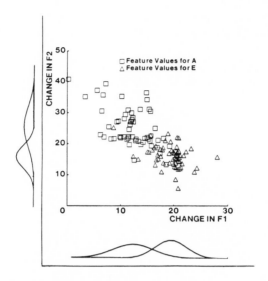

FIG. 15.5. Two-dimensional scatter plot of two frequency-based features for the letters A and E.

seen from the figure, the standard deviation of this feature is about 2.7 times as large when the letter T is presented to the recognizer than when D is presented. The decision boundaries specified by the Bayesian classifier under the assumption that the letters are equiprobable are at the points of intersection of the probability densities. If the variance of a feature differs from class to class, the decision boundary shifts away from the mean value of the class with the greater variance. In a two-class problem, this has the effect of causing observations that fall about halfway between the two mean feature values to be assigned to the decision class producing greater variance in the features, which is what would be desired intuitively.

Covariance of Sets of Features

In order to achieve the best recognition performance possible it is necessary to consider not only the individual means and variances of each of these features but also the covariance of the features as well. The reason for this is shown in Figure 15.5, which displays a two-dimensional histogram of values of features measuring the first and second formant frequencies at the time of vowel onset for the letters A and E. The bell-shaped curves along the coordinate axes of the figure are proportional to the probability density functions characterizing the two features for each of the letters, if we accept the gaussian assumption as valid. The fact that these probability densities overlap quite a bit indicates that recognition performance based on the observed values of either of these features independently would be relatively poor. On the other hand, the observed feature values separate into two well-defined clouds if we consider the histograms as points in a two-dimensional space. This separability indicates that a classifier can be constructed that will achieve good recognition performance for these two letters if it incorporates knowledge of the expected correlation of the two features for each letter, as well as statistics describing the behavior of each of the features considered separately.

If all the letters are equiprobable, the assumption of multivariate gaussian probabilities for the features in the Bayesian classifier leads to a classification rule that essentially minimizes the "distance" in the vector space of the observed feature values from the centroid of the cloud of histogram points observed for the ith letter to be recognized. This measure of distance accommodates differences in variance among the features, as well as correlations of the two features. For example, if the cloud of feature values is ellipsoidal in shape, an observation that falls along the major axis of the ellipse would be closer to the center of the cloud in the sense of the distance measure used by the classifier than a second observation that is equally distant in the usual Euclidean sense, but located along the minor axis. In the two-feature case shown in Figure 15.5, this decision rule partitions the two-dimensional space of possible observations into regions corresponding to each possible decision.

As an example of the improvement in performance that can be obtained by making use of correlation of the feature values, we compared the classification error rate for the letters of the E set with and without considering these correlations. Training on three groups of 28 speakers and testing on 14 other speakers, we observed an error rate of 12.5% for the E-set letters when the features were considered independently, compared to 10.1% errors when the classifier was able to exploit correlations among the features.[4] We expect that the improvement in performance obtained by considering featural correlation will be even greater in discriminating vowel sounds.

Tuning to Individual Speakers

A third way in which variability is important in FEATURE is in dynamic adaptation or "tuning" to the acoustical characteristics of individual speakers. Even though the features used in the system were designed to be speaker independent, the variation of individual feature values for a given letter is

---

[4] The classification procedure used in this evaluation and the evaluation cited in the next section was similar to the procedure described above except that classification decisions are made at each node on the basis of observed values of hand-selected features. In addition, "hard decisions" were made in that only the decision class with the greatest *a posteriori* probability at any given node was considered at subsequent decision nodes.

frequently smaller within a given speaker than from speaker to speaker. For example, across all speakers the average second formant frequency before the onset of the nasal murmur may be 1200 Hz in M and 1800 Hz in N, but a particular speaker may produce average values of 1800 Hz for M 2400 Hz for N. In such cases, the performance of the recognition system can be greatly improved by adapting the statistical parameters of the feature values to the individual speakers.

In our research in dynamic adaptation, we have primarily been concerned with enabling the system to update its estimates of the mean values of the features for a given letter when spoken by a particular individual. FEATURE begins by recognizing utterances according to mean feature values estimated by averaging training data from a representative set of speakers. The system then adapts to the characteristics of an individual speaker after it is informed by user feedback which letter had actually been spoken.

The goal of the dynamic adaptation component of FEATURE is to combine in some optimal fashion the *a priori* information representing the average behavior of all speakers with the *a posteriori* information gained when the system receives samples of speech from the individual presently using the system. We have used another Bayesian technique, maximum *a posteriori* probability (MAP) estimation, to accomplish this task. (Classical MAP estimation has been applied to many types of statistical problems, including estimation of vocal tract length [Kirlin, 1978]). In our dynamic adaptation of the system's representation of the feature mean values to individual speakers, we choose the mean vector M to maximize the *a posteriori* probability

$$p(M|\mathbf{x}) = \frac{p(\mathbf{x}|M)}{p(\mathbf{x})} \tag{3}$$

where $p(\mathbf{x}|M)$ is the conditional probability density for the observed feature values given a particular mean vector for a specific letter, and $p(\mathbf{x})$ and $p(M)$ are the *a priori* probability densities for the mean vectors and the observations, respectively. While this expression is obviously very similar to Equation (1), we note that x now represents the complete set of observed feature values for all utterances presented to the recognition system, rather than just the observations used for a single classification.

The MAP estimate obtained when the mean values of the features as well as the data are assumed to be gaussian is indeed a linear combination of the average across all speakers of the mean values of the features in the training data, and the sample mean of the feature values observed up to the present utterance. The relative weighting of this *a priori* and *a posteriori* information is determined by the ratio of within-speaker variability to across-speaker variability of the observed values of a given feature, and a small value of this ratio indicates that the performance of a given feature is more likely to be improved by dynamic adaptation to individual speakers. Our analysis of these variances indicates that formant estimates and other spectral features derive the most benefit from tuning to individual speakers. The values of features that record temporal events (such as the interval between the beginning of an utterance and vowel onset) tend to be more speaker independent.

An important innovation of FEATURE is that we characterize the mean feature values as random variables that may be correlated from class to class. This approach enables the system to use samples of the letter ⟨M⟩, for example, to update estimates of the expected feature values for the letter ⟨N⟩ as well as ⟨M⟩. As a result, the system adapts more rapidly to individual speakers than it would if all the mean values of the features were assumed to be statistically independent, but at the cost of greater computational complexity and storage requirements.

We have compared the performance of an earlier implementation of FEATURE with and without the use of tuning to individual speakers (Stern & Lasry, 1983). After four presentations of the entire alphabet (with feedback to the system indicating which letter had been presented) the system's error rate using multivariate Bayesian classification alone dropped from 12.5% to 6.1%. Similarly, the error rate for confusing the letters B, D, P, and T dropped from 8.1% to 1.7%, and the error rate for confusing the letters M and N dropped from 8.4% to 4.2%.

CONCLUSION

We have demonstrated that a recognition system based on perceptually-derived features of speech can significantly outperform systems based on more traditional spectral matching approaches, such as dynamic programming, when the recognition task requires that fine phonetic distinctions be performed. Our feature-based system can recognize the letters of the English alphabet with a speaker-independent error rate of about 11%. These error rates decrease considerably when the system is permitted to adapt to the acoustical characteristics of individual speakers. The system achieves an error rate of 16.7% on the confusable E set. In contrast, most template-based systems recognize the English alphabet with an error rate of 15% to 30%, and they classify the E-set letters with error rates of 20% to 40%.

We find it interesting that FEATURE emulates some of the important characteristics of human speech perception. Decisions about phonetic events are based on many different features distributed across both frequency and time. For example, a decision about the letter V is based on onset information, the fricative spectrum, changes in formant frequencies after vowel onset, and several other features. The manner in which these features covary is taken into account when using multivariate statistics.

ACKNOWLEDGMENTS

This research was sponsored in part by the National Science Foundation, Grant MCS–7825824 and in part by the Defense Advanced Research Projects Agency (DOD), ARPA Order No. 3597, monitored by the Air Force Avionics Laboratory Under Contract F33615–78–C–1551.

The views and conclusions contained in this document are those of the authors and should not be interpreted as representing the official policies, either expressed or implied, of the Defense Advanced Research Projects Agency or the US Government.

Many additional researchers in the Carnegie-Mellon University speech group contributed significantly to the software implementations of the FEATURE system, including Michael Phillips, Scott Brill, Andrew Pilant, Philippe Specker, and Robert Brennan. The classifier using automatic feature selection was created and implemented by Alan Rogers.

Victor W. Zue: Comment

In order to comment on the system described in Chapter 15, it is necessary to first understand the state of the art. Today's isolated word recognition (IWR) systems share several features. These systems generally require clear pauses, typically 200 ms, between words and usually operate in a speaker-dependent mode. That is, systems must be trained for a particular speaker's voice. Treating each word as a unit, recognition is performed by matching the parameters of the input signal to the stored templates for the vocabulary items. The stored template that best matches with the input is selected to be the intended word. The scoring algorithm uses time-alignment procedures (the most successful being dynamic programming) designed to account for the inherent variability of the speech signal. These IWR systems usually operate on a small vocabulary of 10 to 200 items.

Despite intensive effort in speech recognition over the past years, there is still a very large gap between human and machine performance. Human speech recognition is robust and flexible: A person can recognize a novel sentence produced by unfamiliar talkers in hostile acoustic environments. In contrast, computer speech-recognition systems typically require training for each speaker, and the performance is very poor for acoustically confusable words. For example, as mentioned by Cole, et al., template-matching systems typically recognize only 60% of the confusable E-set of the letters of the alphabet.

Cole and his colleagues argue that in order to perform fine phonetic distinctions, one must identify and extract acoustic features from the speech signal that are needed to specify phonetic events. Their system, called FEATURE, is designed to recognize the letters of the English alphabets. It is motivated by experimental results in acoustic phonetics, speech perception, and spectrogram reading, indicating the presence of multiple acoustic cues and the trading relations among the various cues. Their approach in the development of the feature-based system involves the following three steps: (1) the acoustic features are determined through studies of various visual displays of a large body of data; (2) algorithms for feature extraction are then created; and (3) classification is done by taking into account interfeature and intrafeature variabilities, using statistical techniques. I think the FEATURE system is one of the most exciting milestones of speech recognition in recent years. Measured in terms of performance, the FEATURE system offers the best recognition results anywhere for the task of alphabet recognition. It constitutes an existence-proof that a feature-based system can outperform the so-called template-matching systems. By incorporating dynamic adaptation through feedback, the system gradually adjusts its performance to a given speaker. This second characteristic of the system is both attractive and essential. Having said this, I now offer some critical comments.

First, Cole contrasts his feature-based approach with the template-matching approach in which the spectrum is used directly for recognition. Strictly speaking, however, this use of the term "feature based" to distinguish such approaches from spectral ones is inappropriate. In the pattern classification literature, template matching refers to techniques for answering questions of the form "Does the input contain an instance of some previously-specified object?" by comparing the unknown with a prototype. Using this definition, feature-based speech-recognition systems which use multivariate gaussian models for classification also perform template matching. Similarly, spectrum amplitudes may be regarded as features so that spectrum-based techniques are "feature-based" as well. What is more important is whether and how much speech-specific knowledge is being utilized for recognition. In the development of the FEATURE system, Cole utilized an enormous amount of speech knowledge by literally examining thousands of spectrograms to discover the acoustic cues. It represents one of the most massive efforts to derive acoustic cues for phonetic contrasts.

One of the most serious problems with a template-matching approach is that it is difficult to define distance measures which are sensitive enough for fine phonetic distinctions but insensitive to irrelevant spectral changes. One manifestation of this problem is that perceptually-unimportant frame-to-frame variations in the spectrum of a long steady-state vowel are given excessive weight. Klatt (Chapter 14) has proposed a number of distance metrics which are intended to be sensitive to phonetic differences and insensitive to irrelevant acoustic differences. Such a distance metric may improve the performance of template-matching systems, since it includes speech knowledge in the measurement of spectral distances.

Second, in a feature-based approach, there are several levels where acoustic-phonetic knowledge can be introduced. On one hand, one must uncover acoustic attributes that are useful in signifying phonetic contrasts. On the other hand, one must also determine how these attributes should be combined to make the phonetic distinction. The FEATURE system selects a set of acoustic attributes that are well motivated. However, the system falls short of specifying the procedure for how these features should be combined for phonetic recognition, and instead classifies the lexical items directly in terms of traditional, statistical techniques for pattern classification. A conclusion that one may draw is that, even with no knowledge about how the acoustic cues should be combined, a set of speech-specific acoustic cues can go a long way in improving system performance.

Third, the FEATURE system is developed for a specific task. Whether the system can be extended to other tasks is not entirely clear. In the system, the four temporal anchors clearly play an important role in the extraction of acoustic attributes. It is doubtful that such anchors can reliably be obtained for a different lexicon. The lexical items of the FEATURE system are relatively simple; i.e., they represent a very small subset of the possible CV and VC combinations used in American English. As consonant clusters and more vowels are introduced, it remains to be seen whether the basic approach is still viable. One task that comes to mind, in order to answer the question of extendibility, is the recognition of a variety of CVs. It would also be of interest to see how system performance degrades when noise, either stationary or transient, is added to the speech signal.

Finally, we come to the question of variability and invariance, which is the theme of this volume. Variabilities in the speech signal can be due to speaker-specific factors, ranging from physiological to sociolinguistic ones. They can also appear as a consequence of contextual influence. The system developed by Cole and his colleagues shows that a judicious selection of well-motivated acoustic attributes will enable variabilities to be captured in the variance and covariance of the feature values. On the other hand, the dependence of system performance on speakers is somewhat alarming. The error rate for the best and worst speaker differ by an order of magnitude. By the authors' own admissions, the performance of their system is still a long way from human performance on the same task.

My comments should not be interpreted as being overly critical of Cole's work. I really intend to point out the magnitude of the problem facing speech-recognition researchers. Cole and his colleagues have made significant contributions to this field. However, there is much much more to be done. Success is more likely to be measured in decades, rather than years.

John Makhoul and Richard Schwartz: Ignorance Modeling

It has become quite clear that our knowledge, either of speech perception or in extracting features that are useful in automatic speech recognition, is very limited. Furthermore, part of that knowledge may, in fact, be erroneous or it may be used erroneously in speech-recognition systems.

Our conclusion from these observations is that, in incorporating our knowledge in a speech-recognition system, we should not neglect to *model our ignorance*. In fact, we believe that, in the last decade or so, high-performance speech-recognition systems have achieved their performance exactly because they had better ignorance models than other systems. We shall demonstrate what we mean by modeling ignorance using some examples.

In template-matching approaches to word recognition, one often computes the similarity of two spectra by using a simple Euclidean type of distance measure. Such distance measures are really ignorance models of perceptual distance between two spectra. Euclidean distances have certain desirable mathematical properties that are found to be useful in recognition, but certainly are not optimal.

In matching the templates of two words, we know that speech changes dynamically in time but don't know exactly how. We use dynamic time warping (Sakoe & Chiba, 1978) as our ignorance model for how speech varies in time. The model basically accepts that we don't know how to warp one word template to compare it to another, so we will try all possibilities (within limits) and pick the warp that gives the minimum distance between templates. This is a mathematical solution with certain desirable properties which result in improved recognition performance, but certainly not optimal performance.

Our final example of an ignorance model, and certainly one of the most powerful, is the probabilistic hidden-Markov model developed at the Institute for Defense Analyses (Baum, 1972) and used most successfully at IBM (Bahl, Jelinek, & Mercer, 1983). At IBM, a phoneme is represented by a hidden-Markov model with a structure that incorporates only a very small amount of speech knowledge. The model parameters are probability density functions that are estimated from training data. One of the major features of the estimation procedure is that while it requires a large amount of training data, computing resources, and storage, it requires relatively little human interaction. The IBM experience has been that, often, a simple but self-optimizing procedure outperforms human intuitions about speech as they are incorporated into automatic recognition systems.

Future speech research should be directed at producing knowledge and intuition that could be incorporated in the design of recognition systems, especially in minimizing the amount of training necessary for optimal performance, and eventually leading to virtually speaker-independent systems. Simultaneously, the search should continue for more sophisticated ignorance models that can make optimal use of what little knowledge we do have.

John Holmes: Comment

Victor Zue has already said much of what I was going to say. The main aspect I am unhappy about in Cole's paper is the presentation of template matching and the use of features as a dichotomy. Even assuming one regards the use of templates in the traditional way involving fairly crude pattern matching, there is no reason why there should not be a lot more speech-specific knowledge put into the patterns that are compared.

If the processes I suggested after Klatt's paper (Chapter 14) were adopted, highlighting in the measurement space such aspects as formant transitions and stop bursts, the template-matching approach would become much more like a feature-based system. I personally believe that the right sort of dynamic-programming algorithm, using a more speech-related measurement space, might have more explanatory power than the type of tree-structured process that Cole and his colleagues have described.

16 Normalization in Vowel Perception

John N. Holmes
Joint Speech Research Unit
Cheltenham, England

INTRODUCTION

Any invariance that exists in speech production targets in normal speech appears to be governed to a large extent by perceptual criteria applied during language acquisition, based on the properties of the acoustic signal as analyzed by the auditory system. For this to be possible there must clearly be some form of perceptual equivalence of men, women and children producing the same phonetic quality, in spite of the manifestly different acoustic signals in these cases. I assume that there is some fairly systematic transformation mapping phonetically equivalent acoustic descriptions between speaker types, and that this transformation might be found either by studying analyses of real speech, or by applying experimental transformations to parametric synthesis data and making subjective judgments about their adequacy.

It is now widely accepted that in the process of language acquisition the child uses acoustic cues derived by auditory feedback to guide the sound production process, and articulatory criteria are not directly involved (Paliwal, Lindsay & Ainsworth, 1983). Even so, the articulatory strategy for particular sounds shows a high degree of uniformity between speakers of a given dialect, but this might be accounted for merely by the fact that the easiest articulation for a particular acoustic effect is the one normally adopted. But there are also many cases where different people develop different articulations for particular sounds, and if the sound quality is acceptable they will not even realize that their articulation may be unusual (Ladefoged, De-Clerk, Lindau & Papçun, 1972). The latter fact is very strong evidence that auditory matching is paramount in language acquisition.

If speech production ability is acquired as a result of auditory matching, in most cases mainly from the mother, but also from the father and other adults, this immediately raises the question of how speech sounds from vocal tracts of very different size and proportions can be in some sense equivalent. Acoustic theory of speech production requires that the average formant frequency interval be inversely proportional to vocal tract length; although it might be possible for a child to match the adult frequency of a single formant without much difficulty, it will obviously not in general be possible to make the frequencies of the lowest two or three formants simultaneously match those of an adult by any physically possible articulation.

A fairly primitive hypothesis is that phonetic equivalence is achieved when the same articulation is used, and all frequencies are scaled by a factor equal to the ratio of vocal tract lengths. Although this hypothesis may be valid as a very rough approximation, there is no reason to believe it could be at all accurate, because the child-to-adult size scaling will normally not be uniform over the whole tract (Bennet & Weinberg, 1979). Whatever the relationship between child and adult articulation, the equivalence clearly has to be in the perceptual domain, although whether the equivalence is innate or learned is not clear. The child could be quite independently matching his/her productions to the adult model, and making judgments about their adequacy entirely from innate auditory criteria. It is also possible that the adult instructor is guiding those judgments in terms of adult auditory equivalence, and in the process is training the child's perception process. Whichever explanation is correct, there is no doubt that mature people do have the ability to make sensible phonetic comparisons between speech sounds from vocal tracts of different size. There is also no doubt that, once the basic ability to use language is fully acquired, speakers of different age, sex and size have no difficulty in producing sounds that are perceived as being phonetically fully equivalent, even to the extent of reproducing quite subtle differences in vowel quality associated with different accents. It seems, therefore, that there must be a systematic relationship between acoustic features that allows the phonetic interpretation of some quite different auditory signals to be equivalent.

The first stage of human auditory analysis consists of a fairly broadly-tuned filtering process (with resolution at any frequency roughly equal to the critical bandwidth, as determined by masking experiments), and from the results of Mathes & Miller (1947) it can be deduced that phase distortion that does not affect the time structure within critical bands has very little auditory effect. Any relationship between speech sounds from different size vocal tracts can therefore be assumed to be concerned with features of the short-term power spectrum, although it is, perhaps, possible that this relationship also depends on what particular speech sound is being heard. There are two obvious ways in whigh this relationship might be investigated. One is to analyze the spectra of a large number of phonetically equivalent speech sounds from a variety of speakers, and to try to deduce some orderly relationship between formant frequencies, spectral shapes, etc. The second method is to generate synthetic speech sounds that are subjectively acceptable representations of the speech of a particular type of speaker, and then to apply a range of transformations to the synthesis parameters and to make subjective judgments as to which transformations retain phonetic quality, while changing perceived speaker characteristics. Choosing transformations for the latter process would, of course, be guided by spectrographic comparison of phonetically equivalent human speech sounds from different speaker types.

STUDIES OF NATURAL SPEECH

It is many years since Potter and Steinberg (1950) presented the hypothesis that a particular pattern of stimulation of the basilar membrane might be identified as a given sound, within limits independent of displacement along the membrane. Quite recently Bladon, Henton and Pickering (1982) reported an investigation into how well this hypothesis is supported by comparison of phonetically-equivalent vowel sounds from male and female speakers of two British dialects of English. To make their results relevant to the Potter and Steinberg hypothesis they processed their measured narrow-band spectra by a "frequency-smearing function" that was specified on a Bark scale and closely modeled the lower levels of processing in the auditory system (Schroeder, Atal, & Hall, 1979). They represented the amplitudes on a scale of loudness, following the finding of Plomp (1970) that psychophysical distance between sounds is highly correlated with differences in loudness-density spectra. The ordinates of the resultant spectral cross-sections represented sones/Bark, and the abscissa scale was in Barks. Bladon et al. (1982) investigated how well this auditory representation of equivalent male and female vowels could be matched after a displacement on the Bark scale. Visual inspection of their loudness-density spectra shows that the female and male versions are very similar apart from a displacement of about 1 Bark, although this similarity is marred by the fact that the resolution of the auditory filter at low frequencies is normally sufficient to separate the harmonics of female speech but not male. The latter effect means that the female spectrum shows a peaky structure in the low-frequency region not seen for male speech, and it is the most obvious cause of the shape difference between male and female vowel spectra. The illustrations in Bladon et al. (1982) showing the difference in shape between male vowel spectra and normalized female spectra are also available in Bladon, Henton and Pickering (1984). To quantify the shift between male and female spectra, Bladon et al. used a distance metric described by Bladon and Lindblom (1981), based on the integrated difference in the loudness density spectra. By plotting this metric against Bark displacement they could find the displacement that gave the closest fit between male and female spectra. On average the displacement giving the best fit was about 1 Bark (roughly the same amount on the Bark scale as the difference between typical male and female values for F_0), but varied between vowels and between the two dialects. However, for the majority of the vowels examined, the curve showing the relationship between fit and displacement had a very broad minimum, making it difficult to be precise about the Bark shift required.

The results of Bladon et al. (1982) give a fair amount of support to the Potter and Steinberg hypothesis, but the departures from the simple Bark shift suggest that, in its simplest form as presented, the hypothesis does not sufficiently well explain the essential similarity between phonetically equivalent vowels for different speakers. Bladon et al. were well aware of the problems and discussed them in some detail.

A major difficulty is the effect of fundamental frequency on the spectrum shape for females, for whom the harmonics are normally resolved in the low F_1 region by the simulated auditory analysis. This fact alone would mean, even if the underlying vocal tract filter functions were identical, that the female speech spectra could not match very well to those of lower-pitched speakers, and this mismatch would tend to broaden the minimum of the curve used to determine optimum Bark shift. As the loudness function that was applied to the amplitudes greatly increases the dominance of F_1 over the higher formants, a low value for the distance metric cannot be achieved without a good F_1 match; yet the F_1 region is just that part of the spectrum whose shape is most disturbed by the higher pitch. In consequence it is quite likely that for certain values of F_0 the harmonic resolution may significantly move the minimum of the spectral-distance/Bark-shift curve. A further factor that will disturb the spectral match will be spectral tilt, caused either by an inherently different form of glottal excitation for a different speaker, or by variation of vocal effort. Although Bladon and Lindblom (1981) have experimentally justified the use of their distance metric for comparing 2-formant with 4-formant vowels at constant F_0, it seems much more doubtful whether this metric is suitable for testing the phonetic equivalence of vowels if other aspects of their quality are very different. For example, there are many common distortions of speech that cause large spectral changes without appreciably affecting phonetic quality. Sharp cut-off band-limiting filters at 300 Hz and 3400 Hz are normally used in public telephone networks, and even within this band the characteristics of earpieces and carbon microphones can cause much greater spectral tilts than normaly occur between male and female speakers. Common experience with these severe spectral shape distortions suggests that phonetic values of vowels are scarcely altered at all, but that other aspects of speech quality, such as would normally be associated with high fidelity reproduction, are almost completely destroyed. This general argument is supported by Carlson, Granström and Klatt (1979),

Klatt (1979b) and Klatt (1982a), who have tested a wide range of distortions
of synthetic vowel sounds with adult male pitch, and established that spectral
slope, high-pass filtering etc., have a great impact on perceived psychophysical quality, but have very little effect on phonetic quality. On the other hand,
phonetic judgments were critically dependent on the frequencies of F_1 and
F_2. The fact that they also found some disturbance to phonetic quality when
they randomized the phases of the spectral components of the vowels suggests that perception models that completely ignore phase could never fully
explain human phonetic judgments. Using the same vowel sounds, Carlson and Granström (1979) have investigated how phonetic differences and
psychophysical differences correlate with various models of the perception
process. Their results showed that a model involving dominance of local
spectral peaks was more successful than all others they tried in predicting
phonetic similarity.

Carlson et al. (1979) did not report any investigation of how their spectral dominance model might be affected by F_0, but such effects are crucial to
male/female normalization. Bladon et al. (1982) and Bladon (1982) discuss
the effect of F_0 on the perception of the F_1 peak in their male and female
vowel data. When they use their process for getting a simulated auditory
stimulation pattern, the position of the F_1 peak for vowels with low F_1 moves
to the nearest F_0 harmonic when F_0 is high enough, and they regard this
peak position as representing the F_1 frequency in their discussion. However,
it seems that human speakers can easily produce pitch glides that cause harmonics to cross the F_1 peak, while maintaining the phonetic quality of vowels.
Bladon (1982) has proposed a fairly complicated process for normalizing the
F_1 peak measured from his spectral representation, depending on the value
of F_0. This complexity might be removed if one could model an assumed
higher level of auditory processing that estimates the true F_1 resonance even
when the harmonics are widely spaced. analysis, auditory

The experiments of Young and Sachs (1979) on the response to vowel
sounds in the auditory nerve of cats suggest that any auditory analysis of
formant frequencies depends on time-synchrony of response in nerve fibers
from near the appropriate place on the basilar membrane, and the central
spectrum model of Srulovicz and Goldstein (1983), combining place and nerve
pulse timing in a central process, explains many results of perception studies.
It thus seems reasonable to assume that the central processing has far more
power for analyzing formant parameters than is possible using the methods of
Bladon et al. (1982). However, until perceptual models have been developed
further and validated for formant perception it is probably safer to study
normalization by experiments in synthesis and perception, rather than by
analysis of human speech production.

SYNTHESIZER REQUIREMENTS

Many studies of vowel perception have been made using synthetic speech, and some of these are directly relevant to the question of normalization. Fujisaki and Kawashima (1968) investigated the roles of F_0 and the formant frequencies for Japanese vowels, and Traunmüller (1981) has studied the effect of the relationship of between F_0 and F_1 on perceived vowel openness. Ryalls and Lieberman (1982) have reported how vowel perception accuracy varies in relation to the F_0 value used for synthesis. All of these studies used terminal-analog synthesizers, but the synthesizers were not capable of copying certain features known to occur in human speech, as explained below.

Because of the problems of defining formant resonances from the spectrum of speech when F_0 is high, it is important to consider whether the phonetically significant features of synthetic spectra will be sufficiently well defined merely by the known resonant frequencies used in their generation. The relative intensities of the lowest two or three harmonics of voiced speech depend critically on the shape of the glottal flow pulse. During normal phonation the main excitation of the F_1 resonance occurs at glottal closure, and the vocal tract will then produce an approximately force-free response at the true resonant frequencies until the glottis opens again. As the glottis opens there is additional, mainly low-frequency, energy added into the vocal tract, but the formant damping increases considerably, particularly for F_1 (Flanagan, 1972). These effects in voiced speech generation mean that the true vocal tract resonances will be better defined by the time structure of the signal immediately after glottal closure than by the harmonic spectrum determined over a longer time window. If human analysis after the broad-band filtering in the cochlea is largely a time-domain process, it follows that any synthesis experiments to test formant-normalization hypotheses need to model the above aspects of natural speech generation. Such modeling should not be important for low values of F_0, where formant bandwidth is comparable with harmonic spacing, but for high-pitched speech the time structure of the formant response could be significantly in error for conventional terminal-analog synthesizers, that do not take into account either the open-glottis increase in formant damping, or the fact that the lowest-frequency components of each glottal pulse enter the vocal tract before the main formant excitation.

The parallel-formant synthesizer of Holmes (1973), modified as described by Holmes (1980), has provision for time-domain representation of glottal pulse shapes and for extra formant damping in open-glottis intervals. It has been adequately established as able to reproduce the perceptual qualities of natural male speech very closely. No attempt has yet been made to produce similarly close copies of female speech, but a small amount of female material has been synthesized using control data derived by automatic analysis.

Engineers who have attempted to analyze formant frequencies for female speech have been aware for many years that the problem of determining the true resonance peaks for speech with widely spaced harmonics is very difficult. However, an engineering process that should give the true resonant frequencies is analysis by synthesis, provided that a synthesis model can be made to approximate speech production closely enough for higher pitched speakers. The analysis-by-synthesis technique of Seeviour, Holmes, & Judd (1976), as developed further by Dupree (1978, 1980) has been used by Dupree (private communication, 1982) on some sentences of female speech. The parameters of the analysis system had not been optimized for female speech, and there were in consequence a number of gross formant measurement errors. However, for those parts of the utterances that were free of gross errors, the formant measurements seemed to vary smoothly in spite of harmonics crossing the spectral peaks, and the resultant resynthesis gave a very close subjective match with the original voice quality. It thus seemed likely that this synthesizer might be more suitable for synthesis experiments relevant to talker normalization than the simpler types used by the authors cited above.

SYNTHESIS EXPERIMENTS

The general trends seen in the natural vowel measurements of Peterson & Barney (1952), Bladon et al. (1982), Bennet (1979) and Fujisaki et al., (1968) all suggest an initial hypothesis that the phonetic quality of vowels (and perhaps of other sounds too) would, within limits, be maintained if all formant resonances were shifted by an equal amount on a Bark scale, accompanied by an F_0 shift roughly in line with the formant shift. However, there seems to be some doubt about the role of F_0 in vowel perception. In machine voice output systems, for example, little harm seems to be done by not providing any change of formant frequencies as F_0 is changed to signal various prosodic features. Yet Traunmüller (1981) and Fujisaki et al. (1968) both seem to support the idea that for correct vowel perception the F_0 value needs to be appropriate for the formant frequencies, and Traunmüller in particular reports very striking changes in phonetic labeling of one-formant vowels as the relationship between F_0 and F_1 is varied. On the other hand, Ryalls et al. (1982) reported that synthetic vowels, using the average adult female formant values from Peterson and Barney (1952), were more accurately identified when synthesized with a typical male F_0 value than with a typical female value. It thus seems that further investigation of the role of F_0 is needed, preferably using a synthesizer that provides a closer model of human speech production than those used in the above experiments.

An initial demonstration of the effect of Bark-scale frequency shift was made using the JSRU rule synthesis system (a text-to-speech system using a hardware version of the Holmes synthesizer). Four sentences were synthesized from text input, with the normal phonetic and prosodic rules that are used for male speech. They were synthesized again with equal constant upward Bark shifts of 0.5, 0.75, 1.0, 1.25, 1.5 and 2.0 Barks applied to all frequency parameters. The upper values took the signals well into the child range for F_0 and the formant frequencies. With 1 Bark shift on all frequencies, the formant frequency pattern and pitch were subjectively appropriate for an adult female voice, and with a 2-Bark shift the results seemed about right for a 10-year old child. However, the female voice quality was much less acceptable than the male quality, which had no frequency shift, either because the simple Bark shift does not adequately represent the change between male and female speech or possibly because the unaltered formant amplitudes did not correctly represent the effect of the different spectrum of a typical female glottal pulse. The success of the synthesis of automatically-analyzed female speech confirms that this defect is not inherent in the synthesizer, so it could perhaps be corrected without too much difficulty by a more elaborate frequency-shift rule or by also modifying the formant amplitudes.

Very careful listening by the author (who has many years of experience with speech synthesis and some formal phonetic training) revealed no obvious phonetic differences between corresponding sounds after modification by any of the various amounts of Bark shift. The equivalence was maintained even to the extent that for a few vowels where the rules were judged to produce sounds slightly different from the intended phonetic quality, the modified vowels were perceived as having a similar amount of phonetic error. However, these judgments were made on meaningful sentences and may have therefore been influenced by linguistic context; the fact that the overall naturalness was not high may have also reduced the sensitivity to small phonetic errors.

In an attempt to get some quantitative measure of how well the simple Bark shift hypothesis is supported for vowels, a pilot experiment has been carried out in which subjects were asked to label isolated synthetic vowels. Although the aim of this experiment was to test the hypothesis that a simple shift of F_0 and all the spectral peaks will maintain phonetic quality, the results could also be interpreted as an assessment of the role of pitch and higher formants in vowel perception, exactly as in the study of Fujisaki et al. (1968). The main differences between this study and that of Fujisaki et al. are as follows:

(i) The experiment reported here used free-choice vowel labeling, with subjects being encouraged to reject vowels whose phonetic quality was not exactly correct. Fujisaki et al. used forced-choice labeling to determine the perceptual boundaries between pairs of vowels on the F_1, F_2 plane.

(ii) The present experiment explored the whole F_1, F_2 plane within the limits of the synthesizer, whereas Fujisaki et al. varied F_1 and F_2 only along lines in the plane previously found to represent particular pairs of Japanese vowels.

(iii) Fujisaki et al. also included whispered vowels.

The vowels for this experiment were generated by the same synthesizer as was used for the previous synthesis of sentences. As the fourth formant in this implementation is fixed, it was switched off and all the tests were made using 3-formant vowels. The values of F_1 and F_2 were chosen in random order at 0.5 Bark intervals to cover the whole of the relevant area of the F_1, F_2 plane. For every value of F_1 and F_2, the frequency of the third formant was calculated according to the algorithm described by Covington and Peikari (1983). The values of K_1, K_2, K_3 and K_4 in their formula were set to 1050, 800, 1400 and 2500 respectively, which were within the ranges they reported for adult male formant data. As the intention was to investigate the effect of Bark-scale frequency shifts, the values of F_3 appropriate for adult male speech were calculated, and then the formants of all vowels for each test condition were subsequently shifted by the same amount, specified in Barks. For this purpose the Hz-to-Bark transformation was that given by Schroeder et al. (1979). This approach was preferred to the alternative of exploring F_1, F_2, F_3 variation directly in three dimensions because it provides the systematic component of F_3 variation according to position on the F_1, F_2 plane, so reducing the number of test tokens needed to explore the effect of F_3 on normalization.

For some conditions F_0 was shifted by the same amount (in Barks) as the formants, and in others it was varied independently. In all conditions F_0 had a falling glide of half an octave from start to finish of each vowel, which was judged to be very similar to the pitch fall an English speaker might use when producing isolated citation-form vowels. The rate of glide was uniform on a logarithmic scale of frequency, and the nominal F_0 for each condition was taken to be the value at the mid-point of each vowel. The vowels were each 400 ms long.

After any required Bark shift, the amplitudes of the formants were calculated to be those that would occur in a conventional cascade synthesizer (Fant, 1959), but the higher-pole correction was varied according to an estimate of vocal tract length based on the average of F_1, F_2 and F_3. In this way the amplitude difference of F_3 between [i] (spread lips) and [u] (rounded lips) was not excessive, as it would have been if the higher-pole correction had been held constant.

The formant amplitudes could also be modified by a frequency-dependent weighting function, to allow different trends in the glottal source spectrum to be represented. The function was specified in dB relative to the 0 Hz value, at 1, 2, 3 and 4 kHz, and was linearly interpolated between these frequencies. The following conditions were tested:

(1) Vowels in which F_3 and F_0 were appropriate for a typical adult male.
(2) As 1, but with F_0 shifted up by 1 Bark.
(3) As 2, but with the F_3 region attenuated by 15 dB.
(4) As 1, but with F_3 shifted up by 0.5 Bark.
(5) As 1, but with F_3 and F_0 shifted up by 0.5 Bark.
(6) As 1, but with F_3 and F_0 shifted up by 1 Bark.
(7) As 1, but with F_3 and F_0 shifted up by 1.5 Bark and with the F_3 region attenuated by 15 dB.

The reduced intensities in the F_3 region were used for some conditions for two reasons:

(i) Vowels in the female and child F_0 ranges sounded too harsh if the unmodified spectrum was used. The reason for this effect may be that human glottal pulses for female and child speech have relatively less high frequency content.
(ii) Between conditions 2 and 3 it was possible to get some indication of the extent to which relative formant amplitudes affect phonetic judgments.

For all conditions the subjects were the same five final-year undergraduate speech science students, who were all phonetically trained and were native speakers of the Received Pronunciation dialect of British English. They were asked to place each vowel into one of six categories; those vowels that were perceived as being phonetically exactly correct as one of the five long monophthongs in the words "heed," "hard," "paw," "zoo" and "serve" in their native dialect were to be labeled appropriately, and the others were to be rejected.

The subjects were also asked, for each condition, to judge the naturalness of the vowels on a 5-point scale, and to estimate the sex and approximate age of the source they would infer if the sounds had been of human origin.

For each condition the vowels that were acceptable occupied five very small regions of the F_1, F_2 plane, each region having a spread of between 1 and 2 Barks, depending on the vowel. Figure 16.1 shows the means of the F_1, F_2 values that were judged acceptable for each vowel in each condition. There were no obvious systematic differences between the judges, so their results were pooled. The values of F_2 were curtailed at 7 and 14.5 Barks because of a limitation of the hardware synthesizer, so it is to be expected in consequence that the mean F_2 values for [ɔ] and [i] will be biased towards the middle of the range. In the case of [i], there were no acceptable vowels in condition 7, presumably because F_2 could not be made high enough.

Subjects obviously differed in their absolute assessment of naturalness, as two subjects used only points 1 to 3 of the 5-point scale, another used only points 3 to 5, and the other two subjects used intermediate values. However, there was a general trend to judge condition 6 as the most unnatural and 3

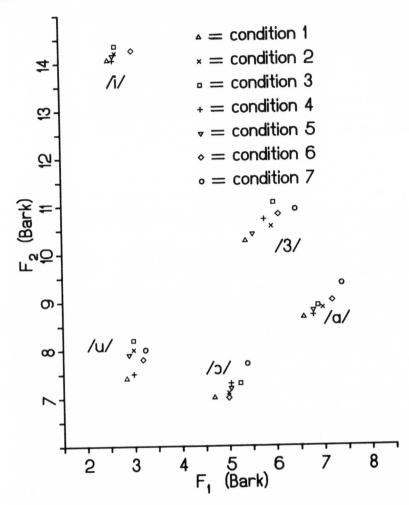

FIG. 16.1. Mean F_1 and F_2 values judged acceptable for five British vowels. The conditions are described in the text.

as more natural than 2. Condition 4 was marginally the most natural, and 1, 3, 5 and 7 were judged about equal.

The sex judgments were unanimously male for 1, 4 and 5, with no great disagreement about age. Condition 5 was judged as young adult, and 1 and 4 as middle-aged. Conditions 2, 3, 6 and 7 all included some judgments of adolescent male and of adult female. In condition 2 only one subject perceived the source as female, whereas in 3, which differed only in intensity of the F_3 region, only one perceived it as male. In condition 7 the one male judgment and three of the female judgments reported the ages as considerably lower than for the same sexes in conditions 2, 3 and 6.

DISCUSSION AND CONCLUSIONS

The experiments here have clearly demonstrated that for isolated citation-form vowels the assessment of phonetic quality by subjects varies as F_3 and/or F_0 are varied. However, the F_1, F_2 values for phonetically equivalent [ɔ], [a] and [3] lie close to diagonal lines in the Bark-scale F_1, F_2 plane, thus suggesting that an approximately constant Bark difference between F_1 and F_2 is necessary if phonetic quality is to be maintained for these vowels. On the other hand, for [u] (with a much lower value of F_1) the change in F_1 was much less than that for F_2, indicating that a different normalization is needed in this case. No clear conclusions could be reached for [i] because all results were very near the F_2 upper limit of the synthesizer. Even for [ɔ], [a] and [3] the differences in the F_1, F_2 positions between conditions was less (in Barks) than the shifts in F_3 and F_0 that caused them. The variation of amplitude of the F_3 region between conditions 2 and 3 seemed to make only a small difference to vowel labeling, in spite of the differences in naturalness and the tendency for one to sound female and the other male. The rather poor naturalness judgments for some of the conditions seem to indicate that in some cases the formant frequencies and/or amplitudes were unrepresentative of any normal human talker.

This pilot study has been far too small in scale to justify any firm conclusions about the form of parameter transformations between speaker types; the original hypothesis does not seem to have been well supported, particularly for [u], but much more work needs to be done to get reliable results that can be established as statistically significant. However, the ability of subjects to make consistent judgments in free choice labeling seems to support the use of formant synthesis as an effective tool for studying phonetic normalization. Many further experiments are planned.

ACKNOWLEDGEMENTS

The author is indebted to Adrian Fourcin and Michael Judd for their help in arranging the tests with subjects at University College, London.

Philip Lieberman: Comment

John Holmes's discussion of normalization focuses on how the formant frequency patterns that are an acoustic cue to the phonetic nature of vowels are normalized by human listeners. As many people have noted, it is clear that the absolute

differences between the formant frequency patterns that specify a *given* vowel of
a particular dialect are usually greater across the population of speakers of that
dialect, than the absolute differences between the formant frequency patterns across
all the vowels of an individual speaker. This pattern of variation is a consequence
of two basic biological principles. There first is a great deal of physical difference
between the supralaryngeal vocal tracts of small children and adults. Everyone is
smaller at birth! At the age when children first begin to produce meaningful words,
close to the start of their second year of life, their vocal tracts are less than half
as long as those of the adults who produce the speech signals on which the child
models her/his utterances. There is no way in which a child can mimic the absolute
formant frequency pattern of adult speech, so from the start of the process of speech
acquisition there must be some "normalization" algorithm present at some neural
level. The child must form an equivalence class between her/his utterances and the
adult productions. Quite apart from the difference in length between the adult and
child vocal tracts, is the different morphology of these vocal tracts. At birth, infants
have a supralaryngeal vocal tract in which the larynx is sited close to the palate.
During quiet respiration the infant's larynx actually locks into the nasopharynx.
There essentially is no pharynx in the direct supralaryngeal pathway from larynx to
lips. Although massive restructuring of the child's supralaryngeal vocal tract takes
place by the third month of life, forming a short pharynx as the larynx descends
into the neck, the full adult supralaryngeal vocal tract configuration, in which the
pharynx is equal in length or somewhat longer than the oral cavity, is not reached
until 12 years.

The second biological principle is the range of genetic variation that typically is
present in mammalian populations. It is obvious that adult humans vary in size.
The length of their supralaryngeal vocal tracts vary in length much as their legs
vary in length. Since formant frequency patterns are acoustic cues for the phonetic
class of a vowel, we must frequency-normalize the acoustic signals of adult speakers.
However, available anatomical data indicate that adult speakers have more or less
the same tongue shapes and pharynx to oral cavity proportions. There may be
some effects of secondary sexual dimorphism in some populations; Caucasoid adult
males thus may in general have somewhat longer pharyngeal lengths than adult
females or adolescent children, but this variation appears to be small compared to
the pattern of ontogenetic variation.

These two biological factors point to two distinct normalization problems. If
the supralaryngeal vocal tracts of a group of speakers have the same general morphology, but differ in size we might expect simple proportional scaling to work
as a normalization procedure. The data of Nearey (1978) demonstrate that simple rescaling, which involves dividing the formant frequencies of a speaker's vowel
utterances by a scaling coefficient, works extremely well for adult males, females
and adolescent children. Nearey's CLH1 procedure makes use of shifts along a log
scale, which is equivalent to dividing the formant frequency pattern by a single
coefficient.

The problem is somewhat different when we have to normalize the utterances
of young children. Preliminary data which we have derived show that different
normalization coefficients for F_1 and F_2 may be necessary in that case since the

children have much smaller pharyngeal lengths than adults. The data that Holmes presents also appear to need different F_1 and F_2 coefficients and it is possible that the pattern of growth across all human adults is somewhat variable. This question can only be answered by obtaining anatomical data.

Since human beings are not automata, completely constrained by their anatomy, some social factors also enter into the normalization problem. The supralaryngeal vocal tracts of 5-year-old boys, for example, are only slightly longer than those of 5-year-old girls. However, 5-year-old American-English speaking boys produce formant frequency patterns that are much lower in frequency than we would expect if the anatomical difference were the only factor. Boys who want to be considered male, talk as though they had longer vocal tracts than they actually have. There is in essence a "male" dialect that is culturally transmitted. It is based on the archetypal secondary sexual dimorphism of the population—adult males are generally larger and hence tend to have longer supralaryngeal vocal tracts that will yield lower formant frequencies. Girls who want to sound male also produce the male dialect as do children play-acting male roles in games like doctor–nurse. A perceptual normalization procedure thus also has to preserve these distinctions since they are perceived by human listeners. A normalization algorithm that wiped out these distinctions would not be equivalent to that found in human beings.

One additional biological principle is manifested in Holmes' data. Human beings like all living organisms, are put together genetically in bits and pieces. The genes that determine the length of the supralaryngeal vocal tract are independent of those that determine the length of the vocal folds in the larynx. It thus follows that there is no absolute correlation between the fundamental frequency of phonation and average formant frequency values. Fundamental frequency thus is not a good candidate for yielding information on formant frequency normalization. Many adult speakers will have long supralaryngeal vocal tracts and small larynxes yielding low formant frequencies and high fundamental frequencies. The reverse pattern also holds. There is a general correlation between F_0 and formant frequency value. Thus F_0's of 1 kHz which can occur in the utterances of year-old children don't occur in the utterances of adult males, but there is no way of predicting the details of the F_0/F_n pattern in the utterances of any particular speaker since the genetic pattern is inherently quantal and uncorrelated.

Finally, it is useful to note that Holmes is operating on formant patterns; this seems to me to be again a biologically correct decision. Formant frequency patterns are derived properties of the acoustic signal that are inherently invariant with respect to the types of gross spectral distortions noted by Mark Liberman. Insofar as human speech evolved as a communications system that would work in the real world, there would be selective pressures to make it resistant to gross spectral variations in the transmission path from the speaker's mouth to the listener's ear. It is not a trivial problem to calculate formant frequency patterns from the raw acoustic signal, but they inherently are insensitive to gross spectral modifications of the acoustic signal such as those that plague systems for automatical speech recognition that operate in terms of the raw acoustic signal.

17

Exploiting Lawful Variability In the Speech Wave

Jeffrey L. Elman and James L. McClelland
Departments of Linguistics and Psychology
University of California, San Diego

INTRODUCTION

A recurring theme in speech perception is the enormous variability one encounters in the acoustic signal. Yet listeners appear able to move beyond this surface variability and retrieve a level of representation which consists of a smaller number of more abstract and perceptually constant elements; moreover, this is done with apparent ease.

Of course, the variability is far from random, and this is key. Many of the alterations in the acoustic form of speech sounds arise out of contextual effects which are predictable, if complex. The problem is not that the signal varies randomly or contains meaningless noise. It is rather that there are many factors which need to be taken into account in the processing of any given sound. A tremendous amount of information is conveyed simultaneously. In our view, the phenomenon which has been described as the "lack-of-invariance problem" is not a problem at all for human listeners. It is precisely the variability in the signal which permits listeners to understand speech in a variety of contexts, and spoken by a variety of speakers.[1] Instead of searching for invariance in the signal, we think it makes more sense to try to understand how it is that listeners deal with the variability which is there.

What is needed is a processing framework which lends itself to the analysis of multiple overlays of information. Machines (serial processors) are not par-

---

[1] We are particularly concerned in this paper with acoustic variability which is predictably conditioned by phonetic context and other linguistic factors. Cross-speaker and within-speaker token-to-token variability, while important phenomena in speech perception, are not directly addressed here.

ticularly effective at integrating information from many sources, at least not in real-time. On the other hand, parallel processing systems—in particular interactive-activation models—are ideally suited to solving this problem.

In this paper we will describe our efforts at applying an interactive-activation approach to the task of performing the mapping from the digitized speech wave to a phonetic level of representation. In the process, we demonstrate how the lawful variability in the speech wave can be treated as a rich source of information, rather than as a regrettable source of noise.

THE INTERACTIVE ACTIVATION FRAMEWORK

The interactive activation framework was laid out by McClelland and Rumelhart (1981). Their paper gives a more detailed description of the basic assumptions and a discussion of the predecessors of the interactive activation approach.

Nodes

Our system is based upon a large number of simple processing elements we call "nodes." Nodes may represent different concepts (e.g., features, phonemes, or words) but are alike in being computationally very simple. Each node has an activation value, which reflects the state of the evidence that the unit the node stands for is present in the input. Each node also has a resting level, toward which its activation tends to decay; and a threshold. Nodes with activation levels below threshold do not influence other nodes. However, once the activation of a node exceeds threshold, it begins to influence the nodes to which it is connected by signaling its activation value to other nodes to which it is connected.

Connections

Connections between nodes can be of two kinds: excitatory or inhibitory. In addition, they may have different strengths associated with them. Excitatory connections have positive strengths, or weights, while inhibitory connections have negative weights. The sign determines whether the connection is excitatory or inhibitory; the absolute value of the weight determines the magnitude of the excitatory or inhibitory effect. The signal from one node to another is simply the product of the output of the sending node times the strength or weight of the connection between the nodes.

The Interactive Activation Process

The interactive activation process is the process of updating the activations of nodes based on the signals they receive from other nodes. This is an iterative process, with each node updating its activation value based on the signals it gets from the other nodes on each iteration or cycle. Each cycle consists of two phases. In the first, a net input to each node is determined, by adding up all the separate signals arising from other nodes. Then, the activations of all of the nodes are updated. The new activation of each node is just the old activation, plus the effect of the net input from other nodes, minus a decay term. If the net input to a node is positive (or excitatory), it will tend to drive the activation value of the node in a positive direction. On the other hand, if the net input is inhibitory, it will tend to drive the activation of the node in a negative direction. However, nodes have restricted dynamic ranges; for each node there is a maximum (arbitrarily set at $+1.0$) and a minimum (usually set at -0.2). If the net input is excitatory, it tends to drive the activation toward the maximum; if negative, toward the minimum. However, the magnitude of the effect is modulated by the distance left to go, so that the activation value always stays in bounds. The decay term tends to restore the activation to the resting level, but does so gradually over many cycles of interactive activation.

THE TRACE MODEL

Overall Structure of TRACE

The TRACE model is an interactive activation model, in that it consists of a set of nodes which interact with each other as described above. In addition to these basic assumptions, the TRACE model makes several key assumptions about the way in which the units are organized and their connections disciplined.

Levels. Nodes in the model are organized into levels. In the TRACE model, there is a feature level, consisting of detectors for acoustic/phonetic features of the speech wave; there is a phonetic level, consisting of detectors for phonemes; and there is a word level consisting of detectors for words.

Time slices. Time is an important variable in speech perception. It would appear to be a trivial observation that not only do we hear sounds, we also know when we heard them; it appears, then, that we keep a record of what units have occurred at each point in time in the input, at least for a short period of time after the input has arrived.

The TRACE. Our view is that the structures in which this perceptual memory resides and those in which current perception is carried out are one and the same. Time in the TRACE model is realized as a series of "frames" or "slices," each of which contains an identical complete set of nodes. There is one slice every 5 msec. The speech input is directed to successive time slices, one after another. Together, these slices make an active processing structure called the TRACE, in which the percept unfolds, and which serves as the working memory representation of the input.

Within each level of the TRACE, then, complete sets of detectors are reduplicated for successive time intervals in a speech stream. Thus the feature level consists of multiple complete sets of feature detectors, one for each 5 msec time-slice of the speech wave.[2] Similarly, the phoneme level consists of a complete set of phoneme detectors for each slice, and the word level consists of a complete set of word detectors for each slice. In the phoneme case, each detector stands for the hypothesis that the phoneme in question is centered below the time slice in question; in the word case, each detector stands (roughly) for the hypothesis that the first phoneme of the word is centered below the time slice in question.

Connections. The levels serve to discipline the interactions between the units. Between-level connections are exclusively excitatory, and are bidirectional. Quite simply, there is a mutually excitatory link between mutually consistent nodes on adjacent levels. Thus, feature nodes excite nodes for phonemes in which they occur in corresponding time slices, and phoneme nodes excite nodes for the features they contain. Similarly, phoneme nodes excite nodes for words in which they occur, and word nodes excite nodes for the phonemes they contain. Words are of course spread out over several phonemes, so for example the node for the word "cat" starting in a given slice will have mutually excitatory connections to [k] in the same and neighboring slices, [æ] in the next few slices, and [t] in the next few slices after that. Within-level connections are exclusively inhibitory, and are again bidirectional. Each node, when active, tends to inhibit all those nodes on the same level which are mutually inconsistent with it. Thus, for example, the nodes for different phonemes in the same time slice are mutually inhibitory. Word nodes are mutually inhibitory in proportion to the extent of their overlap in time.

Exploiting lawful variability

The values of the weights associated with the connections between the feature nodes and the phoneme nodes determine the extent to which a particular pattern of feature values will activate a particular phoneme. Context (adjacent) phonemes alter the feature patterns associated with a particular phoneme

---

[2] Although features are computed every 5 msec, the computation may involve reference to input from other frames. The feature ABRUPT, for instance, is calculated as the rate of change of power across a window 15 msec wide.

in a lawful way. We can exploit this regularity by allowing the detectors for these context phonemes to alter the weights appropriately for phonemes in neighboring slices, so that when the contextually-appropriate feature pattern occurs, the right phoneme will be activated. We will consider how this is done in more detail below.

A Detailed Look at the Feature and Phoneme Levels

Thus far we have described the TRACE model very generally, to give the reader a sense of its basic structure. Since in this paper we will be applying the model to the problem of exploiting the lawful variability in the speech wave, we will be focusing our attention on the feature and phoneme levels. The following section describes the input to the feature level, and is followed by two more which describe the feature and phoneme levels in more detail. Following these sections, we describe some simulations which demonstrate the ability of the model to exploit the variability in the speech wave, using the weight-modulation scheme described above.

Input to the Feature Level. The input to the feature nodes is simply the output of a speech preprocessor. In the preprocessor, digitized speech is preprocessed and converted to a set of values along each of several feature continua, at successive 5 msec. slices. Thus, the input to the model is simply a set of real-valued parameters, one for each feature continuum, for each 5 msec slice of speech.

Calculation of the feature parameter values input to the feature detectors is carried out through standard numerical techniques. We avoid incorporating this stage of processing into the model simply to speed up the simulation and not because we do not believe it can be done more profitably in an interactive activation framework. For the present we focus attention on the next stage of processing, in which feature-node activation values must be mapped to phonemes, to show how the tuning of these mappings on the basis of context can help the perceptual mechanism exploit lawful variability.

The output of the preprocessor is fed to the feature level nodes one time slice at a time, simulating the temporal flow of real speech. The successive sets of feature parameters are directed to successive slices at the feature level, so that each slice captures the parameters of a single 5 msec of speech.

Feature level. At the feature level, each feature continuum is processed by a group of eight nodes, each of which responds maximally to a different value along that feature continuum. Thus, each node may be called a feature-value detector. One such detector might respond best to very high values of a feature, while another would have a response function favoring slightly lower values. The response function for each of the eight nodes is determined by the statistical properties of our data base. We first determine the frequency of occurrence for each value along a feature continuum. This distribution is

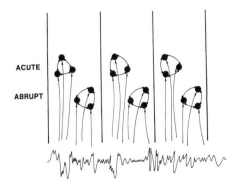

FIG. 17.1.   Three time slices at the feature level. Input comes from
the speech signal and excites the feature detector nodes. (Only two of 16
detector sets are shown; in reality each set has eight rather than three
nodes.)

used to calculate "octiles," and then the midpoints of the octiles are used
as the response peaks for the eight feature value detectors. Each detector
responds best to its peak value, and the response functions fall off linearly
on both sides, reaching half their maximum at the peak of the neighboring
detector on either side. Thus the detectors respond to overlapping ranges of
values along the continuum.

The eight nodes have two types of "outgoing" connections. There are
inhibitory connections between the nodes, so that the node which responds
to high values on the continuum will inhibit the nodes which detect lower
values. The eight nodes also have excitatory connections to phonemes nodes.

In Figure 17.1 we illustrate how the TRACE model appears at the feature
level. Three time slices are shown here. The left-most slice is the earliest in
time. As time proceeds, successive slices are activated by the portion of the
speech input which corresponds to that point in time. Note that the figure
is simplified: only two feature banks are shown. Also, each bank is shown as
having only three detectors rather than eight.

Some discussion is in order here about our choice of feature continua.
Several factors governed their selection; in all cases, we assumed that feature
values were continuously scaled rather than discretely valued (as in binary
features). First, we needed features which have clear acoustic correlates.
Note that this does not mean that the features have invariant realizations
across different contexts, simply that there be some algorithm for computing
the feature value at every instant in time. Second, insofar as was possible, we
wished to find features which had a linguistic motivation. We used several
features which have been proposed by Jakobson, Fant, and Halle (1952);
these features have proven useful in describing a number of common linguistic
phenomena. Third, because it is our belief that much of the variability in the

TABLE 17.1

Distinctive Features in Present Use

power	log rms power
pitch	fundamental frequency of source
alpha	total LPC error; measures predictability of signal; distinguishes speech and silence
edr	error dynamic range; voiced from voiceless
abrupt	change in rms power over time; stops/vowel transitions
diffuse	second moment of LPC spectrum
acute	gross concentration of energy in spectrum
consonantal	smoothed euclidean spectral difference; detects stop bursts and consonantal transitions, as opposed to slower changing vowel formants
spectrum[3]	total energy in each section of the spectrum divided equally in three on a log scale
formant[3]	the values of the first three formants
loci[2]	the hypothetical formant onsets, back-extrapolated from the actual formant onsets (at voicing) to the stop release; provides a context-sensitive measure of the place of articulation of consonants

speech signal can be exploited to provide additional information, we looked for features which seemed especially susceptible to variation which could be predicted on the basis of context.

Our current set of continua is described in Table 17.1. There is a bank of eight detectors for each continuum. We thus have a set of eight detectors which respond to different values of the feature ABRUPT, another eight which respond to ACUTE, and so on. We make no claim that this is the "right" set of features; indeed, we are quite sure the human perceptual system uses a much richer set. The set we have chosen does, however, allow us to begin to test or central theoretical claims about how variability may be exploited with real speech input.

Phoneme Level. The 128 feature nodes in each time slice connect to nodes at the next higher (conceptual) level; these latter nodes represent phonemes.

There has been considerable controversy about the psychological and linguistic reality of phonemes and a variety of other units have been proposed, including transemes, context-sensitive allophones, syllables, and demisyllables. We do not wish to take a strong position on this issue. We do note that many of the criticisms of the phoneme stem from its lack of invariance across different environments, and that some of the alternatives are claimed to "solve" this problem to some degree. In reality, many of these solutions are not solutions at all; they solve the problem of invariance either (1) by making the units sufficiently big that they incorporate much of the context into them; or (2) by making the units extremely small or highly context-specific. The problem with the first solution is that one can never truly "freeze in" enough of the context to guarantee an invariant form for the unit. Both solutions make it difficult to capture the intuition shared by many speakers that the acoustically different bilabial stops in "ball" and "crib" are the same sound. In any event, we feel that the approach we have taken in the TRACE model is to some extent independent from specific representational issues, and that at the very least, we can demonstrate that the lack of invariance is not, in and of itself, a reason to reject a phonemic representation, since the solution we propose to the invariance problem shows how varying input can be mapped in a contextually appropriate way onto the phoneme level.

There are several important differences between the feature and phoneme nodes. Feature values tend to change more rapidly than phoneme values and so they must be more labile. This is accomplished in two ways. First, whereas there are feature nodes for every 5 msec time slice (this seems a reasonable time grain) phoneme level time slices are spaced at 15 msec intervals. Thus phoneme-level slices span three feature level time-slice windows. Second, the receptive fields of phoneme nodes span several slices at the feature level, so that phonemes in successive slices have overlapping "windows" on the feature level. Connections between feature nodes and two phoneme nodes are shown in Figure 17.2. Stronger connections are shown as solid lines and weaker connections with dotted lines. (Note also the convention that excitatory links end in arrows and inhibitory connections end with filled circles.)

The exact nature of the feature-to-phoneme node connections is complicated by the fact that different phonemes have different durations. There are differences in the intrinsic duration of different phonemes. Thus, phoneme nodes must collect input over varying extents of feature nodes. Stop nodes, for example, might have "windows" six feature traces wide whereas vowel nodes might have windows 12 traces wide (or wider). Or the duration of

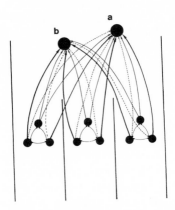

FIG. 17.2. Connections between feature detector nodes and phoneme nodes. Each detector has a connection to every phoneme, but the strength of the connection varies as is appropriate.

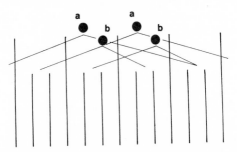

FIG. 17.3. Phoneme nodes have receptive fields which span several slices at the feature level, so that phonemes in successive slices have overlapping "windows" on the feature level.

stops may differ significantly from one another as a function of factors such as their place of articulation. In Figure 17.3 we see sample windows over which several phoneme nodes collect input.

The windows are represented by triangular functions, such that input from slices further in time from the phoneme node's "home slice" has a weaker effect than input from time slices right under the phoneme node. The area under the triangles of different widths is normalized, so that the detectors for phoneme nodes of different width are equally excitable. Without this normalization, longer phonemes would receive more excitation than shorter ones, artificially biasing the model to hear longer phonemes. Obviously this explanation only hints at a general solution to the problem of duration. One problem is that some features of the same phoneme spread further than others. We have adopted the present scheme primarily for simplicity.

Mapping from the Feature Level to the Phoneme Level. Previous versions of interactive activation models have assumed that the connections between nodes are fixed. For example, McClelland and Rumelhart (1981) in the interactive activation model of reading, had fixed excitatory connections of fixed strength between feature and letter nodes, and between letter and word nodes. However, there is a major problem with using fixed connection strengths in mapping of feature level information to the phoneme level; it is in fact the major topic of this volume. The problem is the lack of an invariant relationship between the feature values which are obtained for a given phoneme across different contexts. We have already remarked that the major problem which the lack of invariance presents is not that the variation is random or represents noise. In most cases, the causes for the variation are well-understood. Most importantly, they can often be predicted. Because of their lawful nature, it should be possible to use the context to adjust the mapping from the feature to the phoneme level.

At first this may seem like an impossibility. How can we use what we know about one phoneme to help us identify another, when each depends on the other? The answer demonstrates one of the main strengths of the interactive activation approach. These models do not have to wait until sufficient evidence has accumulated to identify a phoneme unambiguously before that phoneme can alter the processing of the phonemes around it. Interactive activation allows for on-going retuning, such that the contextual effects are immediate and direct, and grow in strength as evidence for the identity of the phonemes in the context is accumulated. An example will show how this might work.

In the model, the detector nodes for the values of the ACUTE feature project to—among other phonemes—nodes for the stop consonants [b], [d], and [g]. The strength of the connections between any given stop node and the eight ACUTE nodes depends on the observed characteristics of that stop. The alveolar stop, for instance, has stronger connections to the nodes which respond to the high end of the ACUTE feature continuum (because its spectrum is typically tilted toward the high end of the spectrum).

However, there are circumstances in which the spectrum of other stops may be shifted toward higher ACUTE values; contiguity to the vowel [i] is one such situation. In Figure 17.4 we can compare the values of ACUTEness that were detected during the stop closure of the bilabial stops [b] when it preceded different vowels. The upper trace in this figure shows how ACUTEness varies with time. The arrows indicate the moment in time when each bilabial stop is released. (For convenience in locating the stop, spectrograms are included at the bottom.) Thus the degree to which detectors for high-ACUTE should excite a given stop should depend not only on the input present during the stop but also the context. Similar sensitivities to context are also found for other feature continua, including the two LOCUS continua. Based on

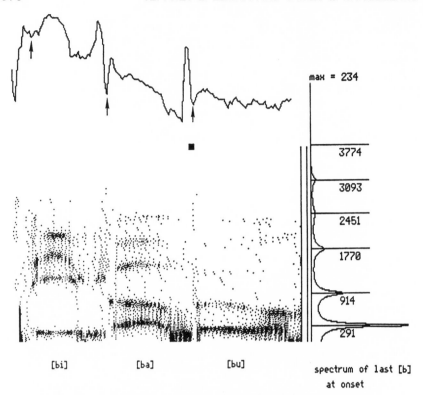

[bi]   [ba]   [bu]   spectrum of last [b]
                                                at onset

FIG. 17.4. Spectrograms of the syllables [bi], [ba], [bu]. The trace at
the top indicates the time-changing values for ACUTEness of the signal.
Arrows indicate the moment of release for the three bilabial stops.

previous work, we had initially hoped that these continua would be less
context sensitive than the others. However, even the values of the LOCUS
parameter as extracted by our preprocessor vary lawfully from context to
context.

This lawful variability is dealt with in TRACE in a relatively direct manner. Quite simply, phoneme nodes have connections which modulate the
strengths of the interconnections between feature nodes and phoneme nodes
in adjacent time slices. An illustration of this is shown in Figure 17.5. Here
we see connections between ACUTE feature detectors and one of three stops.
(Again, for simplicity we show only three of the eight feature detectors, and
we omit the connections between each of these detectors and the other two
stops.) The actual values for ACUTE which are observed for each stop are
heavily influenced by the vowels which occur later in time. So, phoneme
nodes for the vowels [a], [i], and [u] in slice eight are allowed to modulate the
weights of the feature-to-stop connections. In essence, the set of weights is

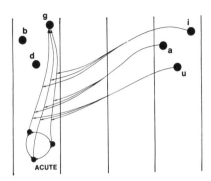

FIG. 17.5. An example of how contextual effects are dealt with in the model. The phoneme nodes for the vowels [a], [i], and [u] are able to modulate the strength of the connections between ACUTE feature nodes and the nodes for the stops [b], [d], and [g]. (This is shown here only for the connections to the velar stop.) This allows the model to compensate for the effect that the vowel has on the spectrum of the stop.

the sum of the sets of weights appropriate for each vowel. The magnitude of the contribution made by each vowel-appropriate set is determined by the activation level of the detector for that vowel in surrounding slices. Thus, if only one vowel is active in the context, the feature to phoneme weights will be dominated by the weights appropriate for the consonant in question when it occurs with that vowel. If several vowels are partially active, the feature to phoneme weights will reflect a composite of the weights appropriate for each vowel. When no vowels are active, the weights are a composite of the sets appropriate for each vowel.

The weight-modulation scheme represents an important increment in the computational capabilities of the nodes, relative to earlier interactive activation models. Not only can they excite and inhibit other nodes, they can also determine how strongly one node can excite or inhibit another. In general, this is an extremely powerful addition to interactive activation models because it allows them to behave in a more sharply context-sensitive fashion than might otherwise be possible. The idea of modulating the weights was introduced by Hinton (1981), and is now being applied to a number of different problems in which the mapping from one level of description onto another is highly context dependent.

SIMULATIONS AND EXPERIMENTS

The TRACE model has been implemented as a program written in the C programming language on a VAX 11/750 digital computer. There are actually two versions of this program; one accepts real speech input and the other processes simulated (speech-like) input. The first version is used to test the operation of the feature and phoneme interactions, and the second, not considered here, is used to explore the properties of the phoneme and word-level interactions. Here we present only the results of simulations using the real-speech model, focusing on the way in which the TRACE model exploits lawful variability by using variable weights to improve its identification of phonemes in context.

Context Effects on Stop Identification

We have tested the model by presenting it with 25 tokens of each of the syllables [ba], [bi], [bu], [da], [di], [du], [ga], [gi], [gu]. These tokens were uttered by the same speaker whose speech was used to tune the connections between the feature detectors and phoneme nodes, but the test tokens were not part of the training set.

We have tested the model under two different conditions. In one, called the "fixed weight condition," a fixed set of weights were used linking the feature and phoneme levels. In the other, called the "variable weight condition," the weight modulation scheme described above was used. In both cases, the weights were calculated using the perceptron convergence procedure (Rosenblatt, 1962). For the fixed-weight condition, the training data for each target phoneme included instances of all three vowel contexts. For the variable-weight condition, the training was carried out separately for each of the three contexts. Thus, the best compromise set of weights that could be found using the perceptron convergence procedure was used in the fixed-weight condition, while for the variable-weight condition, the best set of weights was found for each of the three vowel contexts.

In Figure 17.6 we see the results of presentation of one of the [ba] tokens to the model. The columns represent every phoneme slice, indexed by the feature slice it is centered over. Time begins at feature-slice 0 and continues to feature-slice 57. Since each feature slice lasts 5 msec, the columns display activity occurring at 15 msec intervals.

Of interest is the changing pattern of activation of the phoneme nodes. We show this by using letters to designate phonemes whose activations have passed threshold; the height of the letter in the column indicates the relative activation of that phoneme node. Because activity within a time slice continues even after the input is directed to later slices, we can look at the state of the trace at several different points in time. Figure 17.6 only shows activity at the points in time when the input is directed at slice 6 (30 msec) and slice 21 (105 msec). As mentioned previously, the TRACE is both perceptual representation and working memory, in that it contains a record of the past back to the beginning of the trace which can continue to evolve as it processes

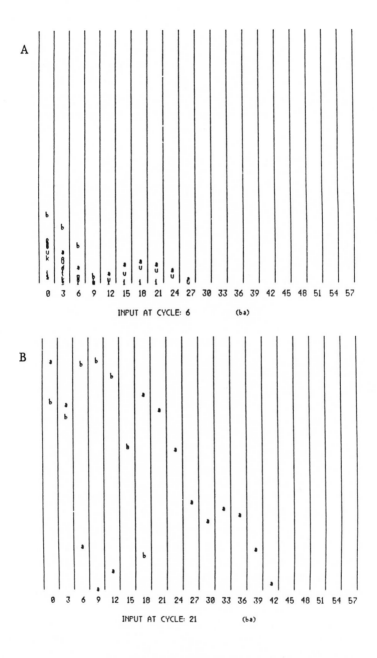

FIG. 17.6. Activation levels of phoneme nodes at 30 msec (a) and 105 msec (b) with presentation of [ba]. Vertical columns correspond to 5 msec time slices; every third slice is shown. The activation level of a phoneme is shown by its height within a column.

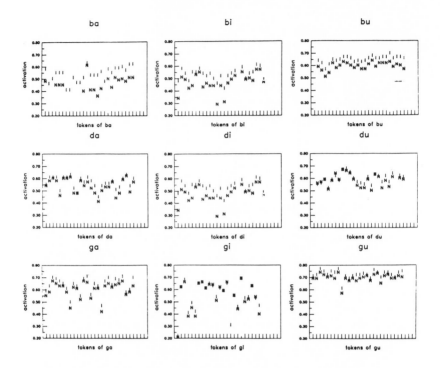

FIG. 17.7.   Results of presenting 25 tokens of each of the syllables [ba],
[bi], [bu], [da], [di], [du], [ga], [gi], [gu] to the model. Results for each
token are shown along the horizontal axis; activation level is given along
the vertical axis. The letter I marks activation levels when context effects are handled by node interactions.The letter N indicates results when
interactions are turned off.

information arriving further down the trace. There is no sharp distinction
between the structures which are responsible for on-going perception, and
those traditionally called short-term perceptual "memory."

All phonemes are below threshold before the input is presented to
TRACE. In Figure 17.6a we see that by approximately 30 msec after release
of the beginning of the sound, the bilabial stop has become quite active. We
also see that there are vowels which have become active in later traces—
traces which in fact have not yet received speech input. The system is able
to anticipate the presence of the vowels because in fact the speech that is
"heard" in Trace 6 contains strong cues as to vowel identity. By 105 msec
(Figure 17.6b) the [b] has become clearly established, and the identity of the
vowel is clear. Note that although there are clear "winners," at no point is
TRACE forced to make a definitive decision about the nature of the perceived

sounds. Perception is treated as a graded phenomenon, and it is possible for the perceptual system to entertain several candidate interpretations for the same stretch of input simultaneously.

The results shown in Figure 17.6 describe the time-course of activation of phoneme nodes for a single token of the syllable [ba] in the variable weight condition. Summary results of the simulation runs from both conditions are shown in Figure 17.7. The nine panels show, for each of the syllable types, the level of activation attained at timeslice 35 (125 msec) by the target stop node in the variable mapping condition (labeled "I") and in the fixed mapping condition ("N"), for each of the 25 different speech tokens used in each condition. In nearly every case these interactions were of at least some benefit, increasing the activation level achieved by the correct target phoneme. There are some syllables where the difference is not very great, ([du], [gi]) but even here there is an advantage for the variable weight condition, particularly for those tokens which do the most poorly in the fixed-weight condition. (In cases where a column contains no N, the activation of the correct phoneme was below .2, the minimum value shown in the figure).

Table 17.2 shows the percentage of different tokens of the stop-vowel pairs in which the correct consonant was more strongly activated than either of the other two, for the fixed and variable mapping conditions. In all cases, TRACE's performance was better with the variable mapping in place. In nearly every case, performance was near perfect with variable mappings. When the context was allowed to modulate the weights, performance was 90% correct; when the context was not allowed to modulate the weights, and the fixed set of weights was used, performance was only 79% correct. The only syllable which presented serious problems was [bi].

It should be noted that the fixed set of weights used in the fixed weight condition was not the average of the weights used for the three different vowel contexts. It was the best set we could find to discriminate between the classes of sounds when the model was forced to find one set of weights to use in all contexts, given the feature set we were using, and the scheme of weight determination described above.

Of course, it might be possible to do better with a different feature set and/or a different procedure for choosing the weights. Whenever there are invariant features, it would seem likely that the perceptual system would exploit them, and if researchers find such features we would certainly want to incorporate them into our model. Our point is simply that the weight modulation scheme employed here provides a way of exploiting lawful variability which cannot be captured in invariant features. Our simulation simply shows that, given a particular set of features, the addition of weight modulation can result in improvements in performance.

TABLE 17.2

Number of Correct Identifications in 25 Trials
Variable Weight and Fixed Weight Results
(Percentage Correct)

| [ba] | | [bi] | | [bu] | |
variable	fixed	variable	fixed	variable	fixed
25	17	14	13	25	20
(100)	(68)	(56)	(52)	(100)	(80)
[da]		**[di]**		**[du]**	
variable	fixed	variable	fixed	variable	fixed
24	21	21	20	23	21
(96)	(84)	(84)	(80)	(92)	(84)
[ga]		**[gi]**		**[gu]**	
variable	fixed	variable	fixed	variable	fixed
22	21	24	22	25	24
(88)	(84)	(96)	(88)	(100)	(96)

Overall percentage correct for variable weight condition: 90
Overall percentage correct for fixed weight condition: 79

Context Effects on Vowel Identification

Much has been made of the lack of invariance in acoustic specification of stops, but it is also true that vowels sometimes exhibit great variability as a function of their context. During the course of building the feature detectors, we became aware of environments where this was particularly true. In Figure 17.8, we see running spectra of three tokens of the vowel [u]. These tokens were excised from the syllables [bu], [du], and [gu]. In each case they begin 150 msec after the release of the stop, which is beyond the point where the obvious consonantal transitions have occurred. The clear differences in these spectra impelled us to modify TRACE in a way for vowels which resembled what we did for the stops. We permitted stop nodes in early traces to interact with certain connections between nodes for features and vowels in later traces (this was allowed to happen only for those feature-vowel combinations where

[u]   [u]   [u]

from [bu]   from [du]   from [ɘu]

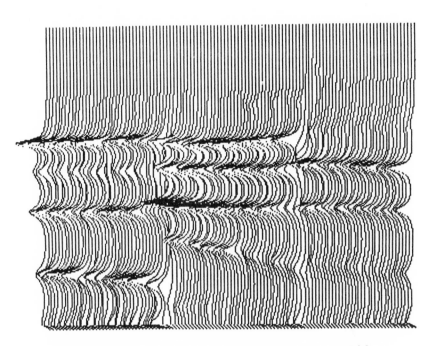

FIG. 17.8. Running spectra (at 5 msec intervals) of the vowel [u], excised from [bu], [du], and [gu]. The initial 200 msec of each syllable was removed, deleting all of the consonantal formant transitions. Spectra are noticeably different.

we observed there to be significant context effects). As was the case with the vowel node effects on feature-stop interactions, the modulations were adjusted to compensate for the observed contextual effects.

These interactions provide important information to the model, and illustrate how contextual effects may be exploited in the recognition process. Figure 17.9 shows how the model responds to input consisting of the final 200 msec of a [gu] token; the initial 175 msec were deleted. Although perceives a vowel at all points in time, during the first few traces the stop node [g] has become somewhat active.

Presumably, human listeners would be able to take advantage of this information as well. To test this, we presented subjects with a series of vowels which had been extracted from the final 200 msec of CV syllables which

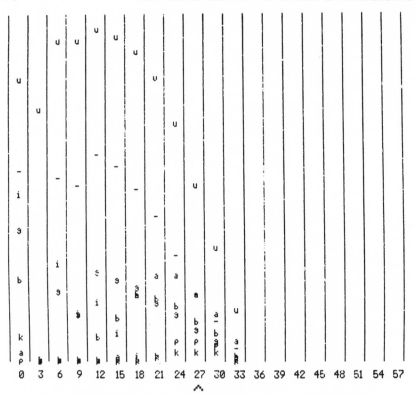

FIG. 17.9.   Activation levels of phoneme nodes at 135 msec with presentation of [u] excised from [gu] context. Although the [u] node dominates,
evidence for the context is present and the [g] node is highly activated.

combined the stops [b], [d], and [g] with the vowels [a], [i], and [u] (the initial
175 msec were deleted). Subjects were told that they would hear a series
of vowels which had been recorded in a CV context, with the C digitally
removed. They were asked to guess what the missing C was. The confusion
matrix of subjects' responses for the vowels extracted from syllables [bu],
[gu], [du] is presented in Table 17.3. We see that subjects were often able to
recover the identity of the missing consonant. These preliminary data provide nice support for the notion that TRACE's attempt to take advantage
of variability—rather than trying to ignore it—corresponds to the approach
human perceivers take.

TABLE 17.3

Response Probabilities for Identifying Preceeding Stop
from Steady-state Portion of the Vowel

Response	Original syllable		
	bu	du	gu
b	.61	.01	.33
d	.10	.97	.24
g	.28	.01	.43

Note: Response probabilities are based on 70 observations for each vowel.

WHEN EXPLOITATION OF LAWFUL VARIABILITY IS NOT ENOUGH

The speech stream contains more information than most approaches successfully exploit, but sometimes it does not contain enough to specify the correct sequence of phonemes uniquely. In these cases, the model's ability to exploit top-down input from the word level to the phoneme level causes the model to prefer lexically acceptable alternatives consistent with the input to lexically unacceptable alternatives. In a forthcoming paper (McClelland and Elman, in preparation), we show how the simulated-speech version of the TRACE model can identify words and use word-level activations to bias phoneme-level activations. Strikingly, the model does not require any word-boundary information. It can pick out the sequence of words from the pattern of phoneme-level activations (where this is not ambiguous), just as the phoneme level picks out the sequence of phonemes from the pattern of feature level activations.

CONCLUSION

Our view on invariance in speech differs from that of some of the other contributors to this volume. We see the lack of acoustic invariance in the speech signal as a positive thing. This variability provides listeners with a rich source of information. We do not deny that it may be possible to transform the acoustic data so as to recover some properties which remain relatively invariant across contexts. But we doubt that this will be true of all aspects of the signal, or that many transformations can be carried out without regard for the context. What we hope we have demonstrated here is that the interactive activation framework embodied in the TRACE model provides a powerful way to process complex contextual interactions.

Hopefully, it also provides greater insight into the ways in which human listeners perceive speech. Despite the simplicity of our distinctive features, TRACE's overall level of performance on the perceptual identification tasks was 90%.

An important reason for the success of the TRACE model is the basic architecture of the TRACE itself. The TRACE allows activations at different points in time to exert mutual influences. Both context which comes before a section of the input, and context which comes after it, can influence the final configuration of activations over the section of the input and therefore the interpretations which that input receives. Local coarticulatory influences of one phoneme on another can be handled by weight modulation, while constraints arising from the lexical and, of course, higher levels not yet implemented can be handled via top-down excitation. Thus, the model is capable of filling in a missing phoneme at the beginning of a word based on the rest or the word, and with higher levels would be able to exploit information from subsequent words. Models which work in a more strictly left-to-right mode cannot cope as easily with backward as well as forward contextual influences, without invoking reprocessing. Yet is is clear that backward contextual influences are crucial if we are to account either for the effects of local phonetic context or lexical and semantic context on phoneme identification. Experiments by Isenberg, Walker, Ryder, & Schweickert (1980) have shown that such backward effects can extend to the preceding word.

We also note that the model provides a solution to a problem which has been troublesome to many recognition schemes. Typically, one of the first tasks undertaken by models of speech recognition is the segmentation of the input. This is made difficult by the frequent lack of obvious segment boundaries. The process is usually fraught with errors which are then compounded at later stages of processing. In contrast, the TRACE model does not attempt an explicit parsing of the input into segments. It recognizes that segmental information is blended across broad stretches of input. Nonetheless, while recognizing the essentially continuous nature of the acoustic input, the model does maintain a level of representation which consists of discrete units (phonemes); it is simply the case that the detectors for these inputs do not require a segmented input, but simply respond to the appropriate pattern or something close to it wherever it occurs in the speech stream.

ACKNOWLEDGEMENTS

This work was supported by contract N00014-82-C-0374 from the Office of Naval Research. We wish to thank Thomas H. Ward for help in development of the signal processing software used by the model, and Paul S. Smith for assistance in carrying out experiments.

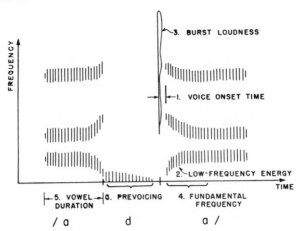

FIG. 17a.1. Analysis of the [d] phoneme in [ada].

Dennis H. Klatt: Comment

A spreading-activation model of speech perception has a great deal of attraction to me because of my interest in artificial intelligence models that began in graduate school many years ago. This is the most ambitious, most specific, and most powerful of the attempts to use neural analogies to formulate a realistic model of auditory perception. Yet there are interesting ways in which the model appears to me to be totally wrong. Consider for example the problem of recognizing the [d] phoneme in the utterance [ada] shown in Figure 17a.1.

There are many cues that contribute to the decision, and they are distributed over a considerable interval of time. For example, to decide whether the consonant is a [t] or a [d], one has to consider at least six more-or-less distinct cues, ranging from the duration of the preceding vowel and the extent of the VC formant transitions to the presence of voicing energy during closure, burst intensity, presence of aspiration, amount of low frequency energy present at voicing onset, and CV formant transition extent.

In the model of Elman and McClelland, there are a set of acoustic feature detectors that, by and large, examine what is going on locally—which appears consistent with the view implied in Figure 17a.1 that these six separate cues must be detected and then integrated in the decision process. However, there are problems in dealing with the natural variability in the durations of acoustic events such as those shown in the figure.

Problem 1 is to compute the value of a cue over the proper interval of time. Take for example the detector whose job it is to detect the presence or absence of a voice-bar (cue 6 in Fig. 17a.1) over some interval of time. If the closure interval is short, as it may sometimes be, and the detector is simply looking for low-frequency energy over a fixed predetermined time interval, energy from the vowels may falsely indicate a voicebar in what is really a voiceless plosive. Elman and McClelland propose to solve this problem by postulating multiple feature detectors, each examining a time interval of different length or different location. If the closure interval is long, then one instantiation of the detector, the one attending to the time interval just after closure, has the right answer at its output, but how does the next level of feature integrating phoneme detectors know which of the multiple instances of each detector to believe?

Problem 2 is to put together the information distributed over time when the temporal location of each cue can vary by as much as it does in normal connected speech. It is well known that a vowel such as [a] can vary in duration over a range from 50 to 300 ms or more depending on the postvocalic consonant, syllable stress, and position of the syllable in the word and in the phrase (Klatt, 1976), and that the duration of a consonant such as [d] (excluding flaps) can vary from 30 to 150 ms or more. How does one then integrate the VC transition cue with the CV transition cue without requiring each detector to say, in effect, "I am giving the best answer of all the VC detector instantiations scattered along the time axis"?

Expressed in another way, problem 2 boils down to an inability in this type of model to treat time as an independent dimension[1] in order to note the *sequence* of acoustic events and then ask if the event sequence is one expected for [d]—only secondarily asking if the events are separated in time by complex relationships unique to [d]. It is exactly this idea of gremlins monitoring the input for a specified sequence of acoustic events required to see [d] and other phonetic segments that led me to formulate Scriber (and then LAFS) as plausible functional models of speech perception (Klatt, 1979). Until a spreading activation model can perform computations similar in kind to those of Scriber and LAFS, I do not believe that it can be taken seriously as a realistic model of perceptual processing.

Problem 3 is that many kinds of context sensitivities and cue trading relationships known to affect perception are not possible to realize in this type of model. One can approximate virtually any tendency in individual cases, which makes it hard to document this as a serious deficiency. However, I believe that the indirect way in which knowledge of phonetic context must be incorporated by a weighting scheme is a hint that some perceptual peculiarities ought to exist, i.e. some relationships would be unlearnable in the sense the perceptrons are known to be limited in the kinds of generalizations that they can make—whereas listeners seem to know everything that is regular in speech acoustic phonetics.

Jeffrey L. Elman, and James L. McClelland: Response

Klatt is correct to point out that the way in which the speech signal varies with changes in speech rate poses important challenges to our approach. However, we believe that the basic interactive activation framework, and in particular the mechanisms we have described for exploiting lawful variability, can meet the challenge. The fundamental point is that the variation in the speech wave as a function of rate and stress is lawful. Just as we were able to exploit this lawful variability by modulating the pattern of connections between feature and phoneme levels as a

---

[1] One can perhaps devise counters to measure the length of vowels or other events.

function of local phonetic context, so we anticipate we will be able to modulate these same connections as a function of on-going speech rate, and even momentary changes in rate. In principle such a mechanism is more powerful than the time warping presently preferred, because it treats the temporal structure of speech as more than just a succession of events at unspecified intervals. There is regularity in the exact details of the way in which speech compresses (and distorts) as it is produced with greater and greater haste, and we believe our approach will be able to exploit this regularity quite effectively. We hope to report progress in demonstrating these points in the near future.

Leigh Lisker: Comment

We seem generally to be in thorough agreement as to what the identity of a word is, while we worry about what the phoneme is; at the same time, we usually think that we need the phonemes in order to decide what the word is. In the oral presentation of their paper, McClelland mentioned a hypothetical case of "barricade" and "parakeet" which is of interest when we consider the question of phoneme perception. I am struck by the expression he used: "along comes the *icade*, so you know that it was a [b], and if it was *akeet* you know it was a [p]." This situation suggests that we decide what the phoneme was on the basis of having identified the word. We tend to think of the phonemes as known, on the basis of which we want to explain how we manage to get the words of a speech message; McClelland's way of looking at the matter of speech perception is in some sense precisely backwards.

Jeffrey L. Elman, and James L. McClelland:
Response

Lisker's comment reflects a vision of the perceptual mechanism which predates the kind of model we are proposing. Models conceived within the context of this older vision viewed phoneme-level processing as a process which assigns identities to phonetic segments in an all-or-nothing fashion, in a sequence of discrete events. In such models, it is of course impossible to see how phoneme identification can be influenced by word recognition if the word is to be recognized on the basis of the output of this very phoneme-identification process. However, our model does not share this implicit assumption that phoneme processing is a series of discrete events. Instead, we see the process of forming representations at the phoneme level as one that takes place slowly and continuously in time, with partial information being passed on to other levels as it is available, and with information being assimilated from other levels as they make information available to the phoneme level. Thus, it is perfectly plausible and reasonable to assume that phoneme level processes can make available information such as "the first phoneme is [p] or [b]; the second [u] and the third [l]" to the word level; and for the word level to use this information to decide that the string must begin with a [p] (since no words in English begin with [bul]). More generally, Lisker appears to be confusing two issues: Whether a process is influenced by information received from another (contingency), and whether a process can only start once another has finished (seriality). Over the years, this assumption has often been held in a number of fields, but it is far from necessarily true. Indeed it is possible for processing to be parallel and at two different levels, and for each level to be contingent on the other, as long as it is possible for each to share partial tentative results with the other. Mechanisms which use this type of parallel-contingent processing are capable of exploiting mutual constraint between different processing levels quite effectively.

O. Fujimura: Comment

The use of phonemes as the basic segmental units for this scheme is not the best choice. Basically, one would like to have a concatenative string of units as the abstract representation of the signal in such a way that the inventory of units (nodes) to be compared at each time sample represents a truly competitive paradigm. Often, however, a time slice represents a syntagmatic combination of phonemic segments, for example, a consonant plus vowel. The consonant and the vowel in such cases (not only in transition, but also in quasi-stationary parts of the signal) do not compete with each other, as the candidate for that slice. Moreover, a non-contiguous interaction (between syllable nuclei ignoring intervening consonants, for example) must be handled. While the network manipulation *can* handle such intersegmental interactions and constraints, it tends to make the framework excessively powerful and computationally intractable. If the phonological units themselves are chosen more naturally for the paradigmatic phonetic structures of speech, the scheme should work more efficiently and algorithm should be substantially simpler. I recommend the use of demisyllables (Fujimura, 1979; Fujimura and Lovins, 1978) as better units for this purpose (of course, at the cost of more units in storage, which I think is justifiable). Then, most of strong and often *ad hoc* intersegmental interactions are already built in in the stored patterns, and noncontiguous interactions can be handled by general interactions between values of specific features (such as vocalic features of contiguous, perhaps only stressed, syllables).

Michael Studdert-Kennedy: Comment

Assessing the perceptual value of coarticulatory effects may be a delicate matter, as the model of Elman & McClelland suggests. For example, Lehiste and Shockey (1972) found that listeners to a VC fragment, cut at the closure of a V_1–stop–V_2 disyllable, could not identify the vowel that had followed in the original utterance. However, if we want to characterize subtle properties of the information in the signal as it accumulates to determine a response, it may not be enough simply to see whether the response occurs or not. Several experiments by Martin and Bunnell (1981, 1982) using [(C)VCV] spondee frames, have shown that reaction time increases and accuracy of indentification decreases for the second vowel, if it has been cross-spliced to follow a context other than that in which it was spoken. Alfonso and Baer (1982) found that listeners can often identify the final stresses vowel in disyllables of the form [əp V p], from information in the initial unstressed vowel alone. Both these studies also showed systematic and predictable acoustic differences in preceding vowel as a function of following context. Finally, Fowler (1981) showed that listeners can discriminate among medial stressed vowels, gated from trisyllables of the form [V b ʌ b V], as a function of the context in which they were originally spoken. (See also, Chapter 6.) None of these results could have occurred if listeners were not sensitive to acoustic changes reflecting articulatory adjustments within one syllable preparatory to execution of the next.

18

Phonological Evidence for Top-down Processing In Speech Perception

John J. Ohala
University of California, Berkeley

INTRODUCTION

The simplest form of processing of an encoded signal involves a direct translation of the incoming ciphers into the final usable form. This suffices when the signal is relatively noise-free and unambiguous. If the signal cannot be taken at face value because it is noisy, which is to say, variable or ambiguous, then more complicated forms of processing are necessary. Any form of processing that relies heavily on the receiver's own internal knowledge sources and algorithms is called "top-down processing." Given the great amount of variability speech scientists have found between the physical parameters of speech and the ciphers which they assume are present in the signal, speech would seem to be a prime example of a signal requiring top-down processing. Nevertheless, in spite of the great amount of research done on this problem, it is still possible to raise questions about the degree of top-down processing necessary in speech.

Speech may seem variable because we haven't identified the correct units yet. If the units are allophones or even syllables or parts of two adjacent syllables—the inventory of such units would be quite large, of course—then much of what is now considered variation (in phonemes) will simply disappear. It is also possible that we have not yet discovered the proper kind of measurements to make on speech to uncover the regularities and constancies that are believed to be present in it. Rather than absolute values of various parameters—e.g., formant frequencies, VOT, vowel duration—perhaps it is some higher-order relations—ratios, rates of change of the parameters—that should be measured (Ladefoged & Broadbent, 1957; Miller, 1982; Pickett &

Decker, 1960). It is also possible that there is a relatively simple relation between the underlying invariant ciphers and the variable acoustic signal, such that little top-down processing is necessary. Such might be the case if the invariant units existed at the neuromotor level, with the "smear" that is evident being a property of the physical constraints of the articulatory system. In this case, a relatively simple analysis-by-synthesis system (which included a model of the speech articulators) which should be successful at extracting the ciphers.

The possibilities are endless and sorting our way through them is very challenging. Nature may even have misled us in our search by setting decoys: The phonemes may well be real units at some level at which speakers and listeners process or store speech (Jaeger, 1980)—thus their intuitive appeal—but they may not be the units used to encode and decode speech. As an example of another case of mismatch in the ciphers used to encode a signal and the "content" of the signal, consider the DNA strands which at some level of analysis transmit units such as "limbs," "tissues," and "hair color," but whose immediate units of encoding are the sequences of the molecules of adenine, cytosine, guanine, and thymine.

In this chapter, I will present phonological evidence for what I believe is a quite complex form of top-down processing in speech perception which demonstrates that the listener must draw upon very detailed knowledge of the phonetic facts of speech. It is evidence whose value does not depend crucially on our knowing what the transmitted units of speech are.

THE ARGUMENT

The speech signal is noisy and therefore ambiguous in the sense that it consists of a mixture of what the speaker intended to encode and transmit *plus* various details that are presumably not intended. Examples of the latter are the small perturbations in F_0 following voiced and voiceless obstruents (Hombert, Ohala & Ewan, 1979) or the variation in vowel-formant frequencies as a function of the vowel, the consonantal environment, and the amount of time allotted to execute the segmental sequences containing the vowel (Lindblom, 1963). The vowel [u], for example, when flanked by dental or alveolar consonants, shows a consistent tendency to have its F_2 raised, making it more like the vowels [ɯ], [ɨ], or even [y], the high-front rounded vowel. This is particularly true if the vowel is short. (It is not the case, however, that the articulation actually changes into these more front vowels, rather that the apical constriction coarticulated with the [u] produces a raised F_2; see Ohala 1974a, 1981b).

Although there is evidence that this type of consonantally-induced formant perturbation actually improves the intelligibility of speech (Strange,
Verbrugge, Shankweiler & Edman, 1976), from another point of view these
distortions represent noise in the signal which listeners have to be able to
factor out: Their own productions of words which they have heard with such
a distorted /u/ should not be articulated with the similar-sounding vowels
[ɯ], [ɨ], or [y] but rather must have genuine /u/'s.

If the listeners-turned-speakers purposely incorporated these mechanical-
ly-caused, fortuitous details in their speech, such features would presumably
be exaggerated, would appear even in the most careful articulatory style,
and would sound sufficiently different from the speech of those from whom
they had (imperfectly) learned the words as to be noticeable and therefore to
constitute a *sound change*. Sound changes—variations in pronunciation from
one generation to the next—do occur but not with the frequency that would
be expected if listeners were unable to differentiate the intended speech from
the noise added by the vocal mechanism itself.

We must assume, therefore, that listeners can factor such noise from the
speech signal and reconstruct the intended signal. They must utilize detailed phonetic knowledge to accomplish this bit of top-down processing.
The contents and structure of this knowledge is anyone's guess. It may be as
hypothesized by the motor theory of speech perception (Liberman, Cooper,
Shankweiler & Studdert-Kennedy, 1967) although the evidence in support
of this model has not been overwhelming. More simply, it could just be
a rather detailed list represented perhaps as a series of if-then statements,
such as those in some expert systems (Shortliffe, 1976), e.g., "if a vowel
with relatively high F_2 appears near [+acute] consonants, then it might be a
back vowel." Such statements could even include something like Lindblom's
(1963) equations which predict achieved formant frequency of vowels given
the target frequency, the formant frequencies of the surrounding consonants,
and the duration of the vowel, except that the equations would solve for target formant frequencies given the other variables. For the present argument,
however, all that is important is the assumption that listeners can "undo"
the distortions in speech—how they accomplish this remains to be seen.

Figure 18.1 gives a schematic representation of the encoding, distortion,
reception, and reconstruction of the articulatory aspect of the speaker's message. Here the slashes and square brackets have their usual meaning of
marking "underlying" or "lexical" forms versus "surface-phonetic" forms, respectively. The /ut/ which the speaker intends to utter gets distorted by
articulatory constraints into something which sounds like [yt] and is received
as such by the listener. The listener then refers to phonetic knowledge as suggested above, factors out the distortion, and reconstructs the intended /ut/.
In the listener's own most careful pronunciations of the same sequence—i.e.,
when the distorting influence if the articulators is at a minimum—the /ut/

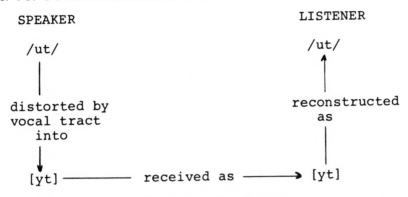

FIG. 18.1. Listener Reconstructs Distorted Message.

will sound more like |ut]. (Also, the listener's psychological judgements about the vowel should be that it is the "same" vowel as that in, say, "move," where consonantal distortions are not very prominent.)

There is experimental evidence supporting this model. Ohala, Kawasaki, Riordan, and Caisse (forthcoming; see also Ohala, 1981b) asked listeners to identify as either /i/ or /u/ a range of very short synthetic, steady-state vowels between (and including) /i/ and /u/ when they appeared in the consonantal contexts /f_p/ and /s_t/. Listeners' crossover from /u/ to /i/ was more towards the front of this continuum when the consonantal context was /s_t/ than when it was /f_p/. Apparently they discounted some of the "frontness" of the vowel stimuli when they appeared in the environment of apical consonants since these consonants, but not labials, would be likely to introduce a "fronting" distortion on a vowel such as /u/. Also, Kawasaki (1978, In press) showed that listeners perceived phonetically nasalized vowels as being less nasal when these vowels appeared near nasal consonants as opposed to when they appeared near nasal consonants attenuated in amplitude or deleted entirely. Apparently when the nasal consonants are present and perceptually evident they take some of the "blame" for the nasalization and the vowels seem more "oral" than they actually are. Other studies by Mann and Repp (1980) and by Fowler (1981b) yield similar results.

THE EVIDENCE OF SOUND CHANGE

From materials testing in structural engineering to aphasiology, it is an accepted strategy to try to understand the workings of a system by seeing how it behaves when it breaks down. We can use the same strategy to study speech perception: Many sound changes, I maintain, represent a breakdown of the speech-perception process.

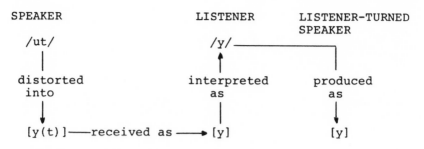

FIG. 18.2.   Distorted Message Received by Listener.

The ability of listeners to factor out distortions in speech rests on their being able to credit the distortions to some other source. If, for some reason, listeners are unable to blame the distortions on something else, it follows that they will not be able to factor them out. These distortions will then be taken as part of the intended signal. This is represented schematically in Figure 18.2, which follows the same graphical conventions as Figure 18.1. The sequence of events is identical to those in Figure 18.1 up to the point that the utterance is received by the listener. In this case the [t], perhaps because it was weakly articulated or unreleased, is missed by the listener who receives only (what sounds like) [y]. Since the listener hears nothing else to blame the frontness of the vowel on, the signal is interpreted as /y/; in the listener's own most careful articulations he or she would utter it that way. If this person's speech is copied by others, one has a sound change within the given speech community.

This is not just a hypothetical scenario. There is prima facie evidence that a large class of sound changes originate in just this way.

Table 18.1 presents evidence (from Michailovsky, 1975) which seems to be best accounted for by the mechanism just described. Here Written Tibetan is taken to represent the older pronunciation, while Lhasa Tibetan represents the modern pronunciation. The data show, first, a loss of the final consonant. When the lost consonant was a dental and the preceding vowel was front, or when the vowel was back and the consonant nondental, there was no change in vowel quality. However, when a dental was lost and the vowel was originally back, the vowel quality changes to a front vowel (rounded if the original vowel was rounded, unrounded otherwise).

Many other sound changes have a similar pattern, i.e., where the conditioning environment is lost simultaneously with the manifestation of the conditioned change. For example, tonal contrasts have developed in many languages when a voicing distinction in prevocalic consonants was lost, e.g., Chinese (Hombert, et al., 1979). As mentioned above, the voicing contrast in consonants has been shown by modern synchronic phonetic studies of nontonal languages like English and French to cause a perturbation of the F0

TABLE 18.1

Phonological Data from Tibeto-Burman
(From Michailovsky, 1975; transcription simplified)

Written Tibetan		Lhasa Tibetan	English Gloss
ɡɲid	>	ɲi:	"sleep"
drel	>	tʰe:	"mule"
nub	>	nu:	"west"
tʰog	>	tʰɔ:	"roof"
BUT:			
skad	>	qɛ:	"language"
bod	>	pʰø:	"Tibet"
bdud	>	ty:	"demon"

on following vowels. These perturbations must be the "seeds" of the sound change which actually took root in Chinese after the loss of the voicing contrast in consonants.

It is not possible to maintain, though, that all conditioned sound changes involve a simultaneous loss of the conditioning environment. Vowel harmony results from phonetic factors that are more or less similar to those described above for Tibeto-Burman, except that it is a neighboring vowel rather than a neighboring consonant which conditions the change, yet in vowel harmony the conditioning segments are not lost. Still, it must be true of all such cases, whether the conditioning environment is lost or not, that the sound changes occurred because listeners did not make the "connection" between the conditioner and "conditionee," i.e., they failed to appreciate the causal relationship between the source of the phonetically-caused distortion and the distortion itself. Naturally, when they do not detect the source of the distortion this failure is understandable, but such failure could happen in other ways as well (cf. Ohala, 1981b).

There are visual analogues to the scenarios represented in Figures 18.1 and 18.2. When we view familiar objects under colored light—e.g., the greenish cast of fluorescent lights or the reddish cast of the setting sun—we do not "see" the effects of this color distortion; we factor it out by reference to our experience and environmental cues. When, however, we take a photograph of these same objects, the finished photograph shows the color distortion very noticeably, because we fail to invoke the same corrective processes.

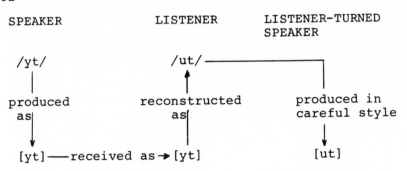

SPEAKER   LISTENER   LISTENER-TURNED
                                                SPEAKER

/yt/   /ut/

produced   reconstructed   produced in
as   as   careful style

[yt]——received as→[yt]   [ut]

FIG. 18.3. Listener Incorrectly Reconstructs and Repeats Message.

Consider now the scenario schematized in Figure 18.3. Here the speaker intends to utter /yt/ and the physical signal is minimally distorted so that the listener receives [yt]. However, the listener thinks that this [y] is really an /u/ distorted by the flanking [t]. The listener therefore reconstructs /ut/ and, in his or her own most careful speech, would also produce [ut]. This would be another sound change but one which goes in the opposite direction to that in Figure 18.2.

Again, this is not a hypothetical case. Such sound changes occur. Darden (1970) described a case where, in the history of the Russian language, a front vowel /a/ shifts to the back vowel /a/ in the environment of palatal or palatalized consonants, precisely the environment where one would expect to find a fronting of back vowels. Presumably listeners interpreted the [a] as a distorted [a] and so they reconstructed it as the latter.

Another probable example fo the same type of sound change can be found in the history of Shona, a southern Bantu language.

TABLE 18.2

Phonological Data from Shona (From Mkanganwi, 1972).

Proto-Bantu		Pre-Shona		Shona	English Gloss
*-bua	>	*-bwa	>	-bɣa	"dog"
*-mu-	>	kumwa	>	kumɣa	"to drink"

Table 18.2 provides relevant data (from Mkanganwi, 1972). Here a labial-velar glide /w/ changed to a /ɣ/ (voiced velar glide or fricative) in the environment of preceding labial consonants. Listeners must have assumed that the labial part of the labial-velar glide was a predictable distortion intro-duced by the preceding labial consonant and therefore factored it out. Since

the velar component could not be accounted for as a distortion created by any neighboring segment, it was preserved.

These two examples are cases of *dissimilation*: Given two segments sharing one or more phonetic features, the values for some or all of these features change in one segment so that the two become more phonetically different. These cases are instances of "contact (or immediate)" dissimilation, since the dissimilating environment is immediately adjacent to the dissimilated segment. I propose that all cases of dissimilation proper,[1] even dissimilation "at a distance" can be analyzed in a similar way. Some examples of this type of dissimilation are given in Table 18.3.

Cases (a) through (h) illustrate dissimilation as a process. Cases (i) through (k) are examples of "preventive" dissimilation, where an expected assimilatory change fails to materialize in an environment where dissimilation would have reversed the sound change if it had occurred. Cases (l) and (m) are examples of phonotactic constraints which have a dissimilatory character; how they originated, whether by dissimilation as a process or preventative dissimilation, is unknown.

What prevented a proper understanding of such sound changes up to now was the belief that they represented "action at a distance," a notion which is as troublesome to linguistics as it is to physicists (see Sturtevant, 1935). However, it is not necessary to invoke "action at a distance" for these cases; they all involve dissimilation of phonetic features which are known to be able to spread beyond the immediate segment they are initially attached to, i.e., such features as aspiration, labialization, retroflexion, glottalization, pharyngealization, palatalization, and place of articulation. Assuming that in the case of dissimilation discovered by Grassman (1863), the aspiration (breathy voicing) was spread throughout the words affected—i.e., that a narrower phonetic transcription of the pre-Sanskrit word for "bind" would be [b̤ e̤ n̤ d̤]—we need only hypothesize that listeners erroneously interpreted the aspiration after the first stop as being a distortion introduced by the second stop and that they therefore "removed" the aspiration from the first. In the cases of preventative dissimilation, the listeners must have removed the phonetic features—extreme palatal constriction in the cases (i) and (k)— which would have provided the environment for the sound change.

There is another sound pattern, not thought of as dissimilatory, which may also be explained by the mechanism outlined here. Schourup (1973), Ruhlen (1975), and Beddor (1982), working independently in cross-language surveys on the sound patterns exhibited by nasalized vowels, arrived at a common conclusion: While distinctively nasal mid-vowels tended to lower in

---

[1] "Proper" because I wish to eliminate certain classes of sound changes which have been improperly labeled dissimilatory, e.g., the epenthetic /b/ in *number*, ultimately from Latin *num(e)rus* is due to assimilatory denasalization, not dissimilation of continuancy (Ohala, 1981b).

TABLE 18.3

Examples of Dissimilation at a Distance
(Full references may be found in Ohala 1981b)

LANGUAGE	FEATURE DISSIMILATED	EXAMPLE
(a) IE > Sanskrit	aspiration	*benḍ- > banḍ- "bind"
(b) IE > Cl. Greek	aspiration	*t^{h}rik^{h}os > trik^{h}os "hair"
(c) Proto-Bantu > Sukuma	aspiration	*takun- > -dak^{h}un "chew"
(d) Latin > Italian	labiality	quīnque > cinque "five"
(e) Anc. Chinese > Cantonese	labiality	*pjam > pin "diminish"
(f) Proto-Quichean > Tzutujil	low F$_2$	*k'aq > k'^{y}aq "flea"
(g) Proto-Quechumaran > Quechua	glottalization	*t'ant'a > t'anta "bread"
(h) Latin > Provençal	"r"-ness	meretrīce > meltritz "courtesan"
(i) Pre-Mam > Mam	palatality	*k'išbisa > k$^{'j}$išbisa- (for expected *tš'išbisa-)
(j) Sanskrit	retroflexion	sarsrāɳa (for expected *sarʂrāɳa)
(k) Vulgar Latin > Span. dial.	palatality	plattea > plaza (for expected *chaza) "city square"
(l) Arabic	place of articulation	$*(\begin{bmatrix} C_1 \\ \alpha \text{ p. artic.} \end{bmatrix} \begin{bmatrix} C_2 \\ \alpha \text{ p. artic.} \end{bmatrix} \begin{bmatrix} C_3 \\ \alpha \text{ p. artic.} \end{bmatrix})$
(m) Yao	labiality	$*(C^w \; V \; \begin{bmatrix} C \\ \text{labial} \end{bmatrix})$

the vowel space (in comparison with cognate oral vowels or with the quality reconstructed for them at earlier periods), contextually nasalized mid-vowels showed the *opposite* pattern, that of raising. Acoustic phonetic theory and some experimental results (Fujimura & Lindqvist, 1971; House, 1957; House & Stevens, 1956) seem to suggest that one of the effects of nasalization on vowels (at least non-low vowels) is to raise F_1, thus producing a lowering of the vowel in the auditory vowel space. Therefore, when there is no nasal consonant near, as in the case of a distinctively nasal vowel, the nasalization and its distorting effects cannot be factored out; listeners, if they hear the vowel as having any different quality, will hear it as lower. On the other hand, if there is a nasal consonant nearby, as in the case of a contextually-nasalized vowel, listeners would be alerted to try to factor out some of the distortions caused by the nasalization. In doing this, they can either factor out just the right amount of apparent vowel lowering and therefore reconstruct the intended quality, or they may "overdo" it and end up reconstructing a vowel with a higher position on the vowel space. This is quite speculative, I admit, but fortunately it is a question that lends itself to empirical investigation.

Although there are still some details to be worked out,[2] this account of dissimilation has a great deal to recommend it from the phonological as well as the phonetic literature. The speech-perception experiments described above have, in essence, demonstrated dissimilation in the laboratory: In the study by Kawasaki (1978, In press), listeners in effect "removed"—i.e., dissimilated—some degree of nasalization from a vowel when it appeared in the environment of flanking nasal consonants. Also, although sound changes which are assimilatory at base—e.g., those exemplified in Table 18.1 and schematized in Figure 18.2—often show the loss of the conditioning environment at the same time as the conditioned change, instances of dissimilation apparently never do. This is explained by the account given here since dissimilation requires that listeners detect some segment that they can "blame" for what they mistakenly regard as distortions in speech.

There is also a visual analogue of dissimilation: camouflage. A brown, black, and white specked quail blends in with the similarly-colored terrain which it inhabits. Viewers could be looking directly at the patch of speckles contributed by the quail and yet not notice it because they attribute that speckled pattern to the terrain. In the same way, we can assume that the pre-Sanskrit listeners heard the aspiration after the first stop in */bend/ but didn't notice it because it was camouflaged by the aspiration from the second stop.

The preceding treatment of these types of sound change differs in an important way from previous ones. These mechanisms are minimally teleo-

---

[2] See Ohala, 1981b for a discussion of additional phonological evidence and possible counterevidence.

logical, i.e., the changes did not occur because a speaker decided to make articulation easier, perception easier, or grammars simpler. They happened because of innocent misapprehensions on the part of listeners. The only teleology involved is the goal of the listeners-speakers doing their best to convey to their listeners the pronunciation of words that they think their listeners use and recognize themselves. It assumes no more mental "baggage" than that which we must assume is necessary for speech to be perceived accurately.

CONCLUSION

I have presented evidence that speech perception is performed by a type of top-down processing involving references to detailed phonetic knowledge. The speech signal as received by the listener consists of a mixture of the purposely encoded elements (which have to be extracted for the sake of accurate re-encoding when the listener becomes the speaker) and distortions caused by the physical constraints of the encoding machinery (which must be factored out). This top-down processing usually works successfully and transparently but reveals itself in those few cases where the mechanism fails to work. Such transmission errors are preserved in the record of sound changes of the languages of the world.

There are at least two important implications of this kind of phonetic-level top-down processing for the issue of invariability in speech processes. First, it suggests that speech *is* highly variable at the phonetic level. If it weren't, listeners would have no reason to construct the elaborate knowledge base that allows them to factor out fortuitous variability. It therefore suggests that the search for "higher-order" invariability in the units of speech will not provide a complete solution to the variability problem. Second, it is presumably no secret to the speaker that listeners have these reconstructive rules. This leaves open the possibility, as previously proposed by Lindblom (1983a), that speakers are aware of how much variability in speech production they can get away with and still be intelligible. Logically, there have to be invariant representations for *some* sort of units of speech somewhere in the link between speaker and hearer, but the bulk of evidence indicates that it is not likely that we will find it outside the brains of these two.

ACKNOWLEDGEMENTS

My thanks to Ian Catford, Paul Kiparsky, Phil Lieberman, and, especially, Jon Allen for helpful comments on the conference version of this chapter and to my Phonology Laboratory colleagues for help and advice, especially

Michelle Caisse, Haruko Kawasaki, Carol Riordan, and Steve Pearson. This research was supported in part by grants from the National Science Foundation and the Committee on Research, University of California, Berkeley.

Jonathan Allen: Comment

I will first summarize Ohala's paper and then give my comments on it. His paper deals with one particular constraint which can be used in speech perception for which Ohala gives quite a bit of evidence. In my summary I will use some of his wording, although not always exactly quoted.

Ohala states that top-down processing of a signal implies that the receiver makes reference to a separate internal knowledge source when deriving the message. So, for example, when a speech signal comes into the receiver, a knowledge source is utilized in order to yield the final perception which comes out as a message. In fact, I suspect Ohala would agree that there are probably multiple knowledge sources involved here, but only one is dealt with in his paper. He goes on to say that such a mechanism for active perception is necessary if the incoming signal is noisy but still has enough redundancy in it to enable the listener to reconstruct the message intended by the sender. Key words here are "reconstruct" and "intended." The idea is to try to understand how it is that we can avoid the effects of the noise in the incoming message in order to perceive what was intended by the sender.

The incoming speech signal, according to this description, consists of two parts; that which the speaker intended to encode and the so-called nonintended perturbations. These last are "automatic consequences of gestures not actively controlled by the speaker." One example is the so-called F_0 perturbation due to consonant voicing; the fact that F_0 rises and then has a little exponential falling tail coming out of an unvoiced consonant, and the symmetrical opposite coming out of a voiced consonant. Another results in the problem which many people have in constructing speech-recognition systems and accounting for perception, namely the fact that [u] in the environment flanked by two [d]s has F_2 rising considerably; that is, there can be a very substantial fronting of the vowel in that particular environment. The thesis of the paper is that these nonintended perturbations, or those that are introduced automatically by the articulatory apparatus in a way that presumably is beneath the level of the speaker's intentions, have somehow got to be factored out or removed.

There is an additional consequence of this effort to factor out perturbations introduced by the articulators. For example, as Ohala points out in some detail, there may be a problem of incorporation of fortuitous detail leading to exaggerated speech. Thus, if a listener hears [u] as intended in an environment flanked by two [d]s and just mimics that, but doesn't understand that the intended segment was [u], then presumably that would lead to an exaggerated articulation which might, going far enough, actually lead to a sound change. Listeners have two possible choices. Either they understand, through some perception of the environment, that what was actually there physically was not what was intended and somehow undo that distortion, or they don't have such a recognition, leading to sound change. That can happen due to, for example, the environment that would suggest that you have to factor this change out being lost or attenuated in some way.

How is a listener actually going to reconstruct this intended signal? Ohala suggests, first very generally, that one particular way of doing it would be to utilize a phonetic knowledge source, indicating that this corresponds to top-down processing. Ohala gives as an example the use of Lindblom's (1963) treatment of vowel reduction in which equations are worked out characterizing the achieved vowel-formant frequency as a function of the *intended* target frequency, the formants of the consonantal environment, and the time, if this is in an interconsonantal environment, for the vowel to actually be realized. Ohala suggests that listeners might be able to utilize this functional relationship and solve for the target frequency given the actual physically achieved vowel-formant frequencies. This is one way, in the particular situation of the fronting of [u], that could be used to actually solve for the intended target. The model that arises from this is characterized by Figure 18.1. The speaker's intention is distorted, or in this case the vowel is getting fronted by the action of the vocal tract. It's actually "heard" as that fronted form; but because of the listener's knowledge of the coarticulation of the vocal tract, it gets reconstructed to give the original vowel [u].

One conclusion from this discussion is the view of some sound changes as being due in part to a failure of the speech-perception system, that is, the failure to appreciate the contextual environment that would trigger the listener to factor out or undo these changes. Listeners won't be able to factor out these distortions if, to use Ohala's words, they can't "blame" them on something else. For example, the conditioning environment may be attenuated or lost, and, in fact, Ohala tends to use sound change as a window for looking upon this factoring-out process. The fact that it doesn't happen when a sound change takes place gives us a view as to how this process takes place. As an example from Tibeto-Burman, the loss of final dental consonants led to no change in a vowel if it was originally front; on the other hand, back vowels became front, that is they didn't get "undone" by listeners as being back, and instead they began to be perceived as front vowels. In fact, the rounding that was either present or absent in the back vowels was preserved when they moved forward. As another example, it is known in the literature that an effect of nasalization on vowels is to raise F_1. On the other hand, if there is no contextual nasal there to do it, in other words there is a distinctively nasal vowel, listeners will hear a lower vowel. But if there is a contextual nasal, they will tend to hear the vowel opening correctly, or perhaps, as Ohala suggests, as higher than intended.

The conclusion of his paper, then, is that listeners do have to use knowledge of the way the articulators work to factor out changes in order to perceive correctly. Sound change, being a failure of that process, actually gives us a view of how that has happened over time.

My own comments tend to be focused not on the actual relationships that were found by Ohala but on the inference of control strategies, which I don't think is justified. Ohala mentions "top down," and in repeated readings of the paper, I've never found that phrase to be essential to the arguments presented in any way. I believe that we really have to take a much more neutral position. All that can be said is that listeners somehow integrate the effects of many different constraint domains, not just articulatory constraints, but other constraints such as phonotactic, lexical, or syntactic. These different constraint domains come together to form the percept in a way that I don't think we understand. Now in formal systems, such as programming systems, the notion of top-down and bottom-up strategies for parsing, for example, is a well-defined notion. There is nothing wrong with it there. But I don't believe that in the kind of human behavior mentioned in Ohala's paper either of these is suggested.[1]

The next thing I want to focus on is allophonic variation, which Ohala comments on in his paper. I certainly believe that every level of linguistic structure has its impact on the surface phonetic reality, particularly morphemes, metrical feet, syllables, and particular features involved in a phoneme. I mention those in connection with the work done by Church (1983). Church developed a context-free grammar with production rules that actually generate these allophones. In other words, given the detailed linguistic structure of what is to be produced, one can write rules in a formal context free grammar that will produce the allophones that one actually observes in a detailed narrow phonetic transcription. Then you can build, as Church did, a parser that will look at this narrow phonetic transcription and reveal all possible lexical items that are implied by the phonetic transcription. In effect, the parser utilizes the constraints provided at each of these structural levels. It's a nested context-free grammar that utilizes all of those constraints. They happen to be formalized in terms of a context-free grammar; that's because we know how to do context-free parsing, but that certainly isn't the only way it could be done.

The key thing I want to stress here is that, in this view, allophones don't represent distortions at all. So there is nothing to be factored out. The underlying phonemes also play no explicit role in the perceptual modeling. That's not to say that these phonemes don't have their place, and that listeners wouldn't like to be able to separate them from the lexical items once these items are found. But they don't play any explicit role in the perception process according to this type of modeling. Allophonic variation is strongly related to the linguistic structures, some of which I have mentioned here, and we can utilize it to find out what was said. This is an example of how I think the kinds of facts that Ohala discussed in his paper can be put into a formal framework that we can actually exploit.

The next point I want to discuss is aimed at a more neutral view of control in perception. I wonder if there is a distinction between "conditioner" and "conditionee." That is, from the point of view of perception, is it necessary to establish or claim a direction of causality? In other words, is there a conditioning environment that somehow conditions one particular element? Or is it only necessary to observe and utilize some form of co-occurrence relation, i.e., that the two things happen

---

[1] I tend to feel, incidentally, in discussions of speech-recognition that go on all the time, that this whole issue of top down versus bottom up is a red herring. Some people say both are going on, or that one is going on. I don't think it's a very useful notion, and I don't think it's important for what Ohala wants to say either. We don't have any accurate characterization of the actual control strategy used by humans.

together or don't happen together. Certainly the combinatorics of these relations can get very large. For example, in Lisker's study of "rapid" and "rabid" and all the many correlates involved in that single-feature distinction, one really wants to know the co-occurrence relationships, rather than any view of causality. I don't feel that we have to look at the data presented in this paper in terms of a conditioner acting on a conditionee. I don't see the need for that directionality, and am perfectly happy to deal with it from a more neutral point of view. I would again suggest that in a grammatical representation, the so-called arrow that we print in writing down productions of these rules facilitates an expansion of the detail, but it doesn't imply any causal direction at all. It's a mistake to read that in.

Lastly, most of the evidence in the paper cited for the relation of sound changes and perception centered around vowels, and one wonders if these arguments can be expanded and generalized to give us even more insight in broader contexts.

Paul Kiparsky: Comment

Ohala's idea that dissimilation arises by the undoing of assumed assimilation is a very interesting one. It makes sense of some of the otherwise unexplained properties of dissimilation. The first has to do with its "structure-preserving" character. Dissimilation processes generally operate in the lexical phonology, so that their outputs exist as independent phonemes in the language. For example, dissimilation of aspiration occurs in languages with distinctive aspiration (Grassmann's Law in Greek and Sanskrit[1]) but it does not occur in English or to my knowledge in other languages with postlexical aspiration. Ohala's theory supports these facts, because a speaker would not be led to assume that a form is derived by some assimilation process unless he or she can impute to it an unassimilated representation which could plausibly occur in its own right, one which would have to be made up of actual phonemes of the language occurring in places where they are allowed to occur by its phonotactics. Most of the cases in Ohala's list of dissimilation processes are structure-preserving in this sense, in some cases nontrivially so (for example, in Slavic [č] caused backing of [æ] to [a] but [e] was not backed by this rule because it had no phonemic back counterpart). In this respect, dissimilation is quite different from assimilation, which is a typical source of new allophones.

Secondly, if dissimilation is based on speakers' apprehension of a form as assimilated, its site is inherently in the lexicon and it follows that it should partake of the idiosyncrasy of all lexical phenomena. Dissimilatory sound changes should therefore be characteristically sporadic, unlike sound changes of the ordinary sort, which originate as postlexical rules, and are mostly of the completely general and mechanical neogrammarian type. That certainly seems to be true. Dissimilation is usually mentioned in discussions of sound change along with metathesis and

---

[1] Leonard Bloomfield, *Language* (New York 1933), pp. 349–351, Paul Kiparsky, "On Comparative Linguistics: the Case of Grassmann's Law." In Thomas A. Sebeok (ed.) *Current Trends in Linguistics*, Vol. 11 (The Hague 1973).

a few other types as one of the so-called "minor sound changes" for which the neogrammarian regularity thesis is waived.

John J. Ohala: Response

I thank Jon Allen for his very clear and constructive review of my paper. Regarding my use of the term "top-down" to describe the kind of processing that gives rise to dissimilation, I used it not so much in a technical sense but rather as a synonym for "interpretive" or "done with reference to accumulated phonetic knowledge."

I appreciate Paul Kiparsky's presentation of additional phonological evidence in support of my account of dissimilation. With reference to another point raised let me say that I'm not sure that dissimilation *should* be found predominantly in a more formal style of speech in contrast to assimilation. Assimilatory processes, as I've suggested, feed dissimilation. Put another way: It is because assimilatory processes exist that listeners have had to develop perceptual strategies to deal with coarticulation. Therefore, dissimilation should be manifest most in the same styles of speech that assimilation is. Possible evidence supporting this—although, I admit it may be subject to other analyses—is the substandard pronunciations of the following English words (where the form in square brackets gives the dissimilated form): *February* [fɛbjuɛri], *library* [laɪbɛri], *surprise* [səpraɪz], *performance* [pəfɔrmɛns].

I agree with those who maintain that the factors which lead to sound change can be found, potentially, at any stage in the speech chain. Chapter 18 dealt primarily (but not exclusively) with the perceptual side, but I have not neglected the articulatory and aerodynamic aspects in other papers (see also Ohala, 1974a, 1975, 1978, 1979, 1980, 1982a, 1982b, 1983; Ohala & Riordan, 1979). Regarding the possible contribution of articulatory or neuromotor constraints to cases of dissimilation like Grassmann's Law (the dissimilation of aspiration in Sanskrit and Greek), I have considered it but I really see no evidence for it. If the difficulty of executing two glottal abductions within a short time span was to manifest itself here, wouldn't one expect the *second* of these two aspirated consonants to become deaspirated, not, as happens to be the case, the *first*? In fact, in the majority of cases of dissimilation at a distance, it is the first of two similar segments which suffers the change. Plausibly this happens because assimilation, which, feeds dissimilation, is usually anticipatory (Javkin, 1979). I would guess that listeners know this and so are particularly on guard against phonetic distortion due to anticipatory assimilation. Sometimes they overreact but do so with the bias noted.

19

SOURCES OF INHERENT VARIATION IN THE SPEECH PROCESS

William Labov
University of Pennsylvania

The systematic analysis of variation has always been a concern of phonetics, but until recently it has not been pursued at more abstract levels of linguistic structure. As long as the theory of speech perception and production looked to a one-to-one, or one-to-many, relationship between linguistic elements and their physical realizations, this was not a major problem. But the weight of the evidence points to a many-to-one relation between linguistic and physical representations; a recognition system that employs probabilistic weighting of variable features in a multivariate model; parallel processing of the signal at many levels; and interrupts that inform the processing at one level of results obtained at another.

The following contribution draws on a form of linguistic description that may be useful in developing such an approach to speech perception. Discrete category boundaries are not assumed: Instead, the degree of categorization of phonetic substance is the main topic of linguistic inquiry. This approach takes spontaneous speech as its data, rather than introspection and formal elicitation. It uses inferential rather than deductive methods, proceeding from the known to the unknown rather than from the unknown to the known.

If we were to accept every variation that we find as an irreducible part of linguistic structure, we would have abandoned the search for invariance, and committed ourselves to an endless and profitless charting of small frequencies. The appropriate treatment of variation remains a central problem of linguistics and phonetics. In an effort to throw some light on the problem, I will review the types of variation that are normally encountered in the speech signal at the phonetic level and then at more abstract levels of phonology. At each point, the first and most critical step is to recognize the source of the variation encountered, to distinguish variation inherent in linguistic structure from artifacts of the eliciting situation, errors of measurement, and the effects of mixing heterogeneous systems.

PHONETIC VARIATION

I will be dealing here with phonetic variation as shown in the dispersion of acoustic measurements and the correlation of these measurements with impressionistic phonetics. The data will be drawn from work at the Linguistics Laboratory at the University of Pennsylvania, where the analysis of linguistic change and variation is based on acoustic measurements of spontaneous speech recorded in the field. Our main focus has been on vowels, and in particular, stressed-vowel nuclei. The discussion of variation in this section will therefore be limited to this one area of phonetic study.

Measurement Error as a Source of Variation

In the study of change in progress, we necessarily develop a strong interest in estimating the accuracy of our measurement. We have to consider three distinct kinds of reliability: within utterances, across utterances within speakers, and across speakers. The first kind is essential in locating relative maxima and minima of formant trajectories, which we need as a best estimate of relative height or fronting. Broad-band spectrograms are quite reliable in this respect: that is, in locating the temporal location of any points of inflection in formant trajectories. To study the dispersion within the vowel system, we need to estimate across-utterance reliability for the central tendencies of the "same" vowel in Hertz. As early as 1948, Lisker examined the minimal dispersion of vowels heard as the same. It is not a simple matter to estimate which parts of this dispersion is due to uncertainty of measurement and which part to variation in production.

The LPC algorithm for isolating the supraglottal spectrum from the glottal spectrum represents a sizeable advance in speed, accuracy, and information, including data on formant amplitudes and bandwidths. Repeated measurements of the same utterance give us a high degree of reliability. But it is more difficult to estimate reliability across utterances. We can synthesize test signals; but the noise or information that differentiates spontaneous speech from the control vowels will differ from one utterance to another. The problem is complicated by the presence of gross errors, or failures of the algorithm to locate plausible formant peaks. Even with moving average smoothing procedures, such failures occur with even the best recordings and increase rapidly as signal-to-noise ratio falls. Several proposals have been put forward for the automatic detection and elimination of gross errors, based on continuity and

WILLIAM LABOV

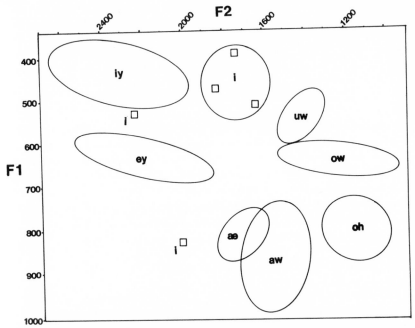

FIG. 19.1.   Multiple norms for /i/ in the vowel system of Lucy R.

most probable formant locations (Lennig, 1978; McCandless, 1974). If the
suspect reading lies beyond the possibilities of human articulation, this is a
reasonable move. Otherwise, the identification of gross errors can be quite
problematic, since many speakers show multiple norms.

Figure 19.1 shows the main outlines of the vowel system of Lucy R., and
a second generation Puerto Rican speaker from Philadelphia. As in other
diagrams used here, it is a doubly linear two-formant plot. The focus here is
on short [i]. There are five tokens plotted:

	F_1	F_2
his	387	1748
been	475	1859
six	511	1617
hidden	533	2243
him	828	1997

Been, six, and *hidden* are in the vicinity of the means for the white population, with a dispersion appropriate to their consonantal environment. But
hidden is in front, peripheral position, close to long [iy] tokens, and *him* is at

the other extreme, close to low central [æ] tokens. In the procedures we used prior to 1982, tokens like *hidden* and *him* would in all probability be set aside as gross errors. But in the current procedure, each token in the chart is stored as a full word, and all suspicious pairs are checked by auditory comparison of neighboring tokens. This diagram is drawn from a test made to compare the two methods of analysis. Only one norm was drawn on the chart made by the earlier method. But auditory comparison with our current techniques convinced us that *hidden* does have a vowel nucleus close to [iy], and *him* close to [æ]. Further study indicates that many second generation Puerto Rican speakers like Lucy R. have three norms: a Spanish-influenced target; a typical Philadelphia target; and a low-overcorrected target, maximally opposed to Spanish influence.

From this experiment and other evidence we have come to the conclusion that auditory comparison of the vowels in a system is an essential step in validating an analysis. We will return to the question of multiple norms as a source of variation in "Variation in Normative Targets" below.

Variation Due to Stress and Timing

A number of instrumental studies have confirmed what is evident to the ear: In English and many other languages, the positions of vowel nuclei vary with stress and duration. In most dialects, rapidly articulated vowels in checked position with durations of 150–200 msec are highly centralized. Nuclei that approach the peripheral position of the cardinal vowels are limited to highly stressed vowels, in free position, of much longer duration: up to 500 msec. Centralization has been associated with the influence of surrounding consonants, under the reasonable observation that a certain amount of time is required for the tongue to reach its programmed target.

A numerical estimate of this source of variation is provided by a sizeable body of data drawn from a single speaker in Philadelphia, whose speech was recorded during an entire day (Hindle, 1980). A stepwise regression analysis of the vowel /aw/, which shows the largest social variation in the system, shows a moderate F_2 effect for duration measured in centiseconds, even within the set of primary stressed vowels. The regression coefficient for F_1 is a small one, $-.34$, while the F_2 coefficient is 1.79. This means that a vowel 100 msec longer than another would not be measurably higher but would show a detectable (17.9 Hz) shift frontwards towards the peripheral target. Differences in fundamental frequency, on the other hand, had no effect on the formant position of /aw/.

It would seem reasonable to take fully stressed vowels of maximum duration as benchmarks for the description of a vowel system, and we have followed that policy over the years. Maximal duration certainly gives us the best view of the target. But there is no general association between

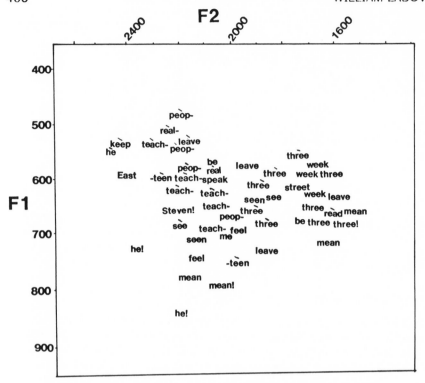

FIG. 19.2. Distribution of /iy/ for Marie Colville, 39, Bethnal Green.

peripherality and target position.

In the course of sound change, there are many processes that raise vowels along a front peripheral track, as in the case of /aw/ just discussed. But there are equally many processes, in English and other languages, that move vowel targets along nonperipheral tracks. Figure 19.2 shows measurements of the /iy/ vowel of a Cockney speaker, a 39 year old woman born in Bethnal Green in London. Here the target of the free vowel has shifted to a highly centralized position, following the chain-shifting pattern we have called the "Southern Shift." The most highly stressed, free vowels are the most centralized, with glides (not shown) that move towards high front position. Where /iy/ is constrained by a following consonant or consonant clusters, or receives secondary stresses, the nucleus is located closer to high-front position.

This type of centralized target is not unique to London. It is typical of many English vowel systems that follow the "Southern Shift": In Southern England, Philadelphia, the coastal South, Appalachia, Texas, Australia. It provides testimony that there is no universal connection between peripheral position and fully articulated vowels. The direction of variation from the

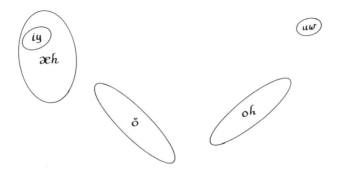

FIG. 19.3. Elliptical distributions of vowels in Northern Cities shift:
Flo Danowski, 39, Buffalo.

norm caused by reduced stress and duration is the product of the specific
organization of targets and their histories.

Effects of Change in Progress

Most sound changes in progress move at right angles to the stress/time dimension. As a result, many of our measurements of vowel systems of individuals show elliptical shapes for vowels involved in change. The extent of
variation along this axis can be several times greater than variation due to
stress.

Figure 19.3 shows the vowel system of a 39-year-old woman from Buffalo,
New York, a characteristic example of the "Northern Cities shift" (Labov, In
press; Labov, Yaeger & Steiner, 1972). Three vowels are actively involved in
the shift: tense /æh/, including all short [a] words, has almost completed the
move to upper mid-position; behind this, short open /o/ in got or God, has
moved to low center and (especially before /t/) to mid-front position; third,
long open /oh/ in soft, loss, or thought, is becoming shorter, and is moving
slowly towards a nonperipheral low central position. The distributions of
these vowels follow the path of the change. On the other hand, /iy/ and
/uw/ remain in a stable, peripheral position and show compact, roughly
globular distributions.

Phonetic Dispersion. Much of the variance within these distributions is
due to the dispersion of phonetic allophones within the phoneme. Figure 19.4
shows this phonetic variation in the vowel system of a 13-year-old boy from
Detroit, where the Northern Cities Shift is somewhat less advanced than in
Buffalo. The triangles represent tense [æh]. The solid triangle represents
short [a] before nasals in *man, hand, hands*: They are the most advanced,
in lower high position. Initial /m/ in *mass* has a smaller but substantial
effect. Following velars lead to lower F_2 positions; similarly for initial /r/.

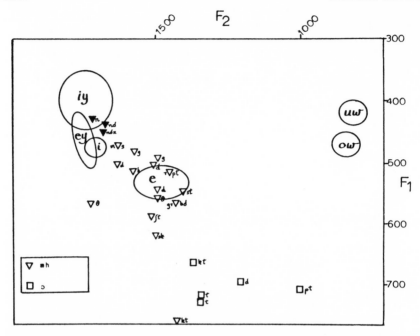

FIG. 19.4.   Phonetic conditioning in the raising of (æh) and fronting of
(ɔ) in the vowel system of Chris Adamo, 13, Detroit.

Following clusters retard the change most, and the /kt/ cluster in *act* gives
the lowest vowel of all, in low-front position.

Short /o/ shows the allophonic dispersion characteristic of this change,
with the frontest vowels before /t/ as in Figure 19.3, and the backest vowels
before labials.

These phonetic effects apparently operate in stable vowels at a lower level.
They would normally be overridden by random target errors, errors of measurement, and effects of stress and style, so that they may not be distinguishable in the tighter distributions of stable vowels.

The Effect of Social Interaction

Interviews can approach the range of variation found in speech, but in principle they cannot wholly overcome the effects of observation in shifting the
speaker towards normative targets (Labov, Yeager & Steiner 1972:26). Furthermore, they can only approximate the range of conditioning effects that
are responsible for the variation found in everyday speech. On the other
hand, direct recordings of social interaction rarely have the sound quality
needed for accurate acoustic measurements.

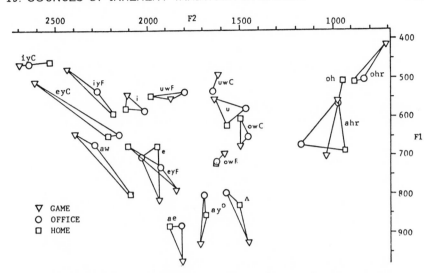

FIG. 19.5.   Mean formant values of Carol Myers in the three settings: GAME, OFFICE, and HOME.

Our best approach to the effects of social interaction on vowel realization is through a series of recordings made by Arvilla Payne for the Philadelphia study of a woman we call Carol Meyers. She is a 39-year-old member of the suburban Philadelphia speech community who worked in a travel agency. She was recorded with a Nagra IV-S and a Sennheiser 405 microphone for a total of ten hours: at the travel agency; at dinner at home; and in a bridge game with four close friends. Hindle (1980) mapped the realization of 5,000 vowels spoken by Carol Meyers in the course of these three sessions. Figure 19.5 and Table 19.1 show the mean values of her stressed vowels in the three contexts. For many vowels, there is a large and significant difference between the bridge game, where the most advanced Philadelphia forms are used, and the other two situations.

In Philadelphia, two thirds of the vowel system participates in a stratified series of sound changes: completed; old and almost completed; mid-range; new and vigorous; and incipient (see "Phonetic Variation Across the Speech Community," below). The greatest contextual shifts in Figure 19.5 occur for the fourth class, changes that are new and moving vigorously in the speech community as a whole:[1]

---

[1] Here the parenthesis notation indicates linguistic variables, which may range within or across the boundaries of the phonemic units indicated by / /. [ ] is used as always to indicate phonetic notation, and italics to indicate orthography that reflects historically intact word classes.

TABLE 19.1

Mean Formant Values for Carol Meyers in Three Settings:
Game [G], Home [H], Office [O][a]

	F_1			F_2			N		
	G	O	H	G	O	H	G	O	H
aw	645	674	802	2399	2290	2097	13	42	11
ayO	930	802	857	1710	1691	1621	18	79	9
ahr	569	673	689	974	1173	932	6	18	3
oh	701	567	506	1032	968	948	4	19	5
ohr	419	502	509	701	833	897	4	19	9
æhN	520	664	769	2625	2529	2593	4	6	1
æh$	415	518	350	2674	2508	2674	1	3	1
æhF	601	611	—	2456	2333	—	17	2	0
iy#	475	533	591	2439	2278	2191	5	41	5
iyC	465	463	458	2993	2645	2536	6	26	5
ey#	792	735	676	1892	1935	2108	7	28	4
eyC	512	646	652	2613	2156	2214	2	31	6
ow#	697	716	722	1587	1620	1625	22	46	21
owC	677	652	608	1495	1455	1498	6	16	2
uw#	554	538	547	1869	1798	1982	11	31	4
uwC	489	536	—	1640	1647	—	2	7	—
i	538	585	576	2108	2015	2119	12	55	10
e	817	706	676	1938	2019	1945	4	62	9
æ	974	882	883	1804	1807	1880	10	48	8
/<	925	797	829	1450	1576	1500	8	17	9
u	554	576	623	1636	1465	1565	4	15	4

KEY

____# free vowel   ____C checked vowel
____N free vowel   ____F before fricatives   ____$ before stops

[a]From Hindle (1980), Table 4.2.

(aw) the fronting and raising of the nucleus of /aw/
(eyC) the fronting and raising of the nucleus of checked /ey/
(ay0) the centralization of the nucleus of /ay/ before voiceless consonants

For those changes where females are in the lead, Carol Meyers' style shift follows the direction of the change. (aw) and (eyC) shift towards high-front peripheral position in the bridge game. The differences in Hertz for (aw) show a regular progression:

	F_1	F_2
Game	-131	238
Office	-76	71
Home	$-$	$-$

On the other hand, (ay0), the third new and vigorous change, is a male-dominated process. Here Meyers shifts in the opposite direction from (aw) and (ey): In the bridge game, she uses more open vowels, though the sound change is moving in the direction of centralization.

One interpretation of the data is that in interaction with her female peers, Carol Meyers presents herself as more Philadelphian and more female; at the office, as less local and less female. This implies that her behavior is finely tuned to the status of each sound change in the community. A second possibility is that she responds to social situations by a single alteration in phonetic setting. When she is more expressive in the bridge game, she uses more peripheral vowels; when she is less expressive and more constrained, all vowels move away from the periphery. A key variable to check this possibility is (æh): the height of the tensed short /a/ words. In Philadelphia, unlike the Northern cities, short /a/ words are split into a lax and a tense phoneme in a complex distribution that we will consider below. The raising of (æh) to high-front position is an older process in Philadelphia sound shifts, almost completed and sometimes corrected in formal styles. Carol Meyers does not show any significant raising of (æh) in the bridge game, which she would have to do if her shifts were the automatic products of a single change in articulatory setting. We can conclude that the variation shown by Carol Meyers in interaction with various speakers is adjusted to the status of individual variables in the vowel system.

Social Correction in Formal Styles.

Most linguists and phoneticians draw their data from controlled styles: translations of sentence and pronunciation of standard sentences and words. In many cases, this is the only possible procedure when the investigator is approaching problems for the first time, or measuring articulation under special

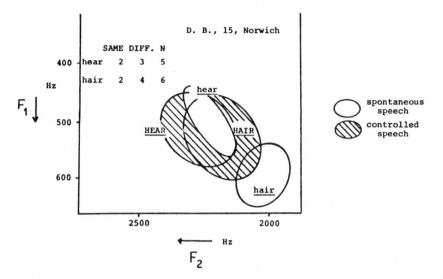

FIG. 19.6.   Distribution of (ihr) and (ehr) in spontaneous and controlled
production of *hear* and *hair* for David B., 15, Norwich, England.

conditions. When spontaneous speech is used, it is most likely to be quite
careful, as the subject unconsciously adjusts to the formal setting and to the
professional status of the experimenter. In such circumstances, it is especially useful to know how much of the variation found in speech is the result
of stylistic correction.

In this discussion, I'll be concerned only with the contrast between spontaneous speech and controlled styles (texts, word lists, minimal pairs, commutation tests). Differences between styles of spontaneous speech are sometimes
important, as the previous section showed; but they are minor compared with
what can happen to linguistic data when we move from the normal use of
the speaking faculty to speech produced on demand. The direction of correction in such formal circumstances depends on the interaction of the cognitive
system and the normative system of the speaker. In past publications, many
examples have been given of radical changes in the phonological systems under the pressure to correct stigmatized forms. For example, in New York
City, the distinction between the two phonemes /æh/ and /æ/ almost dis-
appears in reading word lists, though the result is never as systematic as in
the case of true mergers (see Figures 1a and 1b in Labov, 1981). Figure 19.6
shows an even more dramatic collapse of the distinction of /ihr/ and /ehr/
in Norwich, England (from Yaeger, 1975).

This is one of the many cases of near-merger that have been identified since
the first discussion of this phenomenon in Labov, Yaeger & Steiner (1972).
Trudgill (1983) points out that younger speakers in Norwich maintain a reg-

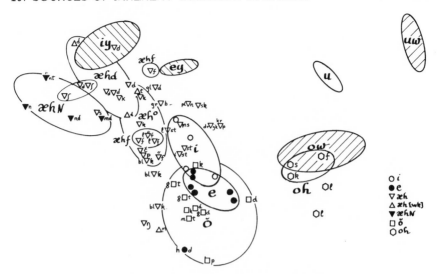

FIG. 19.7a.   Northern Cities Shift: Carol Muche, 23, Chicago.

ular distinction in production between /ihr/ in the word class of *hear* and /ehr/ in the word class of *hair*, but cannot label this difference when they are confronted with minimal pairs. Figure 19.6 shows Yaeger's measurements of these word classes from an interview I conducted in 1971 with a 15-year-old boy in Norwich. In spontaneous speech, there is a clear distinction between /ihr/ and /ehr/, but in reading word lists there is almost a complete merger. This shift does not reflect any stigmatization of the distinction; but rather that the stable distinction made in unreflecting production cannot be maintained when it is subjected to conscious introspection.

This correction in formal style is not a universal characteristic of vowel systems. It is specific to the particular status of an opposition and the stance taken by members of a particular speech community towards the phonetic forms involved. We can profitably contrast New York City with Chicago in this respect. In Chicago, the raising of short /a/ is a general feature of the Northern Cities Shift, socially stratified to some degree but rarely corrected in speech. In the terminology adopted in sociolinguistic studies, it is an "indicator" rather than a "marker" of social status. When working-class speakers read word lists, there is no movement towards a prestige norm. Figure 19.7a shows the spontaneous speech pattern of a young woman of Polish background. Her (æh) vowels cover a large part of the front vowel space from lower mid to lower high. In reading (Figure 19.7b), the nuclei are concentrated in upper-mid position. Formal style concentrates articulation at the vernacular target, rather than departing from it. In reading style,

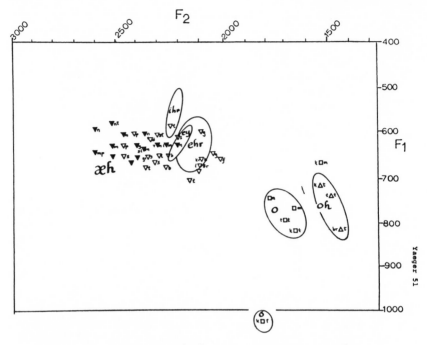

FIG. 19.7b.   Coalescence of (æh) classes in controlled speech (reading
style) of Carol Muehe, 16, Chicago (Labov, Yaeger & Steiner, 1972).

there is a loss of information on the range of phonetic conditioning that
occurs in spontaneous speech, but the phonological system is not confused.

Variation in Normative Targets.

Up to this point, we have been considering variation around a single norm.
But Figure 19.1 illustrated a heterogeneous situation that is not uncommon:
multiple norms of a native speaker. Middle-aged speakers will sometimes
show a few nuclei far removed from their normal distributions, which turn
out to coincide with the main concentration of vowels used by their children. Speakers of urban Scots dialects often show multiple norms for [u:]
in *house*, *out*, or *about*. In Scots, this vowel has never followed the path of
the Great Vowel Shift, though in middle-class speech, the norm is a diphthong with a centralized nucleus in imitation of Southern English. Figure
19.8 shows Yaeger's measurements of the /ū/ vowels of a 14-year-old youth
who I interviewed in the Calton district of Glasgow, in 1971. Three norms
are displayed. There is the older vernacular [u:] in high back position; the
newer fronted vernacular form [y:] in nonperipheral high-front position; and
two examples of the standardizing norm $\bar{u}_2$, a dipthong with a central nu-

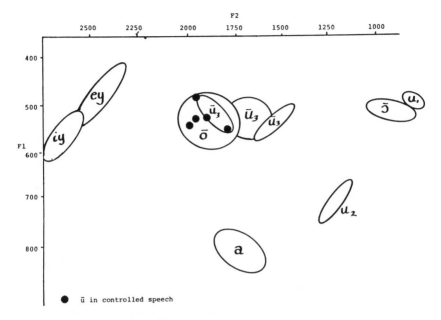

● ū in controlled speech

FIG. 19.8. Distribution of (ū) norms in *house* and *about* in spontaneous speech of Totty R., 14, Glasgow.

cleus. The controlled forms in the word lists are well to the front of the /ū₃/ vowels. There is a clear parallel to the Chicago, Illinois situation, where controlled speech was more in the direction of current sound change than spontaneous speech. But here there is an additional complication. Glasgow boys are overtly against the posh norm. As one boy from the Calton said to me, "When people say [əᵘt], we slog 'em!"

Phonetic Variation Across the Speech Community

So far, we have been considering variation in the speech of an individual. But as the last three sections show, it isn't possible to understand this variation by itself: It is only against the pattern of the speech community that we can interpret the variation shown by the individual, distinguishing measurement error from phonetic conditioning, stylistic variation, interactional effects, or the presence of discrete norms.

The study of phonetic variation across the speech community requires more than validity and reliability of measurement. It also involves a solution to the normalization problem. The study of sound change in progress in Philadelphia compared three techniques of normalization, to find one which would eliminate variation due to differences in vocal-tract length without eliminating information on social variation (Hindle, 1978; Labov, 1978). The

TABLE 19.2

Regression Coefficients for Four Philadelphia
Sound Changes: Neighborhood Study [N = 116]

	Old (æhN)		Mid-range (owC)	(aw)		New and Vigorous (eyC)		(ayO)
	F_1	F_2	F_2	F_1	F_2	F_1	F_2	F_1
Mean	582	2162	1395	691	1956	577	2152	729
Age		1.2	3.5#	2.3#	5.2#	1.3#	3.9#	2.1#
Female			60		89#		49	-36★
Occupation								
Skilled			101*		82★	30★	128#	
Clerical	-50★	-137#						
Managerial	-56★	-175#			-91		-92	
Professional	-106	-90#			-193#		-106	
Mobility								
Upward	30			28				
Downward			-136★	-67	-148★	73#		

KEY

Plain figures, $p < .05$

★ $p < .01$

# $p < .001$

log-mean normalization explored by Neary (1977) was selected, and used to transform the mean values of 116 Philadelphia speakers to a common reference system. These mean values were then submitted to stepwise regression programs that derive coefficients for a number of independent variables independent of the order of their entry into the program (Efroymson, 1966). Table 19.2 illustrates the results for five vowels: the raising and fronting of tense (æhN) before nasals, an older change now moving slowly and strongly stigmatized; the fronting of checked (owC), the fronting of checked /ow/, a middle-range change in progress; and three new and vigorous changes, the fronting and raising of (aw), the fronting and raising of checked (eyC), and the centralization of voiceless (ay0). For each vowel, the regression coefficients and significance are shown for a selected range of independent variables.

The signs of the coefficients are re-assigned in this table to register the relation to the change. Positive means favoring the original direction of the change, negative means disfavoring it. For sex, positive means favoring females, negative means favoring males.

From these figures we can see that women lead in the raising of (aw) and checked (eyC), and men in the centralization of (ay0), a result confirmed in several parallel studies. The curvilinear pattern that is the principal hypothesis of the study is illustrated in the coefficients for occupation. For the new and vigorous changes, the most advanced speakers and the greatest rate of change in apparent time is found among upper working-class speakers with skilled occupations. Unskilled workers and unemployed are the reference level for the stepwise regression; they lag behind, along with the upper occupational groups. Consistent with this are the coefficients for upward and downward mobility, which respectively favor and disfavor changes in progress. The stigmatized character of (æhN) is shown by the increasing negative coefficients with higher occupational classes.

In Figure 19.9 the age coefficients are used to display graphically the relative rate of change in apparent time of all vowels in the system. A vector is drawn through the mean value for each vowel, with the head of the arrow showing the expected value for speakers 25 years younger than the mean, and the tail the expected values for speakers 25 years older than the mean. The thickness of the arrow represents the significance of the coefficients. Here the completed changes like (ahr) show no vectors at all; mid-range changes like the fronting of (ow) show small vectors; the new and vigorous change (aw), (eyC), and (ay0) are represented by the largest arrows; and new and incipient changes like the lowering of (e) show barely significant effects.

Displays such as Figure 19.9 provide the necessary background for the interpretation of individual variation such as that shown for Carol Meyers in Figure 19.6.

Individual versus Particular Explanations.

In recent years, there has been a powerful tendency to provide "universal" explanations for phonetic variation, even when only a few examples in a small number of languages have been available. Whether or not this practice is fruitful, the types of variation discussed above indicate that we are most likely to arrive at general tendencies which interact with each other, rather

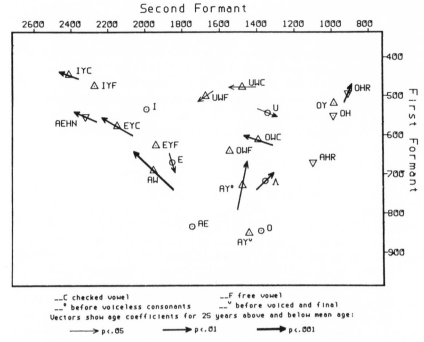

FIG. 19.9. Change of Philadelphia vowels in apparent time: Mean values & age vectors for 116 neighborhood speakers.

than absolute universals that uniquely determine the direction or extent of variation.

The Northern Cities Shift and Southern Shift discussed above conform to general principles of chain shifting that govern the behavior of vowels over a wide range of languages and language families. In chain shifts, tense or long vowels rise; lax or short nuclei fall; and back nuclei move to the front (Labov, Yaeger & Steiner, 1972). There are no clear exceptions to the first principle. Yet in Philadelphia, we can see that the course of the Southern Shift has been interrupted, and a retrograde movement set in motion. The fronting and raising of (eyC) reverses the centralization and lowering of /ey/ which dominated Philadelphia speech before World War II. It is now one of the most vigorous elements in the Philadelphia series of sound changes.

In the raising of (aeh) in the Northern Cities, we generally find that following velars are associated with lower F_2 positions and a more conservative overall position of words like *bag* and *smack* in the sound change. But in Chicago, we have the reverse (Callary, 1975; Labov, In press); following velars are among the most advanced elements in the change. Other examples of such language-specific reversals of expectation will be cited in the discussion of discrete phonological variables to follow.

PHONOLOGICAL VARIATION

Most of the analyses of variation in the past two decades have been concerned with binary data at a more abstract level than the continuous phonetic variation already discussed. On the phonological level, these concern the deletion or insertion, shortenings and lengthenings, and monophthongization and diphthongization of segments. The variation concerns the frequency distribution of the phenomena. Probabilistic models and stochastic concepts are required, based upon the closed algebras of formal linguistics. But the same issues arise as in the previous section: accuracy of measurement, sources of error, reliability of controlled styles versus spontaneous speech, and the utility of universal principles versus general tendencies that interact in language-specific ways. I will briefly discuss one such process that has been studied in detail: the simplification of final consonant clusters in English.

These studies require multivariate analyses, since the variation is conditioned by a variety of phonological, grammatical, and social factors. Special techniques for the analysis of linguistic variation have been developed to take into account two particular properties of linguistic structure. First, it is impossible to fill all cells of a matrix for an ANOVA-type analysis, since in principle most intersections of linguistic features will be empty. Secondly, internal linguistic constraints typically show independent behavior, and the working assumption of independence can be used to test the fit of the model to the observations. The VARBRUL programs of Sankoff and Labov (Sankoff & Labov, 1979) have been the major tools used in the analysis of linguistic variation, though in recent years principle component analyses, multidimensional scaling, and other transformations have been introduced. The VAR-BRUL programs are iterative maximum likelihood algorithms that derive the overall probability of a rule application from a model combining the independent contributions of mutually exclusive groups of environmental factors. In recent years, VARBRUL programs have been expanded to include techniques for selecting significant factors through stepwise regression on the output; to handle trinary as well as binary data; to discover any divisions of the speech community that will improve the likelihood of the analysis.

The Group and the Individual

Early reactions to reports of inherent variation showed that it was difficult for many linguists to absorb the concept of a random variable and to accept the existence of inherent variation. One positive result of these discussions was the stimulus to publish more data on the behavior of individuals, to permit closer comparison of the individuals and the group. A number of such studies have shown that the individual generally mirrors the pattern of the community.

TABLE 19.3

Comparison of Group and Individual Factor
Probabilities for Philadelphia $-$T,D Deletion

	Joanne H.	19 Philadelphians
Number of tokens	566	2886
Input probability	.93	.87
Following segment		
obstuent	1.00	1.00
liquid	.75	.77
vowel	.21	.40
pause	.04	.19
Grammatical status		
monomorphemic	1.00	1.00
ambiguous	.87	.97
past	.10	.44

^{a}From Guy (1980).

Table 19.3 is from Guy's (1980) study of $-$t,d deletion in New York and Philadelphia. The left column is a study of Joanne H., an individual who was recorded over an extended period, like Carol Myers. The figures represent the contributions of individual factors to the probability P of deletion applying in the multiplicative application model:

$$P = p(0) \times p(1) \times p(2) \ldots p(n)$$

where P is the probability of the application of the rule in any particular case, $p(0)$ is an input probability and the various $p(i)$ represent the weighting for the factor present in each mutually exclusive set: the following segment, grammatical status, etc. The right column shows a group run that combines 19 speakers who were recorded in single interviews with more limited data. It is evident that the individual and the group follow similar patterns in the

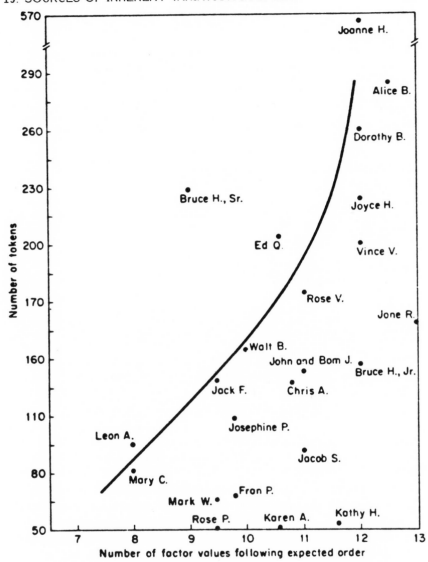

FIG. 19.10.   Relation of frequency of individual cells to agreement with community norms for −t, d deletion in Philadelphia (from Guy, 1980).

ordering of factors within each group. Fluctuations as with any random variable are related to sample size. Figure 19.10 shows the relation of sample size for each individual analysis to the degree of agreement with the community norm. The vertical axis shows the amount of data for each individual: the number of consonant clusters that could be simplified by the process. The

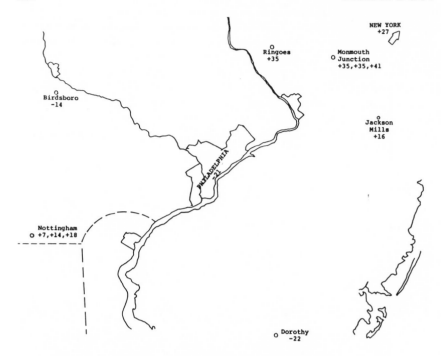

FIG. 19.11.   Differences between effects of following pause and vowel on
—t, d deletion for six towns in Pennsylvania and New Jersey.

horizontal axis shows the number of environmental effects—like the effect of
the following segment—which agreed with those found in the majority of the
speakers examined and predicted by the general theory. Other studies show
that the actual probability weights themselves converge to a single value as
sample size increases.

Language-specific and Universal Constraints. All studies of final consonant
deletion deal with the influence of the first consonant of the next word, if
one follows. They all show a tendency to simplify syllable structure, so
that deletion is favored more by a following obstruent that a following vowel
(Guy, 1980). The intermediate position of liquids and glides depends upon
their articulation, but in general the result can be predicted by the tendency
to simplify consonant clusters in the direction of a CVC or CV syllable.
Whether this in turn is controlled more by articulatory difficulty or acoustic
salience remains to be determined.

Most studies also report on the effect of a following pause. Here there is
no single prediction to be made from phonetic theory. Consonant clusters
can be articulated more easily by releasing the last member; thus following
pause should disfavor deletion. On the other hand, a final consonant can

be assimilated to silence, and in this sense it can be argued that pause will favor deletion. Apparently this ambiguous situation holds for native speakers as well as linguists, since we find widespread variation across dialects. Figure 19.11 shows the geographic variation in the effect of final pause as we proceed from New York to Philadelphia. The figure show the difference between the probability contributed by pause and by a following vowel. Individual communities are quite stable, but across communities there is a gradient. In New York, final pause is treated more like an obstruent. In Philadelphia and the surrounding region, final pause constrains deletion even more than a vowel does.

OVERVIEW

This review has pointed to a number of sources of variation in speech production and in the underlying linguistic structures. Errors in measurement and perception must be considered at every level of analysis. When these are controlled, there appears a fine-grained phonetic variation, where neighboring articulations jointly influence each other. There is a consistent pattern of variation that is the result of differences in stress and timing, so that different articulation come closer than others to the normative targets. These targets themselves vary, producing additional sources of variation. In the early stages of change in progress, there will be continuous shifts of target norms with the age of the speaker; in later stages, there may be discrete shifts of norms as older speakers imitate younger norms, as stigmatized forms are corrected to prestige patterns, and speakers adopt multiple norms for a given phoneme.

Consistent patterns of variation are found in more abstract rules of the language, which assign category status or control the realization of forms at a lower level. The structure of the underlying process can be traced by estimations of the probability of rule application and the contribution to that probability of individual features of the environment.

Paul Kiparsky: Comment

What is the site of the orderly variation discovered by Labov in the application of optional rules? There are two possible answers. One view, which I believe Labov has held for many years, is that the patterning of variation is an irreducible statistical component of linguistic knowledge. The other is that it results from speakers striving (whether unconsciously or consciously) to optimize their speech according to the kinds of functional considerations we have discussed at this conference:

simplifying their articulation, making their output maximally comprehensible, and taking account of whatever social values they discover are attached to the various options—goals which may be weighted in different ways depending on the circumstances. From these, the speakers, as it were, compute a result which yields the kind of systematic statistical picture that is observed in the speech community.

To pose the question so sharply is of course an oversimplification. Probably no one would endorse the second view without certain qualifications. For one thing, it may be that the variation starts in language use but eventually becomes encoded in the grammar at some point and begins to lead a life of its own there. Secondly, it may be that a speaker has to learn such things as the basic frequency of a rule from observation and superimposes on it the functionally governed pattern of inherent variation.

Recent work, most of it by Labov himself and his associates, suggests to me that the second view with these qualifications is still an excellent bet. A priori it is certainly the preferable position, because it implies limits on possible variation. One fact which supports it is that very little dialectal variation has been found in this domain. If you have a speech community where an optional deletion of final consonants is favored if the following word begins with a consonant, you won't find another in which it is the other way round.

Moreover, one can give fairly plausible explanations for the kinds of patterns that have been observed. For example, the frequency with which final [t] drops in New York and Philadelphia was found to depend on the nature of the following consonant: There is deletion most often when the following word begins with an obstruent, less often before a liquid, still less often before a glide, and least of all before a vowel. As Raj Singh has pointed out, this immediately recalls the sonority hierarchy that has been proposed as a universal basis for syllable structure, suggesting that deletion applies to syllable-final stops, so that the likelihood with which a consonant is deleted depends among other things on the likelihood with which it is resyllabified with the onset of the next word, this being in turn determined by sonority.

There is apparent counterevidence, but it needs to be looked at more closely. For example, in the t-deletion case, the behavior of the prepausal environment seems problematic. In New York, pauses favor deletion like obstruents, but in Philadelphia there is even less deletion before pauses than there is before vowels.[1] Do we have a case of irreducibly arbitrary patterns of variation? Perhaps, but these facts alone do not establish it. Suppose for example that deletion effects stops which are unreleased (hence syllable-final) and that New York and Philadelphia differ in whether stops are released before pause. If stops in Philadelphia are released before pause, they are not candidates for deletion and therefore show maximal stability. In any case it is worth keeping in mind that apparently chaotic patterns of variation may result from the interaction of general principles with rules of grammar. Until that avenue of explanation is exhausted, it would be premature to ascribe variation to a statistical component of grammatical knowledge.

---

[1] See the study by G. Guy cited in Labov's paper.

W. Labov: Response

Kiparsky's remarks direct us to the central question in our thinking about variation: how much of the variance is to be attributed to general principles of human physiology or psychology, and how much is the result of historical—that is, social—events? Kiparsky's own thinking has consistently directed out attention to the former, with good reason: linguistic analysis fundamentally concerned with extracting redundancy from linguistic description. Furthermore, historical and social explanations will necessarily yield the right of way to physiological explanations, if they can be found.

Yet we would all agree that an accurate and useful description of a language must strike the right balance of general and particular statements. We have to take into account the ways that speech communities have exploited the choices open to them through the historical patterns of settlement, in-migration and commerce. The problem takes on a particularly pressing form for speaker-independent speech recognition projects. If the diversity of American vowel systems were entirely the result of general laws of development, a recognition algorithm could be constructed by applying the inverse of these laws. Our current view of the English vowel systems (Labov in press) shows that the major dialect areas have become increasingly differentiated over the past century by the operation of chain shifts in opposing directions, with opposing developments of glides and targets. Whether a single base form can be constructed for such diverse vowel systems is still a remote possibility, but it seems more likely that distinct templates have to be made available to a recognition device.

The probabilities associated with consonant cluster simplification may also be useful in speech recognition. From the outset, we have been sensitive to the application of Saussure's sonority hierarchy to the effect of a following segment on $-t,d$ deletion in English. A single set of instructions should give a recognition routine the optimal predictions for the effect of the following segment on deletion. But there is no general explanation that will unambiguously predict the effect of pause. It follows that the effect of a pause on consonant cluster simplification is available for specific dialect differentiation. The fact that we have found dialect diversity in this area does not contradict the importance of general explanations, but rather complements it. Kiparsky's suggestion on consonant release is an important one. We have not yet found any major differences in consonant release between New York and Philadelphia. The study of consonant release, and its relation to resyllabification, is part of our current program for better understanding of dialect diversity in American English.

20 Toward a Phonetic and Phonological Theory of Redundant Features

Kenneth N. Stevens, Samuel Jay Keyser, and Haruko Kawasaki
Center for Cognitive Science and
Research Laboratory of Electronics
Massachusetts Institute of Technology

INTRODUCTION

This study investigates the role of redundant features in natural language. When a certain feature marks a distinction in a language, one or more "redundant" features may accompany that feature. Examples are discussed that suggest that certain types of redundant features strengthen the acoustic representation of distinctive features and contribute additional properties that help the listener to perceive the distinction. Some specific hypotheses are then set forth regarding the properties of redundant features and of distinctive features enhanced by redundancy. For example, it is hypothesized that only certain feature pairings play a role in this enhancement process, and that these pairings or linkings are determined by the properties of the speech-production and perception systems; that enhancement by redundant features can be realized in a continuous rather than quantal fashion; and that redundant features are more likely to come into play when the perceptual distinctions signalled by distinctive features are weak. It is further hypothesized that the linking of features for the purpose of enhancement plays an important role in determining the morphophonemic alternations in language.

DISTINCTIVE FEATURES AND REDUNDANCY

There exists a small set of 20-odd phonetic features that are available for signalling distinctions between words in language (Chomsky & Halle, 1968a; Jakobson, Fant, & Halle, 1963; Jakobson and Waugh, 1979; Ladefoged, 1975). These features are normally organized into bundles that form segments, and words are constituted from sequences of segments or from matrices of features. These features serve the function of organizing segments into classes. Our point of view is that, when a word is spoken, a particular acoustic property appears in the sound whenever a given feature is being used to identify the word, and thus to distinguish it from other words. This acoustic property is invariant in the sense that it is independent of the context of other features and segments in which the given feature occurs.

The acoustic properties that are used to define the inventory of features are determined by the characteristics of the human auditory system and of the speech-generating system. There are some acoustic properties to which the auditory system responds in a distinctive way, and there are certain acoustic properties that the speech-production mechanism is capable of generating without requiring excessive precision in the control of the articulatory structures (Stevens, 1972). For example, forming a complete closure in the vocal tract and then releasing that closure gives rise to an abrupt increase in amplitude of the sound over a range of frequencies, and the auditory system seems to respond in a distinctive way to this kind of abrupt amplitude change, in contrast to a more gradual change. Thus, a clear distinction can be made between continuant consonants such as [f, s, v, z] and stop consonants such as [p, t, b, d]. Or, when a vowel is formed with a fronted position for the tongue body, the second-formant frequency is high and close to the third formant, whereas for a backed tongue-body position, the second formant is low and close to the first. It has been postulated that there is a critical separation of two formants that divides vowel-like stimuli into two classes that give rise to two distinct kinds of auditory response (Chistovich & Lublinskaya, 1979). These are just two examples of the role played by these quantal principles in establishing an inventory of features.

While all of the 20-odd features are used distinctively in different languages, any given language does not employ all of the features to signal distinctions between words, and certainly does not use the features in all combinations. In principle, assuming 20 features, then 2^{20} combinations of these features are possible, but any one language uses only a small fraction of these combinations. A consequence is that there is a potential for redundancy (Jakobson, Fant, & Halle 1963; Jakobson & Waugh 1979). That is, it is possible that a minimal distinction between words can be carried not by not just one feature but by some combination of features. This redundancy could provide the listener with additional acoustic cues that could be used to reduce the possible confusion between words, particularly in situations in which there is noise or in which the speech is not clear for some other reason.

Among the approximately 2^{20} combinations of features that are theoretically possible, some cannot occur simply because of constraints on the sound-generating system. That is, some acoustic properties cannot be produced unless others are produced at the same time. For example, the generation of a nasal vowel or consonant (i.e., a segment with the feature [+nasal]) requires that negligible pressure be built up in the vocal tract (i.e., the feature [+sonorant]). In other words, the feature [+sonorant] is required if the sound is to contain the property that indicates the feature [+nasal]. As another example, the feature [strident] can only operate to signal a distinction in segments that are [−sonorant]. That is, it is necessary to build up pressure behind a constriction in order to provide an acoustic property appropriate for the feature [+strident]. These kinds of redundancy are inherent in the speech-production process, and a speaker has little freedom as to whether or not to implement them. They are also inherent in the speech-perception process since the detection of one of the features (e.g., [nasal]) requires that other features (e.g., [sonorant]) be present to act as a carrier for the feature. Ascribed to such physiological and perceptual constraints, this type of redundancy should be and indeed is observed cross-linguistically.

The redundancy just discussed is rooted in the intrinsic nature of the vocal tract and the auditory system. It is impossible for one feature to be implemented unless a second feature or feature-set is implemented. There is, however, another kind of redundancy which takes advantage of the fact, noted above, that languages select only a subset of the available combinations of distinctive features. In other words, some features are redundant in particular contexts by virtue of their not having been selected to do distinctive duty in some language. For example, the feature [back] is not distinctive for the system of obstruent consonants in English. Do such features simply remain unused or does the speech-perception process and the phonological system make use of them in some systematic way? It is suggested that features which have become available in this fashion can be used to enhance the perceptual cues for distinctive features in a given language. In the process of achieving this goal of strengthening the existing acoustic property, the redundant feature results in the introduction of a new acoustic property that co-occurs with the already present property, or may, in some contexts, exist in place of the property associated with the distinctive feature.

As will be seen below, enhancement by redundant features of the primary distinctions marked by distinctive features takes a variety of forms. There appear to be some classes of distinctive features that require the help of redundant features and others that do not. Such classes of features need to be identified and accounted for, and the mechanisms whereby enhancement is achieved through the introduction of redundant features needs to be clarified. Furthermore, exploring the ways in which redundant features interact with distinctive features may help to clarify the motivations for some synchronic patterns and historical changes which are not readily accounted for by current phonological theory.

EXAMPLES OF REDUNDANCY
AS AN ENHANCING MECHANISM

Below are examples of cases where redundant features are utilized for enhancing primary distinctions. We describe four of these examples in some detail, and then list a few additional examples with only a brief discussion of each.

Enhancement of [back]

We define the feature [back] by beginning with a neutral configuration of the tongue body in the front-back dimension, illustrated in Figure 20.1a. The spectrum envelope for a vowel with this vocal-tract configuration is shown in Figure 20.1b. The second formant is midway between the first and the third. Fronting or backing of the tongue body while maintaining the tongue height about the same causes a raising or lowering of the frequency of the second formant, and the effect on the overall spectrum shape is shown in the figure. When the tongue body is displaced back in the mouth, the second formant moves downward in frequency, and becomes closer to the first than to the third formant, as the figure shows. The result is a valley in the spectrum between F_1 and F_2 that is not as deep as it was for the more neutral configuration, a weaker spectral peak for F_3, and a deeper valley in the spectrum between F_2 and F_3. On the other hand, a forward movement of the tongue body in the mouth leads to a deeper valley in the spectrum between F_1 and F_2, a shallower valley between F_2 and F_3, and a raising of the amplitude of the spectral peaks corresponding to F_2 and F_3 (and possibly F_4). The second formant F_2 has an affinity with F_1 for back vowels and with F_3 (and F_4) for front vowels.

For the nonlow vowels—i.e., for a nonlow position for the tongue body—backward displacement of the tongue body, without lip rounding, leads to a modest lowering of F_2. However, F_2 still remains some distance away from F_1—the difference is in the range 560–800 Hz. This separation of F_1 and F_2 can be observed for the unrounded back vowels [ɯ] and [ʌ] in Figure 20.2, which shows formant frequencies for several rounded and unrounded vowels in Korean (Han, 1963). A further lowering of F_2—i.e., a further decrease in the distance between F_2 and F_1—can be achieved by rounding the lips. Formant frequencies for these rounded back vowels are also shown in Figure 20.2, and we see that the spacing between F_2 and F_1 is reduced by 300 Hz or more by rounding. Thus the acoustic property corresponding to the feature [+back]—i.e., a closer proximity of F_2 to F_1 than to F_3—is enhanced by the feature [+round] for these nonlow vowels. The effect of rounding on the spectrum of a back vowel is illustrated in Figure 20.1c. It is suggested that introduction of the feature [+round] brings F_2 and F_1 close enough that

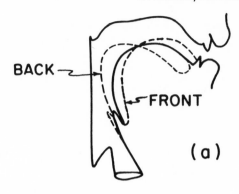

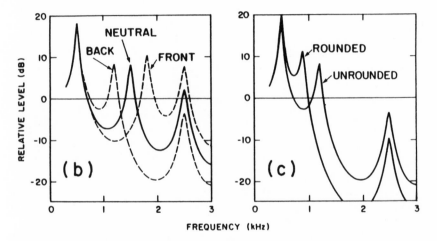

FIG. 20.1. (a) Schematization of midsagittal section of vocal tract for
a neutral vowel (solid contour), and for a back and front tongue-body
position. (b) Idealized spectrum envelopes corresponding to the three
tongue-body configurations in (a). (c) Approximate effect of lip rounding
on the spectrum envelope for a back vowel. (A small downward shift in
F_1 that could also accompany rounding is not shown.)

the two-peaked spectral prominence caused by these formants is interpreted
by the auditory system as a single peak whose frequency is at the center
of gravity of the prominence, as proposed by Chistovich and Lublinskaya
(1979). The feature [round], then, can effect an enhancement of the feature
[back] for these nonlow vowels.

For vowels that are [+high], additional factors can come into play to enhance the front-back distinction. Vowels having the feature [+high] are characterized by a low first-formant frequency and by a high tongue-body position

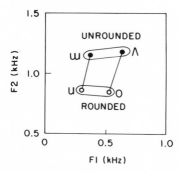

FIG. 20.2. First and second formant frequencies for two unrounded (closed circles) and two rounded (open circles) back vowels in Korean. (Data from Han, 1963.)

that forms a relatively narrow constriction in the oral portion of the vocal tract. For a vowel that is [+high, −back], F_2 is close to F_3, and both F_2 and F_3 can be increased still further by raising the tongue blade against the roof of the mouth. The front part of the tongue forms a narrow channel with the hard palate, and this configuration causes F_3 to come close to F_4. Thus the "center of gravity" of the broad spectral peak formed by F_2, F_3, and F_4 becomes quite high, between F_3 and F_4 (Carlson, Fant, and Granström 1975). The spectrum resulting from this relatively extreme tongue configuration is shown in the left panel in Figure 20.3. Raising of the tongue blade is the articulatory correlate of the feature [+coronal]. In effect, then, we are using the feature [+coronal] to enhance the feature [−back] for high vowels. The acoustic consequence of this enhancing feature is to produce a diffuse and upward sloping spectrum at high frequencies, similar to the acoustic correlate of [+coronal] for stop consonants (Blumstein & Stevens, 1979).

In the case of [+high, +back] vowels, the feature [+back] can be enhanced by rounding the lips as discussed above. Even further lowering of F_2 toward F_1 can be achieved by greater narrowing of the lip opening, i.e., by introducing the feature [+labial]. The spectrum for the vowel with these properties is shown in the right panel of Figure 20.3. The diffuse and downward sloping spectrum that results is similar to the acoustic correlate of [+labial] for stop consonants. Thus the feature [+labial] (as well as [+round]) is used to enhance the feature [+back] for high vowels.

Enhancement of [distributed] and [anterior]

The feature [distributed] appears to be distinctive in some languages for consonants that are [+coronal], i.e., consonants that are produced by raising the tongue blade. From the point of view of articulation, a [-distributed]

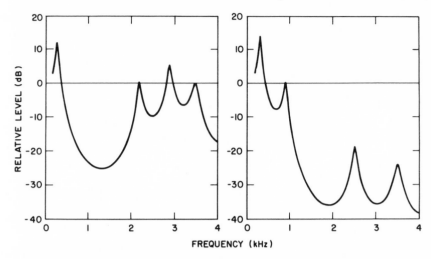

FIG. 20.3. Idealized spectrum envelopes for a high front vowel (left), and a high back rounded vowel (right).

consonant is formed by making a constriction with the apex or tip of the tongue, so that the constriction is quite short. On the other hand, a more extended area of the surface of the tongue blade is used to form the constriction for a [+distributed] consonant, and the length of the constricted region is somewhat greater. This distinction is sometimes called apical/laminal. A dental or palatal consonant is laminal or [+distributed], whereas an alveolar or retroflex consonant is apical or [-distributed]. Drawings that schematize these different configurations of the tongue blade are given in Figure 20.4.

Release of the short apical constriction, involving only movement of the tongue tip, is presumably accomplished much more rapidly than release of the longer laminal constriction. The apical release can be accomplished by a forward and downward movement of only the front part of the tongue blade, whereas the laminal release requires a downward movement of a substantial part of the tongue, including the tongue body. Acoustically, the apical release shows a much more abrupt onset than does the laminal release. This abruptness is a consequence of the very rapid increase in size and decrease in acoustic impedance (proportional to ratio of constriction length to constriction area), which causes a very rapid rise in the frequency of the first formant (F_1), probably of just a few msec duration. The laminal release is slower and the constriction is longer, and, as a consequence, the rise in F_1 would tend to be slower. This slow release and slow rise in F_1 leads to a relatively slow increase in amplitude following the release.

This difference in the release characteristics is illustrated in Figure 20.5, which shows waveforms and spectrograms at the release of the so-called den-

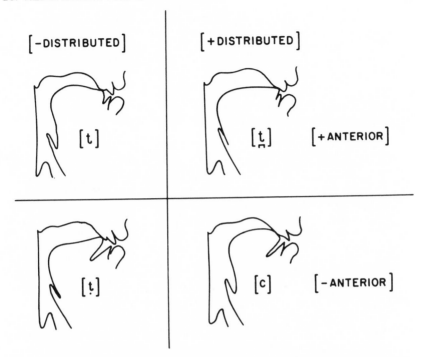

FIG. 20.4.   Schematized versions of midsagittal sections showing positions of the tongue blade for several coronal consonants. The two sketches on the right represent laminal consonants (i.e., [+distributed]), and the two on the left are apical (i.e., [−distributed]). The anterior-nonanterior distinction is schematized on the two rows. The estimates of the configurations in the vicinity of the tongue blade and tongue tip are based on midsagittal sketches and other articulatory data reported by Perkell (1969) (for [t]), Ladefoged and Bhaskararao (1983) and Wierzchowska (1965) (for [t̪]), Perkell, Boyce, and Stevens (1979) (for the palatoalveolar configuration), and Dixon (1980) (who shows sketches of all four configurations). The tongue-body shape posterior to the tongue blade has been estimated, with the constraint that the midsagittal length of the dorsal tongue surface is about the same in all cases. This constraint results in a more backed tongue body for the upper-right and lower-left configurations than for the other two. These estimated tongue-body shapes are also based on acoustic data of the type shown in Figure 20.6 and described in the text. There are differences in the positioning of the lateral surfaces of the tongue blade that are not shown in these midsagittal sections.

tal (laminal) and alveolar (apical) consonants [t̪] and [t], which contrast in Malayalam) (Ladefoged, 1971) and in a number of Australian languages (Dixon, 1980). The slightly faster rise in F_1 for the apical is evident from the spectrogram and the more abrupt rise in amplitude followed immediately by a decay can be seen on the waveform for the apical. Similar acoustic properties can be seen for the palatal stop consonant [c], which is [+distributed]

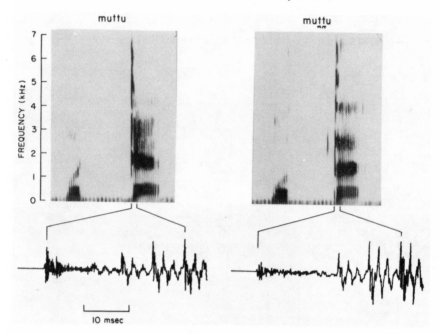

FIG. 20.5.   These spectrograms and waveforms show the distinction between dental [t] and apical [t] in Malayalam. The waveforms at the bottom
illustrate the difference in abruptness of the release for the two consonants.
The spectrograms above illustrate differences in F_2 immediately preceding and following the consonantal closure, indicating a difference in tongue
body position for the two classes of consonants.

and the retroflex [t], which is [−distributed], as well as for the corresponding
pairs of nasal consonants.

Closer examination of the acoustic data for distributed and nondistributed
consonants reveals that another property comes into play for the distribu-
ted/nondistributed contrast, and we interpret this additional property to be
the result of. the introduction of enhancing or redundant features. In the
spectrograms in Figure 20.5, we observe marked differences in the frequency
of F_2 immediately preceding the implosion and also immediately following
the release. F_2 is considerably higher for the [−distributed] alveolar than for
the [+distributed] dental, reflecting a more fronted tongue-body position for
the [−distributed] member of the pair. Examples of data from measurements
of F_2 at four points preceding and following the closure, for several different
utterances, are shown in Figure 20.6 for three speakers. The kinds of differences shown in Figure 20.6, as well as the release characteristics illustrated
in Figure 20.5, have been observed in many examples of intervocalic stops
and nasals produced by Malayalam speakers.

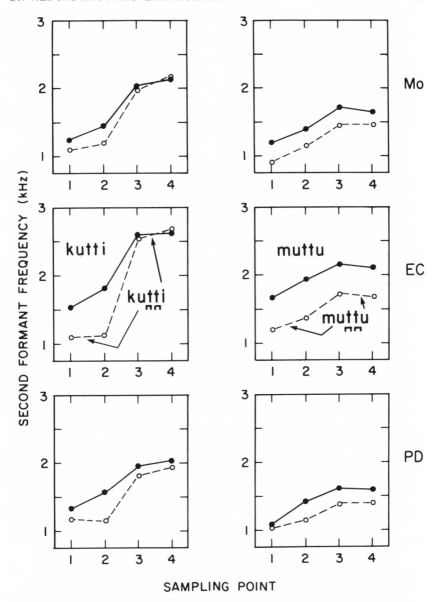

SECOND FORMANT FREQUENCY (kHz)

SAMPLING POINT

FIG. 20.6. Data on second formant frequency sampled at four points preceding and following the consonantal closure for the word pairs [kutti-kutti] (left) and [muttu-muttu] (right) in Malayalam, spoken by two male speakers and one female (EC). Each point represents average data from two utterances. The sampling points are: (1) 30 msec prior to consonant closure; (2) as consonant closure; (3) at onset of voicing; (4) 30 msec after onset of voicing.

We suggest, then, that the feature [back] is playing an enhancing role for these coronal consonants: [+back] enhances [+distributed] and [−back] enhances [−distributed]. A fronted tongue-body presumably provides a favorable posture from which the apico-alveolar constriction can be achieved, whereas a backed tongue-body position provides a posture that favors formation of the dental or interdental constriction. Formation of the dental or interdental constriction requires that lateral edges of the tongue blade make contact with the alveolar ridge over an extended region from the central incisors to the molars. This mode of contact in turn can be achieved more readily if the surface of the tongue blade is lowered. Since the tongue is a noncompressible mass, this tongue blade lowering may only take place if the tongue-body is displaced backward. The sketches in Figure 20.4 show how these configurations might appear in the midline. They indicate more backed tongue-body configurations for [t̪] than for [t].

We conclude from these observations that the feature) [back] is introduced to enhance the feature [distributed] for these coronal consonants. Not shown in Figure 20.6 are data indicating a small but consistent difference between F_1 at points 3 and 4 (following the release) for the apical and laminal consonants, with F_1 for the apical being lower. We interpret this difference as indicating a slightly higher tongue-body position for the apical. (The sketches in Figure 20.4 reflect this difference.)

In several Australian languages, there is a series of four coronal consonants, defined by the two features [distributed] and [anterior] (Dixon 1980). For a [−anterior] consonant, the constriction formed by the tongue blade is posterior to the alveolar ridge, and is produced in such a way as to create a space under the tongue blade, as shown in Figure 20.4 above, leading to a low-frequency resonance of the acoustic cavity in front of the constriction. This resonance usually appears to be associated with the third formant of the adjacent vowel. Thus, for example, the languages Kaititj and Alyawarra have two [+distributed] stop consonants: a [+anterior] consonant [t̪] and a [−anterior]) consonant [c]. Spectrograms illustrating these two consonants are shown in Figure 20.7. Acoustic analysis shows that there is a strong F_3 peak in the noise for the [c], in relation to the corresponding spectral peak for the vowel, but this peak (and in fact the entire burst) is weaker for the [t̪]. Two other acoustic properties are evident, however, in addition to the property corresponding to the feature [anterior]. First, the palatal stop is affricated, so that it has a [+strident] component. Second, the second formant at the onset of the vowel is much higher for the palatal than it is for the dental. This acoustic property can be taken as evidence that the palatal is [−back] whereas the dental is [+back]. These properties are evident in many exemplars of these consonants in different contexts. We have already provided an articulatory rationale for the backness of dental configurations. Fronting of the tongue-body for palatal configurations permits the tongue

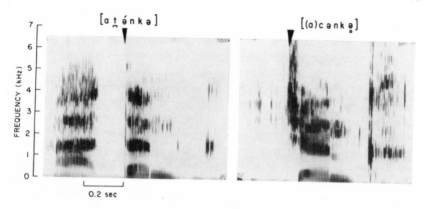

FIG. 20.7. Spectrograms of the words [at 'ənkə] (top) and [(a)cənkə̥] produced by a speaker of Kaititj. These spectrograms illustrate the contrast [±anterior] for these two laminal consonants. The stop release for the [t] and [c] are indicated by arrows at the top of the spectrograms. We thank Peter Ladefoged for making available the recording from which this spectrogram was made.

blade to bunch up into the palatal arch, as Figure 20.4 shows. We surmise, then, that the features [strident] and [back] are playing an enhancing role to provide additional perceptual cues for the feature [anterior] for the [+distributed] consonants. We shall observe later that the role of [back] in enhancing [anterior] has consequences in certain alternations that occur in Lardil, another Australian language.

Enhancement of the Voiced-voiceless Distinction

The basic acoustic correlate of the distinction voiced/voiceless is usually considered to be the presence or absence of low-frequency periodicity in the sound. Vocal-fold vibration is maintained by appropriately adjusting the configuration and state of the vocal folds and by creating a flow of air through the glottis. For example, the low-frequency periodicity usually is observed during the labial closure interval for *rabid* but not for *rapid.* We restrict our discussion here to the voiced/voiceless distinction for consonants, where there appears to be an opportunity for several redundant features to play a role in enhancing this property that signals the presence or absence of low-frequency periodicity due to vocal-fold vibration.

One of the enhancing mechanisms is the feature of length. The feature [-voice] can be enhanced by increasing the duration over which there is lack of low-frequency periodicity. This increased duration of the closure interval for a voiceless consonant relative to that for a voiced consonant has been observed (Peterson & Lehiste, 1960), and is known to provide a cue for distinguishing word pairs like *rapid-rabid* (Lisker, 1957). On the other hand, the duration of the vowel preceding a voiceless consonant can be decreased relative to that for a voiced consonant, again enhancing the property corresponding to the feature [−voice] (Denes, 1955; House & Fairbanks, 1953). This effect is especially strong when the voiceless consonant is in utterance-final position. Both of these duration changes increase the proportion of the syllable duration within which there is lack of low-frequency periodicity. It is assumed that the perception of voicelessness is enhanced if there is an increase in the relative duration of the portion of the syllable without low-frequency periodicity. (See, for example, Port, 1981a and Port & Dalby, 1982.)

Another feature that is available to enhance [−voice] is [+spread glottis]. Adjusting the configuration of the vocal folds so that they are abducted along much of their length can contribute to the inhibition of vocal-fold vibration during the constricted interval. If the glottis is spread at the instant of release of the consonantal constriction, then aspiration noise will occur for a period of time (usually a few tens of msec) until the vocal folds are maneuvered to a more adducted configuration for which vocal-fold vibration is possible. Thus the time interval within which no vocal-fold vibration occurs extends a few tens of msec beyond the release of the constriction (Lisker & Abramson, 1964), and the property of lack of low-frequency periodicity is enhanced. This mode of enhancement is effective in syllable- or word-initial position for which there may not be an opportunity to use a lengthened voiceless interval prior to consonant release as a means to enhance [−voice]. In word-initial position in English, the presence or absence of low-frequency periodicity does not distinguish between voiced or voiceless stops (e.g., [pel] and [bel]). This is a case, then, where an enhancing feature (aspiration or [spread glottis] in this example) provides the primary acoustic evidence, and the acoustic property corresponding to the underlying distinctive feature is not present. (Phonological arguments, for example the plural rule in English, argue for the view that it is voicing which is distinctive in English, and not aspiration.)

Vocal-fold vibration during the closure interval can also be inhibited by increasing the stiffness of the vocal folds. With increased stiffness of the vocal folds, greater pressure across the glottis is needed to initiate vibration. This increased stiffness is usually achieved by increasing the length of the vocal folds, thereby stretching them. Evidence for this increased stiffness comes from examination of the fundamental frequency (F_0) immediately following the release of a voiceless consonant (cf. House & Fairbanks, 1953; Jeel, 1975; Lehiste & Peterson, 1961; Löfqvist, 1975; Slis & Cohen, 1969). For many languages, there is an increased F_0 during the first few glottal periods following the release of a voiceless consonant, but not for a voiced consonant. Thus the feature [+stiff vocal folds] (or a feature similar to this that causes a raised F_0 during a vowel) acts as an enhancing feature for [−voice] for obstruent consonants.

Enhancement of the feature [+voice] can be achieved by increasing the amplitude of the low-frequency sound during the constricted interval, thus increasing the audibility of the low-frequency periodicity. In the case of stop consonants, this increased amplitude can be obtained by opening the velopharyngeal port during the initial part of the closure interval. That is, the feature [+sonorant] is introduced to enhance [+voice], and the [sonorant] feature is implemented with [+nasal]. The resulting nasal murmur has a higher amplitude at low frequencies than does the normal prevoicing that results from sound transmission through the neck tissues. During the latter part of the closure interval, the velopharyngeal port is closed so that intraoral pressure can be built up to obtain the appropriate obstruent release. This prenasalization is used in the production of the intervocalic voiced stops [d] and [g] in the Tosa dialect of Japanese. In the Tokyo and other dialects, the opposition between [k] and [g] is sometimes realized intervocalically as that between [k] and [ŋ]. In this instance as well, the distinctive feature) [+voiced] is enhanced by the redundant feature [+nasal] (Kawasaki, 1981; Oishi & Uemura, 1975).

In the prenasalized example just given, the low-frequency amplitude of the sound is increased by preventing a buildup of intraoral pressure during a portion of the closure interval for the consonant. Significant pressure buildup can also be prevented either by expanding the volume of the vocal tract during the closure interval, or by not making a complete oral closure, thus allowing air to pass through the constriction. While this method enhances the audibility of the low-frequency periodicity, it also reduces or even eliminates the friction noise that occurs at the consonant release. The reduction of intraoral pressure during the closure interval can be viewed as another consequence of the introduction of the feature [+sonorant].

Enhancement of [continuant] by [strident]

The acoustic correlate of the feature [−continuant] is a relatively abrupt onset of sound pressure, preceded by an interval in which the sound pressure is relatively low. Thus for a consonantal segment characterized by the feature [+continuant], there is some acoustic energy in the constricted interval for the consonant, and possibly an onset that is not so abrupt. For the feature [+strident], the acoustic correlate is a relatively high level of turbulence noise, so that in some part of the high-frequency range the noise exceeds the level of the vowel. The production of stridency is achieved by directing a rapid air stream against some obstacle, thus creating an increased level of turbulence. The acoustic correlate of stridency is illustrated in Figure 20.8, which shows spectrograms of the utterances a *sin* and a *thin* in English, as

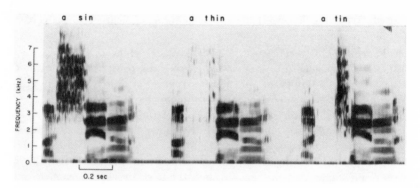

FIG. 20.8. Spectrograms of three utterances: *a sin* (left), *a thin* (middle),
and *a tin* (right).

well as the utterance *a tin*, which contains a stop consonant which is inherently [−strident] (although in this example some stridency is introduced
following the release, thereby enhancing the acoustic cue for the [+anterior]
stop, as noted under "Other Examples" below). The weaker noise for the [θ]
is quite evident in these utterances. This acoustic correlate of stridency is
also supported by perceptual experiments (Heinz & Stevens, 1961; Stevens,
1981a). It is reasonable to assume, then, that [+strident] is a candidate for
enhancing the feature [+continuant] for obstruent segments. The presence
of the relatively high level of noise during the constricted interval serves to
accentuate the contrast with a [−continuant] or stop consonant, for which
the sound pressure during this interval must be minimal. A consequence of
this observation would be that, for a language with just one labial fricative,
that fricative would tend to be labiodental, or strident (with the upper lip
acting as the "obstacle" against which the air stream is directed). Examination of the Stanford Archive (Crothers, Lorentz, Sherman, & Vihman, 1979)
supports this prediction, since it reveals that, among 68 languages that have
a single voiceless labial-fricative phoneme, 62 have the strident labiodental
[f] and only six have the nonstrident bilabial [Φ]. Likewise, coronal fricatives would tend to be strident; i.e., a language would tend to have [s] rather
than [θ], if there were just one coronal fricative. There may also be a tendency to avoid fricatives produced with a place of articulation (such as velar)
that does not allow for stridency, since there is no readily available obstacle
against which to direct the air stream.

Other Examples

[coronal] and [strident]. In English the stop consonant [t] is distinguished
from [p] and [k] by the feature [coronal]. The acoustic correlate of this feature
appears as a spectrum amplitude that increases with increasing frequency

(Blumstein & Stevens, 1979). Some speakers introduce affrication into the burst for |t| in some phonetic environments, as in the example in Figure 20.8 above. In effect, the feature |strident| is introduced to produce greater high-frequency energy immediately following the consonant release, and thus acts to enhance the |coronal| feature. In this context the feature |strident| is redundant.

/high/ and diphthongization. In English and in Swedish, the long [+high] vowels |i| and |u| are diphthongized to |iy| and |uw|, respectively (Fant, 1973; Jones, 1966). It can be argued that the diphthongization toward |y| or |w| accentuates the acoustic attribute associated with |+high|—i.e., a low first-formant frequency—since these offglides cause a movement of F_1 to an even lower frequency. (Presumably the entire vowel is not shifted toward |y| or |w| because a degree of syllabicity must be retained, and this requires that F_1 not be too low near the vowel onset.) This accentuation of the feature [high] is accomplished by the introduction of a nonsyllabic offglide toward the middle of the vowel. The acoustic manifestation of this offglide is a falling of the frequency of the first formant and a concomitant reduction in amplitude.

/low tone/ and /constricted glottis/. In several Southeast Asian languages, including Yao and Mandarin, phonemic low/falling/dipping tones are often accompanied by creaky voice (cf. Chao, 1968; Purnell, 1965). Presumably, creaky voice enables the low-frequency vocal-fold vibration needed for low tones to be even lower. This enhancement of the low tone is accompanied by a modified voice quality, associated with the feature [constricted glottis]. (In this respect, creaky voice and diphthongization are alike in that both are introduced midway in a vowel to enhance an acoustic property associated with a distinctive feature.)

/voice/ and /sonorant/. The distinguishing articulatory characteristic of the feature [+sonorant] is that there is essentially no pressure buildup behind a constriction in the vocal tract above the glottis. Thus, essentially no frication noise is generated along the vocal tract above the glottis. The generation of sound during a sonorant interval is achieved with an acoustic source at the glottis, and this source can either be voicing as a consequence of vocal-fold vibrations or aspiration as a consequence of turbulent airflow in the vicinity of a spread glottis. The airflow is much greater for the voiceless or aspirated case than for the voiced case, and this greater airflow during aspiration is more likely to give rise to turbulence noise at a narrow portion of the vocal tract above the glottis. Voicing is the preferred mode of sound generation during a sonorant interval, since it lessens the possibility of generating frication noise. In this sense, then, the feature [+voice] enhances [+sonorant].

IMPLICATIONS OF REDUNDANCY AS ENHANCEMENT

The picture that emerges from the examples and the discussion given is the following. A given language makes use of a set of distinctive features to specify the inventory of segments that make up the lexical items of that language and in terms of which the phonological component of the language is structured. The distinctive features are drawn from a larger inventory of features that are universally available. Associated with each feature is an acoustic property and an articulatory realization. The features from this inventory that are not distinctive within the language are often used to assist in the implementation of the features that are. Each of these enhancing, or redundant, features serves to strengthen the acoustic property associated with a distinctive feature and, in addition, to contribute its own acoustic property. In what follows, we describe three implications that arise out of these examples.

Nonindependence of Features

In all of the examples given above, we observe the pairing of features; namely, a redundant feature enhances a distinctive feature. An immediate question is: What is the basis for this linking of redundant features with distinctive features? It is our view that this pairing is not random, but rather is based upon characteristics of speech production and auditory perception. For a particular distinctive feature, there are only certain redundant features that can enhance or strengthen the acoustic property associated with the distinctive feature. Thus, rounding enhances backness by virtue of its reinforcing the low-frequency spectral prominence resulting from the proximity of F_1 and F_2. If the possible pairings of distinctive and redundant features are based upon the characteristics of the production and perception systems, then it is expected that this affinity between particular features is universal, i.e., it will be observed across languages. While this affinity may lurk, as it were, in the background, a given language may choose not to exploit the affinity. Further work is clearly needed in order to investigate in detail what principles give rise to those pairings.

An implication of this point of view is that redundant and distinctive features are all drawn from the same inventory. That is, among the list of 20-odd features discussed above, potentially any member of the list either can serve as a distinctive feature or can play the role of a redundant or enhancement feature. There is, however, another possibility. A given distinctive feature/redundant feature pair (or set of pairs) may actually represent different acoustic and articulatory manifestations of a single more abstract feature, a so-called "cover feature." Examples of possible candidates for such a feature are the feature [tense] for vowels, or a generalized feature of voicing or tenseness for consonants, which at first glance appear to have a variety of acoustic correlates. In the examples given above, it does not seem to be necessary to introduce this kind of feature. Nonetheless, we would like to keep open the possibility that distinctive feature theory may make use of "cover features" as well as distinctive features that have well-defined simple acoustic correlates such as nasality or stridency.

Discrete and Continuous Manifestations of Features

A second implication which emerges from the examples reviewed above is that each case of enhancement results not only in the introduction of additional acoustic properties, but also in the strengthening of an acoustic property associated with a distinctive feature. An implication is that the acoustic correlate of a distinctive feature can be instantiated with varying degrees of strength. A theory of this kind would represent the merging of quantal theory (Stevens, 1972) with viewpoints which assign a more continuous character to phonetic events (Liljencrants & Lindblom, 1972).

Enhancement and Saliency

The previous two sections concern the nature of enhancement. We would also like to look at the question of when enhancement occurs. The above examples suggest that enhancement may occur when the acoustic property associated with a particular distinctive feature cannot be reliably detected by listeners. That is, enhancing occurs when confusion is likely to exist between utterances that are distinguished only on the basis of that feature. The introduction of a redundant feature in these situations can serve to increase the "perceptual distance" between these utterances (cf. Klatt, 1982a, b), and thus to increase the reliability with which a listener can make the distinction.

In most of the examples given above, redundant features come into play in the presence of features indicating place of articulation or the state of the larynx . One might ask whether these classes of features are less salient perceptually, and are, therefore, most in need of enhancement. In order to answer this question, we will need to explain in a more quantitative way what is meant by "saliency" or "perceptual distance."

PHONOLOGICAL IMPLICATIONS

An important outcome of the discussion of redundancy given above is that there is a linking, or dependency, between phonetic features. According to this view, there are other redundant features associated with certain distinctive features that serve to enhance the acoustic properties that signal the distinctive features. If features are interdependent, then one would expect to find evidence for this interdependence in phonological rules. In fact, rule systems have not been viewed from this perspective. In what follows, two examples are discussed which re-examine two phonological rules from the point of view of enhancement. The first rule comes from Lardil and attempts to show that a well-motivated phonological rule of that language which relates the features [distributed], [anterior], and [back] can be viewed in the light of the discussion above. The second rule comes from English and attempts to demonstrate that the role of stridency in the phenomena of Spirantization and Palatalization is, in fact, an enhancement role of the feature [continuant] by the feature [strident].

[back] and [anterior] in Lardil

We turn first to the Lardil example. The relevant data are drawn from Klokeid (1976), who notes the following distribution in Lardil, an Australian Aboriginal language:

(1)

nominative	accusative	nonfuture	future	
ngawid	ngawij-in	ngawith-ad	ngawith-ur	"stomach"
yarpud	yarpuj-in	yarputh-ad	yarputh-ur	"snake, bird"
ngampid	ngampij-in	ngampith-ad	ngampith-ur	"lumpy"
kaljid	kaljij-in	kaljith-ad	kaljith-ur	"urine"

In Klokeid's (1976) orthography, the symbol j stands for a laminoalveolar coronal while the symbol th stands for a laminodental. Thus, we find in (1) alternations whereby a laminodental appears before back vowels and a laminoalveolar appears before front vowels. This is a pattern that appears to be widespread in Australian languages (Dixon, 1970; Dixon & Blake, 1979, 1981). Klokeid's description, as well as the detailed descriptions of others such as Dixon (1980), makes it clear that the laminodental consonants are [+anterior] while the laminoalveolar consonants are [−anterior]. Klokeid's account also establishes that both of these allophones stem from an underlying /t/ is optionally flapped in word-final position (Klokeid, 1976, pp. 39–40). To account for these alternations Klokeid postulates the following rule:

(2)

$$/t/ \longrightarrow \begin{bmatrix} +\text{distributed} \\ \alpha \text{ anterior} \end{bmatrix} / \text{_____} \begin{bmatrix} +V \\ \alpha \text{ back} \end{bmatrix}$$

This rule states that the apical root-final /t/ becomes distributed and that, furthermore, there is a correlation between backness and anteriority which takes place among the resultant distributed coronals. In particular, back vowels induce [+anterior] coronals while front vowels induce [-anterior] coronals.

As it stands, there is no motivation for the correlation exhibited in (2). Such a motivation can be found, however, in the discussion given earlier and illustrated in Figure 20.4, in which we inferred from acoustic data that, for [+distributed] coronal consonants in some other Australian languages, [+anterior], or dental, consonants are produced with a more backed tongue-body position than are [-anterior], or palatal, consonants. We also argued from anatomical considerations that this front or back positioning of the tongue-body provides a configuration that enhances the ability of the speaker to achieve the acoustic characteristics appropriate for the palatal or dental consonant, respectively. It could also be argued that the reverse is true. That is, for the class of [+distributed] coronal consonants, achievement of a backed tongue-body configuration is enhanced by using a dental (i.e. [+anterior]) tongue-blade articulation, whereas achievement of a fronted tongue-body configuration is enhanced by using a palatal (i.e. [-anterior]) tongue blade articulation. This correlation between [back] and [anterior] can be formalized by hypothesizing the following universal linking convention (cf. Chomsky & Halle, 1968a, pp. 421ff):

(3)

$$[u \text{ back}] \longrightarrow [\alpha \text{ back}] / \begin{bmatrix} \text{_____} \\ +\text{distributed} \\ \alpha \text{ anterior} \end{bmatrix}$$

where [u back] refers to "unmarked for back." This convention states that universally for distributed consonants, the features [back] and [anterior] are correlated whenever they are free to do so by virtue of either one or the other being redundant in the phonology of a given language.

Given linking convention (3), we restate (2) as follows:

(4)

$$/t/ \longrightarrow \begin{bmatrix} +\text{distributed} \\ \alpha \text{ back} \\ \alpha \text{ anterior} \end{bmatrix} / \text{_____} \begin{bmatrix} +V \\ \alpha \text{ back} \end{bmatrix}$$

The value of the feature [back] on the V determines the value of the same feature on the preceding consonant. We assume that linking convention (3) motivates the correlation seen in (4) between [back] and [anterior]. Thus, (4) replicates the correlation that (3) establishes on grounds of enhancement.

If we are correct in supposing that linking conventions are based upon enhancement properties of feature pairs or pair-sets, then we may be able to shed new light on such conventions. In particular, we may be able to sustain the claim that in such conventions, the relevant features that occur in phonological rules do so precisely because they are in an enhancement relationship with one another. In the present case, we have argued that the correlation of [back] and [anterior] is explicable in terms of a prior theory of constraints between the tongue-body, the tongue blade and the mode of making contact with the hard palate.[1]

There is a further consequence of this point of view which is worth considering. In Chomsky and Halle (1968a), markedness and linking conventions were primarily employed in order to provide an evaluation metric for distinguishing between simple and complex lexical entries. This was accomplished by using values such as $+$, $-$, m and u in the underlying specification of feature bundles. Those representations which contained the fewest pluses and minuses and the most u's were the simplest. This metric, it should be noted, is based upon the notion that underlying representations have to be fully specified for all features. Recent work (Kiparsky, 1982) has suggested that this may not be so and that underspecification of features in the lexicon is necessary. In this case, the same kind of metric would hold. Instead of giving the highest valuation to those entries containing the most u's, one would give the highest valuation to those entries containing the most empty cells.

Stridency in English: Spirantization and Palatalization

In English, there is a battery of rules (cf. Chomsky & Halle, 1968a, 223ff) whereby a stem final /t/ or /d/ (in words like *Egypt* and *invade*), when followed by a morpheme beginning with a palatal glide such as [yən], becomes corresponding) [−anterior,+continuant,+strident] segments. Thus, /t/ becomes [š] and /d/ becomes [ž] in *Egyptian* and in *invasion*, respectively. These forms are assumed to derive from the underlying morpheme sequences [Egypt + yən] and [invad + yən].[2] These alternations are in keeping with the tendency noted earlier for [+continuant, −sonorant] segments to be [+strident]; i.e., for stridency to enhance the property of continuancy. In English, stridency is distinctive for [+anterior, +coronal] continuants (e.g., [s] and [θ]), but is redundant for [−anterior, +coronal] segments such as [š]. In

---

[1] The linking conventions discussed above offer one way of formalizing the enhancement relationship. However, one must examine critically whether linking conventions do, in fact, constitute a viable formalism for enhancement or whether some other formalism is required.

[2] The major rules involved in these alternations are Spirantization and Palatalization.

the view proposed here, then, stridency is available for enhancement in this latter context. Thus, we add the feature [+strident] to the list given above for a palatal fricative, resulting finally in [š] or [ž], as in words like *Egyptian* and *invasion*.

As with linking convention (3), we may propose a universal linking convention such as the following:

(5)

$$[u \text{ strident}] \longrightarrow [+ \text{strident}] \ / \ \begin{bmatrix} \text{————} \\ + \text{continuant} \\ -\text{sonorant} \end{bmatrix}$$

This convention marks a nonsonorant continuant as [+strident] unless stridency is being used distinctively for that segment. In particular, in English a palatal fricative is redundantly strident. The convention will operate on the segments /t/ and /d/ after the rules of spirantization and palatalization have applied to render these segments [+strident] as well as [−anterior, +continuant], i.e., [š] and [ž]. Thus, the process of enhancement of continuancy by stridency is captured in our theory through the device of a linking convention which automatically introduces [+strident] when the phonology sets the stage for it.

SUMMARY AND CONCLUDING REMARKS

This paper has been concerned with a relationship between distinctive and redundant features which has been noted in the literature but has not been studied in detail. We have observed that no language utilizes fully the entire set of 20-odd distinctive features which are hypothesized to describe the phonological and phonetic components of human language. A feature in a given language is often distinctive only in the environment of certain other features in that language.

Redundancy appears to be of two types. One type is obligatory, in that certain feature combinations always occur together. This type of redundancy is a direct consequence of the properties of the vocal tract and the auditory system. The other type, which is of interest in this paper, is optional in character, in that it may or may not be selected for use in particular language. We have proposed that languages make use of these redundant features in order to enhance acoustic properties associated with distinctive feature oppositions. Several examples have been given to illustrate how certain features might reasonably be viewed, within the framework of contemporary theories of speech production and perception, as enhancing or being enhanced by other features. Features chosen for detailed discussion included [distributed], [anterior], [back], [voice], [continuant], and [strident]. A number of other features and processes were touched upon in less detail. These examples indicate ways in which the enhancement process may operate. The manipulation of the articulatory mechanisms corresponding to one feature (the redundant or enhancing feature) interacts with the process of producing another feature (the distinctive feature). The redundant feature produces its own acoustic property but the interaction also results in conditions whereby the acoustic property for the distinctive feature is produced with greater strength, with greater reliability, or with less articulatory effort. These examples point toward a *linking* between two or more features: one of these functions distinctively and the other(s) redundantly to enhance the acoustic property of the distinctive feature.

We raise the question as to whether phonological rules associate features which are related in terms of this linking. To shed light on this question, we have discussed two rules in some detail, one drawn from Lardil and the other from English. A conclusion from these and other examples is that this pairing of redundant and distinctive features does seem to play a role in certain phonological rules, and that it might be useful to review phonological rules from the point of view of enhancement linkages. In fact, the theory may be able to account for a significant number of feature pairings that one finds in such rules, particularly those which reoccur from one language to another.

The concepts of redundancy and enhancement that have been introduced here could conceivably form a basis for gaining insight into several areas not considered in this paper:

1. When a redundant or enhancing feature exists alongside a distinctive feature, there is a possibility that the redundant feature can take over distinctive duty, and that the role of the distinctive feature is reduced or even eliminated. The contrast between lexical items is now carried by a different feature and sound change has occurred. Do enhancing or redundant features play a role in indicating what sound changes are possible?

2. A consequence of the fact that some features can enhance others is that certain combinations of features are more likely to occur in certain languages than others. (For example, back vowels tend to be rounded, continuant obstruents tend to be strident, sonorants tend to be voiced and so on.) A further possible consequence is that, in the process of acquiring the phonological aspects of language, a child is more likely to produce and to respond to some feature combinations than others. Is is possible to interpret acquisition data in terms of the feature linking and enhancement processes of the type discussed in this paper?

3. Redundant features may be utilized optionally by speakers in some contexts, since these features are not required to distinguish between words, particularly when the communication link is relatively free of interference.

Thus when redundant features occur, there is an opportunity for variability in the way a particular word is actualized. Some of this variability is at the option of the speaker and some is determined by the context in which the features occur. The concepts of redundancy thus provide us with a framework within which to examine invariance and variability in the speech process— invariance in the relation between features and acoustic properties, and variability in the selection of features to utilize in a particular context and speaking situation.

This paper is offered as a first step in approaching these and other questions.

ACKNOWLEDGEMENTS

Preparation of this manuscript was supported in part by the MIT Center for Cognitive Science under a grant from the A. P. Sloan Foundation's Particular Program in Cognitive Science, in part by Grant No. NS-04332 from the National Institute of Neurological and Communicative Disorders and Stroke, and in part by Grant No. NSF MCS-81-12899 from the National Science Foundation. We would like to thank K. Hale for discussion about Lardil.

Bruno H. Repp: Comment

I find the theory sketched by Stevens, Keyser, and Kawasaki interesting and promising. It has important implications for the description of phonological structure and for the explanation of this structure in terms of articulatory and perceptual principles. Thus the theory must be welcomed as a significant attempt to bridge the often-lamented gap between phonology and phonetics.

Since I am not a linguist, I have little to say about the phonological side of the theory. I also presume that this aspect is less directly relevant to the concerns of this volume. As to the phonetic side, my aim will be to comment on some of the basic assumptions underlying the theory.

One fundamental assumption is that there is a small set of phonetic features that are common to all languages in the world and are in one-to-one correspondence with certain invariant properties in the speech signal. Although this assumption is stated as if it were an established truth, I presume Stevens et al. would agree that it can be decomposed into several semi-independent hypotheses, all of which are in need of further empirical support. These hypotheses are: (1) the number of phonetic features is small; (2) this small set is universal; (3) the acoustic signal contains certain invariant properties; (4) these properties are in a one-to-one relation with phonetic features. None of these component assumptions is universally accepted, and the last two hypotheses in particular cannot be considered well-supported at present and are the subject of ongoing research. Therefore, they are best considered working assumptions, even if they serve as axioms within the present theory.

The main focus of the authors' theory is on acoustic properties of the speech signal. Those critical properties that are taken to carry the distinctive information are assumed to be the joint result of articulatory and perceptual constraints in the evolution of language. On the articulatory side, a preference for certain regions of maximal stability is predicted; on the perceptual side, a maximally distinct sound output will be preferred. These are familiar assumptions, but they are nevertheless very much in need of further empirical support. While pressures toward articulatory and perceptual ease—to the extent that these concepts can be defined clearly—certainly must play a role in speech communication, there are many other factors at work as well. Skilled behavior, of which I take speech to be an instance, often requires the overcoming of preferences inherent in the perceptual and motor systems. In fact, it might be argued that, if this were not so, the behavior in question should not be called a skill. While there are clearly defined physical limits that cannot be exceeded, there is considerable freedom and flexibility within these limits. I agree, however, that in order to discover and describe this flexibility, a good hypothesis to pursue is that the perceptual and motor systems are tightly constrained.

The authors' main concepts are those of feature redundancy and enhancement. Feature redundancy is predicted on purely formal grounds: There are more possible combinations of features than there are phonetic distinctions in a language, even though many feature combinations do not actually occur because of articulatory restrictions, and also because some distinctive features devised by phonologists are by definition dependent on others. In addition to this *necessary* redundancy, however, Stevens et al. point out that "some features are redundant in particular contexts by virtue of their not having been selected to do distinctive duty in some language."

I am slightly confused by the argument here. If a feature is not used at all, then it does not vary and therefore cannot be redundant. In order to be redundant, a feature must exhibit some variation. Whether it performs distinctive duty in that case is apparently decided by Stevens et al. on the basis of phonological theory. However, we know from many perceptual experiments that virtually every acoustic property that covaries with a phonetic distinction can aid a listener in making that distinction; thus, from a perceptual viewpoint, it is not clear how a feature can vary redundantly and at the same time not do distinctive duty. In other words, it seems that the authors must first negate the distinctive perceptual role of certain features in order to be able to introduce purposeful enhancement as a phonological mechanism. This may be a form of theoretical bootstrapping.

It also seems that there are more acoustic properties in the speech signal than there are distinctive features in phonology, notwithstanding all attempts to describe acoustic feature correlates in a maximally integrated fashion. Although the authors clearly assume that there is a one-to-one correspondence between distinctive features and acoustic properties, some of their examples of feature enhancement suggest that they may be willing to consider the perceptual contribution of acoustic properties other than the primary feature correlates.

The feature enhancement hypothesis claims that redundant features may serve to enhance perceptual distinctions. Stevens et al. state that "in the process of achieving this goal of strengthening the existing acoustic property, the redundant feature results in the introduction of a new acoustic property that co-occurs with the already present property." In the specific cases considered, however, a redundant feature generally contributes to the *same* acoustic property as the feature that is assumed to do distinctive duty in the first place. If merely a new acoustic property were added, its effect would not be a strengthening of the existing property but a facilitation of the perceptual distinction according to the principle that two differences are easier to discriminate than one. If I understand the authors correctly, however, they are only concerned with perceptual facilitation due to enhancement of the primary acoustic property, not with facilitation due to several independent acoustic cues. But since they do consider the possibility that a new property due to a redundant feature may replace the original distinctive property, I conclude that redundant features are assumed both to contribute to existing acoustic properties and to introduce new acoustic properties. This seems to contradict the assumption that features are in a one-to-one correspondence with acoustic properties, for how can a single redundant feature contribute to two different acoustic properties? At the very least, it must be assumed that the primary acoustic properties associated with different distinctive features are not independent of each other but overlap in varying degrees. Another way of expressing this is to state that each acoustic property can be analyzed into a number of more detailed acoustic aspects or cues, some of which are shared by several distinctive features.

I will not attempt to discuss the specific examples provided by the authors, except for noting that they are not equally straightforward. In the first two examples, in particular, it is not fully clear to me whether they are cases of necessary feature redundancy due to articulatory linkages or of optional feature enhancement. This may simply reveal my ignorance, however. I would merely like to point out that, in order to claim that acoustic feature enhancement has occurred in a given language, it is necessary to show that: (1) the primary acoustic property can be found in its unenhanced state; and (2) the supposed enhancement indeed results in an acoustic change in the expected direction. It is necessary to keep in mind the possibilities that some optional feature linkages are due to articulatory facilitation that does not substantially alter the acoustic output, or that a predicted acoustic change is counteracted by some other simultaneous adjustments, so that there are no acoustic or perceptual consequences. These are precisely the questions that Stevens et al. are planning to investigate in more detail.

I would like to comment briefly on the third example. It is argued here that, in English stops, the feature [−voice], characterized by absence of low-frequency periodicity, may be enhanced by several other features, all of which extend the acoustic interval during which voicing is absent. These enhancing features include aspiration, shortening of a preceding vowel, and lengthening of the closure interval.

In addition, the authors mention the higher fundamental frequency at voicing onset. This is an acoustic property that, as far as I can see, is not associated with a particular distinctive feature (unless one invokes tones) and that does not directly enhance the primary acoustic property. Another acoustic feature not mentioned by the authors is the higher onset of F_1 at voicing onset for voiceless stops. Although a high F_1 is associated with the feature [low] for vowels, I presume the authors would consider it here as a byproduct of delayed voicing onset and not as an enhancing feature. All these acoustic properties, of course, can be shown to be perceptually salient. There may be additional examples of such satellites accompanying the primary acoustic properties that are the fixed stars of the present theory.

Stevens et al. also argue that, since the presence or absence of low-frequency periodicity is taken to be the primary acoustic correlate of the voicing feature, the enhancing feature of aspiration takes the place of the primary distinctive property in word-initial position in English. It is argued that, for phonological reasons, voicing is distinctive in English, not aspiration. (In support of this point, the authors cite the plural rule, although it applies, of course, only to word-final consonants.) For phonological theory, however, it should make no difference whether the feature that characterizes the voiced-voiceless distinction in all phonetic environments is called [voice], [aspiration], or [omega]. Clearly, so-called voiced stops all have something in common at the level of abstract description, as do so-called voiceless stops. At the acoustic level, however, there are important contextual differences, and Stevens et al. have perhaps gone a bit too far in reifying phonological nomenclature. If there must be a primary acoustic correlate, why not simply take aspiration to be that correlate of the voicing feature for stops in initial position? Apparently, such context-dependent definitions of acoustic correlates are not permitted in the present theory, which strives to maintain the strict one-to-one correspondence of distinctive features and acoustic properties across all positions and contexts. This highly restrictive and purely formal assumption is the lifeline of the present theory. A reformulation in terms of many-to-one correspondences would presumably be considered inelegant and unparsimonious by the authors, and it would reduce considerably the explanatory power of the present theory. The philosophical problem one encounters here is that whether or not something counts as an explanation depends very much on the assumptions one starts out with.

Toward the end of their paper, Stevens et al. mention several implications of their theory. One implication concerns the nonindependence of distinctive features, which is of interest primarily to phonologists. One additional possibility raised by the authors, that of devising "cover features" encompassing a variety of acoustic correlates, would be a significant step toward reconciling the theory of acoustic invariance with other theoretical views. (The next step might be to consider each acoustic property to be the cover term for an array of contextual variants.)

A second implication concerns the continuous, rather than discrete, manifestation of features in the acoustic signal. At first glance, this conclusion seems hardly novel; clearly, there are many sources of variability in the acoustic signal. However, I believe more is being implied. The theory points toward a particular source of systematic variability in the acoustic instantiation of phonetic distinctions across languages (assuming, of course, that distinctive features are universal). Some languages may make use of redundant features and thereby show stronger acoustic correlates of certain features than languages that make little use of the enhancement possibilities. This is an interesting and nontrivial implication. In other words, there may be systematic cross-linguistic variation in the idealized or prototypical acoustic representation of universal features. On the other hand, the variability around the norm that occurs as a function of context and speaking rate, is not of immediate concern to the present theory. The theory operates at a relatively abstract level even as far as the acoustic signal is concerned; hence the term "acoustic invariance" in the face of ubiquitous variability in natural speech. Stevens et al. are dealing with acoustic competence, as it were, not with acoustic performance. This is to be expected in a theory whose basic conceptual ingredients are supplied by phonological theory.

Clearly, the most interesting aspect of the theory of Stevens et al. is its potential explanatory power, even if that power is evident only within the particular framework adopted. On one hand, the theory aims to provide a systematic account of features and acoustic properties that are likely to enhance each other, based on a careful consideration of articulatory maneuvers and their acoustic consequences. On the other hand, the theory should be able to predict (or, rather, postdict) under what circumstances feature enhancement will actually occur in a given language or even for a given speaker, assuming that some specific feature redundancy is not obligatory and universal. Stevens et al. contribute the observation that features in need of enhancement are likely to be those that are difficult to perceive. This seems a reasonable proposal, although perceptual salience needs to be defined more clearly. Still, even a perceptual criterion cannot readily explain differences across languages and individual speakers. One of the most interesting tasks for the future will be the explanation of these variations, by examining the role enhancing features play in the total phonological system of a language, and—in the case of individual differences—how enhancement may be conditioned by individual variations in dialect, anatomy, and articulatory strategies.

In conclusion, it is clear that the theory of acoustic invariance in speech is alive and well. However, on closer inspection it seems that Stevens et al.'s paper presents an expanded theory that, behind a protective screen of orthodox assumptions, makes steps toward providing a systematic account of variability in the speech signal. One day, out of its chrysalis there might emerge a full-fledged theory of acoustic variability.

AFTERTHOUGHT:
INVARIANCE MAY BE A COGNITIVE ILLUSION

Here are a few very general thoughts on invariance: Our cognitive capabilities have evolved to help us deal constructively with the objects and events in our environment. Our cognitive concepts are categorical and enter our consciousness in serial order. We know a fair amount about how our thought processes work because, to the extent that they are open to introspection, they too form part of our environment. However, introspection reveals absolutely nothing about perceptual and (preparatory) motor processes, which are unconscious and are not part of the world that our minds have evolved to understand. The temptation is great to devise theories of speech perception and production whose ingredients are the conscious products of our cognitive analysis of speech and language. We are all born linguists because of our analytic abilities; however, nobody is born with the ability to understand perceptual or motor processes. These processes are likely to operate according to principles that are not immediately obvious to us and that can be understood—if that is possible at all, excluding tautology as a form of explanation—only by discovering and adopting a completely new conceptual framework. The study of complex organic systems may yield such a framework.

The process of perceptual categorization reduces physical variability to a discrete conscious percept. It is the discreteness and constancy of this percept that suggests to us that there might be invariance somewhere in the physical world. However, this may well be an illusion. Of course, to the extent that there is physical invariance, perceptual processes are simply not needed. Therefore, the search for invariance should by no means be abandoned. However, if the search is not successful, we should not be worried but rather turn our attention to models of perceptual categorization in the context of a large knowledge base.

The appropriate functional unit for that enterprise is most likely the meaningful word, and the contributions to this volume by Cohen and by Elman and McClelland (Chapters 24 and 17, respectively) point in the right direction. Underlying these theories is the assumption that our brains are powerful storage devices with the capability of retaining millions of words, including their precise acoustic specifications abstracted from the variable input, and of processing each new input in a highly efficient fashion. How such a vast lexicon is actually represented in the brain we cannot conceive at present, but note that professional musicians store potentially even larger amounts of musical information, complete with acoustic details of timbre, dynamics, and orchestration. It is from this interconnected array of partially similar lexical entries that our knowledge of linguistic units is derived in an analytic manner. *When we talk about the recognition of phonemes or features, we are using a rhetorical device for describing how much information about a word has accumulated and how that information constrains the possible choices from the lexicon.* This also applies to the nonsense material that is frequently used in our experiments and which is wordlike and perceived by analogy to the most similar words we know. We often feel the need to describe to ourselves the process of information accumulation in familiar analytic terms, and this is all right as long as we realize that the perceptual system need not describe anything to itself. Our perceptual mechanisms do not think or talk to themselves, as we do; they simply do their job. Similar arguments apply to speech production, substituting information dissemination for accumulation. Although speech errors are often cited as evidence for the existence of linguistic units in the production process, I suspect that here, too, we are merely using a familiar descriptive device for characterizing phenomena that ultimately can be predicted from a more intimate knowledge of motor planning.

To conclude, it seems to me that the problem of invariance, as juxtaposed with variability, is more apparent than real and stems in large part from our need to talk to each other about what we are investigating, and to investigate what we are talking about. I am not suggesting that we abandon all verbal communication, but that we take our intuitions with a grain of salt and begin to consider, as Elman and McClelland (Chapter 17) have begun to do, classes of models that capture some properties of our nervous system. The power of these models goes way beyond what can be expressed in words, but it can be demonstrated by mathematical arguments and computer simulation. Perhaps paradoxically, our understanding of perceptual and motor processes may be increased by resisting our urge to describe them in familiar terms.

Gunnar Fant:
Comment

Stevens et al.'s study is basic for the theme of our volume and represents a much needed continuation of the work of Jakobson, Fant, and Halle (1952). On the one hand, it is a stimulating contribution to phonological theory. On the other hand, it should sharpen our attention on the perceptual salience of various acoustic properties entering both redundant and distinctive features. In one sense, we are thus back to viewing phonemes and allophones and feature realizations as individuals shaped by their context specific combination of phonological genes. Does perception pick out the entire gestalt rather than each of the underlying genes? Perception could work both ways but it is hard to prove any specific model. As also pointed out by Repp, (Chapter 20a), the way we conceive of the process is already biased by our terminology and metalinguistic projections.

I have a specific comment on acoustic detail properties. The Malayalam alveolar (apical) stop contrasted with the dental (laminar) stop in Figure 20.5 does not only have a higher F_2 locus but also a positioning of F_4 close to F_3 typical of a small retraction of the point of articulation. This modification also occurs in Swedish when a dental is preceded by a phonological constituent [r] which is retained in the spelled form but is otherwise lost in pronunciation. In the example the alveolar stop has a component [−distributed] along the same dimension as the F_3 lowering due to a more retracted [−anterior] articulation. Is this an additional enhancement for the Malayalam [+distributed]? In any case, it would be interesting to have results from synthesis experiments evaluating the various components in the entire pattern contrast. How important are the dynamics of vowel onset and how important is the F-pattern versus time variation? Both are, of course, conditioned by one and the same underlying articulatory gesture.

Patti J. Price: Comment

I'd like to make a few comments about redundancy. I will start with an example: Given two features that are not *both* needed to maintain a distinction, how is it determined which of the two is the redundant one? One could argue that if one is always there and the other is not, then the one that is always there is not redundant. I am not convinced that this situation is typical. Further, there may well be cases in which there are, for example, three features and the occurrence of any two out of the three would be sufficient to maintain the distinction. How would redundancy be described in this case?

The authors outline two types of redundancy, that arising from constraints of the human speech and auditory systems and that arising from language-specific characteristics. I maintain that there is another type of redundancy, namely that arising from our selection of sets of features used to characterize these aspects of language. Because the features are not orthogonal to each other, not all combinations occur, and redundancy is built in: Thus, the choice of the set of features determines some of the redundancies. This is a problem because we don't know or can't agree on how to choose features, i.e., on what counts as evidence for setting up a particular feature. Now, for a diverse set of reasons, people have come up with systems of features that are not orthogonal. One of the reasons that there is no good agreement on what the features are is that devising an orthogonal or elegant system for a given language is a quite different problem from devising a system of all possible features in all possible languages. For some tasks, we want features that can make distinctions as fine as the speech perception and production systems are capable of making. For other tasks we want features that are capable of uniting a great variety of different sets of sounds that are, for various reasons, linguistically "the same." What is elegant and economical for one task is not necessarily so for others. Thus, assuming that there is one set of features for these various tasks implies excess baggage—i.e., redundancy—and, as such, says more about how we are choosing to look at our data than it says about language.

A fundamental problem here is that there is no agreed upon set of criteria (if there is *any* set of criteria) for the existence of a given feature. In the old days, the minimal pair was critical in their definition. If, as the paper by Stevens et al. implies, there are no truly minimal pairs, we may be worse off than before. The distinction between distinctive and redundant features could offer some salvation, but this distinction is blurred since redundant features can become distinctive and vice versa, i.e., in language change.

The paper presents many interesting ideas, the most important of which is, I feel, its aim to capture linguistically significant generalizations about both the discrete and the continuous aspects of language. As with most interesting theories, it also leads to many new problems. This does not detract from its attractiveness.

I'd like to repeat something that was said by the structuralists: It is not the case that all things *are* structured, but we can always impose a structure on them. A variety of structures can be imposed for a variety of reasons. For example, in physics it is often useful to assume that force equals mass times acceleration ($f = ma$).

This is descriptively (and otherwise) adequate for many purposes, but not all. It is inaccurate and inadequate for some purposes and the theory of Relativity was developed to deal with these problems. Inadequacy for some purposes does not preclude usefulness for other purposes. A "unified" theory is, of course, aesthetically appealing, but assuming that we have one may be procrustean. Further, the fact that many different structures are useful, for many different reasons, is an important fact about language, about language as a tool that we use as speakers, and also about language as a source of data for linguists and for speech scientists. Language is flexible enough to accommodate multiple and changing purposes.

John J. Ohala: Comment

Stevens et al. claim that redundant features in speech are present in order to reinforce the primary distinctive features by contributing additional properties that help the listener to perceive the primary distinctions. I see at least two problems with that claim. First, in many of the cases which might be cited, it seems obvious that these redundant features are present due to purely mechanical factors, i.e., the physical constraints of the vocal tract (Ohala, 1981b, 1983b). For example, the shorter duration of voiced obstruents vis-a-vis voiceless obstruents doesn't simply result in more voicing (of the surrounding sonorants), it is also—perhaps principally—motivated by the necessity to keep the closure interval short enough so that voicing can be maintained by the most easily implemented enlargement of the oral cavity so that the accumulating air flow does not reduce the transglottal pressure drop so much that voicing would be extinguished (Ohala & Riordan, 1979). The F_0 perturbation on vowels after voiced and voiceless stops seems to be an automatic consequence of whatever laryngeal gestures are necessary to produce the voicing difference. The greater voice onset time (VOT) before high vowels than before low vowels seems to be due to the fact that the narrower oral constriction for close vowels creates greater resistance to air flow and thus delays the attainment of the transglottal pressure drop required for voicing. Glottalized consonants cause adjacent vowels to be tense or creaky because the constricted glottis condition is anticipated or perseverated. These redundant features *may* serve perception but their presence would seem to be most directly explained by the physical constraints of speech production.

Second, it is not clear to me how many of these redundant features can be seen as reinforcing the primary distinctive feature. How does the high F_0 on vowelbs following voiceless (and, as it turns out, voiced implosive) consonants reinforce the primary features of these segments? How does the greater VOT of stops before high vowels reinforce the primary distinctive feature, presumably [+high] (or [+diffuse])? Given the large number of redundant features in speech, it is not difficult to find some which seem to enhance the primary feature, e.g., nasalization of vowels before nasal consonants, but it is not obvious that Stevens et al.'s hypothesis is sufficiently general to handle all relevant cases.

Stevens. Keyser, and Kawasaki: Response

RESPONSE TO DR. OHALA

We agree that the linking of distinctive and redundant features often originates in the physical constraints of the vocal tract. However, the "physical" theory of redundancy alone does not explain all possible ways in which distinctive and redundant features interact.

The shortening of voiced obstruents does not seem to result from absolute physical necessity, for these consonants could alternatively be pronounced as partially voiced without any change in their closure duration. We hypothesize that the shortening of voiced obstruents is motivated by a perceptual factor, and therefore is employed for the purpose of enhancement. Voiceless stops typically have stronger bursts than voiced ones, and this difference in burst amplitude may serve as one of the cues to the voicing distinction. It can be argued that a strong burst interrupts the representation of periodicity in the auditory system, and thus itself serves as an enhancing property for [−voiced]. A weaker burst, on the other hand, may not interrupt this auditory representation, allowing the percept of periodicity, i.e., voicing. (It is necessary, then, to postulate a feature that has an acoustic correlate a strong burst or a strong onset—possibly the same feature as that discussed in the paper in connection with Figure 20.5.) Electro-physiological studies of the first-order peripheral auditory system suggest that the response of the auditory neurons to an abrupt rise in amplitude is greater in magnitude when such a rise is preceded by a longer silent interval (Delgutte 1982). (A discussion of the consequences of this response characteristic in modelling the auditory processing of speech is given by Goldhor (1983a).) Thus, the shorter is a stop, the less would be the auditory system's response to its burst. In the case of fricatives, a short interval may reduce the percept of noise, thereby enhancing the perceived periodicity. The shortening of voiced obstruents (as well as lengthening of voiceless ones) would therefore maximize the auditory difference between the voiced and voiceless cognates.

As Dr. Ohala stated, a certain physiological constraint seems responsible for the F_0 variations induced by consonantal voicing or voicelessness. And yet this cause-effect relationship alone does not tell us why, for example, the F_0 perturbations last as long as 100 ms after vowel onset in English but last for a considerably shorter interval in such tone languages as Yoruba and Thai and such a pitch-accent language as Japanese (Gandour 1974, Hombert 1978, Kawasaki 1983). Such a cross-linguistic observation suggests that the redundant systematic F_0 variation is exploited to a greater extent where the introduction of such redundancy will not disturb the properties of other phonemic distinctions. We speculated in our paper that one of the redundant features reinforcing the distinctive feature [−voice] is [+stiff vocal cords]. This feature [+stiff vocal cords] inhibits vocal-fold vibration during the consonantal interval, and has the acoustic correlate of high F_0, which is observed at voicing onset. In this sense, we claim that an F_0 perturbation is involved in enhancing the voicing feature, though the relationship between the two is an indirect one. Though Dr. Ohala considers it a mere aerodynamic consequence, the affinity between [−voice] and [+high] in vowels, witnessed in such phenomena as longer VOT's of voiceless stops before high vowels and greater tendency of high vowels toward devoicing, seems to be another kind of enhancement that languages have freedom to implement to varying degrees. The following observations support our claim. First, only a small subset of languages in the world have the processes of high vowel devoicing. Second, EMG and fiberscopic studies have shown that the laryngeal adjustments for devoiced vowels are very different from those for voiced vowels; the former not only lack and adductive movement of the vocal folds but also show active abductive gestures (Hirose 1971). Thus the devoicing in these cases appears to be an active process under control of the speaker. Dr. Ohala raises a valid point when he notes that there seems, at first glance, to be little basis for an argument that [−voice] causes an enhancement of the acoustic correlate of the feature [+high]. A possible argument might be something like the following. The feature [+high] requires that F_1 be low, and this feature is enhanced if the frequency of F_1 is made as low as possible. That is, F_1 is sufficiently low that it has no prominent character that is distinguishable from the source. Devoicing essentially eliminates F_1, creating a perceptual consequence similar to a lowered F_1.

We can cite numerous cases where an enhancing feature is not an automatic consequence of the production of a distinctive feature. Examples are: rounding of [š] in English, rounding of back vowels, diphthongization of high vowels, stridency in coronal consonants, and stridency in continuants. In these cases the redundant or enhancing feature is imposed strictly because it strengthens the acoustic property of the distinctive feature. There is little linkage between the two in their articulatory manifestations.

In short, our counterarguments for a purely physical account of redundancy are: (1) not all redundant features arise due to physical constraints, and (2) physically-induced redundancy can be optionally further exploited for the purpose of enhancement.

RESPONSE TO DR. REPP AND DR. PRICE

We thank Dr. Repp for his insightful and helpful comments. As a consequence of remarks by Dr. Repp and others, we have recognized some inadequacies in our exposition and in some of our arguments, and we have made some revisions in our manuscript. Thus some of the points made by Dr. Repp may already be answered in the paper.

Near the beginning of his comments, Dr. Repp notes that several hypotheses concerning phonetic features, acoustic properties, and invariance form the starting points for the discussion in our paper. He points out that it may be difficult to provide justification for each of these hypotheses when they are examined individually. However, these hypotheses are not independent; any one of them would be difficult to support unless it were made in the context of the others.

In effect, we are choosing to *define* phonetic features as being characterized by invariant acoustic and articulatory attributes. We will not accept a phonetic feature in the inventory of universal features unless we can define an acoustic and an articulatory property for the feature. This requirement is different from a definition of a feature that allows multiple properties to occur when the feature is actualized. For example, according to some definitions, the feature [+voice] can have a variety of acoustic correlates. In our proposed formulation, we account for this apparent variability by postulating that selected additional features can come into play to enhance or even replace the original voicing feature. Each of these additional features has an invariant acoustic property, and in some cases this property can be present with various degrees of strength.

Thus we are proposing a theoretical framework in which there may be variability in the selection of features to be invoked (each with an invariant acoustic correlate) rather than postulating a one-to-many relation between features and acoustic properties. The features that can be utilized, whether in a distinctive or in a redundant role, are all drawn from the same inventory, and all have the potential of serving in a distinctive role in some language.

The question then arises (and Dr. Repp indeed poses this question) as to whether every auditory-acoustic property that is a potential cue for a distinction can be associated with a feature. That is, can this property be associated with an item on the list of features than can function distinctively in language? A complete answer to this question will require a careful and systematic review, across a variety of languages, of the inventory of features and of auditory-acoustic cues that have been proposed by various researchers. An initial review suggests that the list of acoustic cues arising from perceptual experiments can in almost all cases be interpreted as the acoustic correlates of particular features. This finding is not unexpected if we postulate that the inventory of features is intimately related to, and in fact defined in terms of, the capability of the auditory system to respond distinctively to particular acoustic properties and the capability of the articulatory system to be controlled in such a way as to produce these properties independent of the context.

The hypotheses that form the starting point for our discussion can be summarized, then, as follows. We define the features and their acoustic correlates in such a way that invariance in the implementation of a feature is guaranteed. We propose that variability arises in the features that are selected (largely on the basis of rules) to operate in particular utterances, and not in the relation between features and acoustic properties. With appropriate selection of auditorily-based acoustic properties, we believe that the number of features needed to perform these functions is not large—probably about twenty.

We turn next to comment on the question raised by both Dr. Price and Dr. Repp concerning the selection of which features are to be identified as distinctive and which are redundant in a particular situation. In order to focus the discussion of this question, we shall consider two examples.

One example comes from the the language Yawelmani (Archangeli, 1984), which has four vowels. Examination of the articulatory and perceptual characteristics of these vowels indicates that they can be described in terms of the four major vowel features as follows:

	i	u	o	a
high	+	+	−	−
round	−	+	+	−
back	−	+	+	+
low	−	−	−	+

This description is, however, an overspecification, i.e., there is redundancy in this classification of the vowels. In principle, it is possible to distinguish among four vowels using only two features. A similar overspecification in terms of features occurs for three coronal fricatives in English. The fricatives [s] and [š] are classified as [+strident] and [θ] as [−strident], while the feature [anterior] distinguishes [s] and [θ] from [š]. Acoustic evidence also suggests that [θ] is produced with a backed tongue body position, whereas [s] and [š] can be considered as [−back]. Thus we have the following feature representation for these fricatives

	θ	s	š
strident	−	+	+
anterior	+	+	−
back	+	−	−

Again we have redundancy in the representation of these segments in terms of features.

In situations like this, where it appears that a distinction is carried by more than one feature, is there a basis for arguing that a minimal subset of the features is primary or distinctive, while the remaining features are redundant? Examination of the properties of the acoustic signal does not provide a basis for selecting which of the features form the minimal or distinctive set. Each feature is represented by a property in the sound wave, and although some properties may be present with greater strength or greater reliability, there is often sufficient variability that no one of these properties could be selected as representing the primary or most reliable feature based simply on observation of the sound.

We propose, however, that in situations where more than one feature is involved in making a distinction, such as the Yawelmani or English examples just given, some of the features should be considered as distinctive features and the other features are derived from the distinctive features by a set of redundancy rules. We suggest that a native speaker of a language has access to a representation of words in the lexicon in terms of these underlying distinctive features. A full phonetic representation of the words that includes all of the features may also exist, but the additional features are derivable from the distinctive features through the redundancy rules.

The process of determining which features to label as the distinctive features follows several guidelines:

(1) The distinctive features that are selected should be a minimal set. That is, the underlying feature representation should be maximally simple and should not overspecify the segments in the language.

(2) The rules that are used to derive the redundant features should be universal in character. These rules should be maximally simple, and they should be motivated by relationships among the features that are based on universal physiological and perceptual principles. One of these principles is that a system of oppositions for a particular language evolves in such a way that there is maximum perceptual distinctiveness between contrasting utterances (similar to the ideas proposed by Liljencrants and Lindblom, 1972). Thus, for example, if a language has only five vowels, the vowels will tend to distribute themselves in such a way as to be maximally distinctive.

The universal rules in (2) have not yet been worked out in detail, and the notion of simplicity needs to be quantified more precisely. (See Archangeli, 1984, for a recent proposal in this regard.) Consequently we cannot at this time provide a complete account of how a set of distinctive features is selected.

The nature of the arguments can be illustrated, however, with reference to the Yawelmani vowel example just given. The procedure we shall follow is to *postulate* a set of distinctive features, and then show that, with these features as a starting point, a simple and well-motivated set of rules can be written for deriving the redundant features. It can be argued that if an alternative initial set of distinctive features were selected, the redundancy rules that would be necessary would be both less simple and less well motivated in terms of universal principles.

We begin with a description of the Yawelmani vowel system in terms of the distinctive features marked in the following table:

	i	u	o	a
high			−	−
round		+	+	
back				
low				

The features that are not specified in this table are redundant and are specified by a set of rules.

One type of redundancy rule simply fills in the complements of the features that are marked in the underlying representation. In this example, two such rules are needed:

1. [   ] → [+high]

2. [   ] → [−round]

We now need some rules that will fill in the values of the features [back] and [low]. These rules, we suggest, will follow certain general principles related to auditory perception and to articulatory and acoustic phonetics. One of these principles is that the nonhigh vowel in the vowel triangle that is perceptually the most distinct from all other vowels is the vowel labeled as [+low, +back, −round], that is, the vowel [a]. This vowel has the highest possible first formant frequency, and this attribute separates it maximally from other vowels. If this [+low] vowel were [+round], or if it were [−back], the first formant frequency would tend to be lower, and hence the perceptual distance of the vowel from other vowels would be less. Thus there are perceptual grounds for postulating that a vowel that is [−high, −round] is maximally distinct from other vowels if it also has the features [+low, +back]. At the same time, vowels that are *not* [−high, -round] should not be [+low], since the various [+low] vowels are perceptually rather close together. For example, the first and second formant frequencies for the three low vowels [a], [ɔ], and [æ] are relatively close together, and, in a sparse vowel system this clustering of low vowels is to be avoided. These notions of perceptual distinctiveness related to the low vowels can be captured by two ordered rules:

3. $\begin{bmatrix} -\text{high} \\ -\text{round} \end{bmatrix} \longrightarrow \begin{bmatrix} +\text{low} \\ +\text{back} \end{bmatrix}$

4. $[\quad] \rightarrow [-\text{low}]$

Finally it is necessary to fill in values for the feature [back] for the remaining vowels. Here we draw on a relation between the features [back] and [round] that is discussed in the paper we have prepared for this symposium. In the paper it is shown that the acoustic property that indicates backness for a nonlow vowel (proximity of F_2 and F_1) is enhanced if the vowel is rounded. In a similar fashion one might argue that the acoustic property that indicates rounding (tentatively identified as a greater degree of spectral prominence provided by a formant pair) can be most strongly represented in the sound if the vowel is [+back]. That is, rounding can be signaled in back vowels more effectively than it can in front vowels. This relation between rounding and backness is captured by a fifth redundancy rule, which fills in the unspecified values for the backness feature:

5. [round] → [back].

Application of all these rules in order leads to the completely specified matrix of features given in the table above.

Except for the first two rules, which fill in complement values for the underlying features, these rules can be motivated by relations that exist among the four features [high], [round], [back], and [low]. Given a set of underlying features that have been specified, the rules indicate how other features should be marked in order to enhance or to highlight the acoustic and perceptual representation of the underlying features. Attempts to find an alternative solution to the derivation of the Yawelmani vowel system, using a different underlying representation and/or a different set of redundancy rules, lead to a more complex specification, and the rules that are needed to derive the complete feature matrix are less well motivated in terms of natural relations among the features.

This example, then, illustrates the sense in which, in a given language, we would like to specify some features as distinctive and others as redundant.

21

Variability of Feature Specifications

Mona Lindau and Peter Ladefoged
Phonetics Laboratory
Linguistics Department
University of California, Los Angeles

In the early days of distinctive feature theory, features were regarded both as attributes of phonemes and as properties referring to a single acoustic scale (Jakobson, Fant & Halle, 1951). Later work continued this notion of regarding features as a bridge between abstract phonological entities and physical facts (Chomsky & Halle, 1968a). Each feature was defined in articulatory terms, but it was claimed that this was merely a matter of expository convenience, and the definitions could equally well have been made in acoustic terms. In these distinctive-feature theories, each feature was regarded as being, at the same time, an element in phonological theory and a single physical scale. This made it possible to describe contrasts in binary terms and phonetic differences between languages as different values along a particular physical parameter. Some phonologists, for example McCawley (1968) and Postal (1968), recognized the need to incorporate feature interpretation rules as part of the grammar, but they were extremely vague when it came to working out the details and specifying actual values on any of these physical scales. Ladefoged (1975) is the only concrete proposal of a complete set of feature values for a number of segments in a systematic phonetic transcription (and, as we will show, this proposal is wrong). Just as phonologists were vague in their phonetic specifications, so equally, phoneticians who devised their own feature systems (e.g. Fant, 1971, 1983), did not make any attempt to show how specifications in terms of these features could be related to phonological theories of a language.

It is quite explicit in distinctive feature theory that the features are to be equated with specific, observable properties. Jakobson, Fant, and Halle (1951) state: "A distinctive feature cannot be identified without recourse to

464

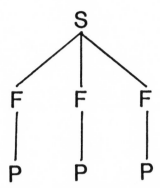

FIG. 21.1. Relationships between segments (S), features (F), and physical parameters (P) in traditional feature theories.

its specific property." Chomsky and Halle (1968a) make it quite plain that "...each feature is a physical scale defined by two points." Although the proposed set of features has been subject to multiple revisions (Chomsky & Halle, 1968a; Halle & Stevens, 1970, 1971; Jakobson, Fant, & Halle, 1951; Jakobson & Halle, 1956; Ladefoged, 1971), there is still a requirement in common to all of these proposed sets of features that each feature is assigned a single, measurable correlate. Most recently this view has been reaffirmed by Stevens (1983): "Each feature is represented in the sound wave as a unique acoustic property to which the auditory system responds in a distinctive way." Each segment, S, is composed of a number of features, F, each of which is related to some physical parameter, P, as sketched in Figure 21.1.

There are several reasons why it seems advisable for a general linguistic theory to permit only a single correlate for each feature. The first is that, without this constraint, features do not have any simple universality. Thus, unless we know that a particular feature always has a particular attribute, we cannot consistently equate descriptions of different languages in terms of that feature. Distinctions in different languages are usually attributed to the same feature by linguists for good phonological reasons. If features were not identified across languages in this way, there would be a tremendous multiplying of categories in the description, and structural similarities in the sound patterns and phonological rules in different languages would undoubtedly be lost. The notion of features and a universal phonetic alphabet would also be needlessly complex and unconstrained, and there are many linguistic universals that we would not be able to capture.

If features do not have a single defining property, then it is possible to describe a sound in more than one way. If feature A can correspond to $x\%$ of property M, $y\%$ of property N, and $z\%$ of property O, and feature B

can correspond to other percentages of these properties, then the possibilities for alternative specifications are present. The possibilities for alternative specifications can be avoided by stating a priori constraints on the permitted many-to-many correspondences that would apply to all phonological descriptions involving these features. But such constraints would be very hard to motivate in terms of a general theory of phonology. Permitting a many-to-many correspondence between features and parameters will almost inevitably permit the possibility of multiple equivalent phonological descriptions. Another reason for requiring a fixed attribute for each feature is that it would be in accordance with a view of human perception that holds that there are specific feature detectors, as proposed by Stevens and Blumstein (1978), Blumstein and Stevens (1979), and Stevens (1983). If this view were correct, it would indeed be a compelling reason for regarding a feature as reflecting a single property. However, there is no case reported of a unique acoustic property that is an invariant correlate of a phonological feature. According to Stevens and Blumstein (1981): "The theory of acoustic invariance has been elaborated most completely for place of articulation in stop consonants." But, without disparaging Stevens' and Blumstein's considerable achievements, their success rate is not very high. The properties proposed for detection of place of articulation are present only in about 83% of initial stops, 75% of final stops if exploded, and 77% of initial nasal consonants. It is also important to note that these numbers exaggerate the success rate in identifying places of articulations, in that the properties for different places of articulation are not mutually exclusive. Thus Stevens and Blumstein found that 83% of initial consonants have the property of the correct place of articulation. But they also found that 25% of all initial consonants have the property of the wrong place of articulation. In other words, 8% of initial consonants have both the correct and one of the incorrect properties. Recent work by Lahiri, Gewirth, and Blumstein (1984) has led to some improvement in these percentages. By allowing the invariant acoustic properties to be both time varying and relative they were able to distinguish bilabial and dental/alveolar stops more than 91% of the time. But this improvement in distinguishing places of articulation is applicable to only one manner of articulation (stop), and only one place in the syllable (initial). Phonological features group sounds in terms of place irrespective of whether they are stops, nasals, or fricatives, and irrespective of whether they are initial or final in the syllable. If correct detection of place of articulation could be achieved in 90% or more of both initial and final positions for stops, fricatives, and nasals, then the feature-detector hypothesis could be considered more seriously.

Stevens and Blumstein (1981) and Stevens (1983) have suggested possible invariant properties for several other phonetic categories. However it is completely clear that there are no reports of the analysis of natural speech that show the presence of truly invariant acoustic properties, however complexly defined, for any phonological feature. Experiments on how listeners perceive synthetic speech are irrelevant to the question of whether there are invariant properties present in natural speech.

It is always possible to argue that the failure to find an invariant property for a particular feature is due to our lack of diligence in looking for it. The claim could be that the invariance is there, but we just have not found it. This is rather like saying that part of the moon is made of green cheese. When we all fail to find the green cheese, it is just because we have not looked in the right places. Of course, there are many occasions in scientific endeavours when it is appropriate to seek structures that are almost certainly present but very difficult to find. This seems to be the situation at the moment in genetics where people are searching for the correlates of inherited characteristics in the structure of the DNA. But the search for invariant properties of phonological features is not like that. In our view, it is more like looking for the particular chemical that will transmute lead into gold.

As an alternative to the notion of each feature having an invariant property, Ladefoged (1981) made specific suggestions for a many-to-many mapping between the features required in a phonological theory and the phonetic parameters necessary for the full linguistic specification of an utterance (the specification that gives all of the facts about an utterance except those that are due to chance circumstances or to its having been spoken by a particular individual). As in previous work (Ladefoged, 1971, 1975), Ladefoged's 1981 paper also stresses the notion that some features are more easily and, from the point of view of phonological rules, more explanatorily characterized in the articulatory domain, and other features provide more explanatory insights when given acoustic definition. Aspects of Ladefoged's views have been criticized by Halle (1982a). But recently Halle himself (Halle, 1983) has advocated a kind of relationship between features and properties which is very different from that given in any of his work cited above. He suggests a many-to-many mapping between phonological features and phonetic parameters.

With a many-to-many mapping between phonological features and physical parameters, the phonological features themselves have become abstract properties: They are entities that emerge from a phonological description. This view is illustrated in Figure 21.2. A segment is still described in terms of features, where the features represent convenient labels for classes of sounds needed by the phonology. Features are connected to physical parameters in a complex, many-to-many relationship.

We will review a number of linguistic phenomena that led us to the conclusion that there is a many-to-many mapping between features and their correlated physical parameters. We have investigated the phonetic properties of many sound classes in a wide variety of languages. In these studies, each language is usually represented by several speakers, so that the results

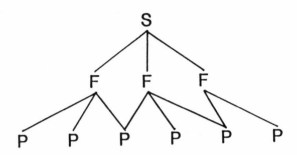

FIG. 21.2. Relationships between segments (S), features (F), and physical parameters (P) proposed here.

are representative of the language. The results demonstrate that articulatory
and/or acoustic correlates of features exhibit considerable variability. This
variability of features occurs both between different languages and between
speakers of the same language.

PLACE OF ARTICULATION

Our view concerning place of articulation is very different from that discussed
above, primarily in that we do not think that there are discrete places of articulation. We recognize that phonological features are needed in many rules
in many languages to specify groups of sounds that can be said to be made
at the same place of articulation. Thus in English, for example, vowels are
lax before consonant clusters, but if the cluster consists of two alveolar consonants, both tense and lax vowels can occur. Or, to take another example,
in many languages nasals are homorganic with the following consonant. It
seems that from a phonological point of view, we need both a cover feature,
PLACE, that enables us to express the notion of "same" or "different" place
in a simple way, and also features for each place, in order to group sounds of
a single place together.

These phonological needs should not lead us into the strait jacket of phonetic invariance. Phonologies consider one language at a time; but when
we consider several languages we see that there are phonetic differences such
that we cannot find invariant characteristics of distinct places of articulation.
Our arguments detailing this point have been given elsewhere (Ladefoged &
Bhaskararao, 1983; Ladefoged & Wu, 1983). Here we will simply note that
x-ray studies show that there is a continuum of possible places of articulation

covering much of the front of the oral cavity. Different languages use different points within this continuum, much as they use different points in the vowel space. It is not possible to find discrete places of articulation such as dental, alveolar, and retroflex. Hindi retroflex [d] occurs at one place, and Telugu retroflex [d] in another. Similarly among fricatives English [s] is very similar to Putonghua [s]; but both are different from both Pekingese [ɕ] and [ʂ] and from English [š]. Tamil [ʂ] is different from all these sounds, despite the fact that linguists often symbolize it in the same way as one of the fricatives of Pekingese. Within this part of the continuum there are five distinct sibilant fricatives: [s, š, (Tamil) ʂ, (Pekingese) ʂ, ɕ], and there is no reason to presume that the continuum could not be split in other ways.

If features are used to describe all these articulations, it is inevitable that they will have to be given ad hoc definitions for each language. As phonologists we will behave as if these are distinct points of articulation. But as phoneticians, we will simply have to specify the sounds of each language in specific ways.

VOWEL FEATURES

The relative nature of the acoustic correlates of vowel quality is well known. The acoustic specification of vowel height, for example, will not be invariant across individuals, but will depend on the person's head size. What is less well known is that the acoustic correlates of the phonological features required for vowels will not be invariant across languages. It is generally agreed that vowel height can be correlated to the first formant (high vowels have a low first formant, and vice versa) and vowel backness to the second formant. But the precise acoustic specification of these features in different languages is not straightforward. For example, most of the world's languages (98%) have a high front vowel transcribed by linguists as [i]. The position in the available acoustic space of this vowel in a particular language depends, among other factors, on the number of vowels in the system. Disner (1983) shows that in the ten-vowel system of Bavarian the [i] has an F_1 centered around 250 Hz. A system with a very small number of vowels, like the Philippine language Tausug with three vowels, will occupy a smaller amount of the available space; in this language [i] has an F_1 centered around 400 Hz. The [i] vowels in the seven vowel systems of Italian and Yoruba are intermediate between those of Bavarian and Tausug, with a mean F_1 around 300 Hz. The Tausug [i] has the same F_1 as the mid vowel phonemes in Bavarian, Italian, and Yoruba. It is, however, still desirable to consider all these [i] vowels as instances of the same feature specifications, as within each system each [i] is the high-front vowel. There will thus be no absolute acoustic invariance corresponding to the feature High; the acoustic correlates will vary from language to language.

ADVANCED TONGUE ROOT

Many African languages have a vowel system that is divided into two harmonizing sets. The two sets have been transcribed by linguists in similar ways for the West African Niger-Congo languages and the East African Nilo-Saharan languages: set 1 vowels are [i, e, o, u], and set 2 vowels are [ɪ, ɛ, ɔ, ʊ]. Early proposals of the phonetic properties for this vowel harmony vary between tenseness, vowel height, and phonation types. Descriptions are quite similar for both language families. Hall, Hall, Pam, Myers, Antell, & Cherono (1974) point out that in both families the direction of vowel harmony is anticipatory: while roots and suffixes may affect each other, prefixes take on the set affiliation of the root. They go on to propose that Proto-Nilo-Saharan borrowed the vowel harmony from Proto-Niger-Congo. Given these structural similarities in the vowel harmony between the two large language families, the same feature should be used to refer to the vowel harmony.

The proposed features for vowel harmony have been of an articulatory nature: ADVANCED TONGUE ROOT (Halle & Stevens, 1970) and EXPANDED PHARYNX (Lindau, 1975, 1979). In many of the Niger-Congo languages, this feature correlates with the size of the pharynx. In Akan, Igbo and Ịjǫ, one set of vowels is produced with a pharynx that is expanded by advancing the tongue root and lowering the larynx, and the other set is produced with a constricted pharynx by retracting the tongue root and raising the larynx. The mechanisms underlying vowel harmony in the Nilo-Saharan languages are however not altogether the same as in the investigated Niger-Congo languages. Different languages make use of different articulatory mechanisms. In Ateso (Nilotic) the tongue root does vary, but no more than can be accounted for by tongue height, and the larynx height does not vary with the harmony affiliation at all. Here vowel harmony is articulatorily confounded with the feature for vowel height. Jacobson (1978) found that in two other Nilotic languages, Shilluk and Dinka, the tongue root differences are not sufficient for distinguishing vowels of different harmony sets. In these languages, there are instead distinct differences in phonation types. Set 1 vowels are breathy, and set 2 vowels have a "tense" or creaky voice. Even within one language, different speakers use different combinations of the above mechanisms to distinguish the two sets. In Dho-Luo (Nilotic) either tongue height or tongue root, with or without vertical larynx displacement, may serve to distinguish the harmonizing sets. In both Ateso and Dho-Luo, one can sometimes also hear a breathy phonation type accompanying the "raised" or tongue-root advanced set. The articulatory correlates for the vowel harmony feature in African languages are thus variable, involving vocal tract shapes, as well as the larynx. Some of the articulatory mechanisms associated with this feature are used for other features as well.

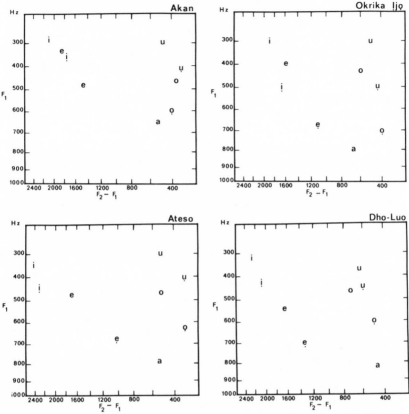

FIG. 21.3. Formant charts of the harmonizing vowels in Akan, Okrika Ijo, Ateso, and Dho-Luo. Set 1 vowels are unmarked, and the set 2 vowels are marked with a dot. The low [a] is neutral to vowel harmony.

Nor is there a unique acoustic correlate of the vowel harmony feature. The different vocal-tract shapes resulting from varying the pharyngeal size have acoustic effects in the frequencies of the first and second formants. Figure 21.3 shows formant charts of two Niger-Congo languages, Akan, and Ijo, and two Nilotic languages; Ateso and Dho-Luo. The chart of Akan represents means of four speakers, and the other languages are represented by one speaker each. In spite of the small number of speakers, there is a general pattern of interest. Each set 2 vowel (marked with a dot) is lower (with a higher F_1) and further back (larger difference F_2-F_1) than its set 1 counterpart. The third formant is not significantly different between the two sets. The acoustic parameters associated with the vowel harmony feature are thus the same as those for features for vowel height and backness. Furthermore, the characteristics of vowel harmony cannot be stated without comparing one vowel relative to another.

REGISTER

Vowel systems in many Mon Khmer languages are characterized by so called registers. The vowels fall in one of two phonological sets, usually referred to as First and Second Register. Historically the registers in many of these languages have a common origin in the loss of a voicing contrast of initial consonants: Voiceless consonants in the protolanguage conditioned First Register vowels, and the voiced consonants conditioned Second Register vowels (Diffloth, 1983). Vowel correspondences in many Mon Khmer languages show the same register affiliation. The same distinctive feature for the registers should thus be used in these languages to capture cross-language similarities in the vowel patterns. We will leave the label for this feature an open question. The phonetic nature of the register feature varies from language to language, and it involves a plethora of parameters. The register distinction may be manifested as differences in vowel quality, including differences in pharyngeal size; diphthongization; duration; phonation types; pitch; or as combinations of these.

Register differences in pharyngeal size, similar to those of vowel harmony in African languages occur in Brôu (Mon Khmer). Formant frequencies of one speaker have been published (Miller, 1967). The nonlow vowels of the first register are lower than their second register counterparts in the same way as the set 2 vowels in African vowel harmony languages are lower than their set 1 counterparts. Thus the Brôu first register vowels could be produced like a set 2 African vowel with a constricted pharynx, and a Brôu second register vowel like a set 1 vowel with an expanded pharynx. This makes sense, given that voiced consonants have a larger pharynx than voiceless consonants. Radiographic data also exist that show differences in pharyngeal size very similar to those in Akan. In addition, however, Brôu vowels also differ in types of diphthongization according to register affiliation. Other Mon Khmer languages realize the First Register as modal phonation and higher pitch, and the Second Register as breathy voice and lower pitch. The Register feature may also be realized as pitch differences alone, as in Kammu (Svantesson, 1983).

The same language may even realize the distinction in different ways for different vowel pairs. Lee (1983) shows that in Mon the Register feature is realized mainly as duration and pitch: First Register vowels are shorter and have a higher pitch than Second Register vowels. There is no overall difference in vowel quality or phonation type. However, the Second Register [e̤] is a higher vowel than the First Register [e], and the Second Register [o̤] is breathy compared to the First Register [o]. The feature for Register must not only be interpreted differently in different languages, but also for different vowels in the same language. In addition, some of the parameters involved are correlates of other features.

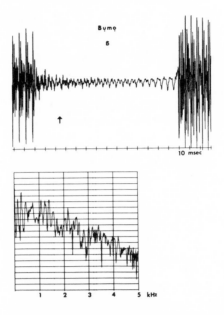

FIG. 21.4. Waveform (top half) and spectrum (bottom half), taken at the arrow, of a labial implosive in Bumọ.

IMPLOSIVES

Several independent phonetic parameters correlate with features of segments that have been called implosive. Lindau (1982) analyzed bilabial and apical implosives from tape-recorded material in five West African languages. These were four Niger-Congo languages—Kalaḅari, Okrika, and Bụmọ (all Ịjọ), Degema (Edoid)—and one Chadic language, Hausa. Articulatory mechanisms were inferred from the acoustic data. The Niger-Congo languages produce implosives with an increasing amplitude of the voicing during the closure in the sound wave, the top half of Figure 21.4. The amount of increase in the voicing tends to covary with the closure duration: The longer the closure duration is, the more the voicing amplitude increases. In Hausa, on the other hand, the relationship between closure duration and the increase of voicing amplitude is generally the opposite. Eight out of 14 Hausa speakers produce implosives of very brief duration with a large increase of voicing amplitude during the closure. These two phonetic variables are part of implosives, but they are independently variable, and different languages will combine them differently.

In addition, phonation types were qualitatively studied by looking at spectra of the implosives. The bottom half of Figure 21.4 shows a waveform of the bilabial implosive in Bụmọ. It is typical of the voiced implosives in the four Niger-Congo languages. The first part of the closure in the waveform displays

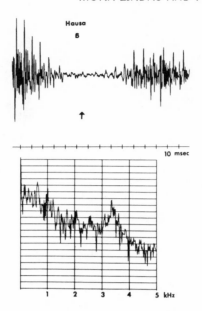

FIG. 21.5.   Waveform (top half), and spectrum (bottom half), taken at
the arrow, of a labial implosive in Hausa.

a considerable amount of high-frequency energy. Below the waveform is a
spectrum of the first 50 milliseconds of the closure, centered at the arrow,
showing a clear formant structure. The high frequency in the waveform is
thus an indication of the upper formants, resulting from excitation of cavity
resonances by the vocal cords vibrating with a relatively sharp closure while
they are being held tightly together in the descending larynx. The first part
of the closure in these languages is thus typically produced with a form of
laryngealization, while the latter part of the closure looks like it is produced
with regular voicing on the waveform.

Hausa implosives differ considerably in the waveform pattern during the
closure. There is also a large amount of individual variation in Hausa. Five
out of the 14 speakers produce no voicing at all during the closure. One
speaker has an implosive very similar to those in the Niger-Congo languages
above. The eight remaining speakers produce an implosive as illustrated in
Figure 21.5. There are highly aperiodic vocal cord vibrations during the
whole closure. The spectrum shows no clear formant structure but there is a
spectral peak around 3500 Hz. This peak cannot be due to cavity resonances
from sharp closures in the vocal cord vibrations. If it were, the lower formants would be apparent as well as one at this high frequency. These Hausa
implosives are thus produced with aperiodic, vocal-cord vibrations. This is
usually also labeled "laryngealization."

In the Niger-Congo languages, the category IMPLOSIVE usually means a rapidly descending larynx with vocal cords vibrating with tight closures at the beginning and continuing with more regular vocal cord vibrations. But in Hausa, the category implosive may mean a voiceless closure, as for five speakers, a type of laryngealized closure with implosion for eight speakers, and a regularly voiced implosive, like in the Niger-Congo languages for one speaker. Thus there are several different physical correlates to the feature IMPLOSIVE in different languages. Within one language, like Hausa, different speakers may produce the implosives in different ways.

It may be argued that the so called implosives in Hausa should not be assigned to an implosive category, but rather to a category of LARYNGEAL-IZATION. This was proposed by Ladefoged (1964). But this will not make the relationship between phonology and phonetics any simpler in Hausa. Hausa has a palatal laryngealized glide ['y] that contrasts with a regular voiced palatal glide [y]. A typical waveform of the laryngealized palatal glide is shown in Figure 21.6. One major characteristic is the very low fundamental frequency, about 35 Hz in this particular glide. Another characteristic is that these sounds are produced with very sharp glottal pulses, resulting in comparatively high amplitude for high-frequency components in the sound. This type of laryngealization is like an extreme version of the type found in the first part of the Bumo implosives.

Even a category LARYNGEALIZED in Hausa will be related to very different modes of phonation in different sound types. The same type of laryngealization will be part of implosives in the Niger-Congo languages and the Hausa ['y], while Hausa implosives are associated with a different type of laryngealization altogether.

RHOTACIZED

The rhotics form a class of phonetically varied sounds that tend to behave in similar ways phonologically. They occupy the same place in consonant systems and in syllable structures. In consonant clusters, the rhotics tend to be vowel adherent. Rhotics participate in the same kinds of rules. They often alternate with each other. In Persian, a trilled [r] has a tap allophone in intervocalic position, and a voiceless trill variant in word-final position. In Fulfulde, a trill is realized as an approximant [ɹ] before a consonant. Postvocalic r's tend to vocalize or get deleted, as in Southern British English, German, Danish, and the Swedish spoken in Skane. Phonetically different rhotics have similar effects on environments: vowels before r's tend to lengthen (English, Swedish), and vowels before and/or after r's tend to lower, as in French and Danish with their uvular r-sound, as well as in Standard Swedish with its apical r-sound.

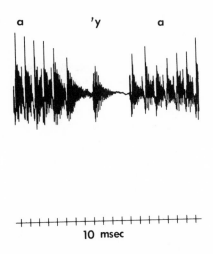

FIG. 21.6.   Waveform of the laryngealized palatal glide in Hausa.

Ladefoged (1975) suggests a feature RHOTACIZED to label the class of r-sounds. But we cannot imagine a unique correlate of this feature in either the articulatory or the acoustic domain. From an articulatory point of view, r-sounds exhibit a wide variety of manners and places of articulation. We find fricatives, trills, taps, approximants, and vowels as realizations of [r], and all may occur as apical or uvular sounds. The American English [r] of the so called "bunched" type is rather unusual: It has two simultaneous constrictions, one at the palate and the other very low in the pharynx (Lindau, 1978).

An acoustic correlate in terms of a lowered F_3 was proposed by Ladefoged (1975) and Lindau (1978). The American English r-sound has a substantially lowered F_3, and so do quite a few other languages, although usually not to the degree found in American English. But uvular rhotics will of course have a raised F_3, approaching F_4. Dental/alveolar rhotics will not always exhibit a lowered F_3, as in the Spanish analyzed by Delattre (1965), and Degema taps (Lindau, 1985).

This class of sounds also exhibits much individual variation. The same speaker may use trills, taps, and approximants, or both apical and uvular r-sounds in free variation. The latter is particularly frequent in border areas between these two types of rhotics. The discussion above shows that there is a many-to-many relationship between features and their correlates for many features. It is even inappropriate to expect phonological features to be in a one-to-one relation to physical scales. Why should they be? Human beings typically classify objects in terms of several physical parameters simultaneously. Objects are called heavy or light, not just according to their mass, but also according to their size and appearance. In the field of categorical perception, it is very difficult to find perceptual attributes that depend on a single physical scale. The pitch of a sound, for example, depends not only on its fundamental frequency, but also on its intensity and duration. The linguist's notion that features are elementary properties is a piece of retrograde psychology. Each feature is associated with variations in many phonetic parameters.

We agree with the standard view that sounds should be described in terms of features in order to describe sound patterns and phonological processes in the languages of the world in the most general and revealing terms. But we regard a feature as a phonological label for a bundle of articulatory and acoustic properties. In most cases we have not found any physical property that constitutes "the phonetic correlate" of a feature. Instead, the situation we often find is that each member in a class of sounds, described by a feature, resembles another member with respect to some property, but it is not the same property that constitutes the resemblance for all members of a class. The relationship between sounds of a class and their phonetic properties is thus more of a "family resemblance" kind (Wittgenstein, 1958) than a kind where all the sounds of one class share a pervading common property. In a family of sounds that functions as a unity within a language and is labelled by a feature, we may find that family member S_1, which resembles S_2, which resembles S_3, which resembles S_4, etc. Although family members S_1 and S_4 may not share any essential phonetic properties, it should still be possible to express their relatedness as a set of steps across other members.

For example, in the class of r-sounds, trills and taps resemble each other in the duration of the pulses involved, tongue-tip trills and uvular trills are similar in the patterns of consecutive pulses, and tongue-tip taps and tongue-tip approximants are close to each other on an articulatory stricture scale. It is thus possible to relate uvular trills to tongue-tip approximants, provided one proceeds in steps across other members of the class of r-sounds.

As we have seen, vowel harmony in African languages and the register distinction in Mon Khmer languages are correlated with several articulatory parameters that are related to each other. Tongue-root movement is part of varying tongue height. Vertical larynx displacement, and possibly tongue-root movement, may be connected to changes in phonation types.

We believe that it is futile to look for the invariance of features in their articulatory and acoustic properties. Rather, the invariance lies in their behavior in classifying sounds in languages, and in their behavior in phonological rules. We view features as rather abstract entities in a complex, but probably statable, relationship to physical scales.

ACKNOWLEDGMENTS:

We would like to thank Arthur House, Gunnar Fant, and the members of the UCLA Phonetics Lab, especially Ian Maddieson, for all their helpful comments and discussions. Kay Williamson helped straighten out our data on African languages. This work was supported in part by a grant from the National Science Foundation and in part by the Swedish Council for Research in the Humanities and Social Sciences.

Sheila E. Blumstein: Comment

Lindau and Ladefoged make the claim that there is a many-to-many mapping between a phonetic feature and a phonetic (physical) parameter, and deny that there may be any single physical property that constitutes a phonetic correlate of a particular feature. For them, membership in a class of sounds is determined by "behavior" in classifying sounds and in the "behavior" of phonological rules.

What is not clear from this account is how/why these distinct physical parameters, many of which undoubtedly have different acoustic/perceptual and articulatory/phonetic manifestations, produce the systematic phonological patterning that is seen repeatedly in natural language. That is, what is the unifying dimension for phonological universals? If there is not acoustic/articulatory commonality for retroflex consonants across languages, for example, why do they behave similarly phonologically, and why do phonologists categorize these supposed different sounds as sharing the common property of retroflexion? It would seem that if there were no principled phonetic bases for phonological categories, then a language would be as likely to have a phonological category including labial and alveolar stops as to have one which includes retroflex type a and retroflex type b. There are obviously some limitations to what sound patterns do occur, and I would like to suggest that these patterns are based on the shared physical dimensions of the phonetic (acoustic) manifestations of the sounds of natural language.

J. C. Catford: Comment

While being very much in sympathy with Chapter 21, I would like to comment on a problem common to all feature-systems. This is the very wide applicability of certain features: *Rhotic* and *retroflex* are cases in point.

Rhotic covers an enormous range of phonetic possibilities including *trills* articulated by any flexible organ—lips, tongue or uvula; alveolar, postalveolar, retroflex, and uvular *fricatives* and *approximants*; and, finally, the curious tongue-bunching of a common type of American [r]. Almost the same sound as this occurs in certain Caucasian languages (particularly Udi and Tsakhur) as a modification of vowels. In the Caucasian languages, this sound has the same depression in the dorsal surface of the tongue, near the uvula, and the same bulging of the root of the tongue into the pharynx as the American [r]. Because of this latter bulging, these sounds in the Caucasian languages are called "pharyngealized." Thus, what is associated with r-sounds in American English, is associated with various kinds of pharyngeal and pharyngealized articulations in the Caucasus. The use of the same feature-term *rhotic* or *rhotacized* conceals a considerable typological difference.

Retroflex provides another example. Any articulation involving raising of the apex of the tongue to the postalveolar position, or even further back, is called *retroflex* in the languages of India—whether it is the extremely retroflex, sublamino-prepalatal, articulations of some Dravidian languages, the mildly retroflex, or mere apico-postalveolar articulation common in Hindi. In India, the term is applied also to the apico-postalveolar fricatives that contrast with lamino-postalveolar fricatives (often called "retroflex" and "palatal," respectively) in Sanskrit, Marathi and a few other languages. In the Caucasus, where a comparable opposition occurs in several languages, the retroflex sounds are generally called "hard" (as opposed to the "soft" palatalized ones). This, of course, is the Russian and Slavic tradition, whereby the slightly retroflex fricatives are associated with nonpalatalized stops, rather than with retroflex stops, as they would be in India.

My own approach is to avoid setting up arbitrary and procrustean features, but to note that the human vocal tract is more or less universal and that there are universal parameters (such as place of articulation): In any given situation, one can derive from observation whatever generalizations are useful in making descriptive or typological statements without being constrained by a preset arbitrary list of features.

22 Features: Fiction and Facts

Gunnar Fant
Royal Institute of Technology
Stockholm, Sweden

INTRODUCTION

These are some personal views on distinctive feature analysis acquired during the course of more than thirty years since my early cooperation with Roman Jakobson and Morris Halle. Most of what I have to say is neither new nor radical and has been expressed in more detail in earlier publications (e.g., Fant, 1973), containing several articles on the subject (e.g., Fant, 1969, 1970). A recent article (Fant, 1983) on Swedish vowels provides additional perspectives. The following is a summary and an attempt to relate feature theory to the topic of this volume.

Distinctive-feature theory has two main purposes. One is to develop a language-universal system of phonetic categories selected to serve phonological classificatory functions. The other is to describe essentials of the speech code, i.e., distinctive dimensionalities and mechanisms of encoding within the speech chain.

It was the great undertaking of Roman Jakobson to attempt to unify these two objectives within the same theoretical frame. Jakobson's influence has been immense. He insisted on absorbing all possible background information from spoken language and research in speech production, acoustics, and perception for this purpose. Still, he was aware of the difficulties of the task and it was he who coined the term "preliminaries" for our joint work. He was always open to new suggestions and could accept new classificatory solutions given new evidence.

Yet there remains in my view an inherent difficulty in reaching a language-universal solution optimal for both purposes. The mechanisms and codes are a unique product of human physiology and, thus, universal while the specific choice of classificatory features for describing a specific language

480

becomes highly dependent on the investigator's phonetic background, the terminology he or she is accustomed to, and to attempts to optimize the feature inventory to simplify descriptions of language structure and usage. One difficulty is that one and the same physical fact may be described in so many different ways. From vowel theory we know that a parametric description in terms of F_1 and F_2 by rotation of coordinates is equivalent to a description in terms of F_2-F_1 and F_1+F_2 which calls for a change in feature labels.

The supposedly happy marriage between phonology and phonetics has its inherent shortcomings and some of us like Peter Ladefoged might argue for a respectful divorce. I am skeptical about the task of formulating a unique ultimate set of classificatory features appropriate for all languages of the world but I do believe in a continued search for insight into universal speech and hearing mechanisms and dimensions and their distinctive role within specific languages. This should at least be our immediate goal.

Jakobson's work has paved the way for the development of the field. His idea of applying tonality features and compactness to consonants as well as to vowels (Jakobson et. al., 1952) relates to basic acoustic and auditory dimensions, such as whether a sound is dominated by high- or low-frequency components and if the energy is concentrated or distributed in the frequency domain. That the auditory system preserves such dimensions is apparent from recent neurophysiological findings (e.g., Sachs, Young & Miller, 1982). This parallelism between consonant and vowel dimensionalities focuses on the output of the speech chain and, thus, on properties essential to the code. The Chomsky and Halle (1968b) approach, on the one hand, is to define features from the production level and not to worry too much about their acoustic and perceptual integrity.

Both systems have their drawbacks. The parallelism within the Jakobson system is not a sufficient basis for all consonant categories and the articulatory base of the Chomsky and Halle system does not explain the code.

FEATURES IN THEORY AND PRACTICE

The stable parts of theory are our real insight in language structure and usage and in the production, acoustics, and perception of speech. This is by no means complete but our knowledge can be tested, updated, and expanded from a solid basis. To me, phonetics is the stable partner of the marriage, while phonology is promiscuous in its experimenting with widely different frameworks and choice of features for describing one and the same inherent phenomenon. I have myself contributed to the phonological diversity by proposing several alternative solutions to the classification of Swedish vowels.

In a pragmatic sense, it does not matter which framework of classificatory features you adopt as long as you know how to handle them phonetically. A column within a feature matrix must first of all serve as an appropriate address for finding a specific phoneme or class of phonemes. In addition, there is the requirement of a maximally simple and direct relation to phonetic events and their ordering in parameter space and time. As an example of pragmatism, Carlson and Granström adopted parts of the Chomsky and Halle feature system for our text-to-speech synthesis program. Labials are accordingly classified as ¦ anterior, coronal, but the program does not have an independent mode of realization of each of these categories. It is the combined presence which triggers labiality. I am, for reasons of principle, against such encoding of phonetically autonomous dimensions by a combination of totally unrelated dimensions. Another example within the Chomsky and Halle system is the minimal distinction of /r/ being [−anterior] and /l/ being [+anterior]. Within the Jakobson, Fant & Halle (1952) system the phoneme /h/ is encoded as [−consonantal], [−vocalic] which I have supported by the roundabout argument that /h/ lacks or has rather weak consonantal attributes (no significant zeros, lack of F-pattern contrast) and is less vowellike than adjacent vowels.

In the Chomsky and Halle (1968b) system, the phoneme /h/ in addition to the [−consonantal], [−vocalic] base is encoded as [+back], [−front] in distinction to the glide /y/ which is labeled [−back], [+front]. This solution obscures the role of the tongue body features which relates to the place of articulation for the /y/ but to the place of the source for /h/ which, of course, can have the same or similar tongue articulation as /y/.

Thus, the hunt for maximum economy often leads to solutions that impair the phonetic reality of features. As a reaction, we could employ traditional phonetic terminology in a feature matrix and abolish the use of minus classifications. Still, we maintain a minimum-average redundancy in the outcome by, on the average, 3 plus-sections needed per phoneme (Fant, 1969). A second stage adding contextual constraints will reduce possible combinations, which is an important consideration in automatic speech recognition.

A simple one-to-one relation between phonetic events and phonological entities is exceptional. Speech segmentation is frequenctly ambiguous and expected events may be missing. A string of several successive phonetic events or segments may carry information about a single phonological segment or distinctive feature, and the converse, a many-to-one relation, introduces a complex set of conditional factors affecting a single phonetic segment or a parameter or cues.

One way out of this dilemma is to develop improved models of speech production which make us more aware of temporal continuities of speech parameters and their constraints induced by physiological, linguistic, situational, and personal factors. Such a view of speech, as a continuous complex vector in space and time anchored in production, must be followed up on the level of the speech wave and speech perception. It will free us from the bonds of segmenting the speech wave with maximal precision prior to recognition, but it will require a more profound insight in the perceptual relevance of rapidly varying speech-vector states.

The articulatory framework should be more or less the same for vowels and consonants, i.e., contain a specification of both main tongue-body configuration and place of articulation which need not coincide exactly with the place of maximum narrowing. Consonants, thus, have an added main tongue-body feature, as introduced by Chomsky and Halle (1968b), and vowels can employ consonantal elements. An example is the extreme palatal narrowing found in the long (tense) Swedish [i:] or [y:] when stressed, while the Swedish long tense [ʉ:] in addition to its extreme narrow lip opening is produced with an apical elevation which advances the place of minimum cross-sectional area anteriorly to that of the vowel [i:] or [y:]. In R-colored vowels, on the other hand, the consonantal modification is a phonologically distinctive element.

The coarticulation model of Öhman (1967a) with separate inputs for vowel and consonant commands is an appropriate starting point for articulatory analysis. His notion (Öhman, 1967b) of redistribution of physiological energy as a result of varying prosodic patterns could be extended to define a dimension affecting scale values of targets and, furthermore, the duration and intensity of phonetic segments and vowel-consonant contrasts. The position of a syllable within a sentence, lexical stress emphasis and deemphasis, and citation forms versus connected speech will all condition such an energy or emphasis factor. It is also related to the tense/lax dimension and has to be followed up by intrasyllabic relations. This is a suggestion for how to organize a search for rules that will predict speech variability.

ARTICULATORY VERSUS ACOUSTIC
PERCEPTUAL ANCHORING: VOWELS

Should distinctive features accordingly be anchored in the articulatory domain? There are examples which point at a single, well-defined, articulatory event conditioning several acoustic cues. Glottal adduction appropriate for voicing not only facilitates the voicing prior to the release of a voiced stop but reduces also the voice onset time (VOT) and lowers the starting point of F_1 in the following vowel. The duration of a previous vowel may also be increased, though marginally only, except when the unvoiced member, in addition, is aspirated (preocclusion aspiration). However, all these cues have one and the same acoustic effect, that of increasing the amount of and continuity of low-frequency energy. The voiced/voiceless, lax/tense, and unaspirated/aspirated distinctions have developed a symbiosis in many languages, like Swedish and English. In my view, it would be against the principle of phonetic reality to consider only one of these features to carry the /g, b, d/ versus the /k, p, t/ distinction.

On the other hand, to back up an output-oriented view, there are examples of a diversity of articulations appropriate for one and the same phoneme, e.g. /r/. In a recent article on Swedish vowels (Fant, 1983), I point out that the short [ɵ] and long [ʉ:], spelled [u], differ drastically in terms of articulation. The [ɵ] is close to a back vowel [o], while [ʉ:] is not less fronted than [i:]. Acoustically, they are also further apart than any two long/short members of a pair, but they still occupy one and the same subspace (see Figure 22.1). In relation to other rounded front vowels, they are extra "flat," i.e., they have a lower $F_1 + F_2'$ than [ö:], [ö] and [y:], [Y].

Complex vowels systems as in Swedish are a challenge to the binary principle since vowels eventually attain mutually adjusted positions within an acoustic space of F_1, F_2', and F_3 or F_1 and F_2 with a tendency of regular spacing in terms of auditory measures, as the Bark unit. Still, I feel it is appropriate to analyze the system in terms of binary distinctions. The basic feature of gravity with the correlate of small $F_2 - F_1$ separating back vowels from front or centralized vowels has a perceptual relevance. Thus, starting out from the vowel [o] and introducing a small forward shift of the tongue to bring F_2 to a location more than 3.5 Bark away from F_1, transcending the boundary beyond which F_1 and F_2 are processed centrally as separate formants, produces a vowel which is perceived as [ɵ]. This is in accordance with the experiments of Chistovich and Lublinskaya (1979). When two formants come closer than about 3.5 Bark they are perceived in terms of a weighted mean value which is the case for grave vowels.

These findings add support to Stevens' (1969) quantal theory. I could also add that the acoustics of speech production acts as a stabilizer for the extreme grave and the extreme nongrave vowels. Once F_2 and F_1 or F_3 and F_2 come closer than about 3 Bark, the distance will change but little with a more extreme back or extreme front articulation. Moreover, the gravity measure will be insensitive to moderate changes in the place of articulation.

Tranmüller (1983) has found that females and males preserve one and the same $F_3 - F_2$ for front vowels. This is mainly a consequence of linear scale of vocal-tract dimensions. A nonuniform difference, such as tha of the relatively shorter female pharynx, would not counteract this trend. In grave vowels, the energy within the F_2 and F_1 modes are fairly equally divided between the front and back of the vocal tract. This is a requirement for proximity. The same is true of F_3 and F_2 of front vowels. The vowel [i] is an exception from this rule since F_2 of [i] has a distinct back cavity and F_3 a front-cavity affiliation. However, the $F_3 - F_2$ measure of [i] is greater than that of other front vowels. The vowel [i] produced with a relatively long pharynx, as in

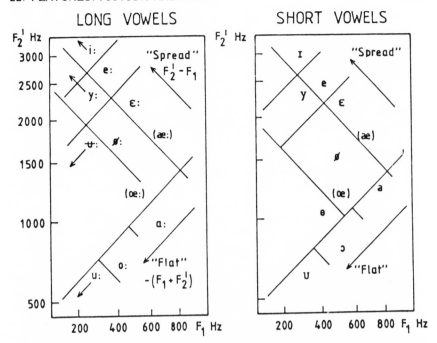

FIG. 22.1.   Swedish long and short vowels within a F_2' versus F_1 frame
with auditory (Bark) adjustment of frequency scales. The [æ] and [œ] are
pre-r allophones of /ø/ and /ɛ/. Observe the relational similarity within
the two groups of vowels. The +45 degree slanting line above the back
vowels corresponds to the critical distance F_2-F_1 3.5 Bark.

male speech, is characterized by a F_3 closer to F4 than to F_2. An additional
stabilizer of F_1 of the vowel [i] is that it can never be lower than the closed
tract resonance frequency of about 200 Hz as set by the wall impedance.
These stability phenomena have been mentioned by Stevens (1969).

Other discrete effects within the Swedish vowel system is the diphthongal
gesture with extreme articulatory narrowing, towards a homorganic consonant, i.e., [i:→j], [u:→ β].

ABSOLUTE VERSUS RELATIONAL INVARIANCE

A fundamental concept in distinctive feature theory, as outlined by Jakobson
et al. (1952), is that of relational invariance. The critical scale value of a
parameter at which a feature shifts from plus to minus is conditioned by the
specific context of preceding, present, and following features within an area
of the distinctive feature matrix and, of course, by prosodic, individual, and

TABLE 22.1

Binary Feature Matrix

Parameter	Feature	[u:] [u]	[o:] [ɔ]	[a:] [a]	[ε:] [ε]	[e:] [e]	[i:] [I]	[y:] [Y]	[ʉ:] [θ]	[ø:] [ø]
$-(F_2-F_1)$	grave	+	+	+	−	−	−	−	−	−
$-(F'_2-F_1)$	flat	(+)	+	−	−	−	−	+	(+)	+
$-(F'_2-F_1)$	extra flat	+	−					−	+	−
F'_2-F_1	diffuse				−	+	(+)	(+)		
F'_2-F_1	sharp				−	+	+	−		

situational factors. The minimum requirement is the presence of a vectorial component along a specific distinctive parameter dimension. A compactness distinction within vowels should therefore, ceteris paribus, always involve a higher F_1 for the compact member. In my 1983 study of Swedish vowels, I have chosen the opposite of compactness, i.e., diffuseness to separate /i/ and /e/ from /ε/. The long Swedish vowels [i:] and [e:] may differ rather little in F_1 whilst the higher F'_2 is the correlate of the sharpness feature assigned to [i:].

Once the acoustic vowel space is normalized with respect to individual and contextual factors, the operation to select a specific vowel may be broken down into a succession of absolute binary decisions in terms of delimiting boundary lines. The sequence of operations is that implied by a coding tree which in my suggestion for Swedish vowels involves [grave], [flat], [extra flat], [diffuse], [sharp] in addition to the long/short distinction (see Table 22.1 and Figure 22.2).

A few words could be said about the marking of redundancies in distinctive feature matrices. I indicate by parenthesis predictabilities from features located lower down in the matrix or in the associated coding tree. Thus, [+extra flat] implies [+flat], and [+sharp] implies [+diffuse]. I use blanks for features that are bypassed in the coding tree, i.e., which are irrelevant or implied by prior branches. Thus, [−flat] implies [−extra flat] and [diffuse] implies [−sharp].

The search for absolute invariance of feature correlates irrespective of context, as pursued by K. N. Stevens, is a challenge (Blumstein & Stevens, 1979. 1980; Stevens, 1980). I have especially in mind his discussion of the correlates of place of articulation of stops. Even though a single spectral section at the early part of a stop release may retain fairly stable "acute," "grave,"

SWEDISH VOWELS

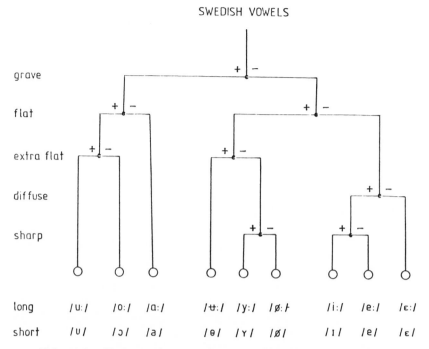

FIG. 22.2.   Distinctive feature coding tree of Swedish vowels.

or "compact" attributes, the specification becomes more precise if we include contextual elements. However, since Stevens allows for temporal contrast effects, one could systematically allow the term "absolute" to mean without reference to phonological identity of the context. This view can then incorporate an integration of cues within a finite window extending sufficiently far in time before and after the stop release to catch transitional phenomena.

The common denominator of an ensemble of velar and palatal stops produced with various degrees of lip rounding is the energy concentration in the F_2' range of the following vowel. In addition to the element of spectral concentration, we thus retain the requirement of a location of the concentration with reference to the F-pattern without having to make a decision about the context. Similarly, the positive going F_2, F_3 versus time transition of labials adds important characteristics to the relative low-frequency dominant spectrum section at the release.

In my view, human speech perception relies on gestalt decoding rather than on isolated short-time spectral patterns or templates. The interdependency of the several cues found within the domain of a single distinction is considerable, as found in many experiments at the Haskins Laboratories. Experience from speech synthesis also indicates that when listeners are confronted with stimuli in a boundary region between phonemes, they may react with different weights to the variation of some of the cues or parameters entering the feature complex. This also speaks for the importance of the complete gestalt or of major cues within the gestalt. The auditory system probably makes efficient use of the entire evidence available. Why should we limit our descriptive work to less precise specifications or to a diluted specification which can operate in all contexts?

Whether this gestalt is anchored in the listener's internalized concept of what a vocal tract can do (Dorman, Lawrence & Liberman, 1979), or whether it is performed by virtue of an experience about auditory patterns in speech is more a matter of preference of verbal phrasing than a real difference.

Sheila E. Blumstein: Comment

I would like to comment on the last point made in the Fant paper. Fant states, "Whether this gestalt is anchored in the listener's internalized concept of what a vocal tract can do... or whether it is formed by virtue of an experience about auditory patterns in speech is more a matter of preference of verbal phrasing than a real difference." One of the primary goals in looking for invariance in speech is to determine how we process speech and language, and to determine what the underlying mechanisms are for such processing. It is not a matter of preference in choosing one anchor over another. It is in effect an empirical issue and a very critical one. If the anchor is expressed in terms of the auditory domain, in terms of the articulatory domain, or in terms of some mental representation mediating the two, then the nature of the mechanisms subserving the use of speech and language will be quite different, as will our models of speech/language processing. For example, the analysis by synthesis model of speech was developed largely because of a failure to find invariant acoustic patterns corresponding to phonetic features. It may turn out that there are indeed invariant auditory patterns as well as invariant vocal tract configurations subserving a common mental representation. However, these are issues which can only be resolved empirically, and which will have critical theoretical consequences.

Nelson Kiang: Comment

In giving us his personal views on distinctive feature analysis, Fant expresses skepticism about basing a complete view of human speech perception on isolated, short-time spectral patterns or templates. He seems to encourage further study of physiological mechanisms as one important direction for future work. As a physiologist, I would like to comment on the outlook for such an approach.

Ultimately, the descriptions of how we process speech or any other auditory stimulus will come from physiology. Unfortunately, we do not know the physiological mechanisms for perceptual constancy which would be fundamental for providing definitive answers to the questions raised in this volume. It is easy to sketch plausible schemes for any well-designed operation but this is different from knowing the actual mechanisms.

After attending this symposium for three days, I am reminded of the debates of the Chinese Naturalists over two thousand years ago about how to account for the properties of material things. Their solution led to the five element theory, in which all the qualities of physical things could be explained as combinations of water, fire, wood, metal, and earth. This theory appeared to be satisfactory in accounting for the diversity of identifiable things as well as differences between specific samples of a type. Today, most modern scientists believe that the building blocks of things are at the atomic and molecular levels, and that invariances in material things are based on similarities in structure at lower levels.

Similarly, the question of what underlies the concept of "species" raised problems for classical biologists. A dog was a dog even though there could be many different kinds of dogs. All attempts to define individual species in terms of key characteristics tended to have an ad hoc quality. Today, most biologists are convinced that the invariances that define species occur at the level of DNA molecules which constitute the building plans for organisms. Certain differences in these molecules will correspond to variations within a species, whereas others will preclude the development of fertile offspring thereby creating distinct species.

In both these examples, the problem is how to account for invariances that define categories and still recognize permissible variations within a category. In each case, the resolution came from a reductionistic approach. Even though the number of cases for which a full synthetic demonstration is available is small, the presently accepted solutions appear satisfactory.

I submit that the search for the bases of invariance in speech perception and production at either acoustic or phonological levels is probably doomed to failure because the invariance must be at neural levels. In taking this view, I do not wish to denigrate the valuable work of the type presented in this volume. Such work will provide factual evidence that will have to be accounted for in any acceptable theory. My present view is that no reasonably realistic neurophysiological formulation to explain speech processing and generation has been proposed at a sufficiently interesting level to warrant detailed analysis. As data from direct studies of the human brain in action become commonplace, the issues raised in this volume will become increasingly relevant to cognitive neuroscientists who will in fact have to account for "gestalt decoding" in terms of specific neural mechanisms. I urge speech scientists to interact with such workers and to insist that their students acquire some familiarity with neurophysiological concepts. By such means, speech studies will receive new revitalizing influences and Fant's cautious optimism will be justified.

Gunnar Fant: Response to Kiang

As speech scientists, we have a tendency to project our preestablished models of language on our models of brain functions, but we are eager to follow the advance of neurophysiology of speech and hearing to learn more and revise our working models. Meanwhile, we resort to available evidence form other stages within the speech chain to fill in the gaps in an overall theory of speech coding and decoding.

Alvin M. Liberman: Comment

My concern is first with invariance only in the conversion from sound to phonetic structure, and then with the facts that such invariance ought, in my view, to take into account.

Because of the way we speak, the acoustic information for a phonetic segment commonly comprises a large number and wide variety of cues, most of them dynamic in form. These cues span a considerable stretch of sound, grossly overlap the cues for other segments, and are subject to a considerable amount of context-conditioned variation.

The phonetic perceiving system is sensitive to all the acoustic cues. None of these cues is truly necessary; all are normally used; and their relative importance bears little relation to their salience as it might be reckoned on a purely auditory basis.

Perception of phonetic structure is immediate in the sense that there is no conscious mediation by, or translation from, an auditory base. Generally, listeners are only aware of the coherent phonetic structure that the cues convey, not of the quite different auditory appearances the cues might be expected to have, given their overlap, context-conditioned variation, number, diversity, and dynamic nature. Thus, taking stop consonants and their dynamic formant-transition cues as a particular example, I note that listeners are not aware of the transitions as pitch glides (or chirps) and also as (support for) a stop consonant; listeners are only aware of the stop. Yet these same formant transitions *are* perceived as pitch glides (or chirps) when—on the nonspeech side of a duplex percept, for example—they do not figure in perception of a phonetic segment.

These facts have two implications. One is that the invariance between sound and phonetic structure should be sought in a general relation between them that is systematic but special, not in particular connections that are occasional and discrete. The relation can be seen to be systematic to the extent it is governed by lawful dependencies among articulatory movements, vocal-tract shapes, and sounds, dependencies that hold for all phonetically relevant behavior, not just for specific and fixed sets of elements. The relation has got to be special because the vocal tract and its organs are special structures that behave, most obviously in coarticulation, in special ways. A second implication is that the special relation between sound and phonetic structure is acted on in perception by a system that is appropriately specialized for the purpose.

If the foregoing assumptions are correct, then the invariance in speech is not unique. Rather it resembles, at least grossly, the kinds of special invariances that are found in many perceptual domains. Accordingly, the system that is specialized for phonetic perception can be seen as one of a class of similarly specialized biological devices. All take advantage of a systematic but special invariance between the "proximal" stimuli and some property of the "distal" object. The result is immediate perception of the properties that make it possible to identify the invariant distal object.

Consider visual perception of depth as determined by the proximal cue of binocular disparity. There is a general and systematic, yet special, relation between the distal property (relative distance of points in space) and the proximal stimulus (disparity). The relation is general and systematic in that it is governed by the laws of optical geometry and holds for all points (within its range) and for all objects, not just for some. The relation is special because it depends on the special circumstances that we have two eyes, that they are so positioned (and controlled) as to be able to see the same object, and that they are separated by a particular distance. Neurobiological investigation has revealed an anatomically and physiologically coherent system that is specialized to process the proximal disparity and relate it to the distal depth. Given that specialization, perception of depth is automatic and immediate; there is no conscious mediation by, or translation from, the double images we would see if, in fact, we were perceiving the proximal disparity as well as the distal property it specifies.

Other perceptual phenomena have the same general characteristics. Auditory localization and the various constancies come immediately to mind, and, if we put aside questions about phenomenal "immediacy," so too do such processes as those that underlie echolocation in bats and song in birds. These are surely specializations if only because each such process, or module, is as different from every other as is the invariant relation it serves. The phonetic module differs from many of the others in at least two ways.

To make one of the differences clear, I would turn again to binocular disparity and depth perception as representative of a large class. In this case the distal object is "out there," a physical thing in the narrow sense of the word "physical," and the invariant relation between its properties and those of the proximal stimulus is determined, as already indicated, by optical geometry and the separation of the eyes. In speech, however, the distal object—a phonetic structure—is a physiological thing, a neural process in the talker's brain, and the invariant relation between its properties and those of the proximal sound is determined in large part by neuromuscular processes internal to the talker but available also to the listener. Thus, the specialized phonetic module might be expected to incorporate a biologically based link between production and perception. Such a link is not part of the disparity module or of the other perceiving modules it exemplifies, though it may very well characterize the "song center" module of certain birds.

A second important difference in the nature of the invariance (and its module) has to do with the question: What turns the module on? In the case of binocular disparity, the answer is a quite specific characteristic of the proximal stimulus—namely, disparity. Notice, however, that disparity has no other utility for the perceiver but to provide information about the distal property, depth. There are, accordingly, no circumstances in which the perceiver could use the proximal disparity as a specification of, or signal for, some other property. Disparity and the depth it conveys do not compete with other aspects of visual perception such as hue or form but complement them. Not so in phonetic perception. There is, first of all, the fact that the speech frequencies overlap those of nonspeech. More to the point, the formant transitions that we don't want to perceive as chirps when we are listening to speech are very similar to stimuli that we do want to perceive as chirps when we are listening to birds. Thus, almost any single aspect of the proximal stimuli can be used for perception of radically different distal objects: phonetic structures in a talker's head or acoustic events and objects in the outside world. The module can hardly be turned on by some specific (acoustic) property of the proximal stimulus. Not surprisingly, then, we find in research on speech perception that the module is not turned on that way, but rather by some more global property of the sound. Thus, just as in the perception of phonetic segments all cues are responded to but none is necessary, so too in identifying sound as speech.

How, then, is the module turned on? What invariant property of the sound causes the listener to perceive that the distal object is a phonetic structure and not some nonlinguistic object or event? I offer a suggestion. Suppose that auditory stimuli go everywhere in the nervous system that auditory stimuli can go, including the language center. The language center has to answer the question: Could these sounds, taken quite abstractly, have been produced by linguistically significant articulatory maneuvers, also taken quite abstractly? If the answer is yes, then the module takes over the purely phonetic aspects of the percept, and the auditory appearances are inhibited. (Auditory aspects that are irrelevant to the phonetic, such as loudness or hoarseness, are perceived as attributes of the same distal object.) If the answer is no, then the phonetic module shuts down and the ordinary auditory appearances of the stimuli are perceived. Hence the common experience of those who work with synthetic speech that when the sound includes configurations that the articulatory organs cannot produce as well as those it can, the percept breaks, correspondingly, into nonspeech and speech. Phenomenally, the nonspeech stands entirely apart from, and bears no apparent relation to, the speech, even though the acoustic bases for these wholly distinct percepts were perfectly continuous. The same arrangement for turning the module on (or off) might account for the fact that certain kinds of acoustic patterns—for example, sine waves in place of formants—can be perceived as speech or as nonspeech depending on circumstances that in no way alter the acoustic structure of the stimulus. It also helps to explain how, as in the unnatural procedures of duplex perception, we can disable the mechanism that forces the choice between speech and nonspeech, and so create a situation in which exactly the same proximal formant transition is simultaneously perceived (in the same context and by the same brain) as critical support for a stop consonant and also as a nonspeech chirp. At all events, there is a kind of competition between phonetic perception and other ways of perceiving sound. A consequence is that the phonetic module produces a more or less distinct mode of perception in a way that modules like depth perception do not. This phonetic mode accommodates a class of distal objects that are distinguished, not only by their role in language, but also by the special nature of the invariant relation by which they are connected to sound.

23

ON THE ORIGIN AND PURPOSE OF DISCRETENESS AND INVARIANCE IN SOUND PATTERNS

Björn Lindblom
Stockholm University

INTRODUCTION

Quantal Nature of Speech

A fundamental property of spoken language is its quantal nature. Linguistic analysis shows that the sound shapes of lexical and grammatical elements are not unanalyzable wholes, but exhibit a quantized organization into combinations of a small number of discrete units such as phonemes (speech sounds, segments, or allophones) and subunits such as distinctive features. "Almost every insight gained by modern linguistics from Grimm's law to Jakobson's distinctive features depends crucially on the assumption that speech is a sequence of discrete entities" (Halle, 1964).

Although the assumption that speech has segmental structure enjoys widespread acceptance both in experimental phonetics and in applied speech research, skeptical voices are nevertheless heard now and then urging that we collect and interpret information on speech processes with a minimum of assumptions about underlying linguistic units (Moll, Zimmerman & Smith, 1976), or that we look for alternatives to concatenative phoneme-based models to improve the performance of rule synthesis and recognition schemes (Fujimura, 1983). The latter view is exceptionally optimistic in that it welcomes new developments in linguistic theory (e.g. nonlinear phonology), whereas the former takes the other extreme and deliberately sets out to ignore linguistic considerations. In general, questioning the linguist's traditional analysis of speech is not entirely uncommon among phoneticians, engineers, and speech scientists whose primary domain is taken to be "observables," such as the signal and the associated speaker/listener behavior, rather than the "unobservable" message structure. Such skepticism has several origins, one being the invariance and segmentation issues which arise from a conflict between the linguistic and physical perspectives on speech and which presumably contribute appreciably toward an underestimation of the weight of linguistic evidence by laboratory workers.

As a background for the following discussion, I will state the invariance and segmentation issues and, from an abundance of examples, I will select a single representative case that typifies how analyses of phonological facts force the conclusion that speech is quantal, that is, featurally and segmentally structured. Let us choose the account of English plural formation given by Halle and Stevens (1979).

According to Halle and Stevens (1979), the plural ending is [iz], [s] or [z] depending on the final consonant of the noun. It is:

(i) [iz] if the noun ends with [s z č ǰ š ž], otherwise
(ii) [s] if the noun ends with [p t k f θ], otherwise
(iii) [z].

The consonants listed in (i) belong to the phonetically defined class of strident and coronal consonants and those of (ii) to the class of voiceless sounds. The rule could therefore be stated in the following alternative way; the plural suffix is:

(i) [iz] if the noun ends with a strident coronal consonant, otherwise
(ii) [s] if the noun ends with a voiceless consonant, otherwise
(iii) [z].

The two formulations make different predictions about the plural of foreign words such as *Bach* and *Reich* which end in nonstrident noncoronal segments, [x] and [ç] respectively, that is in consonant segments that are absent in the English system. The first version would give us [−z] whereas— in agreement with many native speakers' pronunciation—the second would produce [−s]. Halle and Stevens (1979) conclude that such results testify to the psychological reality of the second description and thus to the reality of the feature concept.

English plural formation is an instructive example because, in a rather clear way and in a single process, it demonstrates the roles of feature, segment, natural class, rule order, and rule in phonology. Can phonological regularities be described satisfactorily without postulating such constructs, notably feature and segment? The evidence seems to conclusively preclude an affirmative answer and accordingly supports the hypothesis that speech is featurally and segmentally (=quantally) structured.

Additional evidence for the quantal nature of speech comes from psycholinguistic studies of the performance of speakers and listeners. Speech errors provide a rich source of observations that demonstrate that units that are discrete according to linguistic analysis behave discretely in that they sometimes become detached from their normal context and appear in various patterns of permutation with other related units ("heft lemisphere, Fatz and Kodor, fuwt meeving, glear pluc sky..."; Fromkin, 1973, Appendix). The manner in which different languages convert speech to writing should also be mentioned. For example the Korean *hangul* writing system is said to make a more explicit and systematic use of phonetic features than most orthographies (Tzeng & Wang, 1983).

The Invariance and Segmentation Issues

When articulatory and acoustic events are examined in the light of discrete and invariant linguistic units, the continuous and context-dependent aspects of such events tend to be enhanced. Combining the linguistic-psychological and phonetic-physical perspectives, we obtain the classical but paradoxical picture of speech that underlies formulations of the invariance and segmentation issues:

For a given language there seems to be no unique set of acoustic properties that will always be present in the production of a given unit (feature, phoneme, syllable) and that will reliably be found in all conceivable contexts (INVARIANCE ISSUE).

The speech signal cannot be unambiguously segmented into temporally nonoverlapping chunks corresponding to linear sequences of phonemes, syllables, and words (SEGMENTATION ISSUE).

These problems are evident whenever we compare physical representations of speech with the corresponding linguistic transcriptions. These perspectives define a paradox that remains unresolved after several decades of acoustic phonetic research and that constitutes the theme of this volume.

Themes of the Present Paper

How should the resolution of these issues be approached? I will attempt to suggest some answers to this question by organizing my presentation in two steps.

In the first section, I will look primarily at speech. I accept that the invariance and segmentation issues are genuine issues arising from the incontrovertible but incompatible sets of evidence contributed by phonetics and phonology. This approach amounts to hypothesizing that, as research on the properties of speech signals and speaker-listener behavior progresses and phonetic descriptions become more complete, the paradox will simply disappear. A review of several phonetic lines of inquiry will lead to the conclusion, however, that solutions of the invariance and segmentation problems cannot a priori be expected to reside exclusively in the signal since experimental observations clearly show that listeners rely partly on the explicit stimulus contents, and partly on active hypothesis-driven mechanisms capable of supplying missing, implicit information. Under this analysis, invariance and discreteness would not be expected to have stable phonetic definitions at the levels of feature or segment since primarily they must apply to sound-meaning (percept-meaning) relationships in the grammar and lexicon of a given language: Semantically distinct information must be coded in perceptually distinct form (DISTINCTIVENESS CONDITION). If correct, such a principle puts emphasis on the total context of a phonetic event and is therefore compatible with extensive phonetic variation at the segment and feature sublevels.

In the second section I assume that the invariance and segmentation issues are real problems only so long as speech scientists insist on keeping the phonetic and phonological points of view strictly separate. Under this assumption, the conflict created by juxtaposing the linguistic and physical perspectives could in principle be avoided if we were able to seek a new alliance rather than continue to promote the traditional two cultures represented by phonetics and phonology. Of course, several questions then arise: What would such a unified approach be like? Could such talk be given some substance, or is it merely empty philosophical jargon?

I will demonstrate that this alternative goal appears to come within our reach in a very tangible manner when we begin to investigate—both empirically and theoretically—the "discovery" of the featural and segmental structure of speech by the child. In a sense, every child "solves" the segmentation problem in that, as the transition from prelinguistic vocalization to adult phonological structure is completed, there has been a change from a holistic-continuous to a segmental-discrete mode of coding.

Furthermore, as this "solution" emerges, the phonetics and the phonology of the child develop from a state of close integration to greater autonomy and differentiation (cf. the desired alliance of phonetics and phonology). Therefore I will propose that one way of seeking an approach achieving greater compatibility between phonetics and phonology is to develop a theory that reflects the process of speech development and its transition into adult behavior and that aims at providing an explanatory account of the origins of discreteness and the featural segmental structure of speech. Embarking on such a project might hopefully shed some light eventually also on the invariance and segmentation issues and would seem to emerge naturally from three sources of inspiration.

First, it would assign a role to phonetics within current research on the theory of universal grammar (Chomsky, 1980). Second, such a step would bring the work of the phonetician into line also with that of evolutionary biology. The Darwinian biologist who, confronting any phenomenon in living organisms, has to ask three kinds of questions (Dobzhansky, 1965): (1) "...the question of mechanism (how does it work?)"—cf. on-line behavior of speakers and listeners; (2) the question of adaptation (what does it do for the organism?)"— cf. the role of "function" in shaping speech communication at all levels; and (3) "the twin questions of embryogeny and evolution (how did it come about?)"—cf. the ontogeny and phylogeny of spoken language. As a third related point, linguists often refer to phonological and other linguistic systems as systems "òu tout se tient" and would therefore feel comfortable with anchoring their inquiry within the broader framework of general systems theory (Laszlo, 1972) and other recent developments that attempt to model hierarchical and self-organizing structures studied in physics, biology, and social sciences (Jantsch, 1981).

In a preliminary way, we have begun to trace the origins of discreteness and the featural and segmental structure of speech by undertaking a series of computational experiments in which we attempt to simulate language-like sound patterns. These patterns can be said to be language-like for several reasons. They consist of elements that sound phonetically like natural CV syllables. When looked at collectively as a system, standard linguistic-analysis procedures reveal an organization in terms of features, segment, and phonological rule. However, at no point in the simulations does our theory invoke those concepts explicitly. They arise in a self-organizing way simply as a result of an interaction between vocabulary growth and performance constraints, and exemplify an idea that seems to be fairly novel at least in linguistics—the idea of nondiscrete, implicit structure.

A CLOSER LOOK AT SPEECH

Signal Properties

Here are brief summaries of four standpoints whose common denominator is: Take a closer look at the signal.

1. One possible stance is to dismiss the issues as formulated above as pseudo-problems and to claim that they will disappear once speech scientists succeed in making better and more complete acoustic measurements. On this view, comprehensive information on the acoustic correlates of segmental and prosodic categories—and on the signal microstructure in particular—is still to be acquired. Plainly, we tend to underestimate the rich contents

of the speech wave both with respect to invariance and discontinuous structure.

2. Related to the plea for improved acoustic analyses is the hope that it will be possible to build models that correctly portray the representation of speech in the auditory periphery. Such "auditory spectrographs" might be expected to shed some new light on the segmentation and invariance issues. In fact, to some extent, they already have (Delgutte, 1982).

3. Proponents of theories of direct perception might offer a third related argument. Deriving inspiration from work on visual perception (Johanson, 1975), they would insist that invariance is indeed present in the signal but that speech scientists have so far simply failed to discover the correct dynamic relationships among signal attributes (cf. the experiments on sine-wave speech and discussion by Remez, Rubin, Pisoni & Carrell 1981).

4. Researchers at Haskins Laboratories (Studdert-Kennedy, 1982) have long maintained that we hear speech differently from other sound because we have evolved biologically specialized mechanisms; the implication being that viewing speech signals in the light of such processes would go far towards solving the invariance and segmentation problems. "Speech is special!" (Liberman & Pisoni, 1977).

Clues from Speaker-listener Behavior

There are also important clues from how listeners process signals and how talkers vary their strategy in producing speech. Such considerations bring out counterevidence against the suggestion that taking a closer look at the signal will by itself lead to a complete resolution of the paradox.

First, it is well-known that speech understanding is possible even in the (partial) absence of signal information. Since successful communication is possible in spite of noise and far-reaching and frequent reduction and omission of acoustic cues we have very strong reasons for concluding that the question of invariance is not exclusively or mainly a measurement problem. Such cases of speech understanding motivate the assumption that speech perception is (occasionally or always) based on an active mode of listening in which stimulus-driven and hypothesis-driven processes interact. Thus, successful speech communication presupposes the subconscious application of both linguistic and conceptual knowledge to the interpretation of the signal. It is by means of this top-down strategy that listeners are able to restore, or compensate for, missing or degraded signal information and to perceive physically identical stimuli in different ways depending on the context. Accordingly, if we, as speech scientists, attribute an important role to hypothesis-driven processes, we can begin to see a way of explaining why there should be "no unique set of acoustic properties always present in the production of a given phoneme and that will reliably be found in all conceivable contexts." Consequently, according to adherents of top-down processing, the solution to the invariance problem cannot reside exclusively in the signal.

Second, it is also a matter of common observation that speakers are capable of adjusting their styles of pronunciation according to the sociostylistic and pragmatic demands of a situation. They tend to vary their pronunciation by sometimes overarticulating—to make their speech sufficiently intelligible and audible—and by sometimes underarticulating, when they judge information to be redundant. Such observations bear witness of the output-oriented organization of the speech-motor system and of its considerable reorganizational abilities. Those are key attributes that speech shares with general motor behavior and which are revealed by a substantial body of evidence in the literature. Perhaps with reference to speech, they emerge most clearly from experimentally observed instances of compensatory articulation which show the ability of speakers to achieve sufficient invariance with respect to an intended acoustic target in spite of various factors perturbing production processes (cf. review by Lindblom, 1982).

A Hypothesis about Phonetic Variation

What are the implications of the preceding speech production description for the invariance and segmentation issues? It seems to imply that speech motor control is not organized to generate strictly invariant and clearly segmented acoustic correlates of speech units. Rather, speakers have the freedom to vary, that is to elaborate (overarticulate) or simplify (underarticulate) their speech under the control of communicative and situational constraints. My account suggests the following hypothesis: Phonetic variation originates from the circumstance that the units of speech need be realized in physically explicit form only to the extent that they are tacitly presupposed by the talker to be inferred by the listener's active perceptual mechanisms (for an elaboration of this view, see Lindblom, 1983b). The purpose of the variation is optimization. As the communicative and social-situational demands show short-term time variations, speech is accordingly adapted sometimes to production goals (simplification), sometimes to listener-oriented goals (elaboration).

A CLOSER LOOK AT MESSAGE STRUCTURE

Emergence of the Segment: A Self-organizing Process

Let us digress from linguistics for a brief moment and illustrate the concept of "form and substance" with a few examples from physics, chemistry, and biology (D'Arcy Thompson, 1961). Consider for instance the geometric form of:

- Snow flakes (or other crystal formations).
- The "splash" of a drop hitting the surface of a liquid (Instantaneous photographs reveal regular patterns of circular configurations of droplets that detach and bounce up from the oscillating surface).
- The gradual development of certain chemical reactions that can be observed as colorful, dynamic patterns in a shallow dish, e.g. so-called spiral waves.
- Honeycomb cells with their characteristically hexagonal shape.
- A school of fish escaping the attack of a predator and changing geometrical relationships within the school in quite regular fashions.

These are all arbitrary examples of phenomena that possess certain time-varying geometric properties. They share one characteristic with a host of other physical, biological, and social phenomena: They all arise in a self-organizing way. For such systems there is no initial specification of the resulting form of the process. The shapes of snow-flakes and hexagonal honeycomb cells arise as a result of interaction among various boundary conditions. Their form emerges through indirect causation.

What is the relevance of such cases to linguistics? Are parallels between pattern formation in language, on the one hand, and in other domains, on the other, at best metaphorical? In my opinion, that is not likely. It seems that there may be an important lesson to be learned from such examples. That lesson consists of realizing that it would be totally incorrect to give a scientific account of such nonlinguistic phenomena by describing their geometric form explicitly and directly and in abstracto disregarding the process giving rise to that form and the substance implementing it. They can only be described implicitly and indirectly.

To clarify this point, let us present the termite story (Kugler, Turvey, & Shane, 1982). Termites construct nests that are structured in terms of pillars and arches and that create a sort of "air-conditioned" environment. The form of these nests appear to arise as a result of a simple local behavioral pattern which is followed by each individual insect: The pillars and arches are formed by deposits of glutinous sand flavored with pheromone. (Pheromone is a chemical substance that is used in communication with certain insect species. Animals respond to such stimuli after tasting or smelling them). Each termite appears to follow a path of increasing pheromone density and deposit when the density starts to decrease.

Suppose the termites begin to build on a fairly flat surface. In the beginning the deposits are randomly distributed. A fairly uniform distribution of pheromone is produced. Somewhat later local peaks have begun to appear serving as stimuli for further deposits that gradually grow into pillars and walls by iteration of the same basic stimulus-response process. At points where several such peaks come close, stimulus conditions are particularly likely to generate reponses. Deposits made near such maxima of stimulation tend to form arches. As the termites continue their local behavior in this manner the elaborate structure of the nest gradually emerges (Kugler, Turvey & Shaw, 1982; Prigogine, 1976). In spite of the seemingly purposeful and intricate design of these nests, termites cannot be assumed to have a "mental blueprint" or "target" for the finished product.

Again, what is the relevance of such accounts to linguistics? The point is to demonstrate that:

1. Various types of "structure" can in fact be explained, i.e. they can be deductively derived rather than axiomatically postulated.

2. The explanations, although offered for unrelated physical and biological phenomena, share the property of avoiding the assumption of an explicit dichotomy into form-substance (cf. the description of linguistic structure on the one hand and language performance on the other), "form" being inextricably interwoven with "substance."

3. The interaction of elementary behaviors can give rise to the formation of patterns at macrolevels that exhibit considerable complexity.

4. Although there is obviously more to how people build Gothic arches in cathedrals than how termites build arches in their nests, the termite story—and numerous other similar accounts of "structure"—do teach a lesson relevant to theories of linguistics and human psychology: The structure-causing power of local, "blind" processes can be considerable. Their explanatory value in accounting also for linguistic structure should therefore not be underestimated.

The implication of such accounts is to question the form-substance distinction which is basic in traditional linguistics and which divides the study of pronunciation into two separate domains, phonetics and phonology.

Let us consider two scenarios for how children might discover that words are structured in terms of discrete features and segments and how our early ancestors might have discovered the usefulness of the phonemic principle for mapping an almost unlimited amount of semantic information onto the medium of sound. It seems clear that both for phylogeny and ontogeny speech scientists must reject any explanation that invokes elements of conscious intent. It clearly won't do to attribute to a remote ancestor the following sort of thinking: "Since I have somehow developed all these concepts that I would like to communicate and since the vocalizations that I produce by combining various discrete "features" into segments are communicatively much superior to holistic signals, I will simply invent phonemic coding based on segments and features."

A more reasonable scenario is to assume that the featural and segmental structure of speech arose phylogenetically more or less by accident than as a result of inspired thinking. Our ancestors must have stumbled collectively and blindly over phonemic coding driven by forces that they did not have direct or conscious control over. What speculations could be proposed as to the nature of the phylogeny of phonemic segments?

I will explore a hypothesis that has been discussed by several investigators (Chafe, 1970, 24–29; Hockett & Ascher, 1964; Studdert-Kennedy & Lane, 1980). It suggests that phonemic coding arose in a self-organizing way from an interaction between vocabulary growth and phonetic constraints. As man's conceptual development was dramatically accelerated, a solution to the problem of efficient signal generation and reception seems to have been obtained in parallel.

Vocabulary Growth and Performance Constraints: A Computational Experiment

The basic idea underlying Figure 23.1 is that I begin by specifying a number k which represents vocabulary size. I then feed this number into a computer program that assigns phonetic shape to these elements in a sequential manner and in the presence of certain performance constraints. A phonological analysis of the k phonetic signals is then undertaken. By systematically varying the variables of this "word game," we shall hopefully be able to investigate whether phonological structures could arise from an interaction between vocabulary development and production/perception constraints. Here are some preliminary results.

In the case of the termites, I identified basically two processes: to initiate deposit at random. Deposit next time where scent density exhibits a local maximum; apply recursively. Suppose we attempt to derive the phonetic properties of a small lexicon k of words in a roughly analogous way. Replacing deposits by vocalizations (syllables), we have:

> Select first syllable at random. Select next syllable so as to optimize a performance constraints criterion. Apply recursively until k syllables have been obtained.

Let us develop this analogy in three steps: (1) Define "possible vocalization/syllable"; (2) Define selection process; (3) Define performance constraints and the criterion of optimization!

We shall assume that the syllable is an axiomatically given primitive of our theory. It should also be regarded as a holistic pattern that would resemble a CV sequence if presented on a spectrogram. Note, however, that this resemblance does not in any way imply that it is analyzed as a sequence of two segments. It is a gestalt trajectory coursing through the phonetic (articulatory/acoustic/perceptual) space (straight line with arrow in Figure 23.1) and represents an arbitrary closure-opening gesture in articulatory terms.

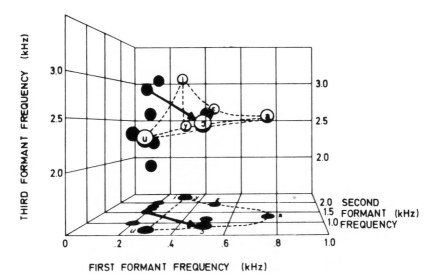

FIG. 23.1.   Definition of possible syllable (possible vocalization).

NOTE:
The three dimensions of the diagram are the first three formant frequencies. The object indicated by dashed contours represents formant patterns for possible open vocal-tract configurations as defined by an articulatory model. A quantization of this space into 19 points was introduced for computational reasons. (Later on, points inside the space will be interpreted phonetically as vowel segments. Note that it is only to make the meaning of the dashed object somewhat easier to grasp that this segmental analysis has been anticipated by introducing spheres for some reference vowel qualities).
The solid spheres pertain to the formant patterns associated with closed vocal-tract configurations, that is with possible closures at various points of articulation along the vocal tract: A quantization into seven steps has been used for the quasi-continuous labial-through-uvular range of places. (Later on, this set will be identified with stop consonant "segments.")
Given the solid spheres and the dashed-contour space, I define possible syllable as a holistic trajectory (straight line with arrow) that runs from an arbitrary solid sphere to an arbitrary point in the open-configuration space.

The assignment of phonetic shape k to distinct meanings can be seen as making a choice from a large inventory of possibilities, that is from the possibilities that the universal phonetic space makes available. For our present purposes, let us simplify by considering only a fragment of these possibilities: n possible syllables (gestalt trajectories as described above). Given these definitions our problem can be stated as a combinatorial one: Select k syllables from a total inventory of n possibilities in the presence of certain performance constraints.

TABLE 23.1

Definition of Performance Constraints in the Simulations

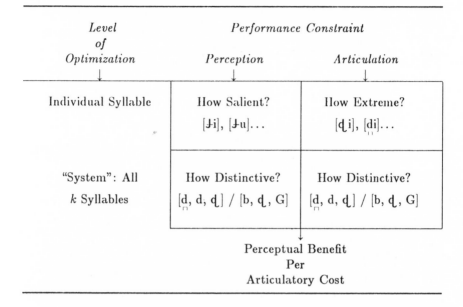

Level of Optimization ↓	Performance Constraint	
	Perception ↓	Articulation ↓
Individual Syllable	How Salient? [ɟi], [ɟu]...	How Extreme? [ɖi], [di]...
"System": All k Syllables	How Distinctive? [ḏ, d, ɖ] / [b, ɖ, G]	How Distinctive? [ḏ, d, ɖ] / [b, ɖ, G]

Perceptual Benefit
Per
Articulatory Cost

<u>NOTE</u>
The optimization criterion represents a quantitative interpretation of perceptual benefit per articulatory cost, which can be broken down into level of optimization—syllable or system—and type of performance constraint—perceptual or articulatory.

Perceptual factors included salience and distinctiveness. The production constraints explored were associated with extremity of articulatory displacement and rate (upper right cell) and sensory discriminability or articulatory distinctiveness (lower right cell). Representative examples are given in terms of phonetic labels.

This task will be unambiguously defined once we have a method for specifying the range of closures (syllable beginnings)and openings (endpoints) that a human vocal tract is capable of producing. In principle, these ranges offer an infinite number of places of articulation and vowel-like configurations. For computational reasons it is necessary to quantize these possibilities into a certain number of discrete points. In the experiments to be reported below I used a seven-point quantization of the trajectory onset space, with articulatory-phonetic labels [b,ḏ, d, ɖ, ɟ, g, G] and a nineteen-point quantization of the endpoint (vowel) space [i, y, ü, ɨ, ɯ, u, e, ø, ə, ɣ, o, ɛ, œ, ʌ, ɔ, æ, Œ, a, ɑ]. This decision is of course arbitrary but provides a sufficiently finely graded sampling of the universal phonetic space. It yields a total of $\underline{n} = 7 \times 19 = 133$ possibilities. The performance constraints were chosen according to Table 23.1.

The selection of a given syllable is optimized at two levels: with respect to the properties of the individual syllable as well as with respect to the system that results from adding a given syllable to those previously selected. Pairs of individual syllables are evaluated in terms of a set of performance constraints and the system in terms of the sum of all such numbers. In the present simulations we have explored the following conditions (For details, see discussion in Lindblom, MacNeilage, Studdert-Kennedy, In preparation). *Perceptual salience* describes the extent of trajectory as calibrated in auditorily motivated dimensions; e.g. a palatal closure followed by an [i] comes out as less salient than a palatal closure changing into [u]. *Extremeness of articulatory gesture* applies both to static configurations and to dynamic events. The static measure is quantified in terms of deviation from neutral position. The dynamic measure is defined in terms of extent of gesture, e.g. [ɟu] represents a more extensive movement than [ɟi]. *Articulatory distinctiveness* is a systems parameter. It is interpreted as sensory discriminability and is computed in terms of "articulatory distance" as specified by an articulatory model (Lindblom & Sundberg, 1971); e.g. a system such as [dV, dV,ɖV] disfavored relative to say [bV,ɖV,GV]. *Perceptual distinctiveness* is calculated for all subsets of syllables and is derived by generalizing experimental results on distance judgements for vowels to holistic syllables (Bladon & Lindblom, 1981); e.g. [dV, dV,ɖV] is less distinctive than say [bV,ɖV,GV].

The numbers that the application of these constraints produces are combined into a single formula which takes both individual syllable properties as well as the collective value of the system into account. In words, the number calculated for each pair of syllables, $\dfrac{L_{ij}}{T_{ij}}$, can be said to represent perceptual benefit per articulatory cost. This formula can be written as:

$$\sum_{i=1}^{k} \sum_{j=2}^{i-1} \frac{1}{\left(L_{ij}/T_{ij}\right)^2} < \text{Threshold}$$

Implicit and Nondiscrete Segments

To simulate the development of the "lexicon," I applied the formula repeatedly for each new syllable to be incorporated into the system and continued this procedure until a system of k syllables had been derived. Since this method would give results that would depend on the syllable chosen for initiating the process I repeated the derivations of systems of k syllables 133 times each time starting from a new syllable. In the present case, k was

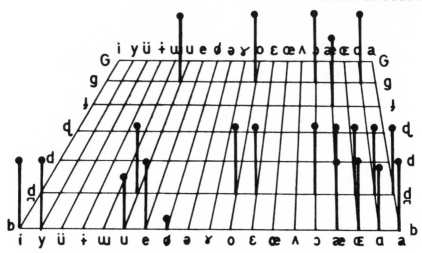

FIG. 23.2.   Results of simulations.

<u>NOTE</u>

Minivocabularies of 24 syllables were derived 133 times (total syllable inventory = 133). Each time a different first syllable initiated the procedure. The diagram shows the probability of finding a given syllable in the pooled set of 3192 (= 133 × 24) syllables. The y-axis represents percent occurrence with the largest vertical lines indicating that the syllable in question occurred in 133 (= 100%) of the simulation runs. The x- and z-dimensions identify the syllables in terms of a phonetic labeling of their beginnings and endpoints.

24. Thus all syllables were equally probable at the start but as soon as the process had been initiated the optimization criterion would come into play and would bias selections.

One way of presenting the results is to investigate how the performance constraints influence the probability of finding syllable x in the subsets of k syllables. By pooling all the 133 subsets of k syllables and by plotting the observations in the form of a distribution diagram, a way of answering that question is obtained. This has been done in Figure 23.2 where we use a 7 by 19 matrix for the 133 syllables and where the largest vertical lines indicate that the syllable in question was observed as occurring in all 133 (=100%) of the simulations. When evaluating these results we should bear in mind the distribution for a corresponding series of derivations in which the enumeration of syllables takes place in a completely unbiased fashion, that is without any performance constraints at all. That experiment would in principle give us a uniform distribution of vertical lines implying that all syllables would be equally probable. As can be seen, the performance constraints make the results deviate markedly from a pattern with completely uniform preferences.

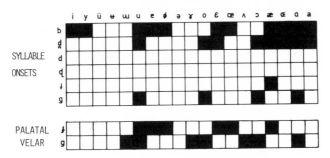

FIG. 23.3.   Results of simulations shown in binary units.

NOTE
Top matrix: The information in Figure 23.2 presented in a binary format. Black cell: This syllable occurred in the derivations. Blank: nonoccurence.

Bottom matrix: The result of initiating simulations with the syllable [ba] and continuing until 48 items had been obtained. The palatal closure was absent in the 24-item vocabularies but is now found to combine with front vowels. The velar is seen to occur with back vowels. In the present theory, this pattern of complementary distribution is not controlled by an explicitly reified phonological rule but is a consequence of the premium that was put on nonextreme articulations in the definition of the performance constraints.

These results can also be arranged in the form of a two-dimensional matrix with rows representing onsets, or closures, and columns vowel-like endpoints. To facilitate analyzing them from a phonological point of view, let us transform the information of Figure 23.2 into a binary format. In the matrix of Figure 23.3 occurrences are marked by a black cell.

From an inspection of the upper matrix of Figure 23.3, it is immediately apparent that certain rows and columns have more than one item. This means that syllables such as [bu, du, gu] contrast. Rows and columns with multiple entries contain syllables that keep one segment constant while varying the other. They identify minimal pairs. Since by definition all syllables have distinct meanings, we might conclude that according to standard procedures these minimal pairs contain distinct phonemes. The existence of [bu, du, gu] appears to suggest that in these derivations [b, d, g] come out as separate phonemic segments. How is that possible? At no point in the derivations have we analyzed the syllables as a sequence of two segments. We have defined our vocalizations as holistic events. Our theory does not invoke segment as an explicit construct. Neither does it use explicit features, although the use of [b, d, g] and a certain subset of vowels implies a systematic favoring of certain articulatory properties, or feature dimensions.

It should be clear from these considerations that there are neither segments nor features in the generation of these phonetic signals and that it is our preceding linguistic analysis that imputes discrete segments and features to them. Just as arches and pillars are implicit in the behavior of the termites, the segments and features represent phonological structure implicitly and nondiscretely present in the process of selecting the phonetic system.

Complementary Distribution as an Implicit Assimilation Rule

As we continue the derivations beyond $k = 24$, we begin to see instances of the palatal closure [ɟ]. It combines with front vowels whereas [g] occurs with back vowels (lower matrix, Figure 23.3). For $k = 48$, the following vocalizations are included in the enumeration initiated by [ba]: Palatal onset: [ɟæ, ɟœ, ɟɛ, ɟø, ɟe, ɟɯ]; velar onset: [ga, gɔ, gʌ, go, gɤ, gu, gɯ]. The vowels are paired with the consonants in a complementary manner: a clear instance of an assimilatory "phonological rule." But note again that "rule" is not a discretely represented construct of our theory. This assimilation process provides another instance of implicit and nondiscrete phonological structure. Instead of using the conventional "rule" notation:

$$
/g/ \rightarrow \begin{cases} [ɟ]/ - \begin{bmatrix} + \text{ Front} \\ V \end{bmatrix} \\ [g]/ - \text{ Elsewhere} \end{cases}
$$

our theory invokes a set of interactive processes that include rewards for CVs having minimal articulatory movement and that make the allophonic variations of the "/g/-phoneme" automatic.

This result raises the general question of whether the acquisition of a sound pattern regularity—as hypothesized by generative phonologists—results in the development of a psychologically real, explicit, and discrete "rule" or whether it takes the form of a "nonrule" (cf. Harms, 1973) that arises as an implicit consequence of various performance conditions. According to the latter alternative, learning "rule x" of a given language would be preferably stated in terms of its indirect causes, that is, applying performance conditions in accordance with demands specific to the language system.

Origins of Quantal Structure

Where do features and segments come from? This question has been addressed perhaps most explicitly by Stevens (1972) in his quantal theory of speech. To a great extent, my work has been inspired by this seminal research and, as illustrated here, similarly attempts to deal with the origins of quantal structure.

According to the present findings, minimal pairs will occur when performance constraints are defined in such a way as to increase the probability of observing syllables that begin or end in the same way at an early stage of the enumerative derivation. In general terms, minimal pairs—and thus segmental and featural structure—could accordingly be caused by any set of performance constraints that have this property. The favoring of syllables with the same onset or endpoint comes about because the search for phonetic shapes is initially constrained to take place near the articulatory rest position (= avoiding extreme articulations). Since sufficient perceptual effects can be achieved, that is the L/T measure is optimized—with near-neutral configurations, syllables initiated from [b] and [d], and to some extent from [ɟ] and [g], are favored over [ɖ]- and [G]-tokens.

The assimilation process and the allophonic alternations arise because of a continuous condition penalizing extreme movements; extremeness of movement in general outweighs the perceptual salience of a gesture. Thus [gi] and [ɟu] may be more salient than [ɟi] and [gu], but that perceptual advantage is not worth the physiological cost. As a result, [ɟi] and [gu] are favored.

SUMMARY AND CONCLUSIONS

Two approaches towards resolving the invariance and segmentation issues have been explored. The first strategy assumes that the solution is in the hands of the phonetician. It hypothesizes that, as research on the properties of speech signals and speaker-listener behavior progresses and phonetic descriptions become more complete, the paradox will simply disappear. However, when the question "what are invariance and discreteness for?" is raised, it is not immediately clear that segments and features must be phonetically invariant and discrete for functional reasons. Formal phonological evidence just shows that they are. Such considerations lead us to the second strategy that takes a new look at message structure by asking: What is the origin and purpose of discrete and invariant message units? How do they arise? Underlying this approach is the suspicion that—although the invariance and segmentation issues seem to be genuine issues since they arise from the incontrovertible but incompatible sets of evidence contributed by phonetics and phonology—they might be avoided if we were able to develop a theory capable of more fully integrating the phonetic and phonological points of view. One way in which such a goal could be attained would be by investigation the "discovery" of the featural and segmental structure of speech by the child.

As a preliminary contribution towards such a program, I demonstrated that:

1. Precursors of featural and phonemic coding can in principle arise in a self-organizing way from an interaction between semantic development (vocabulary growth) and performance constraints.

2. The features, segments, and rules were found to be implicit and nondiscrete properties of the system of holistic phonetic signals.

A comprehensive discussion of the implications of these findings would fall outside the scope of this chapter. They seem to bear on several central topics of linguistic theory: the possibility of defining phonological primes (e.g. distinctive features) deductively, the discovery of such primes by the child, the role of phonetics in developing the concept of markedness (Chomsky & Halle, 1968a, Chapter 9) and the theory of universal grammar (Chomsky, 1980).

The notion of implicit, nondiscrete structure seems applicable to many phenomena studied in physics, biology, and general systems theory, but appears to be in conflict with the evidence from formal phonological analyses of speech. However, it would be premature to reject the implicit and nondiscrete model at this early stage and to state that there is no aspect of adult phonology that needs it.

The theory of implicit, nondiscrete structure is offered here as a novel explanatory idea to be refuted or substantiated in future work. For our present purposes, it has served the purpose of raising the suspicion that the discreteness of linguistic units is an assumption that needs to be supplemented. In order to provide a better theoretical understanding of the dynamics of sound patterns in historical and ontogenetic development as well as in adult on-line performance, linguistics may be forced to develop a theory that is based on a less clear-cut dichotomy between form and substance and that will accommodate instances of discrete and autonomous, as well as nondiscrete and implicit, sound structure. The present study shows that such questions can be addressed. It also suggests that insights about on-line speech processes (invariance and discreteness) may be obtained by studying them directly as well as by attempting to trace their origin and purpose.

Sylvain Bromberger and Morris Halle:
On the Relationship of Phonology and Phonetics

INTRODUCTION

In his paper, Lindblom raises some very fundamental questions about the nature of the objects and properties investigated by phoneticians. Though some people may feel uncomfortable about the abstract character of such questions, it is important that they be boldly pursued. They are not only intrinsically interesting, they are also inescapable. Practice requires that we take a stand on them. By failing to do so openly, we do not avoid them, but simply accept some answers uncritically. And the wrong answers may lead us to work on the wrong problems, or to reject certain lines of investigations for the wrong reasons. Thus, though our comments focus on our disagreements with Lindblom's basic proposal, we would like to make clear at the outset that we applaud the spirit of his paper and that we agree with many of the things in it that we do not discuss.

THE PROBLEM

In the first section of his paper, Lindblom reminds us of facts from phonology and from psycholinguistics that, in his words, "force the conclusion that speech is quantal, that it is featurally and segmentally structured." Then, in the second section, he points out that

(1)

> When articulatory and acoustic events are examined in the light of discrete and invariant linguistic units, the continuous and context-dependent aspects of such events tend to be enhanced. Combining the linguistic-psychological and phonetic-physical perspectives we obtain the classical but paradoxical picture of speech that underlies formulations of the invariance and segmentation issues:

> For a given language there seems to be no unique set of acoustic properties that will always be present in the production of a given unit (feature, phoneme, syllable...) and that will reliably be found in all conceivable contexts (INVARIANCE ISSUE).

> The speech signal cannot be unambiguously segmented into temporally non-overlapping chunks corresponding to linear sequences of phonemes, syllables and words (SEGMENTATION ISSUE). (p. 504)

The problem, thus, is to come to terms with two apparently incompatible "pictures" of speech utterances: the phonologist's picture of these utterances as built out of a finite, hierarchical set of discrete phonological elements (features, phonemes, syllables, words), and the picture of the working phonetician according to which no finite set of phonetic elements corresponding to phonological ones can be recovered from a careful examination of speech tokens. More important, the problem concerns the relationship between the subject matter of phonology and the subject matter of phonetics.

How is one to think of that relationship?

There are basically two ways in which that relationship has been conceived, and we think that the problem requires us to choose between these two ways. We will call them respectively the *physicalist* and the *mentalist* view.

Before embarking on a discussion of these two points of view, we present a brief general remark. The study of speech sounds requires us to think of concrete utterances produced at a certain time by a certain person, i.e. of *tokens*, as instances of more abstract linguistic entities, i.e. *types*. Thus the acoustic event that would be produced at the end of an utterance would be an instance of the word-type 'types'. Sentences, phrases, words, syllables, etc. also fall into types. Each can fall under more than one type. In particular it can fall under a phonological type as well as e.g. under an acoustical type. To theorize about tokens we need a repertoire of types that tokens can instantiate. The difference between those who subscribe to the physicalist point of view and those who subscribe to the mentalist point of view is at heart a difference about the size and nature of that repertoire of types.

THE PHYSICALIST POINT OF VIEW

The physicalist point of view looks upon utterances as instances of only articulatory and acoustical types.

Students of language who adopt this point of view consider utterances (tokens) with two sets of questions in mind: (1) What are the configurations (and sequences of configurations) and activities of the speech organs responsible for their production? (2) What are the characteristics of the observed sound waves? And they look upon the utterances that share certain properties according to the first set of questions as instances of a same *articulatory* type, and upon the utterances that share certain properties according to the second set of questions as instances of a same *acoustical* type.

They believe that their task is to find acoustical and articulatory types peculiar to each language, to determine whether any of these types are common to all languages, to find laws about them, and to seek explanations for these laws.

More specifically, they assume that:

(II)

(a) There exists a finite (relatively small) number of articulatory types s. t. each (normal) utterance will turn out to be a token of one of them or a sequence of tokens of some of them.

(b) And similarly for acoustical types.

(c) Utterances which belong to the same articulatory type belong to the same acoustical type.

(d) This follows from a very simple one-to-one relationship between the articulatory and acoustical characteristics or features on the basis of which types are defined, and hence there exists a set of *phonetic* types definable indifferently in either articulatory terms or acoustical terms.

(e) The rules of phonology can be expressed in terms of these characteristics, and therefore phonology can be done using phonetic types and does not require an ontology or ideology (in the sense of Quine) that goes beyond that required to define *phonetic* types.

Since each utterance has an indefinitely large number of articulatory and acoustical properties in terms of which types can be defined, it is obvious that (II), (a) to (c) above will not hold for *every* choice among these properties. But will it hold for *any*? Is there any set of articulatory or acoustical properties for which (II), (a) to (c) hold? The answer, according to the empirical evidence available so far—and about which Lindblom seems to agree—is negative. This is the heart of the invariance and segmentation issues.

Mitigated forms of the physicalist point of view may replace (d) above with a more complicated proposition. But what characterizes the physicalist position is a consistent refusal to allude to any but articulatory and acoustical properties of tokens and a determination to theorize only about types defined by means of such properties. In other words, from a physicalist point of view, phonological types and features must be identical to phonetic ones; the relationship between them must be that of identity. Hence the segmentation and invariance issues pose a serious problem for phonology: since the traditional units of phonology cannot be defined in exclusively physicalist terms, a physicalist phonology must be created to replace the phonology of the past and it is by no means clear that this can be done.

THE MENTALIST POINT OF VIEW

The mentalist point of view starts from a somewhat different set of presumptions. The mentalist point of view takes seriously the obvious fact that (normally) speech utterances are produced by people intentionally, i.e. each utterance constitutes the carrying out of an intention to say something. The intention is of course very complicated: it is the intention to produce word sequences that have a certain meaning, a certain illocutionary force, a certain syntactic structure, etc, etc. But whatever else it involves, in the cases of interest here it is first and foremost the intention to produce sequences of words, i.e. an intention that can be carried out by moving one's vocal tract in certain ways.

The connection between such an intention and the way it is carried out is a tricky matter. But that is true of most intentions carried out by executing physical acts. Think of the many ways in which the intention of throwing a ball can be executed on any given occasion. Of course, it does not follow that just any type of gesture can count as the carrying out of such an intention. Wriggling one's nose will probably never count as carrying out the intention of throwing a ball. It would nevertheless be absurd to try to define the intention of throwing a ball by specifying in purely physical terms certain trajectories of the arm. No set of necessary and sufficient conditions for being a case of throwing a ball intentionally can be given in purely macro anatomical and physical terms. (We insert the word "macro" because intentions may turn out to be realized as brain states, a matter about which we know nothing.) In other words, the intention to throw a ball is not the same intention as the intention to move one's arm through a certain specifiable trajectory, nor is there a specifiable trajectory s.t. only instances of it can count as the fulfillment of the intention of throwing a ball.

From a mentalist point of view, a speaker of e.g. English has a repertoire of phonological intentions. The intention to utter a certain word, or a sentence, or a longer discourse, is a complex intention—structured by rules—and made up of members of that repertoire. The production of an utterance consists in executing such a complex intention in the light of what the speaker knows about the conditions of utterance and of other desires and intentions that he may have at the time, e.g. the desire to be heard above noise, to save time, etc. as well as the preceding and succeeding intentions. To understand what has been uttered, the hearer must reconstruct the phonological intentions of the speaker. He uses the characteristics of perceived sound waves (as analyzed by his hearing apparatus and mind) and his knowledge of the rules, and his beliefs about the circumstances of utterance.

Articulatory phonetics, from the mentalist point of view, is the study of the gestures and activities produced in the vocal tract *by way of carrying out phonological intentions*, and acoustical phonetics is the study of the resulting sound waves. Thus subscribers to this point of view, like most phoneticians, are not interested in just any set of human movements (or movements in the vocal tract) that result in audible sounds, nor are they interested in the acoustical properties of all the sound waves that humans can produce. And they have a relatively clear criterion by which they demarcate their subject matter: the articulatory facts that interest them are those centrally involved in carrying out phonological intentions, and the acoustical facts that interest them are those involved in the recognition of phonological intentions. The relationship between phonological types (and features) and phonetic ones is not that of identity. It is an instance of the relationship that holds between intention types and physical types.

Given the mentalist picture, the segmentation and invariance issues do not come as a surprise. Nor do they represent the sort of threat that they represent to the physicalist point of view. On the contrary. From a position that distinguishes between phonology and phonetics along mentalistic lines, one would not expect tokens that belong to the same phonological type also to belong to the same articulatory type (one might as well expect all deliberate acts of throwing a ball to involve identical arm trajectories) or the same acoustical type.

Whether acoustical types and articulatory types will coincide (i.e. whether every pair of utterances that comes under the same articulatory description also comes under the same acoustical description) is a question of physics, and involves a different relationship than the relationship with phonological types. The answer, for any interesting typology of utterances, is very likely to be negative. But it does not follow from this that no systematic connections exist between them. On the contrary. If the mentalist point of view is correct, then one should expect systematic connections: after all, articulatory types represent ways in which phonological intentions are executed, and acoustical types represent information on the basis of which these intentions can be recognized! But one should also expect these connections to be complex, and it is unlikely that they will be discoverable without appeal to phonological theory.

The mentalist's appeal to intentions and to phonological elements that are metaphysically distinct from phonetic ones strikes some people as suspicious. But this appeal involves nothing that has not always been implicit in the practice of people who study the sounds of language. In fact, physicalists among phoneticians are all closet mentalists. They all agree that not all acoustical outputs of the human vocal tract are within the province of their science: the sounds emitted in snoring or yawning, in blowing out a candle, or in gargling, though often indistinguishable from speech sounds, and though classifiable under some phonetic types (e.g. the sound of blowing out a candle is indistinguishable from what phoneticians would characterize as a voiceless bilabial fricative, and gargling sounds do not differ physically from uvular trills) are rejected by all phoneticians as outside the purview of phonetics. But on what grounds? Obviously, what systematically distinguishes the set of events that phoneticians study from the others is that the former represent intentions of the speaker to produce words in a language and the latter do not. Thus, at least in their practice the most tough-minded physicalists among phoneticians subscribe to something like the mentalist point of view. But then, why not incorporate that point of view in one's research and theorizing?

Note, by the way, that the very formulation of the issue requires one to classify the units of speech in non-articulatory and non-acoustical terms. Lindblom, for instance, in the passage quoted in (I) above refers to 'discrete and invariant units'. But the units referred to cannot be acoustic types, since that would make his characterization of the invariance issue a self-contradiction. And the phonemes, syllables, and words that he mentions in his characterization of the segmentation issue cannot be acoustically defined phonemes, syllables, and words either, for similar reasons.

Let us then summarize.

The facts mentioned by Lindblom create a problem for the physicalist position. Adherents of that position try to extract from a corpus of utterances phonological features and types that accord with (II), (a) to (e) above, and they have so far failed. Since they do not allow for the possibility that segments of utterances belonging to different phonetic types might nevertheless belong to the same phonological type (and vice versa), and since they do not allow for the possibility that phonological features might have more than one articulatory or acoustical realization, they are caught in a contradiction between the tenets of their position and the empirical evidence.

But these problems do not arise for the mentalist point of view; for that point of view makes a clear distinction between phonological elements and phonetic ones, and allows for the possibility that their joint exemplification in tokens may be governed by very complicated rules. The mentalist must, of course, recognize that little is known about these rules at this point and that much research remains to be done.

LINDBLOM'S SOLUTION

In his paper, Lindblom cites a number of facts and makes a number of remarks that strike us as incompatible with a physicalist resolution of the invariance and segmentation issues. We have already pointed this out about his very formulation of these issues. Later he mentions evidence that lead him to "...the conclusion...that solutions of the invariance and segmentation problems cannot a priori be expected to reside exclusively in the signal since experimental observations clearly show that listeners rely partly on the explicit stimulus contents, and partly on active top-down mechanisms capable of supplying missing, implicit information." And later again he draws the following implication from observations about speech production "...speech motor control in *not* organized to generate strictly invariant and clearly segmented acoustic correlates of speech units."

In spite of this, he seeks a physicalist approach to the resolution of the invariance and segmentation issues. Thus he writes about the approach that he advocates: "...we shall assume that the invariance and segmentation issue are real problems only so long as we insist on keeping the phonetic and phonological point of view strictly separate. Under this assumption then, the conflict created by juxtaposing the linguistic and physical perspective could in principle be avoided if we were able to seek a new alliance rather than continue to promote the traditional two cultures represented by phonetics and phonology."

The alliance Lindblom seeks is essentially a physicalist alliance. It is not an alliance that strives for a theory showing how phonological units (intentions, as we think of them) receive different phonetic realizations (articulatory and acoustical) under different circumstances, or how the rules of phonology are reflected through these realizations, or how acoustical information can serve to reconstruct the phonological intentions responsible for their production.

It is an alliance which treats the units of phonology as illusory by-products of certain general desiderata that govern the process of vocal communication such as the need to keep different messages distinct, economy of effort, etc.. Lindblom likens phonemes and phonological features to the pillars and arches that can be seen in the nests of termites, and he points out that these structures are built by the insects not by following blueprints and plans in which pillars and arches figure explicitly (i.e. that termites lack the intentions to build arches and pillars). Rather the insects follow the procedure of depositing matter at points where there is a maximum concentration of a chemical (pheromone) that is contained in the deposits. "In the beginning the deposits are randomly distributed... Somewhat later local peaks have begun to appear, serving as stimuli for further deposits that gradually grow into pillars and walls by iteration of the same basic stimulus-response process."

Lindblom comments that "in spite of the seemingly purposeful and intricate design of these nests termites cannot be assumed to have a 'mental blue-print' or 'target' for the finished product." He observes further that "although there is obviously more to how people build Gothic arches in cathedrals than how termites build arches in their nests, the termite story... teach(es) a lesson relevant to theories of linguistics." The lesson, according to Lindblom, is that phonemes are not real components of utterances, nor part of the speaker's intention (in our terminology) but that like the arches of the termites, discrete phonemes arise "in a self-organizing way from an interaction between vocabulary growth and phonetic constraints."

Thus, according to Lindblom, the units of phonology are not only illusory aspects superimposed on reality by theory, but, like the arches of the termites (arches are arches, no matter how they might have come about) they are fully specifiable in physicalist terms. The method that generates them requires that they turn out to be describable in articulatory and acoustic terms, and the "alliance" that Lindblom advocates is one that identifies phonological types as phonetic ones. Though Lindblom does not say so explicitly, that is a clear implication of his approach.

Let us turn to that approach.

Lindblom postulates that the primitive vocalizations of an infant are made up of units which are "holistic patterns" that would resemble CV syllables if presented on a spectrogram. A lexicon is then acquired by the child through the application of the following algorithm:

(III)

1. Determine how many meanings you have to represent. Let that number be k.
2. Select next a syllable at random from a given inventory of n possibilities. Let us call it the first syllable.
3. Select a next syllable so as to optimize certain performance constraints criteria.
4. Apply the previous step recursively until k syllables have been obtained. (Let us call a set of k syllables selected that way a k-set.)
5. Apply the steps above recursively until every syllable has served as a 'first' syllable at least once.
6. Pick the k syllables that occur in the largest number of k-sets. (Let us call a set of k syllables selected that way a final k-set.)
7. Assign a different meaning to each member of the final k-set so obtained.

Lindblom makes a number of claims about his algorithm that presumably have a bearing on the invariance and segmentation problem.

His first claim is that the algorithm is a plausible simplified model of how language is acquired by children and developed by language communities, i.e. a theory "that reflects the process of speech development and its transition into adult behavior..." This has a bearing on the issues because Lindblom thinks that "...every child solves the segmentation problem...".

But note that the algorithm does not require information about the language community in which the child is doing his learning. Thus two children growing up in two different language communities that have encoded the same number of meanings (whatever that means) should, according to this theory, acquire the same language; and in general languages that do not differ about the number of meanings they encode will have exactly the same vocabulary (though perhaps with some permutations in the pairing of meanings and sounds.) Furthermore, changes in the number of items in the lexicon should have a drastic effect on the phonology of the language. Both of these implications fly in the face of the known facts of language acquisition.

Lindblom's second claim is that the algorithm does not presuppose features and segments, i.e. that a learner could apply it to a corpus of "gestalt trajectories through the phonetic (articulatory/perceptual) space" without analyzing the members of that corpus (presumably tokens) into segments and features. Lindblom writes "It should be clear... that there are neither features nor segments in the generation of these phonetic signals and that it is our preceding linguistic analysis that imputes discrete 'segments' and 'features' to them. Just as 'arches' and 'pillars' are implicit in the behavior of termites, the 'segments' and 'features' represent phonological structures implicitly and nondiscretely present in the process of selecting the phonetic system." (We will come to that linguistic analysis in a moment.) The suggestion is that features and segments are undetectable in individual tokens but emerge only in the comparison of different tokens and that approaches to the invariance and segmentation issues should take that into account.

This claim strikes us as mistaken. Lindblom's algorithm—in particular the application of the performance criteria in the third step—crucially involves a comparison of the beginnings and endings of syllables. Among the parameters that Lindblom invokes is *perceptual salience*. This he describes as "extent of trajectory in auditorily motivated dimensions, e.g. a palatal closure followed by an [i] comes out as less salient than a palatal closure changing into [u]." To determine the "salience" of a given syllable it is thus necessary to compare its beginning with its ending. But this implies that there is some way of separating the beginning of a syllable from its ending. Thus the segmentation of the syllable is not an *outcome* of the algorithm, but a *condition* for its applicability! The case is quite unlike the case of arches and columns built by termites. Arches and columns can be the outcome of a process that can be described without presupposing anything about the shape of the outcome. But the algorithm in III cannot be thought to have any application without presupposing certain things about its input, and in particular that its input is segmented into phoneme-like units.

The third—and from our point of view the most important—claim that Lindblom makes for the algorithm concerns the final k-sets it yields. These k-sets are held to be themselves amenable to a linguistic analysis that produces quasi-features and quasi-segments for which the invariance and segmentation issue do not arise.

A brief review of that analysis may be helpful. The algorithm that we have described above is first applied to an inventory of discrete syllable-like elements describable in phonetic terms. (Lindblom must assume here—contrary to fact, and contrary to his own statement quoted above—that the segmentation issue does not arise for syllables, but only for units shorter than syllables.) The algorithm assumes that every syllable in the original inventory can be characterized physicalistically in terms of its two termini, its beginning and its ending. In the paper, Lindblom recognizes seven beginning and nineteen ending types, which yield a total repertory of 133 primitive syllables. He represents these termini not with integers or some other arbitrary symbols, but rather with letters drawn from the International Phonetic Alphabet. Thus the seven beginnings are represented with the voiced stop symbols given along the ordinate of the chart (IV) below which we reproduce from Lindblom's paper (top part of Fig. 23.3), and the nineteen endings with the vowels given along the abscissa of the chart.

The algorithm (III) is then applied to select the needed number of distinct syllables from the repertory of 133. It turns out that for $k = 24$ (which one might suppose to represent a fairly early stage in the child's course of language acquisition) the syllables are those indicated with black squares in the chart.

(IV).

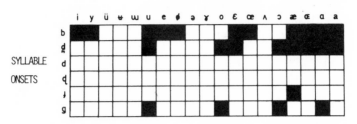

The "linguistic" analysis is now applied to that chart. It proceeds from the fact that the syllables selected form rows and columns rather than diagonal lines (or arrangements that can be turned into diagonals by reordering the points along the axes.) "Rows and columns with multiple entries contain syllables that keep one segment constant while varying the other. They identify *minimal pairs*. Since by definition all syllables have distinct meanings, we must conclude that according to standard procedure the minimal pairs contain distinct phonemes. The existence of [bu du gu] thus appears to suggest that in these derivations [b, d, g] come out as separate *phonemic segments...*" And the analysis proceeds in this way to create quasi-segments. Nothing in the analysis requires departure from the physicalist approach. The types generated by this method are physicalist types.

We do not believe that Lindblom's third claim can be sustained either. Remember that the solution of the problem requires one to find a set of phonological features and segments (at the type level) and a set of phonetic features and segments (at the type level again) such that any two utterances that can be analyzed as containing tokens of the same member of the first set can be analyzed as containing tokens of the same members of the second set. Without going into the details of Lindblom's analysis, we need only notice that the quasi-phonological units generated by that analysis are physicalistic units. As we have seen in chart (IV) above, Lindblom has identified these units with elements from the International Phonetic Alphabet. But that defeats the claim, for if anything is clear, it is that the issues of invariance and segmentation arise most sharply for the elements of that alphabet.

Put very succinctly, our objection runs like this: if Lindblom's method could generate elements that "solve the problem" then the problem would not have arisen. It has arisen. Therefore the method cannot generate elements that solve the problem.

Of course Lindblom could reply that he could have started with a different "inventory" and thereby avoided our objection. But that leaves the matter up in the air until a proper inventory is discovered. We do not believe that such an inventory exists.

CONCLUSION

In this paper, Lindblom invites us to develop a new perspective on the invariance and segmentation issues and to add to the set of facts deemed relevant to their solution. We think that this is an invitation that must be taken very seriously. We also agree with him that pragmatic facts will turn out to be important. However we believe that they will not suffice. We believe that serious work on the theory of intentions and the execution of intentions will also be necessary. Little is known about intentions. We will have to grope in the dark for a while. But that cannot be helped.

Charles Ferguson: Comment

In his paper Bjorn Lindblom, among other things, has sketched a research agenda for child phonologists, and as a practicing child phonologist I would like to comment on the basic points of his presentation and the feasibility of at least some parts of the suggested research agenda.

First of all, I want to make clear that I welcome the position he has assumed and am in agreement with most of the points he makes in his valiant attempt to reorient the thinking of many linguists and speech scientists. My comments will suggest some modifications or complications in his position, not rejection.

I agree that it is time we recognize the probable futility of the search for stable phonetic definitions of invariance and segmentation in terms of features and segments—and, I would add, in terms of syllables and prosodies. This does not mean that the search should be abandoned, but that other lines of research should be more vigorously pursued. I agree that it it time to recognize that the sharp dichotomy between phonetics and phonology may be part of the problem rather than a necessary 'given' for the solution. I think that it is a stimulating and productive notion that sound systems are in large part 'self-organizing' structures and that ontogeny, in some important respects at least, recapitulates phylogeny here. Finally, I agree with Lindblom's implicit claim that understanding the processes of system construction may be more fundamental than identifying a minimal universal list of phonetic features or possible phonological segments.

I have, however, at this point three reservations about the Lindblom position as I understand it. First, I do not see why the syllable is assumed as an axiomatic given. Surely it would be more consistent with his overall position to assume that the given is the vocal symbol or vocabulary item or what could loosely be called the 'word.' Whether in child language development or in the emergence of human language, the first units may be less than or more than a syllable in terms of the usual phonetic analyses. The syllable may indeed be the most important unit in some respects but it too would result from the interaction of boundary conditions just like segments and features. This assumption need not detract from Lindblom's use of the syllable in the kind of modeling he is working with, where for various reasons the syllable is likely to be the best locus for such calculations.

Second, to say that phonological organization results from the interaction of vocabulary growth and performance constraints seem to ignore the important aspect of the conventionalization and persistence of particular sound systems. The Lindblom model must somehow account for the thousands of different languages in the world and for the important effects of the sound structures that occur in the language input processed by the child. Presumably the phonological organization of the language variety the child is acquiring plays a larger and more complex role in the child's phonological development than the physical shape of the surroundings plays in the organization of termites' nests. It is more like the hypothetical case that different populations of the same species of termite traditionally responded differently to the same physical environment in the construction of their nests.

Third, I wish that Lindblom had gone a little further in noting the kind of boundary conditions whose interaction accounts for phonetic variation. He leaves unmentioned, though he is undoubtedly aware of them, all except speaker-oriented simplification and listener-oriented elaboration. Some others may have been equally important in the origin of language as they seem to be in early child phonology. The unmentioned factors include affective expressiveness (which may be neither simplifying nor clarifying), sheer pleasure in play (important in other aspects of child development and probably in human evolution), and socially attributed values of favoring and disfavoring (which may run counter to the others). Failure to mention such factors may be related to the fact that phonologists tend to pay too little attention to these sources of variation in adult sound systems as well.

Just a word about the research agenda. A number of us in various parts of the world (including Lindblom's own lab) are now working in just this field of the emergence of linguistic structure in the child. We have left the delightful period of ages 2–5 where the child is succeeding in building structures that more or less match adult structures, and we are investigating the transition from babbling to speech, which is more challenging to the phonologist and holds promise of more fundamental findings. Two problems plague us that have not been alluded to here. One is the problem of the separation of vocal and non-vocal communication. A meaning that one child expresses orally another child may express gesturally, and some early vocables may have gestures as necessary parts. Our analyses are correspondingly difficult. The other is the unexpectedly large individual differences in phonological development. As a consequence, for the kind of evidence Lindblom wants, we need data from large numbers of children, and yet at this stage of development the child's vocalizations need more contextualization and interpretation on the part of the investigator than at later ages. In other words it is harder to get data suitable for instrumental analysis and at the same time we need much more data. If child phonologists take the Lindblom agenda seriously, this will mean a more large-scale research program in infant 'speech' than any of us have so far imagined.

Robert F. Port: Comment

This comment addresses two interesting themes found throughout Lindblom's chapter. The first is the notion that abstract objects need not be created axiomatically, but could be created by other processes that are "blind" to their own effect. If this approach can be developed, it might offer an alternative way of looking at the invariance problem itself. The second theme is the notion that the shaping principles of language can operate in a number of time frames such that different effects are produced in each frame. In the Chomskyan model of language, the structure of language is formulated as an automaton from axioms representing, in part, the objects from which the system is built: semantic features, syntactic features, and phonetic features. As an empirical model of language, the theory proposes that natural selection provides the real-world counterpart to these mathematical axioms by furnishing the language-learner's mind with innate universal linguistic features.

On the other hand, Lindblom suggests that mental abstractions provided by our genetic inheritance are not the only ones that can exist. Structure can be created without some "authorized" source of the structure; it can evolve. There is no necessity to have the objects of a system postulated as axioms. Instead, other axioms can be employed to construct a situation in which abstract objects can evolve on their own. This does not make the segments and features of Lindblom's system illusory by-products as suggested by Bromberger and Halle (Section 23a). He simply attempts to account for how such objects could have arisen, either in the individual or in human communities. While Lindblom's study attempts to simulate the role of lexical contrast in the creation of a phonological system, in Chapter 25 I attempt to describe other constraints on phonological or phonetic objects that derive from their role as communicative signals in human communities.

Another significant theme that recurs throughout Lindblom's paper is related to the first: There are several time frames for causative principles in language. At least three time scales seem important. First, there is the moment of speaking. Lindblom notes that speakers make moment-by-moment judgments about the relative mix of bottom-up phonetic information that the listener will require as opposed to top-down information from semantic context that is available for word identification. He suggests that the resulting adjustments in carefulness of articulation are based on the principle of economy of effort given a particular communicative need. Of course, one consequence is highly variable productions of words by the same speaker, but the explanatory principles can be seen working in other ways at other levels of structure.

The second time frame is language acquisition in the individual. Lindblom proposes that his "Monte Carlo simulation" be viewed as a metaphor for the child's creation of a true phonological system from a more primitive one in which each word is simply a distinct phonetic event. Similar principles of economy of articulatory effort and communicative efficiency operate at this level as well, although their effects are quite different here than at the moment of speaking. They result, not in token-to-token variation in speech, but rather in a speech-control system for the speaker that employs discrete features and rule-governed context sensitivity, a system that resembles a real-time post-lexical phonology.

The third time frame is the evolution of the language of a community. Here too, similar principles of communicative need and economy of effort interact to yield the grammar and lexicon of a language. As suggested by Lindblom, though not followed up here, the statistical modeling he employed for simulating the child's acquisition should also be applicable. Indeed, such a situation where there are a great many complex causative factors is just the kind of problem for which the Monte Carlo technique has been employed successfully in other sciences. The important point is that the explanatory principles he invokes apply equally in all these time frames— to the speaker in conversation as well as to the child learning a language and to the language itself shaped by centuries of use.

These ideas offer a different way of looking at language, as something other than a rule system. The automaton model of language, although once liberating since it allowed linguists new freedom to describe whatever structure they could find, seems now to be too restrictive since it cuts short an understanding of the origin and nature of the objects (such as phonetic features) that the rule system employs. Much of the "problem of invariance" may result from our having started with an a priori set of mental objects. It may be time now to look more carefully at where these objects come from and what purposes they serve to human communities, and to acknowledge that language is not just an internal system unrelated to anything else we know about our species. The origin of abstract structure in language is a critical theoretical problem to which only one answer has been seriously entertained in recent years: that abstract objects like phonetic features come from innate linguistic competence. Lindblom's contribution is to facilitate our consideration of other possibilities.

24 Invariance and Variability of Words in the Speech Chain

Antonie Cohen
Utrecht University
Utrecht, The Netherlands

INTRODUCTION

An underlying assumption in the study of speech processes is that it involves mappings of human language in which mental activities play a predominant part. From this vantage point, speech communication is seen as a goal-directed activity, in which the situation, knowledge of the world, and the intentions of speaker and listener all contribute in shaping the acoustic signal of speech. The factor "meaning" may have to be considered if we ultimately can account for two processes involved in speech, invariance and variability. A further conclusion to be drawn is that the relation between mental constructs, corresponding to linguistic structures, and acoustic shapes is analogous to the phenomenon described in the literature on gestalt psychology in which invariance can be maintained under numerous transformations.

In order to make the problem of accounting for this intricate relationship between speech and language adaptable to an experimental approach, the notion "word" will be put into focus. The main question that will have to be faced will be what happens to words as linguistic units in the acoustic signal. For this purpose, factors involved both in production and perception of connected speech will have to be considered. This set of factors may best be studied by paying special attention to the role of speech prosody.

My hypothesis is: As we as speech scientists focus on finding out what happens to words in the speech chain we will be better able to produce acceptable, natural sounding synthetic speech and eventually we will be in a better position to tackle the problem of automatic speech recognition. The major problem facing us in the next decade is no longer what it was in the immediate past—i.e. segmentation of the speech chain in phonological segments—but rather that of word identification. The idea underlying this approach is that speech behavior has to do with meaning in terms of intentions to be expressed by the speaker and information to be conveyed to and processed by the listener. The only invariance at stake in speech behavior is anchored through meaning, and in this respect words, as units of meaning each with its phonological structuring, are taken to be suitable candidates for constituting the building blocks of speech. The major claim in this approach is that the recognition of words is a necessary condition for the intention conveyed by the speech message to be properly processed.

Speech is a messy business; it is not an ideal, foolproof message code. However, speech proves to be a tremendously efficient code, established through a long process of evolution and acquired by the individual throughout an extensive period of practice and training. Moreover, listeners have acquired an enormously effective error correcting code which acts as a stabilizer on the unruly waves of everyday speech communication. Humans are adept at drawing on knowledge stored in our mental lexicon in speaking and at making sophisticated guesses about the purport of what reaches our ears. In focusing our attention on words as building blocks, we will advance evidence from the psycholinguistic literature, dealing with speech errors and the way they are corrected, with the use of lexical decision tasks as a research tool, as well as phonemic restoration and tip-of-the-tongue phenomena. This study complements the work of Marslen-Wilson (1980) to the extent that the word is seen as a mediator between the information contained in the acoustic signal and linguistic expectancy.

The trouble with words as linguistic entities, stored as they may be in the mental lexicon, is that they undergo numerous influences once they are uttered in the stream of speech, apart from all such factors as individual characteristics of various speakers. The study of prosody has proved indispensable in building speech-synthesis systems of high-quality speech. It is surely not enough to put one acoustic wordshape after another onto a prerecorded tape, as was shown in early experiments for building a reading machine for the blind by the Haskins Laboratories.

The present situation is different from that of the 1950s and 1960s. There is no longer a need to study the relation between phonemic segments and the acoustic signal of speech, as was the case with numerous experiments involving nonsense syllables. Thanks largely to the advance of technological facilities, we are now in a position to reformulate the main research problem. In order to come up with better synthesis, we ought to know more precisely what happens to the acoustic shapes of words in fluent speech due to prosodic influences. It is necessary to follow up by looking for the perceptual tolerances of pertinent parameter values through listening experiments. Knowledge of these tolerances may help us in addressing the question of what information points in speech help listeners to recognize words in the speech chain. This knowledge may then, we hope, be applied in speech recognition systems, where one of the main problems to be tackled is how to demarcate words in connected speech.

SPEECH AND LANGUAGE

If we wish to take the study of the acoustic signal of speech seriously, in an effort to account for the various processes involved in its generation and interpretation, we might do well to take into consideration that speech events have the ultimate purpose of conveying meaning.

It seems as if this truism has been partly lost sight of in phonetic studies over the last few decades. Most of the work carried out in phonetics laboratories all over the world has had to do mainly with the question of how phonological segments are reflected, as the so-called sounds of speech, in the acoustic signal. From these studies we have acquired a vast amount of knowledge about the intricate way in which these speech sounds are interrelated, so that we now have come to accept that there is no simple one-to-one relationship between abstract linguistic segments and measurable events in the speech chain. Much of this work had been inspired by the linguistic conventions of the time, in which phonemes were regarded to be the ultimate building blocks of linguistic structure, which were claimed to be invariant in the stream of speech. We now know that there is no such invariance, and the problem of the relation between linguistic units, seen as discrete segments, and the continuously varying acoustic signal can be formulated in terms of the phonological segmentation of the speech continuum.

Much of the experimental evidence used to approach this problem has been based on material consisting of nonsense syllables. The link pertaining between speech and language was thus a very tenuous one to the extent that all considerations of meaning were precluded from consideration. In all fairness, it has to be admitted that the linguistic analysis, giving rise to the postulation of phonological segments, is based in itself on the word differentiating characteristics of segments. As such it has to be considered a necessary step in describing the relationship between speech events and linguistic structures. Concentration on this issue bypasses much of what has to be taken into account in studying speech processes in the 1980s. The early work carried out by the Haskins Laboratories, mentioned above should be seen against the background of the pioneering nature in which it was carried out with regard to the technical facility available.

With advancing technology, we are now in a position to handle far larger quantities of speech for experimental purposes, leading to successful applications in the field of speech synthesis. This development has forced us to acknowledge the importance of prosodic features, a topic whose treatment in linguistic studies has been far less developed than that of the segmental aspects of speech. The major role of these suprasegmental features, unlike their segmental counterparts, cannot be captured solely in terms of distinctiveness. We will come back to the role of speech prosody later, when we approach the problem of its influence on the acoustic shape of words in connected speech. Speech events, occurring in real time, demonstrate the working of prosodic features, such as pitch and rhythm, which simply cannot be left out of consideration in studying speech processes and for which, at present, there is no comprehensive linguistic framework.

As in all cases of speech communication, prosodic characteristics are highly dependent on the intentions of a speaker in relation to what he or she has to convey as a message, in terms of meaning, to a listener. Even in the advanced stage of knowledge that we have acquired, thanks to the developments in microelectronics that have led to the sophisticated speech-synthesis systems such as "MITalk" designed by Allen, Klatt and their colleagues at M.I.T., there is always the necessity of a human editor to decide which words in the utterance will have to be made prominent, a decision which is largely taken on pragmatic grounds, involving the knowledge of what went before and which part of the utterance the listener is supposed to focus on.

In the concluding section of this chapter, a plea will be made for investing more research effort in the interplay between what human speakers know about the pragmatic constraints inherent in the shape of speech messages they produce, and their goal of making their intentions interpretable by their listeners. The main criterion for successful communication between human speakers and listeners is a shared language code. But apart from this, speakers will implicitly bring to their task, on the basis of their being a practiced user of the spoken language, a variety of skills embedded in their speech behavior to secure a maximal effect of their speech efforts, such as, for instance, raising the voice to overcome ambient noise. They are made aware of possible disturbances by means of various perceptual feedback channels and they will readily be able to adjust to them. Depending on the actual nature of the speech situation, ranging from intimate conversation to addressing a large crowd, the speakers' awareness of possible disturbances in the speech-communication link will exert a control on their speech production. Looking at speech from the vantage point of the speakers, it is clear that they bring to bear a vast potential of acquired linguistic habits, amounting to their tacit knowledge of the language code, of which they can be made aware when such an awareness is especially called for. Such is the case in puns, in solving crossword puzzles, or in the aesthetic use of language in poetry.

Moreover, speakers will be led by the behavior of their speech partners, which may exert an influence on the type of speech to be produced. Their listeners may or may not be used to the speakers' linguistic idiosyncrasies, their choice of words, their voice qualities. When strangers speak in the street, it is by no means certain that successful communication will be secured in spite of a shared language code. Speakers and listeners have to get adjusted to each other's voice particularities. Although sharing a language code is a necessary condition, it is by no means a sufficient condition for successful speech communication. However, in studying speech processes, we might do well to extend the knowledge of the language code to describe the type of working knowledge which is brought to bear in linguistic performance in speech communication. It is this type of knowledge which has so far remained largely uncharted in linguistic descriptions of the language code.

One of the major components guaranteeing the efficient use of the speech channel in human communication is the awareness and correction of errors, a specific mode of speech behavior capable of adjusting to possible disturbances in the speech link. This capacity is based on an exquisitely tuned complex of feedback loops, both internal and external, with regard to the speaker. (For a good survey, cf. Borden & Harris, 1980.) The study of speech errors (Fromkin, 1973, 1980) has recently provided clear testimony to the presence of an error-correcting code operative both in speaking and listening. Speakers pre-edit their linguistic programs both covertly, in the planning stage, and overtly in their execution, so as to secure efficient and optimal speech communication. Although speech errors are always wont to obtrude themselves, they are mostly corrected by the speakers, though not always consciously (personal observation).

From what we have observed so far about the relation between speech and language, it seems clear that the acoustic signal, as the major focus of attention in studying speech, should be seen in relation to what human language is ultimately all about, the conveyance of meaning. To make this objective at all practicable, we will concentrate on the study of words as linguistic units expressible in terms of phonetic shapes.

WORDS: INVARIANCE IN MEANING, VARIABILITY IN ACOUSTIC SHAPE

When we shift our attention from what happens to phonological segments in the speech stream, as was the case in much phonetic research in the past, to a similar question with regard to words, we do so in the belief that words capture more of the essential function of conveying meaning than segments do, and in this way we will be in a better position to chart the kind of knowledge shared by the partners in a speech communication link. Moreover, it provides us with a suitable context within which to approach the problems of invariance and variability which are the major theme of this volume.

In general, word meanings are taken to be largely invariant, although dictionary entries provide convincing evidence that, even here, the notion of invariance should be taken with a grain of salt. Furthermore, the history of all languages shows clear shifts of meaning in their vocabulary. We are often at a loss to explain precisely what a word means when it is taken out of context. However, quite a few words in the vocabulary are well defined, as e.g. *transubstantiation*. As such, they do not require specific context information to decide upon their meaning. At the other end of the scale are words that do not have a referential meaning in the ordinary sense, such as e.g. the auxiliary "do," which may have no meaning of its own, but derives it from the way it functions in syntactic groups: compare *Does he know?* versus *He does know.*

This is not the place to enlarge on the complexities involved in the study of word meanings proper. For argument's sake, we will confine ourselves to tasks in which knowledge of word meanings is taken for granted. For our purpose, emphasizing the variable acoustic shapes which words assume under the influence of prosody in connected speech, we will not enter into a discussion about linguistic criteria to establish what a word is as a linguistic unit. We will adopt an operational definition; words will be taken to correspond with the items we normally find in print between spaces, including collocations and idioms constituting lexical units, such as *of course* and *once upon a time*, having a unitary meaning.

Before entering on a discussion of the way in which words as linguistic units are represented in the speech code, both in production and in perception, a few preliminary remarks will be made. It is by now a common assumption that we do not signal our intentions as speakers by simply sequencing phonemes like beads on a string, nor do we interpret a speech message in its acoustic shape as so many phonemes strung together. Acoustic word shapes and their meaning present to us an integrated appearance. In a way there is a dual process involved (Polanyi, 1969), to the effect that sounds are transparent vehicles of the word meaning they are supposed to convey. Normally, in concentrating on meaning, language users are hardly aware of the character of the sound shapes, even to the extent that bilinguals may not remember which language they spoke or attended to. We are always bent on interpreting any incoming acoustic signals, a thunder clap, a knock at the door, screeching brakes, or a ringing alarm bell. We do not normally attend to the acoustic details but rather to what they purport to signify to the alerted consciousness. The same applies to the acoustic shapes of words and other linguistic signs in speech. In the words of Neisser:

> The English language is misleading: it allows us to say that we hear *sounds* when we are really hearing events, but makes it unreasonable to say we see *light* when we are really seeing objects.

Actually the two cases are precisely analogous. We see events (or objects) by means of the information available in light, and we hear them by means of the information available in sound [Neisser, 1976; 158].

There is very little that can be called invariant in speech in a veridical sense. The only invariance we might claim is the one based on word types, to be seen as molds in the shape of gestalts, stored in our mental lexicon, determined by the phonological constraints of the language. It is on this basis that certain acoustic shapes can trigger the relevant word-type representation.

Returning to the evidence supplied by the study of speech errors, we may observe that, in the vast majority of cases, a speech program, containing an error in its execution, is stopped at the nearest word boundary after which the correction is effected, resuming at the beginning of the word in which the error occurred (cf. Nooteboom's 1980 study of Meringer's publications). On the listener's side, the operation of the error correcting code was demonstrated by the studies of Warren and Obusek (1971) on the phenomenon of word restoration, in which items of speech had deliberately been obliterated by a disturbing signal, such as a cough.

Complementary to this type of auditory illusion is the effect of verbal transformation (Warren, 1976). This effect refers to the phenomenon that listeners, continuously exposed to hearing repetitions of one word recorded on a closed loop of tape, report hearing a large variety of words differing from the test item. For example, one subject responding to the monosyllable *ripe* under these conditions reported hearing *ripe, right, white–light, right, right–light, ripe, right, ripe, bright–light, right, bright–light*. In these circumstances, listeners can hardly be expected to be aware of the acoustic shape of the word forms as such; in fact, when confronted with a word excised from fluent speech they will be at great pains to recognize it (Pollack & Pickett, 1963).

Further evidence about the ready accessibility of the mental lexicon is provided by auditory lexical decision experiments, which show how efficient the look-up mechanism for words is, enabling skilled language users to determine quickly whether or not a word belongs to their stock of knowledge. Words can be accessed by multiple paths, both as to their acoustic shape and as to meaning. Tip-of-the-tongue phenomena (cf. Browman, 1978, 1980; Brown & McNeill, 1966) testify to the powerful grip listeners have on access paths to their mental lexicon. When confronted with selecting names which share a large stretch of phonological structure, speakers are easily hampered in their decisions, as in the case of *Schubert* and *Schumann*. Actually, proper names are notoriously difficult in perception, especially unfamiliar ones. They denote a single individual, unlike common nouns that denote a class of referents, e.g. *table*.

What holds for single words also applies to idioms and stock expressions, like *as a matter of fact*, and *out of sight, out of mind*. They are "triggered" as a single chunk of linguistic information. Shadowing experiments, in which deliberate mistakes were introduced, revealed that phonological restoration would occur frequently, whereas transpositions in idiomatic and proverbial expressions were hardly ever noticed (Cohen, 1980). Thus we may assume that language users bring to the task of speech communication a firm grip of what words are and how they can be accessed and recognized. The next task will be to see what happens to these pristine forms when they are used in connected speech.

PROSODIC INFLUENCES ON WORDS IN THE SPEECH CHAIN

Having moved outside the region of studying the acoustic shape of words in fluent speech, we will now focus our attention on the factors influencing words both in production and in perception. We have referred to the early efforts of generating speech from prerecorded words. The lack of success of this approach can be explained from the fact that words, in ordinary speech, are subject to influences from what can be called "prosody." One instance of this effect is coarticulation (in the narrow sense of neighboring sounds influencing one another) which has been studied profusely in the literature.

Besides coarticulation, the major effects of prosody can be ranged under the headings of rhythm and intonation. Rhythm refers to alternations in duration dependent on absence or presence of stress, on speech rate, and the position of words in a sentence string. Intonation refers to fluctuations in fundamental frequency of the vocal cords insofar as they can be shown to be relevant to the listener. As such, they can be regarded as being voluntarily programmed by speakers in their efforts to focus attention on specific words and syntactic structures, such as major syntactic boundaries, to guide the listener in breaking up the message into a correct linguistic phrasing. Usually there is an interaction between temporal and pitch cues to bring about the desired effect.

Words are made prominent in an utterance by a suitable pitch accent, whereas major syntactic boundaries are signaled by rises for continuation and falls for termination. Precisely where pitch accents and other prosodic markers are manifested is largely under the speaker's control, and is inspired primarily by the ongoing speech situation, as a result of pragmatic considerations, rather than purely for grammatical reasons (cf. Cutler, 1983).

Experiences with speakers who have undergone laryngectomy, and who were fitted out with an artificial larynx, provides evidence of this strategy. In a study of speech produced with an electrolarynx provided with a semi-automatic pitch control, van Geel (1983) was able to show that users were able to learn how to manipulate the button to use the pitch-accent contours built into the device. Their training consisted of making them aware of where they would normally have provided pitch accents with their previously available voicing mechanism. A close study of their utterances shows that their strategy for triggering the device was largely determined by pragmatic-semantic reasons.

Speakers, in the act of speech communication, use prosodic means at will to make the task for the listener in interpreting the incoming speech signal as manageable as possible. (For an interesting survey of the various factors involved with regard to word recognition see Nooteboom, 1983.) There are a number of indications that in interpreting an incoming speech message, listeners proceed in a word-by-word fashion (cf. Cole & Jakimik, 1980). Indeed, a number of models have been suggested for this purpose, such as the logogen model by Morton (1964) and the cohort model by Marslen-Wilson (1980). In spite of differences in particulars, these models have in common the emphasis of interaction between contextual knowledge and information provided by the acoustic signal.

Returning to the effect of coarticulation, for the optimal use of recognition devices, be they of the logogen or cohort type, listeners are greatly helped in being able to determine where one word ends and the next one begins. It would therefore serve a useful purpose to study more closely the effect of coarticulation across word boundaries (cf. Nakatani & Dukes, 1977). Prosodic features as such may certainly help in delineating words in the speech chain and some successful efforts have been made in this resect at the Centre National d'Etudes des Telecommunications (Vaissiére, 1980) as applied in the field of automatic speech recognition. The system described there uses information of certain intonational features in French for assigning possible prosodic word boundaries. Word endings are usually marked by lengthening of the last vocalic nucleus and they may also be marked by an F_0 peak or continuation rise. Word beginnings are primarily marked by an F_0 rise from the preceding syllable and secondarily by a lengthening of the first consonant, but this can extend to the following vowel.

A similar approach in automatic speech recognition is foreseen by the LAFS model of Klatt (1979a). (LAFS stands for Lexical Access From Spectra.) The system incorporates rules of assimilation and particularly elision for determining word boundaries. Thus there is a precompiled rule specifying [st#s→s] so that the word combination *list some*, pronounced without the intervening [t] gets to be recognized correctly.

More evidence for automatic speech recognition is given by Klatt (1983) and Zue (1983). The latter suggests a recognition device in which preliminary recognition of isolated words is carried out in broad phonetic terms such as vowel, stop, and fricative; the resulting outcome can then be used for lexical access. Within the scope of broad phonetic characteristics stress placement also plays an important part. To sum up, both in human speech communication and in the more sophisticated devices for machine recognition of speech, the influence of prosody on the acoustic shapes of words is playing an important role.

CONCLUSION

It is largely through the cue of meaning, the pragmatic-semantic factor involved in any act of ordinary communication, and the enormously efficient parallel accessibility of our vocabulary that we are capable of handling speech communication. The items to be readied from the mental lexicon are words and collocations, and they are considered to form the building blocks of speech. The way they are actually shaped in the acoustic signal is largely determined by: (1) processes involved in the interplay between the implicit knowledge a speaker has of the ongoing acoustic signal in terms of meaning; (2) the speaker's awareness of situational constraints, such as the amount of ambient noise; and (3) the listener's internalized model of perceptual and interpretative processes.

We know by now something about the influence of prosodic factors in shaping the acoustic characteristics of words in connected speech. There remains, however, a great deal to be known about the proper assignment of prosodic markers, both in terms of fundamental frequency and temporal organization with respect to optimal intelligibility and, in particular, naturalness. More research in this area in human speech communication seems to be required before we can hope to improve the quality of speech produced by machines.

Studying the effects of prosody on the acoustic shape of words and the way they are connected through coarticulation would help us to achieve these goals. If we succeed in establishing what really happens in connected speech, we will be in a better position to tackle the vastly greater problem of automatic speech recognition.

To sum up, possible lines of research include:
1. More attention should be paid to auditory word recognition.
2. More research is needed on the influence of prosodic factors in connected speech on the acoustic shapes of words, including juncture and the assessment of rules for accentuation.
3. With a view to improving human communication or automatic systems of speech synthesis and speech recognition, the role of the normal interaction between speaker and listener should be studied.

Jacqueline Vaissière:

Variance and Invariance at the Word Level

As is well known, the word represents the main point of interaction between all sources of knowledge shared by both the speaker and the listener (Klatt, 1977). Such sources of knowledge include the lexicon which contains the list of available possible words in a language, the syntax, the semantics, and the pragmatics. Those factors constrains sequences of words to form (in the ideal case) grammatically, semantically, and pragmatically correct sentences. The ultimate purpose of speech communication is to convey meaning from speaker to listener. As the basic information-carrying unit, Cohen points out, the word rather than the phoneme might be considered the building block in speech research. As for what concerns invariance at the word level, Cohen considers the listener's point of view and concludes that, "the only invariance we might claim is the one based on word types, to be seen as moulds in the shape of gestalts, stored in our mental lexicon, determined by the phonotactic constrains of the language." Cohen emphasizes the role of other types of information than acoustic information available to the listener to decode the successive words in the message, and cites the LAFS model (Klatt, 1979a) and the Logogen model (Morton, 1964) as possible models for speech perception. From Cohen's mentalist point of view (see Section 23a), the problems of segmentation into phoneme-size units and invariance of phoneme and feature become small relative to the problem of segmentation into word-size units and their invariance. I agree with the views expressed in Cohen's paper, most of which serve to point out the importance of the word as an unit in speech. However, I would like to try to fill in some of the details of these views.

WORD DEFINITION

The paper does not define in enough detail what a "word" is. The definition of the word, either as a unit of meaning or as an acoustic unit, is not clear cut. First, it may refer to the graphic form of the word, and blank spaces are considered boundary markers between successive words. Second, the word may also be defined as the basic unit of meaning, "the morpheme." A "graphic" word, however, may be composed by several morphemes, and morphemes (and not the graphic word) are considered by linguists as the basic unit of meaning. Moreover some words such as the grammatical words (articles or auxiliaries) do not have a meaning by themselves. Third, the separation of the "graphic words" into two word types and the notion of the prosodic word have been introduced by reference to the acoustic level for languages like French and English.

The words of the first type (type A), corresponding typically to function (grammatical) words, are generally very short words in terms of number of syllables, have a reduced duration, an average lower fundamental frequency and are not precisely articulated; the words of the second type (type B), typically lexical words, correspond to a local peak of prominence on one syllable (marked by durational and fundamental frequency contrasts), with a lengthening of the word final syllable, and a strengthening of the word initial phoneme. Depending on the context, a lexical word may however behave as a word of type A and function word as a word of type B. Words of type A and of type B may be regrouped into what is called a single prosodic word (related to the notion of "rhythmic unit," "syntagm," "stress group," or "hat-pattern") primarily characterized by two F_0 movements in opposite direction. Such regrouping obscures the acoustic identity of the component words. Where the prosodic word starts and where it ends is difficult to determine, since there is no solid theoretical basis for such a demarcation.

For example, the two lexical words "petit garçon" are generally regrouped into a single four-syllable prosodic word. The two words may tend to separate however into two different acoustic units in certain circumstances, which depend on the speaker, the style, the rate of speech, the length of the words (shorter words may be regrouped more often), and the frequency of occurrence of the words in the lexicon and in the discourse. Also a long graphic, lexical word has a tendency to "spread" into two prosodic units depending on its morphemic composition (as marked in French by a lengthening of the final syllable of an internal morpheme). Integration or complete separation of two "graphic" words into a single acoustic unit, or separation of a graphic word into two "morphemic" units may not be a binary decision, but may vary along a continuum. In other words, the relationship among graphic words, units of meaning, and prosodic words is not necessarily a one-to-one correspondence.

REPRESENTATION OF THE WORD

Cohen does not express clearly what a gestalt at the level of the word may look like, since by definition, a gestalt must be invariant. A gestalt point-of-view is not incompatible with the view of the word as composed of smaller constituents (phonemes, for example) at least at some abstract level: Such a theory may be equally applied to the syllable, the demisyllable, the diphone, the phone, and the feature. The detailed acoustic shape of a word is known to be influenced by a large number of factors. By pointing out the importance of other sources of knowledge (such as syntax and semantics and phenomena such as phoneme restoration) Cohen suggests a gestalt of high complexity which questions the adequacy of the representation of the word as a string of phonemes.

One principle of phonetic transcription has been to use a set of symbols in the most economical and the most efficient way to represent the various utterances of a language. Linguists postulate two levels, or a continuum of levels, between an abstract representation—a phonemic level—and surface realizations—the phonetic level. A single phonemic symbol, such as the phoneme [R] or the phoneme [l] could be associated with spectrographically very different looking sounds, depending on the position of the phoneme in the syllable (e.g. initial, final, and in cluster) and in the word. It is not clear, for example, if all [R] and [l] allophones share even perceptual equivalence or invariant properties at the acoustic level. There may be some invariant cue across such positions, but the lack of invariance across different syllable and word positions is irrelevant to linguistic theory since the different positional allophones do not contrast with each other. In other terms, such allophones could be treated as separated phonemes, without harm to the theory.

Traditional linguists concern themselves with differences in sound that make a difference in meaning at the level of the utterance. As mentioned by Halle (1964), many properties of speech events have been satisfactorily accounted for in terms of simple sequences of segments, phonemes, and distinctive features. Some prosodic phenomena, such as syllable boundaries and word-stress position in English, may also be minimally distinctive. However, most prosodic phenomena carry no discrete meaning contrast, but rather shades of meaning or information about the organization of the utterance, two notions which are difficult to formalize. The lack of conclusive results concerning prosodic phenomena may not be due to a lack of adequate studies, but to a lack of a linguistic framework for studying them.

When the word is taken as a reference, what seems important for both the listener and the speaker is distinctiveness, not at the level of the phoneme but at the level of the word. Lexical access can be performed by the listener on a partial identification of the features, and it may not be necessary for the speaker to fully realize the acoustic correlates of a feature that, through the hazard of the lexicon, is not distinctive at the word level. The full specification of features is more necessary in short words than in long ones where the burden of distinctiveness can be shared by many features. In nonsense words, whether short or long, the speaker has no possibility to refer to distinctiveness at the word level, and therefore these words tend to be more carefully pronounced. Moreover words can be more or less nonsense: the French word /grup/ is more acceptable as a possible English word than the word /FNAC/, which contradicts the phonotactic constraints of the French language, but still is recognized as a French word (it is an abbreviation for a well-known French store). As pointed out by Cohen, the use of nonsense words is widespread in speech research. We may question the validity of extending the conclusions of such studies to real words.

Not only the lexicon, but also the immediate discourse conditions distinctiveness of both words and non-words. In English, for example, when talking about the abduction and the adduction of the vocal folds, the [b] and the [d] in words like *abducted* and *adducted* may be particularly carefully pronounced since the meanings are contrastive. Once a feature may have become redundant at the word level, the speaker may be more inclined to let articulatory ease suppress some of the distinction, or, on the contrary, to accentuate the distinction in the opposite case. The evolution of the vocabulary items shows a tendency to suppress carriers of redundant information. For example, the word "capital" was formerly an adjective, and used in the phrase equivalent to "capital city." Frequent words tend to reduce their size to a minimal contrastive level ("metro" from "metropolitan"), and their origin is often lost. There may be a strong similarity between the processes leading to suppress redundancy at the level of the lexicon (by suppressing words or abbreviating them) and the processes leading to the reduction of acoustic contrast between the distinctive features in the realization of certain words. It may be argued that the mental representation of certain words (such as frequent words) may be influenced by such a process.

SUPRASEGMENTAL FRAMEWORK
AND SEGMENTAL FEATURES

There is a tendency in contemporary studies to separate the segmental and supra-segmental information contained in the signal and to interpret them separately. The relative duration of the events and the fundamental frequency contours de-livered in parallel with the spectral information provide very useful information for both decoding the segmental information, and for detecting word boundaries, word stress, and word regrouping. However, the word has intrinsic segmental and suprasegmental characteristics which appear concomitantly. Striking similarities related to the word as an acoustic unit have been observed for a number of re-lated and unrelated languages such as English, Swedish, French, and Japanese: word-final syllable lengthening, word-initial consonant lengthening, or word-initial allophones. Similarities also extend to the way with which the words are regrouped into larger units (F_0 rises associated with initiation, F_0 fall and lengthening with termination resetting of the base-line as boundary marker; see Vaissière, 1983a, for references). Such regularities may come from similar ways of representing words in the mental lexicon, and from general processes in composing sentences that are independent of the language spoken. However, there is a lack of knowledge of a large number of languages for definitive conclusions.

The segmental features have to be interpreted depending on their position in the sentence. The word as an unit imposes strong constraints on the acoustic structuring of the utterance. Analysis of the velum behavior in sentences shows the velum to be typically higher in word initial position and in prestressed posi-tion than in other positions for both the nasal consonants (which require an open velopharyngeal port) and the oral consonants (requiring a close velopharyngeal port) (Vaissière, 1983b). A higher position of the velum corresponds to a greater tensing of the levator palatini. It may be hypothesized that the difference in velum height between positional allophones may be due to the superposition of a common suprasegmental feature, let say [+strong], corresponding to a greater tensing at word onsets, rather than to fluctuations associated with each phoneme. With this hypothesis, the aspiration of the so-called tense stops consonants in English [p, t, k] should be considered as being due to the same factor as to the partial devoicing of word initial lax stops [b, d, g], the glottalization of word-initial vowels, the higher position of the velum in word-initial position, or the fact that vowels in sentence context (at least for French) seem to be, ceteris paribus, more precisely uttered if the structuring of the sentence requires them to be uttered in the upper F_0 register of the speaker.

Aspiration, devoicing, glottalization, higher position of the velum or more precise articulation have a common characteristic: a greater tensing of at least one of the articulators, the vocal folds, the velum (levator palitini), or the tongue. Such extra tensing may be contradictory or not to the articulatory requirements of the under-lying segmental feature(s). Less intra- and interspeaker variability in velum height was observed, when the velum was supposed to be low (nasal) and not supraseg-mentally tense (-strong), or high (oral) and suprasegmentally tense (+strong), than in the combination (+nasal), (+strong) or (oral), (-strong) (Vaissière, 1983b). The tensing is not only a function of position in the word, but also a function of the relative importance of the word as an information carrying unit in the sentence context. If a word is sufficiently stressed, it tends to be uttered with an higher fundamental frequency and [p, t, k] may be aspirated even in final or medial position. As a consequence, segmental and suprasegmental characteristics of speech should be considered as intimately connected. Therefore, their separate interpretation should be avoided.

Thus EMG data, articulatory positions, and the acoustic signal may be interpreted as the result of a combination of both segmental features and the suprasegmental framework. The relative importance of suprasegmental variables as compared with the realizations of the segmental features is speaker-dependent, at least for the velum (Vaissière, 1983b). The lack of electromyographic, articulatory, and acoustic invariance for the distinctive features as discussed in this volume may be partly explained first by context-dependent differences in suprasegmental variables, second by a speaker-dependent way of combining suprasegmental influences and the segmental features, and third by unpredictable gestures unrelated to the content of speech (see my comments on speech ready gestures, in Section 10b). Such a lack of observed invariance does not argue against the possible existence of invariance at a more central level, before the integration of the segmental and suprasegmental features into the entire speech event.

CONCLUSION

The acoustic signal is intrinsically highly structured. An important determinant of this structure is the temporal variation of the relative tenseness of the articulatory processes in the realization of a given segmental feature. The word plays a great role in determining this structure and consequently it is a very important unit for interpreting the acoustic correlates of the distinctive features. However, the syllable, the phrase, and the sentence also play important roles; there are no unambiguous criteria to decide which unit is most important. The word is an obvious building block in speech perception and production, but such a view is not incompatible with the use of the phonemes as building blocks for constructing words. So instead of following Cohen's suggestion by "replacing" one building block (the phoneme) by another (the word), it may be more effective to search for an integration of the different acoustic units into a single framework.

Caution is advisable in extending the conclusions of studies of nonsense words to real words. The distinctiveness of a feature at the lexical level may play an important role in its mental representation since there seems to be a natural tendency to reduce redundancy in the communication process.

The decoding of the speech signal by the listener is known to be a complex process involving various types of normalization. This process is far from being fully understood. But our present inability to deal with this problem should not lead to ignoring it in modeling speech understanding, to an underestimation of what is actually contained in the speech signal, and an overemphasis of the role of syntactic, semantic, and pragmatic constraints. No doubt, when the words are not in dictation form but embedded in a context, the pronunciation of the word may become "sloppier" probably because other sources of knowledge constrain the number of possible words in each position so that the full realization of the complete set of features may become redundant. Nevertheless, literate listeners are perfectly able to discriminate meaningful or nonsense words pronounced in isolation and to transcribe them phonetically. One of the problems with invariance is that researchers are still confused about what unit should be invariant or "more" invariant than the others (features, phonemes, allophones, or even words?) and at which level of the communication process (functional invariance, perceptual equivalence, acoustic invariance or articulatory control?). The question of invariance remains the central problem in speech research the importance of which is not reduced by the acknowledgement of the word as an important unit. Even if no invariance will be found in the future, the search for invariance may provide a useful hypothesis and an adequate framework to studying speech.

25 Invariance in Phonetics

Robert F. Port
Indiana University

INTRODUCTION

Since the term "invariance" seems to mean different things to different people, we need a way of discussing the problem that allows for a variety of types of invariance. It seems to me that geometry already has evolved a very useful framework for this purpose that can easily be adapted to the study of speech and language. In this formulation, invariance is defined in terms of specific transformations. This approach makes it possible to specify many abstract properties of an object—in particular, the ones that make it a linguistic-phonetic object—without necessity to describe the properties of the object that differentiate it from others in its space. After presenting this framework, several of the most fully developed theories of the phonetic space will be recast in terms of this descriptive scheme. The final goal will be to present a brief account of a new phonetic theory that will attempt to explain many properties of the phonetic space. This theory will be directly justified in terms of the invariance framework. It will be argued that the phonetic space must have certain properties of invariance in order for phonetic objects to play their role in the communicative function of language.

GEOMETRY AND PHONETICS

The traditional metaphor that speech sounds lie in a "phonetic space" is an excellent one and merits further exploration. The discipline of geometry has dealt with spaces for a long time and mathematicians have some ways of thinking about them that may be useful for phoneticians, linguists, and speech researchers. In this section, I will describe a way of specifying a space that is formal yet does not imply any claims about specific objects or figures in the space. Following this, it will be shown how the concept of isomorphism, which is closely tied to these geometric ideas, can be applied to unify phenomena from different substantive domains.

A major development in thinking about geometric spaces that evolved late in the 19th century is the view of a space, not as a collection of potential objects of a particular type (e.g., points, lines, and circles), but rather as a place where a specific set of rules or transformations apply and in which particular properties remain invariant under those transformations (see Bell, 1945, for discussion). This approach led to clarification of the relationship between, for example, Euclidean geometry and various non-Euclidean geometries. It was found that different types of space could then be defined by the kinds of transformations that can freely operate in the space without modifying figures in the space. In geometry it seems that the transformations and their spaces fall into a nested structure in which more powerful transformation groups include the sets of transformations below them in the hierarchy (of course, this feature is not necessarily relevant to the linguistic problem).

Figure 25.1 illustrates this way of thinking as applied to portions of plane geometry. In the upper panel on the left are listed some of the transformations permitted in the first kind of space (i.e., transformations which do *not* affect the identity of figures). These transformations are known as the "displacements": translation of the figure (a left-right or up-down sliding motion), rotation of the figure, and reflection (left-right or top-bottom mirror image). In the center portion of each panel are the names or pictures of some possible figures in each kind of space. The two equilateral triangles are identical, despite their different orientation in this plane. The test for this identity is that one can employ combinations of the permitted transformations defining the space (that is, displacements) to make the first triangle congruent with the second. The larger equilateral triangle, however, is a different figure since one cannot get from the first, smaller triangle to the larger one with any of the displacement transformations. To the right in this panel are listed some of the properties of figures in this kind of plane that remain invariant under the permitted transformations: distances from any point on a figure to any other point, the angles of any corners, and the property of lying on the same line. It is these properties that determine what can be distinct figures in the space.

If we permit more powerful transformations to occur, then the figures themselves become more abstract. For example, in the second panel, we define a second kind of space in which all the transformations of the first panel are permitted along with the "similarity" transformations which permit both the x and y dimensions to be expanded by the same amount. They permit any object to shrink or expand in constant proportion. In such a space, any equilateral triangle is obviously the same figure as any other equilateral triangle, since one can simply expand or contract one triangle by an

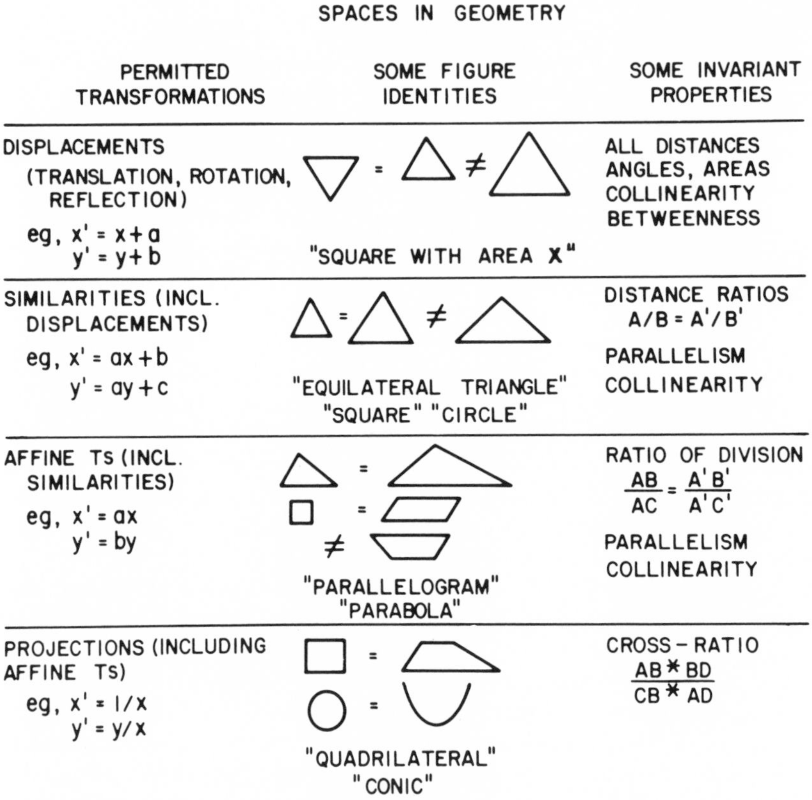

SPACES IN GEOMETRY

PERMITTED TRANSFORMATIONS	SOME FIGURE IDENTITIES	SOME INVARIANT PROPERTIES
DISPLACEMENTS (TRANSLATION, ROTATION, REFLECTION) eg, $x' = x + a$ $y' = y + b$	$\triangledown = \triangle \neq \triangle$ "SQUARE WITH AREA **X**"	ALL DISTANCES ANGLES, AREAS COLLINEARITY BETWEENNESS
SIMILARITIES (INCL. DISPLACEMENTS) eg, $x' = ax + b$ $y' = ay + c$	$\triangle = \triangle \neq \triangle$ "EQUILATERAL TRIANGLE" "SQUARE" "CIRCLE"	DISTANCE RATIOS $A/B = A'/B'$ PARALLELISM COLLINEARITY
AFFINE TS (INCL. SIMILARITIES) eg, $x' = ax$ $y' = by$	$\triangle = \triangle$ $\square = \diagdown$ $\neq \diagdown$ "PARALLELOGRAM" "PARABOLA"	RATIO OF DIVISION $\dfrac{AB}{AC} = \dfrac{A'B'}{A'C'}$ PARALLELISM COLLINEARITY
PROJECTIONS (INCLUDING AFFINE TS) eg, $x' = 1/x$ $y' = y/x$	$\square = \diagdown$ $\bigcirc = \cup$ "QUADRILATERAL" "CONIC"	CROSS – RATIO $\dfrac{AB * BD}{CB * AD}$

FIG. 25.1.   Transformations in Plane Geometry.

appropriate amount to match the other in size and then use the appropriate translations to make them congruent. However, in this kind of plane, an equilateral triangle is still a different figure from any nonequilateral triangle. Some of the invariant properties of this space are the ratio of any two distances (such as the relative length of one side of a triangle with another side), along with parallelism versus nonparallelism of lines and collinearity of points (the property of lying on the same line).

In the affine space of the third panel, different scaling factors of the x and y axis are permitted along with rotation of the axes from perpendicular. Here ordinary intuition may begin to balk a bit at the idea that a square and a parallelogram are the *same* figure. The only invariant distance measure in this plane is the ratio of division (which requires four collinear points to be specified). We are all familiar with figures that have these properties since most time–function graphs (such as a sound spectrogram) are affine figures for which the aspect ratio and absolute size are arbitrary. In a more abstract space, such as the projective space in the bottom panel, the transformations are still more powerful and the invariants still more abstract.

It is possible to talk about spaces in a different way than was proposed by Euclid. His postulates began by asserting the existence of a space occupied by objects such as lines and circles. The properties of Euclidean space were defined in terms of the properties of lines, circles, or triangles. In a similar way, the phonetic space is defined by most current theories (except Ladefoged, 1980) by stating a tentative list of the objects that inhabit it: a particular set of phonetic features or segments. If someone demonstrates that some new feature should be added on the basis of data from a new language, then the space itself has to be expanded as the new features are incorporated. Aside from being totally ad hoc, such theories provide no insight into the reasons why phonetic objects have the properties that they do. My proposal is that the phonetic space might be definable by stating the transformations under which phonetic figures are invariant. Of course, these figures will turn out to have a fair amount in common with the traditional segments and features, but this approach will have the enormous advantage that the reason why they are phonetic objects will be conceptually distinct from the fact of their being phonetic objects. To do this, however, we need a reasonably clear statement of what those transformations are and an account of why we are concerned about these transformations rather than others we might have chosen (since phonetics is an empirical science, which mathematics is not). These matters will be addressed later, because there is another mathematical point to be made.

The mathematical approach suggested here is useful for a second reason. One of the most troublesome difficulties in the definition of phonetic elements is the matter of acoustic versus articulatory definition. Should we describe a particular vowel as articulatorily "rounded" or acoustically "flattened"? Jakobson's solution was to define features that were abstracted away from both substantive domains and which were then provided with both articulatory and acoustic specifications (Jakobson, Fant & Halle, 1952). It seems to me this is roughly the right approach. We want linguistic features that are completely abstract and yet we must assure that they can be specified in both domains in order to be sure they are both pronounceable and perceptible (in order to serve as communicative signals). The concept of isomorphism seems to achieve this effect.

An isomorphism is a kind of equivalence relation in which two sets of objects are asserted to be the same because two conditions hold. First, each object in set S can be placed in one-to-one correspondence with a particular object from set S'. Second, some specific operation (e.g., addition, multiplication, or concatenation) gives correspondingly identical results in both sets. A good example of isomorphic sets is shown in Figure 25.2.

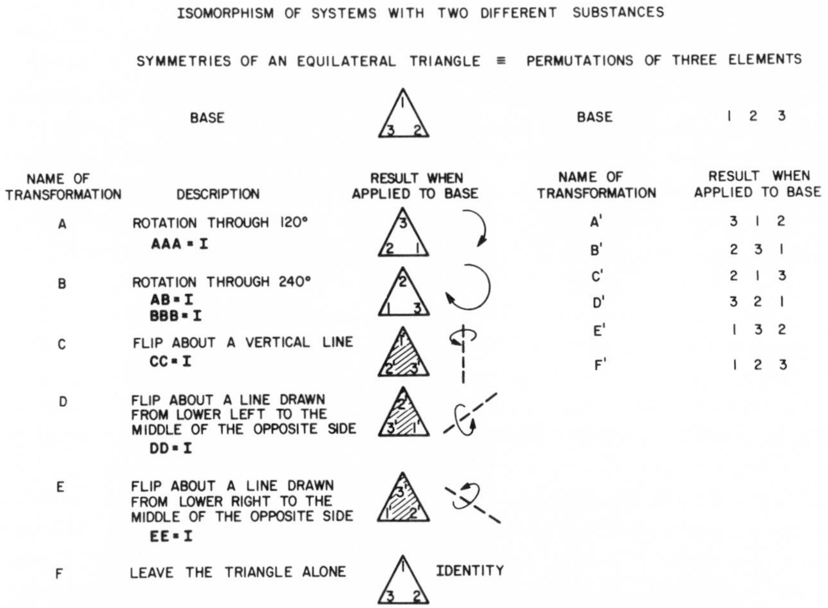

ISOMORPHISM OF SYSTEMS WITH TWO DIFFERENT SUBSTANCES

SYMMETRIES OF AN EQUILATERAL TRIANGLE ≡ PERMUTATIONS OF THREE ELEMENTS

BASE   BASE   1 2 3

NAME OF TRANSFORMATION	DESCRIPTION	RESULT WHEN APPLIED TO BASE	NAME OF TRANSFORMATION	RESULT WHEN APPLIED TO BASE
A	ROTATION THROUGH 120° AAA = I		A'	3 1 2
			B'	2 3 1
B	ROTATION THROUGH 240° AB = I BBB = I		C'	2 1 3
			D'	3 2 1
C	FLIP ABOUT A VERTICAL LINE CC = I		E'	1 3 2
			F'	1 2 3
D	FLIP ABOUT A LINE DRAWN FROM LOWER LEFT TO THE MIDDLE OF THE OPPOSITE SIDE DD = I			
E	FLIP ABOUT A LINE DRAWN FROM LOWER RIGHT TO THE MIDDLE OF THE OPPOSITE SIDE EE = I			
F	LEAVE THE TRIANGLE ALONE	IDENTITY		

FIG. 25.2.   Isomorphism of systems with two different substances. Symmetries of an equilateral triangle ≡ permutations of three elements.

The two sets are the symmetry transformations of an equilateral triangle and the permutations of three elements. The symmetry transformations, or symmetry Ts, of the triangle are the operations that can be performed on it that bring the figure back into congruence with itself. Thus the figure can be rotated 120° to match itself. If this T is repeated three times, the triangle returns to its original or base position. In this particular case, the Ts form a mathematical group (although this is not necessary for isomorphism in general). If not familiar with these transformations, the reader is encouraged to explore the ways in which various combinations of these Ts become equivalent to each other.

If one looks at the permutation transformations of a sequence of three items, it turns out that there is exactly the same number of distinct Ts and they can be grouped into the same subgroups, (A, B), (C, D, E), and F, the identity transformation. Thus we can map symmetry transformation A with the permutation transformation A', B with B', and so on, in a one-to-one fashion. Furthermore, it turns out that under the operation of concatenation of these Ts—i.e., performing various Ts in sequence—the results are exactly the same for both sets. That is, if we perform A, then B, then E, we will end up in the same relationship to the original position of the triangle as if we perform A', then B', then E', and compare the permutation with its original sequence. In this situation, it is said that the two sets (in this case mathematical groups) are isomorphic to each other. In fact, it turns out that there is really only one mathematical group here for which "triangle symmetries" and "three-element permutations" are simply distinct concrete models. The fact that they are each instantiated in totally different substances has no consequences for the abstract properties captured by the group itself.

It may already be clear that the analogy I wish to draw from isomorphism lies in the relation between the acoustic and articulatory domains of phonetics. We do seem to have sets of relatively discrete objects to deal with (the phonological/phonetic segments or features), and the relevant combining operation is apparently similar to concatenation since we make words in any language by producing sequences of these elements. Our goal should be to try to specify what the relevant internal structure of the sets is like. That is, what is the invariant pattern that underlies both articulation and acoustics? A theory of phonetics will have to supply a model to serve the role played by the group structure of symmetry transformations in geometry. A phonetic theory for a particular language is a statement of the relations governing the interaction of the abstract linguistic objects that are modelled both by articulatory gestures and by acoustic patterns. Although the phonetic systems of particular languages do not seem to be mathematical groups (as noted by Cutting, 1983), they are at least closed sets for any particular language. When stated in this way, it is clear that the phonetic system of a particular language will incorporate many structures conventionally viewed as phonological constraints by linguists.

I have described in this section some ways to employ very simple concepts from mathematics which might help us to describe the abstract objects that are words. Too much concentration on the algebraic properties of sentences made from strings of these words has led the field away from one fundamental issue: "What is a word in the articulatory and acoustic domains?" How is it that the same words can be spoken by different people yet be the same? How can words be instantiated both as articulatory gestures and as acoustic patterns? And how is it that they come to be constructed from permutable abstract "sound segments"?

INVARIANCE TRANSFORMATIONS
OF SEVERAL PHONETIC THEORIES

The concept of invariance under specific sets of transformations offers a way of talking about spaces. This mode of description has the advantage that it provides a single set of terms for comparing models that are quite different in their theoretical assumptions and thus may be very helpful for relating different kinds of abstract objects found in speech and language. To illustrate, I will make a first attempt to characterize several versions of the phonetic space by describing the invariance transformations that seem to be implied by the theories. The presentation made in this section is intended as a restatement of well-known theories in new terms that may help us understand their strengths as well as their limitations.

Classical Phonetics

Although it is difficult to find a clear theoretical statement of classical phonetics in modern terms, the general assumptions approximately represent the views of phoneticians such as Sweet (1906), Jones (1940), and Sievers (1901), and are implicit in the project of the International Phonetic Association (IPA, 1952) and in the thinking of most 20th century linguists.

Invariance across Speakers. The use of the phonetic alphabet to transcribe the speech of both adults and children implies an identity of the sounds between all groups of speakers. Thus the fact that a tape recording of a vowel like [a] produced by an adult and one produced by a child sound different to our ears is taken to be irrelevant to a "phonetic" description of those two sounds. This observation can be recast as an invariance transformation by postulating a transformation of the space of speech sounds from the voice of one speaker to that of another speaker. We may say then that this transformation from talker to talker is one under which phonetic objects are invariant in the classical model of phonetics.

This transformation is usually interpreted as extending in principle to the entire human population, thereby justifying attempts to employ the same alphabetic symbols in the transcription of all languages. Although no one has ever claimed to have specified the set in its entirety, it is widely assumed that it can be done in principle.

Gesture-to-sound Invariance. Another property of the standard phonetic space is that objects in it must have both an auditory definition and an articulatory one. The descriptive terms used for speech sounds are normally articulatory (e.g., labial, stop, etc.), and yet it is assumed that one needs only to listen to them to be able to correctly transcribe them. One does not need direct visual contact or other experimentally derived information about articulatory gestures in order to be able to do transcription according to the IPA (1952).

The definition of speech units by their audition auditory properties has been a continual problem for phonetics. Jones (1940) developed the Cardinal Vowels as a solution to this problem. They were to serve as a set of universal reference vowels that would be acquired by ear-training from him or his students. He used articulatory definitions for those vowels that he judged to require articulatorily unique positions (these were basically an extreme

[i]-like vowel and an extreme [a]-like vowel), but used definitions based on auditory judgments (by equal perceptual spacing) for other vowels. Apparently, for Jones, phonetic objects could be defined in either terms; he chose one versus the other depending on which seemed easiest to communicate to other scholars.

What about the case where a single auditory effect can result from several different gestures? The American [r] is such a case since it has two or more quite distinct articulatory positions (in particular, the "bunched" and "retroflexed" positions) that are not differentiable to the ear (Delattre & Freeman, 1968). The conclusion normally drawn in such situations is that these gestures represent a single phonetic event, [r]. If distinct articulatory events map onto a single auditory one, then there can be only a single phonetic object. This property can be restated as invariance under a transformation that transforms equivalence classes of gestures into equivalence classes of auditory events. The equivalence class of gestures is defined as all those which map onto a member of the auditory set. We can capture this property of the classical phonetic space by postulating for it an invariance transformation between gesture classes and (auditory) sound classes. Possible objects in the phonetic space must satisfy this symmetry.

Tempo Invariance. Another invariance transformation occurs between different speaking tempos, since words can have the same transcription across a range of speaking tempos. Thus I can say the word "paper" taking a total time of 250 ms (with a voice-onset-time [VOT] of 50 ms) or pronounce it with a total duration of 140 ms (and a VOT of 35 ms); no change in transcription is required. On the other hand, the converse implication is that if a word, such as "potato," is pronounced at a faster tempo without voicing during the first syllable, then that audible difference must be recorded in the transcription. Thus while the identity of words is also clearly the same at different tempos, their phonetic transcriptions may or may not change. Phonetic symbols themselves are invariant across such transformations in speaking tempos.

Invariance across Changes in Pitch Level. The segmental units of the classical phonetic space can be defined as units that are invariant under certain warpings of the time dimension, as long as they don't involve changes in serial order. Of course, phonetic segments are unaffected by changes in the absolute pitch level and in the range of pitch.

All of the invariances mentioned so far are ones that facilitate the use of phonetic elements for communication with language. If people come in different sizes and different levels of emotional excitement, yet must use the same linguistic signals, then it seems essential that the signals be abstract enough that physical changes in pitch, tempo, and vocal-tract size can not affect the linguistic signals themselves. Still, there are other properties of the classical phonetic space that seem to be somewhat different in character.

Invariance under Permutation of Segments. The kinds of sound units people hear when doing transcription seem to be the same despite changes in adjacent segment identities. Thus we use the same vowel symbols in "bed" as in "Meg," and the same consonant symbol for the [d] in "dig" as in "dog," despite the fact that there are acoustic differences between these segments (Liberman, Cooper, Shankweiler & Studdert-Kennedy, 1967), such as formant transitions that we apparently cannot be aware of auditorily. This property, which is another way of describing the notion of "segment," can be expressed as invariance under a transformation that permutes the order of the sound units, as in ABC→CBA.

Commutation Invariance. In general, phoneticians and linguists agree that many phonetic segments can be broken down into features that can be combined in various combinations to produce the segments themselves. Thus we say that the [+voice] feature in [z] is the same as that in [d], and the fricative property of [f] is also a property of [θ]. This formal property is implicit in any description of consonants and vowels that places them in a matrix, such as the traditional ones of place × manner × voice, or height × backness × rounding. This quality can be expressed as invariance under commutation of the segmental features of the phonetic space (for this use of the term, see Jakobson et al. 1952, p. 1–4). The transformation involved is one that replaces the stop feature of a [d] with the feature fricative or sibilant producing a [z]. Neither the fricative feature nor the place and voicing features are themselves changed by such a replacement.

It is hoped that this set of invariance transformations summarizes fairly well the standard view of the phonetic elements. One advantage of this mode of description is that it will make it easier to compare the different models of speech with each other. Another advantage is that it encourages us to ask *why* speech sounds must have the particular invariants that we observe them to have.

Jakobson's Approach to Phonetics

Jakobson's approach to phonology and phonetics made more powerful constraining assumptions about the invariance properties of phonetic elements. This theory is explicitly based on a view of speech as a structured acoustic communication channel (Jakobson et al., 1952; Fant, 1973). Some of the invariance properties of Jakobson's theory are very similar to those of the classical model of phonetics, while others are more novel. The following is an attempt to recast the model of Jakobson et al. (1952) in terms of some of the most important invariance transformations of its phonetic/phonological space.

Permutation within the Lexicon of Language L; Commutation. These two invariance transformations, which have the effect of specifying segmental features as the basic units of the space, differ fundamentally from classical phonetics in being tied to the lexicon of a particular language, rather than to the perceptual judgments of a trained listener. By relating the notion of the feature to lexical contrast, Jakobson et al. (1952) were able to define the feature in terms of its power to differentiate between objects in the lexicon. The ceteris paribus slogan ("other things being equal") recurs throughout *Preliminaries to Speech Analysis* and reflects this change. Thus the [+tense] feature of [t] in "Tom" is said to be the same ceteris paribus as the [t] in "button," despite the fact that we can easily hear an auditory difference between the [tʰ] and the glottal stop. This invariance is what justifies the distinction between redundant and distinctive features.

Invariance across Speakers of a Language; Invariance across Languages. The invariance of the features across speakers of a language is what ensures their utility in communication. The invariance of the system across languages of the world is perhaps the aspect of the theory that caused the most difficulty. Apparently the rationale for invariance across languages is that human beings are just innately wired up to process language this way. But what satisfies invariance across languages is not, in fact, the same as what satisfies invariance among speakers of a language. The basic system of universal distinctive features—e.g., gravity, compactness, tensity—is supposed to be universal, yet speakers need to know many of the redundant (or nondistinctive) features in order to correctly communicate using speech (Liberman et al., 1967). Thus the ceteris paribus clause, which permitted the features to be defined on the basis of their function in lexical differentiation, prevented them from also accounting for speech production or for lexical access during speech perception. This is simply because keeping lexical items distinct does not require nearly as much substantive detail as basic identification requires (Fant, 1973).

Invariance between Gesture and Acoustics. This invariance between gesture and sound is actually expressed in even broader and bolder terms: "The specification of the phonemic oppositions may be made in respect to any stage of the speech event from articulation to perception and decoding... [p. 13]." But the practical steps that were taken to attempt definition of distinctive features concentrated very sensibly on the articulatory and acoustic stages in the "speech circuit."

The Jakobsonian feature "flat" illustrates clearly that the transformation from articulatory gesture to sound is an invariance transformation of this space. Flatness is defined by a variety of gestures that have the acoustic effect of lowering the higher formants or higher frequency energy of the speech signal. This single, quite abstract acoustic effect can be achieved by any of several gestures that are from this point of view equivalent. Some of these are lip rounding (narrowing the orifice), lip protrusion, and larynx lowering. These distinct motor events are linguistically equivalent because of their identical (or nearly identical) acoustic effects.

One of the most important changes between the features of Jakobson et al. (1952) and the earlier model of classical phonetics is the change from an auditory definition to an acoustic one. Despite Jakobson's hope that phenomenological attributes of speech sounds could find a place in the theory (cf. Jakobson et al., 1952 p. 32 on synthesthesia), Jakobson et al. concentrated on the acoustic domain for description of what previously had been loosely called "sound," but was, in fact an auditory perception of sound. For Jakobson et al., it is not sufficient that two gestures have the same perceptual or auditory effects to be linguistically the same. They must produce acoustic effects that are in some way the same. This change reflects, in part, the discovery by the early 1950s that the acoustic structure of speech does not reveal patterns that are as similar to the auditory experience of speech as had once been hoped (cf. Cooper, Delattre, Liberman, Borst & Gerstman, 1952).

This shift from articulatory-auditory symmetry to articulatory-acoustic symmetry has several important consequences. The most important seems to be that, by specifying acoustics as the domain in which phonetic/phonological objects were to be defined, Jakobson et al. were able to define their lexically distinct features in terms of more abstract sound units (such as flatness, acuteness, and compactness) which might not be directly perceivable in themselves (Who could claim to directly perceive a quality of compactness versus diffuseness of spectrum shape?), but which could be defined in objective acoustic terms. This freedom from the perceptual judgments of phoneticians permitted them to push commutation symmetry for their features toward fewer elements having articulatory definitions that were considerably farther from simple gestures (Jakobson et al., 1952, p. 7). Since acoustics was defined abstractly, gestures too were defined in far more abstract terms. The acoustic similarity (though certainly not identity) of the effects of pharyngeal widening and labialization justified uniting even these two phonetic parameters into a single feature called "flattening" defined by a certain acoustic shaping of the spectrum from its neutral value.

The various symmetries of this space seem to reflect several basic assumptions about the properties of the phonetic/phonological objects: They must be suitable for signalling, be suitable for human brains, and also be maximally efficient for lexical differentiation.

Chomsky and Halle's Theory

In *The Sound Pattern of English*, Chomsky and Halle (1968a) adopted variants of the Jakobsonian feature set for their theory of phonetics and phonology. Since the purposes of their theory differ in fundamental respects from Jakobson's, they changed the theoretical basis of the descriptive model used by Jakobson et al. (1952) in ways that make it more useful as a theory of cognition, but, as I will show below, make it much less useful as a basis for understanding how languages function as instruments of communication. The goal of *The Sound Pattern of English* (*SPE*) is to address the question of what cognitive structures support production and perception of sentences. In order to do this in a formal way, Chomsky and Halle had to postulate a formal alphabet in which to describe linguistic structures in mathematical terms. The *SPE* variants of the Jakobsonian features serve this purpose. They permit the theoretician to get on with the business of figuring out something about the cognitive systems that underlie linguistic abilities.

Chomsky and Halle (1968a) separated the lexical-distinctiveness function of sound features from the speech-transmission function, thereby seeking to avoid the ceteris paribus problem by handling the lexicon with a different but related set of features. The present discussion is concerned only with the invariance properties of the *SPE* phonetic features (Chomsky & Halle, 1968a, Ch. 7).

Permutation Invariance; Commutation Invariance. The effect of these transformations is to define discrete segmental features that can play a role in the cognitive machinery of the grammar. Their other role is to serve as a set of instructions for the machinery of production and as output categories for the perceptual processes. This role is quite different from that played by the Jakobsonian features since the *SPE* features serve, not as an abstract interface between the speaker and hearer, but rather as an interface code between the mind and the body.

Invariance across the Human Species. These features must be "universal" because it is assumed that the features have an innate cognitive origin. Although some aspects of the Jakobsonian features were universal, other aspects were not.

Invariance between "Gesture" and "Auditory Perception." In respect to this invariance, the *SPE* features more closely resemble those of classical phonetics, since the perceptual judgment of the child language-learner (or his professional surrogate, the linguist–phonetician) determines what counts as a phonetic unit. This follows from the view that the phonetic space is a mental space, not a physical one. It embodies what speakers "know" or "intend" about their utterances—"the speaker-hearer's interpretation rather than directly observable properties of the signal [p. 294]." Although Chomsky and Halle assure us that their features also have acoustic correlates (p. 299), it's clear that the theory in no way demands such correlates—indeed it's difficult to see the relevance of acoustics to the theory at all. Features defined in the strictly articulatory terms used in *SPE* are quite appropriate for the cognitive model, since the features exist only in the mind and serve exclusively internal functions, not functions that relate one person with another. Since the *SPE* account of the perception of speech involves reconstruction of the generative processes, an articulatory characterization of the abstract features will serve as well as an acoustic one.

Indeed, there is no innate reason that motivates a requirement in Chomsky and Halle's (1968a) theory that speech sounds be audible at all. Since actual phonetic elements evidently are always audible, this property of phonetic features must be accounted for as an effect of natural selection on the inventory of universal innate phonetic features. Thus the account lies outside the scope of the theory. By concentrating on "linguistic intention," the *SPE* model has almost nothing to say about interpersonal communication with speech sounds. This observation does not challenge the usefulness of the *SPE* phonetic features for research on phonology and other higher linguistic processes. It is just that the theory will not help us understand the communicative aspect of the phonetic space.

The purpose of this volume is to address the problem of variation at the level of physical speech signals, despite invariance at the linguistic level. We are trying to figure out how language can function as a device for communication between people of different sizes who talk at different speeds with enormous idiosyncratic variation in the acoustic form of words. Those concerned with phonetics or speech recognition must directly address what *SPE* ignored: Words or morphemes, whether viewed at the level of articulatory gestures in real time or as physical acoustic signals, apparently do not have alphabetic descriptions that can be constructed from any universal alphabet. A theory of phonetics must provide a way of dealing directly with the invariance of linguistic units in the face of staggering physical variation. We need a definition of a "possible linguistic object" that will provide a basis for analysis of the observed sound structures of individual languages without retreating from physical signals up into the cognitive world and without an a priori constraint on the segmental structure of the objects. The next section will suggest a way that such a theory might be provided.

TOWARD A FORMAL MODEL OF PHONETICS

So far we have sketched out a descriptive scheme for discussing the problem of invariance in speech and have attempted to provide a characterization of several important approaches to the phonetic space in terms of this scheme. As mentioned above, these descriptions are not really statements of the basis of these theories, since it is primarily the rationale for assuming a particular invariance that comprises the substantive theoretical claim. No systematic attempt has been made here to do this for the theories discussed above. In this section, as a new theory is sketched out, a justification for particular invariance transformations will be made where possible.

This theory must be set into a larger framework for discussing language. It is assumed here that language is a phenomenon that is structured by a number of different factors: limitations on human cognitive behavior and memory, limitations based on human anatomy, and the tendency for humans (like other animals) to expend no more effort than necessary for achievement of their goals. One of these factors is the need for language to serve as a communication device for communities of human beings. All of these factors affect the behavior of individual speakers, shape and mold individual languages, and no doubt have affected the gene pool of the human species. This point of view is close to that of Martinet (1955), Diver (1979), and Lindblom (1983).

The particular factor that I wish to explore here is the role of speech sounds as signals for communication in human communities (cf. my earlier discussion, Port, 1981b). What facts about speech can be explained as consequences of this observation? The following is an attempt to provide a framework in which a formal statement of those consequences can be stated.

Rationale

There are several aspects of the human condition that have consequences for any communication system that we might employ. First, we are mutually distinct intelligences separated from each other by the atmosphere. This means that any system we are to employ for communicating with each other must span this interpersonal gap. If we are to employ auditory signals, then we must have (1) a way of generating sound signals; (2) a way of recognizing the signals when they occur in the acoustic channel; and (3) a representation in each communicator of the meaning of each of the signals to be used. This implies, in phonetic terms, that the signals themselves could be described with terminology based either on the articulatory gestures used to generate the acoustic patterns or in terms of the acoustic patterns themselves. With respect to the communication system, these are equivalent. Obviously Morse code signals are neither long and short beeps nor dots and dashes on a page; the signals are abstract enough to be the same signals in both cases. In terms of invariance transformations, this implies that the transformation from horizontal display on a page to beeps in time is an invariance transformation of the Morse code. Similarly, the transformation from articulatory gestures to acoustics must be an invariance transformation of the phonetic space.

Phonetic signals must be invariant between the acoustic signal and the auditory representation of the signal at the receiver end as well. The phonetically critical properties of speech sounds can only be those that are not destroyed by the processes of audition (whether due to lack of resolution or to transformations of the frequency and intensity scales).

Another property of the human condition that is relevant here is that people come in different physical sizes. Due to the laws of physics, human vocal tracts will produce different acoustic effects when gestures that are the same (relative to an individual's anatomy) are produced. If the vocal cavity is used as a resonator and is roughly uniform in diameter from one end to the other, the location of poles in its transfer function will be different for tracts of different length. Similarly, if two vocal tracts are constricted at their midpoints, the effect on the transfer function in absolute value will be different even though it will be the second pole from the bottom that is lowered in each case. Now, if the communicative signals under discussion are to be used by people in different sizes, acoustic effects due to size differences must not affect their definition. That is, speech signals must be invariant under the transformation of the signals from talker to talker. If they were not invariant in this way, some of the signals could only be produced by talkers with vocal tracts of a certain size.

There are also several other invariances that speech sounds seem to have that are not quite so clearly dependent on the communication premise, but also seem to have an influence on the nature of speech sounds. The first of these, and the fourth invariance transformation of phonetics, is invariance over changes in effort or excitability. When humans are in different levels of excitement, they tend to talk at different speeds, with different loudness, or with varying dynamic range. Of course, languages might conceivably have acted to constrain such behavior when speaking. Instead, languages seem to adapt to this human feature by becoming more abstract in such a way that words are invariant under changes in tempo, pitch range, or emphasis. Presumably, this transformation of temporal stretching and compressing provides the invariance property of speech that contributes most to the success of alphabets as descriptive devices for the sounds of human language. Alphabets are also invariant under changes in the spacing and size of the letters.

The final invariance is one that is probably only indirectly related to the communication function of language. This is the fact that words seem to be universally built from smaller sound units that are permutable in different orders. The communication premise clearly makes claims about the properties of speech signals required for transmission of meanings, but there is no a priori reason why words (or morphemes) could not be specified as whole sound units. Of course, Martinet pointed out long ago (1955) that a system in which each morpheme is totally different from each other would be very impractical, since it would make a large vocabulary very difficult for articulatory and perceptual reasons (and conceivably for memory reasons as well). The solution to this problem among humans is that an unlimited vocabulary is built from a very small set of sound units that are distinctive in production and perception. So, even though this is primarily a "human-factors" matter in my judgment, it results in some interesting mathematical properties of speech signals.

In the next section, an attempt will be made to use the properties just mentioned to formally delimit a space of potential objects satisfying those constraints. This space, rather than a universal inventory, will be proposed as the appropriate form of a theory of general phonetics.

Formal Statement

We will sketch a tentative formal statement of the theory. The first step is to define a set of spaces of descriptive parameters for speech,

$$X_i = \{X_1, X_2, \ldots X_n\}.$$

Thus, X_1 might be a space defined by acoustic parameters, X_2 might be a space defined by articulatory measurements or EMG tracings; X_3 might be a space containing symbols of a phonetic transcription. Since they are just parameters relevant to the representation of speech, none of these includes a time dimension or an analog of time (such as sequential strings). Second, we need to define a family of more complex spaces that will consist of sequences (or more generally, time functions) of elements from various X_is. The set of spaces, $A_i = \{A_1, A_2, \ldots A_n\}$, consists essentially of permissible transcriptions or time functions in each X_i. They represent actions or temporal events that occur within X_1, X_2, etc.

A set of mappings or transformations called collectively $S_{i,j}$ (for speech) can now be defined from A_i to A_j. These are mappings from, say, the domain of articulation to acoustics or to transcription. If the transformation $S_{1,2}$ is from the acoustic space A_1 to the articulatory space A_2, then the problem arises that this transformation is many-to-one. But we can define an equivalence relation between objects a and a' in the acoustic space A_1 such that $a = a'$ if and only if

$$S_{1,2}(a) = S_{1,2}(a').$$

That is, if the mapping $S_{1,2}$ of the two acoustic events a and a' yields the same object in A_2, then we say that they are equivalent. Thus identity of result from a transformation is used to define equivalence classes within each space. This allows us to say, for example, that the two modes of production of American English [r] are phonetically identical since the mapping from articulatory actions to acoustic events is one that is used to define classes of phonetic equivalence. The rationale for such a definition of equivalence lies in the requirement for effective communicative signals.

At this point, we can state more generally the constraints of linguistic phonetics in terms of the set S of transformations between these various spaces A. We want be to able to say that phonetic elements have the property that for all i (where i is an index over the descriptive domains A_i), $a = a'$, if and only if there exists a j (where A_j is a different descriptive domain) such that:

$$S_{i,j}(a) = S_{i,j}(a')$$

where S represents all of the transformations involved in the processes of speech communication. Objects having this property are phonetic objects.

The speech transformations S include various mappings involved in speech communication. Thus S can be broken down into various gross components:

$$S = \{T, P, A, E, \ldots\}$$

where T is the transformation from talker-to-talker, P is the series of transformations involved in speech production between intended word through articulatory gesture to the acoustic signal, A represents the corresponding transformations in the auditory system, and E summarizes the various effects of human excitableness.

Depending on our purposes, we might add another invariance transformation, let's call it R, to represent the language-specific constraints under which specific sets F of phonetic objects are invariant. This particular invariance transformation will resemble what linguists call the phonotactics or lexical phonology of a language. The research tasks of the various other sciences of speech and language can be fairly easily reformulated as investigations of the nature of the invariance transformations.

The general theory of phonetics is essentially summarized in equations such as these. In studying a particular language (as opposed to the study of the phonetic space in general), we would want to identify the set F of phonetic signals employed by that community. Aside from the constraints implied in the set S, the equivalence classes of phonetic objects must also, be distinct from one another to be useful for distinguishing lexical items. It is notoriously difficult to provide any formal statement of "how different is different enough." Contrasts that speakers of one language find easy enough, foreigners may find almost impossible either to produce or perceive. Such human-factors problems may have no theoretical solution.

To a considerable extent the resulting objects are likely to resemble the distinctive features and segments of traditional linguistic descriptions, but there are some important benefits from deriving them in this roundabout way rather than simply postulating them. First, although it is difficult to prove they are infinite in number, there is no reason to expect that there is a limited set of possible phonetic objects that could be specified once for all time. Since phonetic theory only specifies the *potential* phonetic space, each language community is free to invent new phonetic objects in this space at any time; the phonetic space is assumed to be formally incomplete. Second, there is no reason to expect that superficially similar phonetic elements (like a given vowel segment or contrast in 'voicing') should be really the same (or even commensurable) across speech communities. The more detailed our phonetic studies, the greater the variety and subtlety of the differences we find between languages (c.f. Chapter 21; Port, Al-Ani & Maeda, 1980). This follows since the phonetic space is so enormously large, the constraints acting on a community in selecting a subset are primarily those of keeping words apart for speakers of that language community (c.f. Chapter 23). Third, there is no reason based on the communication function alone to assume that the sounds must be describable as segments rather than as, say, temporal patterns (c.f., Port & Dalby, 1982), trajectories through some abstract space (modelled perhaps with parameters like F_1, F_2, and F_3, or EMG patterns), or any other structure than can satisfy the phonetic constraints.

In this section, it has been suggested that the simple notion that phonetics provides a signalling space for human beings can be combined with a scheme for describing spaces in general to define the formal properties of a kind of space that is capable in principle of performing this signalling function. It is proposed that communities select subsets of this space for specification of linguistic signals which manifest themselves generally as words.

CONCLUSIONS

At this point, we might ask what exactly the problem of invariance in speech is. It seems to be that linguistic units for the description of sound are invariant under vastly more powerful transformations than are the parameters we measure in physical descriptions of speech. Units like the phoneme are so abstract that stating their invariance transformations in physical terms seems almost impossible. Indeed perhaps the only linguists ever to try to do so are Jakobson, Fant and Halle, (1952). Instead, linguists have attempted to provide an inventory of perceptually defined units to which they tied their phonological units. What seems to be needed is a description of speech sounds that (1) provides explanatory principles for the properties of the linguistic units where possible; and (2) is abstract enough that the defining traits of a phonetic object can be satisfied by patterns in a space of articulatory parameters, acoustic parameters, or whatever other kinds of parameters seem useful.

What I have tried to show is that the problem of invariance in speech is nothing more than the problem: "What is the phonetic form of words?" An answer to this question can only be found by looking into the function that words serve for human communities. A useful way to approach the problem of defining any abstract object is to attempt a description of the transformations under which the object is unchanged.

ACKNOWLEDGMENTS

I am grateful to Jonathan Dalby, Daniel Dinnsen, Marios Fourakis, Osamu Fujimura, Fred Householder, Mark Liberman, Janet Pierrehumbert, William Poser, and especially John Goldsmith for comments and help with this paper. This work was supported by Bell Laboratories and by the National Institutes of Health, Grant No. HD-12511.

REFERENCES

Abbs, J. H. (1971). *The role of the gamma motor system in control of jaw movement for speech.* Unpublished doctoral dissertation, University of Wisconsin, Madison, Wisconsin.

Abbs, J. H. (1972, March). *A kinematic model of speech performance.* Invited lecture presented at the City University of New York Graduate Center.

Abbs, J. H. (1973). Some mechanical properties of lower lip movement during speech production. *Phonetica, 28,* 65–75.

Abbs, J. H. (1979). Speech motor equivalence: A need for multilevel control model. In E. Fischer-Jørgenson, J. Rischel, & N. Thorsen (Eds.), *Proceedings of the Ninth International Congress of Phonetics.* Denmark: Institute of Phonetics.

Abbs, J. H., & Cole, K. J. (1982). Consideration of bulbar and suprabulbar afferent influences upon speech-motor coordination and programming. In S. Grillner, B. Lindblom, J. Lubker, & A. Persson (Eds.), *Speech motor control.* New York: Pergamon Press.

Abbs, J. H., & Eilenberg, G. R. (1976). Peripheral mechanisms of speech motor control. In N. J. Lass (Ed.), *Contemporary issues in experimental phonetics.* New York: Academic Press.

Abbs, J. H., & Gilbert, B. N. (1973). A strain gauge transduction system for lip and jaw motion in two dimensions: Design criteria and calibration data. *Journal of Speech and Hearing Research, 16,* 248–256.

Abbs, J. H., & Gracco, V. L. (1982). Motor control of multi-movement behaviors: Orofacial muscle responses to load perturbations of the lips during speech. *Society for Neuroscience, 8,* 282.

Abbs, J. H., & Gracco, V. L. (1983). Sensorimotor actions in the control of multimovement speech gestures. *Trends in Neuroscience, 6*(9), 391–395.

Abbs, J. H., & Gracco, V. L. (1984). Control of complex motor gestures: Orofacial muscle responses to load perturbations of the lip during speech. *Journal of Neurophysiology, 51*(4), 705–723.

Abbs, J. H., Gracco, V. L., & Cole, K. J. (1984). Sensorimotor contributions to the coordination of multicomponent behaviors: Evidence from recent studies of speech movement control. *Journal of Motor Behavior, 16,* (2) 195–231.

Abbs, J. H., & Hughes, O. (1975, November). *Motor equivalence coordination in the labial-mandibular system.* Paper presented at the Acoustical Society of America Meeting, San Francisco.

Abbs, J. H., & Netsell, R. (1972). *A dynamic analysis of two dimensional muscle force contributors to lower lip movement.* Paper presented at the Acoustical Society of America Meeting, Miami Beach.

Abbs, J. H., & Netsell, R. (1973). *Coordination of the jaw and lower lip during speech production.* Paper presented at the American Speech and Hearing Association Convention, Detroit.

Abbs, J. H., Netsell, R., & Hixon, T. J. (1971). *Variations in mandibular displacement, velocity, and acceleration as a function of phonetic context.* Paper presented at the Acoustical Society of America meeting, Denver, CO.

Abercrombie, D. (1967). *Elements of general phonetics.* Edinburgh: Edinburgh University Press.

Abraham, R. H., & Shaw, C. D. (1982). *Dynamics–The geometry of behavior.* Santa Cruz, CA: Aerial Press.

Al-Bamerni, A. (1983). Effect of speaking rate on nasal coarticulation. In A. Cohen & M.P.R. v.d. Broeke (Eds.), *Abstracts of the International Congress of Phonetic Sciences,* Dordrecht, Holland: Foris Publications.

Al-Bamerni, A. H. & Bladon, R.A.W. (unpublished manuscript). On the role of peak glottal opening.

Alfonso, P. J., & Baer, T. (1982). Dynamics of vowel articulation. *Language & Speech, 25,* 151–173.

Allen, J. (1981). Linguistic based algorithms offer practical text-to-speech systems. *Speech Technology, 1*, 1, 12–16.

Allen, Jont. B. (1979). Cochlear models 1978. In M. Hoke and E. de Boer, (Eds.), *Models of the auditory system and related signal processing techniques*, Scand. Audiol. Suppl. 9.

Archangeli, D. (1984). The structure of Yawelmani. Unpublished PhD thesis, Massachusetts Institute of Technology.

Asanuma, H., & Rosen, I. (1972). Topographical organization of cortical efferent zones projecting to distal forelimb muscles in the monkey. *Experimental Brain Research, 14*, 243–256.

Aslin, R. N., & Pisoni, D. B. (1980). Some developmental processes in speech perception. In G. H. Yeni-Komshian, J. F. Kavanagh, & C. A. Ferguson (Eds.), *Child phonology* (Vol. 2). New York: Academic Press.

Aslin, R. N., Pisoni, D. B., & Jusczyk, P. W. (1983). Auditory development and speech perception in infancy. In M. M. Haith and J.J. Campos (Eds.), *Infancy and the biology of development*. Vol. II of *Carmichael's Manual of Child Psychology* (4th edition). New York: Wiley.

Assman, P. F. (1979). *The role of context in vowel perception*. Master's thesis, University of Alberta, Canada.

Ayala, F. J. (1978). The mechanisms of evolution. *Scientific American, 239*, 56–69.

Baer, T., Bell-Berti, F., & Tuller, B. (1979). On determining EMG onset time. In J. J. Wolf & D. H. Klatt (Eds.), *Speech Communication Preprints, 97th Meeting of the Acoustical Society of America, Cambridge, MA, 1979*. New York: Acoustical Society of America.

Bahl, L. R., Cole, A., Jelinek, F., Mercer, R., Nadas, A., Nahamoo, D. & Picheny, M. (1983). Recognition of isolated-word sentences from a 5000-word vocabulary office correspondence task, *Proceedings ICASSP-83*, 1065–1067.

Bahl, L. R., Jelinek, F., & Mercer, R. L. (1983). A maximum-likelihood approach to continuous speech recognition. *IEEE Transactions Pattern Analysis and Machine Intelligence, PAMI-5*, No. 2, 179–190.

Bailey, P. J., Summerfield, Q., & Dorman, M. (1977). On the identification of sinewave analogues of certain speech sounds. *Haskins Laboratories: Status report on speech research SR-51/52*.

Barlow, S. M., Cole, K., & Abbs, J. H. (1983). A new headmounted lip-jaw movement transduction system for the study of motor speech disorders. *Journal of Speech and Hearing Research, 26*, 283–288.

Barry, W., & Kuenzel, H. (1975). Co-articulatory airflow characteristics of intervocalic voiceless plosives. *Journal of Phonetics, 3*, 263–282.

Barton, D. (1980). Phonemic perception in children. In G. H. Yeni-Komshian, J. F. Kavanagh, & C. A. Ferguson (Eds.), *Child Phonology* (Vol. 2). New York: Academic Press.

Baru, A. V. (1975). Discrimination of synthesized vowels [a] and [i] with varying parameters (fundamental frequency, intensity, duration, and number of formants) in dog. In G. Fant, & M. A. A. Tatham (Eds.), *Auditory analysis and perception of speech*. New York: Academic Press.

Baum, L. E. (1972). An inequality and associated maximization technique in statistical estimation of probabilistic functions of Markov processes. *Inequalities, 3*, 1–8.

Beddor, P. S. (1982). *Phonological and phonetic effects of nasalization on vowel height*. Doctoral dissertation, University of Minnesota.

Bell, E. (1945). *The development of mathematics*. New York: McGraw-Hill.

Bell-Berti, F., & Harris, K. S. (1979). Anticipatory coarticulation: Some implications from a study of lip rounding. *Journal of the Acoustical Society of America, 65*, 1268–1270.

Bell-Berti, F., & Harris, K. S. (1981). A temporal model of speech production. *Phonetica, 38*: 9–20.

Bellugi, U., Poizner, H., & Klima, E. S. (1983). Brain organization for language: clues from sign aphasia. *Human Neurobiology, 2*, 155–170.

Benguerel, A.-P., & Cowan, H. A. (1974). Coarticulation of upper lip protrusion in French. *Phonetica, 30*, 41–55.

Bennett, S. (1981). Vowel formant frequency characteristics of preadolescent males and females. *Journal of the Acoustical Society of America, 69,* 231-238.

Bennett, S. & Weinberg, B. (1979). Acoustic correlates of perceived sexual identity in preadolescent children's voices. *Journal of the Acoustical Society of America, 66,* 989-1000.

Bernstein, N. A. (1967). *The coordination and regulation of movements.* London: Pergamon Press.

Bertanlanffy, L., von (1973), *General Systems Theory.* Penguin, Harmondsworth, England.

Bertoncini, J., & Mehler, J. (1981). Syllables as units in infant speech perception. *Infant Behavior & Development, 4,* 247-260.

Best, C. T., Hoffman, H., & Glanville, B. B. (1982). Development of infant ear asymmetries for speech and music. *Perception & Psychophysics, 31,* 75-85.

Best, C. T., Morrongiello, B., & Robson, R. (1981). Perceptual equivalence of acoustic cues in speech and nonspeech perception. *Perception & Psychophysics, 29,* 191-211.

Best, C. T., & Studdert-Kennedy, M. (1983). Discovering phonetic coherence in acoustic patterns. In A. Cohen and M.P.R. v.d. Broecke (Eds.), *Abstracts of the Tenth International Congress of Phonetic Sciences.*

Bickley, C. (1984a). *Development of vowel articulation in children.* MIT Speech Communication Group Working Papers (Volume 4).

Bickley, C. (May 1984). Acoustic evidence for phonological development of vowels in young children, *MIT RLE Speech Group Working Papers, vol. 4,* 111-124.

Bilger, R. C. (1977). Evaluation of subjects presently fitted with implanted auditory prostheses. *Annals of Otology, Rhinology & Laryngology 86, Suppl. 38.*

Bladon, R. A. W. (1982). Problems of normalizing the spectral effects of variations in the fundamental. *Proceedings Institute of Acoustics Autumn Conference,* A5.1-A5.5.

Bladon, R. A. W. (1983). Speaker normalization by linear shifts along a bark scale, *Proceedings 10th International Congress of Phonetic Sciences.* Utrecht, The Netherlands.

Bladon, R. A. W., Henton, C. G. & Pickering, J. B. (1982). Towards an auditory basis for speaker normalization. *Institute of Acoustics Speech Group Meeting,* Keele, England.

Bladon, R. A. W., Henton, C. G. & Pickering, J. B. (1984). Outline of an auditory theory of speaker normalization: In M. P. R. Van den Broecke & A. Cohen (Eds.), *Proceedings of the Tenth International Congress of Phonetic Sciences.* Dordrecht, Holland: Foris Publications.

Bladon, R. A. W., & Lindblom, B. (1981). Modeling the judgment of vowel quality differences. *Journal of the Acoustical Society of America, 69,* 1414-1422.

Blumstein, S. E. (1973). *A phonological investigation of aphasic speech.* The Hague: Mouton.

Blumstein, S. E. (1981). Phonological aspects of aphasia. In M. T. Sarno (Ed.), *Acquired aphasia.* New York: Academic Press.

Blumstein, S. E. (1983). *Towards a theory of acoustic invariance in speech.* Manuscript.

Blumstein, S. E., Cooper, W. E., Goodglass, H., Statlender, S., & Gottlieb, J. (1980). Production deficits in aphasia: A voice-onset time analysis. *Brain and Language, 9,* 153-170.

Blumstein, S. E., Isaacs, E., & Mertus, J. (1982). The role of the gross spectral shape as a perceptual cue to place of articulation in initial stop consonants. *Journal of the Acoustical Society of America, 72,* 43-50.

Blumstein, S. E., & Stevens (1979). Acoustic invariance in speech production: Evidence from measurements of the spectral characteristics of stop consonants, *Journal of the Acoustical Society of America, 66*(4), 1001-1017.

Blumstein, S. E., & Stevens, K. N. (1980). Perceptual invariance and onset spectra for stop consonants in various vowel environments. *Journal of the Acoustical Society of America, 67,* 648-662.

Blumstein, S. E., & Stevens, K. N. (1981). Phonetic-features and acoustic invariance in speech. *Cognition, 10,* 25-32.

Bonin, G. von (1949). Architecture of the precentral motor cortex and some adjacent areas. In P. C. Bucy (Ed.), *The precentral motor cortex.* Urbana, IL: University of Illinois Press.

Borchgrevink, H. M. (1983). Mechanisms of speech and musical sound perception. In
    R. Carlson & B. Granstrom (Eds.), *The representation of speech in the peripheral auditory
    system*. New York: Elsevier Biomedical Press.
Borden, G. J., & Harris, K. S. (1980). *Speech science primer*. Baltimore, MD: Williams &
    Wilkins.
Bornstein, M. H. (1979). Perceptual development: Stability and change in feature percep-
    tion. In M. H. Bornstein and W. Kessen (Eds.), *Psychological development from infancy:
    Image to intention*. Hillsdale, NJ: Erlbaum.
Bouhuys, A. (1974). *Breathing*. New York: Grune and Stratton.
Bowerman, M. (1982). Reorganizational processes in lexical and syntactic development. In
    E. Wanner & L. R. Gleitman (eds.), *Language acquisition: The state of the art*. Cambridge:
    Cambridge University Press.
Bradshaw, G. L., Cole, R. A., and Li, Z. (1982). Comparison of learning techniques in
    speech-recognition, *Proceedings of the ICASSP IEEE International Conference on Acoustics,
    Speech, and Signal Processing*, 554–557.
Bregman, A. (1978). The formation of auditory streams. In J. Requin (Ed.), *Attention and
    performance, VII*. Hillsdale, N.J.: Lawrence Erlbaum Associates.
Browman, C. P. (1978). Tip of the tongue and slip of the ear: Implications for language
    processing. *UCLA Working Papers in Phonetics, 42*.
Browman, C. P. (1980). Perceptual processing: Evidence from slips of the ear. In V. A.
    Fromkin, (Ed.), *Errors in linguistic performance*. New York: Academic Press.
Browman, C. P., & Goldstein, L. (In preparation). *Towards an articulatory phonology*. Manu-
    script.
Brown, R., & McNeill, D. (1966). The "tip of the tongue" phenomenon. *Journal of Verbal
    Learning Learning and Verbal Behavior, 5*, 325–337.
Bruce, G. & Gårding, E. (1978). A prosodic typology for Swedish dialects. In E. Gårding,
    G. Bruce, & R. Bannert (Eds.), Nordic Prosody. *Travaux de l'Institut de Linguistique de
    Lund, 13*, 219–228.
Buckingham, H. W., Jr. (1979). Explanation in apraxia with consequences for the concept
    of apraxia of speech. *Brain and Language, 8*, 202–226.
Burdick, C. K., & Miller, J. D. (1975). Speech perception by the chinchilla: discrimination
    of sustained [a] and [i]. *Journal of the Acoustical Society of America, 58*, 415–427.
Burling, R. (1959). Language development of a Garo and English speaking child. *Word,
    15*, 45–68.
Butcher, A., & Weiher, E. (1976). An electropalatographic investigation of coarticulation
    in VCV sequences. *Journal of Phonetics, 4*, 59–74.
Callary, R. E. (1975). Phonological change and the development of an Urban dialect in
    Illinois. *Language in Society, 4*, 155–170.
Campbell, R., & Dodd, B. (1979). Hearing by eye. *Quarterly Journal of Experimental Psy-
    chology, 32*, 85–99.
Carlson, R., Fant, G., and Granström, B. (1975). Two Formant Models, Pitch and Vowel
    Perception: In G. Fant & M. A. A. Tatham (Eds.), *Auditory analysis and perception of
    speech*. London: Academic Press.
Carlson, R., & Granström, B. (1975). A text-to-speech system based on a phonetically
    oriented programming language. *Speech Transmission Laboratory, Quarterly Progress and
    Status Report, 1/1975*, 17–26, Royal Institute of Technology, Stockholm.
Carlson, R., & Granström, B. (1979). Model predictions of vowel dissimilarity. *Speech
    Transmission Laboratory, Quarterly Progress and Status Report, 3-4/1979*, 84–104, Royal In-
    stitute of Technology, Stockholm.
Carlson, R. and Granstrom, B. (Eds.). (1982a). *The representation of speech in the peripheral
    auditory system*, Amsterdam: Elsevier Biomedical.
Carlson, R., & Granstrom B. (1982b). Towards an auditory spectrograph.: in R. Carl-
    son & B. Granstrom (Eds.), *The representation of speech in the peripheral auditory system*.
    Amsterdam: Elsevier Biomedical.
Carlson, R., & Granström, B. & Klatt, D. H., (1979). Vowel perception: The relative per-
    ceptual salience of selected acoustic manipulations. *Speech Transmission Laboratory, Quar-*

terly Progress and Status Report, 3 4/1979, 73-83, Royal Institute of Technology, Stockholm.

Carrell, T. D., Pisoni, D. B., & Gans, S. J. (1980). Perception of the duration of rapid spectrum changes: Evidence for context effects with speech and nonspeech signals. *Journal of the Acoustical Society of America 68*, S49.

Chafe, W. K. (1970). *Meaning and structure of language*, Chicago, IL: The University of Chicago Press.

Chao, Y.-R. (1968). *A Grammar of spoken Chinese*, Berkeley, CA: University of California Press.

Chapin, C. (December 1983). *The nature of phonological development: New evidence (A case study of the acquisition of /s/ + stop clusters)*. Paper presented at the Winter meetings of the Linguistics Society of America, Minneapolis MN.

Chapin, C., Tseng, C. Y., & Lieberman, P. (1982). Short-term release cues for stop consonant place of articulation in child speech. *Journal of the Acoustical Society of America, 71*, 179-186.

Chistovich, L. A., Lublinskaya, V. V., Malinnikova, T. G., Ogorodnikova, E. A., Stoljarova, E. I., & Zhukov, S. J. A. (1982). Temporal Processing of Peripheral Auditory Patterns. In R. Carlson & B. Granström (Eds.), *The representation of speech in the peripheral auditory system*. Amsterdam: Elsevier/North-Holland Biomedical Press.

Chistovich, L. A., & Lublinskaya, V. V. (1979). The 'center of gravity' effect in vowel spectra and critical distance between the formants: Psychoacoustical study of the perception of vowel-like stimuli. *Hearing Research, 1*, 185-195.

Chomsky N., & Halle, M. (1968a). *The sound pattern of English*. New York: Harper-Row.

Chomsky, N., & Halle, M. (1968b). The sound pattern of silence in phonetic perception. *Journal of the Acoustical Society of America, 65*(6), 1518-1532.

Chomsky, N. (1980). Rules and Representations. *Behavior and Brain Sciences, 3*, 1-61.

Church, K. W. (1983). *Phrase-structure parsing: A method for taking advantage of allophonic constraints*. PhD thesis, MIT, Cambridge, MA.

Clark, J. E., & Palethorpe, S. (1983). Acoustic and aerodynamic correlates of fricatives. In A. Cohen & M. P. R. v. d. Broeke (Eds.), *Abstracts of the Tenth International Congress of Phonetic Sciences*. Dordrecht, Holland: Foris Publications.

Clark, J. E., Palethorpe, S., & Hardcastle, W. J. (1982). Analysis of English multimodal fricative data using stepwise regression methods, *Working Paper of the Speech and Language Research Centre*, (Macquarie University), *2*, 1-90.

Cohen, A., (1980). Correcting of speech errors in shadowing tasks. In V. A. Fromkin (Ed.), *Errors in linguistic performance*. New York: Academic Press.

Cohen, A., & Nooteboom, S. (Eds.) (1975). *Structure and process in speech perception*. Heidelberg: Springer-Verlag.

Cohen, P. S., & Mercer, R. L. (1975). The phonological component of an automatic speech-recognition system, in D. R. Reddy, (Ed.), *Speech-recognition: Invited papers presented at the 1974 IEEE symposium*. Academic Press, 275-320.

Cole, R. (Ed.). (1979). *Perception and production of fluent speech*, Hillsdale, NJ: Lawrence Erlbaum Associates.

Cole, R. A., & Jakimik, J. (1980). A model of speech perception. In R. A. Cole (Ed.), *Perception and production of fluent speech*. Hillsdale, NJ: Lawrence Erlbaum Associates.

Cole, R. A., Rudnicky, R., Zue, V., and Reddy, D. R., (1980). Speech as patterns on paper. In R. Cole, (Ed.), *Perception and production of fluent speech*, Hillsdale, NJ: Lawrence Erlbaum Associates.

Cole R., & Scott, B. (1974a). The phantom in the phoneme: invariant cues for stop consonants. *Perception and Psychophysics 15*, 101-107.

Cole, R. A., & Scott, B. (1974b). Towards a theory of speech perception. *Psychological Review, 81*, 348-374.

Cole, R. A., & Zue, V. W. (1980). Speech as eyes see it, In R. S. Nickerson, (Ed.), *Attention and performance VIII*. Hillsdale, NJ: Lawrence Erlbaum Associates.

Cole, R. A., Stern, R. M., Phillips, M. S., Brill, S. M., Pilant, A. P., & Specker, P. (1983). Feature-based speaker-independent recognition of isolated letters, *Proceedings ICASSP-83, Vol. 2*, 731-733.

Cooper, F., Delattre, P., Liberman, A., Borst, J., & Gerstman, L. (1952). Some experiments on the perception of synthetic speech sounds. *Journal of the Acoustical Society of America, 24*, 597 606.

Covington, C. D., & Peikari, B. (1983). A formant estimating equation useful in a graphically controlled speech synthesizer. *IEEE Transactions on Acoustics, Speech and Signal Processing, ASSP 31*, 736-738.

Cowan, N., Leavitt, L. A., Massaro, D. W., & Kent, R. D. (1982). A fluent backward talker. *Journal of Speech and Hearing Research, 25*, 48-53.

Crothers, J., Lorentz, J., Sherman, D., & Vihman, M. (1979). *Handbook of phonological data from a sample of the world's languages: A report of the Stanford phonology archive*. Palo Alto, CA: Stanford University.

Crowder, R. G. (1983). The purity of auditory memory. *Phil. Trans. Royal Soc. London, B302*, 251-265.

Crystal, T. H., & House, A. S. (1982). Segmental durations in connected speech signals: Preliminary results. *Journal of the Acoustical Society of America, 72*, 705-716.

Cutler, A. (1983). Semantics, syntax and sentence accent. In A. Cohen & M. P. R. van den Broecke (Eds.), *Abstracts of the Tenth International Congress of Phonetic Sciences*. Dordrecht: Foris Publications.

Cutler, A., & Ladd, D. R. (Eds.), (1983). *Prosody: Models and Measurements*. New York: Springer.

Cutting, J. E. (1983). Four assumptions about invariance in perception. *Journal of Experimental Psychology: Human Perception and Performance, 9*, 310-317.

Cutting, J. E., & Eimas, P. D. (1975). Phonetic feature analyzers and the processing of speech in infants. In J. F. Kavanaugh & J. E. Cutting (Eds.), *The role of speech in language*. Cambridge, MA: MIT Press.

D'Arcy Thompson, W. (1961). *On growth and form* (Abridged Edition). London: Cambridge University Press.

Daniloff, R., Wilcox, K., & Stephens, M. I. (1980). An acoustic-articulatory description of children's defective /s/ productions. *Journal of Communication Disorders, 13*, 347-363.

Daniloff, R., & Moll, K. (1968). Coarticulation of lip rounding. *Journal of Speech and Hearing Research, 11*, 707-721.

Darden, B. J. (1970). The fronting of vowels after palatals in Slavic. *Chicago Linguistic Society, Papers from the regional meeting, 6*, 459-470.

Das, S. K., (1980). Some experiments in discrete utterance recognition. *Proceedings of the IEEE Conference on Acoustics, Speech, and Signal Processing*, 178-180.

Day, R. H., & McKenzie, B. E. (1973). Perceptual shape constancy in early infancy. *Perception, 3*, 315-326.

Delattre, P, & Freeman, D. (1968). A dialect study of American r's by x-ray motion picture. *Linguistics, 44*, 29-68.

Delattre, P. (1965). *Comparing the phonetic features of English, German, Spanish and French*. Heidelberg: Julius Groos.

Delgutte, B. (1980). Representation of speech-like sounds in the discharge patterns of auditory nerve fibers. *Journal of the Acoustical Society of America, 68*, 843-857.

Delgutte, B. (1981). *Representation of speech-like sounds in the discharge patterns of auditory-nerve fibers*. Unpublished doctoral dissertation, MIT, Cambridge, MA.

Delgutte, B. (1982). Some Correlates of Phonetic Distinctions at the Level of the Auditory Nerve. In R. Carlson & B. Granström (Eds.), *The Representation of Speech in the Peripheral Auditory System*. Amsterdam: Elsevier/North-Holland Biomedical Press.

Delgutte, B. (1984). Speech coding in the auditory nerve II: Processing schemes for vowel-like sounds. *Journal of the Acoustical Society of America, 75*, 879-886.

Delgutte, B., & Kiang, N. Y. S. (1984a). Speech coding in the auditory nerve I: Vowel-like sounds. *Journal of the Acoustical Society of America, 75*, 866-878.

Delgutte, B., & Kiang, N. Y. S. (1984b). Speech coding in the auditory nerve III: Voiceless fricative consonants. *Journal of the Acoustical Society of America, 75*, 887-896.

Denes, P. (1955). Effect of duration on the perception of voicing. *Journal of the Acoustical Society of America, 27*, 761-764.

deVilliers, J. & deVilliers, P. (October 1978). *Phonological processes in the One and Two Word stage*. Presented at the Boston University Conference on Language Development.

Dewson, J. H. (1964). Speech sound discrimination by cats. *Science*, *144*, 555–556.

Diffloth, G. (1983). *Proto Mon registers: two, three, four. . . ?* Unpublished ms, University of Chicago.

Dinnsen, D. A. (1980). Phonological Rules and Phonetic Explanation. *Journal of Linguistics*, *16*, 171–191.

Disner, S. (1983). Vowel quality: The relation between universal and language specific factors. *UCLA Working Papers in Phonetics*, *58*.

Diver, W. (1979). Phonology as human behavior. In D. Aaronson and R. Rieber (Eds.), *Psycholinguistic research: Implications and applications*. Hillsdale, NJ: Lawrence Erlbaum and Associates.

Dixon, N. R., and Silverman, H. F., (1981). What are the significant variables in dynamic programming for discrete utterance recognition? *Proceedings of the IEEE Conference on Acoustics, Speech and Signal Processing*, 728–731.

Dixon, R. M. W. (1970). Proto-Australian laminals. *Oceanic Linguistics*, *9*, 79–103.

Dixon, R. M. W. (1980). *The languages of Australia*, Cambridge, UK: Cambridge University Press.

Dixon, R. M. W. & Blake, B. J. (Eds.). (1979). *Handbook of Australian languages* (Vol. I), Amsterdam: John Benjamins.

Dixon, R. M. W. & Blake, B. J. (Eds.). (1981). *Handbook of Australian languages*, (Vol. II), Amsterdam, John Benjamins.

Dobzhansky, T. (1965). Mendelism, Darwinism and Evolutionism, *Proceedings of the American Philosophical Society*, *109*, 205–215.

Doddington, G. (1984). Validation of a large digit data base. In W. A. Lea (Ed.), *Toward robustness in speech-recognition*. Santa Barbara, CA: Speech Science Publications.

Dolmazon, J. M. (1982). Representation of Speech-like Sounds in the Peripheral Auditory System in the Light of a Model. In R. Carlson & B. Granström (Eds.), *The representation of speech in the peripheral auditory system*. Amsterdam: Elsevier/North-Holland Biomedical Press.

Donegan, P. J. & Stampe, D. (1979). The study of natural phonology. In Daniel A. Dinnsen (Ed.), *Current approaches to phonological theory*, Bloomington, IN: Indiana University Press.

Duda, R. O., and Hart, P. F. (1973). *Pattern classification and scene analysis*. New York: Wiley.

Dupree, B. C. (1978). Automatic formant analysis. *Proceedings Institute of Acoustics Spring Meeting*, Cambridge, England.

Dupree, B. C. (1980). The use of tracking rules in automatic formant analysis of speech. *Journal of the Acoustical Society of America*, *68*, S71.

Durand, M. (1955). Du rôle de l'auditeur dans la formation des sons du langage. *Journal de Psychologie Normale et Pathologique*, *52*, 347–355.

Eddington, D. K., Dobelle, W. H., Brackman, D. E., Mladejovsky, M. G., & Parkin, J. L. (1978). Auditory prostheses research with multiple channel intracochlear stimulation in man. *Annals of Otology, Rhinology & Laryngology*, *87*, Suppl. *53*.

Edwards, J., Harris, K. S., & Tuller, B. (1983, November 11). *Components of lingual and labial articulation*. Paper presented at the 106th Meeting of the Acoustical Society of America, San Diego, CA.

Edwards, M. L., & Shriberg, L. D. (1983). *Phonology: Applications in communicative disorders*. San Diego, CA: College-Hill Press.

Edwards, M. L. (1979). *Patterns and processes in fricative acquisition: Longitudinal evidence from six English-learning children.* Unpublished Ph.D. dissertation, Stanford University.

Efroymson, M. A. (1966). Multiple regression analysis. In A. Ralston & H. S. Wilf (Eds.), *Mathematical methods for digital computers*. New York: Wiley.

Eimas, P. D. (1974). Auditory and linguistic processing of cues for place of articulation by infants. *Perception and Psychophysics*, *16*, 513–521.

Eimas, P. D. (1975). Auditory and phonetic coding of the cause for speech: Discrimination of the [r–1] distinction by young infants. *Perception & Psychophysics*, *18*, 341–347.

Eimas, P. D. (1982). Speech perception: A view of the initial state and perceptual mechanisms. In J. Mehler, E. C. T. Walker, & M. Garret (Eds.), *Perspectives on mental representation.* Hillsdale, NJ: Lawrence Erlbaum Associates.

Eimas, P. D. (1985). Some constraints on a model of infant speech perception. In J. Mehler & R. Fox (Eds.), *Neonate cognition: Beyond the blooming buzzing confusion.* Hillsdale, NJ: Lawrence Erlbaum Associates.

Eimas, P. D., & Corbit, J. D. (1973). Selective adaptation of linguistic feature detectors. *Cognitive Psychology, 4,* 99-109.

Eimas, P. D., & Miller, J. L. (1977). *Perception of initial nasal and stop consonants by young infants.* Unpublished study.

Eimas, P. D. & Miller, J. L. (1978). Effect of selective adaptation on the perception of speech and visual patterns: Evidence for feature detectors: In R. D. Walk and H. L. Pick (Eds.), *Perception and experience,* New York: Plenum Press.

Eimas, P. D., & Miller, J. L. (1980a). Contextual effects in infant speech perception. *Science, 209,* 1140-1141.

Eimas, P. D., & Miller, J. L. (1980b). Discrimination of the information for manner of articulation by young infants. *Infant Behavior and Development, 3,* 367-375.

Eimas, P., Siqueland, E. R., Jusczyk, P., & Vigorito, J. (1971). Speech perception in early infancy. *Science, 171,* 304-306.

Elenius, K., & Blomberg, M. (1982). Effects of Emphasizing Transitional or Stationary Parts of the Speech Signal in a Discrete Utterance Recognition System, *Proc. IEEE ICASSP-82,* Paris.

Fant, G. (1959). Acoustic analysis and synthesis of speech with applications to Swedish. *Ericsson Technics, 1,* 3-108.

Fant, G. (1960). *Acoustic theory of speech production.* The Hague: Mouton.

Fant, G. (1962). Descriptive analysis of the acoustic aspects of speech. *Logos, 5,* 3-17.

Fant, G. (1969). Distinctive features and phonetic dimensions. *Speech Transmission Laboratory, Quarterly Progress and Status Report, a, 2-3/1969,* 1-18, Royal Institute of Technology, Stockholm.

Fant, G. (1970). Automatic recognition and speech research. *Speech Transmission Laboratory, Quarterly Progress and Status Report, b, 1/1970,* 16-31, Royal Institute of Technology, Stockholm.

Fant, G. (1971). Distinctive features and phonetic dimensions. In G. E. Perren and J. L. M. Trim (Eds.), *Applications of linguistics.* London: Cambridge University Press.

Fant, G. (1973). *Speech sounds and features.* Cambridge, MA: MIT Press.

Fant, G. (1983). Feature analysis of Swedish vowels— A revisit. *Speech Transmission Laboratory, Quarterly Progress and Status Report, 2-3,* 1-18, Royal Institute of Technology, Stockholm.

Fee, J., & Ingram, D. (1982). Reduplication as a strategy of phonological development. *Journal of Child Language, 9,* 41-54.

Ferguson, C. A., (1975). Sound patterns in language acquisition. *Georgetown University Round Table. on Languages and Linguistics, 1975,* 1-16.

Ferguson, C. A. (1977). New directions in phonological theory: Language acquisition and universals research. In R. W. Cole (Ed.), *Current issues in linguistic theory.* Bloomington, IN: Indiana University Press.

Ferguson, C. A. (1978). Learning to pronounce: The earliest stages of phonological development in the child. In F. D. Minifie and L. L. Lloyd (Eds.), *Communicative and cognitive abilities: Early behavioral assessment.* Baltimore, MD: University Park Press.

Ferguson, C. A. (1983). Reduplication in child phonology. *Journal of Child Language, 10,* 239-244.

Ferguson, C. A., & Farwell, C. B. (1975). Words and sounds in early language acquisition. *Language, 51,* 419-439.

Ferguson, C. A., & Garnica, O. (1975). Theories of phonological development. In E. Lenneberg & E. Lenneberg (Eds.), *Foundations of language development.* New York: Academic Press.

Ferguson, C. A., & Macken, M. A. (1983). The role of play in phonological development. In K. E. Nelson (Ed.), Children's language (Vol. 4). Hillsdale, NJ: Lawrence Erlbaum Associates.

Ferguson, C. A., Peitzer, D. B., & Weeks, T. E. (1973). Model-and-replica phonological grammar of a child's first words. Lingua, 31, 35–65.

Firestone, F. A. (Ed.). (1952). Proceedings of the conference on speech analysis. Journal of the Acoustical Society of America, 24: 581–637.

Fischer-Jørgensen, E. (1954). Acoustic analysis of stop consonants. Miscellenea Phonetica, 2, 42–59.

Fischer-Jørgensen, E. (1972a). PTK et BDG français en position intervocalique accentuée. In A. Valdman (Ed.), Linguistic & phonetics to the memory of Pierre Delattre. The Hague: Mouton.

Fischer-Jørgensen, E. (1972b). Tape cutting experiments with Danish stop consonants in initial position. Annual Report of the Institute of Phonetics, University of Copenhagen, 6, 104–168.

Fitch, H. L. (1981). Distinguishing temporal information for speaking rate from temporal information for intervocalic stop consonant voicing. Haskins Laboratories Status Report in Speech Research, SR-65, 1–32.

Fitch, H., Halwes, T., Erickson, D., & Liberman, A. (1980). Perceptual equivalence of two acoustic cues for stop-consonant manner. Perception and Psychophysics, 27, 343–350.

Flanagan, J. L. (1972). Speech analysis, synthesis and perception (2nd ed.). Berlin, West Germany: Springer.

Folkins, J. W. (1976). Multidimensional lower lip displacement resulting from activation of individual labial muscles: Development of a static model. Unpublished doctoral dissertation, University of Washington.

Folkins, J. W. (1981). Muscle activity for jaw closing during speech. Journal of Speech and Hearing Research, 24, 601–615.

Folkins, J. W., & Abbs, J. H. (1975). Lip and jaw motor control during speech: Responses to resistive loading of the jaw. Journal of Speech and Hearing Research, 18, 207–222.

Folkins, J. W., & Abbs, J. H. (1976). Additional observations on responses to resistive loading of the jaw. Journal of Speech and Hearing Research, 19, 820–821.

Foss, D. J., & Blank, M. A. (1980). Identifying the Speech Codes. Cognitive Psychology, 12, 1–31.

Fourcin, A. J., Rosen, S. M., Moore, B. C. J., Douek, E. E., Clarke, G. P., Dodson, H., & Bannister, L. H. (1979). External electrical stimulation of the cochlea: Clinical, psychophysical, speech-perceptual and histological findings. British Journal of Audiology, 13, 85–107.

Fowler, C. A. (1977). Timing control in speech production. Bloomington, IN: Indiana University Linguistics Club.

Fowler, C. A. (1979). "Perceptual centers" in speech production and perception. Perception and Psychophysics, 25, 375–388.

Fowler, C. A. (1980). Coarticulation and theories of extrinsic timing. Journal of Phonetics, 8, 113–133.

Fowler, C. A. (1981a). A Relationship between coarticulation and compensatory shortening. Phonetica, 38, 35–50.

Fowler, C. A. (1981b). Production and perception of coarticulation among stressed and unstressed vowels. Journal of Speech and Hearing Research, 46, 127–149.

Fowler, C. A. (1983). Realism and unrealism: A reply. Journal of Phonetics, 11, 303–322.

Fowler, C. A. (In press). Segmentation of coarticulated speech in perception. Perception and Psychophysics.

Fowler, C. A., Rubin, P., Remez, R. E., & Turvey, M. T. (1980). Implications for speech production of a general theory of action. In B. Butterworth (Ed.), Language production. New York: Academic Press.

Fowler, C. A., & Turvey, M. T. (1978). Skill acquisition: An event approach with special reference to searching for the optimum of a function of several variables. In G. Stelmach (Ed.), Information processing in motor control and learning. New York: Academic Press.

Fowler, C.A, Rubin, P., Remez, R.E. & Turvey, M. (1980). Implications for speech production of a general theory of action: In B. Butterworth (Ed.), *Language production*. London: Academic Press.

Fromkin, V. (1971). The non-anomalous nature of anomalous utterances, *Language, 47:* 27–52.

Fromkin, V. A (Ed.) (1973). *Speech errors as linguistic evidence*. The Hague: Mouton.

Fromkin, V. A. (Ed.) (1980). *Errors in linguistic performance*. New York: Academic Press.

Fromm, D. (1981). *Investigation of movement/EMG parameters in apraxia of speech*. Unpublished master's thesis, University of Wisconsin-Madison.

Fromm, D., Abbs, J. H., McNeil, M., & Rosenbek, J. C. (1982). Simultaneous perceptual-physiological method for studying apraxia of speech. In R. Brookshire (Ed.), *Proceedings of the Annual Clinical Aphasiology Conference*. Minneapolis, MN: BRK Publishers.

Fujimura, O. (1970). Current Issues in Experimental Phonetics. In R. Jakobson & S. Kawamoto (Eds.), *Studies in general and Oriental linguistics*. Tokyo: Tec.

Fujimura, O., (1976). Syllables as Concatenated Demisyllables and Affixes. *Journal of the Acoustical Society of America, 59,* Supp. No. 1, S55.

Fujimura, O., (1979). An analysis of english syllables as cores and affixes. *Zeitschrift für Phonetik Sprachwissenschaft und Kommunikationsforschung, 4,* 471–476.

Fujimura, O. (1981a). Body-cover theory of the vocal fold and its phonetic implications. In K. N. Stevens & M. Hirano (Eds.), *Vocal fold physiology*. Tokyo: University of Tokyo Press.

Fujimura, O. (1981b). Temporal Organization of Articulatory Movements as a Multidimensional Phrasal Structure, *Phonetica, 38,* 66–83.

Fujimura, O. (1983). *Remarks on speech synthesis*. Tenth International Congress of Phonetic Sciences, Utrecht.

Fujimura, O., Kiritani, S., & Ishida, H. (1973). Computer controlled radiography for observation of movements of articulatory and other human organs. *Computer Biological Medicine, 3,* 371–384.

Fujimura, O., & Lindqvist, J. (1971). Sweep-tone measurements of vocal-tract characteristics. *Journal of the Acoustical Society of America, 49,* 541–558.

Fujimura, O. & Lovins, J. B. (1978). Syllables as Concatenative Phonetic Units. In A. Bell and J. B. Hooper (Eds.), *Syllables and segments*. North-Holland.

Fujimura, O., & Lovins, J. B. (1982). *Syllables as concatenative phonetic units*. Bloomington, IN: Indiana University Linguistics Club.

Fujimura, O., Miller, J. E., & Escolar, G. (1977). Articulatory Feature Detection, *Journal of the Acoustical Society of America, 61,* S48.

Fujisaki, H., & Kawashima, T. (1968). The roles of pitch and higher formants in the perception of vowels. *IEEE Transactions on Audio and Electroacoustics, AU-16,* 73–77.

Fujisaki, H., & Nagashima, S. (1969). A model for synthesis of pitch contours of connected speech. *Annual Report, Eng. Res. Inst., University of Tokyo, 28,* 35–60.

Galaburda, A. M., & Pandya, D. N. (1982). Role of architechtonics and connections in the study of primate brain evolution. In E. Armstrong & D. Falk (Eds.), *Primate brain evolution*. New York: Plenum Press.

Gandour, J. (1974). Consonant types and tones in Siamese. *Journal of Phonetics, 2:* 337–350.

Garnica, O. K. (1971). The development of the perception of phonemic differences in initial consonants by English-speaking children: A pilot study. *Papers and Reports on Child Language Development* (Dept. of Linguistics, Stanford University), *3,* 1–29.

Garnica, O. K. (1973). The development of phonemic speech perception. In T. E. Moore (Ed.), *Cognitive development and the acquisition of language*. New York: Academic Press.

Garnica, O. K., & Edwards, M. L. (1977). Phonological variation in children's speech: The trade-off phenomenon. *Ohio State University Working Papers in Linguistics, 22,* 81–87.

Gay, T. (1977). Articulatory movements in VCV sequences. *Journal of the Acoustical Society of America, 62,* 183–193.

Gentil, M., Gracco, V. L., & Abbs, J. H. (1983). Multiple muscle contributions to labial closure during speech: Evidence for intermuscle motor equivalence. *Proceedings of the 11th International Congress of Acoustics* (Lyon-Toulouse), 11–14.

Gentil, M., Harris, K. S., Horiguchi, S., and Honda, K. (1984). Temporal organization of muscle activity in simple disyllables. *Journal of the Acoustical Society of America, 75*, S23.

Gerstman, L. J. (1968). Classification of self-normalized vowels. *IEEE Transactions on Audio and Electroacoustics.* AU 16, 78–80.

Gewirth, L. (1983). *Variation in the perception and production of word stress.* Unpublished Honors Paper, Brown University, Providence, Rhode Island.

Gibson, J. J. (1966). *The senses considered as perceptual systems.* Boston, MA: Houghton-Mifflin.

Gleitman, L. R., & Wanner, E. (1982). Language acquisition: The state of the state of the art. In E. Wanner & L. R. Gleitman (Eds.), *Language acquisition: The state of the art.* Cambridge: Cambridge University Press.

Godschalk, M., Lemon, R. N., & Kuypers, H. G. J. M. (1983). Afferent and efferent connections of the postarcuate region of the monkey cerebral cortex. *Society for Neuroscience, 9*(Part 1), 490.

Goldhor, R. (1983a). A speech signal processing system based on a peripheral auditory model. *ICASSP 83 (IEEE)*, 1368–1371, Boston, MA.

Goldhor, R. (1983b). The representation of speech in a model of the peripheral auditory system. *Journal of the Acoustical Society of America, 73*, S4.

Goodall, J. (1968). The behavior of free-living chimpanzees in the Coombe Stream Reserve. *Animal Behavior Monographs, 1*, 161–312.

Goodglass, H., & Kaplan, E. (1972). *The assessment of aphasia and related disorders.* Philadelphia, PA: Lea & Febinger.

Gracco, V. L., & Abbs, J. H. (1982). Temporal response characteristics of the perioral system to load perturbations. *Society for Neuroscience, 8*(Part 2), 282.

Grassman, H. (1863). Ueber die Aspiraten und ihr gleichzeitiges Vorhandensein im An- und Auslaute der Wurzeln. *Zeitschrift für vergleichende Sprachforschung auf dem Gebiete des Deutschen, Griechischen und Lateinischen, 12.2*, 81–138.

Greenberg, J. H. (1963). *Universals in language.* Cambridge, MA: MIT Press.

Greenberg, J. H. (1966). Synchronic and diachronic universals in phonology. *Language, 42*, 508–517.

Grieser, D. L. & Kuhl, P. K. (1983). Internal structure of vowel categories in infants: Effects of stimulus goodness. *Journal of the Acoustical Society of America, 74*, Suppl 1, S102–103(A).

Grillner, S. (1975). Locomotion in vertebrates. *Physiological Reviews, 55*, 247–304.

Grégoire, A. (1899). Variations de durée de la syllabe française suivant sa place dans les groupements phonétiques. *La Parole, 9*, 161–176, 263–280, 418–433.

Guy, G. (1980). Variation in the group and the individual: the case of final stop deletion. In W. Labov (Ed.), *Locating language in time and space*, NY: Academic Press.

Gårding, E. (1970). Word tones and larynx muscles. *Working Papers, 3.* Phonetics Laboratory. Department of Linguistics, Lund University.

Gårding, E. (1981). Contrastive Prosody: A model and its application. *Studia Linguistica, 35* (1–2), 146–166.

Gårding, E. (1983). A generative model of intonation. In A. Cutler and D. R. Ladd (Eds.), *Prosody: Models and measurements.* New York: Springer.

Gårding, E., Zhang, J., & Svantesson, J-O. (1983). A generative model for tone and intonation in Standard Chinese. *Working Papers, 25*, 53–65. Phonetics Laboratory. Department of Linguistics, Lund University.

Hall, B., Hall, R. M. R., Pam, M. D., Myers, A., Antell, S. A., & Cherono, G. (1974). African vowel harmony systems from the vantage point of Kalenjin. *Afrika und Übersee, Band LVII, Heft 4*, 241–267.

Hall, R. A. (1938). *An Analytic Grammar of the Hungarian Language.* Language Monographs, 18, Suppl. 14.

Hallé, M. (1964). On the bases of phonology. In J. A. Fodor & J. J. Katz (Eds.), *The structure of language*, Englewood Cliffs, NJ: Prentice-Hall.

Halle, M. (1982). On the relationship of phonologic features to phonetic parameters. In A. S. House (Ed.), *Acoustic phonetics and speech modeling.* Princeton, New Jersey: Institute for Defense Analysis.

Halle, M. (1983). On distinctive features and their articulatory implementation. *Natural Language and Linguistic Theory, 1.1*, 91-105.

Halle, M., Hughes, G. W., & Radley, J.-P. A. (1957). Acoustic properties of stop consonants. *Journal of the Acoustical Society of America, 29*, 107-116.

Halle, M., & Stevens, K. N. (1970). On the feature "Advanced Tongue Root." *MIT Quarterly Progress Report, Research Laboratory of Electronics, 94*, 209-215.

Halle, M., & Stevens, K. N. (1971). A note on laryngeal features. *MIT Quarterly Progress Report, Research Laboratory of Electronics, 101*, 198-213.

Halle, M. & Stevens, K. N. (1979). Some reflections on the theoretical bases of phonetics. In B. Lindblom & S. Öhman (Eds.), *Frontiers of speech communication research*. London: Academic Press.

Halliday, M. A. K. (1979). One child's protolanguage. In M. Bullowa (Ed.), *Before speech: The beginning of interpersonal communication*. Cambridge: Cambridge University Press.

Hammarberg, R. (1982). On redefining coarticulation. *Journal of Phonetics, 10*, 123-137.

Han, M. S. (1963). Acoustic phonetics of Korean. *Technical Report No. 1, ONR 049-183: Contract Nonr 233(80)*. Los Angeles, CA: University of California at Los Angeles.

Harms, R. T. (1973). *Some nonrules of English*. Indiana University Linguistics Club. Reprinted in A. Jazayery, E. Polone, & W. Winter (Eds.) (1978), *Linguistic and literary studies in honor of Archibald A. Hill* (Vol. II). The Hague: Mouton.

Harris, K. S., & Bell-Berti, F. (1984). On consonants and syllable boundaries. In L. Raphael, C. Raphael, & M. Valdovinos (Eds.), *Language and cognition: Essays in honor of Arthur J. Bronstein*. New York: Plenum.

Hartmann, R., Topp, G., & Klinke, R. (1984). Discharge patterns of cat primary auditory fibers with electrical stimulation of the cochlea *Hearing Research, 13*, 47-62.

Hasegawa, A., McCutcheon, M., Wolf, M., & Fletcher, S. (1976). Lip and jaw coordination during the production of /f,v/ in English. *Journal of the Acoustical Society of America, S84*, 59.

Hashimoto, T., Katayama, Y., Murata, K., & Taniguchi, L. (1975). Pitch synchronous response of cat cochlear nerve fibers to speech sounds. *Japanese Journal of Physiology, 25*, 633-644.

Hebb, D. O. (1949). *The organization of behavior: A neurophysiological theory*. New York: Wiley.

Heinz, J. M. & Stevens, K. N. (1961). On the properties of voiceless fricative consonants, *Journal of the Acoustical Society of America, 33*, 589-596.

Helson, H. (1964). *Adaptation level theory*. New York: Harper & Row.

Henke, W. L. (1967). Preliminaries to speech synthesis based on an articulatory model. *Proceedings of the 1967 IEEE Boston Speech Conference*.

Hillenbrand, J. (1983). Perceptual organization of speech sounds by infants. *Journal of Speech and Hearing Research, 26*, 268-282.

Hillenbrand, J. (1984). Speech perception by infants: Categorization based on nasal consonant place of articulation. *Journal of the Acoustical Society of America, 75*, 1613-1622.

Hillebrand, J., Minifie, F. D., & Edwards, T. J. (1979). Tempo of spectrum change as a cue in speech sound discrimination by infants. *Journal of Speech and Hearing Research, 22*, 147-165.

Hindle, Donald (1978). Approaches to vowel normalization in the study of natural speech. In D. Sankoff (Ed.), *Linguistic variation: Models and methods*. New York: Academic Press.

Hindle, Donald (1980). *The social and situational conditioning of phonetic variation*. PhD dissertation, University of Pennsylvania.

Hinton, G. E. (1981). A parallel computation that assigns canonical object-based frames of reference. In *Proceedings IJCAI-7*, Vancouver, B. C.

Hirose, H. (1971). The activity of the adductor laryngeal muscles in respect to vowel devoicing in Japanese. *Phonetica, 23*:156-170.

Hixon, T., Goldman, M., & Mead, J. (1973). Kinematics of the chest wall during speech production: Volume displacements of the rib cage, abdomen, and lung. *Journal of Speech and Hearing Research, 16*, 78-115.

Hixon, T., Mead, J., & Goldman, M. (1976). Dynamics of the chest wall during speech production. Function of the thorax, rib cage, diaphragm and abdomen. *Journal of Speech and Hearing Research, 19,* 297–356.

Hockett, C. (1955). *A manual of phonology.* Baltimore: Waverly Press.

Hockett, C. (1960). The origin of language. *Scientific American, 203,* 89–96.

Hockett, C. F., & Ascher, R. (1964). The human revolution. *Current Anthropology, 5,* 135–147.

Holmberg, T. L., Morgan, K. A., & Kuhl, P. K. (1977). *Speech perception in early infancy: Discrimination of fricative consonants.* Paper presented at the 94th Meeting of the Acoustical Society of America, Miami Beach, FL, December 12–16.

Holmes, J. N. (1973). The influence of glottal waveform on the naturalness of speech from a parallel-formant synthesizer. *IEEE Transactions on Audio and Electroacoustics, AU-21,* 298–305.

Holmes, J. N. (1980). Avoiding unwanted variations of low-frequency gain in the output of a parallel formant synthesizer. *Journal of the Acoustical Society of America, 68,* S18.

Hombert, J.-M. (1978). Consonant types, vowel quality, and tone. In V. Fromkin (Ed.), *Tone: A Linguistic Survey,* 77–111. New York: Academic Press.

Hombert, J.-M., Ohala, J. J., & Ewan, W. G. (1979). Phonetic explanations for the development of tones. *Language, 55,* 37–58.

Houde, R. A. (1968). A study of tongue body motion during selected speech sounds. *SCRL Monograph* (No. 2). Santa Barbara, CA: Speech Communications Research Laboratory.

House, A. S. (1957). Analog studies of nasal consonants. *Journal of Speech and Hearing Disorders, 22,* 190–204.

House, A. S. & Fairbanks, G. (1953). The influence of consonant environment upon the secondary acoustic characteristics of vowels, *Journal of the Acoustical Society of America, 25,* 105–113.

House, A. S. & Stevens, K. N. (1956). Analog studies of the nasalization of vowels. *Journal of Speech and Hearing Disorders, 21,* 218–232.

Huggins, A. W. F. (1975). On isochrony and syntax. In G. Fant & M. A. A. Tatham (Eds.), *Auditory analysis and perception of speech.* London: Academic Press.

Hughes, O., & Abbs, J. H. (1976). Labial-mandibular coordination in the production of speech: Implications for the operation of motor equivalence. *Phonetica, 44,* 199–221.

Hunker, C. J., & Abbs, J. H. (1982). Respiratory movement control during speech: Evidence for motor equivalence. *Society for Neuroscience, 8,* 946.

Huttenlocker, D., & Zue, V. W. (1984). A Model of lexical access based on partial phonetic information, *Proceedings, ICASSP-84* (Vol. 2) 26.4.

Hyman, R., & Frost, N. (1975). Gradients and schema in pattern recognition. In. P. M. A. Rabbit and S. Dornic (Eds.), *Attention and performance V.* New York: Academic Press.

Hyvarinen, J. (1982). Posterior parietal lobe of the primate brain. *Physiological Reviews, 62*(3), 1060–1129.

Immelmann, K., Barlow, G. W., Petrinovich, L., & Main, M. (Eds.), (1981). *Behavioral development.* New York: Cambridge University Press.

Ingram, D. (1974). Phonological rules in young children. *Journal of Child Language, 1,* 49–64.

Ingram, D. (1979). Cross-linguistic evidence on the extent and limit of individual variation in phonological development. *Proceedings of the Ninth International Congress of Phonetic Sciences* (Vol. II). Copenhagen: Institute of Phonetics, University of Copenhagen.

International Phonetic Association (1949). *The principles of the international phonetic association.* London: University College.

Isenberg, D., Walker, E. C. T., Ryder, J. M., & Schweikert, J. (1980, November). *A top-down effect on the identification of function words.* Paper presented at the Acoustical Society of America, Los Angeles.

Itakura, F., (1975). Minimum prediction residual principle applied to speech-recognition. *IEEE Transactions on Acoustics, Speech, and Signal Processing, ASSP-23,* 67–72.

Itoh, M., Sasanuma, S., Hirose, H., Yoshioka, H., & Ushijima, T. (1980). Abnormal articulatory dynamics in a patient with apraxia of speech: X-ray microbeam observation. *Brain and Language, 11,* 66–75.

Itoh, M., Sasanuma, S., & Ushijima, T. (1979). Velar movements during speech in a patient with apraxia of speech. *Brain and Language, 7*, 227-238.

Jacobson, L. (1978). Dho-Luo vowel harmony. *UCLA Working Papers in Phonetics, 43*, 1-121.

Jaeger, J. J. (1980). Testing the psychological reality of phonemes. *Language and Speech, 23*, 233 253.

Jakobson, R. (1968). *Child language, aphasia, and phonological universals.* Transl. by A. R. Keiler. The Hague: Mouton.

Jakobson, R., Fant, G., & Halle, M. (1951). *Preliminaries to speech analysis.* Cambridge, MA: MIT Press.

Jakobson, R., Fant, G., & Halle, M. (1963). *Preliminaries to speech analysis.* Cambridge, MA: MIT Press.

Jakobson, R. & Halle, M. (1956). *Fundamentals of language.* The Hague: Mouton.

Jakobson, R. & Waugh, L. (1979). *The sound shape of language.* Bloomington, IN: Indiana University Press.

Jantsch, E. (Ed.). (1981). *The evolutionary vision: Toward a unifying paradigm of physical, biological and sociocultural evolution,* Boulder, CO: Westview.

Javkin, H. R. (1979, May). Phonetic universals and phonological change. *Report of the Phonology Laboratory, 4.* Berkeley: Phonology Laboratory.

Jeel, V. (1975). An investigation of the fundamental frequency of vowels after various Danish consonants, in particular stop consonants, *Annual Report of the Institute of Phonetics, University of Copenhagen, 9*, 191-211.

Jelinek, F. (1976). Continuous speech-recognition by statistical methods, *Proceedings IEEE, 64*, 532-556.

Jespersen, O. (1913). *Lehrbuch der Phonetik* (2nd ed.). Leipzig: Teubner.

Johanson, G. (June, 1975). Visual motion perception. *Scientific American,* 76-88.

Johansson, G. (1974). Projective transformations as determining visual-space perception. In R. MacLeod & H. Pick (Eds.), *Perception: Essays in honor of James J. Gibson.* Ithaca, NY: Cornell University Press.

Johns, D. E., & Darley, F. L. (1970). Phonemic variability in apraxia of speech. *Journal of Speech and Hearing Research, 13*, 556-583.

Johnson, D. H. (1974). *The response of single auditory-nerve fibers in the cat to single tones: synchrony and average discharge rate.* PhD Thesis, Dept. of Electrical Engineering, MIT.

Johnson, T. L., & Strange, W. (1982). Perceptual constancy of vowels in rapid speech. *Journal of the Acoustical Society of America, 72*, 1761-1770.

Jones, D. (1940). *An Outline of English Phonetics.* New York: Dutton.

Jones, D. (1966). *The pronunciation of English,* (4th ed.). Cambridge, UK: Cambridge University Press.

Jones, D., & Fry, D. (Eds.). (1936). *Proceedings of the Second International Congress of Phonetic Sciences.* Cambridge: Cambridge University Press.

Jones, E. G., Coulter, J. D., & Hendry, S. H. C. (1978). Intracortical connectivity of architectonic fields in the somatic sensory, motor and parietal cortex of monkeys. *Comparative Neurology, 181*, 291-348.

Jusczyk, P. W. (1977). Perception of syllable-final stop consonants by two-month-old infants. *Perception and Psychophysics, 21*, 450-454.

Jusczyk, P. W. (1982). Auditory versus phonetic coding of speech signals during infancy. In J. Mehler, E. C. T. Walker, & M. Garrett, (Eds.), *Perspectives on mental representation.* Hillsdale, NJ: Lawrence Erlbaum Associates.

Jusczyk, P. W. (1985). On characterizing the development of speech perception. In J. Mehler and R. Fox (Eds.), *Neonate cognition: Beyond the blooming, buzzing confusion.* Hillsdale, NJ: Lawrence Erlbaum Associates.

Jusczyk, P. W., Copan, H. C., & Thompson, E. J. (1978). Perception by two-month-olds of glide contrasts in multisyllabic utterances. *Perception & Psychophysics, 24*, 515-520.

Jusczyk, P. W., & Derrah, C. In preparation.

Jusczyk, P. W., Murray, J., & Bayly, J. (1979, March). *Perception of place-of-articulation in fricatives and stops by infants.* Paper presented at the biennial meeting of the Society for Research in Child Development, San Francisco, CA.

Jusczyk, P. W., Pisoni, D. B., Reed, M., Fernald, A., & Myers, M. (1983). Durational context effects in the processing of nonspeech sounds by infants. *Science, 222*, 175–177.

Jusczyk, P. W., Pisoni, D. B., Reed, M. A., Fernald, A., & Myers, M. (1983). Infants' discrimination of the duration of a rapid spectrum change in nonspeech signals. *Science, 222*, 175–177.

Jusczyk, P. W., Pisoni, D. B., Walley, A., & Murray, J. (1980). Discrimination of relative onset time of two-component tones by infants. *Journal of the Acoustical Society of America, 67*, 262–270.

Jusczyk, P. W., Smith, L. B., & Murphy, C. (1981). The perceptual classification of speech. *Perception & Psychophysics, 30*, 10–23.

Jusczyk, P. W., & Thompson, E. (1978). Perception of a phonetic contrast in multisyllabic utterances by two-month-old infants. *Perception & Psychophysics, 23*, 105–109.

Kahn, D. (1978). On the identifiability of isolated vowels. *UCLA Working Papers in Phonetics, 41*, 26–31.

Katz, J. J., & Jusczyk, P. W. (1980, April). Do six-month-olds have perceptual constancy for phonetic segments? Paper presented at the International Conference on Infant Studies, New Haven, CT.

Katz, J., & Jusczyk, P. W. (1980, April). *Do 6-month olds have perceptual constancy for phonetic segments?* Paper presented at the International Conference on Infant Studies, New Haven, CT.

Kawasaki, H. (1978). The perceived nasality of vowels with gradual attenuation of adjacent nasal consonants. *Journal of the Acoustical Society of America, 64*, S19.

Kawasaki, H. (1981). *Voicing in Japanese*. Unpublished manuscript, University of California at Berkeley.

Kawasaki, H. (1983). Fundamental frequency perturbation caused by voiced and voiceless stops in Japanese. *Journal of the Acoustical Society of America, 73*: S88.

Kawasaki, H. (In press). Phonetic explanation for phonological universals: The case of distinctive vowel nasalization. In J. J. Ohala (Ed.), *Experimental phonology*. New York: Academic Press.

Kelso, J. A. S. (1978). Joint receptors do not provide a satisfactory basis for motor timing and positioning. *Psychological Review, 85*, 474–481.

Kelso, J. A. S. (1981). Contrasting perspectives on order and regulation in movement. In J. Long & A. Baddeley (Eds.), *Attention and Performance IX*. Hillsdale, NJ: Lawrence Erlbaum Associates.

Kelso, J. A. S., & Bateson, E.-V. (1983). On the cyclical basis of speech production. *Journal of the Acoustical Society of America, 73*, S76.

Kelso, J. A. S., Holt, K. G., Rubin, P., & Kugler, P. N. (1981). Patterns of human interlimb coordination emerge from the properties of nonlinear limit cycle oscillatory processes: Theory and data. *Journal of Motor Behavior, 13*, 226–261.

Kelso, J. A. S., & Tuller, B., (1984). Functionally specific articulatory cooperation following jaw perturbations during speech: Evidence for coordinative structures. *Journal of Experimental Psychology: Human Perception and Performance, 10*, 812–832.

Kelso, J. A. S., & Tuller, B., (in press). Intrinsic time and speech production: Theory, methodology, and preliminary observations. In E. Keller (Ed.), *Sensory and motor processes in language*. Hillsdale, NJ: Erlbaum.

Kelso, J. A. S., Tuller, B., & Fowler, C. (1982). The functional specificity of articulatory control and coordination. *Journal fo the Acoustical Society of America, 72*, S103.

Kelso, J. A. S., Tuller, B., & Harris, K. S. (1983). A "dynamic pattern" perspective on the control and coordination of articulation. In P. MacNeilage (Ed.), *The production of speech*. New York: Springer-Verlag.

Kent, R. D. (1980). Articulatory and acoustic perspectives on speech development. In A. P. Reilly (Ed.), *The communication game: Perspectives on the development of speech, language, and non-verbal communication skills*. Skillman, NJ: Johnson & Johnson Baby Products Pediatric Round Table Series.

Kent, R. D. (1984). Psychobiology of speech development: co-emergence of language and a movement system. *American Journal of Physiology, 246 (Regulatory, Integrative and Comparative Physiology, 15)*, R888–R894.

Kent, R. D., Carney, P. J., & Severeid, L. R. (1974). Velar movement and timing: Evaluation of a model for binary control. *Journal of Speech and Hearing Research, 17*, 470–488.

Kent, R. D., & Moll, K. L. (1972). Tongue body articulation during vowel and diphthong gestures. *Folia Phoniatrica, 24*, 278–300.

Kent, R. D., & Moll, K. L. (1975). Articulatory timing in selected consonant sequences. *Brain and Language, 2*, 304–323.

Kent, R. D. & Netsell, R. (1971). Effects of stress contrasts on certain articulatory parameters. *Phonetica, 24*, 23–44.

Kent, R. D., & Netsell, R. (1972). Effects of stress contrasts on certain articulatory parameters. *Phonetica, 24*, 23–44.

Kent, R. D., & Rosenbek, J. C. (1983). Acoustic patterns of apraxia of speech. *Journal of Speech and Hearing Research*, 231–249.

Kewley-Port, D. (1980). Representations of spectral change as cues to place of articulation in stop consonants. *Research on Speech Perception, Technical Report No. 3.* Bloomington, IN: Indiana University Press.

Kewley-Port, D. (1983). Time varying features as correlates of place of articulation in stop consonants. *Journal of the Acoustical Society of America, 73*, 322–335.

Kewley-Port, D., & Luce, P. (1984). Time-varying features of initial stop consonants in auditory running spectra: A first report. *Perception & Psychophysics, 35*, 353–360.

Kewley-Port, D., Pisoni, D. B., & Studdert-Kennedy, M. (1983). Perception of static and dynamic acoustic cues to place of articulation in initial stop consonants. *Journal of the Acoustical Society of America, 73*, 1779–1793.

Kewley Port, D. & Preston, M. S. (1972). Early apical stop production: A voice onset time analysis, *Haskins Laboratories Status Report 29/30*, 125–149.

Kiang, N. Y. S., & Moxon, E. C. (1972). Physiological considerations in artificial stimulation of the inner ear. *Annals of Otology, Rhinology and Laryngology, 81*, 714–730.

Kiang, N. Y. S, & Moxon, E. C. (1974). Tails of tuning curves of auditory nerve fibers. *Journal of the Acoustical Society of America, 55*, 620–630.

Kiang, N. Y. S. , Watanabe, T., Thomas, E. C., & Clark, L. F. (1965). Discharge Patterns of Single Fibers in the Cat's Auditory Nerve, *MIT Research Monograph No 35*. Cambridge, MA: MIT Press.

Kimura, D. (1961). Cerebral dominance and the perception of verbal stimuli. *Canadian Journal of Psychology, 15*, 166–171.

Kimura, D. (1967). Functional asymmetry of the brain in dichotic listening. *Cortex, 8*, 163–178.

Kinsbourne, M. (1972). Eye and head turning indicates cerebral lateralization. *Science, 176*, 539–541.

Kiparsky, P. (1982). Lexical morphology and phonology. In *Linguistics in the morning calm*, Seoul, Korea: Hanshin.

Kiparsky, P., & Menn, L. (1977). On the acquisition of phonology. In J. Macnamara (Ed.), *Language, learning and thought*. New York: Academic Press.

Kiritani, S., Itoh, K., & Fujimura, O. (1975). Tongue-pellet tracking by a computer-controlled x-ray microbeam system. *Journal of the Acoustical Society of America, 57*, Part II, 1516–1520.

Kirlin, R.L., (1978). A posteriori estimation of vocal tract length. *IEEE Transactions on Acoustics, Speech, and Signal Processing, ASSP-26*, 571–574.

Klatt, D. (1975). Vowel lengthening is syntactically determined in a connected discourse. *Journal of Phonetics, 3*, 129–140.

Klatt, D. (1976). Linguistic uses of segment duration in English: Acoustic and perceptual evidence. *Journal of the Acoustical Society of America, 59*, 1208–1221.

Klatt, D. H. (1977). Review of the ARPA speech understanding project. *Journal of the Acoustical Society of America, 62*, 1345–1366.

Klatt, D. H. (1979a). Speech perception: A model of acoustic-phonetic analysis and lexical access. *Journal of Phonetics, 7*, 279–312.

Klatt, D. H. (1979b). Perceptual comparisons among a set of vowels similar to /ae/, some differences between psychoacoustic distance and phonetic distance, *Journal of the Acoustical Society of America, 66*, S86.

Klatt, D. (1979c). Synthesis by rule of segmental durations in English sentences. In B. Lindblom & S. Öhman (Eds.), *Frontiers of speech communication research*. New York: Academic Press.

Klatt, D. H. (1980). Speech perception: A model of acoustic-phonetic analysis and lexical access. In R. A. Cole (Ed.), *Perception and production of fluent speech*. Hillsdale NJ: Erlbaum.

Klatt, D. H. (1980). Software for a cascade/parallel formant synthesizer. *Journal of the Acoustical Society of America, 67*, 971–995.

Klatt, D. H. (1982a). Prediction of perceived phonetic distance from critical-band spectra: A first step. *Proceedings IEEE International Conference on Acoustics, Speech and Signal Processing*, Paris, France, 1278–1281.

Klatt, D. H. (1982b). Speech processing strategies based on auditory models. In R. Carlson, & B. Granstrom (Eds.), *The representation of speech in the peripheral auditory system*. New York: Elsevier Biomedical Press.

Klatt, D. H. (1983). The problems of variability in speech recognition and in models of speech perception. In A. Cohen & M. P. R. van den Broecke (Eds.), *Abstracts of the Tenth International Congress of Phonetic Sciences*. Dordrecht: Foris Publications.

Klokeid, T. J. (1976). *Topics in Lardil grammar*, unpublished doctoral dissertation, MIT, Cambridge, MA.

Klovstad, J. W., & Mondshein, L. F. (1975). The Caspers linguistic analysis system, *IEEE Transactions, ASSP-23*, 118–123.

Kohler, K. J. (1983a). Prosodic boundary signals in German. *Phonetica, 40*, 89–134.

Kohler, K. J. (1983b). Stress-timing and speech rate in German: A production model. *Arbeitsberichte des Instituts für Phonetik der Universität Kiel (AIPUK), 20*, 5–53.

Kohler, K. J., Krützmann, U., Reetz, H., & Timmermann, G. (1982). Sprachliche Determinanten der signalphonetischen Dauer. *Arbeitsberichte des Instituts für Phonetik der Universität Kiel (AIPUK), 17*, 1–35.

Kohler, K. J., Schäfer, K., Thon, W., & Timmermann, G. (1981). Sprechgeschwindigkeit in Produktion und Perzeption. *Arbeitsberichte des Instituts für Phonetik der Universität Kiel (AIPUK), 16*, 137–205.

Koopmans-van Beinum, F. J. (1980). *Vowel contrast reduction. An acoustic and perceptual study of Dutch vowels in various speech conditions*. Doctoral thesis, University of Amsterdam.

Kornfeld, J. (1971). What initial clusters tell us about a child's speech code, *MIT RLE Quarterly Progress Report # 101*, 218–221.

Kornfeld, J., & Goehl, H. (1974). A new twist to an old observation: kids know more than they say. *Parasession on Natural Phonology*, Chicago Linguistic Society, 210–219.

Kozhevnikov, V. A., & Chistovich, L. A. (1965). *Speech: Articulation and perception*. Transl. U. S. Department of Commerce. Clearinghouse for Federal Scientific and Technical Information, Washington, DC.

Krebs, J. R., & Davies, N. B. (1981). *An introduction to behavioural ecology*. Sunderland, MA: Sinauer Associates.

Kroodsma, E. E. (1981). Ontogeny of bird song. In K. Immelman, G. B. Barlow, L. Petrinovich, & M. Main (Eds.), *Behavioral development*. New York: Cambridge University Press.

Kubota, K., & Niki, H. (1971). Precentral cortical unit activity and jaw movement in chronic monkeys. In R. Dubner & Y. Kawamura (Eds.), *Oral facial sensory and motor mechanisms*. New York: Appleton.

Kugler, P. N., Turvey, M. T., & Shaw, R. (1982). Is the "cognitive penetrability" criterion invalidated by contemporary physics? *The Behavioral and Brain Sciences, 2*, 303–306.

Kuhl, P. K. (1979a). Speech perception in early infancy: Perceptual constancy for spectrally dissimilar vowel categories. *Journal of the Acoustical Society of America, 66*, 1668–1679.

Kuhl, P. K. (1979b). Models and mechanisms in speech perception: Species comparisons provide further contributions. *Brain, Behavior and Evolution, 16*, 374–408.

Kuhl, P. K. (1980). Perceptual constancy for speech-sound categories. In G. H. Yeni-Komshian, J. F. Kavanagh & C. A. Ferguson (Eds.), *Child phonology, vol. 2, perception.* New York: Academic Press.

Kuhl, P. K. (1981). Discrimination of speech by non-human animals: Basic auditory sensitivities conducive to the perception of speech-sound categories. *Journal of the Acoustical Society of America, 70*, 340–349.

Kuhl, P. K. (1983). Perception of auditory equivalence classes for speech in early infancy. *Infant Behavior and Development, 6*, 263–285.

Kuhl, P. K. (1985). Categorization of speech by infants. In J. Mehler and R. Fox (Eds.), *Neonate cognition: beyond the blooming, buzzing confusion.* Hillsdale, NJ: Erlbaum.

Kuhl, P. K. (in press-a). Perception of speech and sound in early infancy. In P. Salapatek and L. Cohen (Eds.), *Handbook of infant perception.* New York: Academic.

Kuhl, P. K. (in press-b). Comparative studies on the perception of speech: Theoretical contributions to models of speech perception. *Experimental Biology.*

Kuhl, P. K. & Meltzoff, A. N. (1982) The bimodal perception of speech in infancy. *Science, 218*, 1138–1141.

Kuhl, P. K. & Meltzoff, A. N. (1984a). The intermodal representation of speech in infants. *Infant Behavior and Development, 7*, 361–381.

Kuhl, P. K. & Meltzoff, A. N. (1984b). Infants' recognition of cross-modal correspondences for speech: Is it based on physics or phonetics? *Journal of the Acousitcal Society of America, 76*, Suppl. 1, S80(A).

Kuhl, P. K. & Miller, J. D. (1975). Speech perception by the chinchilla: Voiced-voiceless distinction in alveolar plosive consonants. *Science, 190*, 69–72.

Kuhl, P. K. & Miller, J. D. (1978). Speech perception by the chinchilla: Identification functions for synthetic VOT stimuli. *Journal of the Acoustical Society of America, 63*, 905–917.

Kuhl, P. K., & Miller, J. D. (1982). Discrimination of auditory target dimensions in the presence or absence of variation in a second dimension by infants. *Perception & Psychophysics, 31*, 279–292.

Kuhl, P. K. & Padden, D. M. (1982). Enhanced discrimination at the phonetic boundaries for the voicing feature in macaques. *Perception and Psychophysics, 32*, 542–550.

Kuhl, P. K. & Padden, D. M. (1983) Enhanced discriminability at the phonetic boundaries for the place feature in macaques. *Journal of the Acoustical Society of America, 73*, 1003–1010.

Kuksht, M. I. (1975). *Electromyographic, aerodynamic and displacement characteristics of bilabial consonants.* Unpublished master's thesis, University of Washington.

Labov, W. (1978). *The measurement of vowel shifts.* Paper presented to the American Association of Phonetic Sciences, San Francisco, Winter meeting.

Labov, W. (1981). Resolving the Neogrammarian controversy. *Language, 57*, 267–309.

Labov, W. (in press). The three dialects of English. In P. Eckert, (Ed.), *Quantitative analyses of sound change in progress.* New York: Academic Press.

Labov, W., Yaeger, M. and Steiner, R. (1972). *A Quantitative Study of Sound Change in Progress,* U.S. Regional Survey, Philadelphia.

Lacquaniti, F., & Soechting, J. F. (1982). Coordination of arm and wrist motion during a reaching task. *Journal of Neuroscience, 2*, 399–408.

Ladefoged, P. (1964). *A phonetic study of West African languages.* Cambridge, UK: Cambridge University Press.

Ladefoged, P. (1968). The nature of general phonetic theories. In R. J. O'Brien (Ed.), *Georgetown University round table selected papers on linguistics,* Washington, DC: Georgetown University Press.

Ladefoged, P. (1971). *Preliminaries to linguistic phonetics.* Chicago: The University of Chicago Press.

Ladefoged, P. (1975). *A course in phonetics.* New York: Harcourt Brace Jovanovich.

Ladefoged, P. (1980). What are speech sounds made of? *Language, 56*,485–502.

Ladefoged, P. (1981) What are linguistic sounds made of? *Language, 56.3*, 485–502.

Ladefoged, P. & Bhaskararao, P. (1983). Non-quantal aspects of of consonant production: A study of retroflex consonants. *Journal Phonetics, 11*, 291–302.

Ladefoged, P. & Broadbent, D. E. (1957). Information conveyed by vowels. *Journal of the Acoustical Society of America, 29*, 98–104.

Ladefoged, P., DeClark, J., Lindau, M., & Papcun, G. (1972). An auditory-motor theory of speech production. *UCLA Working Papers in Phonetics, 22*, 48–75.

Ladefoged, P. & Wu, Z.-J. (1984). Places of articulation: An investigation of Pekingese fricatives and affricates. *Journal of Phonetics, 12*, 267–278.

Laferriere, M. (1982). *Effects of Stress Differences on Tongue Blade Movement in Vowel Consonant Gestures.* Unpublished paper.

Lahiri, A., & Blumstein, S. E. (1983). Acoustic invariance in speech: Contributions towards an explanation of natural rules in phonology, in preparation.

Lahiri, A., Gewirth, L. & Blumstein, S. E. (1984). A reconsideration of acoustic invariance for place of articulation in diffuse stop consonants: Evidence from a cross-language study. *Journal of the Acoustical Society of America, 76*, 391–404.

Lamel, L. F. and Zue, V. W. (1982) Performance improvement in a dynamic-programming-based isolated word recognition system for the alpha-digit task, *Proceedings of the ICASSP IEEE International Conference on Acoustics, Speech, and Signal Processing*, 558–561.

Lane, H. L. (1965). The motor theory of speech perception: A critical review. *Psychological Review, 72*, 275–309.

Larson, C. R., Byrd, K. E., Garthwaite, C. R., & Luschei, E. S. (1980). Alterations in the pattern of mastication after ablations of the lateral precentral cortex in Rhesus Macaques. *Experimental Neurology, 70*, 638–651.

Lashley, K. S. (1930). Basic neural mechanisms in behavior. *Psychological Review, 37*, 1–24.

Lasky, R. E., Syrdal-Lasky, A., & Klein, R. E. (1975). VOT discrimination by four- to six-and-a-half month old infants from Spanish environments. *Journal of Experimental Child Psychology, 20*, 213–225.

Laszlo, E. (1972). *The systems view of the world.* Oxford: Blackwell.

Lea, W. (Ed.). (1980). *Trends in speech recognition*, Englewood Cliffs, NJ: Prentice-Hall.

Lee, T. (1983). An acoustical study of the register distinction in Mon. *UCLA Working Papers in Phonetics, 57*, 79–96.

Lehiste, I. (1970). *Suprasegmentals.* Cambridge, MA: MIT Press.

Lehiste, I. (1971). Temporal organization of spoken language. In L. L. Hammerich, R. Jakobson, & E. Zwirner (Eds.), *Form & substance.* København: Akademisk Forlag.

Lehiste, I. (1972). The timing of utterances and linguistic boundaries. *Journal of the Acoustical Society of America, 51*, 2018–2024.

Lehiste, I. (1973). Rhythmic units and syntactic units in production and perception. *Journal of the Acoustical Society of America, 54*, 1228–1234.

Lehiste, I. (1977). Isochrony reconsidered. *Journal of Phonetics, 5*, 253–263.

Lehiste, I. (1983). The role of prosody in the internal structuring of a sentence. In S. Hattori & K. Inoue, (Eds.), *Proceedings of the XIIIth International Congress of Linguists.* Tokyo, pp. 220–231.

Lehiste, I. & Peterson, G. (1961). Transitions, glides, and diphthongs. *Journal of the Acoustical Society of America, 33*, 268–277.

Lehiste, I., & Shockey, L. (1972). On the perception of coarticulation effects in English VCV syllables. *Journal of Speech and Hearing Research, 15*, 500–506.

Lehtonen, J. (1970). Aspects of quantity in standard Finnish. *Studia Philologica Jyväskyläensia, 6.*

Leinonen, L., & Nyman, G., II (1979). Functional properties of cells in anterolateral part of area 7 associative face area of awake monkeys. *Experimental Brain Research, 34*, 321–333.

Lempert, H., & Kinsbourne, M. (1982). Effect of laterality of orientation on verbal memory. *Neuropsychologia, 20*, 211–214.

Lenneberg, E. H. (1967). *Biological foundations of language.* New York: Wiley.

Lennig, Matthew (1978). *Acoustic measurement of linguistic change: The modern Paris vowel system.* PhD dissertation, University of Pennsylvania.

Leonard, L. B., Newhoff, M., & Mesalam, L. (1980). Individual differences in early child phonology. *Applied Psycholinguistics, 1*, 7–30.

Leonard, L. B., Rowan, L. E., Morris, M., & Fey, M. E. (1982). Intra-word phonological variability in young children. *Journal of Child Language, 9*, 55–69.

Leopold, W. F. (1947). *Speech development of a bilingual child. Vol. 2. Sound learning in the first two years.* Evanston, IL: Northwestern University Press.

Leopold, W. F. (1953). Patterning in children's language learning. *Language Learning, 5,* 1 14. Repr. in A. Bar Adon & W. F. Leopold (Eds.), *Child language: A book of readings.* Englewood Cliffs, NJ: Prentice-Hall, 1971.

Levy, J. (1974). Psychobiological implications of bilateral asymmetry. In S. J. Dimond & J. G. Beaumont (Eds.), *Hemisphere function in the human brain.* London: Elek.

Lewis, M. M. (1951). *Infant speech: A study of the beginnings of language,* 2nd ed. London: Routledge & Kegan Paul.

Liberman, A. M. (1981). On finding that speech is special. *Haskins Laboratories Status Report on Speech Research, July Dec. 1981,* 107-144.

Liberman, A. M. (1982). On finding that speech is special. *American Psychologist, 37,* 148-167.

Liberman, A. M., Cooper, F. S., Shankweiler, D. P., & Studdert-Kennedy, M (1967). Perception of the speech code. *Psychological Reviews, 74,* 431-461.

Liberman, A. M., Delattre, P. C., & Cooper, F. S. (1952). The role of selected stimulus variables in the perception of the unvoiced stop consonants. *American Journal of Psychology, 65,* 497-516.

Liberman, A. M., Harris, K. S., Kinney, J. A., & Lane, H. (1961). The discrimination of relative-onset time of the components of certain speech and nonspeech patterns. *Journal of Experimental Psychology, 61,* 379-388.

Liberman, A. M., Isenberg, D., & Rakerd, B. (1981). Duplex perception of cues for stop consonants: Evidence for a phonetic mode. *Perception and Psychophysics, 30,* 133-141.

Liberman, A. M., & Pisoni, D. B. (1977). Evidence for a special speech-processing subsystem in the human. In T. H. Bullock (Ed.), *Recognition of complex acoustic signals.* Weinheim, Germany: Chemie GmbH.

Liberman, I. Y., & Shankweiler, D. (1979). Speech, the alphabet, and teaching to read. In L. Resnick & P. Weaver (Eds.), *Theory and practice of early reading,* Hillsdale, NJ: Lawrence Erlbaum Associates.

Liberman, I. Y., Shankweiler, D., Fisher, F. W., & Carter, B. (1974). Explicit syllable and phoneme segmentation in the young child. *Journal of Experimental Child Psychology, 18,* 201-212.

Liberman, I. Y., Shankweiler, D., Orlando, C., Harris, K. S., & Berti, F. B. (1971). Letter confusions and reversals of sequence in the beginning reader: Implications for Orton's theory of development dyslexia. *Cortex, 7,* 127-142.

Liberman, M. C. (1978). Auditory nerve response from cats raised in a low-noise chamber. *Journal of the Acoustical Society of America, 63,* 442-455.

Liberman, M. C. (1982). Single-neuron labelling in the cat auditory nerve. *Science, 216,* 1239-1241.

Liberman, M. C. & Streeter, L. A. (1978). Use of nonsense-syllable mimicry in the study of prosodic phenomena. *Journal of the Acoustical Society of America, 63,* 231-233.

Lieberman, P. (1970). Towards a unified phonetic theory. *Linguistic Inquiry, 1,* 307-322.

Lieberman, P. (1975). *On the origins of language: An introduction to the evolution of human speech.* New York: MacMillan.

Lieberman, P. (1984). *The biology and evolution of language.* Cambridge, MA: Harvard University Press.

Liljencrants, J. & Lindblom, B. (1972). Numerical simulation of vowel quality systems: The role of perceptual contrast. *Language, 48,* 839-862.

Lindau Webb, M. (1983). *Tone and Intonation in Hausa.* Paper presented to the Tenth International Congress of Phonetic Sciences, Utrecht, Holland.

Lindau, M. (1975). Features for vowels. *UCLA Working Papers in Phonetics, 30,* 1-155.

Lindau, M. (1978). Vowel features. *Language, 54.3,* 541-563.

Lindau, M. (1979). The feature expanded. *Journal of Phonetics, 7,* 163-176.

Lindau, M. (1982). Phonetic differences in glottalic consonants. *UCLA Working Papers in Phonetics, 54,* 66-78.

Lindau, M. (1985). The story of [r]. In V. Fromkin (Ed.) *Phonetic linguistics.* New York: Academic Press.

Lindblom, B. (1963). Spectographic study of vowel reduction. *Journal of the Acoustical Society of America*, 35, 1773-1781.

Lindblom, B. (1963). Spectrographic study of vowel reduction. *Journal of the Acoustical Society of America*, 35, 1773-1781.

Lindblom, B. (1982). The interdisciplinary challenge of speech motor control. In S. Grillner, B. Lindblom, J. Lubker, & A. Person (Eds.), *Speech motor control*. London: Pergamon Press.

Lindblom, B. (1983). Economy of speech gestures. In P. F. MacNeilage (Ed.), *The production of speech*. New York: Springer-Verlag.

Lindblom, B. (1983). On the teleological nature of speech processes. *Speech Communication*, 2, 155-158.

Lindblom, B. (1984). Can the models of evolutionary biology be applied to phonetic problems? In M. P. R. v.d. Broecke & A. Cohen (Eds.), *Proceedings of the Tenth International Congress of Phonetic Sciences*, Dordrecht: Foris, 67-81.

Lindblom, B., Lubker, J., & Gay, T. (1979). Format frequencies of some fixed mandible vowels and a model of speech motor programming by predictive simulation. *Journal of Phonetics*, 7, 147-161.

Lindblom, B., MacNeilage, P. F., & Studdert-Kennedy, M. G. (1983a). Self organizing processes and the explanation of phonological universals. In B. Butterworth, B. Comrie & O. Dahl (Eds.), *Explanations of linguistic universals*. The Hague: Mouton.

Lindblom, B., MacNeilage, P., & Studdert-Kennedy, M. (1983b). *The selection theory of phonological pattern formation*. Manuscript.

Lindblom, B., MacNeilage, P., & Studdert-Kennedy, M. (In preparation). *The biological bases of spoken language*, San Francisco: Academic Press.

Lindblom, B. & Rapp, K. (1973). Some temporal regularities of spoken Swedish. *Papers in Linguistics from the University of Stockholm*, 21, 1-59.

Lindblom, B. & Sundberg, J. (1971). Acoustical Consequences of lip, tongue, jaw and larynx movement. *Journal of the Acoustical Society of America*, 50, 1166-1179.

Linville, R. (1982). Temporal aspects of articulation: Some inplications for speech motor control of stereotyped productions. Unpublished doctoral dissertation, University of Iowa, Iowa City, Iowa.

Lisker, Leigh (1948). The distinction between [æ] and [e]: a problem in acoustic analysis. *Language*, 24, 397-407.

Lisker, L. (1957). Closure duration and the intervocalic voiced-voiceless distinction in English. *Language*, 33, 42-49.

Lisker, L. (1978). Rapid vs rabid: A catalogue of acoustic features that may cue the distinction. *Haskins Laboratories, Status Report on Speech Research, SR-54*, 127-132.

Lisker, L. & Abramson, A. S. (1964). A cross-language study of voicing in initial stops: Acoustical measurements," *Word*, 20, 384-422.

Lisker, L., & Abramson, A. (1971). Distinctive features and laryngeal control. *Language*, 47, 767-785.

Local, J. (1983). How many vowels in a vowel? *Journal of Child Language*, 10, 449-453.

Locke, J. (1983). *Phonological acquisition and change*. New York: Academic Press.

Lowerre, B. T., & Reddy, D. R. (1980). The harpy speech understanding system. In W.A. Lea, (Ed.), *Trends in speech-recognition*, Englewood-Cliffs: Prentice-Hall.

Lubker, J. F. (1968). An electromyographic-cinefluorographic investigation of velar function during normal speech production. *Cleft Palate Journal*, 5, 1-18.

Lubker, J. F. (1981). Temporal aspects of speech production: Anticipatory labial coarticulation. *Phonetica*, 38: 51-65.

Luce, P. A., & Charles-Luce, J. (1983). Contextual effects on the consonant/vowel ratio in speech production. *Research on speech perception: progress report no. 9*. Bloomington, IN: Speech Research Laboratory, Indiana University.

Lund, J. P., & Lamarre, Y. (1974). Activity of neurons in the lower precentral cortex during voluntary and rhythmical jaw movements in the monkey. *Experimental Brain Research*, 19, 282-289.

Luschei, E. S., & Goodwin, G. M. (1975). Role of monkey precentral cortex in control of voluntary jaw movements. *Journal of Neurophysiology*, 38, 146-157.

Lyon, R. F. (1982). A Computational Model of Filtering, Detection, and Compression in the Cochlea, *Proc. IEEE ICASSP 82*, Paris.

Löfqvist, A. (1975). Intrinsic and extrinsic F_0 variations in Swedish tonal accents. *Phonetica, 31*, 228–247.

Löfqvist, A., & Yoshioka, H. (1980). Laryngeal-oral coordination in American English obstruent production. *Journal of the Acoustical Society of America, 68*, S102(A).

Löfqvist, A., & Yoshioka, H. (1981). Interarticulator programming in obstruent production. *Phonetica, 38*, 21–34.

Mack, M. and Blumstein, S. E. (1983). Further evidence of acoustic invariance in speech production: The stop-glide contrast. *Journal of the Acoustical Society of America, 73*, 1739–1750.

MacKain, K. S. (1982). Assessing the role of experience in infant speech discrimination. *Journal of Child Language, 9*, 527–542.

MacKain, K. S. (In press). Speaking without a tongue. *National Student, Language and Hearing Association Journal.*

MacKain, K. S., Best, C. T., & Strange, W. (1981). Categorical perception of English [r] and [l] by Japanese bilinguals. *Applied Psycholinguistics, 2*, 369–390.

MacKain, K. S., Studdert-Kennedy, M., Spieker, S., & Stern, D. (1983). Infant intermodal speech perception is a left hemisphere function. *Science, 219*, 1347–1349.

Macken, M. A. (1979). Developmental reorganization of phonology: A hierarchy of basic units of acquisition. *Lingua, 49*, 11–49.

Macken, M. A. (1980). Aspects of the acquisition of stop systems: A cross linguistic perspective. In G. Yeni-Komshian, J. F. Kavanagh & C. A. Ferguson (Eds.), *Child phonology (Vol. 1)*, New York: Academic Press.

Macken, M. A., & Barton, D. (1980a). The acquisition of the voicing contrast in English: A study of voice-onset time in word-initial stop consonants. *Journal of Child Language, 7*, 41–74.

Macken, M., & Barton, D. (1980b). A longitudinal study of the voicing contrast in American English word-initial stops, as measured by voice onset time. *Journal of Child Language, 7*, 41–74.

Macken, M. A., & Ferguson, C. A. (1983). Cognitive aspects of phonological development: Model, evidence, and issues. In K. E. Nelson (Ed.), *Children's language* (Vol. 4). Hillsdale, NJ: Lawrence Erlbaum Associates.

MacNeilage, P. F. (1970). The motor control of serial ordering in speech, *Psychological Review, 77*, 182–196.

MacNeilage, P. F. (1972). Speech physiology. In J. Gilbert (Ed.), *Speech and cortical functioning.* New York: Academic Press.

MacNeilage, P. F. (1980). Distinctive properties of speech control. In G. E. Stelmach & J. Requin (Eds.), *Tutorials in motor behavior.* Amsterdam: Elsevier North-Holland.

MacNeilage, P. F. (1983, October). *Planning and production of speech.* Fourth Silverman Lecture, Central Institute for the Deaf, St. Louis, MO.

MacNeilage, P. F., & DeClerk, J. (1969). On the motor control of coarticulation in CVC monosyllables. *Journal of the Acoustical Society of America, 45*, 1217–1233.

MacNeilage, P. F., Hutchinson, J., & Lasater, S. (1981). The production of speech: Development and dissolution of motoric and premotoric processes. In J. Long & A. Baddeley (Eds.). *Attention and performance IX.* Hillsdale, NJ: Lawrence Erlbaum Associates.

MacNeilage, P. F., Studdert-Kennedy, M., & Lindblom, B. (1984). Functional precursors to language and its lateralization. *American Journal of Physiology, 246 (Regulatory, Integrative and Comparative Physiology, 15)*, R912–R914.

MacNeilage, P. F., Studdert-Kennedy, M., & Lindblom, B. *Primate handedness reconsidered.* Manuscript.

Mann, V. A., & Liberman, A. M. (1983). Some differences between phonetic and auditory modes of perception. *Cognition, 14*, 211–235.

Mann, V. A. & Repp, B. H. (1980). Influence of vocalic context on perception of the [š] vs [s] distinction. *Perception & Psychophysics, 28*, 213–228.

Markel, J. D. (1972). The SIFT algorithm for fundamental frequency estimation, *IEEE Trans. on Audio and Electroacoustics, AU-20*, 367–377.

Marslen-Wilson, W. D. (1980). Speech understanding as a psychological process. In J. D. Simon (Ed.), *Spoken language generation and recognition,* Dordrecht: Reidel.

Marslen-Wilson, W. D., & Welsh, A. (1978). Processing interactions and lexical access during word recognition in continuous speech. *Cognitive Psychology, 10,* 29–63.

Martin, J. G., & Bunnell, H. T. (1981). Perception of anticipatory coarticulation effects. *Journal of the Acoustical Society of America, 69,* 559–567.

Martin, J. G., & Bunnell, H. T. (1982). Perception of anticipatory coarticulation effects in Vowel-Stop Consonant-Vowel Sequences. *Journal of Experimental Psychology: Human Perception and Performance, 8,* 473–488.

Martinet, A. (1955). *Économie de changements phonétiques.* Berne: Francke.

Martinet, A. (1968). Phonetics and linguistic evolution. In B. Malmberg (Ed.), *Manual of phonetics.* Amsterdam: North-Holland.

Massaro, D. M., & Cohen, M. M. (1976). The contribution of fundamental frequency and voice onset time to the /si/-/zi/ distinction, *Journal of the Acoustical Society of America, 60,* 1059–65.

Mathes, R. C., & Miller, R. L. (1947). Phase effects in monaural perception. *Journal of the Acoustical Society of America, 19,* 780–797.

Maxwell, E. (1982). *A study of misarticulation from a linguistic perspective.* PhD dissertation, Indiana University. Distributed by the Indiana Universtiy Linguistics Club, Bloomington, IN.

Maxwell, E. and Weismer, G. (December 1979). *On the acoustic differentiation of /d/ in a deviant phonology.* Paper presented at the Winter meeting of the Linguistics Society of America, Los Angeles CA.

Maxwell, E., & Weismer, G. (1982). The contribution of phonological, acoustic and perceptual techniques to the characterization of a misarticulating child's voice contrast for stops. *Journal of Applied Psycholinguistics, 3,* 29–43.

Mayr, E. (1942). *Systematics and the origin of species,* New York: Columbia University Press.

Mayr, E. (1974). Behavior programs and evolutionary strategies. *American Scientist, 62,* 650–659.

McCandless, S. (1974). An algorithm for automatic formant extraction using linear prediction spectra. *IEEE Transactions on Acoustics, Speech and Signal Processing, ASSP-22,* No. 2.

McCawley, J. D. (1967). The phonological component of a grammar of Japanese. The Hague: Mouton.

McClelland, J. L., & Elman, J. L. (In preparation). The TRACE model of speech perception.

McClelland, J. L., & Rumelhart, D. E. (1981). An interactive activation model of context effects in letter perception. Part I: An account of basic findings. *Psychological Review, 88,* 375–407.

McGurk, H., & MacDonald, J. (1976). Hearing lips and seeing voices. *Nature, 264,* 746–748.

Mehler, J., Barrière, M., & Jasik-Gerschenfeld, D. (1976). La reconnaissance de la voix maternelle par le nourrisson. *La Recherche, 70,* 787–788.

Meltzoff, A. N. (1985). Imitation: Data and theories in the study of infant development. In J. Mehler & R. Fox (Eds.), *Neonate cognition: Beyond the blooming, buzzing confusion.* Hillsdale, NJ: Lawrence Erlbaum Associates.

Meltzoff, A. N., & Moore, M. K. (1977). Imitation of facial and manual gestures by human neonates. *Science, 198,* 175–178.

Menn, L. (1971). Phonotactic rules in beginning speech. *Lingua, 26,* 225–251.

Menn, L. (1976). Evidence for an interactionist-discovery theory of child phonology. *Papers and Reports on Child Language Development, 12,* 169–177.

Menn, L. (1978a). Pattern, control, and contrast in beginning speech: a case study in the development of word form and word function. Bloomington, IN: Indiana University Linguistics Club.

Menn, L. (1978b). Phonological units in beginning speech. In A. Bell & J. B. Hooper (Eds.), *Syllables and segments.* Amsterdam: North-Holland.

Menn, L. (1979). Transition and variation in child phonology: Modeling a developing system. *Proceedings of the Ninth International Congress of Phonetic Sciences* (Vol. II). Copenhagen: Institute of Phonetics, University of Copenhagen.

Menn, L. (1980). Phonological theory and child phonology. In G. H. Yeni-Komshian, J. F. Kavanagh, & C. A. Ferguson, (Eds.), *Child phonology* (Vol. 1). New York: Academic Press.

Menn, L. (1983, March). *Language acquisition, aphasia and phonotactic universals.* Paper presented at 12th Annual University of Wisconsin-Milwaukee Linguistics Symposium.

Menn, L. (1983). Development of articulatory, phonetic, and phonological capabilities. In B. Butterworth (Ed.), *Language production* (Vol II.) London: Academic Press.

Menyuk, P. (1977). *Language and maturation.* Cambridge, MA: MIT Press.

Menyuk, P. (1978). Linguistic problems in children with developmental aphasia. In M. S. Wyke (Ed.), *Developmental dysphasia.* London: Academic Press.

Menyuk, P. (1979). The measurement of linguistic competence over the first five years of life. In R. Kearlsey and I. Sigel (Eds.), *Infants at risk: Assessment of cognitive functioning.* Hillsdale NJ: Lawrence Erlbaum Associates.

Menyuk, P. (1980). The role of context in misarticulations. In G. Yeni-komshien, J. Kavanagh, & C. Ferguson (Eds.), *Child phonology, Vol I.* New York: Academic Press.

Menyuk, P., & Menn, L. (1979). Early strategies for the perception and production of words and sounds. In P. Fletcher & M. Garman (Eds.), *Language acquisition.* Cambridge: Cambridge University Press.

Menzerath, P., & de Lacerda, A. (1933). *Koartikulation steuerung und lautabgrenzung.* Bonn: Ferdinand Dümmlers Verlag.

Merzenich, M. M., Michelson, R. P., Petit, R. C., Schindler, R. A., & Reid, M. (1973). Neural encoding of sound sensation evoked by electrical stimulation of the acoustic nerve. *Annals of Otology, Rhinology and Laryngology, 82,* 486–503.

Michailovsky, B. (1975). On some Tibeto-Burman sound changes. *Berkeley Linguistic Society, Proceedings of the annual meeting, 1,* 322–332.

Miller, C. L., Morse, P. A., & Dorman, M. (1977). Cardiac indices of infant speech perception: Orienting and burst discrimination. *Quarterly Journal of Experimental Psychology, 29,* 533–545.

Miller, G. A. (1977). *Spontaneous apprentices.* New York: The Seabury Press.

Miller, J. D. (1967). An acoustical study of Broŭ vowels. *Phonetica, 17,* 149–177.

Miller, J. D. (1982). A phonetically-relevant auditory-perceptual space. *Journal of the Acoustical Society of America, 72,* S64.

Miller, J. D., Engebretson, A. M., & Vemula, N. R. (1980). Observations on the acoustic description of vowels as spoken by children, women, and men, *Journal of the Acoustical Society of America, 68,* 533(A).

Miller, J. D., Wier, L., Pastore, R., Kelly, W., & Dooling, R. (1976). Discrimination and labeling of noise-buzz sequences with varying noise-lead times: An example of categorical perception. *Journal of the Acoustical Society of America, 60,* 410–417.

Miller, J. L. (1977). Properties of feature detectors for VOT: The voiceless channel of analysis. *Journal of the Acoustical Society of America, 62,* 641–648.

Miller, J. L. (1980). Contextual effects in the discrimination of stop consonants and semivowels. *Perception and Psychophysics, 28,* 93–95.

Miller, J. L. (1981). Effects of speaking rate on segmental distinctions. In P. D. Eimas & J. L. Miller (Eds.), *Perspectives on the study of speech,* Hillsdale, NJ: Lawrence Erlbaum Associates.

Miller, J. L. & Baer, T. (1983). Some effects of speaking rate on the production of /b/ and /w/. *Journal of the Acoustical Society of America, 73,* 1751-1755.

Miller, J. L., & Eimas, P. D. (1979). Organization in Infant Speech Perception. *Canadian Journal of Psychology 33(4),* 353–367.

Miller, J. L., & Eimas, P. D. (1983). Studies on the categorization of speech by infants. *Cognition, 13,* 135–165.

Miller, J. L., & Grosjean, F. (1981). How the components of speaking rate influence perception of phonetic segments. *Journal of Experimental Psychology: Human Perception and Performance, 1,* 208–215.

Miller, J. L., & Liberman, A. M. (1979). Some effects of later-occurring information on the perception of stop consonant and semivowel. *Perception & Psychophysics, 25,* 457–465.

Miller, M. I., & Sachs, M. B. (1983). Representation of stop consonants in the discharge patterns of auditory nerve fibers. *Journal of the Acoustical Society of America, 74,* 502–517.

Milner, B. (1974). Hemispheric specialization: Scope and limitations. In F. O. Schmidt & F. G. Worden (Eds.), *The neurosciences: Third study program.* Cambridge, MA: MIT Press.

Milner, B., Branch, C., & Rasmussen, T. (1964). Observations on cerebral dominance. In V.S. DeReuck & M. O'Connor (Eds.), *Disorders of language* (Ciba Foundation Symposium). London: J. & A. Churchill.

Miyawaki, K., Strange, W., Verbrugge, R., Liberman, A. M., Jenkins, J. J., & Fujimura, O. (1975). An effect of linguistic experience: The discrimination of |r| and |l| by native speakers of Japanese and English. *Perception & Psychophysics, 18,* 331–340.

Mkanganwi, K. G. (1972). The relationship of coastal Ndau to the Shona dialects of the interior. *African Studies, 31,* 111–137.

Moffit, A. R. (1971). Consonant cue perception by twenty- to twenty-four-week-old infants. *Child Development, 42,* 717–731.

Mohr, J. P. (1976). Broca's area and Broca's aphasia. In H. Whitaker & H. Whitaker (Eds.), *Studies in neurolinguistics* (Vol. 1). New York: Academic Press.

Mohr, J. P., Pessin, M. S., Finkelstein, M. D., Funkenstein, S., Duncan, G. W., & Davis, K. R. (1978). Broca aphasia: Pathologic and clinical. *Neurology, 28,* 311–324.

Molfese, D. L. (1977). Infant cerebral asymmetry. In S. J. Segalowitz & F. A. Gruber (Eds.), *Language development and neurological theory.* New York: Academic Press.

Molfese, D. L., Freeman, R. B., & Palermo, D. S. (1975). The ontogeny of brain lateralization for speech and nonspeech stimuli. *Brain and Language, 2,* 356–368.

Moll, K. L., & Daniloff, R. G. (1971). Investigation of the timing of velar movements during speech. *Journal of the Acoustical Society of America, 50,* 678–684.

Moll, K., Zimmerman, G. N. & Smith, A. (1977). The study of speech production as a human neuromotor system: In M. Sawashima and F. Cooper (Eds.), *Dynamic aspects of speech production.* Tokyo: Univ. of Tokyo Press

Moll, K., & Shriner, T. (1967). Preliminary investigation of a new concept of velar activity during speech. *Cleft Palate Journal, 5,* 58–69.

Morais, J., Cary, L., Alegria, J., & Bertelson, P. (1979). Does awareness of speech as a sequence of phones arise spontaneously? *Cognition, 7,* 323–331.

Morasso, P. (1981). Spatial control of movement. *Experimental Brain Research, 42,* 223-227.

Morse, P. A. (1972). The discrimination of speech and nonspeech stimuli in early infancy. *Journal of Experimental Child Psychology, 14,* 477–492.

Morse, P. A., (1976). Speech perception in the human infant and rhesus monkey. *Annals of the New York Academy of Sciences, 280,* 694–707.

Morse, P. A. & Snowden, C. (1975). An investigation of categorical speech discrimination by rhesus monkeys. *Perceptual Psychophysiology, 17,* 9–16.

Morton, J. (1964). A preliminary functional model for language behaviour. *International Audiology, 3,* 1–10.

Moskowitz, A. I. (1970). The two-year-old stage in the acquisition of English phonology. *Language, 46,* 426–441.

Moskowitz, A. I. (1973). The acquisition of phonology and syntax. In K.K.J. Hintikka, J.M.E. Moravsik, & P. Suppes (Eds.), *Approaches to natural language.* Dordrechts, Netherlands: Reidel.

Mountcastle, V. B., Lynch, J. C., Georgopoulos, A., Sakata, H., & Acuna, C. (1975). Posterior parietal association cortex of the monkey: Command functions for operations within extrapersonal space. *Journal of Neurophysiology, 38,* 871–907.

Muakkassa, K. F., & Strick, P. L. (1979). Frontal lobe inputs to primate motor cortex: Evidence for four somatotopically organized 'premotor' areas. *Brain Research, 177,* 176–182.

Munhall, K. (submitted). Relative timing of tongue dorsum movements. *Journal of the Acoustical Society of America.*

Myers, C. S., & Rabiner, L. R. (1981). A level building dynamic time warping algorithm for connected word-recognition, *IEEE ICASSP 81*, 951–955.

Müller, C. G. (1981). Survey of cochlear implant work. *Journal of the Acoustical Society of America*, 70, S52 (Abstract).

Nakatani, L. H., & Dukes, K. D. (1977). Locus of segmental cues for word juncture. *Journal of the Acoustical Society of America*, 62, 714–719.

Nearey, T. (1977). Phonetic feature systems for vowels, PhD. dissertation, University of Connecticut, Storrs, CT.

Nearey, T. (1978). *Phonetic features for vowels.* Bloomington, IN: Indiana University Linguistics Club.

Neary, T. (1977). *Phonetic feature systems for vowels.* PhD dissertation, University of Connecticut.

Neisser, U. (1976). *Cognition and reality.* San Francisco: W. H. Freeman.

Nelson, W. L. (1983). Physical principles for economies of skilled movements. *Biological Cybernetics, 46*: 135–147.

Neville, H. J. (1980). Event-related potentials in neuropsychological studies of language. *Brain and Language, 11*, 300–318.

Neville, H. J., Kutas, M., & Schmidt, A. (1982). Event-related potential studies of cerebral specialization during reading. *Brain and Language, 16*, 316–337.

Newell, A. (1979). Harpy, production systems, and human cognition, In R. Cole, ed., *Perception and production of fluent speech*, Hillsdale, NJ: Lawrence Erlbaum Associates.

Nocerino, N. (1984). *Comparison of several distance metrics in a speech-recognition task*, Masters Thesis, MIT.

Nooteboom, S. G. (1972). *Production and perception of vowel duration.* PhD thesis, University of Utrecht.

Nooteboom, S. G. (1980). Speaking and unspeaking: Detection and correction of phonological and lexical errors in spontaneous speech. In V. A. Fromkin (Ed.), *Errors in linguistic performance.* New York: Academic Press.

Nooteboom, S. G. (1983). Is speech production controlled by speech perception: In M. van den Broecke, V. van Heuven, & W. Zonneveld (Eds.), *Sound structures.* Dordrecht: Foris Publications.

Nusbaum, H. C., Schwab, E. C., & Sawusch, J. R. (1983). The role of "chirp" identification in duplex perception. *Perception & Psychophysics, 33*, 323–332.

O'Brien, J. H., Pimpaneau, A., & Albe-Fessard, D. (1971). Evoked cortical responses to vagal, laryngeal and facial afferents in monkeys under chloralose anesthesia. *Electroencephalography and Clinical Neurophysiology, 31*, 7–20.

Oden, G. C. & Massaro, D. W. (1978). Integration of featural information in speech production, *Psychological Review, 85*, 172–91.

Ohala, J. J. (1974a). Phonetic explanation in phonology. In A. Bruck, R. A. Fox, & M. W. LaGaly (Eds.), *Papers from the parasession on natural phonology.* Chicago: Chicago Linguistic Society.

Ohala, J. J. (1974b). Experimental Historical Phonology. In J. M. Anderson and C. Jones, (Eds.), *Historical linguistics II: Theory and description in phonology*, Amsterdam: North-Holland.

Ohala, J. J. (1975a). Phonetic explanations for nasal sound patterns. In C. A. Ferguson, L. M. Hyman, & J. J. Ohala (Eds.), *Nasalfest: Papers from a symposium on nasals and nasalization.* Stanford: Language Universals Project.

Ohala, J. J. (1975b). The temporal regulation of speech. In G. Fant & M. A. A. Tatham (Eds.), *Auditory analysis and perception of speech.* London: Academic Press.

Ohala, J. J. (1978a). Phonological notations as models. In W. U. Dressler & W. Meid (Eds.), *Proceedings of the 12th International Congress of Linguists, Vienna, August 28–September 2, 1977.* Innsbruck: Inssbrüker Bieträge zur Sprachwissenschaft.

Ohala, J. J. (1978b). Southern Bantu vs. the world: the case of palatalization of labials. *Berkeley Linguistic Society, Proceedings of the annual meeting, 4*, 370–386.

Ohala, J. J. (1979). Universals of labial velars and de Saussure's chess analogy. *Proceedings of the 9th International Congress of Phonetic Sciences, Volume 2.* Copenhagen: Institute of Phonetics.

Ohala, J. J. (1980). The application of phonological universals in speech pathology. In L. J. Lass (Ed.), *Speech and language. Advances in basic research and practice.* New York: Academic Press.

Ohala, J. J. (1981a). The listener as a source of sound change. In C. S. Masek, R. A. Hendrick, & M. F. Miller (Eds.), *Papers from the parasession on language and behavior.* Chicago: Chicago Linguistic Society.

Ohala, J. J. (1981b). Articulatory constraints on the cognitive representation of speech. In T. Myers, J. Laver, & J. Anderson (Eds.), *The cognitive representation of speech.* Amsterdam: North Holland Press.

Ohala, J. J. (1982a). The phonological end justifies any means. *Preprints of the plenary session papers, 13th International Congress of Linguists, Tokyo.* Tokyo: ICL Editorial Committee.

Ohala, J. J. (1982b). Physiological mechanisms underlying tone and intonation. In H. Fujisaki & E. Gårding (Eds.), *Preprints, Working Group on Intonation, 13th International Congress of Linguists, 29 August - 4 September 1982, Tokyo.* Tokyo:

Ohala, J. J. (1983a). The direction of sound change. In A. Cohen & M.P.R.v.d. Broecke (Eds.), *Abstracts of the Tenth International Congress of Phonetic Sciences,* Dordrecht: Foris.

Ohala, J. J. (1983b). The origin of sound patterns in vocal tract constraints. In P. F. MacNeilage (Ed.), *The production of speech.* New York: Springer-Verlag.

Ohala, J. J., Kawasaki, H., Riordan, C., & Caisse, M. (In press). The influence of consonant environment upon the perception of vowel quality. Forthcoming.

Ohala, J. J., & Lorentz, J. (1977). The story of [w]: An exercise in the phonetic explanation for sound patterns. *Berkeley Linguistic Society, Proceedings of the annual meeting, 2,* 133–155.

Ohala, J. J., Lyberg, B. (1976). Comments on "Temporal interactions within a phrase and sentence context." *Journal of the Acoustical Society of America, 59,* 990–992.

Ohala, J. J., Riordan, C. J. (1979). Passive vocal tract enlargement during voiced stops. In J. J. Wolf & D. H. Klatt (Eds.), *Speech communication papers.* New York: Acoustical Society America.

Ohde, R. N., & Sharf, D. J. (1977). Order effect of acoustic segments of VC and CV syllables on stop and vowel identification. *Journal of Speech & Hearing Research, 20,* 543–554.

Ohde, R. N., & Stevens, K. N. (1983). Effect of burst amplitude on the perception of stop consonant place of articulation. *Journal of the Acoustical Society of America, 74,* 706-725.

Öhman, S. E. G. (1966). Coarticulation of VCV utterances: Spectrographic measurements. *Journal of the Acoustical Society of America, 39:* 151–168.

Öhman, S. (1967a). Studies of articulatory coordination, *Quarterly Progress and Status Report, Speech Transmission Laboratory, 1,* 15–20. Royal Institute of Technology, Stockholm.

Öhman, S. (1967b). Word and sentence intonation: A quantitative model, *Quarterly Progress Status Report, Speech Transmission Laboratory, 2/3,* 20–54. Royal Institute of Technology, Stockholm.

Oishi, H. & Uemura, Y. (Eds.). (1975). *Hogen to Hyojungo–Nihongo hogengaku gaisetsu,* Tokyo: Chikuma Shobo.

Oller, D. K. (1980). The emergence of the sounds of speech in infancy. In G. H. Yeni-Komshian, J. F. Kavanagh, & C.A. Ferguson (Eds.), *Child phonology* (Vol. 1). New York: Academic Press.

Oller, D. K. (1981). The emergence of the sounds of speech in infancy. In G. H. Yeni-Komshian et al. (Eds.), *Child phonology, Vol. I, Production.* New York, Academic Press.

Oller, D. K., & Eilers, R. E. (1983). Speech identification in Spanish- and English-learning two-year-olds. *Journal of Speech and Hearing Research, 26,* 50–53.

Oller, D. K., & MacNeilage, P. F. (1983). Development of speech production: Perspectives from natural and perturbed speech. In P. F. MacNeilage, (Ed.), *The production of speech.* New York: Springer-Verlag.

Oller, D. K., Wieman, L. A., Doyle, W., & Ross, C. (1975). Infant babbling and speech. *Journal of Child Language, 3,* 1–11.

Osherson, D. N., & Smith, E. E. (1981). On the adequacy of prototype theory as a theory of concepts. *Cognition, 9,* 35–58.

Osherson, D. N., & Wasow, T. (1976). Task-specificity and species-specificity in the study of language: A methodological note. *Cognition, 4*, 203–214.

Paliwal, K. K., Lindsay, D. & Ainsworth, W. A. (1983). Correlation between production and perception of English vowels. *Journal of Phonetics, 11*, 77–83.

Pastore, R. E., Ahroon, W. A., Buffuto, K. A., Friedman, C. J., Puleo, J. S., & Fink, E. A. (1977). Common factor model of categorical perception. *Journal of Experimental Psychology: Human Perception and Performance, 4*, 686–696.

Perkell, J. S. (1969). Physiology of speech production. *Research Monograph* (Number 53), Cambridge, MA: MIT Press.

Perkell, J. S. (1980). Phonetic features and the physiology of speech production. In B. Butterworth (Ed.), *Language production*. London: Academic Press.

Perkell, J. S. (1983). Individual and possible language-related differences in two aspects of coarticulation: Time of beginning of anticipation and the production of "troughs", *Proceedings of the Tenth International Congress of Phonetic Sciences.* Utrecht, The Netherlands.

Perkell, J. S., Boyce, S. E., & Stevens, K. N. (1979). Articulatory and acoustic correlates of the [s–š] distinction. *Journal of the Acoustical Society of America, 65*, Supplement 1, S24.

Peterson, G. & Barney, H. (1952). Control methods used in a study of the vowels. *Journal of the Acoustical Society of America, 24*, 175–184.

Peterson, G. & Lehiste, I. (1960). Duration of syllabic nuclei in English. *Journal of the Acoustical Society of America, 32*, 693–705.

Pickett, J. M., & Decker, L. (1960). Time factors in perception of a double consonant. *Language & Speech, 3*, 11—17.

Pike, K. L. (1946). *The intonation of American English.* Ann Arbor, MI: University of Michigan Press.

Pisoni, D. B. (1976). Discrimination of brief frequency glissandos. *Research on Speech Perception.* Progress Report No. 3, Indiana University.

Pisoni, D. B. (1977). Identification and discrimination of the relative onset time of two-component tones: Implications for voicing perception in stops. *Journal of the Acoustical Society of America, 61*, 1352–1361.

Pisoni, D. B. (1982). Perception of speech: The human listener as a cognitive interface. *Speech Technology, 1*, 2, 10–23.

Pisoni, D. B., Carrell, T. D., & Gans, S. J. (1983). Perception of the duration of rapid spectrum changes: Evidence for context effects with speech and nonspeech signals. *Perception & Psychophysics 34*, 314–322.

Pisoni, D. & Hunnicutt, S. (1980). Perceptual evaluation of MITalk: the unrestricted M.I.T. text-to-speech system, *ICASSP-80*, 572–575.

Plomp, R. (1970). Timbre as a multidimensional attribute of complex tones: In R. Plomp & B. F. Smoorenburg (Eds.), *Frequency analysis and periodicity detection in hearing.* Leiden: Sijthoff.

Polanyi, M. (1969). *Knowing and being.* Chicago, IL: University of Chicago Press.

Pollack, I., & Pickett, J. M. (1963). The intelligibility of excerpts from conversation. *Language and Speech, 6*, 151–171.

Pols, L. C. W. (1979). Coarticulation and the identification of initial and final plosives. In J. Wolf and D. Klatt (Eds.) *ASA∗50 Speech Communication Papers*, pp. 459–462.

Pols, L. C. W., van der Kamp, L. J. Th., & Plomp, R. (1969). Perceptual and physical space of vowel sounds. *Journal of the Acoustical Society of America, 46*, 458–467.

Pols, L. C. W., & Schouten, M. E. H. (1978). Identification of deleted consonants. *Journal of the Acoustical Society of America, 64*, 1333–1337.

Pols, L. C. W., & Schouten, M. E. H. (1981). Identification of deleted plosives: The effect of adding noise or applying a time window. A reply to Ohde and Sharf. *Journal of the Acoustical Society of America, 69*, 301–303.

Pols, L. C. W., & Schouten, M. E. H. (forthcoming). Plosive consonants identification in ambiguous sentences.

Port, R. F. (1979). Influence of tempo on stop closure duration as a cue for voicing and place. *Journal of Phonetics, 7*, 45–56.

Port, R. F. (1981a). Linguistic timing factors in combination. *Journal of the Acoustical Society of America, 69*, 262–274.

Port, R. F. (1981b). On the structure of the phonetic space with special reference to speech timing. *Lingua, 55*, 181–219.

Port, R. F., Al-Ani, S., & Maeda, S. (1980) Temporal compensation and universal phonetics. *Phonetica, 37*, 235–266.

Port, R. F., & Dalby, J. (1982). C/V ratio as a cue for voicing in English. *Perception and Psychophysics, 2*, 141–152.

Porter, R. (1981). Intended organization of the motor cortex for input-output arrangements. In V. B. Brooks (Ed.), *Handbook of physiology, Section 1* (Vol. II: Motor control, Part 2). Bethesda, MD: American Physiological Society.

Posner, M. I., & Keele, S. W. (1968). On the genesis of abstract ideas. *Journal of Experimental Psychology 8*, 297–314.

Postal, P. (1968). *Aspects of phonological theory.* New York: Harper and Row.

Potter, R. K. & Steinberg, J. C. (1950). Towards the specification of speech. *Journal of the Acoustical Society of America, 22*, 807–820.

Prigogine, I. (1976). Order through fluctuation: Self-organization and social systems. In E. Jantsch & C. H. Waddington (Eds.), *Evolution and consciousness: Human systems in transition.* Reading, MA: Addison-Wesley.

Purnell, H. (1965). Phonology of a Yao dialect spoken in the province of Chiengrai, Thailand," *Hartford Studies in Linguistics, No. 15*, Hartford Seminary Foundation, Hartford, CT.

Rabiner, L. R., Levinson, S. E., Rosenberg, A. E., Wilpon, J. G., (1979). Speaker-independent recognition of isolated words using clustering techniques. *IEEE Transactions on Acoustics, Speech, and Signal Processing, ASSP-27, 4*, 336–349.

Rabiner, L. R. & Wilpon, J. G. (1979) Considerations in applying clustering techniques to speaker-independent word recognition, *Journal of the Acoustical Society of America, 66*, 663–673.

Rabiner, L. R. & Wilpon, J. G., (1981). Isolated word recognition using a two-pass pattern recognition approach. *Proceedings of the IEEE International Conference on Acoustics, Speech, and Signal Processing*, 724–727.

Rand, T. C. (1974). Dichotic release from masking for speech. *Journal of the Acoustical Society of America, 55*, 678–680.

Remez, R. E., Rubin, P. E., Pisoni, D. B., & Carrell, T. D. (1981). Speech perception without traditional speech cues. *Science, 212*, 947.

Repp, B. (1981). On levels of description in speech research. *Journal of the Acoustical Society of America, 69*, 1462–1464.

Repp, B. H. (1982). Phonetic trading relations and context effects: New experimental evidence for a speech mode of perception. *Psychological Bulletin, 92*, 81–110.

Repp, B. H. (1983a). Coarticulation in sequences of two nonhomorganic stop consonants: Perceptual and acoustic evidence. *Journal of the Acoustical Society of America, 74*, 420–427.

Repp, B. H. (1983b). Categorical perception: Issues, methods and findings. In N. J. Lass (Ed.), *Speech and language: Advances in basic research and practice.* New York: Academic Press.

Repp, B. H. (1983c). Phonetic and auditory trading relationships between acoustic cues in speech perception: Further results. *Haskins Laboratories Status Report on Speech Research SR-73*, 121–139.

Repp, B. H., Milburn, C., & Ashkenas, J. (1983). Duplex perception: Confirmation of fusion. *Perception & Psychophysics, 33*, 333–337.

Revoile, S., Pickett, J. M., & Holden, L. D. (1982). Acoustic cues to final stop voicing for impaired- and normal-hearing listeners. *Journal of the Acoustical Society of America, 72*, 1145–1154.

Rietveld, A. C. M. (1975). Untersuchungen zur Vokaldauer im Deutschen. *Phonetica, 31*, 248–258.

Riordan, C. (1977). Control of vocal-tract length in speech. *Journal of the Acoustical Society of America, 62*, 998.

Rosch, E. Principles of categorization (1978). In E. Rosch & B.B. Lloyd (Eds.), *Cognition and categorization*. Hillsdale, NJ: Lawrence Erlbaum Associates.

Rose, S. A., Gottfried, A.W., & Bridger, W. H. (1983). Infants' cross-modal transfer from solid objects to their graphic representations. *Child Development, 54*, 686–694.

Rosenbek, J. C., Wertz, R. T., & Darley, F. L. (1973). Oral sensation and perception in apraxia of speech and aphasia. *Journal of Speech and Hearing Research, 16*, 22–36.

Rosenblatt, F. (1962). *Principles of neurodynamics*. New York: Spartan Books.

Ruhlen, M. (1975). Patterning of nasal vowels. In C. A. Ferguson, L. M. Hyman, & J. J. Ohala (Eds.), *Nasalfest: Papers from a symposium on nasals and nasalization*. Stanford: Language Universals Project.

Ryalls, J. H. & Lieberman, P. (1982). Fundamental frequency and vowel perception. *Journal of the Acoustical Society of America, 72*, 1631–1634.

Sachs, M. B., & Abbas, P. J. (1974). Rate versus level functions for auditory nerve fibers in cats: tone-burst stimulation. *Journal of the Acoustical Society of America, 56*, 1835–1847.

Sachs, M. B., & Abbas, P. J. (1976). Phenomenological model for two-tone suppression. *Journal of the Acoustical Society of America, 60*, 1157–1163.

Sachs, M. B., & Kiang, N. Y. S. (1968). Two-tone inhibition in auditory nerve fibers. *Journal of the Acoustical Society of America, 43*, 1120–1128.

Sachs, M. B., & Young, E. D. (1979). Encoding of steady-state vowels in the auditory nerve: Representation in terms of discharge rate. *Journal of the Acoustical Society of America, 66*, 470–479.

Sachs, M. B., & Young, E. D. (1980). Effect of nonlinearities on speech encoding in the auditory nerve. *Journal of the Acoustical Society of America, 68*, 858–875.

Sachs, M. B., Young, E. D., & Miller, M. I. (1982). Encoding of speech features in the auditory nerve. In R. Carlson & B. Granstrom (Eds.), *The representation of speech in the peripheral auditory system*. Amsterdam: Elsevier Biomedical.

Sakoe, H., & Chiba, S. (1971). A dynamic programming approach to continuous speech-recognition. *Proceedings International Congress Acoustics*, paper 20C-13. Budapest, Hungary.

Sakoe, H., & Chiba, S. (1978). Dynamic programming algorithm optimization for spoken word recognition. *IEEE Transactions Acoustics, Speech, and Signal Processing, ASSP-26*, 43–49.

Saltzman, E. L., & Kelso, J. A. S. (1983). Skilled actions: A task dynamic approach. *Haskins Laboratory Status Report on Speech Research, SR-76*, 3–50.

Sankoff, David, & Labov, W. (1979). On the uses of variable rules. *Language in Society, 8*, 189–222.

Sawusch, J. R., Nusbaum, H. C., & Schwab, E. C. (1980). Contextual effects in vowel perception II: Evidence for two processing mechanisms. *Perception and Psychophysics, 27*, 421–434.

Schell, G. R., & Strick, P. L. (1983). Origin of thalamic input to the supplementary and arcuate premotor areas. *Society for Neuroscience, 9* (Part 1), 490.

Schourup, L. (1973). A cross-language study of vowel nasalization. *Ohio State Working Papers in Linguistics, 15*, 190–221.

Schouten, M. E. H., & Pols, L. C. W. (1983). Perception of plosive consonants. The relative contributions of bursts and vocalic transitions. In M. P. R. van den Broecke, V. J. van Heuven, & W. Zonneveld (Eds.), *Sound structures: Studies for Antonie Cohen*. Dordrecht: Foris Publications.

Schroeder, M. R., Atal, B. S., & Hall, J. L. (1979). Objective measure of certain speech signal degradations based on the masking properties of human auditory perception. In B. Lindblom & S. Ohman (Eds.), *Frontiers of speech communication research*, London: Academic Press.

Schwab, E. C. (1981). *Auditory and phonetic processing for tone analogs of speech*. Unpublished doctoral dissertation, SUNY at Buffalo.

Schwartz. R., Leonard, L., Wilcox, M., & Folger, M. (1980). Again and again: Reduplication in child phonology. *Journal of Child Language, 7*, 75–87.

Scollon, R. (1976). *Conversations with a one year old*. Honolulu: University Press of Hawaii.

Searle, C. L., Jacobson, J. Z., & Kimberley, B. P. (1980). Speech as patterns in the 3-space of time and frequency. in Cole, R. A. (Ed.), *Perception and production of fluent speech.* Hillsdale, NJ: Lawrence Erlbaum Associates.

Searle, C. L., Jacobson, J. Z., & Rayment, S. G. (1979). Stop consonant discrimination based on human audition. *Journal of the Acoustical Society of America, 65,* 799–809.

Seeviour, P. M., Holmes, J. N. & Judd, M. W. (1976). Automatic generation of control signals for a parallel formant speech synthesizer. *Proceedings IEEE International Conference on Acoustics, Speech and Signal Processing,* Philadelphia, PA, 690–693.

Segalowitz, S. J., & Chapman, J S. (1980). Cerebral asymmetry for speech in neonates: A behavioral measure. *Brain and Language, 9,* 281–288.

Seidenberg, M., & Pettito, L. (1979). Signing behavior in apes: A critical review. *Cognition, 7,* 177–215.

Sejnoha, V. (1983). Speaker normalization transformations for automatic recognition. *Journal of the Acoustical Society of America, 74,* S17 (A).

Serniclaes, W. (1979). Sur la dissociation entre periodicité, bruit et frequence fondamentale en tant qu'indices de voisement des occlusives en français. Rapport d'activités de l'Institut de Phonétique de Bruxelles, 13, 71–93.

Shankweiler, D., Liberman, I. Y., Mark, L. S., Fowler, C. A., & Fischer, F. W. (1979). The speech code and learning to read. *Journal of Experimental Psychology: Human Learning and Memory, 5,* 530–545.

Shannon, R. V. (1983). Multichannel electrical stimulation of the auditory nerve in man: I. Basic psychophysics. *Hearing Research, 11,* 157–189.

Shattuck-Hufnagel, S. (1983). Sublexical units and suprasegmental structure in speech production planning. In P. F. MacNeilage (Ed.), *The production of speech.* New York: Springer-Verlag.

Shattuck-Hufnagel, S., & Klatt, D. (1979). The limited use of distinctive features and markedness in speech production: Evidence from speech error data. *Journal Verbal Learning Verbal Behavior, 18,* 41–55.

Shimbamoto, J. S., & Olmstead, D. L. (1978). Lexical and syllabic patterns in phonological acquisition. *Journal of Child Language, 5,* 417–446.

Shinn, P., & Blumstein, S. E. (1984a). On the Role of the Amplitude Envelope for the Perception of [b] and [w]. *Journal of the Acoustical Society of America, 75,* 1243–1252.

Shinn, P. & Blumstein, S. E. (1984b). Perceptual limitations on context-conditioned effects for the perception of [b] and [w], submitted.

Shipman, D. W. (1982). Development of speech research software on the MIT lisp machine. *Journal of the Acoustical Society of America, 71,* S103.

Shipman, D. W. (1983). SPIREX: Statistical analysis in the Spire acoustic-phonetic workstation. *Proceedings of the IEEE ICASSP-83, 3,* 1360–1363.

Shipman, D. W., & Zue, V. W. (1982). Properties of Large Lexicons: Implications for Advanced Isolated Word-recognition Systems. *Proceedings ICASSP-82,* 546–549.

Shortliffe, E. H. (1976). *Computer based medical consultations: MYCIN.* New York: American Elsevier.

Shvachkin, N. K. (1973). The development of phonemic speech perception in early childhood. In C. A. Ferguson & D. I. Slobin (Eds.), *Studies of child language development.* New York: Holt, Reinhart & Winston.

Sievers, E. (1901). *Gründzuge der Phonetik, 5th Ed.* Leipzig: Breitkopf and Härtel.

Simmons, F. B., Mathews, R. G., Walker, M. G., & White, R. L. (1979). A functioning multichannel auditory nerve stimulator. *Acta Otlaryngologica, 87,* 170–175.

Sinex, D. G., & Geisler, C. D. (1983). Response of auditory nerve fibers to consonant-vowel syllables. *Journal of the Acoustical Society of America, 73,* 602–615.

Slis, I., & Cohen, A. (1969). On the complex regulating of the voiced-voiceless distinction, I, *Language and Speech, 12,* 80–102.

Smith, N. V. (1973). *The acquisition of phonology: A case study.* Cambridge: Cambridge University Press.

Smith, R. L. (1979). Adaptation, saturation and physiological masking in single auditory nerve fibers. *Journal of the Acoustical Society of America, 65,* 166–178.

Smith, S. D., Kimberling, W. J., Pennington, B. F., & Lubs, H. A. (1983). Specific reading disability: Identification of an inherited form through linkage analysis. *Science*, *219*, 1345-1347.

Sondhi, M. M. (1968). New methods of pitch extraction, *IEEE Trans. Audio and Electroacoustics, AU-16* 262-266.

Spelke, E. S. (1982). Perceptual knowledge of objects in infancy. In J. Mehler, E. C. T. Walker, & M. Garrett (Eds.), *Perspectives on mental representation: Experimental and theoretical studies of cognitive processes and capacities*. Hillsdale, NJ: Lawrence Erlbaum Associates.

Srulovicz, P. & Goldstein, J. L. (1983). A central spectrum model: a synthesis of auditory-nerve timing and place cues in monaural communication of frequency spectrum. *Journal of the Acoustical Society of America, 73*, 1266-1276.

Stampe, D. (1969). The acquisition of phonetic representation. *Papers from the Fifth Regional Meeting of the Chicago Linguistic Society*, 443-454.

Stark, R. E. (1981). Stages of speech development in the first year of life. In G. H. Yeni-Komshian et al. (Eds.), *Child phonology. Vol. I. Production*. New York: Academic Press.

Stern, R. M., and Lasry, M. J. (1983). Dynamic speaker adaptation for isolated letter recognition using MAP estimation. *Proceedings of the IEEE International Conference on Acoustics, Speech, and Signal Processing*, 734-737.

Stevens, K. N. (1967, November). *Acoustic correlates of certain consonantal features.* Paper presented at Conference on Speech Communication and Processing, MIT, Cambridge, MA.

Stevens, K. N. (1972). The quantal nature of speech: Evidence from articulatory-acoustic data. In E. E. David, Jr. & P. B. Denes (Eds.), *Human communication: A unified view.* New York: McGraw-Hill.

Stevens, K. N. (1975). The potential role of property detectors in the perception of consonants. In G. Fant and M. A. A. Tatham (Eds.), *Auditory analysis and perception of speech.* New York: Academic Press.

Stevens, K. N. (1980). Acoustic correlates of some phonetic categories. *Journal of the Acoustical Society of America, 68*(3), 836-842.

Stevens, K. N. (1981a). Evidence for the role of acoustic boundaries in the perception of speech sounds. *Journal of the Acoustical Society of America, 69*, Supplement 1, S116.

Stevens, K. (1981b). Invariant acoustic correlates of phonetic features. In A. S. House (Ed.), *Proceedings of a symposion on acoustic phonetics and speech modeling.* Princeton, NJ: Institute for Defense Analysis.

Stevens, K. N. (1983). Design features of speech sound systems. In P. F. MacNeilage (Ed.), *The production of speech.* New York: Springer-Verlag.

Stevens, K. N., & Blumstein, S. E. (1978). Invariant cues for place of articulation in stop consonants. *The Journal of the Acoustical Society of America, 64*, 1358-1368.

Stevens, K. N. & Blumstein, S. E. (1981). The search for invariant acoustic correlates of phonetic features: In P. Eimas & J. Miller (Eds.), *Perspectives on the study of speech,* Hillsdale, NJ: Lawrence Erlbaum Associates.

Stevens, K. N.; & Klatt, D. H. (1974). Role of formant transitions in the voiced-voiceless distinction for stops. *Journal of the Acoustical Society of America, 55*, 653-659.

Stockard, C. R. (1941). *The genetic and endocrinic basis for differences in form and behavior.* Philadelphia: Wistar Institute of Anatomy and Biology.

Stoel-Gammon, C., & Cooper, J. A. (1984). Patterns of early lexical and phonological development. *Journal of Child Language, 11*, 247-271.

Strange, W., Verbrugge, R. R., Shankweiler, D. P., & Edman, T. R. (1976). Consonant environment specifies vowel identity. *Journal of the Acoustical Society of America, 60*, 213-224.

Streeter, L. A. (1976). Language perception of 2-month-old infants shows effects of both innate mechanisms and experience. *Nature, 259*, 39-41.

Studdert-Kennedy, M. (1982). On the dissociation of auditory and phonetic perception. In R. Carlson & B. Granström (Eds.), *The representation of speech in the peripheral auditory system.* Amsterdam: North-Holland.

Studdert-Kennedy, M. (Ed.) (1983). *Psychobiology of language*. Cambridge, MA: MIT Press.
Studdert-Kennedy, M., & Lane, H. (1980). Clues from the differences between signed and spoken language. In U. Bellugi & M. Studdert-Kennedy (Eds.), *Signed and spoken language: Biological constraints on linguistic forms*. Weinheim, Germany: Chemie GmbH.
Studdert-Kennedy, M., & Shankweiler, D. P. (1970). Hemispheric specialization for speech perception. *Journal of the Acoustical Society of America, 48*, 579–594.
Sturtevant, E. H. (1935). Vowel assimilation or ablaut in certain Hittite words. *Language, 11*, 175–184.
Summerfield, Q. (1979). Use of visual information for phonetic perception. *Phonetica, 36*, 314–331.
Sussman, H. M., MacNeilage, P. F., & Hanson, R. J. (1973). Labial and mandibular dynamics during the production of bilabial consonants: Preliminary observations. *Journal of Speech and Hearing Research, 16*, 397–420.
Svantesson, J.-O. (1983). *Kammu phonology and morphology*. Travaux de l'institut de linguistique de Lund XVIII. Lund: Gleerup.
Sweet, H. (1874). *History of English sounds*, London: Trübner.
Sweet, H. (1906). *A primer of phonetics*. Oxford: Oxford University Press.
Swoboda, P. J., Morse, P. A., & Leavitt, L. A. (1976). Continuous vowel discrimination in normal and at-risk infants. *Child Development, 47*, 459–465.
Swoboda, P., Kass, J., Morse, P., & Leavitt, L. (1978). Memory factors in infant vowel discrimination of normal and at-risk infants. *Child Development, 49*, 332–339.
Syrdal, A. K. (1982). Frequency analyses of American English vowels. *Journal of the Acoustical Society of America, 71*, S105 (Abstract).
Tallal, P., & Piercy, M. (1975). Developmental aphasia: The perception of brief vowels and extended stop consonants. *Neuropsychologia, 13*, 65–76.
Tekieli, M. E., & Cullinan, W. L. (1979). The perception of temporally segmented vowels and consonant-vowel syllables. *Journal of Speech & Hearing Research, 22*, 103–121.
Thelen, E. (1983). Learning to Walk is Still an "Old" Problem: A Reply to Zelazo. *Journal of Motor Behavior, 2*, 139–161.
Till, J. A. (1976, November). *Infants' discrimination of speech and nonspeech stimuli*. Paper presented at the annual meeting of the American Speech and Hearing Association, Houston, Texas.
Tong, Y. C., Clark, G. M., Blamey, P. J., Busby, P. A., & Dowell, R. C. (1982). Psychophysical studies for two multiple channel cochlear implant patients. *Journal of the Acoustical Society of America, 71*, 153–160.
Traunmüller, H. (1981). Perceptual dimension of openness in vowels. *Journal of the Acoustical Society of America, 69*, 1465–1474.
Traunmüller, H. (1983). Articulatory and perceptual factors controlling the age and sex conditioned variability in formant frequencies of vowels. To be published in *Speech Communication*.
Trehub, S. E. (1973). Infant's sensitivity to vowel and tonal contrasts. *Developmental Psychology, 9*, 91–96.
Trehub, S. E. (1976a). The discrimination of foreign speech contrasts by infants and adults. *Child Development, 47*, 466–472.
Trehub, S. E. (1976b). *Infants' discrimination of multisyllabic stimuli: The role of temporal factors*. Paper presented at the annual convention of the American Speech and Hearing Association, Houston, Texas.
Trevarthen, C. (1979). Communication and cooperation in early infancy: a description of primary intersubjectivity. In M. Bullowa (Ed.), *Before speech*, New York: Cambridge University Press.
Trudgill, Peter (1983). *On dialect: Social and geographic perspectives*. London: Basil-Blackwell.
Tuller, B., Harris, K., & Kelso, J. A. S. (1982). Stress and rate: Differential transformations of articulation. *Journal of the Acoustical Society of America, 71*, 1534–1543.
Tuller, B., Kelso, J. A. S., & Harris, K. (1982a). Interarticulator phasing as an index of temporal regularity in speech. *Journal of Experimental Psychology: Human Perception and Performance, 8*, 460–472.

Tuller, B., Kelso, J. A. S., & Harris, K. (1982b). On the kinematics of articulatory control as a function of stress and rate. *Haskins Laboratories Status Report on Speech Research, SR-71/72*, 81–88.

Tuller, B., Kelso, J. A. S., & Harris, K. S. (1983). Converging evidence for the role of relative timing in speech. *Journal of Experimental Psychology: Human Perception and Performance, 5*, 829–833.

Tuller, B., Kelso, J. A. S. & Harris, K. S. (1984). The timing of articulatory gestures: Evidence for relational invariants. *Journal of the Acoustical Society of America, 76*, 1030–1036.

Tzeng, O. J. L., & Wang W. S-Y. (1983). The first two R's. *American Scientist, 71*, 237–243.

Uldall, E. T. (1971). Isochronous stresses in R. P. In L. L. Hammerich, R. Jakobson, & E. Zwirner (Eds.), *Form & substance*, København: Akademisk Forlag.

Uldall, E. T. (1978). Rhythm in very rapid R. P. *Language & Speech, 21*, 397–402.

Vaissière, J. (1980). La structuration acoustique de la phrase française. *Annali della Scuola Normale Superiore di Pisa, Serie III, vol. X*, 529–560.

Vaissière, J., (1983a). Language-independent prosodic features. In A. Cutler and R. Ladd (Eds.), *Prosody: Models and measurements. Springer Series in Language and Communication, 14*.

Vaissière, J. (1983b). Suprasegmental effect on the velum movements in sentences. In A. Cohen & M.P.R. v.d. Broecke (Eds.), *Abstracts of the Tenth International Congress of Phonetic Sciences*. Dordrecht: Foris Publications.

Van Geel, R. C. (1983). *Pitch inflection in electrolaryngeal speech*. PhD thesis, Utrecht University: The Netherlands.

Verbrugge, R. R., Strange, W., Shankweiler, D. P., & Edman, T. R. (1976). What information enables a listener to map a talker's vowel space? *Journal of the Acoustical Society of America, 60*, 198–212.

Vidal, J. M. (1976). *Empreinte filiale et sexuelle—réflexions sur le processus d'attachement d'après une étude expérimentale sur le coq domestique*. Docteur des Sciences Thèse, University of Rennes, France.

Vihman, M. M., Macken, M. A., Miller, R., Simmons, H., & Miller, J. (In press). *From babbling to speech: A reassessment of the continuity issue*.

Voigt, H. F., Sachs, M. B., & Young, E. D. (1981). Effects of masking noise on the representation of vowel spectra in the auditory nerve. In J. Syka and L. Aitkin (Eds.), *Neuronal mechanisms of hearing*. New York: Plenum Press.

Waddington, C. H. (1966). *Principles of development and differentiation*. London: MacMillan.

Waibel, A., & Yegnanarayana, B., (1981). Comparative study of nonlinear time warping techniques in isolated word speech-recognition systems. *Technical Report CMU-CS-81-125*, Department of Computer Science, Carnegie-Mellon University.

Wajskop, M. (1979). Segmental durations of French intervocalic plosives. In B. Lindblom & S. Ohman (Eds.), *Frontiers of speech communication research*. London: Academic Press.

Wakita, H. (1977). Normalization of vowels by vocal tract length and its application to vowel recognition. *IEEE Transactions ASSP-25*, 183–192.

Walker, A. E., & Green, H. D. (1938). Electrical excitability of the motor face area: A comparative study in primates. *Journal of Neurophysiology, 1*, 152–165.

Walley, A. C., Smith, L. B., & Jusczyk, P. W. (1980). Classification of CV syllables by readers and pre-readers. *Research on Speech Perception*, Progress Report No. 6, Indiana University.

Warfield, D., Ruben, R. J., & R. Glackin. (1966). Word discrimination in cats. *Journal of Auditory Research, 6*, 97–119.

Warren, R. M. (1976). Auditory illusions and perceptual processes. In J. J. Lass (Ed.), *Contemporary issues in experimental phonetics*. New York: Academic Press.

Warren, R. M., & Obusek, C. J. (1971). Speech perception and phonemic restorations. *Perception and Psychophysics, 9*, 358–362.

Waterson, N. (1971). Child Phonology: A prosodic view. *Journal of Linguistics, 7*, 179–211.

Watson, C. (1974). *The role of precentral gyrus in the control of facial movement in Macaca mulatta*. Unpublished doctoral dissertation, University of Chicago.

Watson, J. S. (1972). Smiling, cooing and "The Game." *Merrill-Palmer Quarterly, 18,* 323–339.

Watson, J. S. (1981). Contingency experience in behavioral development. In K. Immelmann, G. B. Barlow, L. Petrinovich, & M. Main (Eds.) *Behavioral development.* New York: Cambridge University Press.

Weismer, G., Dinnsen, D. A., & Elbert, M. (1981). A study of the voicing distinction associated with omitted, word-final stops. *Journal of Speech and Hearing Disorders, 46,* 320–327.

Weismer, G., & Elbert, M. (1982). Temporal characteristics of "functionally" misarticulated /s/ in four- to six-year old children. *Journal of Speech and Hearing Research, 25,* 275–286.

Werker, J. F. (1982). *The development of cross-language speech perception: The effect of age, experience and context on perceptual organization.* Unpublished doctoral dissertation, University of British Columbia, Vancouver, B.C.

Werker, J. F., Gilbert, J. H. V., Humphrey, K., & Tees, R. C. (1981). Developmental aspects of cross-language speech perception. *Child Development, 52,* 349–355.

Werker, J. F., & Tees, R. C. (1983, April). *Changes in categorization of speech sounds.* Paper presented at the Biennial Meeting of the Society for Research in Child Development, Detroit, MI.

Whalen, D. (1982). Perceptual effects of phonetic mismatches. PhD thesis, Yale University, New Haven, CT.

White, G. M., and Neely, R. B., (1976). Speech-recognition experiments with linear prediction, bandpass filtering, and dynamic programming. *IEEE Transactions on Acoustics, Speech, and Signal Processing, ASSP-24,* 183–188.

Wiener, F. M., Pfeiffer, R. R., & Backus, A. S. N. (1966). On the sound pressure transformation by the head and auditory meatus of the cat. *Acta Otolaryngologica, 61,* 255–269.

Wierzchowska, B. (1965). *Wymowa Polska.* Warsaw: Panstwowe Zaklady Wydawnictw Szkolnych.

Williams, L. (1977a). *The effects of phonetic environment and stress placement on infant discrimination of place of stop consonant articulation.* Paper presented at the Second Annual Boston University Conference on Language Development, Boston, MA.

Williams, L. (1977b). Voicing contrasts in Spanish. *Journal of Phonetics, 5,* 169–184.

Williams, L., & Bush, M. (1978). The discrimination by young infants of voiced stop consonants with and without release bursts. *Journal of the Acoustical Society of America, 63,* 1223–1225.

Winitz, H., Scheib, M. E., & Reeds, J. A. (1972). Identification of stops and vowels for the burst portion of /p,t,k/ isolated from conversational speech. *Journal of the Acoustical Society of America, 51,* 1309–1317.

Wittgenstein, L. (1958). *The blue and brown books. Preliminary studies for the philosophical investigations.* New York: Harper & Row.

Woods, W., Bates, M., Brown, G., Bruce, B., Cook, C., Klovstad, J., Makhoul, J., Nash-Webber, B., Schwartz, R., Wolf, J., and Zue, V. (1976). Speech understanding systems. *Final Technical Progress Report,* (Volumes I-V), Report No. 3438. Cambridge, MA: Bolt Beranek and Newman.

Woodworth, R. S. (1938). *Experimental psychology.* New York: Holt.

Woolsey, C. N. (Ed.) (1982a). *Cortical sensory organization* (Vol. 1: Multiple somatic areas). Clinton, NJ: HMANA.

Woolsey, C. N. (Ed.) (1982b). *Cortical sensory organization* (Vol. 3: Multiple auditory areas). Clinton, NJ: HMANA.

Wright, J. (1980). The behavior of nasalized vowels in the perceptual vowel space. *Report of the Phonology Laboratory* [Berkeley], *5,* 127–163.

Yaeger, Malcah (1975). Speaking style: some phonetic realizations and their significance. *Pennsylvania Working Papers, I,* (1).

Yeni-Komshian, G., Cavanagh, J., & Ferguson, C. (1980). *Child phonology,* Vols. I and II, New York: Academic Press.

Yeni-Komshian, G. H., Kavanagh, J. F., & Ferguson, C. A. (Eds). (1981). *Child Phonology.* 2 vols. New York, Academic Press.

Young, E. D., & Sachs, M. B. (1979). Representation of steady-state vowels in the temporal aspects of the discharge patterns of populations of auditory-nerve fibers. *Journal of the Acoustical Society of America, 66,* 1381–1403.

Zaidel, E. (1976). Language dichotic listening and the disconnected hemispheres. In D. O. Walter, L. Rogers, & J. M. Finzi-Fried, (Eds.), *Conference on Human Brain Function.* Brain Information Service/BRI Publications Office, UCLA, Los Angeles.

Zaidel, E. (1978). Lexical organization in the right hemisphere. In P. A. Buser & A. Rougeul-Buser (Eds.), *Cerebral correlates of conscious experience.* Amsterdam: Elsevier/North Holland Biomedical Press.

Zue, V. W, (1976a). *Acoustic characteristics of stop consonants: A controlled study.* Ph.D. Thesis, MIT, Cambridge, MA.

Zue, V. W. (1976, May). Acoustic characteristics of stop consonants: A controlled study. *Technical Report No. 523,* Cambridge, MA: Lincoln Laboratory, MIT.

Zue, V. W. (1983). Proposal for an isolated-word recognition system based on phonetic knowledge and structural constraints. In A. Cohen & M. P. R. van den Broecke (Eds.), *Abstracts of the Tenth International Congress of Phonetic Sciences.* Dordrecht: Foris Publications.

Zue, V. W., & Schwartz, R. (1978). Acoustic processing and phonetic analysis. In W. A. Lea (Ed.), *Trends in speech-recognition.* Englewood Cliffs: Prentice-Hall.

Zwicker, E., & Feldtkeller, R. (1967). *Das Ohr als Nachrichtenempfänger.* Stuttgart: S. Hirtzel Verlag.

Zwicker, E., Terhardt, E., & Paulus, E. (1979). Automatic speech recognition using psychoacoustic models. *Journal of the Acoustical Society of America, 65,* 487–498.

Zwirner, B., & Ezawa, K. (Eds.). (1968). *Phonometrie. Zweiter Teil: Allgemeine Theorie.* (Bibliotheca Phonetica, No. 5). Basel: Karger.

INDEX